Unix Backup and Recovery

Unix Backup and Recovery

W. Curtis Preston

O'REILLY®

Beijing · Cambridge · Farnham · Köln · Paris · Sebastopol · Taipei · Tokyo

Unix Backup and Recovery
by W. Curtis Preston

Copyright © 1999 O'Reilly & Associates, Inc. All rights reserved.
...ica.

...Inc., 101 Morris Street, Sebastopol, CA 95472.

...er O'Leary

Printing History:

November 1999:   First Edition.

Nutshell Handbook, the Nutshell Handbook logo, and the O'Reilly logo are registered trademarks of O'Reilly & Associates, Inc. Many of the designations used by manufacturers and sellers to distinguish their products are claimed as trademarks. Where those designations appear in this book, and O'Reilly & Associates, Inc. was aware of a trademark claim, the designations have been printed in caps or initial caps. The association between the image of an Indian gavial and the topic of Unix backup and recovery is a trademark of O'Reilly & Associates, Inc.

While every precaution has been taken in the preparation of this book, the publisher assumes no responsibility for errors or omissions, or for damages resulting from the use of the information contained herein.

ISBN: 1-56592-642-0   [2/00]

[M]

This book is dedicated to my lovely wife Celynn, my beautiful daughters Nina and Marissa, and to God, for continuing to bless my life with gifts such as these.

—W. Curtis Preston

Table of Contents

Preface

Like many people, I had to learn backups the hard way. I worked at a large company where I was responsible for backing up Unix SVr3/4, Ultrix, HP-UX 8-10, AIX 3, Solaris 2.3, Informix, Oracle, and Sybase. In those days I barely understood how Unix worked, and I *really* didn't understand how databases worked—yet it was my responsibility to back it all up. I did what any normal person would do. I went to the biggest bookstore I could find and looked for a book on the subject. There weren't any books on the shelf, so I went to the counter where they could search the *Books in Print* database. Searching on the word "backup" brought up one book on how to back up Macintoshes.

Disillusioned, I did what many other people did: I read the backup chapters in several system and database administration books. Even the best books covered it on only a cursory level, and none of them told me how to automate the backups of 200 Unix machines that ran eight different flavors of Unix and three different database products. Another common problem with these chapters is that they would dedicate 90 percent or more to backup and less than 10 percent to recovery. So my company did what many others had done before us—we reinvented the wheel and wrote our own homegrown utilities and procedures.

Then one day I realized that our backup/recovery needs had outgrown our homegrown utilities, which meant that we needed to look at purchasing a commercial utility. Again, there were no resources to help explain the differences between the various backup utilities that were available at that time, so we did what most people do—we talked to the vendors. Since most of the vendors just bashed one another, our job was to try to figure out who was telling the truth and who wasn't. We then wrote a Request For Information (RFI) and a Request For Proposal (RFP) and sent it to the vendors we were considering, whose quotes ranged from

$16,000 to $150,000. Believe it or not, the least expensive product also did the best on the RFI, and we bought and installed our first commercial backup utility.

The day came for me to leave my first backup utility behind, as I was hired by a company that would one day become Collective Technologies. Finally, a chance to get out of backups and become a real system administrator! Interestingly enough, one of my first clients had been performing backups only sporadically, but I discovered that they had a valid license for the commercial product with which I was already familiar. (Imagine the luck.) While rolling out that product, they asked me also to look at how they were backing up their Oracle databases. The next thing I knew, I had ported my favorite Oracle backup script and published it. The response to that article was amazing. People around the world wrote me and thanked me for sharing it, and I caught the publishing bug. One of Collective Technologies' mottos is, "If something is broken, fix it!" Normally, we're talking about problems within our own company, but I applied it to the backup and recovery industry . . . and the dream of this book was born.

I Wish I Had This Book

My dream was to write a book that would make sure that no one ever had to start from scratch again, and I believe that my coauthors and I have done just that. It contains every backup tool that I wish I had had when I first entered the Unix business and every lesson and trick that I've learned along the way. It covers how to back up and recover everything from a basic Unix workstation to a complicated Informix, Oracle, or Sybase database. Whether your budget barely stretches to cover the cost of the backup media or allows you to buy a silo bigger than your house, this book has something for you. Whether your task is to figure out how to back up, with no commercial utilities, an environment such as the one I first encountered or to choose from among more than 50 commercial backup utilities, this book will tell you how to do it. With that in mind, let me mention a few things about this book that are unique.

Only the Recovery Matters

As a friend of mine used to tell me, "No one cares if you can back up—only if you can recover." Yet how many backup chapters have you read that dedicate less than 10 percent to recovery? You won't find that in this book. I have tried very hard to ensure that recovery is given treatment equal to that of backups. In fact, many times it is given greater treatment; the Oracle chapter has more than twice as much space dedicated to the recovery as it does to backups!

Products Change

Some people may be surprised that there are no product names mentioned in the commercial backup section. I did this for several reasons, the main one being that products change constantly. It would be impossible to keep this book up to date with the 50 different backup products that are available for Unix. In fact, the book would be out of date by the time it hit the shelves. Instead, this book explains the *concepts* of commercial backup and recovery software, allowing you to apply those concepts to the claims that the vendors are currently making. Up-to-date information about specific products has been placed on *http://www.backupcentral.com.*

Backing Up Databases Is Not That Hard

If you're a database administrator (DBA), you may not be familiar with the Unix backup commands necessary to back up your database. If you're a system administrator (SA), you may not be familiar with the architecture of your particular database platform. Both of these concepts are explained in detail in this book. I explain the backup utilities in plain language so that any DBA can understand them, and I explain database architecture in such a way that an SA, even one who has never before seen a database, can understand it.

Bare-Metal Recovery Is Not That Hard

One of these days you will lose the operating system disk for an important system, and you will need to recover it. This is called a "bare-metal recovery." The standard recovery method described in many backups products' documentation is to install a minimal operating system and restore on top of it. This is the worst possible method to do a bare-metal recovery of a Unix system; among other problems, you end up overwriting some of the system files while the system is running from the very disk to which you are trying to restore. The best ways to do bare-metal recoveries for six different versions of Unix are covered in detail in this book.

The Scripts in This Book Actually Work

Nothing bugs me more than to read a book in which the author talks about a really neat program, only to find out that the program is so full of bugs it won't work. Most of the programs in this book are already running at hundreds of sites around the world. With all the typical "unsupported" disclaimers in place, I do my best to ensure that they continue to work for the people who use them. If you're interested in any of the programs in the book (and on the CD), make sure that you subscribe to the appropriate mailing list on *http://www.backupcentral.com*. I will provide updates as they become available.

How This Book is Organized

This book is divided into six parts:

Part I, *Introduction*

This part of this book contains just enough information to whet your backup and recovery appetite.

Chapter 1, *Preparing for the Worst*, contains the six steps that you must go through to create and maintain a disaster recovery plan, one part of which will be a good backup and recovery system.

Chapter 2, *Backing It All Up*, goes into detail about the essential elements of a good backup and recovery system.

Part II, *Freely Available Filesystem Backup & Recovery Utilities*

This section covers the freely available utilities that you can use to back up your systems if you can't afford a commercial backup package.

Chapter 3, *Native Backup & Recovery Utilities*, covers Unix's native backup and recovery utilities in detail, including *dump*, *tar*, GNU *tar*, *cpio*, GNU *cpio*, and *dd*.

Chapter 4, *Free Backup Utilities*, starts with some simple tools to assist you in your backups, and contains a complete overview of the popular AMANDA utility, which is used to back up many small to medium-sized Unix installations around the world.

Part III, *Commercial Filesystem Backup & Recovery Utilities*

If you have outgrown the capabilities of free utilities, or would just like to take advantage of new backup and recovery technologies, you'll need to look at a commercial product.

Chapter 5, *Commercial Backup Utilities*, is your guide to the hundreds of features available in the over 50 commercial backup products available on the market today, allowing you to make an educated purchase decision.

Chapter 6, *High Availability*, details how, when backups just aren't fast enough, a high availability system is designed to keep you from ever needing to use your backups.

Part IV, *Bare-Metal Backup & Recovery Methods*

A bare-metal recovery is the fastest way to bring a dead system back to life, even if its root drive is completely destroyed.

Chapter 7, *SunOS/Solaris*, contains an in-depth description of the "homegrown" bare-metal recovery procedure that can also be used to back up Linux, Compaq, HP-UX, and IRIX, as well as a detailed Solaris-based example of bare-metal recovery.

Chapter 8, *Linux*, detail how you can perform a bare-metal recovery of a Linux system with a floppy, a backup device, *pax*, and *lilo*.

Chapter 9, *Compaq True-64 Unix*, covers both Compaq True-64 Unix's bare-metal recovery tool and the Compaq version of the homegrown procedure covered in Chapter 7.

Chapter 10, *HP-UX*, covers the *make_recovery* tool, which now comes with HP-UX to perform bare-metal recoveries, along with the HP version of the homegrown procedure.

Chapter 11, *IRIX*, explains how the different versions of IRIX's Backup and Restore scripts work, as well as the IRIX version of the homegrown procedure.

Chapter 12, *AIX*, discusses AIX, a procedure that does not support the homegrown procedure discussed in Chapter 7, but does use *mksysb*, probably one of the oldest and best-known bare-metal recovery tools.

Part V, *Database Backup & Recovery*

This section explains in plain language an area that presents some of the greatest backup and recovery challenges that a system administrator or database administrator will face—backing up and recovering databases.

Chapter 13, *Backing Up Databases*, is a chapter that will be your friend if you're an SA who's afraid of databases or a DBA learning a new database. It explains database architecture in plain language, while relating each architectural element to the appropriate term in Informix, Oracle, and Sybase.

Chapter 14, *Informix Backup & Recovery*, explains both the older *ontape* and the newer *onbar*, after which it provides a logically flowcharted recovery procedure that can be used with either utility.

Chapter 15, *Oracle Backup & Recovery*, explains how to perform Oracle hot backups whether you are using Oracle's native utilities, EBU, or RMAN, and then provides a detailed flowchart guiding you through even a difficult recovery.

Chapter 16, *Sybase Backup & Recovery*, shows exactly how to use the Backup Server utility, including another flow chart to guide you through Sybase recoveries.

Part VI, *Backup & Recovery Potpourri*

The information contained in this part of the book is by no means unimportant; it simply wouldn't fit anywhere else!

Chapter 17, *ClearCase Backup & Recovery*, explains in detail the unique backup and recovery challenges presented by ClearCase.

Chapter 18, *Backup Hardware*, explains the many different types of backup hardware available today, as well as providing criteria that you may use to decide which type of backup drive is right for you.

Chapter 19, *Miscellanea*, covers everything from the oft-debated "live filesystem dumps" question to a few jokes that I found about backup and recovery!

Conventions

The following typographical conventions are used in this book:

`Constant width`
> Is used to indicate command-line computer output, computer-generated messages, and code examples. It is also used when referring to parameters in text.

`Constant width italic`
> Is used to indicate variables in examples and text, and comments in examples.

`Constant width bold`
> Is used to indicate user input in examples.

Italic
> Is used to introduce new terms and to indicate URLs, variables or files and directories, commands, file extensions, filenames, and directory names.

How to Contact Us

We have tested and verified all the information in this book to the best of our ability, but you may find that features have changed (or even that we have made mistakes!). Please let us know about any errors you find, as well as your suggestions for future editions, by writing to:

O'Reilly & Associates
101 Morris Street
Sebastopol, CA 95472
1-800-998-9938 (in the U.S. or Canada)
1-707-829-0515 (international/local)
1-707-829-0104 (fax)

You can also send messages electronically. To be put on our mailing list or to request a catalog, send email to:

nuts@oreilly.com

To ask technical questions or comment on the book, send email to:

bookquestions@oreilly.com

We have a web site for the book, where we'll list examples, errata, and any plans for future editions. You can access this page at:

http://www.oreilly.com/catalog/unixbr/

For more information about this book and others, see the O'Reilly web site:

http://www.oreilly.com

This Book Was a Team Effort

I have never worked with a group of people like the ones I work with at Collective Technologies. Over the past three years, they have answered question after question about the various ways to back up and recover just about everything under the sun. Thanks to them, there is information in this book that would never have been otherwise. They sent me manpages and verified syntax for commands on versions of Unix that I've never even seen. They entered into technical debates about how to compare the architectures of Informix, Oracle, and Sybase. They tested the programs that are included in this book and even wrote a few of them.

By far the greatest contribution that other people gave to this book is that several of the chapters were written by experts in a particular field. I realized about a year ago that I would never finish this book if I didn't ask some of my friends to help. The result was that more than 20 percent of the final book ended up being written by people other than me. Their expertise in a particular area made their chapters far better than anything I could have written on my own. Having said that, please allow me to formally thank all of my coauthors:

AIX bare-metal recovery
    Charles Gagnon and Brian Jensen of Collective Technologies

AMANDA
    John R. Jackson and Alexandre Oliva from the AMANDA Core Development Team

Clearcase backup and recovery
Bob Fulwiler of Seattle, Washington

Compaq/Digital Unix bare-metal recovery
Matthew Huff of Collective Technologies

Dump internals
David Young of Collective Technologies

High-availability systems
Josh Newcomb and Gustavo Vegas of Collective Technologies

HP-UX bare-metal recovery
Steve Ferguson of Collective Technologies

IRIX bare-metal recovery
Blayne Puklich of Collective Technologies

Sybase backup and recovery
Bryn Smith of Collective Technologies

Without these folks, either the book would never have been completed or it would contain substantially less data than the book you see today.

Another group of people that I must thank is my technical reviewers. If every book's author had the team of technical reviewers I had, the world would contain far less misinformation. This book was actually reviewed on an ongoing basis by a number of Collective Technologies people. I set up an RCS system that allowed a team of about 30 reviewers to actually check out my chapters and edit them. They constantly kept me in check, identifying parts of the book that were inaccurate or that needed clarification. You can't imagine the benefit of having such a great team looking over your shoulder. This special ongoing technical review team consisted of:

Scott Aschenbach	Michael Clark	Norman Hill	Jason Perkins
Rusty Atkins	Nancy Cortez	Todd Holloway	Stephen Potter
Ed Bailey	Jim Donnelan	Bill Huff	Jason Stege
David Bajot	William Duffy	Paul Iadonisi	Vince Taluskie
Mike Bush	Steve Ferguson	Brian Jensen	Gustavo Vegas
Enrico Cantu	Henry Ferrara	Eric Jones	Bryce Wade
Paul Chalker	Charles Gagnon	Cliff Nadler	Asim Zuberi

I would like to give a special thank you to every one of you!

Once the final draft of the book was completed, an entirely different set of people did a complete technical review. These people were brutal! I can tell you that this incredibly humbling experience made this book far more technically accurate than it would have been otherwise. All of the technical reviewers did a wonderful job, but I'd like to thank two of them in particular. Gordon Galligher did an extensive technical review of the entire book, even though he got the review copy late and has a newborn baby! Art Kagel, of *comp.databases.informix* fame, reviewed and re-reviewed the Informix chapter until it was right. I even got email at 3:00 A.M. once in which he revealed he'd finally found the answer to a question that had been bugging both of us. The readers owe a big thank you to all of the following people:

Those who reviewed the entire book:

> Brian Epstein
> Gordon C. Galligher
> Mike O'Connor

Those who reviewed selected chapters:

> Clem Akins
> Mark A. Alestra
> Scott Aschenbach
> Greg Bourgoin
> Jeffrey Dykzeul
> Norm Eisenberg
> Lee Gould
> Brian Jensen
> Art S. Kagel
> Cliff Nadler
> Daniel T. Pigg
> Rodney Rutherford
> Liza Weissler

Wow! That's more than 40 technical reviewers! That means that if you find something in this book that's not technically correct, I've got 40 other people to point the finger at! Again, I would like to send a virtual high five to every one of these folks. Whether you helped me with the syntax of one or two commands or reviewed the whole book, I couldn't have done it without you!

I Don't Know It All

If there's one thing I learned while writing this book, it's that I do not know everything there is to know about backups. If you have a better way to do anything listed in this book, have learned any special tricks, or have written any neat utilities that you think would help other people do backups and recoveries, let me know. Email me at *curtis@backupcentral.com.* Your tricks or utilities may be included in the next edition of the book and listed immediately on *http://www.backupcentral.com.*

How Can I Say Thanks?

How can I begin to thank the hundreds of people who helped me?

To God: May any praise for this book go to You alone.

To my wife, Celynn: I say "thank you" for the many nights you spent alone while I pounded away at my keyboard somewhere around the globe. You're a special woman who never gave up on me or my dream. I love you. Can we finally take a vacation that doesn't involve a laptop?

To my older daughter, Nina: I say "Yes! It's finally done!" I know you've spent the last three years wondering when you were ever going to get your daddy back. Well, I'm done. Come give me a hug.

To my baby daughter, Marissa: Maybe you, Nina, Mom, and I can finally spend some time together now!

To my parents: What can I say? You always believed in me. You always used to tell me, "I don't care if you're a ditchdigger. Just be the best darn ditchdigger in the world." Well, being a backup guy is as close as you can get to being a ditchdigger in the computer business, and I "wrote the book" on that.

To my wife's family: Thank you for raising such a wonderful lady. Thank you for treating me as one of your own and supporting us on our quest. *Pahingi ng sinagang?*

To all the teachers who kept trying to get me to live up to my potential: You finally got through.

To Collective Technologies: I never could have done this if it hadn't been for you folks. You truly are a special group of people, and I'm proud to be known as one of you.

To Ed Taylor, Gordon Galligher, Curt Vincent, and anyone else who made the call to bring me on board at CT: What can I say? I'd probably still be swapping tapes if it wasn't for you. (Wait! I *am* still swapping tapes!)

To Jeff Rochlin: How could I forget the guy who taught me how to use my own RFI? Thanks, dude. I hope Mickey's treating you really nice.

To all my SA friends: Thank you for supporting me during this project. As I visited your hometowns in my travels, you welcomed me as one of your own. Only you truly understand what it's like trying to do something like this, and I couldn't have done it without you.

To O'Reilly & Associates: Thank you for the opportunity to bring this much-needed book to market. (Sorry it took me two and a half years longer than it should have!)

To Gigi Estabrook, my editor: We'll have to actually meet one of these days! I don't know how you do this, reading the same book over and over, without letting your eyes just glaze over. You're a great editor, and I could really tell that you put your all into this project. Thank you, thank you, and thank you. (Now don't edit *that* sentence, OK?)

To the reader: Thank you for purchasing this book. I hope you learn as much reading it as I did writing it.

To everyone else: Stop asking me if the book's done yet, all right? It's done!

I

Introduction

Part I consists of the following two chapters:

- Chapter 1, *Preparing for the Worst*, describes the elements that should be part of an overall disaster recovery plan.
- Chapter 2, *Backing It All Up*, provides an overview of the backup and recover process.

1

Preparing for the Worst

One of the simplest rules of systems administration is that disks and systems fail. If you haven't already lost a system or at least a disk drive, consider yourself extremely lucky. You also might consider the statistical possibility that your time is coming really soon. Maybe it's just me, but I lost four laptop disk drives while trying to write this book! (Yes, I had them backed up.)

This chapter talks about developing an overall disaster recovery plan, of which your backup and recovery system will be just a part.

My Dad Was Right

My father used to tell me, "There are two types of motorcycle owners. Those who have fallen, and those who will fall." The same rule applies to system administrators. There are those who have lost a disk drive and those who will lose a disk drive. (I'm sure my dad was just trying to keep me from buying a motorcycle, but the logic still applies. That's not bad for a guy who got his first computer last year, don't you think?)

Whenever I speak about my favorite subject at conferences, I always ask questions like, "Who has ever lost a disk drive?" or "Who has lost an entire system?" Actually, this chapter was written while at a conference. When I asked those questions there, someone raised his hand and said, "My computer room just got struck by lightning." That sure made for an interesting discussion! If you haven't lost a system, look around you . . . one of your friends has.

Speaking of old adages, the one that says "It'll never happen to me" applies here as well. Ask anyone who's been mugged if they thought it would happen to them. Ask anyone who's been in a car accident if they ever thought it would happen to them. Ask the guy whose computer room was struck by lightning if he thought it would ever happen to him. The answer is always "No."

While the title of this book is *Unix Backup & Recovery*, the whole reason you are making these backups is so that you will be able to recover from some level of disaster. Whether it's a user who has accidentally or maliciously damaged something or a tornado that has taken out your entire server room, the only way you are going to recover is by having a good, complete, disaster recovery plan that is based on a solid backup and recovery system.

Neither can exist completely without the other. If you have a great backup system but aren't storing your media off-site, you'll be sorry when that tornado hits. You may have the most well organized, well protected set of backup volumes,* but they won't be of any help if your backup and recovery system hasn't properly stored the data on those volumes. Getting good backups may be an early step in your disaster recovery plan, but the rest of that plan—organizing and protecting those backups against a disaster—should follow soon after. Although the task may seem daunting, it's not impossible.

Developing a Disaster Recovery Plan

Devising a good disaster recovery plan is hard work. You need to build it from the ground up, and it can take months or even years to perfect. Since computer environments are changing constantly, you continually have to test your plan to make sure it still works with your changing environment.

This chapter is not meant to be a comprehensive guide to disaster recovery planning. There are books dedicated to just that topic, and before you attempt to design your own disaster recovery plan, I strongly advise you to research this topic further. This chapter gives an overview of the steps necessary to complete such a plan, as well as discusses a few details that are typically left out of other books. It provides a frame of reference upon which the rest of the book will be based.

There are essentially six steps to designing a complete disaster recovery plan. While you may work on several steps simultaneously, the order listed here is very important. Don't jump into the design stage before understanding what level of risk your company is willing to take or what types of disasters the plan needs to address. Likewise, what good does it do to have a well-documented, well-organized disaster recovery plan based on a backup system that doesn't work? The six steps are as follows:

---

* This book will use the term *volume* instead of *tape* whenever appropriate. See the section "Why the Word "Volume" Instead of "Tape"?" in Chapter 2, *Backing It All Up*, for an explanation.

1. *Define (un)acceptable loss.*

   Before you develop a disaster recovery plan, decide how much you will lose if you don't. That will help you decide how much time, effort, and money to spend on a disaster/recovery plan.

2. *Back up everything.*

   You have to make sure that *everything* is backed up—including data, metadata, and the instructions you'll need to get them back.

3. *Organize everything.*

   You have everything on backup volumes. But can you find the volume you need when disaster strikes? The key to being able to find your backups is organization.

4. *Protect against disasters.*

   Most people think about natural disasters only when creating a disaster recovery plan. There are nine other types of disasters, and you have to protect against all of them. (The 10 types of disasters are covered in Chapter 2.)

5. *Document what you have done.*

   You need to document your plan in such a way that anyone can follow your steps after or during a disaster.

6. *Test, test, test.*

   A disaster recovery plan that has not been tested is not a plan; it's a proposal. You don't want to be in the middle of a disaster and discover that you have forgotten some critical steps.

Step 1: Define (Un)acceptable Loss

A disaster recovery plan is an insurance policy. If you've ever read anything about backups, you've heard that before. I would like to extend that analogy. Consider your car insurance policy. All insurance policies in the United States start with PIP, or personal injury protection. That way if you hit someone and get sued, you are protected. You can then add coverage for collision, personal property, emergency roadside assistance, and rental car coverage. These additional layers of coverage are called *riders.* Just like your car insurance policy, disaster recovery plans may include optional riders. You simply need to decide the types of riders that your company needs, or can afford. How do you do this? You have to look at the potential losses that your company will suffer if a disaster occurs and decide which ones are acceptable or unacceptable, as the case may be. You then select the riders that will protect you against the losses that you have decided are unacceptable. (This analogy is discussed in further detail in Chapter 2, *Backing It All Up.*)

You need to make the same kind of decisions on behalf of your company. If it is unacceptable to lose a single day's worth of data when a disaster happens, then you need to send your volumes to an off-site storage vendor every single day. You must decide what kind of losses your company is not willing to accept, and then insure against those losses with your disaster recovery plan. You cannot design a disaster recovery plan without this step. Every decision that you must make will be based on the information you discover during this analysis. Doing otherwise might cause you to purchase riders that you don't need or to leave out ones that you do need.

Classify Your Data

What is considered an acceptable loss for office automation data may not be considered acceptable when considering your customer database. Some data is easily re-created with effort, while other data is irreplaceable. Look at each type of data that you have and decide whether it can be re-created.

There are several types of re-createable data. Suppose you are a company that sells a software product. You have hundreds of developers working around the clock on a very important product. If disaster hits, they would hate it, but they could re-create their work. The schedule will slip, but with enough time, you could replace the enhancements that they made to the code. As a rule, if data is being created by a single person or group of people, *without interaction from anyone outside your company*, then that data is probably replaceable. *This is not to say that this data should not be backed up.* It means that you might decide not to send volumes off-site for this type of data every single day, since both the volumes and the storage vendor cost money. You might decide to send them off-site only once a week. On the other hand, the cost of re-creating that data must be taken into account, and you may not want to explain to a group of 200 developers why they have to re-create everything they did last week. If that is the case, then you have defined that losing more than one day's worth of anyone's work is unacceptable. Great! That's the purpose of this step.

There are types of data that are always irreplaceable. Suppose that you work in a hospital where patients come in to have MRIs and CAT scans performed in preparation for surgery or medical treatments. These images are stored digitally—there are *no* films. The doctors and surgeons use these images to plan critical operations or delicate treatments. What if a failure occurred that destroyed these images? These scans are often a picture of a progressing illness at a particular point in time. The loss of these images not only would expose the hospital and doctors to possible lawsuits but also could cost someone her life.

There are also financial institutions and brokerage firms that process hundreds of thousands of transactions each day. These transactions can total millions of dollars. A loss of a single transaction could be devastating. Would you want your bank to lose the direct deposit of your paycheck? Would you want your brokerage firm to lose your buy request for that hot new Internet IPO stock?

Examples of irreplaceable data do not have to be so devastating. Suppose a customer asks to have his address changed. You update the system and then you suffer a disaster. Do you even remember which customers called you last week, let alone what they asked for? Probably not. Your customer will sit at his new address awaiting his statement or product while you ship it to the old address. The result is that your credibility is destroyed in the customer's eyes. In today's world, you may end up on *20/20* or *Dateline NBC.*

In some instances, sending your backup volumes off-site daily (or hourly) is sufficient. However, there are situations in which the data is so critical and irreplaceable, the data must be duplicated and sent off-site immediately.

Assign a Monetary Value to Your Data

It is not possible to assign a monetary value to all types of data. How do you decide what an angry customer will cost you? (A truly angry customer can significantly cripple your business—especially if she sues you.) With other types of data, though, it is very easy. If you have five people who will have to redo a week's worth of their work, then the cost is a week's worth of their salaries, plus overhead. There are other things that are more difficult to calculate, such as the loss of productivity due to a drop in morale.

Weigh the Cost

You should not just blindly spend money on a disaster recovery plan that is more expensive than a disaster would be. This sounds like a given, but it can happen if you are not careful. It is possible that there are certain types of losses that you feel are unacceptable, no matter what the cost is to insure against them; that is fine, but make sure that you are insuring against them deliberately—and for all the right reasons.

Step 2: Back Up Everything

This sounds like a given, right? It's not. Certain types of data typically are excluded or forgotten. Many companies cut corners by omitting certain types of data from their backups. For example, by excluding the operating system from your backups, you may save a little media. However, if you find yourself in need of the old */etc/fstab*, you will be out of luck. You may save some money, but you also may be putting your company at risk. It's easier and safer just to back up everything.

There also may be types of data that are forgotten completely. The most common mistake is to back up the data on a system but not to get a "picture" of what the system itself looks like in case you have to rebuild it.

Exclude Lists Good, Include Lists Bad

It is best to have a system that automatically backs up everything, except for a few explicit exceptions specified on an exclude list. If your backup system requires you to update an include list every time a new filesystem is added, you may forget or you may add it incorrectly; the result is that the filesystem does not get backed up. In a disaster, this means the data never comes back. This is why I prefer backup products that automatically back up *all* filesystems. (The concept of include and exclude lists is covered in Chapter 2.)

Databases

Backing up a database requires more work than backing up a normal filesystem. (Actual database backup procedures are covered in Part V of this book.) Theoretically, if you are backing up everything in your filesystems and you are backing up your databases in some manner, you should be able to recover from disaster. Unfortunately, there are scenarios in which you might leave out an essential piece of the disaster recovery puzzle. The only way to ensure that you are prepared to recover your databases in case of a disaster is to back them up to another machine.

In fact, a previous version of my Oracle backup script (see Chapter 15, *Oracle Backup & Recovery*) did not back up the online redologs during a hot backup. All my backup and recovery tests worked fine, until I attempted to restore the database to a different system. We were able to restore all the database files, but the database needed the redologs in order to complete the recovery. Since we had not backed up the redologs, we did not have them to restore. You see, when I was recovering the database to the same system, the redologs were always there. (Of course, I immediately changed the script to address this problem.)

Backups of Your Backups

Whether you are using a homegrown solution that creates flat file indexes of your volumes or a commercial backup product that has a btree index, you need to be able to recover it easily. Think about it. Even if your commercial backup system makes volumes that can be read by native backup utilities, without the database that identifies what's where, you have no idea what system is on what volume. *That means that this database has now become the most important database in your company.* You need to make sure that it is backed up, and its recovery should be the easiest and most tested recovery in your entire environment. Again, you need to test your recoveries on a different system. One problem here is that many of the licenses for commercial backup products are node-locked. This means that you may have problems recovering the backups of one system to another system. Sometimes you can prepare for this in advance with a backup key, although that can *really* cost you. Some products enable recovery but disable backup to a server that is not licensed. This allows you to begin your disaster recovery on a new server, even if the product is not licensed for that particular server.

Another difficulty with a number of commercial products is that the backup of the database does not include any of the executables. In that case, you have two choices. The first choice is the normal backup method, in which case you will have to reinstall the software and any patches prior to restoring its database. The second choice is to run a special *dump, tar,* or *cpio* backup of all filesystems on which the backup software and database reside. (These utilities are discussed in Chapter 3, *Native Backup & Recovery Utilities.*)

Metadata

There are a number of types of metadata that may or may not be backed up by a normal backup system. You need to ensure that each of them is backed up in other ways. This data ranges from things that would be merely helpful in a disaster to those that will be essential. As you look over this list, you may begin to get the idea that a lot of this would be much easier if you standardize your system and disk layout. You would be right.

AIX's LVM, Sun's ODS, Veritas's LVM
> Each of these products is a logical volume manager that allows you to stripe disks together, perform software-based RAID (Redundant Array of Independent Disks) and mirroring, and do many other wonderful things. The problem is that each of these products needs to have its individual configuration stored somewhere. If you are concerned only with rebuilding filesystems, then the physical layout of the system itself may not be that important. You simply need to supply the system with similarly sized disks and recover your data. However, if you are running databases on raw partitions, you had better have a good backup of these configurations, so that you can re-create those raw partitions exactly the way they were before a disaster.

AIX's mksysb, HP's make_recovery
> Some operating systems have special utilities that store all of the appropriate information for you. The only problem with all of these utilities is that you have to use them up front, and you have to do so every time the system configuration changes.

The root slice

    If you are really backing up the root slice, then disaster recovery of a single system is simple. You can recover this data to a properly partitioned drive without installing the operating system. You could then easily accomplish a normal restore of the rest of the filesystems. (Bare-metal recovery is covered in detail in Part IV of this book.)

Partition tables

    Whether or not you are using a logical volume manager, maintaining a printout of the physical layout of all of your disks is a big help. If you're not running LVM, it is essential.

System layout—SysAudit or SysInfo

    A lot of the preceding information is recorded for you if you use the *SysAudit* and *SysInfo* programs.

Step 3: Organize Everything

Good organization is really the key to a good disaster recovery plan. If you have hundreds or thousands of backup volumes but can't find them if you need them, what good are they? There is also the physical layout of the servers themselves. If they are all laid out in a standard way, recovering from a disaster is a whole lot simpler than if each server has its own unique layout.

Standardized Server/Disk Layout

Standardizing the layout of your servers is one of the more difficult things to do, since server configurations and OS configurations change over time. Look at the following list for some of the ways you can standardize, and standardize where you can. Experience has shown that it is worth the trouble to go back and restandardize. That is, it is worth the trouble to reimplement your new standard on your old servers.

The root disk

    This should be your standard everywhere. Keep your OS on one disk if possible. Recovering an OS that is spread out on multiple disks is very difficult. Also, keep the partitioning (or LVM partitioning) of all of your OS disks consistent. You don't want to have to remember, "Oh yeah, this is the one with 1 MB of swap . . ."

Same-size disks

    Partition all of your same-size disks exactly the same way, if possible. Consistency makes swapping them in and out very easy and gives you a lot of flexibility.

Same-function disks

If you have disks that serve the same purpose, partition them in the same way.

Database data disk

Decide on the best way to partition your database data disks, and partition all of them in the same way. For example, you might decide to fit as many 2 GB partitions as you can onto the disk. Anything left over can be used for those small databases that are always lurking around.

Application disk

Usually, the best thing to do here is make it one big disk, while reserving that first cylinder again. (It's a good habit to get into.)

Media Organization

You need to keep track of your backup volumes. You need to be able to find any one of them at a drop of a hat. Here is a list of things you can do to ensure that:

Unique alphanumeric volser#

Regardless of its name, each volume should have a unique volume serial number (volser #), which will identify that individual volume. Its name may change over time, but this number will always refer to that volume and that volume only.

Database to track volser#, name, type, date used, location, "loaned to"

If you have volumes in more than one location, you need a database. If you have people who use your backup volumes, you need a database. If you want to find your volumes ever again, you need a database. It can track a lot of information for you, including to whom you loaned a volume.

Bar code system

Bar codes are useful for more than tape libraries. You can purchase a bar code scanner rather inexpensively and use it to track the movement of your volumes.

Proper media storage

All tape media should be stored in such a way that the spindle, or axle, of the tape wheel, is horizontal—in the same way that a car's axles are horizontal. Do not store tapes so that the axle of the tape reel is pointing upwards. This means that most tapes should be stored on their sides—not laying in a drawer somewhere. Tapes have been known to shift and lose their alignment if stored in that position for too long. (CD-ROM and optical media is less susceptible to this problem.)

Temperature and humidity

The better the climate of your media storage area, the longer the media will last. If the area is just a normal office with unfiltered air and occasionally or even regularly rises to temperatures that feel warm to a human, your media is in the wrong place.

Physical security

Media costs money. If you leave your backup volumes in an unlocked drawer, someone is liable to walk away with them. The cost of the media is not the problem, it's the loss of data that is stored on them. Keep your media secured. Don't let anyone but a select few have access to the media, and ensure that anyone else who is given access is logged. Remember, unless the data on the volume is encrypted, anyone with a backup drive can read it—no matter what file protections exist on your server.

Spot checks and full inventories

Do an occasional inventory spot check of a random sample of volumes, perhaps once a month or quarter. Make sure that they are where you think they are. Then follow it up with a semiannual full inventory of all backup volumes.

For a detailed example of the application of all of the above media organization concepts, see "12,000 gold pieces" in Chapter 2.

Put Electronic Documentation in One Place

A friend of mine used to say, "Online good, paper bad." In the computer world, it is very good to have your documentation online. Online documentation is easier to update and easier to access during normal operations. However, it does have one drawback—it's difficult to read in a disaster. With that in mind, you should put all your documentation eggs in one basket, and make that basket very easy to find.

Output from a system layout program

Run a system layout program (such as the *SysAudit* or *SysInfo* programs discussed in Chapter 4) on a regular basis and store the output in a centralized location. For example, if you have automounter and a central machine called *admin*, you might store all *SysAudit* output in */net/admin/client_name/SysAudit.out*.

Procedures

You need to have well-documented procedures for how to do everything, from day-to-day system administration to how to rebuild your most important servers.

Files on Zip/Jaz/CD-ROM

You also might want to consider having a special backup made of all your documentation. If you can fit such a backup on PC-style media (Zip, Jaz, or CD-ROM), it might make reading it in a disaster much easier, since many peo-

Avoid Those Catch-22 Situations

Planning for a disaster is difficult to do. You have to keep in mind the catch-22 situations that can surprise you. I remember when one of them happened to me. We were quite proud of our media inventory system (see "12,000 gold pieces" in Chapter 2). The database was well defined and constantly updated. We could find any volume at any time—as long as the database was available. What do you suppose we had to do when the system that contained the database went down? It wasn't easy, I tell you, to find that volume. Luckily, we had the volume name and its bar code number on the volume itself. Once our backup software told us which volume it wanted, we simply searched high and low until we found it. After this little scenario, we changed the way our volumes were inventoried. We found out that the off-site storage company had a customer-defined field that we weren't using. All we had to do was feed them the names of the volumes associated with each bar code. That way, the next time we needed a volume and did not have the database, we could ask *them* for it.

ple on your IT staff may carry a laptop. A properly made CD-ROM can be read on either a Unix or Windows machine.

One tar volume

Put all of this documentation (from the system layout information to the actual procedures) in one place, so that you can create one *tar* backup of it. Whether this backup is to CD-ROM or to optical media or to a tape, it should be in one place to allow for easy retrieval.

Make sure that the reader (Word, Adobe Acrobat, browser) is on the volume

You need to make sure that a copy of the executable needed to read your documentation is stored with that documentation. This definitely means backing up a copy of Word, Adobe Acrobat, or whatever document reader you use.

Step 4: Protect Against Disasters

What types of disasters strike your area? I grew up in an area in which an entire city block dropped into a sinkhole. Shortly after that, we were hit by hurricane David. Floods, tornadoes, and earthquakes hit other parts of the world. Your disaster recovery setup should be designed to protect against the types of disasters that affect your area.

You need to get a copy of the *Disaster Recovery Yellow Pages*. This is one of the most useful references that I have seen. These folks have combed the yellow pages of hundreds of cities and found literally thousands of companies that can help you with every phase of disaster recovery planning. They have everything from A to Z, including every kind of company that you could possibly need to recover from a disaster. There are emergency communication services, fire damage reclamation services, emergency medical services, emergency equipment suppliers, and anything else you can imagine. Some of these companies even have computer rooms on trucks that are able to roll out at a moment's notice. The *Disaster Recovery Yellow Pages* publishers have been told by a number of customers that a mere scan of their table of contents has made them rethink their disaster recovery plan. Get yourself a copy for your computer room and one for your vault. Send email to *dryp@datablast.com* for a complete table of contents.

Protect the Media and Documentation

Everyone knows that the best place to store your media is *not* in your computer room, next to the computer being backed up. Yet, that is the most common place where media is stored. You need to do something to protect the media that backs up your computers, or that media will be useless when disaster strikes.

On-site vault systems

There are a number of fire-ready media vaults that you can use to protect your media against fire. This is the best protection for media that is to be stored on-site. Be forewarned, though, they are expensive. Contact Wrightline, Inc., for more information (*http://www.wrightline.com*).

Off-site storage companies

The best protection for your media is to send it to an off-site storage company every day. They will store it in a fireproof vault that will protect against most natural disasters. (If someone wants to blow up your off-site storage company, though, there's not much you or they can do.)

Once you have chosen a storage company, do not assume that your data is being properly protected. It is merely the beginning of a partnership that you must foster. You need to check up on your storage company occasionally to make sure that it is doing what it is supposed to be doing. Chapter 2 has some suggestions on how to do that.

A Cure for What Ails You . . .

Make sure that the location and setup of the vault is appropriate for the types of disasters that strike your area. I remember one off-site storage company that seemed extremely secure. Their vault was actually in an area that had formerly been a bomb shelter during WWII. This thing might have withstood a nuclear attack. There was one problem, though. In that area, the most likely natural disaster was a flood. Make a quick guess as to where bomb shelters are? That's right, below ground level. You get the picture. Again, make sure the storage company is prepared for the types of disasters that strike your area.

Protect the Business

Many disaster recovery plans talk about how to recover the lost data but not how to recover the lost computers, furniture, telephones, or anything else. You need to have a plan to protect all of this, as well as anything else that your company would need to function normally. This is referred to as a business continuity plan, and is a whole other field. Consult the *Disaster Recovery Yellow Pages* for business continuity vendors.

Step 5: Document What You Have Done

While you are working your way through these steps, and certainly once your disaster recovery plan is complete, get it all down in writing. Document every procedure that you can. This is necessary to recover from a disaster—and to recover from the loss of an essential person. (You never know when someone might win the lottery.)

Document in a Portable Format

Again, there are a number of documentation formats. Choose the one that makes the most sense to you.

HTML

This is the documentation of choice for disaster recovery documentation. It is readable on any platform with a browser and therefore extremely portable. You don't even have to edit raw HTML anymore, since you can save as HTML with any modern word processor. This makes doing documentation in HTML much easier. Just make sure that you do the code in such a way that it can be read if the hostname changes. For example, make relative references to the current server rather than hard links to a particular URL. The one downside to using HTML is that it can take up more space than the other options discussed here.

PDF

The two positive things about the Adobe PDF format are its size and its truly platform-independent nature. However, it is not editable in its native format, and not everyone has a PDF reader installed. Still, the PDF format may be a good choice for you, as long as you are aware of its limitations.

Word processor

The word processor format is probably the easiest to manage of all these options. The only difficult part is getting a reader. However, if you choose the Microsoft Word format, any Windows laptop can read it with Wordpad. The only issue with this format is portability, although there are applications that can read Word files on Unix. Since you would have to obtain such an application prior to a disaster, though, I would suggest a more portable format.

Paper copies

Electronic copies of documentation are much easier to keep up to date, so therefore should be your preferred method of documentation. Nevertheless, that doesn't mean that you can't print out a limited number of copies of your manual. If you keep each procedure as a separate file, you can even update your printed manual without having to reprint the entire thing.

Paper versions of your procedures can be *very* helpful in case of a total system failure.

Step 6: Test, Test, Test

The key to successfully recovering from a real disaster is to test your disaster recovery plan. The point of testing is to find things that need updating—and you will always find them. If you find a bad link in your disaster recovery plan, then fix it. Do not consider this test a failure. In fact, perhaps you should consider a test that *doesn't* find something wrong a failure.

Have a stranger test procedures

Don't have the person who wrote the procedure test the procedure. Have someone who is competent, but unfamiliar with your systems, do the test. Perhaps you can hire a consultant to test your procedures; they should be written so that such a person should be able to follow them. Not only is it a great way to find loopholes in your procedures, it is a great way to test what would happen if you lost some essential personnel.

Dream up disasters

This is the fun part. Ask the most pessimistic person you know to dream up disasters for you. See if he can come up with one that you haven't planned for.

Full-test every six months

This is what the contracts of many disaster recovery companies require. Such a test should take a day or so and is well worth your time. One of the problems with this is the availability of personnel. Again, hiring consultants is a good way to get this test done. Just don't use all consultants and no company personnel, because then nobody in-house will learn much from the test.

D/R companies will require a test

This is a great way to force you to do a test. If you have a contract with a disaster recovery company, they will require you to test your plan. If you don't test your plan, you are in breach of contract and the D/R company cannot be held responsible. There's something about paying money to a company for nothing that forces you to do what they want you to do—test!

Put It All Together

This chapter merely scratches the surface of disaster recovery planning. There are other books on the subject; look for books in print that have "disaster recovery" in their titles. Remember that prior proper planning prevents pitifully poor performance during a disaster that destroys, demolishes, and devastates your company. The chapters that follow describe in detail one element of a disaster recovery plan—the backup and recovery of your data.

2

Backing It All Up

In Chapter 1, *Preparing for the Worst*, we looked at disaster recovery as a whole. The nuts and bolts of backup and recovery are but a small part of the overall disaster recovery picture. Before we begin looking at the details of how to perform certain types of backups, let's look at backups in general.

Don't Skip This Chapter!

The casual reader might assume that this chapter is an introduction to basic backup concepts. While that is, in fact, the purpose of this chapter, it is also true that many seasoned administrators are unfamiliar with the ideas presented here. One reason for this is that administrators find themselves constantly being pulled away from "mundane" activities like backups for things that are *thought* to be more "important"—like installing new servers and figuring out why the systems are running slowly. Also, many administrators may go several years without ever needing a restore. (The need to use your backups on a regular basis would undoubtedly change your ideas about their importance.)

I wrote this book because backups (and recoveries) have been my primary area of emphasis for several years, and I would like to share the lessons I've learned from this focused activity. This chapter provides an overview of how your backups should work. It also explains many basic, yet extremely important, concepts upon which any good backup plan should be based and upon which any implementation discussed in this book will be based.

There are many stories in this book, like the one in the following sidebar. Each is a true story that really happened to someone I know. These are not urban legends or horror stories passed on from admin to admin. These are firsthand encounters with disaster. Why is that important? Each story makes a point, and it was not just made up to make that point. The things that I warn about in this book really happen. This can be a very tough job if you are not prepared, so read closely.

Why the Word "Volume" Instead of "Tape"?

Most backup utilities were written originally to back up to tape, and most people do back up to tape. Therefore, most books and manpages talk about backing up to tape. However, many people are backing up to CDs or magneto-optical disks. These media types have many advantages, since they act more like disk drives than tape drives. Random access of backup data is easier, and you can read them using any block size you wish, since they do not record interrecord gaps as tape drives do.*

Since many people are no longer using tape, this book will use the more generic word "volume" whenever appropriate. You'll also find the term "backup drive" instead of "tape drive." Again, that is because the backup drive could be a CD burner, especially if you're a Linux user. The book uses the words "tape" and "tape drive" only when they are necessary and appropriate.

Why Should You Read This Book?

If you've been doing system administration for some time, you may be asking yourself this question. There are many answers. Perhaps self-preservation is your primary motivator. You'd like to make sure you don't lose your job the next time that a disk drive goes south. Perhaps you've already got a decent backup system, but you'd just like to make it better. Maybe you are looking for some new ideas on how to deal with upcoming backup and recovery needs. What follows are some of the reasons *I* think you should read it.

You Never Want to Say These Words

"We lost only a few days' worth of data." I swore the day I said that that I would never say those words again. From that day forward, I was convinced of the importance of backups. I never again assumed anything, and I began to study everything I could about backup technology. This book represents my attempt to compile what I have learned into a single volume, and it is written so that no one who reads it should ever need to utter the preceding statement. In my opinion, *no amount of data loss is acceptable.* I would also wager that you would be hard-pressed to find an end user who would feel much different. Whether it's a spread-sheet that one person created, or a customer database representing hours, or days

---

* See "How Do I Read This Volume?" in Chapter 3, *Native Backup & Recovery Utilities.*

The One That Got Away

"You mean to tell me that we have absolutely no backups of *paris* whatso-ever?" I will never forget those words. I had been in charge of backups for only about two months, and I just knew my career was over. We had moved an Oracle application from one server to another about six weeks earlier, and there was one crucial part of the move that I missed. I knew very little about database backups in those days, and I didn't realize that I needed to shut down an Oracle database before backing it up. This was accomplished on the old server by a *cron* job that I never knew existed. I discovered all of this *after* a disk on the new server went south.

"Just give us the last full backup," they said. I started looking through my logs. That's when I started seeing the errors. "No problem," I thought, "I'll just use an older backup." The older logs didn't look any better. Frantically, I looked at log after log until I came to one that looked as if it were OK. It was just over six weeks old. When I went to grab that volume, I realized that we had a six-week rotation cycle, and we had overwritten that volume two days ago.

That was it! At that moment, I knew that I'd be looking for another job. This was our purchasing database, and this data loss would amount to approxi-mately two months of lost purchase orders for a multibillion-dollar company.

So I told my boss the news. That's when I heard, "You mean to tell me that we have *absolutely no backups* of *paris* whatsoever?" (Isn't it amazing how I haven't forgotten its name? I don't remember any other system names from that place, but I remember this one.) I felt so small that I could have fit inside a 4-mm tape box. Fortunately, a system administrator worked what, at the time, I could only describe as magic. The dead disk was resurrected, and the data was recovered straight from the disk itself. We lost only a few days' worth of data. Our department had to send a memo to the entire company saying that any purchase orders entered in the last two days had to be reentered. I should have framed a copy of that memo to remind me what can happen if you don't take this job seriously enough. I didn't need to, though—its image is perma-nently etched in my brain.

Some of this book's reviewers said things like, "That's pretty bold! You're writ-ing a book on backups, and you start it out with a story about how you messed up. Some authority you are!" Why did I include it? Through all the years, and all the outages, this one sticks in my mind. Perhaps that's because it's the only one that almost "got me." Had it not been for the miraculous efforts of a won-derful administrator named Joe Fitzpatrick, my career might have been over before it started. I include this anecdote because:

—Continued—

- It's the one that changed the direction of my career.

- There are several valuable lessons that I learned from it, which I discuss in this book.

- It could have been avoided if I had had a book like this one.

- You must admit that it's pretty darn scary.

of sales invoices and the efforts of hundreds of people—ask the person who needs the data how much data loss they think is acceptable. Every statement, every opinion, every story, and every chapter in this book are based on the premise that any data loss is unacceptable. Let me state that again for emphasis.

 With the technology that is now available, there is no reason for any data to be lost—*if* backups are given the proper attention and priority that they need.

Backup Technology Has Evolved

If you've been doing backups for a while, you know that this hasn't always been the case. Just a few years ago, if you couldn't do it with *dump, tar, cpio,* and your standard database backup utilities, you couldn't do it. The demand for midrange computers has grown astronomically in the last few years, and the need for bigger databases, larger filesystems, long filenames, and long pathnames grew proportionally. As things typically go in the backup world, large filesystems and huge databases were designed and shipped long before the utilities to back them up effectively were available. This created a large market for commercial backup utilities: one or two such products emerged, and scores of others eventually followed.

Many of these early products were just GUIs and volume management built on top of existing native backup utilities, and the GUI layers often added a significant level of functionality. Other companies felt that these native utilities had many limitations that could not be fixed without abandoning them altogether. Those companies chose to develop custom, or even proprietary, backup methods. They attempted to overcome the limitations that products that were based on *dump* and *tar* could not. Not all of these proprietary backup products did well, however, which sometimes left customers in the lurch with scores of backup volumes that could be read only by a deprecated product. Administrators who have been burned by a bad commercial utility often prefer a tool that uses native utilities.

Administrators can now choose from an almost dizzying number of backup products to fit a number of environments. Picking the right one can be difficult. Some are better than others, and some are simply a waste of money. However, there are very few systems or environments that are not being addressed with one product or another. Some solutions may require you to get closer to the bleeding edge of technology, and probably will cost quite a bit, but they are available. Sometimes options available with a particular backup product may even determine what platform is best for your very large database (VLDB) or Network File System (NFS) file server. This is a first in the industry: there are now hardware and software platforms that sell better because they are easier to back up. Instantaneous, up-to-the-minute restores that are invisible to the user are now available—for the right price.

How Serious Is Your Company About Backups?

I've heard it all. I've been accused of caring only about backups. It's been said that I think the whole world revolves around a cartridge reel. I've said that someday the world's going to crash, and I'm going to have the backup. The question is: how serious are *you* about protecting your data? To help you come to a decision in this matter, let's talk about what will happen if you don't have good backups.

What Will Lost Data Cost You?

To answer this question, you need to consider what kind of data you are backing up. This is a perfect time to include people who may not consider themselves computer people. Get input from other departments to answer this question. When all those 1s and 0s come together, just what kind of stuff are we talking about? Do you use manual accounting methods, or are your company's financial records stored in some accounting software somewhere? When a customer calls in and orders something, do you jot that down on a carbon-copied order form, or do you enter it in some sort of order processing program? What about things like budgets, memoranda, inventories, and any other "paperwork" that you throw around from day to day? Do you keep copies of every important memo that you send, or do you depend on the computer for that?

If you're like most people, you have grown quite dependent on these things we call computers. You forget how much of your work has been saved in the form of little magnetized bits spread out across a bunch of spinning platters. Maybe you work in an environment in which you've never lost a disk, so you've never had to do a restore. Maybe you've never fat-fingered a key and deleted an important file. If that's the case, then remember what my dad used to say. Motorcycle riders come in two types—those who have fallen and those who will fall. The same is true of disk drives. If the rabid dog of disaster hasn't bitten you, trust me, it's scratching at your door right now!

So what would you lose if you lost data? To quantify this, we need to examine the types of systems that may reside in your environment. Most of what you could lose is very tangible—and quantifiable in monetary terms—and might surprise you.

Lost customers

This is quite possibly the most tangible and most devastating of all losses. If you've got your entire customer database on a computer somewhere, how will you know who they are if that computer dies? So you might actually "lose" your customers and never find them again. You also could lose customers who depend on data that is on one or more of your computers; if the customer finds out that you have lost his data, he will undoubtedly be less than impressed with you. The degree to which this data loss affects him may not even be relevant to him—he knows that you lost a little bit of data, and "He who is faithful with little will be faithful with much." The customer might leave just because he no longer feels that your company is competent.

Orders

Whatever service or product your company provides, you have some way of keeping track of requests for that product or service. Again, chances are that the method is computer based. Data loss may mean several hours, days, or even weeks of lost orders. These may be orders that your salespeople worked very hard to get!

Morale

Think about how you would feel if you were one of the salespeople whose orders were lost. You spent days or weeks working on a bunch of sales, and now they're gone forever. Maybe you should go somewhere else where your hard work doesn't go to waste. The better the salesperson, the better the chance that she may jump ship if you lose her sales. What about the average employee? If your computers have a reputation for going down and a reputation for losing data, it gives the employees a feeling of helplessness. Maybe they should go somewhere where they have the proper equipment to do their jobs.

Image

What about your standing in the industry? News of a major data loss undoubtedly spreads. This news may get to competitors, whom you can trust to use it against you at any opportunity. The news also may get to a regulatory agency that is in charge of your type of company. For example, if you work for a bank, it would be a terrible thing for the OCC to find out that you had a major data loss. They may decide to take a really close look at your affairs. Nobody wants that kind of attention!

Budget

It takes only one story of lost data to give your computer department an internal reputation for data loss. Try as you might, that reputation may stay for a while. You're only as good as your last restore. (A friend of mine said, "You're only as good as your *worst* restore.") If people don't trust your backups, they will duplicate your backup efforts. Employees will spend time and money backing up their systems locally. Each person may decide to buy his own backup drive and backup software or even to come up with his own in-house script. Their backups will be inefficient and costly at best and subject them to further data loss at worst. When everybody takes matters into her own hands, you can lose quite a bit of money in lost people-hours and extra hardware.

Time

How many people do you have supporting your computers? How much of their efforts will you lose if your development system loses data? I know of many companies that have many contract programmers writing code all the time. If the system on which they are storing this code loses their code, how much money will you have wasted on their work? In fact, no matter what department you look at, if they do their work on a computer and you lose that data, you can lose considerable time, and money, in lost work.

What Will Downtime Cost You?

When planning your backup and recovery program, you may have several options that will affect the *speed* of the recovery. The faster the recovery, the more the backup system will cost you. What you must ask yourself before deciding on these types of options is, "What will downtime cost?" When thinking about this, I'm reminded of a copier machine commercial from a few years ago. "When your copier goes down, do people just say, 'That's all right, we'll just use carbon paper!'" If one of your main systems goes down, can your people continue working, or does your entire company come to a standstill? If it comes to a standstill, are your people salaried, so that sending them home saves you no money?

Customer perception

A customer hates to hear, "Please call back, our computers are down," or "Connection not responding." Depending on your type of business, they might just decide to go elsewhere. The longer your systems are down, the more customers will hear this message.

Employee perception

Nobody wants to work at a company where the computers are always going down. The more your employees depend on your systems, the truer this becomes. If you were a salesperson who couldn't use your contact database for a day or so, how happy would you be?

Time

> Again, you lose time. You lose headway, and your salaried employees who depend on the down system are effectively being paid to do nothing.

You Can Find a Balance

Using a system that has no backups is like driving a car 100 miles an hour down a busy road the day after your insurance policy expires. Likewise, having a three-node, highly-available cluster for a noncritical application is like having full coverage on your 20-year-old, fifth car. Just as insurance plans have different levels of coverage and riders to cover various types of damage, different backup methodologies provide different levels of recoverability.

Don't Go Overboard

Not all environments need up-to-the-minute data recoverability. For many environments, recovering the systems up to last night's backups is acceptable. For some environments, recovering the system even up to last week or month is OK. Spending thousands of dollars and hundreds of hours implementing the greatest backup solution in the world is a waste—if you don't need that level of coverage. This usually is not the problem for most sites; on the contrary, most sites don't spend nearly enough money or effort on their backup and recovery system. In other cases, however, money sometimes is wasted on an unnecessarily elaborate system.

Recoverability requirements also vary from machine to machine within the same company. The amount of work that would be lost, or the possibility of adversely affecting a customer, may determine these requirements. For example, it may be considered acceptable for an employee or two to lose a day's work spent on a few word processing documents. That is, unless it was your Senior Vice President's secretary who was working on the departmental budget, in which case your mileage may vary. And, it would probably be totally unacceptable for you to lose even one hour's worth of entries into the company-wide sales database used by hundreds of people.

The point is that *your backup requirements are determined by your recoverability requirements.* The difficulty comes in finding (and using) a tool capable of providing you with the level of recoverability that you need. Consider users' home directories for a minute. If they are local to each user's workstation, a loss of one user's disk in the afternoon would mean that one user would lose a few hours of work. However, if user directories are located on an NFS file server that serves thousands of users, you could potentially lose several thousand hours of work if you use only traditional backup tools. If that loss would be considered unacceptable, then you need to examine the newest trend in backups—the *snapshot.* Snapshot software allows you to take a "picture" of your filesystem at a single point in time and then use that picture to back up that filesystem. If the backup references the filesystem via this snapshot, it will back up a consistent picture of the filesystem as it looked at the time the snapshot was taken. (Snapshots are discussed in more detail in Chapter 19, *Miscellanea.*) Snapshot software costs money, of course, but it provides a level of functionality just not possible otherwise.

Sometimes the tool you need comes with your operating system or database platform, but it's just not being used properly. Sometimes backup tools aren't being used at all. For example, if you have a production Oracle database, combining nightly hot backups with archived redologs will provide you with up-to-the-minute recoverability. However, if you lose a disk that is part of a database that doesn't use archiving, you will lose all work since the last cold backup. See Part V for more information.

If you have a production instance of any kind and are not using the transaction logging feature of your database engine, turn on logging as soon as possible!

Therefore, while it is necessary to find the appropriate utility to give you the degree of recoverability that you require, it is also necessary to use it.

Get the Coverage That You Need

Some environments cannot afford even one minute of downtime, and they should pay for the best backup coverage—whatever it costs. This is because of the great loss that they will incur if they ever lose their systems for even a short period. (I know of one company that claims that they lose $20,000 a minute when their systems are down.) On the other hand, if you are in an environment that can afford downtime, then spending huge amounts of money for an immediately available *hot site** is a complete waste of money.

Consider Table 2-1. No one should depend on a car, or a computer, without having *at least* the basic level of coverage. If the only car that you own is uninsured, and some drunk driver runs into you and totals it, how would you recover from such a loss? Similarly, if your computer systems have critical information stored on them, how will you recover when a hard drive crashes and all that data is lost? What some people forget is that the opposite of this equation is true as well. If you have a third car that happens to be a 20-year-old (nonclassic) junker, you

---

* A hot site is a place where you have computers standing by to do an immediate recovery of your environment.

probably will get only liability coverage on it. The reason for this is that you could live without that car if it were to be destroyed today. Spending hundreds of extra dollars a year to insure a $50 car just doesn't make sense. Likewise, if the computers that you are managing are in an environment in which you can do without them for a few days, do you really need hot-swappable, mirrored drives? Pick an appropriate level of protection for your environment.

You need to balance the cost of a particular backup implementation against the projected monetary loss of the outage from which it protects you. For example, assume that you are evaluating two backup choices. The first option involves sending copies of your backup volumes to an off-site vendor for storage at a cost of $100 a month. (I'm just making up numbers here.) The second option is an immediately available standby machine in another city that receives up-to-the-minute replication data from your production machine; let's say this option costs you $2000 a month.

Your company is located in Utopia where no natural disasters have ever occurred, your disks are all mirrored, and you have determined that a day's worth of downtime would cost only $100. Do you really want to spend $24,000 a year to protect against something that probably will never occur? If your building were blown up by terrorists, wouldn't the day-old off-site copies serve just as well? Your company would suffer an extra day or so of downtime, but you have already determined that this is affordable. The $1200 a year solution is probably much more appropriate for this environment.

However, are you protecting yourself from everything that you should be? Are you in an area that is prone to natural disasters and yet have no protection against that sort of event? Maybe you need to consider a different type of off-site storage. If you have a customer base that needs the data on your computers on a regular basis, have you provided for quick recovery in case of a failure? Perhaps you should be considering a hot site or multiple-site mirroring of your database servers. Table 2-1 is a good overview of the various levels of coverage. (Some of these analogies are a bit of a stretch, but I believe they illustrate the point.)

Table 2-1. Comparison Between Automobile Insurance and Computer Backups

	Automobile Insurance	Computer Backups
Minimum coverage	Collision and liability (just keeps you from losing your shirt if you run into someone).	Regular nightly backups (keeps you from losing your job when a disk drive dies)
Getting back exactly what you lost	Replacement cost coverage (would pay the cost of *replacing* the car).	Filesystem snapshot software Database transaction logs
Unexpected disasters	Comprehensive coverage (vandalism, acts of God, etc.).	Journaling filesystems Uninterruptable Power Supplies (UPS)

Table 2-1. Comparison Between Automobile Insurance and Computer Backups (continued)

	Automobile Insurance	Computer Backups
Get me driving now	Rental car coverage (you get a car if your car is in the shop due to an accident).	RAID Mirroring Using hot-swap drives High-availability (HA) system
Major disasters	Another company will pick up your policy and replace your car if both your car and your insurance company are destroyed in an earthquake. (OK, it's a stretch, I know.)	Sending copies of your backup volumes to off-site storage, in case both your computer room and media library are destroyed Sending your backups via a dedicated network to a large storage system at your off-site storage vendor
Maximum protection	The insurance company not only agrees to the conditions listed earlier, but also agrees to store another car of the same model in another state that you can use at any time if all cars in your state are destroyed. (Whoa, I'm *really* out there, now!)	Real-time mirroring to a hot-swappable system at another site of yours Sending your backups via either network or courier to a hot-site vendor

The Impossible Job That No One Wants

Would anyone reading this book say that losing data is OK? I don't believe so. Then why do we treat backups so lightly? Sometimes I feel like Rodney Dangerfield when I'm arguing for better backups—"I tell ya, I don't get no respect, no respect." Backups often aren't considered during systems design. When a new server is purchased, does anyone ask for the impact on the current backup methodology? Some IS departments do not even have control over the purchase of new systems, since they are sometimes bought by other cost centers. Have you ever tried to explain to another department manager why his 300-gigabyte database server isn't going to get backed up to the standalone, uncompressed 2-gigabyte DDS drive that came with it? (I have!)

Another often-overlooked issue is backup personnel. Have you ever tried to find the person in charge of backups? It's often an extra duty that gets passed around, in a manner similar to the way my sister and brother and I argued over whose turn it was to wash the dishes. If you are lucky enough to have a dedicated person, it's usually the most junior person that you have. I know, because that's how I got my first Unix job. In fact, that's how *many* people get their first Unix jobs. How can we give such a low priority to something so important? Perhaps we should change that. Will one book change this long-standing hiring tradition? Probably not, but maybe it will help. At the very least, if the person in charge of backups has this book, that person has a complete guide to accomplishing the immense task that lies ahead.

What's the big deal, you say? With modern computer systems and reliable disk drives, why are backups still so important? Because computers still go down, that's why. Companies also are placing more reliance than ever on computers functioning reliably. I don't care how good your Unix vendor is or how reliable your disk drives are or even if you have Dogbert himself as your network administrator, systems go down. Murphy's law thrives in computer systems. Not only will your computer systems go down occasionally, they will do so at the time most inconvenient to you and your customers. At that moment, and that moment will come, it is the job of the backup person to replace the data on the disk or disks that have stopped the show. "How long will it take?" is a typical question. The only acceptable response is "it's already done."

Who wants to be the person who messed up the restore and caused the customer database to be offline for three extra hours? Who wants to be the person who has to send a memo to the entire company saying that any purchase orders entered in the last two days have to be reentered? Who wants to be the person who has that in mind every day, as she is checking the results of last night's backups? If you do your job well and no data is lost, then you are just doing what you're supposed to do. If you mess up, you're in big trouble. Who wants that job? No one, that's who.

You're reading this book because you've got the impossible job that nobody wants. Whether you've been doing it for a while or have just started down the backup road, you can see that the task that lies ahead is an immense one. The volume of data is tremendous, the nature of the data changes constantly, and the utilities at your disposal never seem to be up to the job. I know because I've been there. I've spent months trying to implement "solutions" from operating systems and database products that weren't ready. I've seen companies spend money on expensive commercial utilities, only to buy the wrong utility for their application. I've watched newer and bigger servers roll in the door, without a single backup drive among them. I've also spent long nights and weekends in computer rooms trying to recover data in a "reasonable" amount of time. Unfortunately, "reasonable" is defined by the end user who has no idea how difficult this job is.

There are now solutions to almost every backup problem out there. If you run a small shop with just a few systems, all of which are the same operating system, there's a solution for you. If you work in a huge shop with hundreds of boxes with various flavors of Unix and NT or just a few multiterabyte databases, there's a solution for you. The biggest part of the problem is misinformation. Most people simply do not know what is available, so they either suffer without a solution or settle for an inferior one—usually the one with the best salesperson. This book will describe the solutions currently available to you and then show you how to choose the right solution for your environment.

The six important questions that you have to ask yourself (and others) continually are why, what, when, where, who, and how.

Why?

Why are you protecting yourself against disaster? Does it really matter if you lose data? What will the losses be?

What?

What are you going to back up, the entire box or just selected filesystems? What else, besides normal filesystems, should be included in a backup?

When?

When is the best time to back up your system? How often should you do a full backup? When should you do an incremental backup?

Where?

Where will the backup occur? Where is the best place to store the backup volumes?

Who?

Who is going to provide the hardware, software, and installation services to put this system together?

How?

How are you going to accomplish it? There are a number of different ways to ensure yourself against loss. Investigate the different methods, such as off-site storage, replication, mirroring, RAID, and the various levels of protection each of these provides. (Each of these topics is covered in detail in later sections of this book.)

Deciding What to Back Up

Experience shows that one of the most common causes of data loss is that the lost data was never configured to be backed up. The decision of *what* to back up is an important one.

Plan for the Worst

When trying to decide what files to include in your backups, take the most pessimistic technical person in your company out to lunch. In fact, get a few of them together. Ask them to come up with scenarios that you should protect against. Use these scenarios in deciding what should be included, and they will help you plan the "how" section as well. Ask your guests, "What are the absolute worst scenarios that could cause data loss?" Here are some possible answers:

- An entire system catches fire and melts to the ground, leaving an unrecognizable mass of molten metal and blackened, smoking plastic.

- Since this machine was so important, you, of course, had it replicated to another node right next to it. Of course, that machine catches fire right along with this one.

- You have a centralized server that controls all backups and keeps a record of backup volume locations and what files are on what volumes, and so on. The server that blew up sits right next to this "backup server," and the intense heat took this system with it.

- The disastrous chain reaction continues, taking out your DHCP server, NIS master server, NFS home directory server, NFS application server, and the database server where you house the inventory of all your backup volumes with their respective locations. This computer also holds the telephone database listing all service agreements, vendor telephone numbers, and escalation procedures.

- You haven't memorized the number to your new off-site storage vendor yet, so it's taped to the wall next to your backup server. You realize, of course, that the flames just burnt that paper beyond recognition.

- All the flames set off the sprinkler system and water pours all over your backup volumes. Man, are you having a bad day . . .

What do you do if one of these scenarios actually happens? Do you even know where to start? Do you know:

- What volume was last night's backup on?

- Where you stored it?

- How to get in touch with the off-site storage vendor to retrieve the copies of your backup volumes?

- Once you find that out, will your server and network equipment be available to recover?

- Who you call to get replacement equipment at 2:00 A.M. on a Saturday?

- What the network looked like before all the wires melted?

First, you need to recover your backup server, since it has all the information you need. OK, so now you found the backup company's card in your wallet, and you've pulled back every volume they had. Since your media database is lost, how will you know which one has last night's backup on it? Time is wasting . . .

All right, you've combed through all the volumes, and you've found the one you need to restore the backup server. Through your skill, cunning, and plenty of help from tech support, you restore the thing. It's up and running. Now, how many disks were on the systems that blew up? What models were they? How were they partitioned? Weren't some of them striped together into bigger volumes, and weren't some of them mirroring one another? Where's that information stored? Do you even have a *df* output of what the filesystems looked like? Man, this is getting complicated . . .

Didn't you just install that big jumbo kernel patch last week on three of these systems? (You know, the one that stopped all those network broadcast storms that kept bringing your network down in the middle of the day.) You did make a backup of the kernel after you did that, didn't you? Of course, the patch also updated files all over the OS drive. You made a full backup, didn't you? How will you restore the root drive, anyway? Are you really going to go through the process of reinstalling the operating system, just so you can run the *restore* command and overwrite it again?

Filesystems aren't picky about size, as long as you make them big enough to hold the data that you restore to them, so it's not too hard to get those filesystems up and running. But what about the database? It was using raw partitions. You know it's going to be much pickier. It's going to want */dev/rdsk/c7t3d0s7* and */dev/dsk/ c8t3d0s7*, and */dev/dsk/c8t4d0s7* right were they where and partitioned just as they were before the disaster. They also need to be owned by the database user. Do you know which drives were owned by that user before the crash? Which disks were those again? If restoring the root drive included reinstalling the operating system, how will you know what UID the database user was?

It could happen.

 The catch-22 situations above are covered in Part IV.

Take an Inventory

Make sure you can access essential information in the event of a disaster.

Backups for your backups

Many companies have begun to centralize control of their backups, which I think is a good thing. However, once you centralize storage of all your backup information, you have a single point of failure for your entire backup plan. Restoring this server would be the first step in any multisystem outage. For things like media inventory, don't underestimate the value of an inventory printed on paper and stored off-site. That paper may just get you out of a catch-22. Given the single-point-of-failure factor, the recovery of your backup server should be the easiest and best-documented recovery that you have. You may even want to investigate creating a special *dump* or *tar* backup of that data to make it even easier to recover during a disaster.

What peripheral devices did you have?

Assuming you back up */dev* on a regular basis, you might have a list of all the device *names*, but do you know what models they are? If you have all Brand-X 2.9-gigabyte drives, then you have no problem, but many servers have a mixture of drives that were installed over time. You may have a collection of 1-GB, 2-GB, 2.01-GB, 2.1-GB, 2.9-GB, 4-GB, and 9-GB drives, all on the same system. Make sure that you are recording this in some way. Most Unix systems record this already, by the way, usually in the */var/adm/messages* file, so hopefully you're backing *that* up.

How were they partitioned?

This one can *really* get you, especially if you have to restore the root drive or a database drive. Both of these drives are typically partitioned with custom partitions that must be repartitioned exactly the same as before for a proper restore to occur. Typically, this partition information is not saved anywhere on the system, so you must do something special to record it. On a Solaris system, for example, you could run a *prtvtoc* on each drive, and save that to a file. There are scripts that capture much of this information; two of them—*SysAudit* and *SysInfo*—are covered in Chapter 4, *Free Backup Utilities*.

How were your volume managers configured?

There are a number of operating-system-specific volume managers out there such as Veritas Volume Manager, Solstice (Online) Disk Suite, and HP's Logical Volume Manager. How is yours configured? What devices are mirrored to what? How are your multidisk devices set up? Unbelievably, this information is not always captured by normal backup utilities. In fact, I used Logical Volume Manager for months before hearing about the *lvmcfgbackup* command. (*lvmcfgbackup* backs up the LVM's configuration information.) Sometimes if you have this properly documented, you may not need to restore at all. For example, if the operating system disk is crashed, you simply put the disks back the way they were and then rebuild the stripe in the same order, and the data should be intact. I've done this several times.

How are your databases set up?

I have seen many database outages. When I ask a database administrator (DBA) how her database was set up, the answer was almost always, "I'm not sure . . ." Find out this information, and record it up front.

Did you document how you set up NFS, NIS, DHCP, etc.?

Document, document, document! There are a hundred reasons to properly document things like this, and recovery from a disaster is one of them. Good documentation is definitely part of the backup plan. It should be regularly updated and available. No one should be standing around saying "I haven't set up NIS from scratch in years. How do you do that again? Has anyone seen my copy of O'Reilly's *NFS and NIS* book?" Actually, the best way to do this is to automate the creation of new servers. Take the time to write shell scripts that will install NIS, NFS, and *automounter*, and configure them for your environment. Put these together in a toolkit that gets run every time you create a new server. Better yet, see if your OS vendor has any products that automate new server installations, like Sun's Jumpstart or HP's Ignite-UX.

Do you have a plan for this?

The reason for describing the earlier horrible scenarios is so that you can start planning for them now. Don't wait until there's 20 feet of snow in your front yard before you start shopping for a snow shovel! It's going to snow; it's only a question of when. Take those pessimists out to lunch, and let them dream of the worst things that could happen, and then plan for them. Have a fully documented, step-by-step plan for the end of the computer world as you know it. Even if the plan needs a little modification when you actually have to use it, you will be glad you have a starting point. That will be a whole lot better than standing around saying, "What do we do now? Has anyone seen my resume?" (You did keep a hard copy of it, right?)

Know what's on your boxes!

The best insurance against almost any kind of loss is for the backup/recovery person to be familiar with the systems that he is protecting. If a particular server goes down, you should know immediately that it contains an Oracle database and should be running for those volumes. That way, the moment the server is ready for a restore, so are you. Become very involved in the installation of any new system or database. You should know what database platforms you are using and how they are set up. You should know about any new filesystems, databases, or systems. You need to be very familiar with every box, what it does, and what's on it. This information is vital, so that you can include any special backups for that type of system.

Are You Backing Up What You Think You're Backing Up?

I remember an administrator at a previous employer who used to say, "Are we getting this on tape?" He always said it with his trademark smirk, and it was his way of saying "Hi" to the backup guy. His question makes a point. There are some glo-

bal ways that you can approach backups that may drastically improve their effec-
tiveness. Before we examine whether to back up part or all of the system, let us
examine the common practice of using include lists and why they are dangerous.
Also, we will cover some of the ways that you can avoid using include lists. What
are include and exclude lists? Generically speaking, there are two ways to back up
a system:

*   You can tell your backup system to back up everything, except what is in an
    exclude list, for example:

    ```
    Include: *
    Exclude: /tmp /junk1 /junk2
    ```

*   You can tell your backup system to back up what is in an *include list,* for
    example:

    ```
    Include: /data1 /data2 /data3
    ```

Looking at these examples, ask yourself what happens when you create */data4*?
Someone has to remember to add it to the include list, or it will not be backed up.
This is a recipe for disaster. Unless you're the only one who adds filesystems and
you have perfect memory, there will always be a forgotten filesystem. As long as
there are other administrators and there is gray matter in your head, something
will get left out.

However, unless you're using a commercial backup utility, it takes a little effort to
say, "Back up everything." How do you make the list of what systems, filesystems,
and databases to back up? What you need to do is look at files like */etc/vfstab* (or
its equivalent on your operating system) and parse out a list of filesystems to back
up. You can then exclude any filesystems that are in any exclude lists that you
have.

Oracle has a similar file, called *oratab,* which lists all Oracle instances on your
server.[*] You can use this file to list all instances that need backing up. Unfortunately, Informix and Sybase databases have no such file unless you manually
make one. I do recommend making such a file for many reasons. It is much easier to standardize system startup and backups when you have such a file. If you
design your startup scripts so that a database does not get started unless it is in
this file, then you can be reasonably sure that any databases that anyone cares
about will be in this file. This means, of course, that any important databases will
be backed up without any manual intervention from you. It also means that you
can use the same Informix and Sybase startup scripts on every system, instead of
having to hardcode each database's name into the startup scripts.

---

[*] You can install an Oracle instance without putting it in this file. However, that instance will not get
started when the system reboots. This usually means that the DBA will take the time to put it in this file.
More on that in Chapter 15, *Oracle Backup & Recovery.*

How do you know what *systems* to back up? Although I never got around to it, one of the scripts I always wanted to write was a script that monitored the various host databases, looking for new systems. I wanted to get a complete list of all hosts from */etc/hosts*, Domain Name System (DNS), and Network Information System (NIS), and compare it against a master list. Once I found a new IP address, I would try to determine if the new IP address was alive. If it was alive, that would mean that there was a new host that possibly needed backing up. This would be an invaluable script, and would make sure that there aren't any new systems on the network that the backups don't know about. Once you found a new IP address, you could use *queso* to determine what kind of system it is. *queso* gets its name from an abbreviated Spanish phrase that means "What operating system are you?" It sends a malformed TCP packet to the IP address, and the address's response to that packet reveals which operating system it is based on. (*queso* is covered in Chapter 4.)

Back Up All or Part of the System?

Assuming you've covered things that are not covered by normal system backups, you are now in a position to decide whether you are going to back up your entire systems or just selected filesystems from each system. These are definitely two different schools of thought. As far as I'm concerned, there are too many gotchas in the selected-filesystem option. Backing up everything is easier and safer than backing up from a list. You will find that most books stop right there and say "It's best to back up everything, but most people do something else." You will not see those words here. I think that not backing up everything is very dangerous. Consider the following comparison between the two methods.

Backing up only selected filesystems

Save media space and network traffic

The first argument that is typically stated as a plus to the selected-filesystem method is that you have to back up less data. People of this school recommend having two groups of backups, operating system data and regular data. The idea is that the operating system backups would be performed less often. Some would even recommend that they be performed only when you have a significant change, like an operating system upgrade, patch installation, or kernel rebuild. You would then back up your "regular" data daily.

The first problem with this argument is that it is outdated; just look at the size of the typical modern system. The operating system/data ratio is now significantly heavy on the data side. You won't be saving much space or network traffic by not backing up the OS even on your full backups. When you consider incremental backups, the ratio gets even smaller. Operating system partitions will have almost nothing of size that would be included in an incremental backup, unless it's something important that should be backed up! This includes things like */etc/passwd, /etc/hosts, syslog, /var/adm/messages*, and any other files that would be helpful if you lost the operating system. Filesystem swap is arguably the only completely worthless information that could be on the OS disk, and it can be excluded with proper use of an exclude list.

Harder to administer

Proponents of piecemeal backup would say that you can include important files like the preceding ones in a special backup. The problem with that is that it is so much more difficult than backing up everything. Assuming you use exclude lists for the regular backups (as discussed before), you have to remember to do manual backups every time you do something major. Also, there is the matter of files like */etc/passwd* that change every day. You need to back them up, and they are included in the filesystems that you've excluded. That means you have to do something *special* for them. *Special is bad.*

Easier to split up between volumes

One of the very few things that could be considered a plus is that if you split up your filesystems into multiple backups, it is easier to split them between multiple volumes. If a *dump* of your system will not fit on one volume, then it is easier to automate it by splitting it into two different include lists. However, in order to take advantage of this, you will have to use include lists rather than exclude lists; then you are subject to their limitations discussed earlier. I also suggest that if you have systems that are larger than your backup drives, it is a good time to consider a commercial backup utility.

Easier to write a script to do it than to parse out the /etc/vfstab or /etc/oratab

This one is hard to argue against. However, if you do take the time to do it right the first time, you never need to mess with the include lists again. This reminds me of another favorite phrase of mine, "Never time to do it right, always time to do it over." Take the time to do it right the first time.

The worst that happens? You overlook something!

In this scenario, the biggest benefits are that you save some time spent scripting up front, as well as a few bytes of network traffic. The worst possible side effect is that you overlook the filesystem that contained your boss's budget sheet that just got deleted.

Backing up the entire system

Complete automation

Once you go through the trouble of creating a script or program that works, you just need to monitor its logs. You can rest easy at night knowing that all your data is being backed up.

The worst thing that happens? You lose a friend in the network department

> You may increase your network traffic by a few percentage points, and the people looking out after the wires might not like that. (That is, of course, until you restore the server where they keep their DNS source database.)

Backing up selected filesystems is one of the most common mistakes that I find when evaluating a backup configuration. It is a very easy trap to fall into, because of the time it saves you up front. Until you've been bitten though, you may not know how much danger you are in. If your backup setup uses include lists, I hope that this discussion convinces you to rethink that decision.

Deciding When to Back Up

This might appear to be the most straightforward topic. Everybody backs up their system every night, right? What's the big deal? Actually, this could more aptly be titled "What levels do I run when?" It's always a big question. How often do you run a full backup? How often do you run incremental backups? Do you run various levels of incrementals that back up just today's changes or continuous incremental backups that back up everything since the last full backup? Everyone has his own answers to these questions. The only thing that is a definite is that there should be *at least* some level of incremental backup every night. Before any further discussion on the topic, let's define some terms.

Backup Levels

The following are various backup levels:

Level 0
> A full backup.

Level 1
> An incremental backup that backs up everything that has changed since the last level 0 backup.

Levels 2–9
> Each level backs up whatever has changed since the last backup of the next lowest level, e.g., a level 2 backs up everything that changed since a level 1, or since a level 0, if there is no level 1.

Incremental
> Usually, a backup that behaves like levels 1–9. Also used by some products to mean the same as a level 1, backing up all changes since a level 0.

Differential
> A type of "incremental" backup, in the generic sense, which backs up only what has changed since the last differential. This term is usually found in soft-

ware that does not use the numbered level concept. Such software would use the terms "full," "incremental," and "differential." In this type of setup, you would use a full backup to get the entire system, an occasional incremental to get all changes since that full backup, and differentials each night to catch only the changes since the previous day. In some backup products, repeated level 9s will act like differential backups.

It should be noted that not all backup products agree on these terms. Some use the term "incremental" to refer to what is described here as "differential." They may then use the term "cumulative incremental" to describe an incremental backup that backs up all changes since the last level 0. Make sure you become familiar with your product's terminology.

A question that I am often asked is, "You want me to back up every night?" What they really mean is, "Even on the weekend?" Nobody's working on the weekend, right? *Right* . . . except for your noisiest customer last weekend. You know the customer I'm talking about: the one who calls your boss instead of the help desk when there's a problem. And if your boss isn't in or doesn't fix the problem fast enough, this customer will call your boss's boss. Well, last weekend this customer was really behind so she spent the entire weekend at work, working around the clock on next year's budget. She finally got it straightened out at about 1:00 A.M. Monday. At around 4:00 A.M., the disk where her home directory resides stopped working. (Everything dies Monday morning, doesn't it?) You haven't run a backup since Friday night. Your phone is ringing, and it's your boss. Any guesses as to what he wants to talk to you about? Do *you* want to be the one to tell this customer that you could have saved her file, but you don't run backups on the weekend?

Which Levels Do You Run and When?

There are several schools of thought on this one. The following are some suggested backup schedules.

Weekly schedule: all full (level 0) backups

Example 2-1 contains a backup schedule for the paranoid (not that paranoid is a bad thing). You perform a level 0 backup every day onto a separate volume. (Please don't overwrite yesterday's good level 0 backup with today's possibly corrupt level 0 backup!) If your system is really small, then this schedule might work for you. If you have systems of any reasonable size, though, this schedule will not be very scalable. It's also really not that necessary with today's commercial backup software systems.

Example 2-1. All Full Backups

Sunday	Monday	Tuesday	Wednesday	Thursday	Friday	Saturday
0	0	0	0	0	0	0

Weekly schedule: weekly full, daily level 1s

The advantage to the schedule in Example 2-2 is that throughout most of the week you would need to restore only two volumes—the level 0 and the most recent level 1. This is because each level 1 will back up all changes since the level 0 on Sunday. Then over the weekend you run a differential backup that catches all changes on Saturday, just in case your friend is working. Another advantage of this type of setup is that you get multiple copies of files that are changed early in the week. This is probably the best schedule to use if you are using simple utilities like *dump*, *tar*, or *cpio*, since they require you to do all the volume management. A two-volume restore is *much easier* than a six-volume restore—trust me!

Example 2-2. Weekly Full Backups, Daily Level 1s

Sunday	Monday	Tuesday	Wednesday	Thursday	Friday	Saturday
0	1	1	1	1	1	2

Weekly schedule: weekly full, daily leveled backups

The advantage of the schedule in Example 2-3 is that it takes less time and uses less media than the preceding schedule. There are two disadvantages to this plan. First, each changed file gets backed up only once, which leaves you very susceptible to data loss if you have any media failures. Second, you would need six volumes to do a full restore on Friday. If you're using a commercial backup utility, the latter is really not a problem, though, since these utilities do all the volume management for you.

Example 2-3. Weekly Full Backups, Daily Leveled Backups

Sunday	Monday	Tuesday	Wednesday	Thursday	Friday	Saturday
0	1	2	3	4	5	6

Weekly schedule: monthly full, daily Tower of Hanoi incrementals

One of the most interesting ideas that I've seen is called the *Tower of Hanoi* backup plan. It's based on an ancient mathematical progression puzzle by that name. The game consists of three pegs and a number of different sized rings inserted onto those pegs. A ring may not be placed on top of a ring with a smaller radius. The goal of the game is to move all of the rings from the first peg to the third peg, using the second peg for temporary storage when needed.[*]

One of the goals of most backup schedules is to get changed files on more than one volume, while reducing total volume usage. The Tower of Hanoi (TOH) accomplishes this better than any other schedule. If you use a TOH progression for your backup levels, most changed files will get backed up twice—but only twice. Here are two different versions of the progression. (They're related to the number of rings on the three pegs, by the way.)

```
0 3 2 5 4 7 6 9 8 9
0 3 2 4 3 5 4 6 5 7 6 8 7 9 8
```

The mathematical progressions above are actually pretty easy. Each consists of two interleaved series of numbers (e.g. 0 2 3 4 5 6 7 8 9 interleaved with 3 4 5 6 7 8 9). Let's put this with some days to explain how it works. Please refer to Example 2-4.

Example 2-4. Basic Tower of Hanoi Schedule

Monday	Tuesday	Wednesday	Thursday	Friday	Saturday	Sunday
3	2	5	4	7	6	0

It starts with a level 0 (full) on Monday. Suppose that a file is changed on Tuesday. The level 3 on Tuesday would back up everything since the level 0, so that changed file would be included on Tuesday's backup. Suppose that on Wednesday we change another file. Then on Wednesday night, the level 2 backup must look for a level that is lower, right? The level 3 on Tuesday is not lower, so it will reference the level 0 also. So the file that was changed on Tuesday, as well as the file that was changed on Wednesday, gets backed up again. On Thursday, the level 5 will back up just what changed that day, since it will reference the level 2 on Wednesday. But on Friday, the level 4 will not reference the level 5 on Thursday; it will reference the level 2 on Wednesday.

Note that the file that changed on Wednesday was backed up only once. To get around this problem, we use a modified TOH progression, dropping down to a level 1 backup each week, as shown in Example 2-5.

Example 2-5. Monthly Tower of Hanoi Schedule

Su	Mo	Tu	We	Th	Fr	Sa	Su	Mo	Tu	We	Th	Fr	Sa	Su	Mo	Tu	We	Th	Fr	Sa	Su	Mo	Tu	We	Th	Fr	Sa
0	3	2	5	4	7	6	1	3	2	5	4	7	6	1	3	2	5	4	7	6	1	3	2	5	4	7	6

---

[*] For a complete history of the game and a URL where you can play it on the Web, see *http://www.math. toronto.edu/mathnet/games/towers.html*.

If it doesn't confuse you and your backup methodology,* I recommend the schedule depicted in Example 2-5. Each Sunday, you will get a complete incremental backup of everything that has changed since the monthly full backup. During the rest of the week, every changed file gets backed up twice—except for Wednesday's files. This protects you from media failure better than any of the schedules mentioned previously. You will need more than one volume to do a full restore, of course, but this is not a problem if you have a sophisticated backup utility with volume management.

"In the Middle of the Night . . ."

This phrase from the Billy Joel song indicates the usual best time to do backups. Backups should be scheduled in such a way that they do not run during normal business hours. Sometimes you cannot avoid it, but it should not be a regular occurrence. There are two main reasons for this:

Integrity

> Unless you work in a 24×7 shop, nighttime is the time when the files are the most stable. (Of course, there could be batch jobs running that are manipulating data as well, so not all files will be stable.) If you are backing up during the day, then files are changing and probably also are open. Open files are more difficult to back up. Some backup packages handle open files better than others, but some cannot back them up at all. Also, if the file is changing throughout the day, you will not be sure what version you actually get on your backup.

Speed

> Another reason for not doing backups during the day is that the network is much busier, hence slower, during the day. The throughput of your backups will slow significantly when your network is being used for normal traffic. If this is a problem at night as well, you might consider using a special network just for your backups. Doing backups during the day can significantly affect the speed of your other applications, and it is not good practice to regularly slow down your systems while people are using them.

---

* This is always the case for any recommendation in this book. If it confuses you or your backup methodology, it's not good! If your backups confuse you, you don't even want to try to restore! Always Keep It Simple SA . . . (K.I.S.S.).

Of course, in today's global and Internet economy, "night" is relative. If you are in a shop in which the systems are accessed 24×7, you will have to do things quite differently. You may want to look at Chapter 5, *Commercial Backup Utilities* to see what commercial products are doing to help meet this type of challenge.

Deciding How to Back Up

Once you've decided *when* you're going to back up, you have to decide *how* you are going to back up the data. But first, look at what types of problems you are protecting yourself from.

Be Ready for Anything: Ten Types of Disasters

As stated earlier, how you want to do your restores determines how you want to do your backups. One of the questions that you must ask yourself is, "What are you going to protect yourself from?" Are the users in your environment all "power users" who use their computers intelligently and never make dumb mistakes? Would your company lose a lot of essential data if the files on your users' PCs are accidentally deleted? If a hurricane takes out your whole company, would it be able to continue doing business? Make sure that you are aware of all the potential causes for data loss, then make sure your backup methods are prepared for all of them from which you want to protect yourself. The most exhaustive list of potential causes of data loss that I have seen was in another O'Reilly book called *Practical Unix and Internet Security*, by Simson Garfinkel and Gene Spafford. Their list, with my comments attached, follows:

User error

    This has been, by far, the biggest percentage of restores in every environment that I have seen. "Hey, I was sklocking my flambality file, and I accidentally pressed the jankle button. Can you restore it, *please*?" This one is pretty easy, right? What about the common question: "Can you restore it as of about an hour ago?" There is one backup method that can handle this. There are systems that come with snapshot technology built in. There is at least one software product that can give you this capability on a standard Unix box. Snapshots, which are discussed in Chapter 19, give you the ability to do what users already think you're doing—backing the servers up all day, as often as you want. You can do this with almost no CPU overhead if you have the right software solution.

System-staff error

>   This is less common than user error (unless your users have root), but when it happens, oh boy, does it happen! What happens when you *newfs* your Informix raw device or delete a user's home directory? These restores need to go *really fast*, since they're your fault. As far as protecting yourself from this type of error, the same is true here as for user errors—either typical nightly backups or snapshots can protect you from this.

It Does Have a Happy Ending (Almost)

I never had a server melt down to nothing, but I have lost entire servers, configuration and all. Luckily, I had their configuration saved. I also remember a time when we lost the server that contained our Informix database that listed all data about our volumes and their locations. I remember saying "How do I get out of this one?" Luckily, we sent a printout of each day's volumes along with our off-site shipment. I asked for all of that day's volumes, along with that printout. *Whew!*

What's that? You think that I'm a mean and vicious person who just gave you nightmares for the next week? You have no idea how you would get that information if you needed it? You say that you're going to lose sleep for a while? Good! Better to have lost sleep than lost data. One of the main purposes of this book is to scare you. A complacent person in charge of backups is a dangerous thing. The preceding scenario includes several catch-22 situations and wipes out data that is not normally caught by standard backups.

Hardware failure

>   Most books talk about protecting yourself from hardware failure, but they usually don't mention that hardware failure can come in two forms: disk drive failure and system-wide failure. It is important to mention this, because it takes two entirely different methods to protect yourself from these failures. Many people do not take this into consideration when planning their data protection plan. For example, I have often heard the phrase "I thought that disk was mirrored!" when a filesystem is corrupted by a system panic. Mirroring does not protect you from a system-wide failure. As a friend used to say, if the loose electrons floating around your system decide to corrupt a filesystem when your system goes down, "mirroring only makes the corruption more efficient." Snapshots, however, will not protect you from hardware failure—unless you have the snapshot on a backup volume.

"How Were the Backups Last Night?"

I suppose I've heard thousands of administrator-error horror stories, like people typing `rm -r /*` . I remember a guy who wanted to delete a junk file in */bin* called *?*&(&^JI($SF))FS%$#T*, or something like that. He typed `rm /bin/?*`. But there's one story that I witnessed firsthand that still makes me laugh.

A consultant was given the task of cleaning up our home directories. Apparently, my company was very good about deleting logins for people who had left the company, but we weren't very good about deleting their home directories. The consultant wrote a program that basically did the following:

1. *cd* into */home1*

2. *find*, looking for directories that did not match an entry in the password file and were not owned by root

3. *rm –r* that directory

Each user's home directory was located under a directory that was the first letter of her login. For example, the home directory for *cpreston* was in */home1/ c/cpreston*. The scenario went something like this. The idea was that */home1/ c* would be owned by root and thus would not be deleted. Unfortunately, over the years, an administrator or two would *cd* into */home1/c/cpreston* and try to correct an ownership problem. To do that, the administrator would type *chown cpreston .*. Well, if you've ever done that as root, you know that *.** includes *..*, which in this case would be */home1/c*. Thus, the */home1/c* ends up being owned by me!

The consultant did not foresee this and so would interpret */home1/c* as a user's home directory and look for the user called "c" in the password file. Of course, there was no such user, so the program said `rm -r /home1/c`. I'm not sure when my friend realized what was happening, but I do remember being on my way out the door and getting a weird phone call. "How were the backups of */home1* last night?" my friend asked—very sheepishly and very mysteriously. "Fine, as always," was my response, "Why?" There's something beautiful about the power that the backup guy yields at that magic moment when someone *really* needs some files restored. Up to that point, you're the guy who comes in early and stays late, watching the backup drives spin. In one moment, you're transformed into the most important person they know! *Cool.*

Disk drive failure

Protecting your systems from disk drive failure is relatively simple now. Your only decision is how safe you want to be. Mirroring, often referred to as RAID 1, offers the best protection, but it doubles the cost of your initial drive and controller hardware investment. That is why most people choose one of the other levels of RAID (Redundant Arrays of Independent Disks), the most popular being RAID 5. (RAID 5 volumes protect against the loss of a single drive by calculating and storing parity information on each drive.) All RAID levels are covered in detail in Chapter 6, *High Availability.*

System-wide failure

Most of the protection against system-wide failure comes from good system administration procedures. Document your systems properly. Use your system logs and any other monitoring methods you have at your disposal to watch your systems closely. Respond to messages about bad disks, controllers, CPUs, and memory. Warnings about hardware failures are your chance to correct problems before they cause major disasters. Another method of protecting yourself is to use a journaling filesystem. Journaling treats the filesystem much like a database, keeping track of committed and partially committed writes to the filesystem. When a system is coming up, a journaling filesystem can roll back partially committed writes, thus "uncorrupting" the filesystem. Journalling filesystems are covered in detail in Chapter 6.

Software failure

Protecting yourself from software failure can be difficult. Operating system bugs, database bugs, and system management software bugs can all cause data loss. Once again, the degree to which you protect yourself from these types of failures depends on which type of backups you use. Taking frequent snapshots is the only way to truly protect yourself from losing data, possibly a lot of data, from software failure.

Electronic break-ins, vandalism, and theft

These three causes of data loss are really beyond the scope of this book, but their impact on your system is not. If you do lose data due to any one of these, it's really no different from any other type of data loss. If you want to really protect yourself from losing data in this manner, I highly recommend reading the book from which I borrowed this list, *Practical Unix and Internet Security.*

Natural disasters

Are you prepared for a hurricane, tornado, earthquake, or flood? If you're not, you're not alone. Imagine that your entire state was wiped out. If you are using off-site storage, is their facility close to you? Is it prepared to handle whatever type of natural disasters occur in your area? For example, if your office is in a flood zone, does your data storage company store your backups on the first floor? If they're in the flood zone as well, then your data can be lost in one good rain. If you really want to ensure yourself against a major natural disaster, then you should explore real-time, off-site storage at a remote location, discussed later in this chapter.

Other disasters

I remember when we used to test our disaster recovery plan at one company. We would pretend that some sort of truck blew up on the street that ran by our data center. The plan was to recover to an alternate building. This would mean that we would have to have off-site storage of media and an alternate site that was prepared to accommodate all our systems. A good way to do this is to separate your production and development systems and place them in different buildings. The development systems can then take the production systems' place, if the production systems are damaged or if power is interrupted to the production building.

Archival information

It is a terrible thing to realize that a very important but rarely used file is missing. It is even more terrible indeed to find out that it has been gone longer than your retention cycle. For example, you keep your backups for only three months, after which you reuse the oldest volume, overwriting any backups that are on that volume. If that is the case, then any files that have been missing for more than three months are *impossible* to recover. No matter how insistent the user is about how important the files are, no matter how many calls he makes to your supervisors, you will *never* be able to restore the files. That is why you should archive your volumes on a regular basis. A normal practice is to set aside one full backup each month for a few years. How many years is up to you. If you're going to keep your archives for a long time, make sure you read the sidebar called "Are You Keeping Your Archives Too Long?"

High Availability Versus Disaster Recoverability

These two goals do *not* automatically go hand in hand. I'll define both terms to explain what I mean:

High availability

High availability (HA) is your company's ability, in the event of an essential system outage, to provide continuous computer service to those who need it. Techniques such as redundant power supplies, redundant controllers, RAID, and hot-standby systems are the building blocks for today's high-availability systems. Most of these systems are based on mirroring disks between two systems that share a common hostname. If the primary system goes down, the other system takes over, providing continuous service to the end user. Most high-availability systems are built upon the idea of having these two systems sitting right next to each other, although HA across a LAN/WAN is becoming more commonplace every day.

Are You Keeping Your Archives Too Long?

Most states have laws that govern how long certain types of documentation are allowed to be kept in a company's files. For example, a state may say that your personnel department can keep disciplinary paperwork for only two years. If an employee believes that her chances for a promotion are reduced because of a disciplinary action that is more than two years old, she can sue for damages. Many lawsuits have been filed based on these laws.

What happens when the disciplinary action "paperwork" is actually a file on someone's computer? The laws extend to the computers too, and the files must be deleted. But what if that file is on an archive volume that is being kept forever? Many companies have backup policies that dictate that one volume per system per year is kept "forever." In recent years, some companies have lost lawsuits because of policies like this.

The only way around this is to exclude from regular backups any directories that contain this type of information and archive them using a different schedule that conforms to the document retention laws of your state. I admit this is a pain. You will never read that I think that doing something special for anything is a good thing, but in these litigious times, this one should not be overlooked.

Disaster recoverability

Disaster recoverability is your company's ability to recover from a major disaster, such as an earthquake or fire, that destroys a large portion of your network. In order to recover from a disaster such as this, you need to have a plan that includes backup systems at another site. You also need to have a full set of backups stored at an off-site location. You would then take those volumes and use them to restore the backup systems until they look like your original network. There are many variations on this theme, but this is a basic plan.

As you can see, your ability to provide continuous service in the event of a system outage does not necessarily reflect your ability to recover from a major disaster. A major disaster would destroy both systems of a highly available pair. Hopefully this will not always be the case. (If you are interested in having a highly available, disaster-resistant network, check out Chapter 6.)

It is possible to have some level of disaster recoverability *and* high availability. When trying to decide between the two, consider them analogous to an investment portfolio. Any good financial adviser will tell you that the first thing you should do is to save up three to nine months of salary and have it in a liquid form so that it is immediately available. This would be your emergency fund. That is why it is kept liquid, so you can get to the money easily in an emergency. If you immediately start putting all your savings into a retirement plan, then you may suffer a large penalty if you need it in an emergency.

A basic disaster recovery plan is essential and should be the first thing that you plan for outside of normal backups. If your entire building is destroyed by fire, who cares that you had a dual-host, fail-over, fault-tolerant NFS server? You will sustain an irretrievable data loss. All records of your company's entire existence will be destroyed. Once you have protected yourself from that by *at least* storing a set of archive volumes at an alternate location, you can start considering a high-availability system—if it makes good business sense for your company.

Automate Your Backup

If you work in a shop with a modest budget, you probably looked at this heading and said, "Sure, if I could afford it." Although automation that involves expensive jukeboxes and autochangers is nice, that is not the type of automation I am talking about. There are two types of automation. One type allows your backups to complete an entire cycle without requiring any manual intervention from you, such as ejecting and loading new volumes. This type of automation can make things much easier but can also make them much more expensive. If you can't afford it, a less expensive alternative is to have your backup system notify you when you need to do something manually. At the very least, it should notify you if you need (or forgot) to change a volume. If things aren't going right, you need to know. Too many times people look at their backup logs only when they need to do a restore. That's when they find out that their backups have failed for days or weeks. A slightly intelligent backup could email you or page you if things don't go the way you expect them to go.

The second type of automation is actually much more important. This type of automation refers to how your backups "think." Your backup process should know what to back up without your telling it. If a DBA installs a new database, your backups should know about it. If a system administrator installs a new file-system, your backups should automatically include it. This is the type of automation that is essential to safe backups. A good backup system should not depend on a human brain to remember to do something.

Plan for Expansion

Another common problem happens as a backup system grows over time. What works for one or two boxes doesn't necessarily work for 200. As the volume of data grows, the need for a standardized backup script becomes greater and greater. This is a problem because most administrators, as they are writing their shell script to back up five or six boxes, do not think ahead to the time when there may be many more. I can remember my early days as the backup guy. I had 10 or 11 systems, and the "monster" was an Ultrix box. It was "huge," we said in those days. (It was almost 8 gigabytes!) The smallest tape drive we had was a 10-GB (with compression) Exabyte. We used the big 10-GB tape drive for the 8-GB system. We had what I considered to be a pretty good in-house backup script that worked without modification for two years.

Then came the HPs. The *smallest* system was 20 GB, and the biggest was much bigger than that. But these big systems came with this little 2-GB (6 with compression) DDS drive. Our backup script author never dreamed of a system that was bigger than a tape. One day I woke up, and our system was broken. I then spent months and months hacking up that shell script to support splitting the filesystem into two tapes. Eventually I gave up and bought a commercial product. My point is that if I had thought of that ahead of time, I might have been able to overcome the limitation without losing so much sleep.

When you are designing your backup system—or your computer room, for that matter—plan on your systems getting bigger and more numerous. Plan for what you will do when that happens—trust me, it *will* happen. It will be much better for your mental health (not to mention job security) if you can foresee the inevitable and plan for it when you design the system the first time. Your backup system is something that should be done right the first time. And if you spend a little time dreaming about how to break it *before* you design it, you can save yourself a lot of money in antacids and sleeping pills.

Don't Forget About mtime, atime, and ctime

Unix records three different times for each file. The first is *mtime*, or modification time. The *mtime* value is changed whenever the contents of the file have changed, such as when you add lines to a log file. The second is *atime*, or access time. The *atime* value is changed whenever the file is accessed, such as when a script is run or a document is read. The last is *ctime*, or change time. The *ctime* value is updated whenever the attributes of the file, such as its permissions or ownership, are changed.

Administrators use *ctime* to look for hackers, since they may change permissions of a file to try to exploit your system. Administrators also monitor *atime* to look for large files that have not been accessed for a long time. (Such files can be archived and deleted.)

Backups change atime

You may be wondering what this has to do with backups. You need to understand that any backup utility that backs up via the filesystem will modify *atime* as it reads the file to back it up. Almost all commercial utilities, as well as *tar, cpio,* and *dd,* have this feature. *dump* reads the filesystem via the raw device, so it does not change *atime.*

The atime can be reset—with a penalty

A backup program can look at a file's *atime* before it backs it up. After it backs the file up, the *atime* obviously will have changed. It then can use the *utime* system call to reset *atime* to its original value. However, changing *atime* is considered an attribute change, which means that it changes *ctime.* This means that when you use a utility like *cpio* or *gtar* that can reset *atime,* you change *ctime* on every file that it backs up. If you have a system that is watching for *ctime* changes, it will think that it's found a hacker for sure!

Make sure that you understand how your utility handles this issue.

Keep It Simple, SA

K.I.S.S. Have you seen this acronym before? It applies double or triple to backups. The more complicated your backup scheme is, the more likely it is to fail. If you do not understand it, you cannot implement it. Remember this every time you consider adding a new bell or whistle to your backup system. Every change puts your data at risk. Also, every change you make might make your backup system that much more complex—and more difficult to explain to the new backup person. One of the heads of support for a commercial backup product said that he sees the same thing over and over again. One person gets to know the software really well, and writes various scripts to automate this and that. Backups become a well-oiled machine—until they are turned over to the trainee. The trainee doesn't understand all the bells and whistles, and things start breaking. All of a sudden, your data is in danger. Keep that in mind the next time you think about adding some cool new feature to your backup script.

This next comment also relates to the previous section about "thinking big." One of the common judgment errors is to not automate in the beginning. It's so much easier to just put a hardcoded include list in a file somewhere or put it in the *cron* entry itself. However, what that creates is many different backup methods. If each box has its own special customized backup system, it is very hard to monitor your backups and explain them to the new person.

Remember, special is bad. Just keep saying it over and over again until you believe it.

It's not such a big deal when you have two or three systems, but it is when you grow to 200 systems. If you have to remember every system's idiosyncrasies every time you look at your logs, things will inevitably get out of control. Exceptions for each system also can mean that things get overlooked. Do you remember that nine months ago you excluded */home** on *apollo*? I hope so, if *apollo* just became your primary NFS server, and it now has seven home directories.

If you cannot explain your backups to a stranger in less than a few hours, then things are probably too complex. You should look at implementing things like centralized logging, standardized backup scripts, and some level of automation.

Storing Your Backups

It doesn't do any good to make really good backups, only to have your backup volumes destroyed, lost, or misplaced. You need to have a well-defined process for storing your media.

Storage in General

If you've read this far, you know that I consider your backups to be very important. If your backups are important, then isn't the media on which they reside just as important? That goes without saying, right? Well, you'd never know it from most volume "libraries." Volume "piles" is probably a more accurate term. How many computer rooms have you seen that have volumes spread out all over the place? They get stacked, piled, fall behind the systems, and a DLT cartridge works really well as a coaster for a coffee mug. (We wouldn't want to get any coffee rings on the new server, right?)

Have you ever really needed a volume and couldn't find it? I've been there. It's a horrible feeling to know that you've got the file on a volume, but can't find the darn volume! Why, then, do we treat our backup volumes like so much dirty laundry? Organize your backup volumes! Label them, catalog them, give them unique names or numbers, and put them in some sort of logical order in some sort of storage container. Do it, or the backup demon will come to haunt you!

Your ability to perform a large recovery quickly is directly related to how well organized your media is.

On-Site Storage

What about that media cabinet that you're using for your on-site volume storage? You don't have one, you say? You're using a file cabinet, you say? Well, use something, but if you can afford it, there are a number of companies that make storage containers for media. They also make cabinets that can withstand fire. Spend the money—you'll be glad you did. Doing a restore is so much less stressful when you can find the volume with no problem. Remember, though, that fireproof does not mean heat-proof. These types of media safes are meant to withstand brief fires that are quickly extinguished by a sprinkler system. If a fire burns for long right next to the container or raises the temperature in the room significantly, the volumes may be no good anyway. (This is another good reason why you also must store volumes off-site.)

Have the most well-organized person in your office design your media storage system. Here's an idea. Ask your best administrative person to take a look at your storage system and compare it to his filing cabinet. Explain that you want an honest evaluation.

12,000 gold pieces

A financial institution where I once worked had an inventory of more than 12,000 pieces of media, and we never lost one. How did we do it, you ask? We treated every volume as if it were a piece of gold. Our inventory system was built on a number of things:

- Each volume had a unique numeric identifier.

- This number was in the form of a bar code placed on *every volume*. (Labeling some 500+ $5^1/_4$-inch original installation floppies that came with our AT&T 3b2/1000s was no joy, I assure you, but we did it with the help of a team of temporaries!)

- Each volume's number, name, purpose, media type, date used, and location were stored in an Informix database.

- Every volume movement was tracked by that database. When a volume was taken to another building for a backup or restore, that was recorded in the database. If a volume was sent to our off-site storage vendor, that was stored in the database. If an administrator borrowed a backup volume or installation CD, it was recorded in a field called "Loaned to:".

- For momentary moves of media out of the media library for restores, there was a manual log. For daily, high-volume moves, we used a bar code scanner with a shell script that automatically updated the database.

- We did a complete inventory every other quarter and a spot-check inventory once a month. If the spot-check inventory turned up too many errors, it was time for another full inventory.

- During the inventory we checked every volume against a printout of the database and every entry in the printout against an actual volume. (The latter half of the inventory was when we had to go hunt down errant administrators who had squirreled away backups or installation media in their drawers.)

- The volumes were stored in Wrightline media cabinets and were behind locked doors. Only the backup operators had access to the volumes. (These were the same operators who were held responsible if something came up missing.)

- The inventories were called "self-audits," and there was also an annual internal audit by the audit department, as well as the external audit by the OCC (Office of the Comptroller of Currency). They would comb through our logs, looking for inconsistencies. They had a knack for finding entries that looked a little weird and saying, "Let me see this one . . ."

- This entire process was thoroughly documented, and they are still following these procedures to this day, although they've probably improved them a bit.

The OCC takes this whole issue of data protection very seriously. (The OCC, by the way, is the group that has the power to say you can no longer be a bank. You want to make sure that they are happy with your procedures.)

Off-Site Storage

Once you have organized the media that you are storing on-site, it's time to consider off-site storage. There are two ways to store your data off-site:

- The typical method of sending copies of your volumes to someone

- Real-time off-site storage

The latter is more expensive but is much easier to use during a disaster. That is, of course, what off-site storage is meant to prepare you for—the destruction of your media and/or the building that holds it. If you have a complete set of backups in another location, you would be able to recover from even the worst local disaster.

Choosing an off-site storage vendor

Choosing an off-site storage vendor is as important a task as choosing your backup software. Choosing the wrong vendor can be disastrous. You depend on that vendor as your last line of defense, which is why you are paying them. Therefore, their storage and filing procedures need to be above reproach. They need to be better than the scenario I described in "12,000 gold pieces." Their movement-tracking procedure must be free of holes. Here is a list of things to consider when choosing an off-site storage vendor.

Individual media accountability

The first storage vendor I ever used stored all of my volumes inside cases. They never inventoried the individual pieces of media. It was up to me to know which volume was in which case. When I needed a volume from one of the cases, they had to go in and get it. Once that was done, there was no log of where that volume actually existed. Both you and the storage vendor should be tracking the location of every volume.

Bar-coded, location-based inventory

Again, each volume should have a bar code that allows your storage vendor to scan every volume in and out. They should scan volumes into their vault when they arrive and scan them out when they give them back to you.

Electronic double check

If you are keeping track of every volume's location, and so are they, you should double-check each other. One or both of you can print out an export of your database that shows volume locations. You can write a program that cross-checks the location of every volume against the other inventory. I can't tell you how many times such a program has saved me. It's great to find an error when it happens, instead of weeks later when you need a volume that got misplaced.

Testing your chosen vendor

See if your vendor is on their toes. One tricky thing you can do is to see if they will leave you alone in the vault. You are a customer of this company, so ask them if you can do an inventory of your media alone. See if they will allow you unrestricted access to the inside of the vault. If they leave you alone inside the vault with no supervision, you have access to other companies' media. That means that at certain times, other companies may have access to your media. Run, don't walk, from this company.

Make surprise inspections. Make spot checks. Ask for random volumes back, and see how quickly they can find them. Ask for volumes you just sent them. Volumes in the process of being inventoried are the hardest to find, but they should be able to do it. If you regularly send them five volumes a day with an inventory, put four volumes in one day, but list five on the inventory. See if they notice. If they don't, raise a ruckus! Their procedures should protect you from these types of human errors. If they don't, then those procedures need to be improved. Don't make a complete pain of yourself, but do be unpredictable. If you become predicable, you may be overlooked. Keeping them on their toes will make them remember you—and how important you think your volumes are. (By the way, your ability to make surprise inspections and spot checks should be spelled out in your contract. Make sure that it is OK for you to do this. If it is not . . . well, you know what to do.)

They will be storing two types of volumes for you, those that rotate in and out and those that stay there indefinitely. As you rotate the cyclical volumes in and out, they will be inventoried. Your archive volumes are another story. If a volume has been there for two years and never touched, how do you know that it's OK? You should make a full inventory of those volumes at least once, preferably twice, every year.

Send the original, keep the copies. One of the things that you should regularly test is your copy procedure. If you are sending volumes off-site, you have the option of sending them originals or copies. Send them the originals. When it comes time for a restore, use your copy. If things go wrong, you can always go get the original. This process validates your copy procedure every time you do a restore. You can correct flaws in the process before disaster strikes. I can remember several times when a volume was eaten in a drive, or had soda spilled on it, and we needed that off-site copy really badly. That is the wrong time to find out your copy procedure is no good!

Using real-time off-site storage

One of the latest trends is what I am calling real-time off-site storage. This is expensive, but it's a beautiful thing. If you can afford it, I highly recommend it. The premise is that the storage company is connected to you through a dedicated connection, such as a T3 or ATM connection. You then send your backups directly to an automated media library at their site. One of the best things about this method is that you can inventory your jukebox anytime using your backup software. Any good jukebox uses bar codes to identify its volumes, and if it uses bar codes, the jukebox inventory takes only a minute or so. The only question you need to ask yourself is, "What happens if *they* burn to the ground?" All your data could be lost. Don't let this happen. Make sure that this storage company is not the only location for your backed-up data.

Testing Your Backups

I wish there were enough to say about this to make it a separate chapter, because it's that important. I can't tell you how many stories I have heard about people who wait until they need a major restore before they test their backups. That's when they find out that they've been using the wrong device or the wrong blocking factor or that the device had I/O errors. This point cannot be stated strongly enough. If you don't test your backups, then you are guaranteed to get a surprise sooner or later.

Test Everything!

It is important to test every type of restore. If you are testing filesystem backups, make sure you:

- Restore many single files. Can you find the needle in the haystack?

- Restore an older version of a file.

- Restore an entire filesystem, and compare your results with the original. Are they the same size, and so on?

- Pretend that an entire system is down, and try to re-create it.

- Pretend that a particular volume is bad, and force yourself to use an alternate backup.

- Retrieve a few volumes from your off-site storage vendor.

- Pretend that your backup server is destroyed, and try to recover from that. (This one's tough!) This test is extremely important if you are using a commercial backup utility. Some products do not plan for this well, and you can find yourself in a real catch-22 situation.

If you are testing database restores, make sure you:

- Restore part of your database, pretending that you lost only one data file or disk drive, if this option is available.

- Restore the entire database onto another server; this is where you learn about files that you are not including.

- Restore the database up to a point in time, earlier than the present time (this is helpful to recover from a DBA or user error).

- Pretend that last night's backup failed, and force yourself to use an older backup. Theoretically, if you have saved all your transaction logs to a backup volume, you should be able to use a backup that is weeks old and roll it forward to the present time using those logs. This is another strong argument for using transaction logs.

Test Often

As I said earlier, sit around one day with some really pessimistic people and ask them to dream up scenarios for you to test. Test your ability to recover from each of these scenarios *on a regular basis*. What works this month might not work next month. The only thing that is guaranteed to remain constant is change. Management changes, hardware changes, networks change, and OS and database versions change. Every change you know about should make you want to perform a test of the affected area.

Monitoring Your Backups

If you are not monitoring your backups, they are not doing what you think they are doing—guaranteed. This is one pot that will not boil if you don't watch it. Every backup should have a log that is examined daily. This can be automated as well. For example, here's how I automate the monitoring of *dump* backup logs:

Give me a summary

> *dump* gives a whole bunch of messages that I couldn't care less about, `Pass I`, `Pass II`, `% done`, etc. When I'm monitoring the dump backups of hundreds of filesystems, most of that is so much noise. What I really want to see is what got dumped, where it went, when it went, what level it was, and the ever-popular `DUMP IS DONE` message. To get a summary of just these lines, the first thing I do is use *grep –v* to exclude the phrases I don't want, leaving only a few lines. This is much easier to review.

Show me anything weird

> You can do this in either of two ways. If you know the phrases that show up when things go wrong, then *grep* for those. Another way is to use *grep –v* to remove all lines you're expecting, and see what's left. If there's nothing, then great! If there are lines left over, they are probably errors. You may see lines like `I/O Error`, `Write error`, or something else you don't like to see in your backups.

You Can Always Make It Better

I don't care how good your backups are; they can always be better. You could spend every waking hour tweaking and improving every piece of your backup program, know everything there is to know about backups, and they could still be better. My backups will never be good enough. There's always a new bell or whistle on some other backup package, a bigger or smarter jukebox, a faster backup drive, or some scenario I thought of that I'm not covering. You must realize, however, that every change you make is a potential for data loss. A common thread that you will find in this book is that every time the human being enters into the equation, things can go wrong. You may be the best shell or Perl hacker in the world, and you will still make mistakes.

"Don't Fix What Ain't Broken . . ."

You've heard it before, but given the risk that each change makes, it goes double in the backup world. As you read this book or some magazine, or talk to other administrators, you will undoubtedly come up with a list of things that you wish you were doing. Concentrate on the *holes*, or scenarios that your backup and recovery plan just does not cover. Worry about the fact that none of your volumes is stored off-site before you think about working on that cool menu program you've been wanting to write for your restores. Make sure you're covering all the bases before you start redecorating the stands. Before you consider making a new change, ask yourself if something else is more important or if the change is really necessary and worth the risk.

Following Proper Development Procedures

Don't make a new change on your backup script and then roll it out to all your machines at once. Test it on a development system, or better yet, on a system that you don't normally back up. That way you aren't putting any backups in jeopardy. Another good practice is to test the change in parallel with what you're already doing. The bigger the change, the more important it is to do a parallel conversion. This is especially true if you're using a new method, rather than just enhancing your current one. Don't stop using your old method until you're sure that the new one works! Follow a plan similar to this:

- Test the syntax of your new script somewhere where it really won't hurt anybody if it does something like, oh, crash the system!

- Test the operation on a small scale on one system, using it in the same manner as you would in production. For example, if you are going to do both remote and local backups with this program, test both on a small scale.

- Try to simulate every potential error the program might encounter:

    — Eject a volume in the middle of the backup.

    — Write-protect a volume.

    — Reboot the system you are backing up while it is backing up.

    — Drop the network connection and power down a disk drive.

    — Know the program and the errors for which it is testing, and simulate each one to test that section of your program.

- Test on a small number of systems, preferably in parallel with your current method.

- When you roll it out to all systems, definitely do so in parallel. One of the ways you can do this is to squeeze all your backups onto as few volumes as you can, then use the leftover drives to do the new backup in parallel. Your network guys might hate you, but it's really the only way to do a true parallel conversion. When I converted to my first commercial backup utility, I ran in this mode for almost a year.

- Only after you've tested and thoroughly documented your new system should you turn off the old method. Remember to keep documentation and programs around to restore data from the old system until all the old volumes have been recycled into the new system.

- Also consider your archive volumes. If you have volumes that are five years old, are you going to be able to read them on a new vendor's backup solution? Will you even be able to read them in version 14 of your current software when your company began writing the archive volumes in version 2? Will the media itself even be readable?

- This gets into a whole other subject. Media life. Even if you could still theoretically read the volumes 12 versions later, the volumes are probably bad. If you have *long*-term archives, you need to make fresh copies of them at some set interval.

Unrelated Miscellanea

We were going to call this section "Oh, and by the way," but that seemed like a really weird heading.

Protect Your Career

One of the reasons that backups are unpopular is that people are worried that they might get fired if they do them wrong. People do get in trouble when restores don't go right, but following the suggestions in this section will help you to protect yourself from "recovery failure fallout."

Self-preservation: document, document, document

Have you ever tried to go on vacation? If you're the only one who understands the restore process or the organization of your media, you can bet that you will be called if a big restore is required. Backups are one area of system administration in which inadequate documentation can really get you in trouble. It's hard to go on vacation, get promoted, or do anything that would pull you away from the magical area that only you know. Your backups and restores should be documented to the point that any system administrator can follow them step-by-step in your absence. That is actually a good way to test your documentation—have someone else try to use it.

The opposite of good documentation is, of course, bad, or nonexistent, documentation. Bad documentation is the surest way to help you find a new job. If you do ever manage to take a real vacation in which you don't carry a beeper, check you voice mail, or check your email, watch out. Murphy's law governs vacations as well. You can guarantee yourself that you, or more accurately, your coworkers, will have a major outage that week. If they crash and burn because you left them no clue as to how to perform a restore, they will be looking for you when you return. You will not be a popular person, and you just might find yourself combing through the want ads.

You Can Run, but You Can't Hide

A number of times the lack of documentation caused me to lose personal time. I remember one vacation during which I spent two to three hours on the phone every day. I remember spending long nights in computer rooms because no one knew which button to press next. But none of those memories is as strong as the time when my wonderful daughter, Nina, was born. Right about now, you're probably saying "Aaah, that's sweet." It's not what you think. Yes, she has given me a whole other reason to get up every day, but that's not what this story's about.

The hospital in which my wife gave birth was about two blocks from my office building. I knew that. My coworkers knew that. (Anybody who looked out the window knew that!) The day Nina was born, we lost a major filesystem. I knew it was on a backup volume, and I knew I was *off duty*. I left my beeper, which is normally welded to my side, at home. I did not call in to work. I knew the process was documented. The problem was that they weren't reading the documentation. "Call Curtis!" I was standing in my wife's hospital room, talking about our wonderful child, when the phone rang. Those guys tracked me down and called me in the hospital! They asked me to come in, but since I knew the system was documented well, the answer was *"No!"* This is an example of the lengths to which someone will go to find you if you *don't* have proper documentation or if they have not been shown how to use it.

Documentation is also an important method of letting your internal customers know what you are doing. For example, if you skip certain types of files or filesystems, it is good if you let people know that. I can remember at least one very long conversation with a user who really didn't want to hear that I didn't back up */tmp*! "I never knew that TMP was short for temporary!"

Strategy: make backups an integral part of the installation process

When a new system comes in the door, someone makes sure that it has power. Someone is responsible for the network connection, assigning an IP address, adding it to the NIS configuration, and installing the appropriate patches. All of those things happen because things don't work if they don't happen. Unfortunately, no one will notice if you don't add the machine to your backup list. That is, of course, until it crashes and they need something restored. You have the difficult task of making something as "unimportant" as backups become just as natural as adding the network connection.

 A new system coming in the door is usually the best test machine for a complete server recovery/duplication test. Not many people miss a machine that they don't have yet.

The only way that this is going to happen is if you become very involved in the whole process. Perhaps you are a junior person, and you never sit in on the planning meetings because you don't understand what's going on. Perhaps you *do* understand what's going on but just *hate* to go to meetings. So do I. If you don't want to attend every meeting yourself, just make sure that someone is looking out for your interests in those meetings. Maybe there's an ex-backup operator that goes to the meetings who will be sympathetic to your cause. Have briefings with him, and remind him to make sure that backup needs are being addressed, or to let you know about any new systems that are coming down the pike. Occasionally go to the meetings yourself, and make sure that people know that you and your backups exist; hopefully they will remember that the next time they think about installing a new system without telling you. Never count on this happening, though. You've got to be ever-diligent looking for new systems in need of backup.

New installations are not the only thing that can affect your backups. New versions of the operating system, new patches, new database versions, all have the potential of breaking your backups. Most system administrators bring in a new version of their operating system or database and run it on a new box or development box before they commit it to production. Make sure that your backup programs run on the new platform as well. I can think of a number of times that new versions broke my backups. Here are a few examples:

- HP-UX 10.20 supports file sizes greater than 2 GB, but the *dump* manpage says that *dump* will not back up a filesystem with large files.

- Informix 7.1.x switched the order in which *ontape* asked its questions. My script used a here document,* and it was expecting the questions in the old order, of course, and just didn't work all of a sudden. (This one surprised me, because it wasn't a major upgrade. We went from 7.1.3.ud1 to 7.1.3.ud3, or something like that.)

- Oracle changed significantly from Version 6 to 7. As I recall, they maintained backward compatibility, but there was a slew of new ways to do things that had to do with backups.

- An operating system upgrade introduced a SCSI_TIMEOUT variable into the kernel that even support didn't know about. The result was that, when I issued an *mt . . . fsr* command that took longer than 60 minutes, it just timed out and went back to the prompt. (I had really old 8200 8-mm drives, which did not support fast file search; an *fsr* that took more than an hour was actually very common.) This one surprised me as well, because my backups worked just fine. It was only when I went to restore that I had the problem. I ended up tweaking an include file somewhere and rebuilding the kernel.

- Another operating system upgrade introduced a new "feature" that limited to 64K the number of records you could skip with the *fsr* command. My commercial backup utility just stopped dead in its tracks. This one actually took some coding on the OS vendor's end, resulting in a kernel patch. It was a bit difficult to accomplish, because they considered it an enhancement and not a bug fix.

The longer I think about it, the more stories I come up with. If you've been doing this for a while, I'm sure you have a few of your own. Suffice it to say that OS and application upgrades can and do cause problems for the backup person. Test . . . test . . . test . . .

Get the Money Your Backups Need

This final section has absolutely nothing to do with backups. It has to do with politics, budgeting, money, and cost justifications. I know that sometimes it sounds as if I think that backups get no respect. Maybe you work at Utopia Inc., where the first thing they think about is backups. The rest of us, on the other hand, have to fight for every volume, drive, and piece of software that we buy in order to accomplish this increasingly difficult task of getting it all on a backup volume.

Getting the money you need to accomplish your task can sometimes be very difficult. Once a million dollar computer is rolled in the door and uncrated, how do

---

* A here document is a way to call a command within a script and answer the questions that it will ask you.

you tell the appropriate department that the 2-GB backup drive that came with it just isn't going to cut it? Do you know how many hoops they went through to spend a million dollars on one machine? You want them to spend how much more?

Be ready . . .

The first thing is to be prepared. Be ready to justify what you need. Be ready with information such as:

- Statistics on recoveries that you have performed

- Any numbers that you have on what downtime and lost data would cost the company

- Numbers that demonstrate how a purchase would help reduce staff costs

- Numbers that demonstrate how the current backup system is being negatively impacted by growth or new applications

- Cost comparisons between the one-time cost of an expensive jukebox and the continuing cost of the manual labor required to swap volumes every night; (also be prepared to explain how jukeboxes reduce the chance for human error and how that helps the company as well)

- A documented policy that every new gigabyte results in a surcharge of a certain amount of money

- A well-designed presentation of what service your backups will provide and the speed at which you can recover data[*]

- A letter all ready to go, with which your boss is comfortable, that explains very matter-of-factly what they can expect if they don't provide the funding you need

Make a formal presentation

The more expensive your solution is, the more important it is that you make a formal presentation, especially if you are in a corporate environment. A formal technical presentation has three parts: an executive summary, an overview section that goes into more detail, and then a technical specifications section for those who are *really* interested.

Executive summary

This should be one page and should explain on a very high level what is proposed in the rest of the presentation. Global figures and broad descriptions are good; do not go into too much detail. This is made for the VP who needs to

---

[*] Don't commit yourself to unrealistic restore times, but if the new system can significantly improve restore times, show that!

do the final sign-off but has 20 other presentations just like it to review at the same time. Basically, state the current problem and describe your solution.

General section

Go into detail in this section. Use plenty of section headings, allowing your readers to read ahead and skim over it if they like. Headings also allow the people who read only the executive summary to look up any specific area that they are not clear on. The outline of the general section should match that of the executive summary. You can include things like references to other publications, such as magazine reviews of a particular product, but do not quote them in detail. If they are relevant, you can attach copies in the technical section. Make sure you demonstrate that you have thought this through and that it is not just a stopgap measure. Put a high-level comparison between the option you chose and the other options available, and explain why you chose the one you did. Describe how it allows for future growth and how much growth it will allow before you must reconsider. Also explain what plans you have for the old methodology and what conversion method you are going to use, such as running both in parallel for a while. Tables are also good. If you can use real numbers, it is much more effective—just make sure you can back them up. If anyone believes that the numbers are made up, it will totally invalidate the report. Try to compare the up-front cost of your solution with the surprise cost of lost data.

Technical specifications

Go wild. If anyone has made it this far, they're either really interested or a true computer techie just like you! If this report is the cost justification for a new backup drive, find a table that compares the relative cost per MB of all the various options. Include hard numbers and any white papers that are included with the proposed product. If you think it is relevant, but possibly too long and boring, this is the place to put it.

Good Luck

The chapters that follow explore in depth the various methods that you may employ to back up your systems. Most of these topics also are covered in documentation from the appropriate vendor; this book is not meant to be a replacement for that documentation. I try to explain things that are not covered in the documentation and possibly address some subjects more frankly than a manual provided by the vendor can.

Welcome to the world of backups.

II

Freely Available Filesystem Backup & Recovery Utilities

Part II consists of the following two chapters:

- Chapter 3, *Native Backup & Recovery Utilities*, describes the backup utilities that are part of a standard Unix distribution.
- Chapter 4, *Free Backup Utilities*, discusses additional, free utilities that can support a backup/recovery plan.

3

Native Backup &
Recovery Utilities

Native utilities are the backup utilities that you find in a standard Unix distribution. I'll admit that these utilities are rather boring. They do nothing fancy and they have many limitations, some of which have been there since they were originally written to back up a PDP-11 to a 9-track tape. (In sixth and seventh edition Unix, it was still called *restor*—a throwback to the Multics days.) Some of these utilities have bugs that persist to this very day. (They've finally fixed the "tape-rewinding" bug in *dump*, but only on some Unix versions.)

Yet these native backup utilities do have a few features that have not been duplicated by commercial backup vendors. These features will always be there, and they don't cost extra. They also work *basically* the same everywhere, with only a few minor differences. Whether you're just starting out in the backup world or you're an experienced systems administrator, you need to be familiar with these utilities.

An Overview

This chapter describes the benefits and pitfalls of several utilities. *dump* and *restore* are usually the best option if they are available. After *dump* and *restore*, *cpio* has the best functionality, but it is slightly less user friendly than its cousin *tar*. *tar* is incredibly easy to use and is much more portable than either *dump* or *cpio*. If you have to back up raw devices or perform remote backups with *tar* or *cpio*, *dd* will be your new best friend.

This chapter begins with an overview of each of these backup utilities. It then goes into detail about the syntax for each command for both backup and recovery. Finally, near the end of the chapter, there is an invaluable comparison chart that can be used as a quick reference guide for comparing *dump*, *tar*, and *cpio*.

The dump and restore Utilities

If you are responsible for backing up at least one Unix server, can't afford a commercial backup product, and don't want to trust your mission-critical backups to a public domain utility, then hopefully your version of Unix supports the commands *dump* and *restore*. You can't beat their flexibility and versatility for backing up and restoring an entire system. *dump* and *restore* are relatively sophisticated commands, with simple interfaces whose essential options are the same on most Unix systems. Some versions of Unix have changed the name and a few of the features of *dump*, but most of the changes are minor.* *dump* can even be found on Unix-like systems such as Linux† and Network Appliance boxes. Even if you don't plan on using *dump* for backups in the future, chances are you've got several *dump* volumes in a cabinet somewhere that you may need to read someday. When you do need to read those volumes, hopefully you will have this book handy.

The cpio Utility

If you do not have *dump* or you can't use the version you have, then *cpio* is your next best choice. *cpio* has been around longer than any other backup utility and has some very important features that other commands do not have. First, there are a few things that *cpio* will not do for you that *dump* can. *cpio* cannot:

- Perform incremental backups without the use of *touch* files and *find*

- Leave both *atime* and *ctime* unchanged after a backup (see the section on *mtime, atime,* and *ctime* in Chapter 2, *Backing It All Up*)

- Perform an interactive restore, like the *-i* option in *restore*

cpio can be a very powerful backup tool. The main thing that sets it apart is its ability to accept the list of files to be backed up from standard input.

 Some newer versions of *tar* support listing the files via standard input, but most native versions of *tar* do not support it. See "Backing Up with the dump Utility" in this chapter for more details.

---

* Some, however, include *major* modifications, and in some respects *dump* is not really *dump* at all! *Let the user beware!* Make sure you read the manpages for your version of *dump*.

† Remember that Linux is just like Unix, but it doesn't carry the Unix brand. Therefore, it is Unix-like.

Why isn't cpio more popular?

If *cpio* is so wonderful, why is *tar* more popular? The most probable reason is that the basic operations of *tar* are much simpler (and more standard) than the same operations in *cpio*. For example, every version of *tar* supports *tar cf device* and *tar xf device*, whereas *cpio* sometimes supports the *−I* and *−O* options and sometimes does not. If you add all the *cpio* options available on all the various versions, you would find more than 40 of them. There are also some arguments that use the same letter but have completely different functions on different versions of Unix. However, I believe that if you use only the options that are standard on most (if not all) platforms, *cpio* can have almost the same simplicity as *tar*—almost.

The tar Utility

If you need to back up your entire system on a regular basis, *dump* is probably your best choice if it is available. Your second best choice is *cpio*, since you can use it with *find* to perform incremental backups. But if you're like most people, you do a whole lot of backups that don't need this level of functionality. You may want to make a quick backup of a user's home directory. The user has a huge directory that you would love to delete, but the only way she'll let you back up her directory is if you give him a copy of it on a tape or CD. You don't care about *atime*; you don't want to do regular, incremental backups; you just want to get the stuff onto a backup volume, and you want it to be easy for someone else to get it off the backup volume. In this case, *tar* is your best bet.

There are some things that *cpio* can do for you that most native versions of *tar* can't (GNU *tar* does not have these limitations, thanks to a lot of work from a lot of people. See the sidebar on GNU *tar* later in this chapter.):

- Accept a list of files to back up from *stdin*. (Again, a few native versions of *tar* support this. See the section on *tar* later in this chapter for more details.)

- Reset *atime* of the files it backs up, although this changes *ctime*. The native versions of *tar* are not able to reset *atime*, but the GNU version of *tar* can.

Although *tar* hasn't been around as long as *cpio*, it has gained much wider acceptance. This is perhaps its greatest feature. Nearly everyone knows how to read a *tar* volume, and if they don't it's really easy to show them how. If it is a *tar* file on disk or even a compressed *tar* file, programs like WinZip* can automatically

---

* WinZip is a registered trademark of Nico Mak Computing, Inc. You can download a demo version from their web site at *http://www.winzip.com*.

decompress it and read what's inside. (WinZip cannot open a *cpio* archive.) It is also much more portable between Unix platforms than *dump* or *cpio*.*

The dd Utility

The *dd* command is not a backup command used by most people. It is a very low-level command and is designed for copying bits of information from one place to another. It does not have any knowledge of the structure of the data it is copying—it doesn't need to. Therefore, unlike *dump*, *tar*, and *cpio*, it is not used to copy a group of files to a backup volume. It can copy a *single* file, a *part* of a file, a raw *partition*, or a part of a raw partition, and can even copy data from *stdin* to *stdout* while modifying it *en route*. Again, although it can copy a file, it has no knowledge of the filename or contents once it has done so. It simply copies the bytes that are in the place from which you told it to copy. It then puts those bytes where you told it to put them.

Although it is rather simplistic in this manner, it is extremely flexible. It can copy files or partitions regardless of format. It can translate data between two different platforms, such as EBCDIC to ASCII, or big endian to little endian.† A perfect example of *dd*'s flexibility is the Oracle backup script included in Chapter 15, *Oracle Backup & Recovery*. Oracle data is allowed to be in files in the filesystem or on raw disk partitions. Since the script could not predict which configuration each DBA would use, it used *dd*, since it is able to copy both files and raw partitions. That way the DBA can use whichever configuration makes most sense for his application, and the script will automatically back up either configuration. It even backs up a mixed configuration, where some of the data sits on files and some sits on raw partitions. This is the kind of flexibility that *dd* gives you.

Other Utilities

There are other native backup utilities that are less well known or are available only on certain platforms. The most popular among these are listed here:

pax

The portable archive exchange, or *pax*, utility produces a portable archive that conforms to the Archive/Interchange File Format specified in IEEE Std. 1003.1-1988. *pax* also can read and write a number of other file formats such as *tar* or

---

* The DJGPP project, a port of *gcc* and the GNU tools and utilities suites to MS-DOS and Windows, made *cpio* its portable archive standard and has ported both GNU *cpio* and GNU *tar* to DOS and Windows as 32-bit executables.

† The concept of big endian/little endian is explained in detail in "The Little Endian That Couldn't" later in this chapter.

cpio. Like many things in the Unix world, *pax* has a group of devoted followers that swear it's the best way to go.

fbackup

The *fbackup* utility is available only on HP-UX and is the utility that HP's System Administration Menu (SAM) supports. Backups made with this utility can be read only on another HP-UX machine using *frecover.* Although the utility does have several advantages over traditional *cpio* and *tar,* I do not like its complete lack of portability. Even though you can't use SAM to perform a *dump, cpio,* or *tar* backup, I believe the portability of these three commands is worth the extra effort that it takes to use them.

The explanation of *dump, tar, cpio,* and *dd* that follow are not meant to replace the manpages for those commands on your particular version of Unix. The syntax here should work on most Unix platforms, but you definitely should become familiar with the manpages for your Unix platform(s). They may contain anything from minor to major caveats for that particular OS. In some cases, vendors document an extra feature or two. Always stay up to date with the manpages for your backup command—whatever it is.

Backing Up with the dump Utility

For many environments, *dump* may be all you need to ensure good-quality backups. To use *dump* and *restore* for regular system backups, you need to understand the following:

- How to use *dump* to back up a filesystem (with the appropriate options)

- How the backup ends up on the volume

- How to get the table of contents of a *dump* volume

- How to manipulate the volume and restore from a backup created by *dump*

- The limitations of *dump* and *restore*

- What you should be doing if you are using *dump* on a regular basis

The first thing to understand is what your *dump* command is and what its options are. See Table 3-1 for a listing of *dump* commands on various Unix versions. What follows is essentially a unified manpage for these *dump*-like commands on specific operating systems.

Table 3-1. dump-Like Commands on Different Unix Versions

HP-UX 9.x HP-UX 10 SunOS IRIX	Solaris	SCO	Network Appliance	AIX	Linux	SGI	Tru64 Unix
(r)dump	*ufsdump*	*xdump*[a]	*dump*	*backup* and *rdump*	*dump*	*dump* and *xfsdump*[b]	*dump* and *vdump*

[a] SCO's *xdump*, a link to *xbackup*, works only with XENIX filesystems. There is another command, called *backup*, which is really a link to *cpio*, which works with non-XENIX filesystems. SCO's *xdump* is also missing two options—the *b* "blocking factor" and the *n* "notify" options—which are standard on other Unix systems. SCO's *xdump* does not support remote devices. Its companion, *xrestore*, is also quite different from the other versions of *restore*.

[b] SGI's *xfsdump* is the least standard *dump*-like command. It does not "work and play well" with other *dump* commands. For example, it rewinds the tape before it starts (regardless of the device you use), makes multiple tape files per dump, and does not support remote devices on non-SGI systems. One of the ways to get around some of these errors is to pipe the output of *xfsdump* through *dd*.

---

dump and restore Save the Day

It had been a long, hard week and we were trying to finish up a few things so we could go home. That's when we got the call. That's *always* when you get the call. A very important directory, which contained a seldom used but essential utility, was missing from the system. "No problem," I said, "we've got it on tape." So I thought. When I went to recover the files, I realized that this directory had been missing for a while. In fact, it had been missing for so long that it had not been backed up by the commercial utility we were using. You can imagine the feeling that was in my stomach.

I looked up on the old filing cabinet where we kept a pile of poorly organized, inadequately labeled, and almost forgotten *ufsdump* tapes. But right now, they were the most important tapes in the world, since they had been made before we started using the commercial utility. I put those tapes in the drive, one by one, using the *table of contents* option of *ufsrestore*, in hopes that one of them would be the right one. The stack was getting shorter and shorter. Finally, one of the tapes looked like it could be the one. I switched modes, using the *interactive* option, and there it was. I selected the directory and extracted it. The directory was saved, and the customer never even knew that we almost weren't able to restore the data. That was one day I was really glad that I knew *dump* and *restore*. (I also learned how important it was to archive monthly full backups.)

Syntax of the dump Command

Let's start with the basic *dump* commands:

```
# dump levelunbdsf blkg-factor density size device-name file_system
```

The following are examples of running this command:

- Command to create a full backup of */home* to a local tape drive called */dev/rmt/0cbn*:

  ```
  # dump 0unbdsf 126 141000 11500 /dev/rmt/0cbn /home
  ```

- Command to create a full backup of */home* to an optical or CD device called */backup/home.dump*:

  ```
  # dump 0unbdsf 126 141000 11500 /backup/home.dump/home
  ```

- Command to create a full backup of */home* to the remote tape drive */dev/rmt/0cbn* on *elvis*:

  ```
  # (r)dump 0unbdsf 126 141000 11500 elvis:/dev/rmt/0cbn /home
  ```

The preceding commands are comprised of three options (*0*, *u*, and *n*) that do not require arguments and four options (*b*, *d*, *s*, and *f*) that do require a "companion" argument.

The *dump* command accepts as its first argument a list of options, then each option's argument is placed on the command line in the same order in which the options are listed. This is illustrated in Figure 3-1.

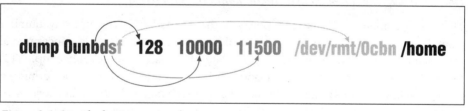

Figure 3-1. Sample dump command

The Options to the dump Command

The *dump* utility has seven main options that are available on most platforms:

0–9

    Specifies the level of backup that *dump* should perform.

b

    Specifies the blocking factor that *dump* should use.

u

    Tells *dump* to update the *dumpdates* file.

n

Tells *dump* to notify the members of the operator group when a *dump* is completed.

d and s

Tell dump how large the backup volume is. *dump* uses these numbers to estimate how much "tape" is available.

f

Tells *dump* what device to use.

W, w

These little-used options tell *dump* to perform a dry run that tells you what filesystems need to be backed up.

If you are using *dump* for regular system backups, you should be using most of the preceding options. It is important to note that many of these options have default values—eliminating the need to specify that option and its argument in the *dump* command. For example, the default backup level is usually 9. The problem with the default values is that they vary between operating systems and may also vary even on the same operating system, depending on factors such as media type. It is better to specify each of these options the same way on all your *dump* backups, to make restores at a later date easier.

The *dump* utility options are described in detail below.

Option: specifying a complete or incremental backup (0-9)

The first argument that you can specify is the *dump* level. You use any number from 0 to 9. (See Chapter 2 for an explanation of backup levels.) Incremental dumps refer to the *dumpdates* file for the date of the last lower-level backup. (This file is discussed later under the *–u* option.) For example, if you are performing a level-5 backup, *dump* backs up all files that have changed since the last level-4 or lower backup. It gets the date of this backup from *dumpdates* (usually */etc/dumpdates*). Since the *dumpdates* file is needed for incremental backups, you must use the *–u* option to update it. (The *–u* option is discussed later.)

Option: specifying a blocking factor (b)

The *b* option specifies the number of blocks to write in a single output operation. This refers to the *number* of physical blocks. The *size* of the entire block that *dump* will write depends on the size of the physical block multiplied by the blocking factor. For most versions of Unix, the physical block size for *dump* is 1024 bytes. So, if you specify a blocking factor of 10, the size of the actual block that *dump* will write is 10,240, or 10K. This option is not available on SCO. (See the section, "What is a block and why should I care?" at the end of this chapter for more information about block sizes.)

There was at least one flavor of Unix that allowed you to change the blocking factor for *dump* but not for *restore*. This means that you would be allowed to make *dump* volumes that you could not read! Make sure that your flavor of *restore* allows you to change the blocking factor. (The particular flavor of Unix was Ultrix, and they have now added code to the *restore* command that automatically detects block sizes up to 32K. They then limited *dump* to a blocking factor of 32. This sounds like the wrong way to go, but at least it *works*.)

Option: updating the dumpdates file (u)

The *−u* option causes *dump* to update the *dumpdates* file for the filesystem that you backed up. (The *dumpdates* file is usually */etc/dumpdates* but is */var/adm/dumpdates* on HP-UX 10.x.) This is a plain text file that lists each filesystem's raw device and the date that the last backup of each level was taken on that device. Here is an example */etc/dumpdates* file taken from a Solaris box:

```
/dev/rdsk/c0t1d0s0          0 Thu Sep 30 23:07:22 1999
/dev/rdsk/c0t1d0s0          1 Sun Oct  3 02:49:51 1999
/dev/rdsk/c0t3d0s0          0 Wed Oct 20 00:31:49 1999
/dev/rdsk/c0t3d0s0          1 Fri Oct 29 01:33:33 1999
/dev/rdsk/c0t3d0s0          5 Sun Oct 31 00:28:14 1999
/dev/rdsk/c0t3d0s4          0 Thu Jul 22 17:41:25 1999
/dev/rdsk/c0t3d0s4          1 Sun Jul 25 01:01:24 1999
```

You can see that device *c0t1d0s0* had a level-0 backup on September 30, 1999, and a level 1-backup on October 3, 1999. Device *c0t3d0s0* had a level-0 backup on October 20, 1999, a level 1 on October 29, and a level 5 on October 31.

There are a few important things to note about the *dumpdates* file. (See Table 3-2 for the various names and locations of the *dumpdates* file.) The first time you run *dump* on a system, you must first create an empty *dumpdates* file, and it must be owned by root. If it is not there or is not owned by root, *dump* does not create it. Your dump will continue, but it will complain. Note that *dumpdates* is updated only if the entire dump completes successfully. If there are any errors that cause *dump* to abort, then *dumpdates* will not be updated. This means that it is a good file to use for an automated script that checks to see if your dumps worked.

You might not want to use the *−u* option when making a special "one-time" backup volume, since doing so will change the behavior of other backups. For example, if you are making a one-time level-0 backup for someone and used the *−u* option, your automated level-1 backups would reference that level-0 backup that has been given to someone else and is not a part of your normal backup pool.

Table 3-2. Locations and Names of the dumpdates File

HP-UX 9.x, SunOS, Solaris, AIX, Linux, IRIX	HP-UX 10.0	SCO
/etc/dumpdates	/var/adm/dumpdates	/etc/ddate

The *dumpdates* file, whatever it may be called, can be viewed or modified with a standard text editor. You might want to do this, for example, if you know that this week's level-0 backup has been eaten by a hungry tape drive. You don't have time to rerun a full level 0 again, but you want some sort of backup. However, if you run a level 1, it will reference this week's level 0-backup, which you know is no good. You can edit the level-0 line for the appropriate filesystems, changing the date to the date of last week's level 0 that has not been eaten. Your level 1s will then reference that last week's level 0, rather than this week's level 0, which was destroyed. This can allow you to sleep a little better after that level 0 is destroyed, without having to rerun a complete level 0.

Option: notifying your backup operators (n)

The *n* option causes *dump* to notify everyone in the operator group, as specified in the */etc/group* file, if a *dump* backup requires attention. This notification looks similar to a wall message. (This option is not available on SCO.) A *dump* backup may require attention when any of the following occurs:

- A *dump* backup reaches the end of a tape, or your CD fills up.

- A backup drive is malfunctioning, causing write errors.

- There are difficulties reading from the disk drive.

Option: specifying density and size (d and s)

The density (*d*) and size (*s*) options do not affect *how* data is written to the backup media. The *dump* command uses them only to determine how much data can fit on a given volume and to determine when it has reached the logical-end-of-tape (LEOT, or the point at which *dump* thinks the volume is full) before it reaches the physical-end-of-tape (PEOT). *dump* then prompts the operator to switch volumes. The logic behind this is to keep the volume from hitting PEOT, since older versions of *dump* do not handle this well. Here is a quick explanation of these two flags:

d (density). By specifying a density, you are telling *dump* how much data will fit on one inch of tape. (This value is really a throwback to the nine-track tape days, but *dump* uses it in combination with the *s* option to figure out how large the backup volume is.) If you want to make sure that *dump* uses the entire volume, use a large value like 80,000.

s ("tape" size in feet). This option tells *dump* how long the tape is. It then calculates how much data will fit on the tape using the values provided for size and density. If you want to make sure that *dump* uses the entire volume, use a large value like 500,000. Using 80,000 as the density and 500,000 as the size effectively tells *dump* that your volume is capable of storing 480 GB! (Yes, this and the *d* option both seem silly if you're backing up to disk or CD, but they are important. See the following section, "Do I have to use the s and d options?," for more information.)

In actual practice, these options are very difficult to use and yield very little value. Most people fake *dump* out by using values that make *dump* think that it will never run out of tape. This causes *dump* to use the entire volume and lets it discover the PEOT if or when it gets that far. There are many reasons for this:

- The *dump* command can now detect and handle PEOT. (*dump* used to abort upon reaching PEOT.) In Solaris, they even have an option that causes the tape to eject, and if you are using an autochanger, it then inserts the next tape. On Solaris, therefore, *dump* could then continue without intervention.

- The calculations work only if it is the only backup that *dump* has put on the volume (e.g., each time you use *dump*, you tell it that the tape is 10,000 feet long. If you have already put at least one backup on the volume, it is no longer 10,000 feet long).

- If you were to use "real" values, you would probably have a small density value with a very large size value. Many Unix versions tell you that doing this can cause problems. (I'm serious. You have to make them up!)

- If you want *dump* to actually stop before PEOT, you need to underestimate the values, which results in using less space than the volume actually has. (Some budgets necessitate using every inch of every volume that you paid for.)

- Adding compression into the calculation really complicates the process, since compression is one area where the phrase "your mileage may vary" really applies.

Do I have to use the s and d options?

A few newer versions of *dump* have done away with these options and provided a new *size in kilobytes* option that you can use to specify the size of the volume in kilobytes. Even so, I personally use the *s* and *d* options with every *dump* command I run so that I don't have to remember how different versions work. You will find this is a common theme throughout this book: the more things you can

---

Avoid Creating a dump Backup Across Multiple Volumes

By "across multiple volumes," I mean that this is a single *dump* backup that starts on one volume, runs until it hits LEOT or PEOT, and then continues on another volume. For example, if you have a 4-GB DDS tape drive and are backing up a 2-GB filesystem and a 3-GB filesystem, the first *dump* backup would fit on the tape. The second one would fill up the rest of the tape, requiring you to insert a second tape to allow *dump* to finish. (See Figure 3-2.)

In my opinion, creating a backup in this manner is asking for trouble. If you have no choice, then you must do it, but it raises some questions and adds difficulty to your restore. For example, you have to load tape 1 and start reading it before you can load tape 2. It's already hard enough to do a restore in the first place! Also, I start wondering about how safe the files are that are stored near the end of the first tape. Are you sure they're safe? The *dump* command can be funny sometimes.

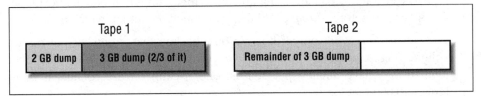

Figure 3-2. Example of a multiple-volume dump backup

do the same everywhere, the fewer things you have to worry about. The more per-host and per-OS customization you do, the more trouble you can get into. (For example, the *size in kilobytes* option uses a different letter on each version of Unix that supports it!) In this case, using the archaic *size* and *density* options actually makes writing shell scripts much easier, since you can use the same options on most versions of Unix.

What happens, then, if you don't use either the *s, d,* or *size in kilobytes* options? On some Unix flavors, *dump* uses the default values for size and density (except for AIX, which has apparently done away with these options altogether). Unfortunately, the default values usually are set to work with a nine-track tape. (Solaris has changed its default values to be slightly more sensible.) If this happens, *dump* will think it needs several volumes. The output of *dump* will look something like the following:

```
DUMP: Estimated 5860 blocks (3006KB) on 39.00 tapes.
```

Notice that it thinks it's going to need 39 tapes. This is what can happen if you do not use the size and density options to specify the capacity of the volume. As mentioned before, you can easily disable this feature by setting these values to some ridiculously high figure, so that *dump* never thinks that it's run out of tape. (I personally use numbers like 1,000,000 for both.)

Option: specifying a backup device file (f)

The *f* option specifies the name of the backup device to which you are sending the data. (This "device," of course, could be either an actual tape device or a file sitting on a disk, optical platter, or CD.) If you are expecting to use the hardware compression feature of your tape drive, make sure that you choose the device that supports compression. If you want to send the data to a drive on another system, use the format *remote_system_name:device*. Most versions of Unix support using remote devices in *dump*.

Remote devices require that the host with the remote device trust this host via the */.rhosts* file. If you try to use a remote device from a nontrusted system, you might get the dreaded message:

```
Permission Denied
```

To test if you are a trusted host, try issuing the following command as root:

```
rsh remote_system uname -a
```

If it does not work, then you need to put a line with this system's name in the remote system's *~root/.rhosts* file.

 The use of *rsh* and */.rhosts* files is a major security hole, and many sites no longer allow their use! Don't go creating */.rhosts* files everywhere and blame it on me. Make sure you investigate whether you are allowed to use *rsh* at your site before you start using it. If you are not allowed to use *rsh*, you might want to look at implementing *ssh* as a drop-in replacement for *rsh*. See "Using dd and rsh (or ssh) as a Conduit Between Systems" later in this chapter for more information.

Unfortunately, in today's mixed environments, you don't always know what other systems think a particular system's name is. The remote system might be using DNS, NIS, or a local hosts file. When you *rsh* to a system, it initially sees you as an IP address. It then does a *gethostbyaddr()* and tries to resolve that address into a name. Depending on how your particular system is set up, it may consult DNS, NIS, or the local */etc/hosts* file—the order in which it consults these sources also varies with your setup. If it uses the local hosts file or NIS for address resolution, it may or may not appear with a fully qualified domain name such as *apollo.domain.com*. If it uses DNS, then it will appear with the fully qualified domain name. It is important to know this, since this is the name that you must put into the *.rhosts* file. Suppose your system is called *apollo*, and the remote system is *elvis*. If you want to *rsh* from *apollo* to *elvis*, you should try the easy step first. On *elvis*, you would enter this command:

```
echo apollo >>/.rhosts
```

If that doesn't work, then *apollo* appears as something else to *elvis* (e.g., *apollo.domain.com*). To find out for sure, you can telnet to *elvis* from *apollo*, then use commands like *last, who, tty,* or *netstat* and look at the field that lists the system from which you came. If it turns out to be *apollo.domain.com*, then put that into the */.rhosts* file on *elvis*. (For example, at one client site, it would appear as *apollo.DOMAIN.COM*.) Once you have put the correct name in */.rhosts*, the *rsh* should work.

Option: displaying which filesystems need to be backed up (W and w)

The *W* and *w* options of *dump* are available on most Unix systems and display information about which filesystems need to be backed up. Usually the *w* option displays information on all filesystems, while the *W* option lists only those filesystems that need to be backed up, based on the backup level you have chosen. These options have slight variations between Unix flavors, so read the appropriate manpage.

Other options: interesting options for Solaris's ufsdump utility

Solaris's *ufsdump* has a few options not found in other versions of Unix. It supports the *−l* (autoloader), *o* (off-line), *a* (archive file), and *v* (verify) options:

- The *l*, or autoloader, option ejects the tape if it reaches PEOT before *dump* is done. It then waits up to two minutes for the next tape to be inserted. This works well with sequential autoloaders.

- The *o*, or offline, option merely ejects the tape at the end of the backup, protecting the tape from being overwritten by another process.

- The *a*, or archive file, option writes *dump*'s table of contents to *archive_file* (as well as writes it to the volume, as all *dump* commands do). This file can then be used by *ufsrestore* to see if a file is on a given volume without having to mount that media.

- The *v*, or verify, option compares the backup to the actual filesystem. While this may sound good in theory, it requires the filesystem to be unmounted, which is not practical in many applications.

What a dump Backup Looks Like

This section explains one primary difference between *dump* and its cousins, *tar* and *cpio*. *dump* writes a table of contents at the beginning of each volume, while *tar* and *cpio* do not.

dump records an index on the volume

The index is read during an interactive restore, allowing you to do commands like *cd* and *ls* on this table of contents, viewing and selecting files that you want for the restore. (The *restore* utility is discussed later in this chapter.) This interactive restore feature is one of *restore*'s biggest advantages over *tar* and *cpio*. There is one important thing to note about this index: it is made at the beginning of the backup, before it has tried to actually back up anything. The presence of the index makes the interactive restore efficient, since you don't have to read the whole volume before you can see what's on it. But the fact that it's created before the backup data is written, and possibly minutes or hours before the data is written to tape, means that files made during the backup are not included, and files deleted during the backup are listed on the index but are not actually on the volume.

Using the index to create a table of contents

You can create a table of contents of a *dump* volume by physically reading the contents of the index that *dump* creates and seeing what *dump* intended to write to the volume. Also, it is important to mention that this reading of the volume in no way guarantees the integrity of the actual file on the volume, any more so than an *ls –l* on a file in a directory verifies its integrity. You may be wondering why this discussion is included here, in the section about *dump*; it is because making this table of contents should be a part of every *dump* backup that you take. Having said that, how does one create a table of contents of a *dump* file? First, what does a "*dump* file" really mean? Perhaps an illustration would help. See Figure 3-3.

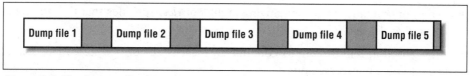

Figure 3-3. The format of a dump tape

A volume created by *dump* may have multiple *dump* files, sometimes called "partitions," on it. Each file ends in an end-of-file (EOF) mark, symbolized in Figure 3-3 by shaded areas.

You have two options if you want to obtain a table of contents for "Dump file 3" in Figure 3-3:

- You can tell *restore* to read the third file on a tape using the *s* option; this causes *restore* to skip files 1 and 2 and read file 3. (This option does not apply to disk-based *dump* backups.)

- You can manually position the tape (using *mt* or *tpctl*) so that it is sitting at the beginning of that file. You then tell *restore* to read it as if it were the first file on the tape.

 You must know the blocking factor in which the volume was written. If you are not sure, then try the default by not specifying a blocking factor. If that doesn't work, see "How Do I Read This Volume?" near the end of this chapter.

The first method is the easiest, since it involves only one step. The syntax of the command is as follows:

```
$ restore tsbfy file blocking-factor device
```

To read the third dump file on the tape with a blocking factor of 32, use the following command:

```
$ restore tsbfy 3 32 /dev/rmt/0cbn
```

- The *t* option tells *restore* to read the volume index and give you a table of contents.

- The *s* option, and its accompanying argument *3,* tells *restore* to read the third *dump* file on a tape.

- The *b* option, and its accompanying argument *32,* tells *restore* that you used a blocking factor of 32 when you wrote this *dump* file.

- The *f* option, and its accompanying argument *dev,* specifies that the *dump* file is on that device.

- The *y* option tells *restore* to continue in the case of errors, instead of asking you if you want to continue.

If you do choose to manually manipulate the tape, as in the second option, you need to be familiar with your Unix version's magnetic tape command. This is usually *mt.* It has five options—*status, rewind, offline, fsf,* and *fsr*—four of which you might use when manipulating *dump* tapes. The format of the command is:

```
$ mt -t device argument
```

If you are planning to position the tape, make sure you are using a *nonrewinding* device, such as */dev/rmt/0n*. Otherwise, it will rewind as soon as you finish positioning it!

Some versions of *mt* use a *–f* instead of a *–t*. The `device` argument is the no-rewind tape device that you are using, such as */dev/rmt/0n*. Then specify one of the following for `argument`:

status

This gives you the *ioctl* status of the tape device. It does not require an accompanying argument.

rewind

This rewinds the tape to the beginning. This option is spelled *rew* on some versions of Unix. It does not require an accompanying argument.

offline

This ejects the tape from the tape drive. This option is spelled *offl* on some versions of Unix. It does not require an accompanying argument.

fsf x

This is short for "forward space file." It positions the tape forward *x* file marks, where *x* is a number greater than 0. (If you do not specify a value for *x*, it defaults to 1.) If you are at the beginning of the tape, you are at file 1, so if you want to be at file 3, you need to go forward two files. This requires an *fsf 2*, as in *mt –t* device *fsf 2*.

fsr x

This is short for "forward space record," and is not needed when manipulating *dump* tapes. (If you do not specify a value for *x*, it defaults to 1.)

The following are examples of how to use the *mt* command. To rewind the tape */dev/rmt/0cbn*, issue the command:

```
# mt -t /dev/rmt/0cbn rewind
```

To forward the tape */dev/rmt/0cbn* to the second file on the tape, issue the command:

```
# mt -t /dev/rmt/0cbn fsf 1
```

To eject the tape */dev/rmt/0cbn*, issue the command:

```
# mt -t /dev/rmt/0cbn offline
```

To get the status of the tape */dev/rmt/0cbn*, issue the command:

```
# mt -t /dev/rmt/0cbn status
```

Once you position the tape to the proper file, you simply use the same *restore* command as before, leaving off the *s* option and its argument:

```
$ restore tbfy 32 /dev/rmt/0cbn
```

Whichever method you use, the table of contents is sent to standard output, which you should redirect into a file. One important thing to note about this output is that the name of the filesystem dumped to this volume is not in the output. This table of contents is relative to that filesystem, whatever its name was. For example, if you backed up */var*, and you were looking for */var/adm/messages*, the output would look something like this:

```
345353   ./adm/messages
```

I recommend that you create a table of contents for each *dump* volume when you make it and store this output in a file that matches the name of the volume. Obviously you should use a unique name, like:

```
./dump.system.filesystem.level0.Oct19.1999
```

Saving the tables of contents in this way is very handy when you're searching for a file, and you can't seem to find it on any volume. A quick *grep* of all the *dump* files shows you which volume you need.

Automating Your dump Backups: The hostdump.sh Utility

If you are using *dump* for your regular system backups, like any backup methodology, it should be automated. Simply putting a single-line *dump* command in *cron* is not enough; you need a script that includes at least the following features:

- Sanity and return-code checks to ensure that *dump* and *restore* are doing what you think they're doing

- An "intelligent" way of deciding which filesystems to back up, rather than just an include list (see "Are You Backing Up What You Think You're Backing Up?" in Chapter 2 for more information on include lists)

- Some method of dealing with hosts that won't fit on a single volume

- Creation of a table of contents by reading the volumes after the backup and saving the table of contents to a file (once again, this table of contents can be used when you are looking for a particular file. If you name the table of contents the same as the volume, simply *grep* for the filename out of *table-of-contents*, and you've got the names of the volumes that have the file you are looking for)

This section presents *hostdump.sh*, a shell script that has grown over the years to include all of the preceding features, as well as a few more. It was first written several years ago to back up Ultrix boxes, and it has grown to support many other Unix versions. The script currently supports almost every version of Unix that I could find that uses some form of *dump*. It should run unmodified on each version of Unix listed at the top of the program. I continue to update it based on reader input, including bug fixes and adding other Unix versions. The script is available on the web site listed in the front of the book and is included with the accompanying CD-ROM.

If your version of Unix is supported by *hostdump.sh*, it's pretty much plug-and-play. All you have to do is put in a volume, give it a device name and a hostname, and it does the rest. *hostdump.sh* backs up all the hosts that you list to the device that you specify. It automatically determines the names of all the filesystems and their filesystem types. If the filesystem type supports *dump*, it calls the appropriate command. If it is an unknown filesystem or one that does not have a good *dump* command, *hostdump.sh* uses *cpio*. The script also puts two extra *tar* files on the volume. The first is a header put on the first partition of the tape* that lists all the filesystems on the volume and the commands that were used to back them up. After all backups are done, it then rereads the table of contents of each of the backups and places that information into another *tar* file at the end of the volume. (The *tar* file at the beginning of the volume contains detailed instructions on how to find and read the *tar* file at the end of the volume, including which partition it will be placed on.)

To back up one or more Unix systems, simply tell the script what level of backup to perform, what device to use, what file to log to, and what systems to back up. To do this, issue the following *hostdump.sh* command:

```
# hostdump.sh level device logfile system_list
```

For example, to perform a level 0 backup of *apollo* and *elvis* to */dev/rmt/0cbn* on *apollo* and log it to */tmp/backup.log*, issue the following command on *apollo*:

```
# hostdump.sh 0 /dev/rmt/0cbn /tmp/backup.log apollo elvis
```

hostdump.sh automatically determines the names of all the filesystems and backs them up to the backup drive device that you specify. Sometimes you don't want to back up an entire system. To back up less than the entire system, add, after the system name, the name of the filesystem(s) that you want. To back up more than one filesystem, simply list them in the order that you want them backed up. (You will need to continue to specify the name of the system that contains the filesystem as well.)

```
# hostdump.sh  level device logfile system:/filesys system:/filesys
```

---

* Or a separately named file for a disk-based backup.

For example, to perform a level-0 backup of *apollo* and *elvis*'s root drive to */dev/ rmt/0cbn* on *apollo* and log it to */tmp/backup.log*, issue the following command on *apollo*:

```
# hostdump.sh 0 /dev/rmt/0cbn /tmp/backup.log apollo:/ elvis:/
```

The arguments to the *hostdump.sh* command are:

level
A valid *dump* level between 0 and 9.

device
A nonrewinding tape device, such as */dev/rmt/0n* or */dev/nrmt0*, or a file on disk, CD-ROM, or optical platter. (The script tests to see if the device you specify is actually a no-rewind device.)

logfile
This is an absolute pathname to a log file that will contain *stdout* and *stderr* from the *hostdump.sh* script. This pathname should be a name that can be associated with the volume. When I use this script for production backups, I name the volumes and the log files after the name of the system, backup drive, and level. You could use something like this:

```
/backuplogs/apollo.DevRmt0n.Level0.12.13.1999
```

system1 [system2 ... systemx]
This is a list of one or more systems that you want the script to back up. Each system you list is written to the volume, in the order in which they are listed. The script automatically looks at each system's *fstab* file, and creates a list of filesystems to be backed up. The locations of various *fstab* files are shown in Table 3-3. Except for AIX's */etc/filesystems* and SCO's */etc/default/filesys*, they all have the same format, listing all the information about a particular filesystem in one white-space-delimited line. AIX's and SCO's files each have their own unique format.

Table 3-3. Locations and Names of the fstab File

Unix Flavor	Location of fstab File
AIX	*/etc/filesystems*
BSDI, DG-UX, FreeBSD, Next, Tru64 Unix, Irix, Ultrix, SunOS, Convex, Linux, HP-UX 10+	*/etc/fstab*
HP-UX 8.x, 9.x	*/etc/checklist*
SCO Openserver	*/etc/default/filesys*
Solaris, SVr4	*/etc/vfstab*

system:/filesys [system:/filesys]

If you are backing up the whole system, it is best to use the preceding option and have *hostdump.sh* figure out which filesystems to back up. But if you want to limit the filesystems included, you can list as many as you want in this format.

system1 system2 system3:/filesys system4:filesys

You also can mix and match the options like this. Any systems that are listed without an accompanying filesystem name receive a full backup. Any systems that have a filesystem listed after them have only that filesystem backed up.

Including or excluding special-case filesystems

You may have filesystems that are listed in the *fstab* file that you want to exclude on a regular basis. Or you may want to back up the */tmp* filesystem, which is normally excluded by *hostdump.sh*. *hostdump.sh* can handle both of these special cases. If you want to exclude filesystems that normally would be included, you put that filesystem's name in a file called *fstab.exclude* on the system where you want to exclude it. (For *fstab,* you need to substitute whatever that version of Unix calls the *fstab* file. For example, you would use */etc/vfstab.exclude* on Solaris.) To include filesystems that are not in the *fstab* file or are normally excluded by *hostdump.sh*, put that filesystem's name in a file called *fstab.include* on the system where you want to include it.

For example, assume that, on a Solaris system called *apollo*, you want to exclude the */home* filesystem. Normally it would get backed up since it is in */etc/vfstab*. Suppose also that you want to include the */tmp* filesystem. In order to do this, you would create two files on *apollo*.

One would be called */etc/vfstab.exclude*, and it would contain the entry:

    /home

The second file would be called */etc/vfstab.include*, and it would contain the entry:

    /tmp

Handling systems bigger than a single volume

hostdump.sh, like the *dump* and *restore* commands, was not originally designed with today's systems in mind. The script was first written to back up Ultrix systems (the largest of which was 7 GB at the time) to 8-mm compressed drives (the smallest of which was 10 GB). The original author* never envisioned a system in

---

* The credit for the first version of *hostdump.sh* goes to Andrew Blair. Although almost none of the original code remains, the original logic of the script does. It's quite possible that many of my ideas about how backups should be done go all the way back to this script. Thanks, Andrew!

which the disk was bigger than a volume. Then the company started ordering HPs that shipped with 20 GB of disk and one 4-GB DDS tape drive! Something had to be done.

 This is where backup philosophy enters again. Please remember the essential elements of a good backup:

— Automation (should not require me to swap volumes in the middle of the night)

— Intelligence (should figure out for itself what to back up; include lists are bad)

— Comprehensive (don't forget anything)

The easiest thing would be to scrap the original idea of looking at the *fstab* and give *hostdump.sh* a list of filesystems to back up. That would be an easy option to include, and the job would get done. Essentially, that's what I've done, but with a twist. I recommend accomplishing this in the following manner:

- Use *hostdump.sh* in the usual manner, but exclude enough filesystems in *fstab.exclude* so that what is left will fit on one volume.

- You then run *hostdump.sh* twice. The first run will back up the filesystems that are in the *fstab* file, but aren't in *fstab.exclude*. The second run will back up only the filesystems that are listed on the command line. (An example of how to do this follows.)

 This works because the default operation of *hostdump.sh* is to back up what is listed in the *fstab* file, excluding what is listed in the *fstab.exclude* file. However, if you specify filesystems on the command line, it will ignore both *fstab* and *fstab.exclude* and back up only the filesystems that you specify.

Why is it important to do it this way? It goes back to the second essential element of a good backup—intelligence. Say, for example, that you had only two include lists. You tell *hostdump.sh* to back up /, /usr, /var, /opt, and /home1 on one volume and /home2 and /home3 on another. What happens when you add /home4? Unless someone or something tells the backup program, it will never get backed up. You'll never know it either, until someone asks you to restore */home4/ yourboss/really-important-presentation-to-the-board-of-directors.doc*. So, whenever you are in a situation like this, whether you are using this program or not, you need to find a way to back up the entire system on one backup drive (excluding certain filesystems), then back up the excluded filesystems on another volume.

That way, when you add */home4*, it will be included automatically on the first volume. The worst thing that could happen is that the new */home4* fills up your first volume, and you have to manually add it to the second volume and exclude it from the first.

To use this option, run *hostdump.sh* a second or third time, specifying the filesystems that were excluded in *fstab.exclude*. It is easier to explain this option with an example. In this example, *elvis* is the name of the Solaris system you want to back up. You are using *hostdump.sh* for the first time, and you know that a full backup will fit onto three different volumes. You have divided the filesystems equally, as follows:

> Volume 1: OS filesystems (*/, /usr, /var, /opt, etc.*), */home1*
> Volume 2: */home2, /home3,* and */home4*
> Volume 3: */home5* and */home6*

Now, take the following steps:

1. Back up the whole system, excluding */home2–6*, on the first volume.

    a. Create a file on *elvis* called */etc/vfstab.exclude* containing the following lines:

    ```
    /home2
    /home3
    /home4
    /home5
    /home6
    ```

    b. Then run this command every night:

    ```
    #  hostdump.sh level device1  logfile1 elvis
    ```

    c. This will back up the entire system, excluding what is in */etc/vfstab. exclude.*

2. Back up the other filesystems on other volumes. Run these two commands every night:

    ```
    # hostdump.sh level device2 blocking-factor logfile2
      elvis:/home1 elvis:/home2 elvis:/home3 elvis:/home4
    # hostdump.sh level device3 blocking-factor logfile3
      elvis:/home5 elvis:/home6
    ```

The *hostdump.sh* program is included on the accompanying CD-ROM.

Restoring with the restore Utility

While writing this section, one phrase kept coming to mind. "The *time* to take Dramamine is too *late* to take Dramamine." The same thing applies to learning how to use the *restore* utility. You need to become very familiar with the various

ways in which you can use *restore* to retrieve data from a backup created with
dump. If you are in the midst of a critical restore as you read this, don't worry—
this section is organized with that scenario in mind and includes every trick available in *restore*.

 This next section assumes that you know the volume was made with
dump and that you know its block size. If you do not know this
information, please skip ahead to "How Do I Read This Volume?"
near the end of this chapter.

Is the Backup Volume Readable?

To make sure that you know the format and block size of a tape, try listing its
table of contents. The following command produces the table of contents of a volume created with *dump*:

```
$ restore tbfy block_size device-name
```

For example, to read the table of contents of a *dump* tape (made with a blocking
factor of 32) on */dev/rmt/0cbn*, issue the following command:

```
$ restore tbfy 32 /dev/rmt/0cbn
```

If that works, then the rest is easy. (If not, read "How Do I Read This Volume?"
later in this chapter.

Blocking Factor

Sometimes, however, as mentioned earlier in this chapter, *dump* can write in a
blocking factor that *restore* cannot read. This problem is usually very simple to get
around. Once again, you will need the block size in which the volume was written. Determine the volume's block size as discussed in Chapter 19, *Miscellanea*.
Assume that the block size of the volume is 65536. Use *dd* to read the volume,
and pipe the output of *dd* to *dump*, giving "-" as the file argument. This tells
restore to read its data from standard input.

```
# dd if=device-name bs=64k|restore tfy -
```

Why does this work? The blocking of data while writing to a volume drive actually changes how the data physically resides on the volume. The *restore* command needs to understand the blocking format to be able to read the volume.
However, if you use *dd* to read the data from the volume, the data is put into a
pipe. The *dd* command effectively sets the block size of the pipe to 1, allowing
restore to use any block size when reading it.

Byte-Order Differences

The *dump* backup format is very filesystem-specific. If you have byte-order differences, the versions of *dump* and *restore* are probably also different. The easiest, and possibly the only, thing to do is to find a system that has the same operating system as the one that made the volume. That is because reversing the byte order may allow you to read the *dump* header but, depending on the *dump* format, it may render the restored files useless.

Different Versions of dump

Unfortunately, this issue will only get worse with time. The *dump* command is tied heavily to the filesystem, and *dump* generally works with only one type of filesystem. The problem with this is that Unix vendors keep trying to improve the filesystem, so there are many Unix vendors who have more than one type of filesystem. If *dump* exists at all on your version of Unix, it may support only the older filesystem types. In some cases, there are multiple versions of *dump*. For example, IRIX has both *dump* and *xfsdump*. Each version of *dump* also has its own version of *restore*. Different versions of *restore* may or may not be able to read a backup written by another version of *dump*. This is yet another area where your mileage definitely will vary.

Probably the best example of the changing nature of *dump* is SGI's XFS filesystem and its *xfsdump* command. On the surface, it looks like the old *(efs)dump* command with a few new options. However, this could not be further from the truth. Assume for a minute that you are using a homegrown program that uses *dump*.* You then add the new XFS filesystem that you just installed to *xfsdump*'s include list. The first thing that *xfsdump* does is *rewind the tape*, whether or not the no-rewind device was chosen. It then attempts to read the first block of data on the tape. Depending on the complexity of the script that called *xfsdump*, the first file on the tape could be an electronic label that the script put on the tape, or it could be the first *dump* backup that went to the tape. In the latter case, *xfsdump* will say, "This is not an *xfsdump* backup . . . I will overwrite it." If it *is* an *xfsdump* backup, *xfsdump* will not overwrite it but will append to it.

Another thing about *xfsdump*, perhaps its most "interesting" feature, is that it writes multiple tape files per *xfsdump* backup. Typically, each *dump* backup creates one tape file on the tape, but *xfsdump* uses an algorithm to determine how many files it should place on the tape. This supposedly makes recovery quicker, but it also makes it completely incompatible with almost all homegrown shell

---

* For example, *hostdump.sh*.

scripts. (The *hostdump.sh* program, described above, has figured out how to work with this "feature" of *xfsdump*.)

The best thing to do here is be prepared. Know which versions of *dump* and *restore* you use, and experiment with them to see if they can read each other's volumes. If you are talking about two versions of *dump* on the same system, it probably will either always work or never work. Remember to test, test, test.

Syntax of the restore Command

Once you can read a *dump* volume, you need to decide what data needs to be read and how to read it. This section discusses commonly used arguments to *restore* and when to use them.

Essentially, there are four things you might want to do with a *dump* volume:

- Read the table of contents to verify its contents
- Restore an entire filesystem
- Restore selected files
- Perform an "interactive" restore

The first three uses of *restore* can take their data from standard input. These are the appropriate ways to use the command if you must pipe data to them, such as the preceding *dd* example. The interactive restore works well only when it can see the whole *dump* file or tape. The syntax of a normal *restore* command is as follows:

```
$ restore [trxi]vbsfy blocking-factor file-number device-name
```

The Options to the restore Command

How *restore* behaves depends on what types of arguments you pass to it.

Determining the type of restore

The first argument to *restore* specifies what *type* of restore to perform. You may specify only one of four possible arguments:

t   Tells *restore* to display a table of contents of the volume.

r   Specifies that the entire contents of the volume should be restored to the current working directory.

x   Tells *restore* to extract only the files listed at the end of the command.

i   Allows you to perform an interactive restore.

Determining how the restore behaves

The rest of the arguments are optional and specify how it will behave while it performs a restore:

v   Specifies verbose output.

s   Tells *restore* to skip some number of tape files before it begins reading the tape.

b   Allows you to specify the blocking factor of the volume you are reading.

f   Specifies the filename of the backup drive (or disk file) you are using.

y   Tells *restore* to attempt to recover from read errors.

The following sections explain these options in more detail.

Option: creating a dump volume table of contents (t)

The *t* option is used to see what files are contained on a *dump* volume. This is a good command to include in any automated shell script that controls your *dump* backups. It is also handy on the backend if you are unsure of things such as the case or exact locations of the filenames. You can extract the list of files on any *dump* volume into a file, then use tools like *grep* to find the files you are looking for. For example:

```
# restore tfy device >/tmp/dump.list
```

The preceding command reads the table of contents of the *dump* backup on **device**, and sends its output to */tmp/dump.list*. The following command searches */tmp/dump.list* for the phrase `filename`.

```
# grep filename /tmp/dump.list
3455          ./somedirectory/filename
```

Option: performing a complete (recursive) filesystem restore (r)

The *r* option is designed to restore an entire filesystem by reading the *entire contents* of a *dump* volume into a filesystem. This should be used only if you are absolutely sure that you want to restore the entire filesystem. It requires that you start with the level-0 *dump* file and then optionally read in any incremental backups. It writes the file *restoresymtable** and references that file when reading the incremental restores. An incremental *dump* records the time of the lower-level *dump* on which it was based. Since the *r* option is designed to restore an entire filesystem, it does not allow you to read an incremental *dump* that is based on a *dump* volume that has not been read yet. For example, suppose that you have three *dump* backups, a level 0 from Monday, a level 1 from Tuesday, and a level 2

---

* This file is called *restoresmtable* on some Unix versions.

from Wednesday. If you read the level 0 using the *r* option and then try to read the level 2 without reading the level 1, *restore* will complain.

You should remove the *restoresymtable* file when the entire restore is complete. (Do not remove it until you have read all levels of your backup tapes, however.)

To use this option, you first *cd* into the filesystem that you want to restore. You then load the level-0 backup and execute the following command:

```
# restore rbvsfy blocking-factor file-number device-name
```

For example, to restore the entire contents of a *dump* tape that was made with a blocking factor of 32 and is sitting in */dev/rmt/0cbn*, issue the following command:

```
$ restore rvbfy 32 /dev/rmt/0cbn
```

After this command completes, load any incremental backups, starting with the lowest-level backup, and execute the same command again. Do this until you have loaded the most recent incremental backup. If you have more than one *dump* volume of the same level, you need to load only the most recent one. For example, if you make a level 0 once a month and make level-1 backups the rest of the month, to restore the entire filesystem you need to load only the original level 0 and then the latest level 1.

Option: restoring files by name (x)

You can use the *x* option if you know the exact name and path of the file(s) you want to restore. (Not all *restore* versions that I tested support using wildcards in the include list, so you do need to know the *exact* filenames.) It basically makes *restore* work like *tar*, allowing you to list on the command line the files to be extracted. Keeping in mind that all *dump* backups are made with relative pathnames, you need to *cd* into the filesystem where you want the file(s) to reside. You then execute the following command to extract file(s) from the backup:

```
# restore xbvsfy blocking-factor file-number device-name ./dir/file1 ./dir/file2
```

For example, to restore the files */etc/hosts* and */etc/passwd* from a *dump* tape that was made with a blocking factor of 32 and is sitting in */dev/rmt/0cbn*, issue the following command:

```
$ restore xvbfy 32 /dev/rmt/0cbn ./etc/hosts ./etc/passwd
```

Option: restoring files interactively (i)

This is the option that differentiates *restore* from *tar* and *cpio*. When *dump* makes a backup, it stores at the beginning of the dump an index of what it is about to back up. (As with the other *restore* modes of operation, you should *cd* into the filesystem where you want the restored files to reside before you execute the *restore* command.) The interactive option simulates mounting the *dump* volume and establishes a mock shell where you can use the following commands: *cd, ls, pwd, add, delete,* and *extract*. You can use these commands to maneuver around the directories listed on the *dump* volume much as if you were moving around a filesystem.

When you see a file that you want to include in your restore, you simply enter *add filename*. Most versions of *restore* also support shell wildcards here, too, so you can also enter *add *pattern**. Once a file is selected for a restore, an asterisk appears next to it the next time you ask for a file listing with *ls*. If you notice that you have added a file that you do not want to restore, just enter *delete filename* or *delete *pattern**. This, of course, does not delete the file from the volume; it merely drops that file from the list of files to be extracted. Once you have selected the files that you want to restore, simply type **extract**.

restore then asks a question about which volume to start with. This question is relevant only if you are restoring a few files that are spread across multiple tapes. Because the files are dumped in inode order, you can put the last tape in first, and *restore* can read the first file's inode number and tell immediately if it needs to read anything on that tape; if so, it has to read only up to the last inode on that tape. If it still needs to read files off the other tapes, put them in the drive in decreasing order, and again it will know if it has to read those tapes—and how much of them to read. If you put tape 1 in first, it will simply read the tapes sequentially. If you are restoring a filesystem, this works just fine.

If you are restoring a few files from a dump backup that spans multiple tapes, put the tapes in the drive in reverse order and answer with the appropriate number. If you have only one tape or are just going to read the tapes sequentially, just enter the number 1.

The file(s) that you selected are then restored into the directory where you were when you entered the *restore* command. (It will, of course, make any directories that it needs to restore the files.) Once the restore has completed, it asks you, "set owner/mode for '.'?" Many people don't understand what this question means. Assume that you backed up */home/curtis*, which was owned by the user *curtis*. If you are restoring that home directory to */tmp*, answering "Yes" results in the */tmp* being owned by the user *curtis*! Therefore, be careful when restoring files to alternate locations and answering "Y" to this question. Answering "No" results in the directory permissions being left as they are.

Example 3-1 is a sample *restore* session. Most of the extra verbose comments that you see here, such as block size, the date that *dump* made the volume, and other messages, are the result of adding the verbose (*v*) option (the verbose option is discussed later in this section). In this session, the file */etc/passwd* is selected and restored to */tmp/etc/passwd*. (That is because I am sitting in the */tmp* directory when I start the restore.)

Example 3-1. Sample restore Session

```
# cd /tmp
# ufsrestore ifvy /tmp/dump
Verify volume and initialize maps
Media block size is 126
Dump    date: Wed Jan 29 23:57:30 1999
Dumped from: Wed Jan 29 19:30:08 1999
Level 9 dump of / on apollo:/dev/dsk/c0t0d0s0
Label: none
Extract directories from tape
Initialize symbol table.
ufsrestore > ls
.:
     2 *./            2 *../         11395  devices/   28480  etc/

ufsrestore > cd etc
ufsrestore > ls
./etc:
 28480  ./             2 *../         28562  dumpdates   28486  passwd

ufsrestore > add passwd
Make node ./etc
ufsrestore > ls
./etc:
 28480 *./             2 *../         28562  dumpdates   28486 *passwd

ufsrestore > extract
Extract requested files
You have not read any volumes yet.
Unless you know which volume your file(s) are on you should start
with the last volume and work towards the first.
Specify next volume #: 1
extract file ./etc/passwd
Add links
Set directory mode, owner, and times.
set owner/mode for '.'? [yn] n
ufsrestore > q
# ls -lt /tmp/etc/passwd
-rw-r--r--   1 root       sys        34983 Jan 29 23:54 /tmp/etc/passwd
```

Option: restoring files to another location

All filenames on a *dump* backup volume have a relative pathname. In other words, if you back up */home*, which includes */home/mickey* and */home/mouse*, the listing would look like this:

```
    15643   ./mickey
    12456   ./mouse
```

So, restoring the files to an alternate location is very easy. Simply change directories to something other than the original mount point (e.g., */home1*) and start the restore from there. *restore* creates directories as needed. If you change the directory */home* to */tmp* in the preceding example, it creates */tmp/mickey* and */tmp/mouse.*

Option: requesting verbose output (v)

The *v* option does not require an argument and results in a verbose output. It will display a lot of extra information, such as the date and level of the backup, as well as the name of each file as it is restored.

 The *s*, *b*, and *f* options require an argument. These options work just as their counterparts in the *dump* command do. (This is not to say that the *s* option performs the same function in both commands, though.) You list all the options you want to use in a list of all options just after the *restore* command, then you list each option's accompanying argument in the same order as you listed the options. For example, to use the *s*, *b*, and *f* options, you issue the following command:

```
# restore tbfsy blocking-factor device-file file-number
```

Option: skipping files (s)

The *s* option is used to read a *dump* backup other than the first one on a tape. When you issue multiple *dump* commands to a non-rewinding tape device, each becomes a separate; file pairs are separated by an EOF (end-of-file) mark. You cannot read all of these in one stroke with a single command. (If you were restoring, you probably wouldn't want to, since each probably is a backup of a separate filesystem.) You have to read each backup with a separate *restore* command. There are two scenarios here. You can:

- Consecutively read every filesystem from the tape, such as when you want a table of contents of the entire tape.
- Read a certain filesystem from a tape.

Reading multiple filesystems consecutively may be accomplished by simply executing several *restore* commands in a sequence, using the nonrewinding tape device. Whether this works for you depends on how your system's tape device driver functions. After a successful execution of a *restore* command, the tape may stop at the end of the file just after the EOF mark. If it is a Berkeley-style device, it may stop at the end of the file just *before* the EOF mark. In that case, the next *restore* command would fail. You sometimes can fix this by executing one forward space file command (e.g., *mt –t device fsf 1*). This would position the tape just after the EOF mark. You could then execute your next *restore* command.

Reading a certain filesystem's *dump* backup from tape can be accomplished one of two ways. You can:

- Position the tape to the appropriate *dump* file using *mt* or *tctl* and then execute your *restore* command with no *s* argument.

- Rewind the tape, and use the *s* option to tell *restore* which file to read. It then forwards the tape to that file and reads it. It requires an argument, from 1 to *n.* This value should be the number of the file that you want to read from the tape. The first backup on the tape is numbered 1, so issuing the command *restore tsf 1 device* is functionally the same as *restore tf device*.

Please note the difference between *mt* and *restore*. The way *mt* and *restore* number the tape files is off by one. If you want to tell *mt* to go to the second file on tape, you issue the command *mt –t device fsf 1*. If you want *restore* to read the second dump volume on the tape, you issue the command *restore [irtx]s 2*. This has confused more than one system administrator!

Option: specifying a blocking factor (b)

The *b* option is used to explicitly tell *restore* what blocking factor *dump* used when writing the volume. It requires an argument that is a numeric value, normally between 1 and 126, or the highest blocking factor that your version of *dump* supports. This blocking *factor* is multiplied by the *minimum block size* that your version of *dump* supports. The minimum block size is usually 1024 but may be 512. (Check your version's manpages.) Many versions of *restore* can now automatically detect most common blocking factors, so you may not even need this option. If you determine that you have a blocking factor that your version of *restore* cannot automatically detect, then use it to tell *restore* which blocking factor was used. If you are using *dd* to read the data and pipe it into *restore*, then you do not need to use the *b* option. (See "What is a block and why should I care?" near the end of this chapter for more information about tape blocks and their role in backup and recovery.)

Option: specifying a backup drive or file (f)

The *f* option is used quite often, and it tells *restore* to read from the device specified in the accompanying argument, instead of the default tape drive for your version of Unix. The argument may specify any of the following:

/dev/rmt/0

> A local device name (e.g., */dev/rmt0, /dev/rmt/8500compressed*)

/backup/dumpfile

> Any backup file that was created by *dump*

`remote_host:`*/dev/rmt/0*

> A remote device, by specifying a hostname prior to the device*

"_"

> Standard input, such as when reading from *dd*, or a *dump* sent to standard output

Option: specifying no query during restore (y)

Normally, when *restore* encounters an error in the file, it stops and asks you if you want to continue. If you add the *y* option, it does not ask you this question and tries to continue as best it can when it encounters an error.

Limitations of dump and restore

dump and *restore* have many capabilities. A good shell script can automate their use and can provide a very good safety net for that time when your disk goes south. However, these utilities do have their limitations:

- There is no way to get a consistent picture of an entire filesystem at any given moment in time.

- The *dump* command sometimes can be very silent about open files and other problems, although it will complain with a "bread error" if things get really confused.

- When files are skipped, *restore* actually can make you think they are on the volume.

- You do need to write scripts to work with *dump*, and scripts can have errors.

- There are multiple versions of *dump*, not all of which play well with one another.

- Like all native utilities, *dump* and *tar* do not have online indexes like those that are available with commercial utilities.†

---

* Not all versions of *restore* support the use of remote hosts.

† Solaris's version of *dump* does have an *a* option that performs some level of indexing, but it definitely isn't the same as what you'd get with a commercial product.

As long as you keep these issues in mind, you can get by for a long time using *dump* and *restore* and avoiding having to spend anything extra for commercial software. Have fun!

Features to Check For

The script described earlier, *hostdump.sh*, is the result of many years of tuning and enhancing and incorporates the efforts and ideas of many people. While it may not be the best backup script available, it does do several things that many shell scripts do not. Make sure that whatever backup script you use does the following:

Lots of error checking
> I have seen too many shell scripts over the years that assume things. Do not assume that a simple command worked just because it always does. When you are automating things, check the return code of *everything*. If you can anticipate what will cause a given error, try writing the script so that it will fix it first before completely giving up.

Notification, notification, notification
> I cannot emphasize this enough. If your script sees something that it isn't used to seeing, then you should be notified. All good activities also should be logged, so that you may go check those logs to make sure everything worked. Too many restores have failed because someone didn't read their backup logs. If you do have a script that notifies you when things go wrong, don't assume that nothing is wrong if you don't get mail. What if *cron* is down? What if some minor change that you made to the script causes it to abort without a notification? What if *sendmail* was or is down? *Never assume anything.*

Proper checking of an rsh command
> Too many scripts check the return code of the *rsh* command and not the return code of the command that was executed on the remote machine. Try this sometime. Issue this command:
>
> ```
> $ rsh remote-system do_stuff ; echo $?
> ```
>
> where **remote-system** is a system that you can *rsh* to, and **do_stuff** is a command that does not exist on that system. You will see that the command that you issue fails on **remote-system**, but the *rsh* returns a successful return code of 0. That is because the *rsh* succeeded, whether or not the command it issued succeeded or not. That is why you see syntax like the following:
>
> ```
> rsh apollo "ls -l /tmp/* ; echo \$?>/tmp/ls.success"
> SUCCESS=`rsh apollo cat /tmp/ls.success ; rm /tmp/ls.success`
> if [ $SUCCESS -eq 0 ] ; then
>   #everything worked
>   echo "Everything worked."
> else
> ```

```
       echo "Something bad happened!"
    fi
```

This shows you the return code of the remote command, instead of just the *rsh* command.

The preceding syntax does not work with *csh*, since it does not allow output redirection in the same way. One way to get around the *csh* problem is to create a small script that you *rcp* over. That script can explicitly call */bin/sh*, so you can be sure you are getting that shell. (The *hostdump.sh* script uses this method.)

Get the table of contents from the backup volume

You always should reread your backup volumes, for two reasons. The first is that it is the best verification that the backup worked, short of actually restoring the data. The second is that you can store these tables of contents into a file and use those files during an actual restore to find out which volume has the file you are looking for.

The best way to verify that the *dump* volume is intact is to list the table of contents with the verbose option turned on, sort by inode number, and restore the last file. This reads the whole volume and ensures that the dump is intact all the way to the last file.

Backing Up and Restoring with the cpio Utility

cpio is a powerful utility, but it makes you do more of the work than *dump* does. This means you need to know a little bit more about how it works if you want to use it for regular system backups. You need to understand:

- How to use *find* with *cpio* to do full and incremental backups of a filesystem, while leaving the access time (*atime*) of the files unmodified
- What arguments give you the best results.
- How to use *rsh* to send a *cpio* backup to a remote backup drive.
- How to get a table of contents of that volume
- How to manipulate a tape drive and restore from a backup created by *cpio*

One good thing about *cpio* is that its name is usually *cpio*. (A great advantage over *dump* to be sure!)

Let's start with the basic syntax of *cpio*, followed by some example commands.

cpio's backup syntax is as follows:

```
cpio -o [aBcv]
```

cpio's restore syntax is as follows:

```
cpio -i [Btv] [patterns]
```

The following example command creates a full backup of */home* to a local tape drive:

```
$ cd filesystem
$ touch level.0.cpio.timestamp
```

The preceding command is optional, but it makes incremental backups possible.

```
$ find . -print|cpio -oacvB > device
```

Of course, the *device* in the preceding command also could be a local file if you are backing up to an optical or CD device. This command creates an incremental backup of */home* to a local tape drive:

```
$ cd /home
$ touch level.1.cpio.timestamp
$ find . -newer level.0.cpio.timestamp -print \
  |cpio -oacvB > device
```

This command creates a full backup of */home* to a remote tape drive:

```
$ cd /home
$ find . -print|cpio -oacvB \
  |(rsh remote_system dd of=device bs=5120)
```

Syntax of cpio When Backing Up

The *cpio* command takes its list of files from standard input (*stdin*) and by default sends its data stream to standard output (*stdout*). To provide a list of files to back up, use anything that generates a list of files:

- *ls* or *find* (e.g., *ls | cpio –oacvB*)

- Creating an include file, then sending it to the *stdin* of *cpio*

   (e.g., *cat /tmp/include | cpio –oacvB*, or *cpio –oacvB </tmp/include*)

You will see that all the preceding references generate an include list with a path that is *relative* to the current working directory. This is done automatically with *dump*, but with *cpio*, you can use either relative paths (e.g., *cd /home;find .*) or absolute paths (e.g., *find /home1*). However, using absolute paths severely limits your restore flexibility. If a table of contents of your *cpio* file shows */home1/ directory/somefile*, you can restore it only to */home1/directory/somefile*. (Sometimes it is possible to use *chroot* to fix this, but it is very tricky!) On the other hand, if the table of contents shows *./home1/directory/somefile* or *home1/ directory/somefile* you could restore it to anywhere you want by changing to another directory and running the restore from there. Therefore you should always use relative paths when creating include lists for *cpio* or *tar*. (GNU *tar* has an option to suppress absolute paths during a restore, but it is probably better to develop a habit of using relative paths when creating include lists for either of these backup utilities.)

Using *find* is the usual method for making regular system backups, mainly because it can make *cpio* perform incremental backups. Before beginning a full backup of a filesystem or directory, create a timestamp file in the top-level directory. For example, in the native version of *cpio*, if you want to do incremental backups of */home1*, create a file called */home1/level.0.cpio.timestamp*. You then perform the full backup, using a *find* command that lists the entire contents of that directory or filesystem (e.g., *find . –print*). When it is time for a level-1 backup, you create the file */home1/level.1.cpio.timestamp*, and use a *find* command that looks for files newer than */home1/level.0.cpio.timestamp* (e.g., *find . –newer level.0. cpio.timestamp*). The *level.1.cpio.timestamp* file then can be used to do a level-2 backup, by using a *find* command that looks for files newer than that file. You can use this technique to generate as many levels of backups as you wish.

The Options to the cpio Command

There are six options that should be used when making regular *cpio* backups. The first five usually are listed all at once (e.g., *–oacvB*), and the last one usually is listed as a separate argument (e.g., *–C 5120*). (Note the *–B* and *–C* options are mutually exclusive—they cannot be used together.)

o   The *o* option specifies that a backup should be created.

a   The *a* option resets *atime* to its value before the backup.

c   The *c* option tells *cpio* to use the ASCII header format.

v   The *v* option results in verbose output.

B, C
    The *B* and *C* options let you specify the block size.

In addition, you can specify a device or file to which *cpio* will send its output, rather than sending it to *stdout*. All of these options and more also are available in the GNU version of *cpio*, as is the ability to use remote devices.

Option: specifying the output mode (o)

The *o* option is one of the three modes of *cpio* (*o*, *i*, and *p*) and is the one used for creating a backup. This would be listed as the first of several arguments.

Option: restoring access times (a)

One of the differences between *dump* and *cpio* is that *dump* backs up directly using the disk device, whereas *cpio* must go through the filesystem. Therefore,

Use GNU cpio If You Can!

This is supposed to be a chapter on the native versions of the commands that reside on Unix, but there are many public domain utilities that add significant functionality to their native predecessors. GNU *cpio* is a perfect example, and there are three very good reasons for using it if you can:

- The native *cpio* utility is *not* very portable, even when it says it is. However, if you write a backup using GNU *cpio*, you always will be able to read it as long as you have GNU *cpio* on your system—no matter what platform it is.

- The portable ASCII format also has limitations. For example, it cannot handle a filesystem with more than 65,536 inodes. The *newc* header format available in GNU *cpio* has overcome this limitation.

- It supports remote devices just like *dump*! All you have to do is enter:

    ```
    -O remote_host:/device_name.
    ```

GNU *cpio* is available at *http://www.gnu.org*.

when *cpio* reads a file to back it up, it changes its access time (*atime*). System administrators typically use this value to see when a user has last used a file by looking at it in some way. Files that have not been accessed in a long time are not being used and typically are removed from the system as part of a cleanup process. If your backup program changes the access time of a file, it appears as if all files are used every night. This option to *cpio* can reset *atime* to its original value.

Option: specifying the ASCII format (c)

When *cpio* backs up, it can send the data to the backup device using a number of header formats. These formats can be very platform dependent, and therefore not very exchangeable between systems. The *most exchangeable* format (although not completely exchangeable) is called the *ASCII* format. The *c* option tells *cpio* to use this format. As mentioned in the sidebar "Use GNU cpio If You Can!," this format may not be as interchangeable as you might think. If you are really concerned with portability, you should consider using GNU *cpio*. If you can't use it, you should try transferring *cpio* files between the different flavors of Unix that you have. At least you will know where you stand. Either way, using the *c* option can't hurt.

Option: requesting verbose output (v)

The *v* option causes *cpio* to print the list of files that it backs up to standard error (*stderr*). The actual data of the *cpio* backup will go to standard out (*stdout*). (The backup data will always go to *stdout,* unless your version of *cpio* supports the −*O* option, which can specify an output file or device.)

Option: specifying a blocking factor of 5120 (B)

The *B* option simply tells *cpio* to send its data to *stdout* in blocks of 5120, instead of the default block size of 512. This can help the backup to go faster. However, it is nowhere near the large blocking factors that many modern backup drives prefer. You should therefore use the *C* option listed next if it is available on your system. The two options are mutually exclusive. (See "What is a block and why should I care?" near the end of this chapter for more information about tape blocks and their role in backup and recovery.)

Option: specifying an I/O block size (C)

The *C* option does require an argument and allows you to specify the actual block size. If you are on AIX, the value is a blocking *factor,* which will be multiplied by the minimum block size of 512. Most other Unix versions allow you to specify the value in bytes.* Either way, you can set this value to be quite large, allowing *cpio* to perform much better with modern backup drives. Once again, this option is mutually exclusive with the *B* option and usually is listed separately with its argument, as in the following example:

```
$ find . -print|cpio -oacv -C 129024 >device
```

Option: Specifying an output device or file (O)

Some versions of *cpio* allow you to specify a −*O device* argument, which causes the output to go to *device.* (This option is not always available.) All versions of *cpio,* however, default to sending the backup data to *stdout.* Once again, for simplicity, you don't have to use the −*O* option even if it is available. To specify a backup device, simply redirect *stdout* to a file or device. This method always works, no matter what version of Unix you are using.

Backing up to a remote device (piping to an rsh command)

The native version of *cpio* does not automatically support remote devices in the way that *dump* does. (The GNU *cpio* version does do this.) So, in order to backup to a remote backup drive, you need to replace the >*device* option with a pipe to an *rsh* command:

```
| rsh remote_system dd of=device bs=5k
```

---

* This time, it's HP that's the strange one! They do not have a similar method for setting block size, and the −*C* option on HP does something totally different, causing it to use checkpoints. It has nothing to do with blocking factor at all. (The feature isn't such a bad idea, but couldn't they have used another letter?)

Notice that it is piped to a *dd* command on the remote host. Since the input file is *stdin*, you need only to specify the output file (*of=*) and the block size. You want to specify the 5K block size, because that is readable by any version of *cpio*.

Restoring with cpio

The same rules apply to *cpio* as to any other *restore* command. I hope that you aren't sitting there with a *cpio* volume in your hand that contains your very critical system backup, and you've never restored with *cpio* before. Remember, test, test, test, and practice, practice, practice! OK, now that I'm off my soapbox, don't worry. Restoring from a *cpio* volume isn't that hard, although there are a number of possible challenges that you may face when trying to read a *cpio* volume.

> This next section assumes that you know the volume was made with *cpio* and that you know its block size. If you do not know this information, please skip ahead to "How Do I Read This Volume?" at the end of this chapter.

Different versions of cpio

Just because you know that a backup volume was written in *cpio* format doesn't mean you will be able to read it easily. This is because, although most versions of *cpio* are *called cpio*, they don't always produce the same format. Even the ASCII header that is intended to provide portability is not readable among all platforms. If you just want to see if you can read the volume, try a simple *cpio –itv < device*. If that works, then you're golden! If it doesn't work, you might get errors like:

```
Not a cpio file, bad header
```

or:

```
Impossible header type
```

> GNU *cpio* can save you hours of work. If you have GNU *cpio*, you could skip this whole section. The following is an excerpt from the GNU *cpio* manpage, "By default, *cpio* creates binary format archives, for compatibility with older *cpio* programs. When extracting from archives, *cpio* automatically recognizes which kind of archive it is reading and can read archives created on machines with a different byte-order."

Byte-order problems

If you are reading the volume on a type of platform that is different from the one on which the volume was written, you might have a byte-order problem, and you probably will get the first of the two preceding errors. The *b*, *s*, and *S* options to *cpio* are designed to help with byte-order problems:

```
$ cpio -itbv < device
# Reverse the order of the bytes within each word.
$ cpio -itsv < device
# Reverse the order of the bytes within each half word.
$ cpio -itSv < device
# Swap half word within each word
```

Reversing the byte order may allow you to read the *cpio* header, but it may render the restored files useless. If the volume was not made with the *c* option, your best bet is to restore it on a system with the same byte order. (Consult "How Do I Read This Volume?" near the end of this chapter for more information about byte-order.)

Wrong header type

If you don't have a byte-order problem, the *cpio* data might have been written with a different type of header. Some versions of *cpio* can automatically detect some of the headers, but they can't detect all of them, and some versions of *cpio* can detect only one type automatically. You may have to experiment with different headers to see which one it was written in. If this is your problem, you are probably getting the "Impossible header type" error. (Again, GNU *cpio* is able to detect any header type automatically.) Try some of the following commands:

```
$ cpio -ictv <device
# Try reading the incoming data in ASCII format
$ cpio -itv -H header <device
# Try reading with a header of value header
```

The value *header* could be *crc*, *tar*, *ustar*, *odc*, and so on. Consult your manpage. This option is not available everywhere.

```
$ cpio -ictv -H header <device
# Combining ASCII and header options
```

Strange block size

Finally, the *cpio* volume could have been written with a block size other than what *cpio* expects. If the block size of your *cpio* backup is 5 K, you can try telling *cpio* to use that block size by adding the *B* option to any of the preceding commands (e.g., *cpio –itBv*). If the block size is not 5 K, you can get *cpio* to use it by adding a *–C blocksize* at the end of the *cpio* command (e.g., *cpio –itv –C* 5120). (See "What is a block and why should I care?" near the end of this chapter for more information about tape blocks and their role in backup and recovery.)

Full or partial restore, or table of contents only?

Once you determine that you can read the *cpio* backup volume, you have several choices of what to do with it:

- Restore the contents into the current directory or filesystem.
- Restore files that match the pattern you specify. This "pattern" can be the ouput of a command, as shown in the following examples.
- Do either of the preceding while interactively renaming the files.
- Read the table of contents.

cpio's Restore Options

Before doing any of the preceding, you have several options available to read from a *cpio* volume. Many of these are the same options that you used to create a *cpio* volume, such as (*B*) for 5-K blocks, (*c*) to read an ASCII-based header, and (*v*) to give verbose output. In addition, you have the following:

i   The *i* option starts out the restore options string and tells *cpio* that it is in input mode.

t   If the *–i* option is followed by a *t, cpio* generates a table of contents. It does not actually restore anything from the volume.

k   The *k* option tells *cpio* to attempt to skip bad spots in the volume.*

d   The *d* option causes *cpio* to make directories as needed.

m   The *m* option tells *cpio* to restore the original modification times of the files when they were backed up. Otherwise, *cpio*'s default action is that the modification times of a restored file is set to the time of the restore.

 Note that *cpio*'s default action in this regard is the opposite of *tar*'s default action.

---

u   This option tells *cpio* to unconditionally overwrite all files.

---

* This option is also in GNU *cpio* for compatibility reasons with legacy shell scripts but is actually ignored. GNU *cpio always* attempts to skip bad spots on the tape. Therefore, if you are using *gcpio*, you can drop this option. Some other versions do not have the option at all.

"*pattern*"

This restores files that match the pattern.

ƒ "*pattern*"

This restores files except those that match the pattern.

r　This tells *cpio* to interactively rename files. If any files are restored, the user is asked to rename each file as it is restored. If the user enters a null value, the file is not restored.

Telling cpio Which Device to Use

Unlike *tar* or *dump, cpio* does not take the name of the backup device as an argument.* You must feed *cpio* the data through *stdin.* You can do this the hard way by using *dd* or *cat:*

```
$ dd if=device bs=blocksize | cpio -options
```

Alternatively, you can simply redirect *stdin* to read from the device:

```
$ cpio -options < device
```

Examples of a cpio Restore

The only question now is what options are needed. The easiest way to explain this is to show you example commands for the things that you can do with a *cpio* volume. There are several "optional" options listed in these example commands. Many of these options, while not required, make the operation easier or more robust. Some of the options may not be applicable to your particular application, so feel free to not use them.

Listing the files on a cpio volume

The following command reads the *cpio* volume in (*B*) blocks of 5120 bytes, uses the (*c*) ASCII format when reading the header, (*k*) skips bad spots on the volume when possible, lists only the (*t*) table of contents with a (*v*) verbose (*ls –l*) style listing:

```
$ cpio -iBcktv < device
```

Doing an entire filesystem restore

The following command reads the *cpio* volume in (*B*) blocks of 5120 bytes, uses the (*c*) ASCII format when reading the header, and makes (*d*) directories where needed. It (*k*) skips bad spots on the volume when possible, retains the original

---

* Unless you want to use the *–I* option supported by some versions of *cpio.* Once again, though, this book concentrates on those options that work almost everywhere.

file (*m*) modification times, (*u*) unconditionally overwrites files, and (*v*) lists the names of the files that it recovers as it reads them:

```
$ cpio -iBcdkmuv < device
```

Of course, you can do the same thing, but without the (*u*) unconditional overwrite:

```
$ cpio -iBcdkmv < device
```

Doing a pattern-match restore

To restore files that match a certain pattern, simply list the pattern(s) you are looking for after the command:

```
$ cpio -iBcdkmuv "pattern1" "pattern2" "pattern3" < device
```

The *pattern* uses filename expansion wildcards, not regular expressions.* Filename expansion wildcards work like the ones on the command line (e.g., **ome** will find both *home1* and *rome*). The *cpio* command is the only native restore utility that supports wildcard restores like this. For example, if you want to restore all of the files that were in my home directory (*/home1/curtis*), you could type:

```
$ cpio -iBcdkmuv "*curtis*"
```

 Quoting the pattern like that causes the filename expansion to be applied to the files in the archive. If you don't quote the pattern, the shell will expand the wildcard for you, and *cpio* will only see a list of filenames that currently exist on the system that match that pattern **curtis**. If you have deleted some of these files, or if you are in a different directory, the results will not be what you are expecting!

To restore all files *except* those matching a certain pattern, use the *f* option, and list the excluded pattern(s):

```
$ cpio -iBcfdkmuv "pattern1" "pattern2" "pattern3" < device
```

Renaming files interactively

The following is the same command as that in the "Doing an entire filesystem restore" section but prompts the user to interactively (*r*) rename any files that are restored:

```
$ cpio -iBcdkmruv < device
```

---

* For learning more than you ever though possible about regular expressions, I highly recommend O'Reilly's book *Mastering Regular Expressions*, by Jeffrey Friedl. Understanding what they are and what they do is an eye-opening experience, and makes your use of tools like *grep*, *sed*, *awk*, and *vi* much more fruitful.

The following is the same command as one in the "Doing a pattern-match restore" section but prompts the user to interactively (*r*) rename any files that are restored:

```
$ cpio -iBcdkmruv "pattern" < device
```

Other useful options

b, s, S

These options are used to swap bytes when you have byte-order problems. Use them as a last resort, since I've yet to see them used with unqualified success. There is one scenario in which they might come in handy: you are trying to read a volume that was made on a little-endian machine, but you're on a big-endian machine. (See "How Do I Read This Volume?" near the end of this chapter for more information on this.) The person making the *cpio* backup did not use the *−c* option, so the only way that you can read the volume is to perform a byte swap:

```
$ dd if=device bs=10240 conv=swab | cpio -options
```

But you discover, after doing that, that the words within the backup are now backward from the order in which you need them, resulting in restored files that couldn't be read. Allegedly, you could have *cpio* swap the words for you as they are restored. Notice the addition of the *b* option to the regular *cpio* command:

```
$ dd if=device bs=10240 conv=swab | cpio - iBcdkmubv < device
```

The *b* option is the equivalent to using both the *s* and *S* options together. The problem here is that all this byte-swapping is going on without *dd* or *cpio* knowing what the format of the file is. What if the expected eight-byte words aren't eight bytes at all? What if they're 10? Again, I have not met anyone who has used these options with complete success, so if you do, send me an email!

6   The *6* option reads a Unix sixth-edition archive. Use it for reading *really old* *cpio* backups.

Restoring to a different directory

If you made your backup volumes using relative pathnames, this is not a problem. Simply *cd* to the directory where you want to restore and issue your *cpio* restore commands from there. If you don't know if the volume was written with relative pathnames, enter the command *cpio −itv < device* and look at the filenames. If they start with a /, then the volume was made with absolute paths. In that case, you can do one of two things:

Use a symbolic link

If you are on Unix, you should have the *chroot* command available. If you are on a non-Unix platform or do not have the *chroot* command available, you may have to be more creative. If you have to restore to a different directory and the backup was made with absolute pathnames, you might create a symbolic link from */home2* to */home1* (e.g., *ln –s /home2 /home1*). That way, any files that are supposed to go into */home* will actually go into */home2*. This works only if */home1* is not mounted on that system. If */home1* is already present; you must *unmount* it. This, of course, is a pain, which is why you should be making your backup volumes with relative pathnames.

Use GNU cpio

This is really the best option. GNU *cpio* has a no-absolute-pathnames option that removes the leading slash (/) from any absolute paths and restores the files relative to the current directory.

Using cpio's "Directory Copy" Feature

If you need to move a directory from one place to another, you can try this little-used feature of *cpio*. Issue the following command:

```
$ cd old-directory ; find . -print | cpio -padlmuv new-directory
```

This moves *old-directory* to *new-directory*, resetting (*a*) access times, creating (*d*) directories when needed, (*l*) linking files when possible, retaining the original (*m*) modification times, (*u*) unconditionally overwriting all files, while giving a (*v*) verbose output of the files that get copied.

 Some versions of Unix also have a *–L* option that causes *cpio* to follow symbolic links, copying the directories and files to which they point, instead of the symbolic link itself. If you use this option, make sure that the *find* command that is feeding *cpio* its file list uses the *–follow* option. If you do not, you will get unpredictable results.

If you were to compile a list of all the options that are available on all Unix platforms, it would be very long. Depending on your platform, there may be a lot of other neat options that can make *cpio* more useful for you. There are also a number of extra features in GNU's version of *cpio*. Make sure you read the manpage for your version of *cpio*. Please be aware that if you use any of the options that affect how the *cpio* backup is *written*, it may reduce its portability.

Backing Up and Restoring with the tar Utility

tar is the most popular backup utility discussed in this chapter. Many of the files that you download from the Internet are in *tar* or compressed *tar* format.

Although it usually isn't used for daily backup and recovery, you are sure to find several uses for the *tar* utility.

As mentioned earlier, *tar* cannot preserve the access times of files that it backs up. If this is important to you, the GNU version of *tar* is able to do this.

Syntax of tar when Backing Up

The basic *tar* command is as follows:

```
$ tar [cx]vf device pattern
```

Now let's look at some example commands. To create an archive of a directory called *pattern*, use the command:

```
$ tar cvf device pattern
```

To do the same thing, but with a blocking factor of 20, use the command:

```
$ tar cvbf 20 device pattern
```

To do the same thing, but to have *tar* verify the data as it writes it (available only in GNU *tar*),* use the command:

```
$ gtar cvWbf 20 device pattern
```

To create an archive of everything in the current directory starting with an "a", use the command:

```
$ tar cvf device a*
```

The Options to the tar Command

tar has two great advantages. The first is the level of acceptance that it has received. The second is its short list of options—there really are not very many:

c   The *c* option tells *tar* to *create* an archive (to make a backup).

v   The *v* option tells *tar* to be *verbose*. It lists the name and size of each file as it is being archived.

W   The *W* option, available only in GNU *tar*, tells *tar* to attempt to verify the files as it writes them.

---

* Yet another reason why you should be using *gtar* if you are performing regular system backups with *tar*.

b blocking-factor

> This option tells *tar* to read and write in blocks of *n* bytes, where *n* is the value of the *blocking-factor* (that you specify) multiplied by the minimum block size (for that operating system). This will normally be 512 but could be 1024. The resulting value, referred to as the *block size,* can range from 512 to 10,240. A block size of 10,240 would normally mean a blocking *factor* of 20, since 20 times 512 is 10,240. There is a default value for *b* if you do not specify it. This default value if usually 20 but could be as little as 1. (See "What is a block and why should I care?" near the end of this chapter for more information about tape blocks and their role in backup and recovery.)

f device

> This option tells *tar* to write to the device specified in the *device* argument, instead of the default tape device for that platform. This *device* could be a file on disk or optical platter, a tape drive, or standard output (*stdout*). If you are using GNU *tar*, it also could be a remote system's tape drive. (See the sidebar about GNU *tar*.) To send the data to *stdout*, enter a dash (-) where the device name should be. (Using - is not available on all platforms.)

pattern

> This is what generates the include list for *tar*. Again, it is based on filename expansion syntax, so to back up everything starting with an "a", you enter "a*" as that argument. You can put any filename here, including a directory; that causes everything in that directory to be archived.

Listing files on standard input

Most versions of *tar* do not support listing the files to be archived on standard input, like *cpio* does. However, some newer versions of *tar* have added this functionality with a new flag that allows you to specify a file that contains a list of files to be backed up. If you want to specify the names of the files to be backed up via standard input, and your version of *tar* allows you to specify an include list, you can accomplish this by using named pipes. For example, suppose you wanted to run a *find* from */home/curtis* and back up all the files that you find there. First, we need to create a named pipe:

```
# mknod p /tmp/$$.namedpipe
```

Next we run the *find* command and send its output to */tmp/$$.namedpipe*:

```
# cd /home/curtis ; find . -print >/tmp/$$.namedpipe
```

Now we tell *tar* to read */tmp/$$.namedpipe* as the list of files to be included:

```
# tar cvf /dev/rmt/0cbn -I /tmp/$$.namedpipe
```

This causes *tar* to see the result of the *find* operation as the list of files to be included. A partial list of the native versions of *tar* that support this feature are listed in Table 3-4.

Table 3-4. Versions of tar That Support an Include List

Operating System	Flag
AIX	*-L*
DG-UX, SunOS, Solaris	*-I*
FreeBSD, Linux, GNU *tar*	*-T*

Syntax of tar When Restoring

A *tar* backup is very easy to read. Even if you used a blocking factor when you created the *tar*, you don't need it for the restore. *tar* automatically figures it out. (Did I hear you say "How beautiful . . ."?) To read a backup written with *tar*, enter:

    $ **tar xvf** *device*

or:

    $ **tar xvf** *device pattern*

The *x* flag tells it that you are extracting (restoring) from the *tar* file. The *v*, *f*, and **device** arguments work the same way as they do when making a backup.

Restoring selected parts of the archive

When restoring, you can specify the filename(s) that you want to restore by listing one or more **pathnames** after the device name. It is important to note, however, that the pathname must match the name in the *tar* archive *exactly*, or it will not be restored. Unlike in *cpio*, wildcards are not supported in *tar*. However, if you specify a directory name, everything in that directory will be restored. Remember, your specification must match the directory name exactly.

Consider the following example. There is a subdirectory called *home*, and we will create a *tar* archive of it, called *file.tar*. One could enter *tar cvf file.tar home* or *tar cvf file.tar ./home*. Watch how that affects what you must do to restore from it:

    $ **tar cvf home.tar ./home**
    a ./home/ OK
    a ./home/myfile OK
    a ./home/myfile.2 OK

Note that, if it was backed up with *./home*, it must be restored with
./home.

```
$ tar xvf home.tar home
tar: blocksize = 5
$ tar xvf home.tar ./home
tar: blocksize = 5

x ./home, 0 bytes, 0 tape blocks
x ./home/myfile, 0 bytes, 0 tape blocks
x ./home/myfile.2, 0 bytes, 0 tape blocks
```

This time it will be backed up with *home* as the pattern:

```
$ tar cvf home.tar home
a home/ OK
a home/myfile OK
a home/myfile.2 OK
```

Notice again that if it was backed up with *home*, it must be restored with *home*.
The pattern of *./home* will not work:

```
$ tar xvf home.tar ./home
tar: blocksize = 5
$ tar xvf home.tar home
tar: blocksize = 5
x home, 0 bytes, 0 tape blocks
x home/myfile, 0 bytes, 0 tape blocks
x home/myfile.2, 0 bytes, 0 tape blocks
```

If you don't know the name of the file you want to restore, and you don't want to
restore the entire archive, you can create a table of contents and look for the file
there. First, make a table of contents of the archive:

```
tar tf device >somefile
```

If you do that with the archive in the preceding example, you would have a file
that looks like this:

```
home/
home/myfile
home/myfile.2
```

If you knew you were looking for *myfile*, you could *grep* for that out of this file:

```
# grep myfile somefile
home/myfile
home/myfile.2
```

You would now know that you should enter:

```
$ tar xvf device home/myfile
```

Tricking tar into using wildcards during a restore

There is a trick that works most of the time on tape and should work all of the time for *tar* files on disk. You issue two *tar* commands at once:

```
$ tar xvf device `tar tf device | grep 'pattern'`
```

If you are using this trick with a tape drive, make sure you use the rewind device, or it won't work! You also might want to add the *sleep* command to give the tape time to rewind:

```
$ tar xvf device `tar tf device | grep 'pattern' ; sleep 60`
```

Changing ownership, permissions, etc. during a restore

The default actions of *tar* can vary from system to system, but most versions of *tar* support the following three options during a restore:

m   Normally, restored files retain the modification times that they had when they were archived. This option changes the modification times to the time of the restore. This is the opposite of the behavior for the *cpio* command.

tar's default treatment of modification times during a restore is the opposite of *cpio*'s.

o   This option tells *tar* to make you the owner of any files that you restore. This is the default behavior for users other than root. Unless this option is used, files extracted by root take on the user and group identifiers saved in the *tar* file.

p   By default, *tar* normally does not restore all file attributes. File permissions are determined by the current *umask*, instead of the permissions of the original files. Also, the *setuid* and *sticky bits* are not restored for any files not owned by the user. This option tells *tar* to use the permissions of the original files, including any special attributes like *setuid*. (You must be root to set the *setuid* and *sticky bits* on other users' files.)

One important thing to note is that while GNU *tar* can read an archive created by any other version of *tar*, the reverse is not necessarily true. Certain native versions of *tar* cannot read archives created with GNU *tar*.

Use GNU tar If You Can

GNU *tar* is an extremely popular utility. Besides being able to read an archive written by any other version of *tar*, it adds a significant level of functionality. Here are some of its most popular advancements:

- The *–d* option performs a *diff* compare between the archive and a filesystem. It does this by reading the tape, and comparing its contents against the files that it finds in the filesystem. Any differences will be reported.

- The *–a* option resets access times (*atime*).

- The *–F* option runs a script when *tar* reaches the end of a volume. This can be used to automatically swap volumes with a media changer.

- The *–Z* and *–z* options automatically pass the archive through *compress* or *gzip*, respectively.

- The *–f* option supports remote device names.

- By default, GNU *tar* suppresses a leading slash on absolute pathnames while creating or reading a *tar* archive. (You can suppress this with the *–p* option.)

GNU *tar* is available at *http://www.gnu.org*.

Some Other Neat Things About tar

tar has many options, and you should read the manpages to find them all. It can come in very handy.

Finding everything that's under the directory

Sometimes things underneath a directory are not what they seem. If you are creating "one last archive" of a directory before deleting it, you might want to follow any symbolic links that you come across. This is what the *–h* option is for. Make sure you've got lots of tape!

Using tar to move a directory

As discussed earlier, *cpio* has a built-in command to move directories. The problem is that many people do not remember its syntax when the time comes. However, you also can use *tar* to move a directory. You do this by first *cd*ing to one level above the directory you are going to move:

```
$ cd old-dir ; cd ..
```

You then use *tar* and a set of parentheses to create a subshell that "untars" the directory into its new location. (Note the use of the *p* flag to ensure that *tar* creates the new directory with the same permissions as the old one.)

```
$ tar cf - old-dir | (cd new-dir ; cd .. ; tar xvpf - )
```

The - option for the *tar cf* tells it to send its data to *stdout*. (We omit the *v* option to prevent writing the filenames to the display twice.) The "-" option on the *tar xvf* tells it to look at *stdin* for its data. Surrounding the *cd old-dir ; tar xvf -* with parentheses creates a sub shell so that the directory *old-dir* is extracted into *new-dir*.

I have seen people try to move a user's home directory by *cd*ing into that directory and creating a *tar* of "*". The problem with this is that it does not include the "." files like *.profile*, *.cshrc*, or *.netscape*. I have then seen the person say, "Oh, I need to use '.*', not '*'!" Remember always, and never forget, that the expression '.*' matches the string '..' (the parent directory). *That means that the archive will also include the directory above it.* That's why it is much easier to go a level above, and *tar* the directory. (Another way to do this would be to make an archive of ".". I prefer the former because it shows what directory the files came from.)

The syntax may seem a bit difficult, but it is very portable. It could be made a little shorter by saying:

```
$ cd parent ; tar cf - old-dir | (cd new-parent ; tar xvpf - )
```

In this example, *parent* is the directory above the *old-dir*, and *new-parent* is the parent directory of the new location. For example, if you were moving */home1/fred* to */home2/fred*, *parent* would be */home1*, *old-dir* would be *fred*, and *new-parent* would be */home2*. Make sure you mean what you type. One of the problems with *tar* is that you get very familiar with typing *tar cvf*. Then one day you need to do a *tar xvf* and accidentally type a *c* instead of an *x*. Guess what happens. Your archive is ruined, and there is no way to fix it. This is one of the most common questions on Usenet, and there's never been a good answer to it.

Restoring to an alternate location

If you make your *tar* archives with relative pathnames, then restoring to an alternate location is very easy. Simply change directories to something other than the original mount point (e.g., */home1*), and start the restore from there. *tar* creates directories as needed.

If you did not create the *tar* archive with relative pathnames, you can use GNU *tar* to take off the leading slash.

Read the *cpio* section about relative pathnames and why they are important.

Backing Up and Restoring with the dd Utility

As far as backup utilities go, the *dd* utility is about as featureless as they come. However, it has certain applications for which it is uniquely suited.

Basic dd Options

The basic syntax of *dd* is as follows:

```
# dd if=device of=device bs=blocksize
```

The preceding options are used almost every time you run *dd*; they are explained in the following sections.

Option: specifying the input file

The *if=* argument specifies the input file or the file from which it is going to copy the data. This is the file or raw partition that you are going to back up (e.g., *dd if=/dev/dsk/c0t0d0s0* or *dd if=/home/file*). If you want *dd* to look at *stdin* for its data, you don't need this argument.

Option: specifying the output file

The *of=* argument specifies the output file or the file to which you are sending the data. This could be a file on disk or an optical platter, another raw partition, or a tape drive* (e.g., *dd of=/backup/file, dd of=/dev/rmt/0n*). If you are sending to *stdout*, you don't need this argument.

Option: specifying the block size

The *bs=* argument specifies the block size, or the amount of data that is to be transferred in one I/O operation. This value normally is expressed in bytes, but in most versions *dd* also can be specified in kilobytes by adding a *k* at the end of the number (e.g., 10 K). (This is different from a blocking *factor*, like *dump* and *tar*

---

* Of course, a tape drive is another raw device as well.

use, which is multiplied by a fixed value known as the minimum block size. A blocking *factor* of 20 with a *minimum* block size of 512 would give you an *actual* block size of 10,240, or 10 K.) It should be noted that when reading from or writing to a pipe, *dd* defaults to a block size of 1.

Changing block size does not affect how the data is physically written to a *disk device*, such as a file on disk or optical platter. Using a large block size just makes the data transfer more efficient. When writing to a *tape device*, however, each block becomes a *record*, and each record is separated by an interrecord gap. Once a tape is written with a certain block size, it must be read with that block size or a multiple of that block size. (For example, if a tape were written with a block size of 1024, you must use the block size of 1024 when reading it, or you may use 2048 or 10,240, which are multiples of 1024.) Again, this applies only to tape devices, not disk-like devices. (See "What is a block and why should I care?" near the end of this chapter for more information about tape blocks and their role in backup and recovery.)

Option: specifying the input and output block sizes separately

When specifying block size with the option *bs=*, you are specifying both the incoming and outgoing block size. There are situations in which you may need a different block size on each. This is done with the *ibs=* and *obs=* options. For example, to read a tape with one block size and create a tape with another, you could issue a command like this:

```
# dd if=/dev/rmt/0 ibs=10k of=/dev/rmt/1 obs=64k
```

Option: specifying the number of records to read

The *count=n* option tells *dd* how many records (blocks) to read. You can use this to read the first few blocks of a file or tape to see what kind of data it is, for example (see the following section). You can also use it to have *dd* tell you what block size a tape was written in (see below).

Using dd to Copy a File or Raw Device

You can use *dd* as a backup command, since it can copy the bits in a file or raw device to another location. You even can pipe the bit stream through *compress*, allowing you to store a compressed copy of the data. (*dump*, *tar*, and *cpio* do not have this capability, although GNU *tar* does.) The best example of using *dd* as a backup command is the hot-backup script for Oracle, *oraback.sh* (see Chapter 15 for more information about *oraback.sh*). Since Oracle can use both raw partitions and files for its database files, the script could not predict which command to use. However, *dd* supports both of them!

Using dd to Convert Data

The *dd* command also can be used to convert data from one format to another in one pass.

Converting data to go into another command

Again, this is done by using a different input and output block size (*ibs=*, *obs=*). If a command, such as *restore*, can read only certain block sizes, and you have a volume that was written in another block size, you can use *dd* to read the volume and pipe the results of *dd* into *restore*.

Converting data that is in the wrong format

Although you may think of *dd* as a bit copier, it also can manipulate the format of the data, such as converting between different character sets, upper- and lower-case, and fixed-length and variable-length records.

conv=ascii
> Converts EBCDIC to ASCII

conv=ebcdic
> Converts ASCII to EBCDIC

conv=ibm
> Converts ASCII to EBCDIC using the IBM conversion table

conv=lcase
> Maps US ASCII alphabetic characters to their lowercase counterparts

conv=ucase
> Maps US ASCII alphabetic characters to their uppercase counterparts

conv=swab
> Swaps every pair of bytes; can be used to read a volume written in different byte order

conv=noerror
> Does not stop processing on an error

conv=sync
> Pads every input block to input block size (*ibs*)

conv=notrunc
> Does not truncate existing file on output

conv=block
> Converts input record to a fixed length specified by *cbs*

conv=unblock
> Converts fixed-length records to variable length

conv=..., ...
> Uses multiple conversion methods separated by commas

Using dd and rsh (or ssh) as a Conduit Between Systems

Most other backup commands can only read or write from *stdin*, whereas *dd* can do both at the same time. This makes *dd* very versatile and the only native backup utility that can be used to pass a stream of data from one command to another or from one system to a device on another system, using *rsh* or *ssh*. This can work either way.

Reading a backup on a remote device

The *restore*, GNU *tar,* and GNU *cpio* commands can read the remote device by simply giving it *remote_host:remote_device* as the device name. However, the native versions of *tar* and *cpio* do not support such an option. Therefore, you need some way to do this with these commands. You simply *rsh* a *dd* command to the remote system and read its data stream on the local system:

```
# rsh remote_host "dd if=device ibs=blocksize"| tar xvBf -
```

> Again, when reading a tape volume using *dd*, you normally have to specify a block size. If you do not, it uses a block size of 512, which generates an I/O error unless the tape volume was written with that block size. Also notice the quotes around the remote *dd* command. In this command, the quotes actually are not necessary, since the pipe is executed on the local system. In other, more complicated commands, such as one where there is a pipe to be executed on the remote system, quotes such as this around the remote command make things work properly. (In this instance, it merely makes it more readable.)

Writing a backup to a remote device

This one is a bit trickier. You may have to create a subshell* with embedded *rsh* and *dd* commands and pipe the output of the local backup command to that:

```
# tar cvf - . | (rsh remote_system dd of=device obs=block_size)
```

Putting parentheses around the remote command creates the subshell. Notice that you must specify the remote block size, and you need to be careful when doing

---

* Your mileage will vary. Not all versions of Unix require you to create a subshell.

so. If you want to create a volume that can be read by *tar*, make sure you use a block size that *tar* can understand, such as 10,240. (This is usually the biggest block size *tar* can read or write, and this is done by specifying a blocking *factor* of 20 in *tar*.)

If you are not able to use rsh

If you are not able to use *rsh*, you may look into using *ssh* as a drop-in replacement for *rsh*. The *ssh* command uses a much more secure authentication mechanism and allows you to do the same type of commands as *rsh* does without the security holes that *rsh* brings. However, using the remote device feature of GNU *tar*, GNU *cpio*, or *dump* assumes the use of *rsh*. If you are not allowed to use *rsh* but can use *ssh*, you can use commands like the following to integrate *dump*, *tar*, and *cpio* with *ssh*.

To read tapes on remote hosts:

```
# ssh remote_host "dd if=device bs=blocksize"| tar xvBf -
# ssh remote_host "dd if=device bs=blocksize"| restore rvf -
# ssh remote_host "dd if=device bs=blocksize"| cpio -itv
```

To create backup tapes on remote hosts:

```
# dump 0bdsf 64 100000 100000 - \
  | ssh remote_host "dd if=device bs=64k"
# tar cvf - | ssh remote_host "dd if=device bs=10k"
# cpio -oacvB | ssh remote_host "dd if=device bs=5k"
```

Using dd to Determine the Block Size of a Tape

This is kind of a neat trick. If you tell *dd* to read one block of data and then write it to disk, you can look at the size of that block to see what the block size of the tape is. Since you don't know the block size, start by using the largest block size that your operating system supports for that device, which is usually 128 K or 256 K, although it could be higher:

```
# dd if=device bs=128k of=/tmp/junk count=1
```

This tells *dd* to read data, using a block size of 128 K, until it gets to the first inter-record gap. If the block size is smaller than 128 K, it stops there. If it's bigger than 128 K, *dd* will interpret it as an I/O error and complain. Just increase the block size value and try again. (Try 256 K this time.) This process creates a file called */tmp/junk*. The size of that file is the block size of the tape!

Using dd to Figure out the Backup Format

Here's another trick. Use the same command as in the preceding section to create the file */tmp/junk*, then issue the command:

```
# file /tmp/junk
```

This uses /etc/magic to determine the file type. If it is *tar* or *cpio*, it usually comes back and tells you so. If it can't guess the file type, it just says "data," which isn't very helpful.

Comparing tar, cpio, and dump

A few years ago, John Pezzano from Hewlett-Packard did a paper comparing native backup products. It is the best one that I have seen, so I asked his permission to update it and include it in this book. It is Table 3-5.

Table 3-5. Conversion of Native Utilities

Feature	tar	cpio	dump
Simplicity of invocation	Very simple (*tar c files*)	Needs *find* to specify filenames	Simple—few options
Recovery from I/O errors	None—write your own utility	Resync option on HP-UX will cause some data loss	Automatically skips over bad section
Back up special files	Later revisions	Yes	Yes
Multivolume backup	Later revisions	Yes	Yes
Back up across network	Using *rsh* only	Using *rsh* only	Yes
Append files to backup	Yes (*tar −r*)	No	No
Multiple independent backups on single tape	Yes	Yes	Yes
Ease of listing files on the volume	Difficult—must search entire backup (*tar −t*)	Difficult—must search entire backup (*cpio −it*)	Simple—index at front (*restore −t*)
Ease and speed of finding a particular file	Difficult—no wildcards, must search entire volume	Moderate—wildcards, must search entire volume	Interactive—very easy with commands like *cd*, *ls*
Incremental backup	No	Must use *find* to locate new/modified files	Incremental of whole filesystem only, multiple levels
List files as they are being backed up	*tar cvf 2>logfile*	*cpio −v 2>logfile*	Only after backup with *restore −t > logfile* (*dump* can show % complete, though)
Back up based on other criteria	No	*find* can use multiple criteria	No

Table 3-5. Conversion of Native Utilities (continued)

Feature	tar	cpio	dump
Restore absolute pathnames to relative location	Only by using *chroot*	Limited with *cpio −I*	Always relative to current working directory
Interactive decision on restore	Yes or no possible with *tar −w*	Can specify new path or name on each file	Specify individual files in interactive mode
Compatibility	Multiple platform	Multiple platform with ASCII header, not always portable	Readable between *some* platforms, but cannot be relied on
Primary usefulness	Individual user backup, transfer files between filesystems	System backup, transfer files between filesystems	System backup
Volume efficiency	Medium, usually limited to 10 K block size	Medium, usually only 5 K block size, but can specify larger size on some OSes	High, can usually specify up to maximum block size of device
Wildcards on restore	No	Yes	Only in interactive mode
Simplicity of selecting files for backup from numerous directories	Low—must specify each independent directory, subdirectories included	Medium—*find* options	None—will back up one and only one filesystem
Specifying directory on restore get files in that directory	Yes	No—must use *path/***	Yes
Stop reading tape after a restored file is found	No	No	Will stop reading tape as soon as last file is found
Track deleted files	No	No	If you restore with *-r*, files deleted before last incremental dump will be deleted
Filesystem efficiency	Better	Worst (files get a *stat* from both *find* and *cpio*)	Best
Limit on path length (tests done with Solaris native utilities 7/99)	155 characters. Complains "prefix is greater than 155 characters." *gtar* has slight workaround	255 characters. Doesn't complain. Just truncates pathname to 255 *chars*	1056 characters.

Table 3-5. Conversion of Native Utilities (continued)

Feature	tar	cpio	dump
Likelihood that file exists in TOC but not in archive	Low	Low	Medium (since TOC is made first)

Standard Unix backup utilities may not be very sexy or even full of features, but if you get to know them, they will always be there. Some of the "seminative" commands (e.g., *tar*) are also very helpful, but they are not always available. Therefore, a good working knowledge of the truly native commands can come in very handy when you're in a jam or when someone hands you an unknown volume and says "Can you read this?"

How Do I Read This Volume?

If you're a system administrator long enough, someone eventually will hand you a volume and ask "Can you read this?" They don't know what the format is, or where the volume came from, but they want you to read it. Or you may have a very old backup volume that you wish you could read but can't. How do you handle this? How do you figure out what format a volume is? How do you read a volume that was written on a different machine? These are all questions answered in this chapter. There are about 10 factors to consider when trying to read an unknown or foreign volume, half of which have to do with the hardware itself— whether or not it is compatible. The other half have to do with the format of the data. If you are having trouble reading a volume, it could be caused by one or more of these problems.

Prepare in Advance

If you've just been handed a volume and need to read it right now, ignore this paragraph. If you work in a heterogeneous environment and might be reading volumes on different types of platforms, read it carefully now. Reading a volume on a platform other than that on which it was created is always difficult.

In fact, except for circumstances like a bad backup drive or data corruption, the only sure way to read a volume easily everytime is to read it on the machine that made it. Do not assume that you will be able to read a volume on another system because the volume is the same size, because the operating system is the same, or even if the utility goes by the same name. In fact, don't assume anything.

If it is likely that you are eventually going to have to read a volume on another type of system or another type of drive, see if it works *before* you actually need to do it. Also, if you can keep one or two of the old systems and drives around, you will have something to use if the new system doesn't work. (I know of companies that have 10- or 15-year-old computers sitting around for just this purpose.) If you test things up front, you might find out that you need to use a special option to make a backup that can be read on other platforms. You may find that it doesn't work at all. Of course, finding that out now is a lot better than finding it out two years from now when you really, really, really need that volume!

Wrong Media Type

Many media types look similar but really are not. DDS, 8mm, DLT, optical, 3×90, and other drives all have different generations of media that work in different generations of drives. If the volume is a tape and its drive has a Media Recognition System (MRS), it may even spit the tape back out if it is the wrong type. Sometimes MRS is not enabled or not present, so you assume that the tape should work because it fits in the drive. Certain types of media are made to work in certain types of drives, and if you've got the wrong media type for the drive that you are using, the drive will not be able to read it. Sometimes this is not initially obvious, since the drive reports media errors.

Problems involving incompatible media types sometimes can be corrected by using the newest drive that you have available. That is because many newer drives are able to read older tapes created with previous generations of drives. For example, a DDS-3 can read tapes that were made with the 1.6-GB DDS drives of years past. However, this is not always the case and can cause problems; for example, an AIT drive is an 8-mm drive, but it can read only AIT tapes. Exabyte's Mammoth drive can read the older non-AME tapes, but you must immediately clean the drive after doing so. Some drives can read tapes from only one or two generations ago; for example, a TR-3 drive can read TR-2 tapes but not TR-1s.

Bad or Dirty Drive

If the drive types and media types are the same but one drive cannot read the other drive's tapes, then the drive could be defective or just dirty. Try a cleaning tape, if one is available. If that does not work, the drive could be defective. It also is possible that the drive that wrote the tape was defective. A drive with misaligned heads, for example, may write a backup image that can't be read by a good drive. For this reason, when you are making a backup volume that is going to be stored for a long time, you should verify right away that it can be read in *another* drive.

Try, Try Again

During a restore, I came across a tape that kept on saying it was blank. Of course the info on the tape was needed for someone who accidentally deleted an important file. After several tries in all four tape drive units in the jukebox, it finally was able to be recognized and read. The restore was done without any further complications. After a lot of breath holding, prayer, and profanity, I realized the moral was—if you at first don't succeed, try, try again!

—Ed Lam

Different Drive Types

This is related to the media-types problem. Not all drives that look alike are alike. For example, not all DDS-2 drives are labeled that way. Not all drives that use hardware compression are labeled as such, either. The only way to know for sure is to check the model numbers of the two different drives. If they are different manufacturers, you may have to consult their web pages or even call them to make sure that the two drive types are compatible.

Wrong Compression Setting/Type

Usually, drives of the same type use the same kind of compression. However, some Value Added Resellers (VARs) sell drives that have been enhanced with a proprietary compression algorithm. They can get more compression with their algorithm, thus allowing the drive to write faster and store more. One such VAR is Contemporary Cybernetics, which claims a 5-to-1 compression ratio with their algorithm. This is more than twice what the Lempel-Ziv (DCLZ) algorithm claims. If all of your drives are from the same manufacturer, this may not be a problem—as long as the vendor stays in business! But if all your drives aren't from the same manufacturer, you should consider using an alternate compression setting if they have one, such as IDRC or DCLZ.* Again, this goes back to proper planning.

The Little Endian That Couldn't

Differences exist among machines of different architectures that may make moving volumes between them impossible. These differences include whether the machine is big-endian, little-endian, ones complement, or twos complement. For

---

* Typically, IDRC is found in Exabyte 8-mm drives and DLT drives, and DCLZ is found in DDS drives. Newer IBM drives and AIT 8-mm drives use a different algorithm.

They Used What Kind of Compression?

One day we needed to restore from some older tapes and were having trouble reading them. The drives kept complaining about I/O errors every time we tried to read one of these tapes. After further research, we found out that the tapes had been made on a particular brand of tape drive using their proprietary compression algorithm. Unfortunately, this company no longer made the drive. Luckily, we were able to find some refurbished drives that could read the tapes. The first thing we did was to copy them to a tape drive that used a standard compression algorithm.

—Mike Geringer

---

example, Intel-based machines are little-endian and RISC-based machines are big-endian. Moving volumes between these two types of platforms may be impossible.

Most big Unix machines are big-endian, but Intel x86 machines and older Digital machines are little-endian. (See Table 3-6.) That means that if you are trying to read a backup that was written on an NCR 3b2 (a big-endian machine), and you are using a backup drive on an NCR Intel SVr4 (little-endian) box, you may have a problem. There is also the issue of ones-complement and twos-complement machines, which are also different architectures. It is beyond the scope of this book to explain what is meant by big-endian, little-endian, ones complement, and twos complement. The purpose of this section is merely to point out that such differences exist and that if you have a volume written on one platform and are trying to read it on another, you may be running into this problem. Usually, the only way to solve it is to read the volume on its original platform.

Table 3-6. Big- and Little-Endian Platforms

Big-Endian	Little-Endian
SGI/MIPS, IBM/RS6000, HP/PA-RISC, Sparc/RISC, PowerPC, DG Aviion, HP/Apollo (400, DN3xxx, DN4xxx), NCR 3B2, TI 1500, Macintosh, Alpha[a]	DECStations[b], VAX, Intel x86

[a] I have heard that Alpha machines can actually be switched between big- and little-endian, but I can't find anyone to verify that. But Digital Unix is written for a big-endian alpha, so yours will probably be big-endian.

[b] These are the older DEC 3x00 and 5x00 series machines that run Ultrix.

Most backup formats use an "endian-independent" format, which means that their header and data can be read on any machine that supports that format. Usually, *tar* and *cpio* can do this, especially if you use the GNU versions. I have read GNU tar volumes on an Intel Unix or Linux (i.e., little-endian) box that were written on

HPs and SUNs (i.e., big-endian machines). For example, it is quite common to *ftp* *tar* files from a Unix machine to a Windows machine, then use Winzip to read them. Again, your mileage may vary, and it would help if you test it out first.

Some people talk about reading a volume with *dd* and using its *conv=swab* feature to swap the byte order of a volume. This may make the header readable but may make the data itself worthless. This is because of different byte sizes (eight bits versus 16 bits) and other things that are beyond the scope of this book. Again, the only way to make sure that this is not causing your inability to read a volume is to make sure that you are reading the volume on the same architecture on which was written.

Block Size (Tape Volumes Only)

Tape volumes are written in different block sizes, and you often need to know the block size of a tape before you can read it. This section describes how block sizes work, as well as how to determine your block size.

What is a block and why should I care?

When a program reads or writes data to or from a device or memory, it is referred to as an *I/O operation*. How much data is transferred during that I/O operation is referred to as a *block*. Since the actual creation of each block consumes resources, a larger block usually results in faster I/O operations (i.e., faster backups). When an I/O operation writes data to a disk, the block size that was used for that operation does not affect how the data is physically recorded on the disk; it affects only the performance of the operation. However, when an I/O operation writes to a tape drive, each block of data becomes a tape block, and each tape block is separated by an interrecord gap. This relationship is illustrated in Figure 3-4.

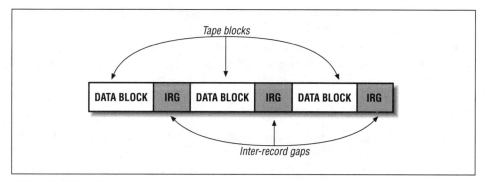

Figure 3-4. Tape blocks and interrecord gaps

All I/O operations that attempt to read from this tape must understand its block size, or they will be unsuccessful. If you use a different block size, three potential scenarios can occur.

Block size is a multiple of the original block size

For example, a tape was recorded with a block size of 1024, and you are reading it with a block size of 2048. This scenario is actually quite common and works just fine. Depending on a number of factors, the resulting read of the tape may be faster or slower than it would have been if it used the original block size. (Using a block size that is too large can actually slow down I/O operations.)

Block size is larger than the original block size (but not a multiple)

For example, a tape was recorded with a block size of 1024, and you are reading it with a block size of 1500. What happens here depends on your application, but most applications will return an I/O error. The read operation attempts to read a whole block of data, and when it reaches the end of the block that you told it to read, it does not find an interrecord gap. Most applications will complain and exit.

Block size is smaller than the original block size

For example, a tape was recorded with a block size of 1024, and you are reading it with a block size of 512. This will almost always result in an I/O error. Again, the application attempts to read a block of 512 bytes, then looks for the interrecord gap. If it doesn't see it, it complains and exits.

Interrecord gaps actually take up space on the tape. If you use a block size that is too small, you will fill up a lot of your tape with these interrecord gaps, and the tape actually will hold less data.

Each tape drive on each server has an optimal block size that allows it to stream best. Your job is to find out which block size gives you the best performance. A block size that is too small will decrease performance, whereas a block size that is too large may decrease performance as well, as the system may be paging or swapping to create that large block size. Some operating systems and platforms also limit the maximum block size.

Determine the blocking factor

Use the trick described earlier under "Using dd to Determine the Block Size of a Tape" to determine your block size. If you're reading a *tar* or *dump* backup, you'll need to determine the blocking factor. If the backup utility is *tar*, then the blocking factor usually is multiplied by 512. *dump*'s blocking factor usually is multiplied by 1024. Read the manpage for the command that you are using and determine the multiplier that it uses. Then, divide the block size by that multiplier. You now have your blocking factor.

For example, you read the tape with *dd*, and it says the block size is 32,768. The manpage for *dump* tells you that the blocking factor is multiplied times 1024. If you divide 32,768 by 1024, you will get a blocking factor of 32. You then can use this blocking factor with *restore* to read the tape.

AIX and its 512-byte block size

Some operating systems, such as AIX, allow you to hardcode the block size of a tape device. This means that no matter what block size you set with a backup utility, the device will always write using the hardcoded block size. During normal operations, most people set the block size to 0, allowing the device to write in any block size that you specify with your backup utility. (This is also known as "variable block size.") However, during certain operations, AIX automatically sets the block size to 512. This normally happens when performing a *mksysb* or *sysback* backup, and the reason this happens is that a block size of 512 makes the *mksysb/ sysback* tape look like a disk. That way, the system can boot off the tape, since it effectively looks just like the root disk. Most *mksysb/sysback* scripts set the block size back to 0 when they are done, but not all do so. You should check to make sure that your scripts do, to prevent you from unintentionally writing other tapes using this block size.

Why can't you read, on other systems, tapes that were written on AIX (with a block size of 512)? The reason is that AIX doesn't actually use a block size of 512. What AIX *really* does is write a block of 512 bytes and then pad it with 512 bytes of nulls. That means that they're really writing a block size of 1024, and half of each block is being thrown away! Only the AIX tape drives understand this. This means that a tape written with a block size of 512 can be read only on another AIX system.*

However, if you set the device's hardcoded block size to 0 (variable), you should have no problem on other systems—assuming the backup format is compatible. Setting it to 0 makes it work like every other tape drive. The block size you set with the backup utility is the block size the tape drive writes in. (If you want to check your AIX tape drive's block size now, start up *smit* and choose *Devices*, then *Tape Drives*, then *Change Characteristics*, and make sure that the block size of all your tape drives is set to 0!)

You can even set the block size of a device to 1024 without causing a compatibility problem. Doing so will force the device to write using a block size of 1024,

---

* I have often thought about writing a Perl program to read such a tape and throw away the nulls but just haven't gotten around to it!

regardless of what block size you specify with your backup utility. However, this is a "normal" block, unlike the unique type of block created by the 512-byte block size. Assuming that the backup format is compatible, you should be able to read such a tape on another platform. (I know of no reason why you would *want* to set the block size to 1024, though.)

To set the block size of a device back to 0, run the following command:

```
# chdev -1 device_name -a block_size=0
```

Unknown Backup Format

Obviously, when you are handed a foreign volume, you have no idea what backup utility was used to make that volume. If this happens, start by finding out the block size; it will come in handy trying to read an unknown format. Then, use that block size to try and read the volume using the various backup formats, such as *tar*, *cpio*, *dump*, and *pax*. I would try them in that order, since foreign volumes are most likely going to be in *tar* format, since it is the most interchangeable format.

One trick to finding the type of backup format is to take a block of data off of the volume and run the *file* command on it. This often will come back and say *cpio* or *tar*. If that happens, great! For example, if you used the block size-guessing command shown previously, you would have a file called */tmp/sizefile* that you used to determine the block size of the tape. If you haven't made this file, do so now, then enter this command:

```
# file /tmp/sizefile
```

If it just says "data," you're out of luck. But you just might get lucky, especially if you download from the Internet a "robust" *magic* file:

```
# file -f /etc/robust.magic /tmp/sizefile
```

In this case, *file* will help to reveal the format for commands and utilities not native to the immediate platform.

Different Backup Format

Sometimes, two commands sound the same but really aren't. This can be as simple as incompatible versions of *cpio*, or at the worst, completely incompatible versions of *dump*. Format inconsistencies between *tar* and *cpio* usually can be overcome by the GNU versions, since they automatically detect what format they are reading. However, if you are using an incompatible version of *dump* (such as *xfsdump* from IRIX), you are out of luck! You will need a system of that type to read the volume. Again, your mileage may vary. Make sure you test it up front.

A Day Late and a Dollar Short

In the mid-1980s, I was told that data needed to be recovered from a machine that had been decommissioned in the mid-1970s. I was told the name of the machine and about where the tapes were stored, so I started digging.

When I found the tapes, once I scrounged a tape drive with low enough density to be able to read them, I discovered that they were in a *dump* format that was no longer supported! I found the source code for the original *restore* program (the BSD 4.1 one in this case), downloaded it to my machine (SunOS 4.0.1 in this case, a BSD 4.3-like system), and started working on porting the old program. No good. I soon realized it would take me weeks to do it; the filesystem and *dump* formats had changed that much.

There *had* to be a different way, so I searched the data vaults for more tapes. Luckily, I found another stack of tapes, marked as being in *tar* format. I had lucked out! Most of these tapes were still readable, and the data came off the first try.

Moral of the story: when you decommission a machine, make an archival copy of the data in every format you can, on every type of media you can. Some, like *dump*, are very efficient but might not be supported someday, while others like *tar* and *cpio* have stayed around year in and year out. Times change, media change, formats change, so make as many variations as you can for your data to be retrievable as long as possible.

This made me a big fan of using *tar* for archival purposes, but that makes excellent sense. Its name stands for Tape ARchiver, after all.

—Doug Freyburger

Damaged Volume

One of the most common questions I see on Usenet is, "I accidentally typed *tar cvf* when I meant to type *tar xvf*. Is there any way to read what's left on this volume?" The quick answer is No. Why is that?

Each time a backup is written to a tape, an end-of-media (EOM) mark is made at the end of the backup. This mark tells the tape drive software, "There is no more data after this mark—no need to go any further." No matter what utility you try, it will always stop at the EOM mark, because it thinks this is the last backup on the tape. Of course, the tape could just be damaged or corrupted. One of the tricks I've seen used in this scenario is to use *cat* to read the corrupted tape:

```
# cat <device >/tmp/somefile
```

This just blindly reads in the data into */tmp/somefile*, so you can read it with *tar*, *cpio*, or *dump*.

The badtar utility

There is a utility written by Mike Williams called *badtar* that is designed to read damaged *tar* volumes. It is enclosed on the CD and also can be found on the web site *http://www.backupcentral.com.* Here are some quotes from the *README* file:

> The following program can be used to extract files from a tar tape that contains read errors. It is known to work for BSD systems. It is used as a filter whose output should be piped into tar thus

```
# badtar -f /dev/rmt16 -l log_file | tar xf -
```

> This program is not perfect. It cannot read what cannot be read, but it will continue over read errors, pad files to suitable lengths when blocks are missing, ignore files whose header tar blocks are mangled etc.

Reading a "flaky" tape

One of the fun things about being a backup specialist is that everyone tells you their favorite backup and recovery horror stories. One day a friend told me that he was having a really hard time reading a particularly flaky tape. The system would read just so far into the tape and then quit with an I/O error. However, if he tried reading that same section of tape again, it would work! He really needed the data on this particular tape, so he refused to give up. He wrote a shell script that would read the tape until it got an error. Then it would rewind the tape, fast-forward (*fsr*) to where he got the error, and try again. This script ran for two or three days before he finally got what he needed. I had never heard of such dedication. I told my friend Jim Donnellan (*sparky@colltech.com*) that he had to let me put the shell script in the book. The shell script in Example 3-2 was called *read-tape.sh* and actually did the job. Maybe this script will come in handy for someone else.

Example 3-2. The read-tape.sh Script

```
# !/bin/sh

DEVICE=/dev/rmt/0cbn
# Set this to a non-rewinding tape device

touch rawfile
# The rawfile might already be there, but just in case
while true ; do

 size=`ls -l rawfile | awk '{print $5}'` # Speaks for itself

 blocks=`expr "$size" / 512`
 # Ditto. 512 was a good blocksize for 4mm DAT. Just be consistent
```

Example 3-2. The read-tape.sh Script (continued)

```
full=`df -k . | grep <host> | awk '{print $6}'`
# Unfortunately, this only gets checked once per glitch. Maybe a fork?

echo $size
# Just so I know how it's going

echo $blocks

echo $full

if [ $full -gt 90 ] ; then
    echo "filesystem is filling up"
    exit 1
fi

mt -f $DEVICE rewind
# Let's not take chances. Start at the beginning.

sleep 60
# The drive hates this tape as it is. Give it a rest.

mt -f $DEVICE fsr $blocks

# However big rawfile is already, we can skip that on the tape

dd if=$DEVICE bs=512 >> rawfile # Let's get as much as we can

if [ $? -eq 0 ] ; then
 # If dd got clipped by a tape error, there's still work to do,
 echo "dd exited cleanly"

 # if not, it must have gotten to the end of the file this time
 # without a hitch. We're done.
 exit 0
fi

done
```

Send me your tips!

If you've got tips on how to read corrupted or damaged volumes, I want to hear them. If I use them in later editions of the book, I will credit your work! (I also will put any new ones I receive on the web site for everyone to get immediately.)

Multiple Partitions on a Tape

This one is more of a gotcha than anything else. Always remember when a backup is sent to tape, it could have more than one partition on that tape. If you are reading an unknown tape, you might try issuing the following commands:

```
# mt -t device rewind
# mt -t device fsf 1
```

Then, try again to read this backup. If it fails with "I/O error," then there are no more backups. (That's the EOM marker again.) If it doesn't fail, try the same commands that you tried in the beginning of the tape to read it. Do not assume that it is the same format as the first partition on the tape. For example, *hostdump.sh*, a program included in this book, puts a *tar* header on the front of every *dump* tape. Also understand that every time you issue a command to try and read the tape, you need to rewind it and fast-forward it again using the two preceding commands.

If at First You Don't Succeed . . .

Then skydiving probably is not for you! That doesn't mean that you have to stop trying to read that volume. Remember that the early bird gets the worm, but the second mouse gets the cheese. The next time you're stuck with a volume you can't read, remember my friend Jim and his flaky tape.

4

Free Backup Utilities

Whether you have a small budget or no budget, there are many utilities that are available to help you automate your backups. This chapter provides an overview of the following utilities:

- *hostdump.sh*, a plug-and-play backup script
- *infback.sh*, an Informix backup utility
- *oraback.sh*, an Oracle backup utility
- *syback.sh*, a Sybase backup utility
- *star*, a very fast implementation of *tar*
- *SysAudit*, a system configuration backup utility
- *SysInfo*, another system configuration backup utility
- *queso*, a program to determine, via a LAN connection, the operating system type of a server
- *nmap*, another network probing tool with a lot of added functionality

Then, we discuss in detail one of the most popular free backup utilities, the Advanced Maryland Automatic Network Disk Archiver, or AMANDA.

The hostdump.sh Utility

As discussed in Chapter 3, *Native Backup & Recovery Utilities*, the *hostdump.sh* utility is a plug-and-play backup script that supports more than 20 versions of Unix. The main purpose of *hostdump.sh* is to get a "quick-and-dirty" backup of a system before doing anything else to it. To use it, simply make sure there's a volume in the drive, then invoke *hostname.sh* with a device name and one or more hostnames, and it does the rest. The *hostdump.sh* utility backs up all the hosts that you list to the device that you specify. It automatically determines the names of all the filesystems, as well as their filesystem types. If it is a filesystem type that supports *dump*, it calls the appropriate command. If it is an unknown filesystem, or one that does not have a good *dump* command, it uses *cpio*. The *hostdump.sh* utility also puts two extra *tar* files on the volume. The first file is a header that lists all the filesystems on the volume and the commands that were used to back them up. After all backups are done, it then rereads the table of contents of each of the backups and places that information into a second *tar* file at the end of the volume. Detailed instructions on how to read the *tar* file at the end of the volume are also in the header file on the first partition. *hostdump.sh* is covered in detail in Chapter 3.

The infback.sh, oraback.sh, and syback.sh Utilities

These three programs do both cold and hot backups of Informix, Oracle, and Sybase, respectively. They are written in the Bourne shell, which is compatible with every Unix system. These scripts run on nearly every Unix platform because they use GNU's *config.guess*. They all have some method of creating a complete list of database instances on a server and then automatically backing up every instance found. All three scripts support these features:

- Backup to disk or tape

- Automatic detection of database configuration

- Backup of databases on filesystems or raw partitions

- Mail-based success and error notification

These scripts can be found on the CD and at *http://www.backupcentral.com*. They are discussed in detail in Part V of this book.

A Really Fast tar Utility: star

The *star* utility is the fastest known implementation of *tar*. It has been tested at speeds exceeding 14 MB/s. (This is more than double the speed that *dump* gets.) *star* development started in 1982 and is still in progress. *star*'s main advantages over other *tar* implementations are:

FIFO

> This is a "double-buffering" system that keeps the tape streaming. This gives you faster backups than you can achieve with *dump*, if the size of the filesystem is > 1 GB.

Sophisticated diff

It has a user-tailorable interface for comparing *tar* archives against file trees.

Longer pathname length

You may archive pathnames up to 1024 bytes, as you can with *dump.*

Does not clobber files

More recent copies on disk will not be clobbered from the backup volume. This may be the main advantage over other *tar* implementations. This allows automatic repair of a corrupted filesystem. (You can check for differences after doing this with the *diff* option.)

Automatic byte swap

star automatically detects swapped archives and transparently reads them the right way.

star is available from *ftp://ftp.fokus.gmd.de/pub/unix/star.*

Recording Configuration Data: The SysAudit Utility

The *SysAudit* utility, originally written by Robert Err and updated by David Young, discovers and records system configuration information such as:

- Disk partitioning information
- Volume manager configuration
- Filesystem configuration

It records this information in a file that can later be cross-checked against the current configuration. If SysAudit detects a change in the configuration, it can notify you. *SysAudit* is available at *http://www.backupcentral.com.*

Although the *SysAudit* utility isn't quite as sophisticated as the *SysInfo* utility described next, it does provide information that *SysInfo* does not. Specifically, it shows you how your disks are partitioned, which is something that will come in quite handy if you lose your entire system.

Displaying Host Information: The SysInfo Utility

SysInfo is a utility from Magnicomp that supports several different Unix platforms and is available at *http://www.magnicomp.com/sysinfo/sysinfo.shtml.* The following is Magnicomp's description of this utility:

> *SysInfo* displays various types of information about a host's hardware and operating system (OS) software. It is intended to provide information in both human readable and program parsable formats. System Administrators can use *SysInfo* to obtain hardware asset information and OS configuration information. Programs that use *SysInfo* can obtain this information in a platform independent manner. The amount of information displayed varies by operating system. Here are some of the types of information that may be provided (varies by platform):
>
> *   Host name
> *   Host name aliases
> *   Host network addresses
> *   Host ID
> *   System serial number
> *   Manufacturer of the system's hardware
> *   System model name
> *   CPU type
> *   Application architecture
> *   Kernel architecture
> *   Amount of main memory
> *   Operating system name
> *   Operating system version
> *   Kernel version
> *   A variety of information about devices
> *   A variety of different kernel parameters
> *   A variety of different system configuration parameters

Performing Remote Detections: The queso Utility

The *queso* utility performs remote operating system detection by sending a malformed TCP packet and observing how a particular host responds to it. The name is a shorthand version of the Spanish phrase, "Que Sistema Operativo?," which means "What is your operating system?" *queso* is used by the Internet Operating System Counter, a survey of operating system usage on the Internet (*http://www. leb.net/bzo/ioscount/index.html*). *queso* can be used to monitor the network, looking for new hosts that may be candidates for backups. You might be wondering how *queso* does what it does. This is what the author of *queso* had to say about that:

> How we can determine the remote OS using simple tcp packets? Well, it's easy, they're packets that don't make any sense, so the RFCs don't clearly state what to answer in these kind of situations. Facing this ambiguity, each TCP/IP stack takes a different approach to the problem, and this way, we get a different response. In some cases (like Linux, to name one) some programming mistakes make the OS detectable.

queso is available at *http://www.apostols.org/projectz/queso.*

Mapping Your Network: The nmap Utility

The Network Mapper, or *nmap*, is quite a bit more sophisticated than *queso*. Whereas *queso* can be passed only a single IP address or hostname, you can tell *nmap* to scan an entire range of IP addresses, such as your entire Class B network. Although it does detect the operating system of remote systems, it also can be used to detect security holes in your network. Here is a quote from the *nmap* web site that explains how it works:

> *Nmap* is a utility for port scanning large networks, although it works fine for single hosts. The guiding philosophy for the creation of *nmap* was TMTOWTDI (There's More Than One Way To Do It). This is the Perl slogan, but it is equally applicable to scanners. Sometimes you need speed, other times you may need stealth. In some cases, bypassing firewalls may be required. Not to mention the fact that you may want to scan different protocols (UDP, TCP, ICMP, etc.). You just can't do all this with one scanning mode. And you don't want to have 10 different scanners around, all with different interfaces and capabilities. Thus I incorporated virtually every scanning technique I know into *nmap*. Specifically, *nmap* supports:
>
> * Vanilla TCP connect() scanning,
> * TCP SYN (half open) scanning,
> * TCP FIN, Xmas, or NULL (stealth) scanning,
> * TCP ftp proxy (bounce attack) scanning
> * SYN/FIN scanning using IP fragments (bypasses packet filters),
> * UDP raw ICMP port unreachable scanning,
> * ICMP scanning (ping-sweep)
> * TCP Ping scanning
> * Remote OS Identification by TCP/IP Fingerprinting
> * Reverse-ident scanning
>
> *Nmap* also supports a number of performance and reliability features such as dynamic delay time calculations, packet timeout and retransmission, parallel port

scanning, detection of down hosts via parallel pings. *Nmap* also offers flexible target and port specification, decoy scanning, determination of TCP sequence predictability characteristics, and output to machine parsable or human readable log files.

nmap is available at *http://www.insecure.org/nmap.*

Since both *queso* and *nmap* can be used in a malicious way, please obtain written permission before running them on your network. You don't want your boss or client to think that you are trying to hack them!

AMANDA

AMANDA, the Advanced Maryland Automated Network Disk Archiver, is a public domain utility developed at the University of Maryland. It is as advanced as a free backup utility gets and has quite a large user community. With an installed base of at least 1500 sites, AMANDA is easily the most popular free backup utility of its type; therefore I am covering AMANDA in detail.

AMANDA allows you to set up a single master backup server to back up multiple hosts to a single backup drive. (It also works with a number of stackers.) AMANDA uses native *dump* and/or GNU *tar*, and can back up a large number of workstations running multiple versions of Unix. Recent versions also can use SAMBA, described later in this chapter, to back up Microsoft Windows (95/98/NT/ 2000)-based hosts. AMANDA is freely available software maintained by the AMANDA Users Group. More information about AMANDA can be found at *http:// www.amanda.org.*

This section was written by John R. Jackson with input from Alexandre Oliva. John has done system administration and operating systems and application development for more than 20 years on everything from peripheral processors to supercomputers. He currently works for the Purdue University Computing Center. Alexandre is a PhD student in computer science at the Institute of Computing of the State University of Campinas, Brazil, where he used to work as a system administrator and started to use and develop Amanda. John and Alexandre are members of the Amanda Core Development Team and may be reached at *jrj@purdue.edu* and *oliva@dcc.unicamp.br.*

AMANDA was written primarily by James da Silva at the Department of Computer Science of the University of Maryland around 1992. The goal was to be able to back up large numbers of client workstations to a single backup server machine.

AMANDA was driven by the introduction of large capacity tape drives, such as ExaByte 8 mm and DAT 4 mm. With these drives and the increased number of personal workstations, it no longer made sense to back up individual machines to separate media. Coordinating access and providing tape hardware was prohibitive in effort and cost. A typical solution to this problem reaches out to each client from the tape host and dumps areas one by one across the network. But this usually cannot feed the tape drive fast enough to keep it in streaming mode, causing a severe performance penalty.

 Since AMANDA is optimized to take advantage of tape drives, we will use the word *tape* throughout this section. However, that doesn't mean that you couldn't use it with an optical or CD-ROM drive.

The AMANDA approach is to use a "holding disk" on the tape server machine, do several dumps in parallel into files in the holding disk, and have an independent process take data out of the holding disk. Because most dumps are small partials, even a modest amount of holding disk space can provide an almost optimal flow of dump images onto tape.

AMANDA also has a unique approach to scheduling dumps. A "dump cycle" is defined for each area to control the maximum time between full dumps. AMANDA looks at that information, and at statistics about past dump performance, and estimates the size of dumps for this run to decide which backup level to do. This gets away from the traditional, static "It's Friday so do a full dump of */usr* on client A" approach and frees AMANDA to balance the dumps so the total runtime is roughly constant from day to day.

 This section is based on AMANDA Version 2.4.2. Updated versions of this section will be available with the AMANDA source code.

AMANDA Features

AMANDA is designed to handle large numbers of clients and data, yet is reasonably simple to install and maintain. It scales well, so small configurations, even a single host, are possible. The code is portable to a large number of Unix platforms. It calls standard backup software, such as vendor-provided *dump* or GNU *tar*, to perform actual client dumping. There also is support for backing up Windows-based hosts via SAMBA. There is no Macintosh support yet.

AMANDA provides its own network protocols on top of TCP and UDP. It does not, for instance, use *rsh* or *rdump/rmt*. Each client backup program is instructed to write to standard output, which AMANDA collects and transmits to the tape server host. This allows AMANDA to insert compression and encryption and also gather a catalog of the image for recovery. Multiple clients are typically backed up in parallel to files in one or more holding disk areas. A separate tape-writing process strives to keep the tape device streaming at maximum throughput. AMANDA can run direct to tape without holding disks, but with reduced performance.

AMANDA supports using more than one tape in a single run but does not yet split a dump image across tapes. This also means it does not support dump images larger than a single tape. AMANDA currently starts a new tape for each run and does not provide a mechanism to append a new run to the same tape as a previous run, which might be an issue for small configurations.

AMANDA supports a wide range of tape storage devices. It uses basic operations through the normal operating system I/O subsystem and a simple definition of characteristics. New devices usually are trivial to add. Several tape changers, stackers, and robots are supported to provide truly hands-off operation. The changer interface is external to AMANDA and well documented, so unsupported changers can be added without a lot of effort.

Either the client or tape server may do software compression, or hardware compression may be used. On the client side, software compression reduces network traffic. On the server side, it reduces client CPU load. Software compression may be selected on an image-by-image basis. If Kerberos is available, clients may use it for authentication, and dump images may be encrypted. Without Kerberos, *amandahosts* authentication (similar to *.rhosts*) is used, or AMANDA may be configured to use *.rhosts* (although *rsh*, *rlogin*, and *rexec* are not themselves used). AMANDA works well with security tools like TCP wrappers (*ftp://info.cert.org/pub/network_tools*) and firewalls.

Since standard software is used for generating dump images and software compression, only normal Unix tools such as *mt*, *dd*, and *gunzip/uncompress* are needed to recover a dump image from tape if AMANDA is not available. When AMANDA software is available, it locates which tapes are needed and finds images on the tapes.

AMANDA is meant to run unattended, such as from a nightly *cron* job. Client hosts that are down or hung are noted and bypassed. Tape errors cause AMANDA to fall back to "degraded" mode in which backups are still performed but only to the holding disks. They may be flushed to tape by hand after the problem is resolved.

AMANDA has configuration options for controlling almost all aspects of the backup operation and provides several scheduling methods. A typical configuration does periodic full dumps with partial dumps in between. There is also support for:

- Periodic archival backup, for purposes such as taking full dumps to a vault away from the primary site

- Incremental-only backups in which full dumps are done outside of AMANDA, such as for very active areas that must be taken offline, or no full dumps at all for areas that can easily be recovered from vendor media

- Full dumps, such as of database areas that change completely between each run or critical areas that are easier to deal with during an emergency if they are a single-restore operation

It's easy to support multiple configurations on the same tape server machine, such as a periodic archival configuration along side a normal daily configuration. Multiple configurations can run simultaneously on the same tape server if there are multiple tape drives.

Scheduling full dumps is typically left up to AMANDA. They are scattered throughout the dump cycle to balance the amount of data backed up each run. It's important to keep logs of where backup images are for each area (which AMANDA does for you), since they are not on a specific, predictable, tape (e.g., the Friday tape will not always have a full dump of */usr* for client A). The partial backup level also is left to AMANDA. History information about previous levels is kept and the backup level automatically increases when sufficient dump size savings will be realized.

AMANDA uses a simple tape management system and protects itself from overwriting tapes that still have valid dump images and from tapes not allocated to the configuration. Images may be overwritten when a client is down for an extended period or if not enough tapes are allocated, but only after AMANDA has issued several warnings. AMANDA also can be told to not reuse specific tapes.

A validation program may be used before each run to note potential problems during normal working hours when they are easier to correct. An activity report is sent via email after each run. AMANDA also can send a report to a printer and even generate sticky tape labels.

There is no graphical interface. For administration, there is usually only a single simple text file to edit, so this is not much of an issue. For security reasons, AMANDA does not support user-controlled file recovery. There is an *ftp*-like restore utility for administrators to make searching online dump catalogs easier when recovering individual files.

Future Capabilities of AMANDA

In addition to the usual enhancements and fixes constantly being added by the AMANDA Core Development Team, three main changes are in various stages of development.

- A new internal security framework will make it easier for developers to add other security methods, such as SSH (Secure Shell) (*ftp://ftp.cs.hut.fi/pub/ssh/*) and SSL (Secure Socket Layer).

- Another major project is a redesign of how AMANDA runs the client *dump* program. This is currently hardcoded for a vendor *dump* program, GNU *tar* or SAMBA *tar*. The new mechanism will allow arbitrary programs such as *cpio*, *star*, and possibly other backup systems. It also will add optional predump and postdump steps that can be used for locking and unlocking and snapshots of rapidly changing data such as databases or the Windows Registry.

- The third major project is a redesign of the output subsystem to support non-tape media such as CD-ROM, local files, remote files via tools like *rcp* and *ftp*, remote tapes, and so on. It also will be able to split dump images across media, handle multiple simultaneous media of different types such as writing to multiple tapes or a tape and a CD-ROM, and handle writing copies of images to multiple media such as a tape to keep on site and a CD-ROM or duplicate tape for archiving.

  In addition, the output format will be enhanced to include a *file-1* and a *file-n*. The idea is to put site-defined emergency recovery tools in *file-1* (the first file on the output) that can be retrieved easily with standard non-AMANDA programs like tar, then use those tools to retrieve the rest of the data. The *file-n* area is the last file on the output and can contain items such as the AMANDA database, which would be complete and up-to-date by the time *file-n* is written.

AMANDA Resources

AMANDA may be obtained via the *http://www.amanda.org* web page or with anonymous FTP at *ftp://ftp.amanda.org/pub/amanda/*.

A typical release is a *gzip*-compressed *tar* file with a name like *amanda-2.4.1.tar.gz*, which means it is major Version 2.4 and minor Version 1. There are occasional patch releases that have a name like *amanda-2.4.1p1.tar.gz* (release 2.4.1 plus patch set 1). Beta test prereleases have names like *amanda-2.5.0b3.tar.gz* (third beta test prerelease of 2.5.0).

Some operating system distributions provide precompiled versions of AMANDA, but because AMANDA hardcodes some values into the programs, they may not match the configuration. Work is being done to move these values to runtime configuration files, but for now AMANDA should be built from source.

The AMANDA web page contains useful information about patches not yet part of a release, how to subscribe to related mailing lists, and pointers to mailing list archives. Subscribe to at least *amanda-announce* to get new release announcements or *amanda-users* to get announcements plus see problems and resolutions from other AMANDA users. The *amanda-users* mailing list is a particularly good resource for help with initial setup as well as problems. When posting to it, be sure to include the following information:

- AMANDA version

- OS version on the server and client(s)

- Exact symptoms seen, such as error messages, relevant sections of email reports, debugging and log files

- Anything unusual or recent changes to the environment

- A valid return email address

Finally, the *docs* directory in the release contains several files with helpful information, such as a FAQ.

Installing AMANDA

After downloading and unpacking the AMANDA release, read the *README, docs/ INSTALL,* and *docs/SYSTEM.NOTES* files. They contain important and up-to-date information about how to set up AMANDA.

Install related packages

Several other packages may be required to complete an AMANDA install. Before continuing, you should locate and install packages your environment will need. In particular, consider the following:

GNU tar 1.12 or later   *www.gnu.org*
    The GNU version of the standard *tar* program with enhancements to do partial backups and omit selected files. It is one of the client backup programs AMANDA knows how to use.

SAMBA 1.9.18p10 or later   *www.samba.org*
    SAMBA is an implementation of the System Message Block (SMB) protocol used by Windows-based systems for file access. It contains a tool, *smbclient*, that AMANDA can use to back them up.

Perl 5.004 or later   *www.perl.org*

> *Perl* is a scripting programming language oriented toward systems program-
> ming and text manipulation. It is used for a few optional AMANDA reporting
> tools and by some tape changers.

GNU readline 2.2.1 or later   *www.gnu.org*

> The GNU *readline* library may be incorporated into interactive programs to
> provide command-line history and editing. It is built into the AMANDA
> *amrecover* restoration tool, if available.

GNU awk 3.0.3 or later   *www.gnu.org*

> The GNU version of the *awk* programming language contains a common ver-
> sion across platforms and some additional features. It is used for the optional
> AMANDA *amplot* statistics tool.

gnuplot 3.5 or later   *ftp://ftp.dartmouth.edu/pub/gnuplot/*

> This *gnuplot* library (which has nothing to do with the GNU tools; see the
> accompanying *README*) is a graph-plotting package. It is used for the
> optional AMANDA *amplot* statistics tool.

Be sure to look in the AMANDA *patches* directory and the patches section on the
web page for updates to these packages. SAMBA versions before 2.0.3, in particular, must have patches applied to make them work properly with Amanda. Without the patches, backups appear to work, but the resulting images are corrupt.

When AMANDA is configured, locations of additional software used on the clients, such as GNU *tar* and SAMBA, get built into the AMANDA programs, so additional software must be installed in the same place on the AMANDA build machine
and all the clients.

Perform preliminary setup

A typical AMANDA configuration runs as a user other than root, such as backup or
amanda, given just enough permissions to do backups. Often, direct login as the
user is disallowed. To use the vendor dump program instead of GNU *tar*, the
AMANDA user must be in a group with read access to the raw disk devices. Membership in this group should be tightly controlled since it opens up every file on
the client for viewing.

There are two ways to link AMANDA and the raw device group membership.
Either put the AMANDA user in the group that currently owns the raw devices, as
the primary group or as a secondary, or pick a new group for AMANDA and
change the group ownership of the devices. AMANDA (actually, the vendor *dump*
program) needs only read access, so turn off group write permission. Turn off all
"world" access.

AMANDA runs GNU *tar* under a *setuid*-root program that grants the needed permissions. The GNU version of *tar* must be used with AMANDA. Vendor-supplied versions (unless they originated from GNU and are at least Version 1.12) do not work because AMANDA depends on additional features.

Configure the AMANDA build

Use the AMANDA user and group for the *--with-user* and *--with-group* options to *./configure*. For instance, to use amanda for the user and backup as the group:

```
# ./configure --with-user=amanda --with-group=backup ...
```

No other options are required for *./configure*, but all the possibilities may be seen with *./configure --help*. Don't get carried away changing options. The defaults are usually suitable and some require experience with AMANDA to fully understand. Leave *--with-debugging* enabled so debug log files are created on the clients. They take very little space but often are necessary for tracking down problems.

The normal build creates both tape server and client software. The tape server host often is backed up by AMANDA and needs the client parts. However, the clients usually do not need the tape server parts. A little disk space and build time may be saved by adding *--without-server* to the *./configure* arguments when building for them.

The default security mechanism uses a file formatted just like *.rhosts* but called *amandahosts*. This keeps AMANDA operations separate from normal *rsh/rcp* work that might use the same user. It is not recommended, but *.rhosts* and *hosts.equiv* may be used by adding *--without-amandahosts* to the *./configure* arguments.

The TCP ports used for data transfer may be restricted with *--with-portrange* to use AMANDA between hosts separated by a firewall. A typical entry would be:

```
# ./configure --with-portrange=50000,50100 ...
```

This does not affect the initial UDP requests made from the tape server to the clients. The amanda UDP port (typically 10080) must be allowed through the firewall.

If more than just a few *./configure* options are used, they may be put in */usr/local/share/config.site* or */usr/local/etc/config.site* to keep them the same from build to build. An example is in *example/config.site*.

Build and install AMANDA

After *./configure* is done, run *make* to build AMANDA, then *make install* to install it. The *make install* step must be done as root because some AMANDA programs require system privileges.

Unless the base location is changed, AMANDA installs into these areas:

/usr/local/sbin
> Programs administrators run

/usr/local/lib
> Libraries

/usr/local/libexec
> Private programs only AMANDA uses

/usr/local/man
> Documentation

Now is a good time to read the main *amanda* manpage. It provides an overview of AMANDA, a description of each program, and detailed configuration information.

The following programs must be *setuid*-root (which *make install* as root does). The first group (*amcheck*, *dumper*, and *planner*) run on the tape server machine and need a privileged network port for secure communication with the clients. The others are utility routines optionally used on the clients, depending on the *dump* program used and operating system type.

sbin/amcheck
> AMANDA sanity checker program

libexec/dumper
> Client communication program

libexec/planner
> Estimate gathering program

libexec/killpgrp
> Used to kill vendor *dump* programs that run as root

libexec/rundump
> Setuid wrapper for systems that need to run the vendor *dump* program as root

libexec/runtar
> Setuid wrapper to run GNU *tar* as root

All these programs are installed with world access disabled and group access set to the AMANDA group from *--with-group*. Be sure all members of that group are trustworthy since *rundump* and *runtar* in particular give access to every file on the system.

If AMANDA software is made available via NFS, be sure the mount options allow setuid programs. Also, if GNU *tar* is used, root needs write access to */usr/local/var/ amanda/gnutar-lists* (or the *--with-gnutar-list* value to *./configure*) to store information about each partial level.

If the build has trouble or AMANDA needs to be rebuilt, especially with different *./configure* options, the following sequence makes sure everything is cleaned up from the previous build:

```
# make distclean
# ./configure ...
# make
# make install          (as root)
```

Problems with the *./configure* step sometimes can be diagnosed by looking at the *config.log* file. It contains detailed output of tests *./configure* runs. Note that it is normal for many of the tests to "fail" as part of *./configure* determining how to access various features on the system.

A common problem when using the GNU C compiler is not reinstalling it after the underlying operating system version changes. *gcc* is particularly sensitive to system header files and must be reinstalled or have its *fixincludes* step rerun (see the *gcc* release installation notes) if the operating system is upgraded. Running *gcc --verbose* shows where *gcc* gets its information and contains an indication of the operating system version expected.

AMANDA needs changes to the network services and *inetd* configuration files. The *client-src/patch-system* script should be able to set up systems in most cases. It currently does not handle systems that deliver service entries via YP/NIS. If the script does not work, add the following entries to the services file (e.g., */etc/services*) or YP/NIS map:

```
Amanda          10080/udp
Amandaidx       10082/tcp
Amidxtape       10083/tcp
```

Each client needs an entry in the *inetd* configuration file (e.g., */etc/inetd.conf*) like this, substituting the AMANDA user for *Amanda* and the full path to the AMANDA *libexec* directory for *PATH*:

```
amanda dgram udp wait Amanda /PATH/libexec/amandad amandad
```

The *amanda* service is used by all AMANDA controlling programs to perform functions on the clients.

The tape server host needs entries like these if the *amrecover* tool is to be used:

```
amandaidx stream tcp nowait Amanda /PATH/libexec/amindexd amindexd
amidxtape stream tcp nowait Amanda /PATH/libexec/amidxtaped amidxtaped
```

The *amandaidx* service provides access to the catalogs, while *amidxtape* provides remote access to a tape device. After every *inetd configuration* file change, send a HUP signal to the *inetd* process and check the system logs for errors.

Configuring AMANDA

Once installed, AMANDA must be configured to your environment.

Decide on a tape server

The first thing to decide is what machine will be the AMANDA tape server. AMANDA can be CPU-intensive if configured to do server compression, and almost certainly network and I/O-intensive. It typically does not use much real memory. It needs direct access to a tape device that supports media with enough capacity to handle the expected load.

To get a rough idea of the backup sizes, take total disk usage (not capacity), *Usage*, and divide it by how frequently full dumps will be done, *Runs*. Pick an estimated run-to-run change rate, *Change*. Each AMANDA run, on average, does a full dump of *Usage/Runs*. Another *Usage/Runs*Change* is done of areas that got a full dump the previous run, *Usage/Runs*Change*2* is done of areas that got a full dump two runs ago, and so on.

For example, with 100 GB of space in use, a full dump every seven runs (e.g., days), and estimated run-to-run changes (new or altered files) of 5 percent:

```
100 GB / 7              = 14.3 GB
100 GB / 7 * 5%         =  0.7 GB
100 GB / 7 * 5% * 2     =  1.4 GB
100 GB / 7 * 5% * 3     =  2.1 GB
100 GB / 7 * 5% * 4     =  2.9 GB
100 GB / 7 * 5% * 5     =  3.6 GB
100 GB / 7 * 5% * 6     =  4.3 GB
                        = 29.3 GB
```

If 50 percent compression is expected, the actual amount of tape capacity needed for each run, which might be on more than one tape, would be 14.7 GB. This is very simplistic and could be improved with greater knowledge of actual usage but should be close enough to start with. It also gives an estimate of how long each run will take by dividing expected capacity by drive speed.

Decide which tape devices to use

Unix operating systems typically incorporate device characteristics into the file-name used to access a tape device. The two to be concerned with are "rewind" and "compression." AMANDA must be configured with the nonrewinding tape device, so called because when the device is opened and closed it stays at the same position and does not automatically rewind. This is typically a name with an *n* in it, such as */dev/rmt/0n*. On AIX, it is a name with a *.1* or *.5* suffix.

Put the AMANDA user in the group that currently owns the tape device, either as the primary group or as a secondary, or pick a new group for AMANDA and change the group ownership of the device. AMANDA needs both read and write access. Turn off all "world" access.

Decide whether to use compression

Optionally, dump images may be compressed on the client, the tape server, or the tape device hardware. Software compression allows AMANDA to track usage and make better estimates of image sizes, but hardware compression is more efficient with CPU resources. Turn off hardware compression when using software compression on the client or server. See the operating system documentation for how hardware compression is controlled; on many systems it is done via the device filename just like the nonrewinding flag. AIX uses the *chdev* command.

Decide where the holding space will be

If at all possible, allocate some holding disk space for AMANDA on the tape server. Holding disk space can reduce backup time by significantly allowing several dumps to be done at once while the tape is being written. Also, for streaming tape devices, AMANDA keeps the device going at speed, and that may increase capacity. AMANDA may be configured to limit disk use to a specific value so it can share with other applications, but a better approach is to allocate one or more inexpensive disks entirely to AMANDA.

Ideally, there should be enough holding disk space for the two largest backup images simultaneously, so one image can be coming into the holding disk while the other is being written to tape. If that is not practical, any amount that holds at least a few of the smaller images helps. The AMANDA report for each run shows the size of the dump image after software compression (if enabled). That, in addition to the *amplot* and *amstatus* tools, may be used to fine-tune the space allocated.

Compute your dump cycle

Decide how often AMANDA should do full dumps. This is the "dump cycle." Short periods make restores easier because there are fewer partials but use more tape and time. Longer periods let AMANDA spread the load better but may require more steps during a restore.

Large amounts of data to back up or small capacity tape devices also affect the dump cycle. Choose a period long enough that AMANDA can do a full dump of every area during the dump cycle and still have room in each run for the partials. Typical dump cycles are one or two weeks. Remember that the dump cycle is an upper limit on how often full dumps are done, not a strict value. AMANDA runs them more often and at various times during the cycle as it balances the backup load. It violates the limit only if a dump fails repeatedly and issues warnings in the email report if that is about to happen.

By default, AMANDA assumes it is run every day. If that is not the case, set "runs per cycle" (described later) to a different value. For instance, a dump cycle of seven days and runs per cycle of five would be used if runs are done only on weekdays.

Normally, AMANDA uses one tape per run. With a tape changer (even the *chg-manual* one), the number of tapes per run may be set higher for extra capacity. This is an upper limit on the number of tapes. AMANDA uses only as much tape as it needs. AMANDA does not yet do overflow from one tape to another. If it hits end of tape (or any other error) while writing an image, that tape is unmounted, the next one is loaded, and the image starts over from the beginning. This sequence continues if the image cannot fit on a tape.

Runs per cycle and tapes per run determine the minimum number of tapes needed, called the "tape cycle." To ensure the current run is not overwriting the last full dump, one more run should be included. For instance, a dump cycle of two weeks, with default runs per cycle of 14 (every day) and default tapes per run of one, needs at least 15 tapes (14+1 runs times 1 tape/run). Using two tapes per run 30 tapes (14+1 runs times 2 tapes/run). Doing backups just on weekdays with a dump cycle of two weeks, runs per cycle of 10, and two tapes per run 22 tapes (10+1 runs times 2 tapes/run).

More tapes than the minimum should be allocated to handle error situations. Allocating at least two times the minimum allows the previous full dump to be used if the most recent full dump cannot be read. Allocating more tapes than needed also goes back further in time to recover lost files. AMANDA does not have a limit on the number of tapes in the tape cycle.

Copy and edit the default configuration file

Pick a name for the configuration (the name *Daily* will be used for the rest of this section). Create a directory on the tape server machine to hold the configuration files, typically */usr/local/etc/amanda/Daily*. Access to this directory (or perhaps its parent) should be restricted to the AMANDA group or even to the AMANDA user.

Each tape assigned to a configuration needs a unique label. For this example, we'll use the configuration name, a dash, and a three-digit suffix, `Daily-000` through `Daily-999`. Do not use blanks, tabs, slashes (/), shell wildcards, or nonprintable characters.

AMANDA limits network usage so backups do not take all the capacity. This limit is imposed when AMANDA is deciding whether to perform a dump by estimating the throughput and adding that to dumps that are already running. If the value exceeds the bandwidth allocated to AMANDA, the dump is deferred until enough others complete. Once a dump starts, AMANDA lets underlying network components do any throttling.

Copy the template *example/amanda.conf* file to the configuration directory and edit it. Full documentation is in the *amanda* manpage. There are many parameters, but probably only a few need to be changed. Start with the following (some of which are described later):

org
: This string will be in the subject line of AMANDA email reports.

mailto
: Target address for AMANDA email reports.

dumpuser
: Same as *--with-user* from *./configure*.

dumpcycle
: The dump cycle.

runspercycle
: The runs per cycle.

tapecycle
: The tape cycle.

runtapes
: Number of tapes to use per run.

tapedev
: The no-rewind tape device if a changer is not being used or if the manual changer is being used.

tapetype
: Type of tape media.

netusage
: Network bandwidth allocated to AMANDA.

labelstr
: A regular expression (*grep* pattern) used to make sure each tape is allocated to this AMANDA configuration. Our example might use `Daily-[0-9][0-9][0-9]`.

The following parameters probably do not need to be changed, but look at their values to know where AMANDA expects to find things:

infofile
: Location of AMANDA history database. Older versions of AMANDA used this as the base name of a database file. Newer versions use this as a directory name.

logdir

Directory in which AMANDA logs are stored.

indexdir

Location of optional AMANDA catalog database.

Configure the holding disk

Define each holding disk in an *amanda.conf holdingdisk* section. If partitions are dedicated to AMANDA, set the *use* value to a small negative number, such as −10 MB. This tells AMANDA to use all but that amount of space. If space is shared with other applications, set the value to the amount AMANDA may use, create the directory, and set the permissions so only the AMANDA user can access it.

Set a *chunksize* value for each holding disk. Negative numbers cause AMANDA to write dumps larger than the absolute value directly to tape, bypassing the holding disk. Positive numbers split dumps in the holding disk into chunks no larger than the *chunksize* value. Even though the images are split in the holding disk, they are written to tape as a single image. At the moment, all chunks for a given image go to the same holding disk.

Older operating systems that do not support individual files larger than 2 GB need a chunk size slightly smaller, such as 2000 MB, so the holding disk still can be used for very large dump images. Systems that support individual files larger than 2 GB should have a very large value, such as 2000 GB.

Configure tape devices and label tapes

AMANDA needs to know some characteristics of the tape media. This is set in a *tapetype section*. The example *amanda.conf*, web page, and *amanda-users* mailing list archives have entries for most common media. Currently, all tapes should have the same characteristics. For instance, do not use both 60-meter and 90-meter DAT tapes since AMANDA must be told the smaller value, and larger tapes may be underutilized.

If the media type is not listed and there are no references to it in the mailing list archives, go to the *tape-src* directory, *make tapetype*, mount a scratch tape in the drive, and run *./tapetype NAME DEV* where *NAME* is a text name for the media and *DEV* is the no-rewind tape device with hardware compression disabled. This program rewinds the tape, writes random data until it fills the tape, rewinds, and then writes random data and tape marks until it fills the tape again. This can take a very long time (hours or days). When finished, it generates a new *tapetype* section to standard output suitable for adding to the *amanda.conf* file. Post the results to the *amanda-users* mailing list so others may benefit from your effort.

When using hardware compression, change the *length* value based on the estimated compression rate. This typically means multiplying by something between 1.5 and 2.0.

The *length* and *filemark* values are used by AMANDA only to plan the backup schedule. Once dumps start, AMANDA ignores the values and writes until it gets an error. It does not stop writing just because it reaches the *tapetype length.* AMANDA does not currently use the *tapetype speed* parameter.

Once the *tapetype* definition is in *amanda.conf,* set the *tapetype* parameter to reference it.

Without special hardware to mount tapes, such as a robot or stacker, either set the *tapedev* parameter to the no-rewind device name or set up the AMANDA *chg-manual* changer. The manual changer script prompts for tape mounts as needed. The prompts normally go to the terminal of the person running AMANDA, but the changer may be configured to send requests via email or to some other system logging mechanism.

To configure the manual changer, set *tapedev* to the no-rewind tape device and set *tpchanger* to *chg-manual.* To send tape mount prompts someplace other than the terminal, which is necessary if AMANDA is run from a *cron* job, see the *request* shell function comments in *changer-src/chg-manual.sh.in.*

Another common tape changer is *chg-multi.* This script can drive stackers that advance to the next tape when the drive is unloaded, or it can use multiple tape drives on the tape sever machine to emulate a changer. The *chg-multi* script has a configuration file and a state file. Put the path to the configuration file in the *amanda.conf changerfile* parameter. There is a sample in *example/chg-multi.conf.* It has the following keyword/value pairs separated by whitespace:

firstslot
> Number of the first slot in the device.

lastslot
> Number of the last slot in the device.

gravity
> Set to 1 if the device is gravity fed and cannot go backward, otherwise set to 0.

needeject
> Set to 1 if the tape needs to be ejected to advance to a new tape, otherwise set to 0.

multieject
> Set to 1 if sending multiple ejects causes the changer to advance through the tapes, otherwise set to 0. If set to 1, *gravity* also must be set to 1, because the

script currently does not handle carousels that wrap back around to the first tape after the last one. Also, *needeject* must be set to 0.

ejectdelay

Set to a number of seconds of extra delay after ejecting a tape if it takes a while before the next tape is ready.

statefile

Set to the path to a file *chg-multi* builds and maintains with the current state of the changer.

slot

Repeat as needed to define all the slots and corresponding tape devices. The first field after *slot* is the slot number. The next field is the no-rewind tape device name. For changers that have a single tape device, repeat the device name for each slot. To emulate a changer by using multiple tape devices, list a different no-rewind tape device for each slot.

chg-multi also may be used as a framework to write a new changer. Look for **XXX** comments in the script and insert calls to commands appropriate for the device. Make any source changes to the *changer-src/chg-multi.sh.in* file. That file is processed by *./configure* to generate *chg-multi.sh*, which turns into *chg-multi* with *make*. If *chg-multi.sh* or *chg-multi* is altered, the changes will be lost the next time AMANDA is rebuilt.

A third popular changer is *chg-scsi*. It can drive devices that have their own SCSI interface. An operating system kernel module may need to be installed to control such devices, like *sst* for Solaris, which is released with AMANDA, or *chio*, available for various systems. As with *chg-multi*, set the *amanda.conf changerfile* parameter to the changer configuration file path. There is a sample in *example/chg-scsi.conf*. The initial section has parameters common to the entire changer:

number_configs

Set to the number of tape drives connected to this changer. The default is 1.

eject

Set to 1 if tape drives need an explicit eject command before advancing to the next tape, otherwise set to 0.

sleep

Set to the number of seconds to wait for a tape drive to become ready.

changerdev

Set to the device path of the changer. This may be set in the *amanda.conf* file instead of here if preferred.

Following the common parameters is a section for each tape device:

config
> Set to the configuration number, starting with 0.

drivenum
> Set to the tape drive number, usually the same as the configuration number.

dev
> Set to the no-rewind device name of the tape drive.

startuse
> Set to the number of the first slot served by this drive.

enduse
> Set to the number of the last slot served by this drive.

statfile
> Set to the path to a file *chg-scsi* will build and maintain with the current state of this drive.

Test any changer setup with the *amtape* command. Make sure it can load a specific tape with the *slot NNN* suboption, eject the current tape with *eject*, and advance to the next slot with *slot next*.

Tapes must be prelabeled with *amlabel* so AMANDA can verify the tape is one it should use. Run *amlabel* as the AMANDA user, not root. For instance:

```
# su amanda -c "amlabel Daily Daily-123 slot 123"
```

Configure backup clients

After tapes are labeled, pick the first client, often the tape server host itself, and the filesystems or directories to back up. For each area to back up, choose either the vendor *dump* program or GNU *tar*. Vendor *dump* programs tend to be more efficient and do not disturb files being dumped but usually are not portable between different operating systems. GNU *tar* is portable and has some additional features, like the ability to exclude patterns of files, but alters the last access time for every file backed up and may not be as efficient. GNU *tar* also may deal with active filesystems better than vendor *dump* program, and is able to handle very large filesystems by breaking them up by subdirectories.

Choose the type of compression for each area, if any. Consider turning off compression of critical areas needed to bring a machine back from the dead in case the decompression program is not available. Client compression spreads the load to multiple machines and reduces network traffic but may not be appropriate for slow or busy clients. Server compression increases the load on the tape server machine, possibly by several times since multiple dumps are done at once. For either, if GNU *gzip* is used, compression may be set to **fast** for faster but less aggressive compression or **best** for slower but more aggressive compression. Set *compression* to none to disable software compression or use hardware compression.

Pick or alter an existing *dumptype* that matches the desired options, or create a new one. Each *dumptype* should reference the **global** *dumptype*. It is used to set options for all other *dumptypes*. For instance, to use the indexing facility, enable it in the **global** *dumptype* and all other *dumptypes* will inherit that value.

The indexing facility generates a compressed catalog of each dump image. These are useful for finding lost files and are the basis of the *amrecover* program. Long dump cycles or areas with many or very active files can cause the catalogs to use a lot of disk space. AMANDA automatically removes catalogs for images that are no longer on tape.

Create a file named *disklist* in the same directory as *amanda.conf* and either copy the file from *example/disklist* or start a new one. Make sure it is readable by the AMANDA user. Each line in *disklist* defines an area to be backed up. The first field is the client hostname (fully qualified names are recommended), the second is the area to be backed up on the client, and the third is the *dumptype*. The area may be entered as a disk name (*sd0a*) a device name (*/dev/rsd0a*) or a logical name, (*/usr*). Logical names make it easier to remember what is being backed up and to deal with disk reconfiguration.

To set up a Windows client, set the hostname to the name of the Unix machine running SAMBA and the area to the Windows share name, such as *//some-pc/C$*. Note that Unix-style forward slashes are used instead of Windows-style backward slashes.

Enable AMANDA access to the client from the tape server host (even if the client is the tape server host itself) by editing *.amandahosts* (or *.rhosts*, depending on what was set with *./configure*) in the AMANDA user home directory on the client. Enter the fully qualified tape server hostname and AMANDA user, separated by a blank or tab. Make sure the file is owned by the AMANDA user and does not allow access to anyone other than the owner (e.g., mode 0600 or 0400).

For Windows clients, put the share password in */etc/amandapass* on the SAMBA host. The first field is the Windows share name, the second is the clear text password, and the optional third field is the domain. Because this file contains clear text passwords, it should be carefully protected, owned by the AMANDA user, and allow only user access. By default, AMANDA uses SAMBA user *backup*. This can be changed with *--with-samba-user* to *./configure*.

Test and debug setup

Test the setup with *amcheck*. As with all AMANDA commands, run it as the AMANDA user, not root:

```
# su amanda -c "amcheck Daily"
```

Many errors reported by *amcheck* are described in *docs/FAQ* or the *amcheck* manpage. The most common error reported to the AMANDA mailing lists is self-check request timed out, meaning *amcheck* was not able to talk to *amandad* on the client. In addition to the ideas in *docs/FAQ*, here are some other things to try:

- Are the AMANDA services listed properly in */etc/services* or a YP/NIS map? The C program in Example 4-1 uses the same system call as AMANDA to look up entries.

Example 4-1. A C Program to Check the AMANDA Service Numbers

```c
# include <stdio.h>
# include <string.h>
# include <netdb.h>

main (
    int argc,
    char **argv)
{
    char *pn;
    char *service;
    char *protocol = "tcp";
    struct servent *s;

    if ((pn = strrchr (*argv, '/')) == NULL) {
        pn = *argv;
    } else {
        pn++;
    }
    if (argc < 2) {
        fprintf (stderr, "usage: %s service [protocol]\n", pn);
        return 1;
    }
    service = *++argv;
    if (argc > 2) {
        protocol = *++argv;
    }
    if ((s = getservbyname (service, protocol)) == NULL) {
        fprintf (stderr, "%s: %s/%s lookup failed\n", pn,
          service, protocol);
        return 1;
    }
    printf ("%s/%s: %d\n", service, protocol,
      (int) ntohs (s->s_port));
    return 0;
}
```

Run it on both the tape server and client and make sure the port numbers match:

```
$ cc check-service.c -lnsl -lsocket        (Solaris)
$ a.out amanda udp
amanda/udp: 10080
$ a.out amandaidx
amandaidx/tcp: 10082
$ a.out amidxtape
amidxtape/tcp: 10083
```

- Is there a line in the *inetd* configuration file on the client to start *amandad*?

- Was *inetd* sent a HUP signal after the configuration file was changed?

- Are there system log messages from *inetd* about amanda or *amandad*? For instance, *inetd* complains if it cannot look up the AMANDA services.

- Is */tmp/amanda/amandad/debug* being updated?

- Is the access time on the *amandad* executable (*ls -lu*) being updated? If not, *inetd* is probably not able to run it, possibly because of an error in the *inetd* configuration file or a permission problem.

- Run the *amandad* program by hand as the AMANDA user on the client. It should sit for about 30 seconds, then terminate. Enter the full path exactly as it was given to *inetd*, perhaps by using copy/paste.

Do not proceed until *amcheck* is happy with the configuration.

For initial testing, set the *record* option to no in the global *dumptype*, but remember to set it back to yes when AMANDA goes into normal production. This parameter controls whether the *dump* program on the client updates its own database, such as */etc/dumpdates* for vendor *dump*.

To forget about an individual test run, use *amrmtape* to remove references to the tapes used, then use *amlabel* to relabel them. To completely start over, remove the files or directories named in the *infofile* and *indexdir* parameters, the *tapelist* file named in the *tapelist* parameter, all *amdump.** files in the configuration directory and all *log.** files in the directory named by the *logdir* parameter. These files contain history information AMANDA needs between runs and also what is needed to find particular dump images for restores and should be protected when AMANDA goes into production.

Operating AMANDA

Once configured, you will need to set up the automated use of AMANDA.

Run amdump

The *amdump* script controls a normal AMANDA backup run. However, it's common to do site-specific things as well with a wrapper shell script around *amdump*. *amdump* is meant to run unattended from *cron*. See the operating system documentation for how to set up a *cron* task. Be sure it runs *as the* AMANDA *user*, not root or the installer.

The *amdump* script does the following:

- If a file named *hold* is in the configuration directory, *amdump* pauses until it goes away. This may be created and removed by hand to temporarily delay AMANDA runs without having to change the *cron* task.

- If it looks as if another copy of *amdump* is running or a previous run aborted, *amdump* logs an error and terminates. If an earlier run aborted, *amcleanup* must be run. An *amcleanup* step should be added to the tape server system boot sequence to handle crashes. No backups can be performed after an abort or crash until *amcleanup* is run.

- The AMANDA *planner* program decides what areas to back up and at what level. It does this by connecting to each client and getting estimated sizes of a full dump, the same partial level that was done on the previous run and possibly the next partial level. All clients are done in parallel, but it can take a while to gather all this information.

- The schedule is then passed to the *driver* program that controls actual dumping. It, in turn, starts up several *dumper* processes (based on the *inparallel* amanda.conf parameter) and a single *taper* process. The *taper* process splits into two parts, a reader and a writer, to keep streaming tape drives busy.

- *driver* commands *dumpers* to start backups, telling each its client, area, options such as compression, and whether the result should go to the holding disk or direct to tape. Each *dumper* connects to *amandad* on the client and sends a request describing the dump program to run and options such as whether to do compression or indexing. The image comes back to the *dumper*, which writes it, possibly via the server compression program, into the holding disk or directly to a *taper* connection. If enabled, *dumper* also collects catalog information generated on the client and compresses it into the *indexdir* area. The *driver* also commands *taper* to write files from the holding disk to tape or to prepare to receive an image directly from a *dumper*.

- After backups are done, *amreport* is run to generate the email report. It also renames the log file for the run to a unique *log.YYYYMMDD.N* name.

- Old *amdump.NN* debug log files are rolled so only enough to match the tape cycle are retained.

- The *amtrmidx* program is run to remove old catalogs if indexing has been used.

There are several ways to determine which tapes AMANDA will need for a run. One is to look at the AMANDA email report from the previous run. The tapes used during that run and those expected for the next run are listed. Another is to run *amcheck* during normal working hours. In addition to showing which tapes are needed, it makes sure things are set up properly so problems can be fixed before the real AMANDA run. A third is to use the *tape* suboption of *amadmin*. Without a tape changer, AMANDA expects the first tape to be mounted in the drive when it starts. Automated tape changers should be able to locate the tapes. The *chg-manual* changer prompts for the tapes.

Read AMANDA's reports

An AMANDA report has several sections:

```
These dumps were to tape Daily-009, Daily-010.
Tonight's dumps should go onto 2 tapes: Daily-011, Daily-012.
```

This shows which tapes were used during the run and which tapes are needed next.

```
FAILURE AND STRANGE DUMP SUMMARY:
  gurgi.cc.p /var lev 0 FAILED [Request to gurgi.cc.purdue.edu timed out.]
  gurgi.cc.p / lev 0 FAILED [Request to gurgi.cc.purdue.edu timed out.]
  pete.cc.pu /var/mail lev 0 FAILED ["data write: Broken pipe"]
  samba.cc.p //nt-test.cc.purdue.edu/F$ lev 1 STRANGE
  mace.cc.pu /master lev 0 FAILED [dumps too big, but cannot incremental dump new
disk]
```

Problems found during the run are summarized in this section. In this example:

- *gurgi.cc.purdue.edu* was down, so all its backups failed.

- The */var/mail* problem on *pete.cc.purdue.edu* and *F$* problem on *nt-test.cc.purdue.edu* are detailed later.

- The */master* area on *mace.cc.purdue.edu* is new to AMANDA, so a full dump is required, but it would not fit in the available tape space for this run.

```
STATISTICS:
                             Total      Full      Daily
                           --------  --------  --------
  Dump Time (hrs:min)         5:03      3:23      0:33   (0:14 start, 0:53 idle)
  Output Size (meg)        20434.4   17960.0    2474.4
  Original Size (meg)      20434.4   17960.0    2474.4
  Avg Compressed Size (%)       --        --        --
  Tape Used (%)              137.4     120.0      17.4   (level:#disks ...)
  Filesystems Dumped           90        21        69   (1:64 2:2 3:3)
  Avg Dump Rate (k/s)       1036.5    1304.3     416.2
  Avg Tp Write Rate (k/s)   1477.6    1511.2    1271.9
```

This summarizes the entire run. It took just over five hours, almost three and a half hours writing full dumps and about half an hour for partials. It took 14 minutes to

get started, mostly in the *planner* step getting the estimates, and *taper* was idle
almost an hour waiting on dumps to come into the holding disk.

In this example, hardware compression was used so Avg Compressed Size is not
applicable and Output Size written to tape matches Original Size from the clients.
About 137 percent of the length of the tape as defined in the *tapetype* was used
(remember that two tapes were written), 120 percent for full dumps and 17 percent for partials. The Rate lines give the dump speed from client to tape server and
tape writing speed, all in KB per second. The Filesystems Dumped line says 90
areas were processed, 21 full dumps and 69 partials. Of the partials, 64 were level
1, two were level 2, and three were level 3.

```
    FAILED AND STRANGE DUMP DETAILS:

   /-- pete.cc.pu /var/mail lev 0 FAILED ["data write: Broken pipe"]
   sendbackup: start [pete.cc.purdue.edu:/var/mail level 0]
   sendbackup: info BACKUP=/usr/sbin/ufsdump
   sendbackup: info RECOVER_CMD=/usr/sbin/ufsrestore -f... -
   sendbackup: info end
   |   DUMP: Writing 32 Kilobyte records
   |   DUMP: Date of this level 0 dump: Sat Jan 02 02:03:22 1999
   |   DUMP: Date of last level 0 dump: the epoch
   |   DUMP: Dumping /dev/md/rdsk/d5 (pete.cc.purdue.edu:/var/mail) to standard
output.
   |   DUMP: Mapping (Pass I) [regular files]
   |   DUMP: Mapping (Pass II) [directories]
   |   DUMP: Estimated 13057170 blocks (6375.57MB) on 0.09 tapes.
   |   DUMP: Dumping (Pass III) [directories]
   |   DUMP: Dumping (Pass IV) [regular files]
   |   DUMP: 13.99% done, finished in 1:02
   |   DUMP: 27.82% done, finished in 0:52
   |   DUMP: 41.22% done, finished in 0:42

   /-- samba.cc.p //nt-test.cc.purdue.edu/F$ lev 1 STRANGE
   sendbackup: start [samba.cc.purdue.edu://nt-test/F$ level 1]
   sendbackup: info BACKUP=/usr/local/bin/smbclient
   sendbackup: info RECOVER_CMD=/usr/local/bin/smbclient -f... -
   sendbackup: info end
   ? Can't load /usr/local/samba-2.0.2/lib/smb.conf - run testparm to debug it
   | session request to NT-TEST.CC.PURD failed
   |                 directory \top\
   |                 directory \top\Division\
   |       238 (     2.7 kb/s) \top\Division\contract.txt
   |     19456 (   169.6 kb/s) \top\Division\stuff.doc
   ...
```

Failures and unexpected results are detailed here. The dump of */var/mail* would
not fit on the first tape so was aborted and rerun on the next tape, as described
further in the next section.

The dump of *F$* on *nt-test.cc.purdue.edu* failed due to a problem with the SAMBA configuration file. It's marked STRANGE because the line with a question mark does not match any of the regular expressions built into AMANDA. When dumping Windows clients via SAMBA, it's normal to get errors about busy files, such as *PAGEFILE.SYS* and the Registry. Other arrangements should be made to get these safely backed up, such as a periodic task on the PC that creates a copy that will not be busy at the time AMANDA runs.

```
NOTES:
    planner: Adding new disk j.cc.purdue.edu:/var.
    planner: Adding new disk mace.cc.purdue.edu:/master.
    planner: Last full dump of mace.cc.purdue.edu:/src on tape Daily-012 overwritten
             in 2 runs.
    planner: Full dump of loader.cc.purdue.edu:/var promoted from 2 days ahead.
    planner: Incremental of sage.cc.purdue.edu:/var bumped to level 2.
    taper: tape Daily-009 kb 19567680 fm 90 writing file: short write
    taper: retrying pete.cc.purdue.edu:/var/mail.0 on new tape: [writing file: short
             write]
    driver: pete.cc.purdue.edu /var/mail 0 [dump to tape failed, will try again]
    taper: tape Daily-010 kb 6201216 fm 1 [OK]
```

Informational notes about the run are listed here. The messages from *planner* say:

- There are new *disklist* entries for *j.cc.purdue.edu* and *mace.cc.purdue.edu*.

- Tape `Daily-012` is due to be overwritten in two more runs and contains the most recent full dump of */src* from *mace.cc.purdue.edu*, so the tape cycle may not be large enough.

- The next scheduled full dump of */var* on *loader.cc.purdue.edu* was moved up two days to improve the load balance.

- The partial dump of */var* on *sage.cc.purdue.edu* was bumped from level 1 to level 2 because the higher level was estimated to save enough space to make it worthwhile.

The rest of the notes say *taper* was not able to write as much data as it wanted, probably because of hitting end of tape. Up to that point, it had written 19567680 KB in 90 files on tape `Daily-009`. Another attempt at the full dump of */var/mail* from *pete.cc.purdue.edu* was made on the next tape (`Daily-010`) and it succeeded, writing 6,201,216 KB in one file.

```
DUMP SUMMARY:
                                          DUMPER STATS              TAPER STATS
    HOSTNAME  DISK             L  ORIG-KB OUT-KB COMP% MMM:SS   KB/s MMM:SS   KB/s
    ---------------------------- -------------------------------------- ---------------
    boiler.cc /                 1    2624   2624   --    0:13  200.1   0:02 1076.0
    boiler.cc /home/boiler/a    1     192    192   --    0:07   26.7   0:02  118.5
    boiler.cc /usr              1     992    992   --    0:41   24.2   0:02  514.7
    boiler.cc /usr/local        1     288    288   --    0:09   31.2   0:04   86.3
    boiler.cc /var              1    4256   4256   --    0:21  205.9   0:04 1104.3
```

```
egbert.cc /               1    41952   41952   --    1:26  487.3   0:37 1149.4
egbert.cc /opt            1      224     224   --    0:06   37.5   0:02  136.0
egbert.cc -laris/install  1       64      64   --    0:11    5.8   0:02   49.5
gurgi.cc. /               0   FAILED -------------------------------------------
gurgi.cc. /var            0   FAILED -------------------------------------------
pete.cc.p /               1    13408   13408   --    0:41  328.2   0:08 1600.5
pete.cc.p /opt            1     3936    3936   --    1:04   61.2   0:03 1382.6
pete.cc.p /usr            1     1952    1952   --    0:29   67.0   0:03  584.3
pete.cc.p /var            1   300768  300768   --    2:33 1963.8   2:50 1768.8
pete.cc.p /var/mail       0  6201184 6201184   --   73:45 1401.3  73:47 1400.8
...
```
(brought to you by Amanda version 2.4.1p1)

This section (which has been abbreviated) reports each area dumped showing client, area, backup level, sizes, time to dump, and time to write to tape. Entries are in alphabetic order by client and then by area. This is not the same as the tape order. Tape order can be determined with the *find* or *info* suboption of the *amadmin* command, *amtoc* can generate a tape table of contents after a run, or *amreport* can generate a printed listing. By default, client names are truncated on the right, area names on the left, to keep the report width under 80 characters. This typically leaves the unique portions of both.

Two log files are created during an AMANDA run. One is named *amdump.NN*, where *NN* is a sequence number (1 is most recent, 2 is next most recent, etc.); it is in the same directory as *amanda.conf*. The file contains detailed step-by-step information about the run and is used for statistics by *amplot* and *amstatus*, and for debugging. The other file is named *log.YYYYMMDD.N* where *YYYYMMDD* is the date of the AMANDA run and *N* is a sequence number in case more than one run is made on the same day (0 for the first run, 1 for the second, etc). This file is in the directory specified by the *logdir amanda.conf* parameter. It contains a summary of the run and is the basis for the email report. In fact, *amreport* may be run by hand and given an old file to regenerate a report.

Old *amdump.NN* files are removed by the *amdump* script. Old *log.YYYYMMDD.N* files are not removed automatically and should be cleared out periodically by hand. Keeping a full tape cycle is a good idea. If the tape cycle is 40 and AMANDA is run once a day, the following command would do the job:

```
# find log.????????.* -mtime +40 -print | xargs rm
```

If *--with-pid-debug-files* was used on *./configure*, clients accumulate debug files in */tmp/amanda* (or whatever *--with-debug* was set to) and should be cleaned out periodically. Without this option, client debug files have fixed names and are reused from run to run.

Monitor tape and holding disk status

While *amdump* is running, *amstatus* can track how far along it is. *amstatus* may also be used afterward to generate statistics on how many *dumpers* were used, what held things up, and so on.

When a tape error happens on the last tape allowed in a run (as set by *runtapes*), AMANDA continues to do backups into the holding disks. This is called "degraded" mode. By default, full dumps are not done and any that were scheduled have a partial done instead. A portion of the holding disk area may be allocated to do full dumps during degraded mode by reducing the *reserved amanda.conf* value below 100 percent.

A tape server crash also may leave images in the holding disks. Run *amflush*, as the AMANDA user, to flush images in the holding disk to the next tape after correcting any problems. It goes through the same tape request mechanism as *amdump*. If more than one set of dumps are in the holding disk area, *amflush* prompts to choose one to write or to write them all. *amflush* generates an email report just like *amdump*.

Operating systems vary in how they report end of tape to programs. A no space or short write error probably means end of tape. For I/O error, look at the report to see how much was written. If it is close to the expected tape capacity, it probably means end of tape; otherwise, it means a real tape error happened and the tape may need to be replaced the next time through the tape cycle.

To swap out a partially bad tape, wait until it is about to be used again so any valid images can still be retrieved. Then swap the tapes, run *amrmtape* on the old tape and run *amlabel* on the replacement so it has a proper AMANDA label.

If a tape is marked to not be reused with the *no-reuse* suboption of *amadmin*, such as one that has been removed or is failing, AMANDA may want a freshly labeled tape on the next run to get the number of tapes back up to the full tape cycle.

If a tape goes completely bad, use *amrmtape* to make AMANDA forget about it. As with marking a tape *no-reuse*, this may reduce the number of tapes AMANDA has in use below the tape cycle, and it may request a newly labeled tape on the next run.

Adding tapes at a particular position in the cycle

The following steps let AMANDA know about all tapes, including those that do not have data yet.

- Run *amlabel* on the new tapes.
- Edit the *tapelist* file by hand and move the new tapes *before* the tape to be used just ahead of them. For instance, move `Daily-100` before `Daily-099`.

- Set the datestamp on the new tapes to the same as the previous tape, e.g., make them the same for `Daily-099` and `Daily-100`.

- Update the *tapecycle amanda.conf* parameter if new tapes are being added.

When the cycle gets to the last old tape (`Daily-099`), the next tape used will be the first new one (`Daily-100`). A new option is planned for *amlabel* to do these steps automatically.

Miscellaneous operational notes

Multiple *amdump* runs may be made in the same day, although catalogs currently are stored without a timestamp so *amrecover* may not show all restore possibilities. To redo a few areas that failed during the normal run, edit the *disklist* file by hand to comment out all the other entries, run *amdump*, then restore the *disklist* file.

Use the *force* suboption of *amadmin* to schedule a full dump of an area on the next run. Run this *as the* AMANDA *user*, not root. AMANDA automatically detects new *disklist* entries and schedules an initial full dump. But for areas that go through a major change, such as an operating system upgrade or full restore, force AMANDA to do a full dump to get things back into sync.

AMANDA does not automatically notice new client areas, so keep the *disklist* in sync by hand. AMANDA usually notices areas that are removed and reports an error as a reminder to remove the entry from the *disklist*. Use the *delete* suboption of *amadmin* (as the AMANDA user) to make AMANDA completely forget about an area, but wait until the information is not needed for restores. This does not remove the entry from the *disklist* file—that must be done by hand.

Non-AMANDA backups may still be done with AMANDA installed, but do not let the client *dump* program update its database. For vendor *dump* programs, this usually means not using the *u* flag or saving and restoring */etc/dumpdates*. For GNU *tar* it means the *--listed-incremental flag* (if used) should not point to the same file AMANDA uses.

As with all backup systems, verify the resulting tapes, if not each one, then at least periodically or by random sample. The *amverify* script does a reasonably good job of making sure tapes are readable and images are valid. For GNU *tar* images, the test is very good. For vendor dump images of the same operating system type as the tape server machine, the test is OK but does not really check the whole image due to the limited way the catalog option works. For vendor dump images from other operating systems, *amverify* can tell if the image is readable from tape but not whether it is valid.

Tape drives are notorious for being able to read only what they wrote, so run *amverify* on another machine with a different drive, if possible, so an alternate is available if the primary drive fails. Make a copy of the AMANDA configuration directory on the other machine to be able to run *amverify*. This copy is also a good way to have a backup of the AMANDA configuration and database in case the tape server machine needs to be recovered.

Advanced AMANDA Configuration

Once you have AMANDA running for a while, you may choose to do some additional advanced configuration.

Adjust the backup cycle

Several *dumptype* parameters control the backup level AMANDA picks for a run:

dumpcycle
> Maximum days between full dumps

strategy nofull
> Never schedule (or run) a full dump

strategy incronly
> Only schedule non-full dumps

Note that *dumpcycle* is both a general *amanda.conf* parameter and a specific *dumptype* parameter. The value in a specific *dumptype* takes precedence. To handle areas that change significantly between each run and should get a full dump each time (such as the mail spool on a busy email server or a database area), create a *dumptype* based on another *dumptype* with attributes changed as desired (client *dump* program, compression) and set *dumpcycle* in the new *dumptype* to 0:

```
define mail-spool {
    comp-user-tar
    dumpcycle 0
}
```

To run full dumps by hand outside of AMANDA (perhaps they are too large for the normal tape capacity or need special processing), create a new *dumptype* and set *strategy* to `incronly`:

```
define full-too-big {
    comp-user-tar
    strategy incronly
}
```

Tell AMANDA when a full dump of the area has been done with the *force* suboption of *amadmin*. Take care to do full dumps often enough that the tape cycle does not wrap around and overwrite the last good nonfull backups.

To never do full dumps (such as an area easily regenerated from vendor media), create a new *dumptype* and set *strategy* to nofull:

```
define man-pages {
    comp-user-tar
    strategy nofull
}
```

Only level-1 backups of such areas are done, so wrapping around the tape cycle is not a problem.

To do periodic archival full dumps, create a new AMANDA configuration with its own set of tapes but the same *disklist* as the normal configuration (e.g., symlink them together). Copy *amanda.conf*, setting all *dumpcycle* values to 0 and *record* to no, e.g., in the global *dumptype*. If a changer is used, set *runtapes* very high so tape capacity is not a planning restriction. Disable the normal AMANDA run, or set the *hold* file as described in "Operating AMANDA," so AMANDA does not try to process the same client from two configurations at the same time.

Adjust parallelism

AMANDA starts several *dumper* processes and keeps as many as possible running at once. The following options control their activity:

inparallel
> Total number of *dumpers*

maxdumps
> Maximum *dumpers* for a single client

The default *maxdumps* is one, meaning only one *dumper* is assigned to a client at a time. If a client can support the load, increase *maxdumps* so more than one dump on that client is running at once. Note that *maxdumps* is both a general *amanda.conf* parameter and a specific *dumptype* parameter. The value in a specific *dumptype* takes precedence.

Field four of the *disklist* file is a "spindle number." Areas with the same non-negative spindle number are not backed up at the same time if *maxdumps* is greater than 1. This prevents thrashing on an individual physical disk. Set spindle number to -1 (which is the default) for independent areas that can be done in conjunction with any other area, such as a whole physical disk. If the tape server has multiple network connections, an *amanda.conf interface* section may be set up for each one and clients allocated to a particular interface with field five of the *disklist*. Individual interfaces take precedence over the general *netusage* bandwidth limit and follow the same guidelines described earlier in "Configuring AMANDA": the limit is imposed when deciding whether to start a dump, but once a dump starts, AMANDA lets underlying network components do any throttling.

Individual AMANDA *interface* definitions do not control which physical connection is used. That is left up to the operating system network software. While it's common to give an AMANDA interface definition the same name as a physical connection, e.g., le0, it might be better to use logical names such as back-door-atm to avoid confusion.

The *starttime dumptype* parameter delays a backup some amount of time after AMANDA is started. The value is entered as *HHMM*, so 230, for instance, would wait 2.5 hours. This may be used to delay backups of some areas until they are known to be idle.

Monitor for possible improvements

amstatus may be used to get a summary of *dumper* activity:

```
# su amanda -c "amstatus Daily --file amdump.1 --summary"
...
  dumper0 busy   :   5:52:01  ( 98.03%)
  dumper1 busy   :   0:23:09  (  6.45%)
  dumper2 busy   :   0:13:27  (  3.75%)
  dumper3 busy   :   0:16:13  (  4.52%)
  dumper4 busy   :   0:06:40  (  1.86%)
  dumper5 busy   :   0:03:39  (  1.02%)
    taper busy   :   3:54:20  ( 65.26%)
0 dumpers busy :   0:03:21  (  0.93%)    file-too-large:  0:03:21  (100.00%)
1 dumper  busy :   4:03:22  ( 67.78%)     no-diskspace:  3:40:55  ( 90.77%)
                                         file-too-large:  0:21:13  (  8.72%)
                                           no-bandwidth:  0:01:13  (  0.50%)
2 dumpers busy :   0:17:33  (  4.89%)     no-bandwidth:  0:17:33  (100.00%)
3 dumpers busy :   0:07:42  (  2.14%)     no-bandwidth:  0:07:42  (100.00%)
4 dumpers busy :   0:02:05  (  0.58%)     no-bandwidth:  0:02:05  (100.00%)
5 dumpers busy :   0:00:40  (  0.19%)     no-bandwidth:  0:00:40  (100.00%)
6 dumpers busy :   0:03:33  (  0.99%)         not-idle:  0:01:53  ( 53.10%)
                                             no-dumpers:  0:01:40  ( 46.90%)
```

This says:

- *dumper* 0 was busy almost all the time.

- *dumper* 1 (and above) were not used very much.

- *taper* was busy about two-thirds of the total runtime.

- All *dumpers* were idle less than 1 percent of the total runtime.

- One *dumper* was busy 67.78 percent of the total runtime, and the reason two *dumpers* were not started when one was busy was not enough holding disk space (no-diskspace) 90.77 percent of that time, the next image to dump was too large to fit in the holding disk at all (file-too-large) 8.72 percent of that time, and network bandwidth was exhausted (no-bandwidth) 0.50 percent of that time.

This configuration would benefit from additional holding disk space, which would allow more *dumpers* to run at once and probably keep *taper* busy more of the time.

Other common status indicators are:

`not-idle`
Everything is running that can be.

`no-dumpers`
All *dumpers* are busy, and there are other dumps that could be started.

`client-constrained`
The maximum number of *dumpers* for remaining clients are already running, or all spindles are already in use.

`start-wait`
All remaining dumps are delayed until a specific time of day.

If the tape server machine has multiple tape drives, more than one AMANDA configuration may run at the same time. Clients and holding disks should be assigned to only one configuration, however.

AMANDA waits a fixed amount of time for a client to respond with dump size estimates. The default is five minutes per area on the client. For instance, if a client has four areas to back up (entries in *disklist*), AMANDA waits at most 20 minutes for the estimates. During dumping, AMANDA aborts a dump if the client stops sending data for 30 minutes. Various conditions, such as slow clients, which *dump* program is used and characteristics of the area, may cause timeouts. The values may be changed with the *amanda.conf etimeout* parameter for estimates and *dtimeout* for data. Positive *etimeout* values are multiplied by the number of areas. The absolute value of a negative number is used for the whole client regardless of the number of areas.

Excluding files

GNU *tar* can exclude items from the dump image based on filename patterns controlled by the *dumptype exclude* parameter. A single pattern may be put on the *exclude* line itself, or multiple patterns may be put in a file *on the client*. The *dumptype exclude* line in that case includes a `list` keyword and the path to the file.

Exclusion entries are shell-style wildcard expressions, except * matches through any number of / characters. If a matched item is a directory, it and all its contents are omitted. For instance:

`./usr`
Omit the *usr* directory at the top level of the area and everything under it.

```
core
```
Omit all items named *core*.

```
*/core*
```
Omit all items starting with *core*, e.g., *core, core19970114, corespondent,* or *corexx/somefile* (probably not a good idea).

```
*/test*.c
```
Omit all items starting with *test* and ending with *.c*, e.g., *test.c, testing.c,* or *testdir/pgm/main.c* (probably not a good idea).

```
*.o
```
Omit all items ending with *.o*.

```
*/OLD/*
```
Omit all items within directories named *OLD*, including subdirectories and their contents, but dump the *OLD* directory entry itself.

Restoring with AMANDA

Remember that no one cares if you can back up—only if you can restore.

Configuring and using amrecover

One way to restore items with AMANDA is with *amrecover* on the client. Before *amrecover* can work, AMANDA must run with the *dumptype index* parameter set to **yes** and the **amindexd** and **amidxtaped** services must be installed and enabled to *inetd*, usually on the tape server machine (the default build sequence installs them). Also, add the client to *.amandahosts* (or *.rhosts*) for the AMANDA user on the server machine. Since *amrecover* must run as root on the client, the entry must list root as the remote user, not the AMANDA user. *amrecover* should not be made setuid-root because it would open up catalogs of the entire system to everyone.

For this example, user **jj** has requested two files, both named *molecule.dat*, in subdirectories named *work/sample-21* and *work/sample-22* and wants the versions last modified on the 13th of January. Become root on the client, *cd* to the area, and start *amrecover*:

```
$ su
Password:
# cd ~jj
# amrecover Daily
AMRECOVER Version 2.4.1p1. Contacting server on amanda.cc.purdue.edu ...
220 amanda AMANDA index server (2.4.1p1) ready.
200 Access OK
Setting restore date to today (1999-01-18)
200 Working date set to 1999-01-18.
200 Config set to Daily.
200 Dump host set to pete.cc.purdue.edu.
```

```
$CWD '/home/pete/u66/jj' is on disk '/home/pete/u66' mounted at '/home/pete/u66'.
200 Disk set to /home/pete/u66.
amrecover>
```

At this point, a command-line interface allows browsing the image catalogs. Move around with the *cd* command, see what is available with *ls*, change date with *setdate*, add files and directories to the extraction list with *add*, and so on. The *extract* command starts actual recovery:

```
amrecover> setdate ---14
200 Working date set to 1999-01-14.
amrecover> cd work/sample-21
/home/pete/u66/jj/work/sample-21
amrecover> add molecule.dat
Added /jj/work/sample-21/molecule.dat
amrecover> cd ../sample-22
/home/pete/u66/jj/work/sample-22
amrecover> add molecule.dat
Added /jj/work/sample-22/molecule.dat
amrecover> extract
Extracting files using tape drive /dev/rmt/0mn on host amanda.cc.purdue.edu.
The following tapes are needed: Daily-034

Restoring files into directory /home/pete/u66
Continue? [Y/n]: y

Load tape Daily-034 now
Continue? [Y/n]: y
Warning: ./jj: File exists
Warning: ./work: File exists
Warning: ./work/sample-21: File exists
Warning: ./work/sample-22: File exists
set owner/mode for '.'? [yn] n
amrecover> quit
```

amrecover finds which tapes contain the images, prompts through mounting them in the proper order, searches the tape for the image, optionally decompresses it, brings it across the network to the client, and pipes it into the appropriate *restore* program with the arguments needed to extract the requested items. *amrecover* does not know how to run every client *restore* program. See the *amrecover* manpage for current information. *amrecover* should not be used to do full filesystem recovery with vendor *restore* tools, but does work with GNU *tar*. Vendor tools should be run with the *r* flag for a full recovery, and *amrecover* is oriented toward extracting individual items with the *x* flag. Full filesystem recovery with vendor *restore* should be done with *amrestore*. *amrecover* (actually the *amidxtaped* server) does not know about tape changers, so mount the tapes by hand or use *amtape* if a changer is available.

Using amrestore

The *amrestore* command retrieves whole images from tape. First, find which tapes
have the desired images. The *find* suboption of *amadmin* generates output like
this (abbreviated):

```
# su amanda -c "amadmin Daily find pete u66"
Scanning /amanda...

date        host                  disk              lv tape or file   file status
...
1999-01-12 pete.cc.purdue.edu    /home/pete/u66     1 Daily-032          14 OK
1999-01-13 pete.cc.purdue.edu    /home/pete/u66     1 Daily-033          26 OK
1999-01-14 pete.cc.purdue.edu    /home/pete/u66     1 Daily-034          40 OK
1999-01-15 pete.cc.purdue.edu    /home/pete/u66     1 Daily-000          34 OK
1999-01-16 pete.cc.purdue.edu    /home/pete/u66     1 Daily-001          31 OK
1999-01-17 pete.cc.purdue.edu    /home/pete/u66     0 Daily-002          50 OK
1999-01-18 pete.cc.purdue.edu    /home/pete/u66     1 Daily-003          20 OK
```

The `Scanning /amanda...` message says that *amadmin* looked in the holding
disk (*/amanda*) for any images left there. It then lists all tapes or files in the holding disk that contain the requested area.

The *info* suboption to *amadmin* shows tapes with the most recent images:

```
# su amanda -c "amadmin Daily info pete u66"
Current info for pete.cc.purdue.edu /home/pete/u66:
  Stats: dump rates (kps), Full:  652.0, 648.0, 631.0
                    Incremental:  106.0, 258.0, 235.0
          compressed size, Full: -100.0%,-100.0%,-100.0%
                    Incremental: -100.0%,-100.0%,-100.0%
  Dumps: lev datestmp  tape        file   origK  compK secs
          0 19990117   Daily-002     50  582239 582272  892
          1 19990118   Daily-003     20    3263   3296   31
          2 19981214   Daily-032     21    7039   7072   37
```

Old information may appear, such as 19981214 (14-Dec-1998) in this example.
While it's true this was the last level-2 dump of this area, it is of little interest
because at least one full and one level-1 dump have been done since then. The
compressed size values here may be ignored because this particular configuration
uses hardware compression so no software compression data is available.

A third way to know what tape has an image is to generate a tape table of contents with *amtoc* after each AMANDA run:

```
# partition                          lvl  size[Kb]  method
0  Daily-002                          -         -   19990117
1  boiler.cc.purdue.edu:/usr/local    1        31   normal
2  egbert.cc.purdue.edu:/opt          1       127   normal
3  boiler.cc.purdue.edu:/usr          1        95   normal
...
50 pete.cc.purdue.edu:/home/pete/u66  0    582239   normal
...
```

A printed report similar to the *amtoc* output may be generated automatically by *amreport* for each run with the *lbl-templ tapetype* parameter in *amanda.conf* using the *example/3hole.ps* template.

The *find* and *info* suboptions to *amadmin* need the AMANDA log files and database. These usually are not large amounts of information and a copy should be pushed after each *amdump* run to an alternate machine that also has the AMANDA tape server software installed so they are available if the primary tape server machine dies. Tools like *rdist* (*ftp://usc.edu/pub/rdist/*) or *rsync* (*ftp:// samba.anu.edu.au/pub/rsync/*) are useful.

If AMANDA was built using *--with-db=text* (the default), the database is stored in a set of text files under the directory listed in the *infofile amanda.conf* parameter. Here is the file that matches the *info amadmin* output:

```
# cd /usr/local/etc/amanda/Daily/curinfo
# cat pete.cc.purdue.edu/_home_pete_u66/info
version: 0
command: 0
full-rate: 652.000000 648.000000 631.000000
full-comp:
incr-rate: 106.000000 258.000000 235.000000
incr-comp:
stats: 0 582239 582272 892 916549924 50 Daily-002
stats: 1 3263 3296 31 916637269 20 Daily-003
stats: 2 7039 7072 37 913614357 21 Daily-032
//
```

The first field of each `stats` line is the dump level. The last field is the Volume Serial Number (VSN) and the field just before it is the tape file number. The field with the large number just before that is a Unix epoch time value, which may be converted to text with this *Perl* script:

```
$ cat epoch.pl
#!/usr/local/bin/perl -w
require 'ctime.pl';
foreach (@ARGV) {
  s/,//;
  if (m/[a-fA-FxX]/) {
    unless (m/^0[xX]/) {
      $_ = '0x' . $_;
    }
    $_ = oct;
  }
  print &ctime ($_);
}
exit (0);
$ epoch.pl 916549924
Sun Jan 17  0:12:04 US/East-Indiana 1999
```

Prepositioning the tape to the image with *mt fsf* may significantly reduce the time needed to do a restore. Some media contains an index for very fast file searching compared to the one-file-at-a-time scanning done by *amrestore*. Each tape-location method listed previously also shows the tape file. Use that number with *mt fsf* after a *rewind* to position to a particular image.

amrestore takes client, area, and datestamp patterns as optional arguments to search for matching images. Each argument is a *grep*-style regular expression, so multiple images may match. This also means an image may need a specific pattern. For instance:

```
# amrestore $TAPE pete /
```

finds not just the root area for the `pete` client but images for any client with `pete` someplace in the hostname and a slash anywhere in the area name. Assuming only one client matches `pete`, the following gets just the root area:

```
# amrestore $TAPE pete '^/$'
```

The up arrow (caret) at the beginning says the pattern must start with this string. The dollar sign at the end says it must end there. The quote marks around the pattern protect the special characters from shell expansion.

Without flags, *amrestore* finds every matching image, uncompresses it if needed, and creates a disk file in the current working directory with a name made up of the client, area, and dump level. These images may be used directly by the client *restore* program.

amrestore may be used to generate a tape table of contents by giving it a host pattern that cannot match:

```
# mt rewind
# amrestore $TAPE no.such.host
```

As it searches in vain for *no.such.host*, it reports images that are skipped:

```
amrestore:  0: skipping start of tape: date 19990117 label Daily-002
amrestore:  1: skipping boiler.cc.purdue.edu._.19990117.1
amrestore:  2: skipping egbert.cc.purdue.edu._opt.19990117.1
amrestore:  3: skipping boiler.cc.purdue.edu._.19990117.1
 ...
```

For large images, the *p* flag writes the first match to standard output, which may then be piped into the client *restore* program. This flag also is useful for moving an image across the network. For instance, here is one way to restore a file directly from the tape server (*amanda.cc.purdue.edu*) while logged in to the client:

```
# rsh -n amanda.cc.purdue.edu amrestore -p $TAPE pete ''^/$' ' \
  | gtar xf - ./the-file
```

You may have to tell vendor *restore* programs to use a small blocking factor to handle the arbitrary size chunks of data available through a pipeline:

```
# rsh -n amanda.cc.purdue.edu amrestore -p $TAPE pete u66 \
  | ufsrestore -ivbf 2 -
```

Restoring without AMANDA

The AMANDA tape format is deliberately simple and data can be restored without any AMANDA tools if necessary. The first tape file is a volume label with the tape VSN and date it was written. It is not in `ANSI VOL1` format but is plain text. Each file after that contains one image using 32-KB blocks. The first block is an AMANDA header with client, area, and options used to create the image. As with the volume label, the header is not in ANSI format but is plain text. The image follows, starting at the next tape block, until end of file.

To retrieve an image with standard Unix utilities if *amrestore* is not available, position the tape to the image, then use *dd* to read it:

```
# mt rewind
# mt fsf NN
# dd if=$TAPE bs=32k skip=1 of=dump_image
```

The *skip=1* option tells *dd* to skip over the AMANDA file header. Without the *of=* option, *dd* writes the image to standard output, which can be piped to the decompression program, if needed, and then to the client *restore* program.

Since the image header is text, it may be viewed with:

```
# mt rewind
# mt fsf NN
# dd if=$TAPE bs=32k count=1
```

In addition to describing the image, it contains text showing the commands needed to do a restore. Here's a typical entry for the root filesystem on `pete.cc.purdue.edu`. It is a level-1 dump done without compression using the vendor *ufsdump* program:

```
AMANDA: FILE 19981206 pete.cc.purdue.edu / lev 1
  comp N program /usr/sbin/ufsdump
```

To restore, position the tape at start of file and run:

```
dd if=$TAPE bs=32k skip=1 | /usr/sbin/ufsrestore -f... -
```

As with any backup system, test these procedures while in normal production so the principles and techniques are familiar when disaster strikes.

III

Commercial Filesystem Backup & Recovery Utilities

Part III consists of the following two chapters:

- Chapter 5, *Commercial Backup Utilities*, suggests the elements that you might look for in a commercial utility.
- Chapter 6, *High Availability*, discusses ways in which you can design logical schemes to increase the availability of systems even during recovery.

5

Commercial Backup Utilities

Choosing a commercial backup product is hard work. There are more than 50 products with hundreds of features that change every day. Combine the complexity of the subject matter with the fact that every company's data protection needs are different, and the result is that if two administrators of equal skill from two different companies perform an equally exhaustive search for a backup product, they will arrive at different results because of differences in their companies' specific needs. A product that might not be a good choice for any other company might be the *perfect* choice for yours, simply because it does something no other product does—something that your company needs it to do.

Although there are a few products that come close, there is no single product that meets everyone's needs. That means that neither this chapter nor this book says "pick product X" at any time. This is for a lot of reasons, not the least of which is *change*. The backup and recovery market changes every day. Users' backup and recovery needs change, and what different companies do to meet those needs changes. Add to that the ever-present influence of competition. It's happened more than once that a lesser-known backup product comes out with a new version that significantly changes its standing in the market. This constantly changing nature of the backup and recovery market means that any recommendation you read here could be wrong by the time the book hits the shelves.[*]

There are two reasons why this chapter also is not going to attempt to give you a summary description of the available backup products. The first is, as said, that the information here may be out of data by the time the book is printed. The second reason is bias. I would be lying if I said that I knew all 50+ products equally. I

---

[*] Just to illustrate this point, a few years ago I really liked a particular backup product. It was a very good product that had features that other products still don't have. The company got bought out recently, and the product no longer exists!

know certain products better than others, and those products would receive a more accurate description.

What to Look For

What information should you look for in a backup product, then? This chapter contains several sections that correspond to sections of an exhaustive Request For Information (RFI), which appears at *http://www.backupcentral.com*. Each section describes a particular area of backup and recovery technology. After reading the section, you should be able to understand the corresponding questions in the RFI. You then can use the RFI in a number of ways. Feel free to use it (or excerpts of it) for your own RFI from the backup vendors that you are considering. However, any vendor that wishes to may have its updated RFI response posted on the web site, *http://www.backupcentral.com*. This web site also will be used to cover any new areas of technology that aren't covered in this book.

When looking at a potential backup product, there are several questions that you should be asking:

- Does the product fully support your platforms?
- Does the product back up raw partitions?
- Does the product back up very large filesystems and large files?
- Does the product back up many clients to one drive simultaneously?
- Does the product back up one client to many drives simultaneously?
- Does the product handle data requiring special treatment?
- Does the product have storage management features?
- Does the product reduce network traffic?
- Does the product support a standard or unique backup format?
- How easy is the product to administer?
- How secure is the product?
- How easily does the product perform recoveries?
- How well does the product protect the backup catalog (database, index)?
- How robust is the product?
- How automated is the product?
- Can the product verify its volumes?
- What does the product cost?
- What vendor is selling the product?

These issues are discussed in the following sections.

Full Support of Your Platforms

One of the easiest ways to narrow the list of backup software vendors from which to choose is to find out who supports the platforms you are running. There is no reason that a vendor should have to answer an RFI with 300+ questions if it doesn't support most of your platforms. By the same token, there is no reason you should have to read the answers to 300 responses from more than 50 vendors. (That's 15,000 responses, by the way!) Before getting into the nitty-gritty features, simply find out who supports all or most of the platforms that need to be backed up.

The key word in the previous paragraph is "most." Most shops are becoming increasingly heterogeneous, with a number of Unix variants, Intel-based operating systems, and any number of database-like products. In such a shop, there are always a few boxes that run a "different" version of Unix or a lesser-known database product that most products don't support. (Often, this is because no one has asked them to support it.) A good current example of this is Linux. Commercial backup and recovery companies are just beginning to recognize it as a potential source of revenue. This means that the list of vendors who offer supported client software for Linux is very short. (Some of them offer unsupported versions, though.) During the first cut, include products that back up *most* of the operating systems that you are running. Restricting the search to only those that handle every platform might exclude some very good products or force the selection of the wrong product. Many vendors will consider porting their products to a new operating system or database if a potential customer asks them to do so, although this may come at a cost. (In the final analysis, however, a product that has been supporting a particular platform for a while *usually* supports it better.)

There are many different operating systems out there. There are Unix variants, MacOS, Netware, OS/2, various Windows flavors, and mainframe operating systems. Most of the big products handle almost all of these. There was a time when you had to purchase one product for the Novell servers, one for the MVS mainframes, and yet another for the Unix servers. Today there are products that handle all of those from one console. However, the rush by so many large backup products to support *everything* has left a few holes. There are a number of examples of this. Things that are typically left out in Unix are block special files, character special files, and named pipes. Microsoft's Registry also is occasionally left out, and Novell's NDS gets left out as well. Make sure each product fully supports the platforms they claim to support.

Should You Back Up Device Files?

If a backup product did not back up Windows 2000's Registry, it would not be considered certified by Microsoft. However, there are some prominent Unix backup packages that don't back up special files and named pipes. If the operating system is lost, their typical answer is to "reinstall the operating system and our software, and then start the restore." This takes too much time and involves writing a lot of information twice. If the backup system backed up the special files, there is a much quicker way to recover from the loss of the operating system. See Part IV of this book for more information about such recoveries.

What if a system was able to boot, but the */dev* directory was all messed up? Being able to restore those files can reduce the number of hours of downtime. Does the backup product really need to back up the device files? Yes it does!

Back It Up—All of It!

A production system had a bad disk and lost the programs that ran the application, including the database. The normal backup backed up only the data, not the application software. They could not find the original software. Fortunately, I had a complete tape copy in my desk from testing before production, and we were able to use it to restore the software. (Eventually, the original software also was found, copied, properly stored, and cataloged.)

—Norm Eisenberg

Does It Support DCE/DFS?

In addition to the various operating systems, another factor that may affect your backup software decision is the Distributed Computing Environment (DCE). Prior to deciding on a backup solution, find out if your company has any plans to use DCE. If so, make sure that this computing environment is supported by your backup software. One essential element of DCE compliance would be the method that the product uses for communication. Normally this would mean that it can't use *rsh* for communication between client and server. This, of course, would require the vendor to develop some type of secure communication.

A part of DCE is the Distributed File System (DFS).[*] It is a cousin of MTI's Andrew Filesystem, is distributed by Transarc, and works on quite a few platforms. DFS is much more complicated than NFS and includes data replication, a highly secure system of authentication called Kerberos, and a central (replicated) database that keeps track of all this information. Each piece represents data that needs to be

---

[*] DCE is an *environment*, which may or may not include DFS in any given implementation. DFS requires DCE, but DCE does not require DFS. As long as a backup product communicates with sockets, it probably won't have a problem working in a DCE environment. DFS, on the other hand, must be backed up via its Application Programming Interface (API).

backed up in a special way. At one time, Transarc was working on an API to which some of the vendors were going to port. As of this writing, however, only one company seems to have backup support for DFS. If DFS is to grow in popularity, this has to change. People do not want to be forced to buy a particular backup product because of one application they'd like to use.

Backup of Raw Partitions

Many environments use their commercial backup product to back up raw partitions. A *partition* is a section of disk that may or may not contain a filesystem. Typically, when one refers to a *raw* partition, it is a section of disk that does *not* contain a filesystem. This disk may contain data for a database product, such as Oracle, Informix, or Sybase. It also may be the first part of the root partition of the operating system disk that contains the boot block. Since most backup products are designed to back up files that reside on a filesystem, they may not be able to back up a raw partition.

The ability to back up raw partitions could help when backing up relatively small databases that reside on raw partitions. To back up most databases with a product that supports raw partitions, simply shut down the database and tell the backup software what raw partitions to back up. In order to do this, the backup software needs to be capable of backing up these raw partitions.

The second reason to consider the use of this feature is to back up the root partition of an operating system disk. It's another way to recover the root disk without reinstalling the operating system. There are two essential parts to the operating system disk. The first is the operating system itself, which resides on one or more filesystems on that disk. The second is the boot block (in Unix) or Master Boot Record (in DOS relatives). This tells the system's firmware where to go to find the operating system kernel. This block of data normally resides on the first slice, or root partition, of the operating system disk. It resides *outside* the filesystem and thus would not be backed up by normal procedures. If the backup product is able to back up the raw partition on which it resides, it's possible to recover it without reinstalling the operating system. (This is covered in detail in Part IV of this book.)

Many of the popular backup packages now work with raw partitions. There is one drawback to backing up raw partitions, though. A raw partition is seen as one big file. That means that every time it is backed up, the entire partition will be backed up. With a 100-MB root partition of an operating system, this is not a problem. If it's a multigigabyte raw device, it can fill up quite a lot of backup media very fast. There are products that can intelligently read a raw partition and perform an incremental backup of its contents. This is a new option as of the writing of this book, but it is worth investigation.

Backup of Very Large Filesystems and Files

Large filesystems and files caught many backup products by surprise. For many years, 4-GB filesystems with a maximum of 2-GB files ruled the land. This is because none of the operating systems allowed anything larger. Then came 32-bit operating systems and the terabyte filesystem. It wasn't long after that that some vendors were announcing the ability to create terabyte files. This caused a major problem with some backup vendors, because many design decisions were made assuming there was a 4-GB limit.

There are a few things to consider when investigating if a given product can handle large files and filesystems. Does the vendor have any hardcoded limits that say a file can't be any bigger than *n* bytes? Do they have problems if a filesystem (or file) is bigger than a volume?

Simultaneous Backup of Many Clients to One Drive

This is also a relatively new problem for backup software products. It used to be that the backup drive was the bottleneck in any backup system. For many years, the optimum speed of most backup drives was less than 1 MB per second. Since disks were able to supply data much faster than that, the only other potential bottleneck would be the network. Therefore, even a 10-MB network could stream a backup device at its full speed.

Those days are gone. There are now backup drives that can write three times as fast as many disk drives. Backup drives now use Fast-Wide SCSI, large buffers, and sometimes write multiple streams of data to the drive at once. Fibre-channel backup drives are now available. The result is that many backup drives can write at 10 MB/s or faster. The difficulty with most of these drives, though, is that they are "streaming" tape drives. This means that you must supply them with a steady stream of incoming data equivalent to their maximum throughput. If not, the drive will not stream, resulting in a significantly slower transfer rate than it is capable of. This problem, of course, affects only streaming tape drives. It does not affect backup drives that simulate a disk drive, such as Magneto-Optical, CD, and DVD drives.

All streaming tape drives are designed to write most effectively at their optimum speed. If they are supplied with data at a slower rate than that, the result may be surprising. What begins to happen is referred to as "repositioning." See the "Tape Drives" section of Chapter 18, *Backup Hardware*, for more information on this concept. The drive spends most of its time repositioning and has less time to actually write data. The result is that *it will write at a small fraction of its maximum data rate.*

When would this happen? Consider a single-threaded backup process such as *dump* or *tar.* It will encounter many potential bottlenecks before getting to the drive. The first obstacle is the disk itself, which may not be capable of supplying data at a sufficient rate. Another is the SCSI bus and system to which the drive is connected. It may be busy satisfying other I/O requests, hence impacting the data rate that can be transferred across the bus. The next, of course, is the network. If it's a 10-Mb network, the best possible data rate is less than 1 MB/s. The final possible bottleneck is the system to which the backup drive is connected. Any one of these bottlenecks could slow the data rate to less than the optimal speed for the backup drive. If that happens, a tape drive stops streaming and begins repositioning in order to keep in pace with the incoming data. When this happens, *it becomes the new bottleneck.* What can be done about this? Most commercial backup products solve this problem by implementing multithreaded backups. Multithreaded backups can read data from several systems and several disks at one time and supply the data from all of these threads to the backup drive simultaneously. The data from these different sources is then "interleaved" onto the volume. The backup drive is thus always being supplied with a sufficient stream of data, so it can write at its maximum speed. A cautious administrator learning of this feature for the first time might be worried. Some administrators don't like the fact that their data is spread out all over the volume. However, this feature is really the only way to stream a backup drive that can read or write at speeds faster than a disk. This is why most commercial backup products implement multithreading.

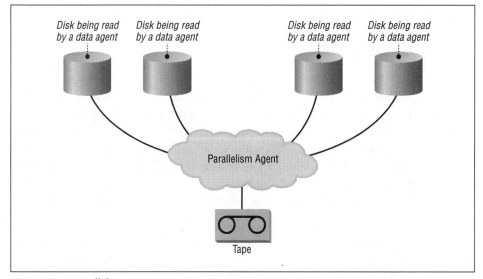

Figure 5-1. Parallelism

Different backup software vendors use different terms for this feature. It often is referred to as "parallelism" or "interleaving." As in Figure 5-1, which depicts parallelism, there are several processes called data agents (DA for short) reading from disks at one time. Those processes feed their data streams to the parallelism agent (PA for short), which does the actual job of interleaving the separate streams together into one stream, which then gets written to the backup drive.

Parallelism can be done in one of two ways.

File-Level Parallelism

Backup software products accomplish the first type of interleaving by leaving the file intact. Each DA would read a file and then tell the PA it was ready to send this file. The PA then would read the entire file from the DA and write it to the backup volume as one contiguous section. The PA then would look to see which DA had the next available file ready. This works fine for small files that are coming from systems that are all the same speed. However, if a DA on a relatively slow system has a large file, it will occupy the PA's time during the transmission of that entire file. The result is that the backup drive may slow down when such large files are backed up. This type of parallelism is illustrated in Figure 5-2.

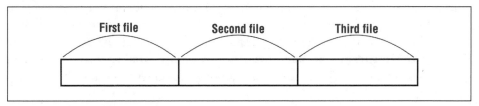

Figure 5-2. File-level parallelism

Block-Level Parallelism

Most backup software products that support parallelism use a method known as *block-level* parallelism, also referred to as *record-level* parallelism. With this method, each file is split into multiple blocks of data. These blocks then are written to the volume in a noncontiguous fashion, interleaved with other blocks of data from other files or systems. This is the most efficient way, since it means that the data needed by the parallelism agent can be taken from any disk on any system that is being backed up by this backup definition, so the PA never has to wait on a DA. Unlike file-level parallelism, no single system or disk can cause a bottleneck.

Notice in Figure 5-3 that each file is split into multiple blocks, labeled "Block 1," "Block 2," etc. File one is a large file and took up many blocks. It was coming from a slow system, which was not able to supply data very fast. File three, on the other hand, came from a much faster system. That explains why blocks 2 and 3 are together. This is why block-level parallelism is so efficient. Faster disks and faster systems will be allowed to send the data as fast as they can to the volume, while slower systems will get a block in every so often. All the while, the volume is recording away.

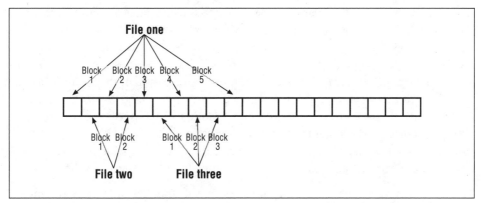

Figure 5-3. Block-level parallelism

There is a downside to block-level parallelism—slower restores. Just how slow the restores will be is determined by how the product handles parallelism during a restore. If the product is using block-level parallelism, then during a restore the backup drive normally will be given a list of instructions like the following:

1. Position to block 1000

2. Read one block of data

3. Position to block 1003

4. Read one block of data

5. Position to block 1010

6. Read one block of data

There is a completely different way to speed up restores of parallelized data. The software could read the volume continuously, disregarding blocks that it doesn't need. (This actually is taking a step back in technology, but unfortunately it's the only way to get some of the modern backup drives to perform well during a restore of interleaved data.) The lesson to learn here is to test every product's ability to restore interleaved data.

Simultaneous Backup of One Client to Many Drives

How does a backup product get a Very Large Database (VLDB) or Very Large System (VLS) onto backup media? This is a slightly different scenario than the one described previously. The many-to-one concept is trying to deal with the fact that there may be thousands of clients but only a few backup drives. Many-to-one parallelism allows 5 or 10 systems to share the same device, so that backup devices are constantly streaming, and backups can be done in a timely manner. In contrast, the situation that calls for one-to-many is a single system that could not possibly back up its files to a single backup drive in one night. Even if one had a backup drive that is capable of 20 MB/s, that is only 72 GB per hour, or 576 GB in an eight-hour period—assuming the drive could be streamed for that long. What if the system contains 6 TB of data? Also, what if the drive is capable only of 5 MB/s? That backup drive could do only 144 GB in an eight-hour period.

The only way to get that kind of speed is to use four 20 MB/s drives simultaneously. (Other combinations would work, of course, but they all require multiple simultaneous backup drives.) However, in order to make that happen, the backup software needs to be able to take the *one system* and send it *to many devices* simultaneously. There are many products that are able to do this. What is important is *how they do it*.

There are two ways to accomplish the one-to-many requirement.

The Do-It-Yourself Plan

The most common way that backup software companies tell you to back up a VLDB or VLS is to configure multiple backup definitions, each of which is a subset of the entire system—then run them simultaneously. For example, there could be one backup definition that backs up everything, excluding */home1* and */home2*. Then there could be a second backup definition that backs up just */home1* and */home2*. The software then would be told to back them up at the same time. That way, two different devices would be operating at the same time—potentially cutting the backup time by as much as half.

The first problem with this method is that it does not adequately leverage the hardware resources. Assume that the two backup definitions are exactly the same size. On full-backup day, both backup drives will be used exactly the same amount of time, and the backup time will be cut in half. However, incremental backups occur much more frequently than full backups. Since each filesystem may have a separate purpose, the size of their incremental backups most likely will vary greatly. On any given night, one backup definition may need to back up 5

GB, while the other may need to back up 20 GB. The 5 GB will finish in one-fourth the time of the 20 GB, leaving its backup drive unused for the remainder of the backup. If the incremental backups could be balanced as well as the full backups are, then the backup drives would be better utilized, allowing for a much smaller backup window.

The second problem is the ever-changing nature of system configurations. Inevitably, data requirements will continue to grow, requiring the creation of a new filesystem, such as */home3*. If the backup definitions are defined as described earlier (using the "everything except" method), the first thing that happens is that the "everything except */home1* and */home2*" definition becomes larger by automatically including */home3*, and its backup will take much longer. If */home2* simply grows in size, the backup times will be skewed in the other direction. Eventually, there will have to be another backup definition to balance the load even further.

The last problem is the human factor. Suppose the backup definitions aren't defined as described earlier. Suppose there is one definition that backs up */, /user*, and */var*. Then there is another that backs up */home1* and */home2*. What happens when */home3* is added? If someone forgets to tell the person responsible for backups, it won't get backed up at all.

This is why backups should never be defined this way. If backup definitions must be split up, always start with an "everything except" backup definition. That way, when a new filesystem is added, it will get backed up automatically.

Of course, there is also the chance for syntax errors. Many of the backup programs allow you to exclude directories by using regular expressions. Regular expressions can be very cryptic, confusing, and easily misused. For example, if someone excluded */home1* with a regular expression, */home10* also could be excluded accidentally if the product uses true regular expressions. (The proper way to exclude */home1* would be to use the regular expression *^/home1$*, where ^ represents the beginning of the string and *$* designates the end of the string.)

If backups are defined by the use of regular expressions, backup definitions must be monitored constantly, adjusting them so that they are all the appropriate size. Some will get bigger, some will get smaller, but they all have to be watched. The more systems there are to do this with, the bigger this effort becomes, and the more likely it is that an error will occur.

Glad Nobody Asked for That One!

As with many warnings, this one comes with its own story. I was using a backup product that required me to create separate backup definitions if I wanted to do one-to-many. The host was so big and my tape drives were so slow that I had to define five separate backup definitions. First, I had a backup definition that included everything except */data1–/data8*. Then I had four more, each of which backed up two of the */datax* filesystems. When the machine's administrator added */data9*, it was backed up automatically by the "everything except */data1–8*" backup. However, when */data10* and */data11* were added, they didn't get backed up at all.

One day I was browsing around and I noticed that I couldn't find any history for the */data10* filesystem. It was only after a frantic call to tech support that I found out the error was mine. When I excluded */data1*, what I actually said was, "exclude all filesystems that matched the regular expression */data1*." Unfortunately */data1* also matches */data10*. For more than two months, there were two filesystems that weren't getting backed up. Luckily, nobody needed a restore. This is why I say to be very careful when excluding filesystems using regular expressions.

A Much Better Method

There is a much better way to back up a VLDB or VLS. Backup products have come a long way since *dump*. With *dump*, one had to essentially say, "back up this filesystem to that backup drive." There is more than one performance problem with this scenario. The first is that it is single-threaded. As mentioned in the many-to-one scenario, it is highly unlikely that a single-threaded backup process is going to even come close to providing a modern backup drive with its optimum data rate. Second, it is not intelligent. What if the filesystem is very large, and the backup needs to go to multiple backup drives simultaneously?

This has been one of the areas in which major advances have been made in the last few years. There are a few backup products that can be set up as follows. First, you have to configure the software so that it knows where the backup devices are. Then it must be told what the names of the backup clients are. It then utilizes many-to-one and one-to-many technology to fully utilize each device, and ensure that the backups complete as fast as possible.

Before explaining how these products work, I must explain the concept of a *thread*. A thread is a single stream of data coming from a client and going to a backup device. When using *dump*, there is one thread reading from the disk on one end and writing to a drive on the other end. When using a commercial backup utility, there may be several threads reading from the system at once. The more advanced utilities typically will not spawn more than one thread per physical disk. Some may spawn more than one thread from a logical disk, if the disk is a logical volume composed of several physical volumes. Also, since a single thread may not stream a tape drive at its full speed, the backup product also may send multiple threads to a backup drive at once, "interleaving" them together into a constant stream of data being fed to the backup drive. This particular section aims to explain backup utilities that are able to dynamically allocate threads to the backup devices that need them.

How is this accomplished? Please refer to Figure 5-4 through Figure 5-6. These three figures are a logical representation of a combination of the dynamic one-to-many and many-to-one concepts. Each disk on the left is meant to logically represent data residing on a single system. Each drive on the right is meant to represent one backup device, such as a tape or optical drive. As this is a logical representation, this is not meant to say that these are network backup drives. These could be network backup drives (mounted on the backup server), or they could be backup drives that are physically connected to the backup clients. The Backup System Control shown in these figures is a logical representation of the backup system that controls all of these data paths. The data paths, or threads, are represented by the curved lines (A–Z and 1–6) connecting the three sections of the drawing. Notice that there are four clients, each of which is capable of supporting eight threads. There are five backup devices, each of which can support four threads.

In the scenario represented in these three figures, the backup system has been configured to start up to eight threads per backup client and to send up to four threads to each backup device. At the beginning of the backup, as illustrated in Figure 5-4, the backup system attempts to start eight threads per client. (For simplicity's sake, this example assumes that each client has enough physical disks to support that many threads.) The first four threads (A–D) are routed automatically by the backup system to the backup device Tape A. Threads E–H are sent to Tape B, threads I–L to Tape C, threads M–P to Tape D, and threads Q–T are sent to Tape E.

Since each of the five drives can support only four threads apiece, a maximum of 20 threads can run at once. That means that threads U–6 must wait. (When a thread must wait like this, there is no data traffic for that thread. Such threads remain in the drawing for illustration purposes.) The system continues backing up in this manner until one of the threads has completed the disk or filesystem that it is backing up.

Assume for this example that threads B, C, E, and I are backing up filesystems that were smaller than the rest. This also could be an incremental backup in which those filesystems had very little changed data. In Figure 5-5, those threads have completed, as represented by their dotted lines. That leaves volume A with only two threads and volumes B and C with only three. Since they are capable of supporting four threads, the backup system attempts to find more threads for them. Threads U–X are now started, as represented by the bold lines, and routed by the backup system to the drives in need of more threads. All five drives once again have four threads apiece.

In the final drawing, Figure 5-6, threads A–T have all finished. That leaves two drives with no threads and three drives with fewer than four. Once again, the backup system recognizes this and activates threads Y–6, as represented by the bold lines, and routes them to the drives in need of threads. However, there are only 12 possible threads at this time, so drives D and E are not needed.

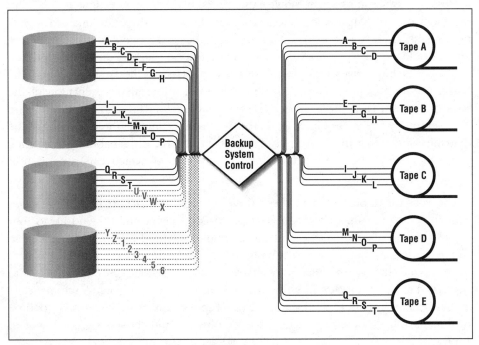

Figure 5-4. One-to-many example (time index 1)

This dynamic method of combining the many-to-one and one-to-many concepts can be implemented with minor variations, depending on which backup product you use. It is very efficient and ensures that all backup devices are running at their optimum speed. The next advancement would be to allow the number of threads going to a device to be dynamic as well. For example, suppose the backup product knows that a given device is supposed to support 10MB/s. The product would make sure that it had enough threads to support this speed, or perhaps one extra. Some drives might need only one or two threads, if the threads are coming from a very fast system with a good link to the drives.

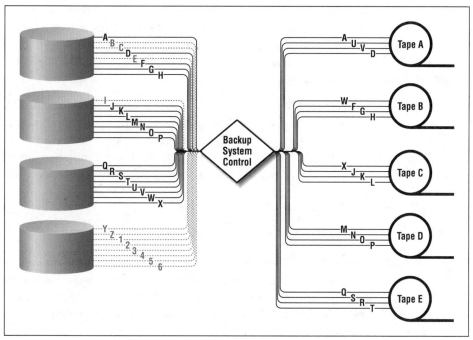

Figure 5-5. One-to-many example (time index 2)

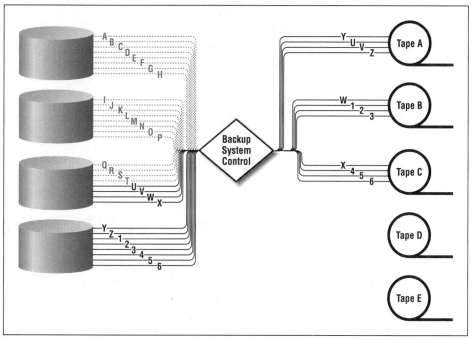

Figure 5-6. Many example (time index 3)

There's another scenario that calls for a one-to-many type backup. There are many products that are able to handle the preceding scenario, but what if it is a single large *filesystem*? Due to modern advancements in filesystems, they can now be a terabyte or more. So now, not only is there 2 TB of data to back up from one system, it all resides in one filesystem.

There is no way to back up a 2-TB system to a 20-MB/s drive in one night. The only way to get that kind of speed is to use four 20-MB/s drives simultaneously, on four separate SCSI channels. However, in order to make that happen, the backup software must be able to take the *one filesystem* and send it *to many devices* simultaneously. As of this writing, this is an area that only one product has properly addressed.*

Data Requiring Special Treatment

All commercial backup products can back up normal filesystem data. However, there is a lot of data that does not reside in a normal filesystem. Some data does reside in a filesystem but still requires special treatment before it can be backed up. Find out how the product that you are considering handles data such as this:

Network-mounted filesystems
> It is sometimes necessary to back up data that resides on a disk that is mounted from another machine.

Data that needs a custom script to back it up
> Some types of data fall in between "normal" filesystem data and database data. If this data is created by a special utility, that utility must be shut off prior to running the backup.

Relational Database (RDBMS) data
> Although some RDBMS data can be backed up using shutdown/startup scripts, there is now a much better way to back up most commercial database products.

The following sections discuss these three needs.

Network-Mounted Filesystems

Why would anyone want to back up via NFS? In almost every shop, there is a client that is not supported by commercial backup software. Perhaps it's an older operating system that is no longer supported. Perhaps the software vendors aren't convinced that the operating system has enough market share. (Remember that these vendors aren't in this for free.) What good does it do to port your software to a platform that no one is using?

---

* Since this may change by the time the book is available, I won't mention the product's name here. See *http://www.backupcentral.com.*

One solution to back up such a client would be to NFS-mount its filesystems to the backup server and back up the data via NFS. Yes, NFS is a horrible way to back up. Yes, there are problems with restoring via NFS. But, as they say, something is better than nothing.

Along with NFS is Microsoft's network filesystem, which uses the Server Message Block (SMB) protocol, and Netware's network filesystem, which uses the Netware Core Protocol (NCP). (Microsoft now calls their network filesystem the Common Internet File System, or CIFS.) These protocols work similarly to NFS, and a supported backup server could mount such drives over the network and back them up that way. (One of the problems with this method is that it will not back up or restore the Access Control Lists (ACLs)—but at least you'll have the data.)

The other issue with NFS-, SMB-, and NCP-mounted filesystems is whether the backup software can exclude them. Imagine what would happen in a heavy NFS environment if the backup product started to back up *all* NFS partitions! Typically, this is avoided by excluding all NFS and SMB mount points, but some products have the capability to selectively back up NFS and SMB partitions. Some products allow you to configure a client in such a way that it will back up all NFS-mounted partitions that it contains.

Custom User Scripts

Up until a few years ago, custom user scripts were the only option available for backing up databases. The backup product would run a special program written by the administrator that shut down the database. The backup product then would back up the files or raw partitions on which the database resides. Finally, the program would restart the database. Depending on the size of the database and the uptime requirements, this approach to database backups may still be a viable solution for some environments.

This method is now used for some types of data that do not fully qualify as "database" data but is dynamic enough that it requires custom handling. Perhaps you use a network-monitoring tool that continually probes the network and stores the result in several interrelated files. Since those files must be backed up at a consistent point in time, the network-monitoring tool will need to be shut down while the backup is running. This can be accomplished by a custom script.

Some backup products even allow you to use a custom script that creates a stream of data that is passed to the product. For example, one product in particular does not natively support the backing up of raw partitions, but it does allow its users to write programs that use a command such as *dd* to pass it the data from that raw partition. The product then writes that data to a backup volume. (Of course, this method requires a custom restore script as well.)

Unix Databases

A few years ago, no commercial backup utilities backed up database data directly. The best you could do was to shut them down with a custom script as discussed in the previous section. However, databases are now so large that this option is no longer viable for many environments. Within the last few years, each of the major database vendors has come out with some sort of Application Programming Interface (API) that commercial backup utilities can use to back up the vendor's database. Oracle7 has the Enterprise Backup Utility (EBU), Oracle8 has its Recovery Manager (RMAN), and Informix 7.21 released their Online Backup and Recovery (*onbar*). Sybase has its Backup Server, which started with System 10 but was made much better with System 11. Each of these utilities has four common traits:

- They can pass a data stream to a third party utility, such as a commercial backup product. (With Informix and Oracle, that's all it can do. Only the Sybase utility also can perform standalone backups.)
- They are capable of doing this while the database is online.
- They are capable of providing multiple, simultaneous threads from the same database.
- Once set up, they can be called from either that commercial backup utility or the database interface. (For example, you can log into the database server as the *informix* user and issue an *onbar* command, and that will automatically start a session with the commercial backup utility. You also can issue a backup command from the backup product and have it call *onbar*.)

There are a number of other databases, such as DB2, Lotus Notes, and SQL Server. Many of them have some method of backing their data up to a commercial backup utility. The question you must ask the backup vendor is, "Which of these databases have you ported to?" Even if you aren't using any database products today, the number of databases that a particular product backs up to demonstrates its level of commitment to the enterprise market.

Also, it should be mentioned that there are other interfaces that do not use the vendor-supplied APIs. Also, some commercial backup utility vendors have independently written their own interfaces to these database products, and these interfaces do not use the database vendor's API either. The preferred method should be to use the vendor-supplied API. Backups and restores done through some other method usually are not supported by the database software vendor.

Windows 2000 Databases

One common backup solution for Windows 2000 products is to back up databases to a file on another disk and then back up that file using standard utilities.

There is nothing technically wrong with this philosophy, and many products have used it over the years to automate backups. One limitation of this method is scalability. What happens when you cannot afford a disk big enough for a second copy of the database? It is no longer rare to find Windows 2000 databases that are 20, 30, or even 60 GB. Backups to disk also require extra CPU time to back up the data twice.

Unfortunately, when some database vendors think of Windows 2000, they think "small." They conclude that it's all right to expect the system administrator to swap volumes and do manual backups every once in a while. That is why companies continue to come out with new databases for Windows 2000 that do not have enterprise-class backup interfaces. This means that a good Windows 2000 systems engineer should diligently:

- Communicate with the database vendors, goading them to develop an enterprise-class interface for their products

- Communicate with the backup software vendor, ensuring that it ports to any database backup APIs that exist

- Communicate with those whose job it is to purchase new database products for Windows 2000, making sure that the backup component is part of the evaluation (choosing a product with an existing API that is already being used by backup vendors can save a lot of time and hassle)

Storage Management Features

One of the latest buzzword phrases in the backup software business is *storage management.* Just as some people think the word "Internet" was invented within the last few years, many think that storage management is a new concept. It actually goes way back to the mainframe days when 3480 tapes were much less expensive than DASD disks. It became necessary to move important, yet unused, data off the expensive disks and onto less expensive 3480 media. (This is one way of *managing* the available *storage*, thus the term *storage management.*) SCSI disks were a lot cheaper, so Unix environments just bought more disks as they needed more storage space. Unfortunately, this "disk is cheap" mentality has led users to create far more and far bigger files than ever before. Within the last few years, though, IS managers have started to become very frustrated with the amount of money they are spending on disk. They believe that there are a number of files that could be moved from disk to a slower storage medium without anyone noticing. This belief has given rise to a demand for storage management in the Unix arena. Just what is storage management, though?

This section examines the two principal storage management concepts that relate to backups:

- Archiving
- Hierarchical storage management

Archiving

The first principal storage management concept we will address is archiving. In most distributed circles, archiving typically has meant backups that are retained for a long time. In the storage management domain, archiving has a slightly different twist: these backups that are saved for a long time must be saved in such a way that different pieces of related data are easy to retrieve.

Once again, this is not a new concept. How many times has a user said, "Can you put this directory on a backup volume before I blow it away for good?" They then want the volume marked with a special label, such as "Informix executables 3/99." That way, if they ever need to roll back to the old version of Informix, all the appropriate data will be on one volume and easy to find. Commercial products have a similar ability. The product can be told, "Archive all of the data described in this archive definition under the heading 'Informix executables 3/99'." Unlike the manual method, commercial products make it very easy to add files from different systems into one archive file. They simply need to be included in the product's archive definition. That way, someone who needs those files years from now, essentially tells the product, "Show me the archived files that match the string 'Informix'." One of the archives listed would be "Informix executables 3/99." The user then could select that archive and restore the needed files. Once again, in this context, the host from which those executables came is irrelevant.

Hierarchical Storage Management

The second principal storage management concept is Hierarchical Storage Management, or HSM. HSM is a horse of a different color. While archiving allows someone to delete files from disk once they have been archived, that is not its primary purpose. Its primary purpose is to make those files easy to find years from now when the user doesn't remember what system they were on. HSM's primary purpose is to automatically monitor filesystems, looking for files that meet certain conditions. In Unix, the parameter that usually is monitored is the *atime* value for each file. If a file's *atime* has not changed, it means that it has not been accessed or used in any way, and a file that meets that condition can be migrated to less expensive media.

In a truly *hierarchical* system, this would involve successively less expensive media types. For example, the file might be moved from a high-speed high-availability system to older, nonmirrored, single-ended disks. It then might be moved to optical disks and eventually to tape. Each of these levels is less expensive than the previous level but also has a longer random-access time. When a file is moved, or "migrated," to a less expensive level, the HSM system leaves a "stub" file behind that has the same name as the original file. If anyone attempts to access the stub file, the original file is retrieved automatically by the HSM system. This is invisible to the end user, other than the extra time taken to access the file. (Some high-speed systems can reduce this time to less than 15 seconds.)

Consider a heavy CAD environment. Engineers may make new drawings every day but want to keep the old ones around for reference. Suppose somebody asks, five years from now, "What parts went into XYZ?" Without an HSM system, the drawing for XYZ would have to remain on disk for years, simply taking up space. Now, if the engineer making the drawing was conscientious about the disk space she was using, she might contact the administrator and ask for her files to be *archived*. (However, most end users are not concerned about the administrator's disk space problems.) An HSM system would proactively monitor this CAD directory and "notice" that this particular group of CAD drawings hasn't been examined for more than a year. It then would migrate them to a less expensive storage medium without any action from the engineer. When the engineer did eventually need this file, all she would have to do is open it up in her CAD application. It would be retrieved automatically. To her, it would appear as if the system was really slow today. If she had been educated about HSM, she might think, "Oh, the file must have been migrated." As long as the file comes back, she probably won't mind the HSM system at all. In an HSM system, there does need to be some education of the user community; they need to know that their files are being migrated. If they do not know, they will call the help desk whenever they experience a delay when retrieving a file. (Make sure that the help desk doesn't tell them how to "cheat" the HSM system. Users have been known to put *touch* * in their login scripts. Not only will this completely invalidate the HSM system; it will significantly increase the size of incremental backups!)

 Implementing an HSM system should be done slowly and methodically with significant help from someone who has set up such a system somewhere else. Unrealistic migration policies and improper end-user education can spell disaster for an HSM system. Many system administrators have been required by their end users to remove or deactivate their HSM systems. HSM *can* work, but so many people have seen poorly configured HSM systems that they have earned a really bad reputation. Step very carefully when moving toward an HSM solution.

Reduction in Network Traffic

One of the best ways to perform backups is to install a completely separate network to carry all the backup traffic. However, many people do not have the funding necessary to set up such a network, so they need to be careful about how their backup system influences the network that it shares. There are a few different things that backup products can do to minimize their impact on the network, whether it is a private one for backups or the corporate backbone.

Keep Backup Traffic at the Subnet Level

One of the best ways for a backup product to reduce the amount of traffic that goes between networks is to distribute the backup devices to the subnet level. Keeping backup traffic on its local subnet results in two benefits. First, backup traffic is distributed, so that no single subnet sees all the traffic. The overall impact to the internal customer (who also is trying to use the corporate intranet) is therefore reduced. The second benefit is that the overall throughput of the backup system will be able to scale with the network as the network grows by the addition of subnets. Consider the drawing in Figure 5-7. There are six different subnets (100.10–100.15), each of which is switched 10 MB (switches not shown). Each of the switches is plugged into a router, which also is plugged into the 100.1 subnet, where the backup server resides.

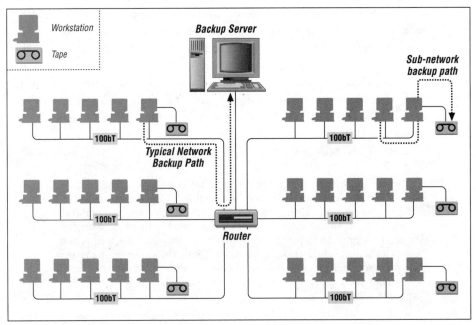

Figure 5-7. Network backup data paths

A typical, network-based backup system causes data to flow in the manner illustrated by the data path on the left. The data path represented by the lefthand dotted line shows that the data goes over the 100.10 subnet, the router, and the 100.1 subnet to the backup server. If all of these six subnets are backed up that way, the total backup throughput could be no higher than the speed of the 100.1 subnet or the router, since all traffic must go through them. This quite possibly would be 10 Mb/s, or 1 MB/s, which is less than the speed of one Exabyte 8500 and one-tenth the speed of a Quantum DLT 7000. The result is that the backup system will never stream the backup drive.

However, if the backup software supports remote devices, the backup traffic can be localized to the subnets, as illustrated on the right. Even without taking advantage of switching technologies, the backup system now has an overall throughput of 6 MB/s instead of 1 MB/s.

Use Client-Side Compression

Backup software products also can use client-side compression to reduce network traffic. This means that files are compressed on the client before they are sent across the network. This is very CPU-intensive on the client end, but the amount of data that actually goes out on the network can be greatly reduced. If the system CPUs are fast and the network is slow, this can improve overall backup throughput and reduce total backup time.

Using client-side compression can slow down restores as well. How much restores are affected varies with the product and the nature of the systems being backed up. Before using compression, test to see how much it affects restore performance. It may be too great a sacrifice.

Incorporate Throttling

Another feature that is difficult to find in backup software products is called "throttling" and can help reduce the effect of the backup traffic on the overall network. Some products allow the administrator to throttle a backup client, that is, to specify how many megabits per second a backup client can send out on the network. That way, even on a 10-Mb network, the backup system would use only a prescribed percentage of the total bandwidth, since that's what it was told to do. This will slow down the backups, of course, but the people trying to use the network will surely appreciate it.

Just What is a Switch Anyway?

If you are not a network guru, you might ask yourself this question. A *switch* is one of the greatest advancements in network technology in a long time. Before the switch, the best that you were likely to see on the local subnet was called "shared Ethernet." This meant that all systems connecting to a hub essentially share the same piece of wire. (Some environments didn't even have a hub and actually did share the same physical piece of wire.) Therefore, since all packets went to each port of the hub, the overall throughput of the LAN was the same as any port on the hub—usually 10 Mb/s.

With the advent of switching technology, when port A talks to port B, they get the equivalent of their own "wire." So while ports A and B are talking, ports C and D can talk as well, unaffected by the traffic on ports A and B. This is because data traffic inside the switch is done in RAM, which allows each port to talk at full speed, resulting in a much greater overall throughput compared to shared 10 Mb. For example, on a 24-port 10-Mb switch, there could be 12 different "pairs" of systems communicating, using two ports each. That is an overall throughput of 120 Mb/s. (Actually, with full duplex switching, you can get 120 Mb/s going both ways, for a total bandwidth of 240 Mb/s. However, this doesn't help backups too much, since we're only trying to go one way.)

What's really nice for backup systems is the 100-megabit "uplink port." Most switches have one or more of these ports. That port can be plugged into a dedicated 100-megabit network card on the system with the backup drives. Ten clients on 10 different 10-megabit switch ports then could back up at the same time, since each one would be able to use the full speed of its 10-megabit port. That incoming traffic is then "funneled" to the one 100-megabit port, allowing the backup system to receive an incoming data stream of up to 100 Mb/s, or 10MB/s, which is the full speed of a DLT 7000 tape drive.

When the 10bT ports in this example become 100bT, the rules change slightly. Each port still gets its own dedicated 100 Mb of bandwidth. However, when you try to combine all those channels into one gibabit uplink port, your mileage will vary. The ability of a backup server to fill a gigabit Ethernet pipe is highly unlikely. (See "Gigabit Ethernet" in Chapter 19, *Miscellanea.*)

Storage Area Networks

The final, and relatively new, traffic reduction feature of backup software products is the storage area network (SAN). I believe that it is safe to say that SANs will soon become a part of every network. The advantages that they offer over traditional LAN or SCSI technology are incredible. Before explaining *what* SANs are, I should explain *why* they are needed.

Conventional wisdom says that to get maximum use out of a large library, you connect it to a dedicated backup server and back up data across the LAN. There are two reasons why this is not always the best solution. The first reason is that even the best network can transmit only so much data. Even if you have a private gigabit Ethernet or OC-12 network just for backups, the best you are going to get is about 600 Mb/s, which is just over two TB in an eight-hour period. What if there is more than two TB of data to back up? Even if you *do* have enough network bandwidth to back up your environment, your backup clients will be working very hard to send that data over the network. This is the other reason that sending large amounts of data over a LAN is not always the best solution. All of the major backup software vendors have worked hard over the last few years to reduce the CPU and memory utilization of *local* backups—not of network-based backups. It is amazing how much data these applications can transfer if they are allowed to do so locally. It's even more amazing how few resources they use to do it.

What this means is that, while the computing industry has gone from centralized to distributed to centralized, the backup industry has gone from distributed to centralized to distributed. Backups were first done in a distributed fashion because it really was the only way to do them. Each server backed up to its tape drive. Then, as servers became more and more distributed, managing their backups created the demand for centralized backup systems. Now, many of the distributed servers have become so large that we need to move their backups back to the server level.

Is there a way to distribute a library's backup drives without giving up the automation offered by a centralized library? There is if you have a storage area network. Just as a LAN allows the sharing of *computing resources*, a SAN allows the sharing of *storage resources*. In the backup and recovery area, this means that multiple servers can have physical access to the same library. If you define a SAN simply as any system that gives multiple servers access to one storage device, you probably already have a SAN in your environment.

One example of a simple SAN is a library with separate SCSI connections for each backup drive. Some backup software packages allow you to connect each backup drive to a separate system, while maintaining central control over the library. This allows each backup client to perform local backups to the drive(s) to which it has access, while giving all clients access to all slots within the library. Up until the latter part of 1998, this was the only kind of SAN that was available for backup and recovery. The problem with this type of SAN is that it allows systems to share the library but does not allow them to share the drives. If a particular drive is physically attached to one system, another system cannot use that drive. Therefore, this type of SAN does not fully leverage the library resource. What if you could physically attach every backup drive to several servers? That would allow every system to have full access to all backup drives when it needs it, such as when it needs to do a full backup.

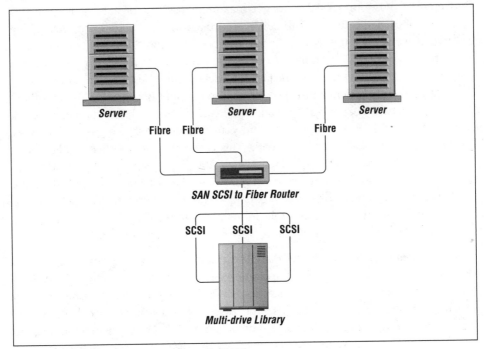

Figure 5-8. A basic storage area network (SAN)

Such access is possible with a true SAN. As illustrated in Figure 5-8, a true SAN uses a "SAN router" to give all servers *virtual* physical access to all peripherals. The router in this illustration is a combination fibre/SCSI router, allowing you to connect the servers to the switch via Fibre Channel and the peripherals to the switch via normal SCSI. (You also could use such a router to connect Fibre Channel peripherals to a SCSI-only server.) A SAN router is then told which servers should have access to which peripherals. A basic router is configured using physical switches and buttons. A more advanced router can be configured via a terminal interface or even via SCSI commands.*

Once the peripherals are attached and the router is configured, all SCSI/Fibre Channel traffic is routed through the SAN router, and each server "thinks" that the library is locally attached to it. This allows the server to take advantage of the recent advancements in backup technology that allow local backups to be much faster (and much easier on the CPU) than LAN-based backups.

---

* Not everyone agrees that the device in the center of Figure 5-8 should be called a "router"; some prefer to call it a "bridge," since it bridges between fibre and SCSI. Since a router communicates at the IP level, simlar to a SAN router, I believe the term router is more appropriate. The major manufacturer of these devices calls them routers. You be the judge.

When people first see a SAN drawing, they don't see much difference between it and a LAN. However, to transfer data across a LAN, a system must build network packets and transmit them via the network interface. The system on the other end must then reassemble those packets into usable information. When a system is communicating with a shared peripheral via a SAN, it uses the same simple SCSI protocols that it would use if the peripheral were locally attached. This is much faster and easier on the CPU.

A truly advanced router can even allow programs such as commercial backup applications to dynamically configure which servers have access to the peripherals. For example, when it is time for a particular server's full backup, the backup application could configure the router in such a way that it can have access to every available backup drive. Of course, it also could do this for a critical restore as well.

A variation on the dynamic configuration method is to configure the router (manually or via some other interface) in such a way that all servers believe that they have access to all peripherals. This would be dangerous under normal circumstances, since all servers may try to simultaneously access the same peripheral. However, if the backup application is SAN aware, it can dynamically assign peripherals to the servers that need them without having to talk to the SAN router. This is an equally effective method of peripheral allocation, as long as the application makes sure that it does not give more than one server access to the same peripheral at the same time.

Serverless Backup

Suppose that you had a very large database that resided on a relatively large server, and every time you ran a backup, you negatively impacted the performance of the database server. What if you could back up the database without actually sending the data through the server that is using the database? If you're willing to accept a completely new type of network design, this is now possible. Consider the drawing in Figure 5-9.

At the top of Figure 5-9, you see two database servers that are connected to a large, multihost-attachable disk array. The backup server also is attached to this array. The databases actually are sitting on top of mirrored partitions inside the large disk array. To accomplish a "serverless backup," the backup server tells the database server that it needs to do a backup of the database. The database server splits off one of the mirrors and tells the backup server that it can back it up. The backup server then backs up the data via its own fibre-channel connection. The entire database

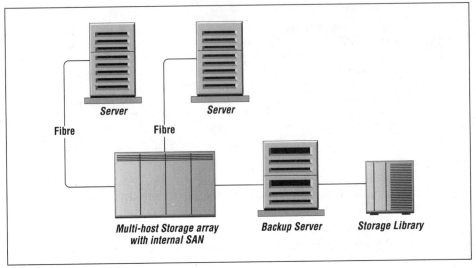

Figure 5-9. Serverless backup

therefore can be backed up without transferring the data through the client that is using it.

This technology also offers another advantage that traditional backup methods cannot. This second mirror can be left disconnected until it is time to back it up again. At that point, it can be quickly resynced to the other side of the mirror. Leaving it disconnected like this gives you an instantly available backup of the entire database. If something were to happen to the production database, you could run a few commands and remount the database using the mirror. All you would need to do is to replay your transaction logs since the mirror was split off. Without this standby mirror, you would have to restore the database before you could replay your transaction logs. Just think of the possible time savings during a large recovery. (This technology is available today for a limited number of platforms, disk arrays, and databases. Contact your backup software vendor.)

SANs Are Here to Stay

SANs, as shown in Figure 5-10, present several advantages over traditional schemes. A SAN would:

- Provide scalable storage devices, which could be shared regardless of platform

- Grant faster data migration, allowing storage redeployment in a highly available, distributed, or centralized environment

- Support higher levels of I/O throughput

- Allow increased performance on backup and restore tasks

- Contribute to better host connectivity, due to offloading the LAN from storage access-related traffic

- Promote sharing of both storage and backup devices across the enterprise

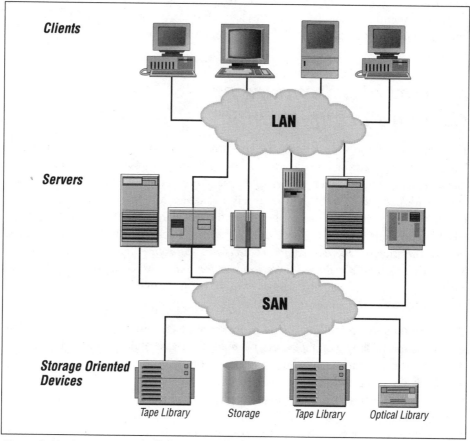

Figure 5-10. Connecting any type of peripheral via a SAN

SANs are composed of several technologies, including network components, storage devices, and interfaces. They can be implemented using current technology, but they also can be configured to take advantage of more modern technologies such as Fibre Channel, which allow it to be used in long-haul connections (over five kilometers). Although this market is in its infancy, a few vendors are offering solutions geared specifically toward implementation of SANs.

When considering SAN technology in the light of the backup and recovery industry, it is the ultimate network traffic-reduction method. It allows SAN-connected hosts to perform local backups, taking advantage of the recent advancements in CPU and memory usage reduction. It does all this while allowing maximum utilization of large libraries. If you have a large environment, and especially if you have very large servers, you definitely should find out which backup applications are SAN aware.

More and more companies are using network-based backups. A properly designed system can make maximum use of both network and backup hardware. A poorly designed system can (at the very least) make the users hate it. At its worst, the backups may not complete at all. This is one area where a lot of planning is well worth it.

Support of a Standard or Custom Backup Format

A *custom backup format* is one that is readable only by a particular commercial backup utility.* Backups made in a custom backup format cannot be read by native backup utilities such as *tar*, *cpio*, or *dump*. Some backup products use a custom format that is published or freely available. Although their backups can't be read with native utilities, a programmer theoretically could write a program that would read their backups. There are also some backup products that are completely proprietary. *In fact, some products are so proprietary that even their own product can't read a volume if the indexes for that volume have expired or been deleted.* A *standard* backup format would be a format that is readable by a standard utility. There are two schools of thought on this subject.

There are those who feel that using proprietary or custom backup formats is dangerous. If the backup volumes can't be read by native utilities, then what do you do when the commercial backup product is broken? They prefer to use utilities that back up using industry standard backup formats such as *cpio* or *tar*.† They provide a sense of security that is just not possible when using a unique backup format. Companies often switch backup products, and when that happens, their old volumes are not readable by the new product. If the volumes were readable by standard utilities, however, they still could be used for restores.

There are several vendors on both sides of this debate. What follows is my best effort to explain the pros and cons of each side. You will have to choose which pros and cons are most important to you.

---

* The word "custom" is more appropriate than "proprietary," because proprietary implies that you are not allowed to know the format.

† As of this writing, the one remaining commercial product that uses the *dump* format just got bought out by a competitor, so the only formats that are probably now available are *tar* and *cpio*.

What is commonly done in this scenario is to keep the old backup system running for restores only. However, I have heard stories of one product whose license will expire if the customer stops paying the company its maintenance fee.

There are also those who say that the old backup formats are just that—old. They served their purpose, but it is time to move on to more sophisticated utilities. There are two problems with native utilities. The first problem is that they are always changing. The *dump* command is filesystem-specific, and different versions of *dump* are incompatible. The *tar* and *cpio* commands also have changed their formats over time and are not always compatible between different operating systems. The second problem is that native utilities have significant limitations, like pathname lengths and the inability to handle open files. The most significant limitation, though, is their inability to generate or receive multiple backup streams.

Native Backup Formats

Longtime system administrators have learned how to use *dump, tar*, and *cpio*. There is a familiarity there that just isn't going to be possible with a unique format. Some people also have been burned by commercial utilities that have come and gone. There have even been a few that have changed their own formats, making their old volumes unreadable by a new version of their own software! This means that concerns about custom and proprietary formats are valid. Since restricting yourself to native utilities will significantly reduce the number of available products, make sure that you properly examine the limitations of these native utilities before doing so. The limitations of each of these utilities is discussed in the following sections.

The dump utility

The *dump* command is a Berkeley contribution and as such is not always included on some pure System V Release 4 systems. (That sure surprised me the first time that happened!) *dump* backs up a filesystem via the raw device, not through the filesystem. It therefore must know the structure of the filesystem that it is backing up, so each new type of filesystem requires a new version of *dump*. Also, a *dump* backup of one filesystem type will not necessarily be readable by the *restore* utility of another filesystem type. There have been a number of new filesystem types over the years. Each new filesystem usually comes with its own version of *dump*, and many of the newer versions are not reverse compatible with the older versions. (See "Different Versions of dump" in Chapter 3, *Native Backup & Recovery Utilities*.) Some new filesystem types don't come with a traditional *dump* command at all.

A backup tool should not rely on a native utility that changes from filesystem to filesystem. The backup volumes are not compatible between platforms, and even within the same platform, such as *(efs)dump* and *xfsdump* on SGI. Also, *dump* is not always available.

The tar and cpio utilities

Unlike *dump, tar* and *cpio* access files through the filesystem just as a user does. Since they are not filesystem dependent, they change much less over time than *dump* does. This may be *tar*'s and *cpio*'s greatest advantage. However, there are different versions of *tar* and *cpio* for each platform, and not all of them are compatible. It also should be noted that most of the commercial backup products that write in a *tar-* or *cpio*-compatible format do not use the actual *tar* or *cpio* command; they have their own command that writes in a format that is readable by *tar* or *cpio*. That way, the commercial product can overcome *tar*'s and *cpio*'s limitations, such as *cpio*'s 255-character limitation and *tar*'s 100-character limit on pathnames. (GNU *tar* and *star* also have overcome some of these limitations. *GNUtar* is covered in Chapter 3, and *star* is covered in Chapter 4, *Free Backup Utilities.*)

Custom Backup Formats

As stated earlier, the camps are divided into those backup products that use a standard format and those products that do not. Further, products that do not use a standard format should themselves be divided into two groups—those that publish their format and those that do not. Theoretically, a programmer who knows the format of the volume could write a program to read it. Most products depend quite heavily on a database that tracks the location of each file or piece of file on the volume. If the database is corrupted or lost, they may not be able to read the volume at all.

Should someone use a product that has a custom backup format? Before purchasing such a product, be sure to ask a few questions. Is the format of this volume completely proprietary, or is there a document explaining how it was written? Is there a standalone utility that allows me to read these volumes even if the catalog is down? If this product made a volume but then later did not know what was on it, could it reread the volume and determine the file sets that went to that volume?

Some backup programs that use custom formats come with a standalone utility that can read the volume without the use of the backup database, providing essentially the same functionality as a native command. *This is a beautiful thing*, but it's harder to come by than you might imagine.

SIDF: a compromise?

The System Independent Data Format (SIDF) was first proposed back in 1993 and has been adopted as an international volume-interchange format. It is being used on a limited basis by a small number of backup products. If a product followed this format completely, not only would it have completely platform-independent volumes, its volumes would be readable by other backup software products. As of this writing, this format is barely gaining acceptance, but I would like to see the effort succeed, as it would make things so much easier for so many people. (Think of it as the equivalent of ASCII for backup volumes.)

It should be noted that there are different "levels of partitioning"* to SIDF, and not all levels can read volumes made with the other levels of partitioning. Theoretically, though, you could write an independent program that would read SIDF volumes. (Learn more about SIDF at *http://www.sidf.org*. As of this writing, the site looks very dated, though.)

While this format may be very promising, it does not appear to be going anywhere. If someone knows differently, feel free to let me know.

A Reality Check

Suppose you had a bunch of volumes that were written in *tar* format, and your backup software has been keeping track of them all. If that software is not functioning properly, how will you know what is on the hundreds, or even thousands, of backup volumes that you have? I suppose you could do a *tar tvf* on all of them and create your own "minicatalog." That's not an easy task to do. Suppose you had 500 or so DLT 7000 tapes. At 10MB/s, it would take you 41 days to read them all. This is just to get a table of contents of these volumes.

A much better solution would be to get a backup system that you trust. Learn how to check the database for inconsistencies. Run those checks every day, and if any inconsistencies are found that can't be fixed, recover the database back to the point in time before it became corrupted. If the backup software allows it, you then have it reread any volumes that have been written to since then.

Ease of Administration

If a person is administering a relatively large backup system, the activities in the following list are performed all the time. How easy is it to do these things with the product you are considering?

Making duplicate volumes for off-site storage
   This feature allows an administrator to make copies of volumes and send the copies off-site.† The right way to do this is to copy from volume to volume, instead of running another backup. The more advanced products allow the copied volume to have its own identity. That way, the copied volume can be

---

* Essentially, different levels of complexity. A more complex level may have more advanced features but may require more work to read.

† Actually, a better method is to send the *originals* off-site. Doing the day-to-day restores from the copies is a constant verification of the copy process. Unfortunately, many products won't allow copies to be made this way.

tracked in the catalog. (Older methods of copying volumes resulted in two copies of the same exact volume. The second volume never actually existed in the product's database; it was just another copy of the first volume.) Some products also allow an administrator to specify the location of the copy volumes so that he will know which volumes are on-site and which volumes are off-site. That way, the software won't ask for the volume that it knows is off-site, if it knows it has another volume on-site that has the same data on it.

Copying a saveset

There is a downside to copying volumes. Depending on the level of volatility of the data and the luck of the draw, the system may or may not fill up a complete volume each night. If copies are being made and sent off-site every day, what happens to the volume that is half full? If it is copied and sent off-site, the software cannot continue to write to the original volume, even though it has more room available. If it did, it would have to copy the entire volume again. Wouldn't it be better if the software knew how to copy last night's backups, or *savesets*, regardless of which volumes happened to receive them?

Saveset copying does just that. It is the ability to say "take all of the files that got backed up last night (the savesets) and put them on these volumes over here, which I will send off-site." Depending on the complexity of the software, last night's backups may have ended up as 100 MB pieces on 20 volumes. Saveset cloning would take those 20 separate 100-MB backups and put them all on one 2000-MB (2-GB) volume. This would be done after the backup, and the data traffic would stay local to the backup system—so it isn't affecting the other CPUs, the network, or the users.

Simultaneous copying of savesets

A very new feature that has begun to appear is the ability to copy the backup as it is being made. This is sometimes referred to as "twinning." If things are set up right, and the software does what it is supposed to do, you actually can make copies in no more time than it takes to make the first backup. The better products would allow the two backup volumes to be different sizes, allowing for differences in compression and different types of media. Perhaps you may want to put your on-site backups on one type of media and put your off-site backups on another type of media.

Consolidating a host's backup

This nifty feature of some backup programs allows for the consolidation of all of the backups for a given host onto a volume or small set of volumes. This makes preparing for a disaster much easier.

Consolidating volumes that have very little data on them

This is just a volume utilization feature. Due to different expiration times of different backups, there may be a large set of volumes, each of which has only a few hundred MBs of data that's still useful. Volume consolidation would consolidate these backups from all of the partially used volumes onto one volume, allowing the source volumes to be reused.

Excluding files

There are always files that should be excluded from backups: files in */tmp*, spool files, core files, etc. The types of files that need to be excluded vary from site to site. Be aware that different products have different methods for excluding files.

Client backup and restore

Some sites may wish to delegate the administration of the backups of a small group of machines to another person, an internal client. (Sometimes it is the internal client, not the administrator, who makes this request.) The client wants to share your backup libraries and resources but also wants to be able to control her own backups and restores. Different products have different capabilities.

My personal preference is to be able to restore to anywhere from anywhere. Some products allow you to restore only to the client that backed up the data. Other products allow you to restore to any authorized client but require you to log in to that client to initiate the restore. This is not so bad if the client that you must log in to is a Unix client, since you can display your X session back to your workstation. If it's a Windows or NT machine, though, you will have to physically go to that machine to initiate the restore. (That is, unless you have one of those remote control packages that allow you to remotely log in to an NT machine.)

I believe that you should be able to restore:

— From the original backup client

— From any authorized backup client

— From the backup server to any authorized client

Interface types

Most products have Java, HTML, Motif, Curses, and/or command-line interfaces. Make sure the product has an interface that is appropriate for your environment. (I also should state the importance of an optional command-line interface in almost any environment; you can't always count on an X display during a disaster recovery, and you also may wish to do your work over a modem connection.)

Notification

How should the administration team be notified when a backup fails or needs attention? There are a number of different methods. The most common method is email. Some vendors even allow different email recipients for different types of messages. Other vendors allow you to write custom interface programs that send reports wherever you would like. Some backup products can even send alpha pages if there is a modem available.

Perhaps the most sophisticated notification method is the use of an SNMP trap. SNMP stands for Simple Network Management Protocol and was originally developed for network hardware so that routers from different vendors could understand one another. SNMP has been expanded to include all types of network monitoring, and it is what most of the commercial network monitoring tools are based on.

Installation and upgrading

Most server installations are pretty automated. The real bear is the installation of client-side software. There are usually two ways that client-side software is installed: manually or automatically. When using the manual method, you first must get the client software to the machine. This is done either by *ftp* or *nfs*. Then you either run an installation script, or perhaps make your own modifications so that the software will start the next time the system reboots. In that case, you also would need to start the software the first time manually, unless you are able to quickly reboot the client. However, if root is allowed to remotely execute commands on other systems, there are a few products that can completely automate the client installation. You simply need to tell the product which clients should get the client software, and it will *rcp* the software over and install it automatically. For most of the packages, this is the only time root needs to be able to *rsh* to a system.

The product is installed once, but it will be upgraded once or twice a year. Therefore, ease of upgrading is another very important feature to consider. Upgrading also may be performed manually or automatically. However, some products (once installed) are able to communicate via their own software and update the software automatically. This means that once the product is installed, *rsh* isn't needed at all. Such products can perform this upgrade automatically, communicating via their own sockets.* Since updating the software on hundreds of clients is the most difficult repetitive task you will do, this feature would be quite handy to have.

Security

Historically, backups and security have had almost completely opposite goals. Things such as *.rhosts* files were absolutely necessary to gain any type of backup

---

* It should be noted that some products don't need to install client software at all. They usually are not very powerful, but they do exist.

automation, and yet they are a well-known security problem. Fortunately, most modern backup products have worked around these problems.

Sockets or rsh?

There are very few products left that communicate via *rsh*. *rsh* has been identified as a security hole, and many sites have disabled it. The products that still use *rsh* usually do not require the ability to *rsh* as root; instead, they set up a special user ID that is used only for that purpose. That way, a *.rhosts* entry needs to be set up only for that user.

Most products now communicate via Berkeley sockets. This means that they need to have some client-side software running with which they can communicate; the process running on the client is called a "daemon."

Encryption?

More and more people are asking for encryption. Encryption can be accomplished in one of three ways. Some software packages encrypt the commands that they send back and forth, so that a rogue server cannot imitate them and perform unauthorized actions, such as request a restore of data it is not entitled to. Another method is to encrypt backup data in transit but then decrypt it as it is being written to a backup volume. This allows backups over an insecure network but does not require an encryption key to read the volume (think of it as a "backup tunnel"). Then, of course, there are software packages that encrypt the data on the volume itself. This is one of the newest areas in backup and recovery, so very few products are supporting this kind of encryption.

Ease of Recovery

I often quote an old coworker of mine, "No one cares if you can back up—only if you can restore."* Ease of recovery and speed of recovery often are overlooked when evaluating backup products. Many small factors can make doing restores either very easy or impossible.

Platform independence

This is a very important factor. Some products have gone to the trouble to ensure that every volume made by every version of their software can be read by every other version, no matter what platform it was made on. If this has been done, and a client is destroyed, its data still can be recovered, even if the replacement version is not of the same type. If volumes are not platform

---

* Ron Rodriguez gets credit for this one. Replacing Ron as "backup boy" was my first job in this field. I have no idea how many times Ron said this, but I guess it sunk in.

independent, an administrator might need to keep a functional machine of each operating system version just for restores.* Having true platform independence also makes doing regular restores much easier.

Parallel restore

This can be a very nice feature. When restoring a large directory or filesystem, the backups for that filesystem may be spread out over several volumes. Some products are able to read all these volumes at once, making the restore actually faster than the backup. When investigating this possibility, you also should find out if these volumes can be loaded in any order.

User restores

Some environments have sophisticated users that who like to be able to do their own restores. If this is true in your environment, then this feature will come in handy. Those who do not want users doing their own restores will want to know whether this feature can be disabled.

Relocated restores

This is *very* important. You sometimes need to restore a file that was originally located on another system. This different location may be a different host or a different directory. Some products do not allow this.

Bare-metal restores

A bare-metal restore is restoring a system from scratch, without even having a functioning operating system. (See Part IV of this book for more information about bare-metal recoveries.) The best example of this is the *mksysb* utility on AIX. *mksysb* allows an administrator to back up the entire system and create a volume from which a system can boot and restore. This volume then can be used to restore the entire system from scratch. This is sort of the Holy Grail of backups—the ability to restore an entire system from nothing. Unfortunately, almost no one does it. Some products do a few special things to make this easier, though.

Multiple versions

This is also very important. A lot of backup products not only track the most recent version of a file that was backed up but also track all versions of the file that are on backup volumes. Sometimes it's necessary to restore a file to the way it looked four days ago.

Tracking deleted files

This one surprises many people. Suppose there is a filesystem that changes quite a bit. New files are added and deleted every day. (A good example of this would be where the Oracle's archived redologs go. Hundreds of files may

---

* Believe me, I know! I know of one place that still keeps around one or two AT&T 3b2s running SVr3 because of all the old *cpio* backups made on QIC drives that are unreadable on other platforms.

be added and deleted every day.) When asking the backup software to restore this filesystem, one might expect that it would restore it the way it looked yesterday. Unfortunately, many products will instead restore all files that were ever located in that directory! It takes extra effort on the part of the software to "notice" that a file has been deleted and to *not* restore it unless told to do so. Failure to track deleted files can make restoring some filesystems very difficult.

Overwriting options

Has a user ever called and said that he blew away half his home directory because he typed *rm -r ** by accident? This user doesn't want the program to blow away everything in his directory by restoring on top of it. A good way to protect against that is to tell the backup software to "restore everything in here, except those files that are newer than what we have on backup." There are a number of other overwriting options, such as unconditional overwrite, prompt before overwrite, and don't overwrite the same exact file.

Protection of the Backup Index

The backup database, or index, keeps track of which files were backed up to which volume. Since the backup system can't restore anything without this index, it becomes the single most important database in your environment. It is also the single point of failure in any backup system. As mentioned earlier, even if a volume is made with a format that is readable by a native utility, you still need the index to know what's on it. The backup index is the greatest invention since someone created volume labels, but if it goes bad, you are out of luck.

Backup indexes usually are located on the central backup server, but they can be spread out to what is sometimes called "slave servers." (A slave server would be one that is allowed to have backup devices.) One of the first questions you might ask is, "How big will this thing get?" The typical answer is .5 percent to 1 percent of the amount of data that is being backed up. That answer is very misleading, completely wrong, and totally irrelevant. The total size of the data that is being backed up has absolutely nothing to do with the database size. Let me state that again.

The total size of the data that is being backed up has absolutely nothing to do with the size of the backup database. It is the number of files being backed up, not their size, that determines the size of the database.

Each file that is backed up becomes a record in the index. That record will be the same size, regardless of how big the file is that was backed up.* The appropriate question, therefore, is, "How many bytes does each new file add to the index (a) the first time it is backed up and (b) any additional times it is backed up during incremental backups?" This number can then be multiplied by *the number of files that are being backed up.* This will show how big the index can get from one full backup. Multiply that number by the number of full backups the system is required to keep online. Using an estimate of a 2–5 percent daily volatility rate,† estimate how big the index will grow from each incremental backup. Multiply that number by the number of incremental backups that the system is required to keep online. Add that to the first number, then multiply by 2. The result will be a pretty realistic, albeit slightly exaggerated, estimate of how big the backup index will get.

Managing the growth of the index is also a big issue. Whatever database format they use, one of the index files may grow larger than what the filesystem permits. If that happens, the index may get immediately corrupted. The backup product should have some method of dealing with this problem. Also, the entire index may get larger than the largest filesystem allowed, so it should be able to spread that data out across multiple filesystems.

Just as the volumes should be platform independent, so should the backup index. You should be able to restore it to any system in which the server software runs and continue working. In order for this to work, the index needs to be completely platform independent. Some products are, and some aren't. Some of them are not platform independent, but they do provide a utility to move the index to other platforms. One of the best tests of this is to attempt to recover a Unix server's backup index to a Windows 2000 server.

Before committing to buying a commercial backup product, test its index restore procedure. Some products can restore the index in a single step, while others require 20 pages of steps. Once you actually purchase a product, test that procedure again. Then test it on a regular basis so that you never hear yourself saying, "My whole world just crashed, including my backup server. Now what am I supposed to do again?"

A couple of minor (but nice) features also are helpful. The first is the ability to change a client's name within the index. If a backup client's hostname changes, and the backup product does not support this feature, there are only two choices. The first choice is to give up all backup history for that host. The second is to pay for another license, since the software will recognize the new hostname as a new client.

---

* Some products do use a variable-length record so that things like the length of the pathname can slightly affect the size of the record, but the size of the file still has no bearing.

† This is actually a huge volatility rate, but most environments don't have any data on the *number* of files that change each day. Even if they've been monitoring their backup software, most reports talk only about how much data was backed up, not how many files were backed up.

Another very nice feature, seen as essential by some, is the ability to reread a volume back into the index. Suppose there is a volume that has been set aside and is now expired out of the index completely. What if the only backup of a file that you need is on that volume? What if you don't know? Some products can perform the restore without having to reread the entire volume, while others can read the volume right back into the index, making it appear as if it were just backed up. Some products are not able to reread that volume at all! One factor that goes into the product's ability to read a volume like that is whether the vendor puts a copy of the index information onto the volume. It's an extra step, but I think it's well worth it. Basically, after every backup, the new portion of the backup index that was created from that backup is placed on the volume. That makes rereading the volume from scratch *much* easier. It is possible to reread a backup volume without placing the index on the volume, but having the index there makes it much easier.

The importance of the backup index, and your familiarity with how it works, cannot be overemphasized. It is the lifeblood of any backup system and should be treated like gold.

Robustness

Horrible things happen to backup systems. Systems reboot and get powered off. Backup drives hang, libraries jam, and networks die. The "robustness" of a product can be measured by how well it deals with these sorts of problems. Can the product reroute backups from a failed backup drive to a good one? Will it even notice that a backup drive or process is hung? Is it able to recover from a client rebooting while the client is being backed up? Will this client rebooting in the middle of its backup corrupt the index?

These are very important considerations. Things will go wrong, and when they do, you want to know the backups are still OK. If the backup product is able to reroute around failures, retry open files, and restart failed backups, the worst that should happen to you is a really long report when you come in the next morning.

Automation

There are some very nice tape and optical libraries out there now. They have bar codes, automatic cleaning, hot-swappable power supplies, field-replaceable drives, and more. How well does this product take advantage of these things? One of the greatest features of using a modern library is to use bar-coded volumes. Put 20 volumes in the library, then tell the backup software to read the bar code and electronically label the volumes according to what the bar code says. That sure beats swapping 20 volumes in and out of backup drives for a half-hour while they get labeled!

Index Horror Stories

Most of my backup horror stories stem from problems with the backup index. My first bad experience was with backing up a large NFS server that was used to store home pages for a large online service's web servers. There were more than three million small files that made the index so large that it often would become corrupted. Even after distributing the index over multiple slave servers, the size still would cause index corruption. As if regular index corruption weren't enough, we often would not catch the corruption until several days later when the backup product would act more strange than usual. Since we were foolish enough to only keep two days' worth of index backups, we could not recover a reliable index. Eventually we ended up dumping the index into ASCII files daily and then backing up those files from a different server with the regular retention schedules.

My other index horror story comes from the same site. In another effort to keep our index small, we stored the index of a backup for only two weeks (even though the data was kept on a backup volume for two months). I had one user who on multiple occasions deleted data after he was done with it, only to determine two and a half weeks later that he really wasn't done with it. Since the records containing those files had expired out of the index, every volume that might have the data had to be reread. One of those restores had me rereading more than 40 DLT 4000 tapes (in a jukebox that held only 28 tapes) while still trying to do regular backups. It took me more than three long days to read the tapes; even then I was not able to retrieve all of the data. Fortunately for my job, it was not mission-critical data.

—Bryce Wade

Volume Verification

Another often-ignored area of backup and recovery software is its ability to verify its own backups. There are plenty of horror stories out there about people who did backups for years or months assuming that they were working just fine. Then when they went to read the backup volumes, the backup software told them that it couldn't read them. The only way to ensure that this never happens to you is to run regular verification tests against your media. There are several different types of verification:

Reading part of volume and comparing it
> There is at least one major vendor that works this way. If you turn on media verification, it forwards to the end of the volume and read a file or two. It compares those files against what it believes should be there. This is obviously the lowest level of verification.

Comparing table of contents to index

This is a step up from the first type of verification. This is the equivalent of doing a *tar tvf*. It does not verify the contents of the file; it verifies only that the backup software can read the header of the file.

Comparing contents of backup against contents of filesystem

This type of verification is common in low-end PC backup software. Basically, the backup software looks at its backup of a particular filesystem, then compares its contents against the actual contents of the filesystem. Some software packages that do this will automatically back up any files that are different than what's on the backup or that do not exist on the backup. This type of verification is very difficult, since most systems are changing constantly.

Comparing checksum to index

Some backup software products record a checksum for each file that they back up. They then are able to read the backup volume and compare the checksum of the file on the volume with the checksum that is recorded in the index for that file. This makes sure that the file on the backup volume will be readable when the time comes.

Verify, Verify, Verify!

We were using commercial backup software to back up our file servers and database servers. One day, a multimillion-dollar client wanted some files back that were archived about a year and a half ago. We got the tapes and tried a restore. Nothing. We tried other tapes. Nothing. The system administrator and her manager were both fired. The company lost the client and got sued. The root cause was never identified, but they had definitely never tried to verify their backups.

—Eugene Lee

Cost

The pricing aspect of backup software is too complex to cover in detail here, but suffice it to say that there are a number of factors that may be included in the total price, depending on which vendor you buy from:

- The number of clients that you want to back up

- The number of backup drives you wish to use

- What type of backup drives you want to use (high-speed devices often cost more)

- The number of libraries and the number of drives and slots that they have

- The size of the systems (in CPU power)

- The speed of backup that you need

- The number of database servers you have

- The number of different *types* of databases that you have

- The number of other special-treatment clients (MVS, Back Office) that require special interfaces

- The type of support you expect (24×7, 8×5, etc.)

Vendor

There is a lot of important information you need to know about a company from which you plan to purchase such a mission-critical product as backup software. How long have they been providing backup solutions? What kinds of resources are dedicated to the products' development? What type of support do they have? Are they open to suggestions about their product?

Get the name of at least one reference site and talk to them. Be aware, it is very hard for companies to come up with references. A lot of clients do not want to be a reference, just for political and legal reasons. Be flexible here. Don't require the salesperson to come up with a reference site that is exactly like your environment.

If you do get a reference site, make sure that you get in touch with them. The number one complaint of salespeople is that they go through the trouble of obtaining reference sites, only to have the customer never call them.

The Internet is also a wonderful asset at a time like this. Search for the product's name in the Usenet archives at *http://www.deja.com.* (Make sure you search the complete archives.) Look for names of people who say good and bad things, and then email them. Also, do general searches on all search engines. Try one of the megasites like *http://www.dogpile.com* that can search several other sites for you. A really good product will have references on consultants' web sites. A really bad product might even have an "I hate product X" web site. Read everything with a grain of salt, and recognize that every single vendor of every single product has a group of people somewhere who hate it and chose someone else's product. Some clients have been through three backup products and are looking for a fourth.

Conclusions

Picking a commercial backup utility is a hard job. The only one that's harder is writing one. The data provided here covers a lot of areas and can be confusing at times. Be sure to compare the headings here with the questions that are in the RFI at *http://www.backupcentral.com*. The questions may help to explain some of the finer points.

The RFI that I use is extensive; it has more than 300 questions. Its main purpose is to put all vendors on a level playing field, and I have used it many times to evaluate backup software companies. Although it is extremely difficult to word a single RFI to cover the entire backup product industry, this is my best attempt at doing so. Most of the questions are worded in such a way that a "Yes" answer is considered to be a good answer, based on my opinion, of course. Even though you may not agree with me on every point of the RFI, you should find it very useful in evaluating backup software companies. This RFI is not biased toward any particular product. It *is* biased toward how I believe backups should work. You may find that some of the questions are looking for features that you believe you may not need, especially the more advanced enterprise-level features like dynamic parallelism. I would submit that you might need them at some point. You never know how your environment will grow. For example, my first commercial backup software setup was designed to handle around 20 machines with a total of 200 GB. Within two years, that became 250 machines and several terabytes. You just never know how big your environment is going to grow. However, if you are simply looking for a backup solution for a small environment, and you are sure that it will never grow much larger, feel free to ignore questions about such features.

The same goes for any other features that you know you will never need. If you know that you're never going to have an MVS mainframe, then don't worry about a company's response to that question. If you know that you're never going to have connectivity between your company and the Internet, then don't worry about how a product deals with firewalls.

I also should mention that there are special-use backup products that serve a particular market very well but may not have some of the other enterprise-level features that I consider to be important. For example, there is a product that does a great job of backing up Macintoshes. They do that job better than anybody else, because they've done it longer than anybody else. (There are other products that back up Macintoshes, but they do not "think" like a Macintosh environment thinks.) This product does just that. For a purely Macintosh environment, that product might be just the product for you. (Of course, if you have a purely Macintosh environment, you probably wouldn't be reading this book.)

The RFI is available at *http://backupcentral.com.*

6

High Availability

Good backup and recovery strategies are key to any organization in protecting its valuable data. However, many environments are starting to realize that while a system is being recovered, it is not available for general use. With a little planning and financial backing, you can design and implement logical schemes to make systems more accessible—seemingly all the time. The concept of *high availability* encompasses several solutions that target different parts of this problem.

 This chapter was written by Gustavo Vegas of Collective Technologies, with input from Josh Newcomb of Motorola. Gustavo may be reached at *gustavo@colltech.com*, and Josh may be reached at *jnewcomb@paging.mot.com*.

What Is High Availability?

High availability (HA) is defined as the ability of a system to perform its function without interruption for an extended length of time. This functionality is accomplished through special-purpose software and redundant system and network hardware. Technologies such as volume management, RAID, and journaling file-systems provide the essential building blocks of any HA system.

Some would consider that an HA system doesn't need to be backed up, but such an assumption can leave your operation at significant risk. HA systems are not immune to data loss resulting from user carelessness, hostile intrusions, or applications corrupting data. Instead, HA systems are designed in such a way that they can survive *hardware* failures, and some software failures. If a disk drive or CPU fails, or even if the system needs routine maintenance, an HA system may remain available to the users; thus it is viewed as being more *highly available* than other systems. That does not mean that its data will be *forever available*. Make sure you are backing up your HA systems.

Overview

Systems are becoming more critical every day. The wrong system in an organization going down could cost millions of dollars—and somebody's job. What if there were software tools that could detect system failures and then try to recover from them? If the system could not recover from a hardware failure, it would relinquish its functionality (or "fail over") to another system and restart all of its critical applications. This is exactly what HA software can do.

Consider the example of two servers in the highly available configuration depicted in Figure 6-1. This is an illustration of what is called an *asymmetric* configuration. This kind of configuration contains a primary server and a takeover server. A *primary server* is the host that provides a network service or services by default. A *takeover server* is the host that would provide such services when the primary server is not available to perform its function. In another type of configuration called *symmetric*, the two servers would provide separate and different services and would act as each other's takeover server for their corresponding services. One of the best-suited services to be provided by an HA system is a network file access service, like the Network Filesystem, or NFS. In the example in Figure 6-1, each server has an onboard 100-megabit Ethernet interface (hme0) and two Ethernet ports on two quad fast Ethernet cards (qfe0 and qfe1). These network card names could be different for your system depending upon your hardware and operating system. qfe0 and hme0 are being used as the *heartbeat links*. These links monitor the health of the HA servers and are connected to each system via a private network, which could be implemented with a minihub or with a crossover twisted-pair cable. There are two of these for redundancy. qfe1 is used as the system's physical connection to the service network, which is the network for which services are being provided by the HA system. The two shared disk arrays are connected via a fiber-channel connection and are under volume management control. These disk arrays contain the critical data.

Such a design allows for immediate recovery from a number of problems. If Server A lost its connectivity to the network, the HA software would notice this via the heartbeat network. Server A could shut down its applications and its database automatically. Server B could then assume the identity of Server A, import the database, and start the necessary applications by becoming the primary server. Also, if Server A was not able to complete a task due to an application problem, the HA software could then fail over the primary system to the takeover server.

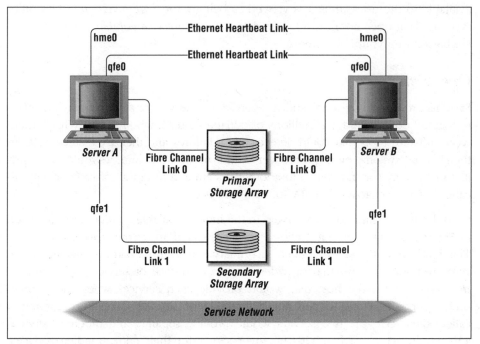

Figure 6-1. Asymmetric configuration

The takeover server would be a system that absorbs the applications and identity of the primary server.

Highly available systems depend on good hardware, good software, and proper implementation. The configuration in Figure 6-1 is an example of a simple configuration and may not necessarily be suitable for your organization but may help to get you started.

How Is HA Different from Fault-Tolerant Solutions?

A fault-tolerant system uses a more robust and hardware-oriented configuration than does a high-availability system. Fault-tolerant systems usually include more than two systems and use specific-purpose hardware that is geared to withstand massive failures. They also are designed around a voting system in which the principle of quorum is used to make decisions, and all processing units involved in computations run the same processes in parallel.

On the other hand, high available solutions typically are software oriented. They combine duplication of hardware on the involved systems with various configuration techniques to cope with failures. Functions usually are run in only one of the systems, and when a failure is realized, the takeover system is signaled to start a duplicate function. The asymmetric configuration is possible in this scenario.

Good examples of fault-tolerant systems are found in military and space applications. Companies like Tandem (now Compaq) and Stratus market this type of system. Sun Microsystems has a division that specializes in providing fault-tolerant systems.

How Is HA Different from Mirroring?

Mirroring is really the process of making a simultaneous copy of your critical data that is instantly available online. Having data written redundantly to two disks, two disk groups, or even two different disk arrays can be highly beneficial if an emergency occurs. Mirroring is a primary ingredient in the recipe for data recovery and should be part of your total backup and disaster recovery plan. However, having a system highly available is much more than just installing software; it is creating an environment in which failures can be tolerated because they can be recovered from quickly. Not only can the system's primary data storage fail, but also the system itself can fail. When this happens, HA systems fail over to the takeover system with the mirrored data (if necessary) and continue to run with very minimal downtime.

Can HA Be Handled Across a LAN/WAN?

In general terms, high availability can be handled even across a local or wide area network. There are some caveats to the extent, feasibility, and configuration that can be considered in either case, however. Currently available commercial solutions are more geared to local area network (LAN) environments; our example depicted in Figure 6-2 is a classical example of HA over a LAN.

Conversely, a wide area network (WAN) environment presents some restrictions on the configuration that may be used. For instance, it would be cumbersome and costly to implement a private network connection for the heartbeat links. Additionally, a WAN environment would require more support from the network devices, especially the routers.

As an illustration, we will show you how to use routers to allow the activation of a takeover server in such a way that it uses the same IP address as the primary server. Naturally, only one host can use a particular IP address at one time, so the routers will be set up as a kind of automatic A/B switch. In this way, only one of the two HA systems can be reached at that IP address at any one time. For the switchover to be automatic, the routers must be able to update their routing databases automatically. When the switchover is to occur, Router R3 will be told not to route packets to its server, and Router R4 will be told to start routing those packets to the takeover server. Because the traffic is turned off completely, only the HA server and its takeover counterpart should be behind Routers R3 and R4, respectively. All other hosts should be "in front" of R3 or R4 so that they continue to receive packets when the router A/B switch is thrown.

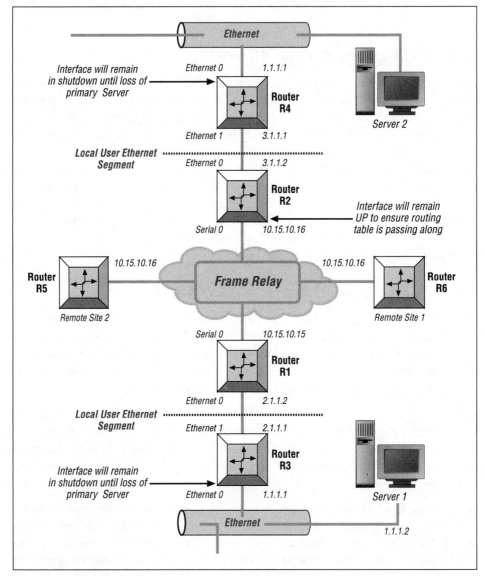

Figure 6-2. HA over a LAN

In order to accomplish this feat, the routing protocol must be a dynamic protocol, one capable of updating routing tables within the routers without human intervention (please refer to Figure 6-2). We have laid out a structure in such a way that the primary server resides behind Router R3, a layer-3 routing device. Local traffic flows between R1 and R3. R1 is the gateway to the WAN. The takeover server is located behind R4, which remains inactive as long as no failures of the primary server are detected. R2 is the WAN gateway for the takeover server.

If a failure is detected on the primary server, R3 would be disabled and R4 would be enabled, in much the fashion of the switch described earlier. At this point, the routers will begin to restructure their routing tables with new information. R4 will now pass to R2 routing information about the takeover server's segment, and R3 will announce to R1 the loss of its route, which will in return announce it to the WAN. Some protocols that deal with routing may require users to delete the primary server's network from a router's tables and to add the takeover server's network to the router, which will now support the takeover server's segment. By using R1 as a default gateway for the primary server's segment, the routing switchover should happen more quickly.

In order to get the mission-critical data from one point to another, a product such as Qualix DataStar, which can provide remote mirroring for disaster recovery purposes, should be used. Its use will enable an offsite copy at the fail-over location.

A more sophisticated solution for a WAN environment could be implemented using two servers mirroring each other's services across the network by running duplication software such as Auspex's ServerGuard. Network routers could be configured in such a way that they would manage the switching of IP addresses by using the same philosophy as in regular HA. Cisco has developed just such a protocol, called Hot Standby Routing Protocol (HSRP).

Another possibility is to use SAN technology to share highly available peripherals. Since SAN peripherals can be attached via Fibre Channel, they could be placed several miles away from the system that is using them.

Why Would I Need an HA Solution?

As organizations grow, so does the need to be more proactive in setting up systems and procedures to handle possible problems. Because an organization's data becomes more critical every day, having systems in place to protect against data loss becomes daily more desirable. Highly available designs are reliable and cost-effective solutions to help make the critical systems in any environment more robust. HA designs can guarantee that business-critical applications will run with few, if any, interruptions. Although fault-tolerant systems are even more robust, HA solutions are often the best strategy because they are more cost-effective.

HA Building Blocks

Many people begin adding availability to their systems in levels. They start by increasing the availability of their disks by using volume management software to place their disks in some sort of RAID* configuration. They also begin increasing filesystem availability by using a journaling filesystem. Here is an overview of these concepts.

Volume Management

There are two ways to increase the availability of your disk drives. The first is to buy a hardware-based RAID box, and the second is to use volume management software to add RAID functionality to "regular" disks.

 The storage industry uses the term "volume management" when talking about managing multiple disks, especially when striping or mirroring them with software. Please don't confuse this with managing backup volumes (i.e., tapes, CDs, optical platters, etc.).

The amount of availability that you add will be based on the level of RAID that you choose. Common numbered examples of RAID are RAID-0, RAID-1, RAID-0+1, RAID-1+0, RAID-10 (1+0 and 10 refer to the same thing), RAID-2, RAID-3, RAID-4, RAID-5, and RAID-6. See Table 6-1 for a brief description of each RAID level. A more detailed description of each level follows.

Table 6-1. RAID Definitions

Level	Description
RAID:	A disk array in which part of the physical storage capacity is used to store redundant information about user data stored on the remainder of the storage capacity. The redundant information enables regeneration of user data in the event that one of the array's member disks or the access data path to it fails.
Level 0	Disk striping without data protection. (Since the "R" in RAID means redundant, this is not really RAID.)
Level 1	Mirroring. All data is replicated on a number of separate disks.
Level 2	Data is protected by Hamming code. Uses extra drives to detect 2-bit errors and correct 1-bit errors on the fly. Interleaves by bit or block.

---

* Redundant Array of Independent Disks. I believe that the original definition of this was Redundant Array of Inexpensive Disks, as opposed to one large very expensive disk. However, this seems to be the commonly held definition today. Based on the prices of today's RAID systems, "Independent" seems much more appropriate than "Inexpensive."

Table 6-1. RAID Definitions (continued)

Level	Description
Level 3	Each virtual disk block is distributed across all array members but one, with parity check information stored on a separate disk.
Level 4	Data blocks are distributed as with disk striping. Parity check is stored in one disk.
Level 5	Data blocks are distributed as with disk striping. Parity check data is distributed across all members of the array.
Level 6	Like RAID-5, but with additional independently computed check data.

The RAID "hierarchy" begins with RAID-0 (striping) and RAID-1 (mirroring). Combining RAID-0 and RAID-1 is called RAID-0+1 or RAID-1+0, depending on how you combine them. (RAID-0+1 is also called RAID-01, and RAID-1+0 is also called RAID-10.) The performance of RAID-10 and RAID-01 are identical, but they have different levels of data integrity.

RAID-01 (or RAID-0+1) is a mirrored pair (RAID-1) made from two stripe sets (RAID-0), hence the name RAID-0+1, because it is created by first creating two RAID-0 sets and adding RAID-1. If you lose a drive on one side of a RAID-01 array, then lose another drive on the other side of that array before the first side is recovered, you will suffer complete data loss. It also is important to note that all drives in the surviving mirror are involved in rebuilding the entire damaged stripe set, even if only a single drive were damaged. Performance during recovery is severely degraded unless the RAID subsystem allows adjusting the priority of recovery. However, shifting the priority toward production will lengthen recovery time and increase the risk of the kind of catastrophic data loss mentioned earlier.

RAID-10 (or RAID-1+0) is a stripe set made up from n mirrored pairs. Only the loss of both drives in the same mirrored pair can result in any data loss, and the loss of that particular drive is $1/n$th as likely as the loss of *some* drive on the opposite mirror in RAID-01. Recovery involves only the replacement drive and its mirror so the rest of the array performs at 100 percent capacity during recovery. Also, since only the single drive needs recovery, bandwidth requirements during recovery are lower and recovery takes far less time, reducing the risk of catastrophic data loss.

RAID-2 is a parity layout that uses a Hamming code* that detects errors that occur and determines which part is in error by computing parity for distinct overlapping sets of disk blocks. (RAID-2 is not used in practice—the redundant computations of a Hamming code are not required, since disk controllers can detect the failure of a single disk.)

---

* A Hamming code is a basic mathematical Error Correction Code (ECC).

RAID-3 is used to accelerate applications that are single-stream bandwidth oriented. All I/O operations will access all disks since each logical block is distributed across the disks that comprise the array. The heads of all disks move in unison to service each I/O request. RAID-3 is very effective for very large file transfers, but it would not be a good choice for a database server, since databases tend to read and write smaller blocks.

RAID-4 and RAID-5 compute parity on an interleave or stripe unit (an application-specific or filesystem-specific block), which is a data region that is accessed contiguously. Use of an interleave unit allows applications to be optimized to overlap read access by reading data off a single drive while other users access a different drive in the RAID. These types of parity striping can require write operations to be combined with read and write operations for disks other than the ones actually being written, in order to update parity correctly. RAID-4 stores parity on a single disk in the array, while RAID-5 removes a possible bottleneck on the parity drive by rotating parity across all drives in the set.

While RAID-2 is not commercially implemented, and RAID-3 is likely to perform significantly better in a controller-based implementation, RAID levels 4 and 5 are more amenable to host-based software implementation. RAID-5, which balances the actual data and parity across columns, is likely to have fewer performance bottlenecks than RAID-4, which requires access of the dedicated parity disk for all read-modify-write accesses. If the system fails while writes are outstanding to more than one disk on a given stripe (for example, multiple data blocks and corresponding parity), a subsequent disk failure would make incorrect data visible without any indication that such data is incorrect. This is because it is impossible to compute and check parity in the corruption of more than one disk block. For increased reliability, parity RAID should be combined with a separate log, to cache full-stripe I/O and guarantee resistance to multiple failures. However, this log requires that additional writes be performed. If generally addressable nonvolatile memory (NVRAM) or a nonvolatile Solid State Disk (SSD) is available, it should be used for log storage. If neither of these possibilities exists, try to put the log on a separate controller and disk from the ones used for the RAID array.

The most appropriate RAID configuration for a specific filesystem or database tablespace must be determined based on data access patterns and cost versus performance tradeoffs. RAID-0 offers no increased reliability. It can, however, supply performance acceleration at no increased storage cost. RAID-1 provides the highest performance for redundant storage, because it does not require read-modify-write cycles to update data, and because multiple copies of data may be used to accelerate read-intensive applications. Unfortunately, RAID-1 requires at least double the disk capacity of RAID-0. Also, since more than two copies of the data can exist (if the mirror was constructed with more than two sets of disks), RAID-1 arrays may be constructed to endure loss of multiple disks without interruption. Parity RAID allows redundancy with less total storage cost. The read-modify-write it requires, however, will reduce total throughput in any small write operations (read-only or extremely read-intensive applications are fine). The loss of a single disk will cause read performance to be degraded while the system reads all other disks in the array and recomputes the missing data. Additionally, it does not support losing multiple disks and RAIDcannot be made redundant.

Journaling Filesystem

When a system crashes, it sometimes can take a very important filesystem with it. Journaling (or "intent-based") filesystems keep this from happening by treating the filesystem more like a database. They do this by implementing a sequential transaction log on disk to commit write operations. (The sequential nature of the write operations speeds up disk activity, because very few seek operations are needed.) Although different journaling filesystems perform this logging in slightly different ways, changes to the filesystem are logged permanently on an additional log structure on the disk.

The most important issues to be resolved are how to retrieve information from the log and how to manage free space on disk in order to avoid fragmentation. There are a number of methods used in log filesystems to expedite data access. One such method is a structure commonly called an *extent*. Extents are large contiguous sets of blocks, allocated during the creation of a file. The initial extent has an associated index block, much like the Unix inode, but the index needs to have only a pointer to the first block of the extent and a note on its size. When a file needs to grow larger than one extent, another extent can be allocated and the index block updated to contain the first block address and size of this new extent. In this way, even a very large file can be accessed directly. In the case of an extremely large file, the last few entries of an index block may have pointers used for indirect addressing.

Choosing the right extent size is essential for this type of filesystem. If the extents are too small, the filesystem could suffer from performance penalties associated with having a fair number of block indexes stored per file. If the extents are too big, large amounts of disk space may not be usable; this is called *internal fragmentation*. In order to address the problem of extent size, some implementations allocate extents based on the I/O pattern of files themselves, on a per-case basis.

Extents also can be compressed and empty disk space reclaimed by a cleaning process. Such a process would move extents to a smaller set of clean extents. After this operation is completed, the migrated extents could be marked as clean and later utilized for new data or further cleaning. The cleaning process usually is implemented to run between some thresholds or watermarks that depend on disk space availability.

Checkpoints

A checkpoint is a position in the log that indicates a point at which all filesystem structures are stable and consistent. After all modified information—including the index block, data blocks, and so on—is written to the log, the system writes a checkpoint region to a fixed block on disk. This region contains the addresses of all the blocks of the index block map and extent usage table, as well as the current time and a pointer to the last written extent. All this information is handy at startup time and particularly after a system failure, since it shows the last recollection of a completed filesystem operation. Checkpoints can be performed at different points in time, but the best configuration would probably take into account a threshold of data written to the log; this would minimize the overhead necessary to perform a checkpoint.

Checkpoints are a great advantage if you need to recover from a system failure. The checkpoint is the "starting point" that the filesystem starts from after a system failure. It then uses the roll-forward mechanism, described next, to recover consistent data written to the log since the last checkpoint.

Rolling forward

In theory, a checkpoint alone can give a consistent view of the system after it is reinitialized. However, if the checkpoint is not performed soon enough, some entries in the log may be discarded, although they contain valid information. The roll-forward mechanism is a good vehicle to save as much data as possible. When invoked, this mechanism uses the information usually available in the extent summary blocks to recover recently written data. If a summary block indicates the presence of a new index block, the system updates the index block map read from the checkpoint segment, so that the index block map refers to the new copy of the index block. This operation automatically incorporates newer blocks into the recovered filesystem. Index blocks are always written last. Therefore, if blocks are discovered for a file, without a newer copy of the index block for that file, the operation assumes that the new version of the file is incomplete and discards the new data blocks.

Using the checkpoint and roll-forward mechanisms, it is possible to speed up the file consistency check operation, usually performed on Unix systems upon startup by the *fsck* command. Integrity of the filesystem is preserved, and write operations to the filesystem are minimized, all while speeding up consistency checks.

Commercial HA Solutions

High-availability products have been maturing rapidly over the last couple of years and are becoming a standard in disaster recovery configurations. These solutions can alleviate the problems that occur when a server and/or application crashes, by having a fail-over server ready for such a circumstance. Commercial HA solutions provide readily available tools to configure systems in the HA fashion, saving you time and implementing a supported environment.

Currently Available HA Products

There are many competitive high-availability software products on the market today; deciding which one to purchase can be tough. The following list of features is a quick take on the types of questions to ask your potential HA vendor:

Clustering capability
> How many servers can be clustered together? If more than two servers, can any server fail over to any other server?

Load-balancing capability
> If two servers are serving the same function in an HA configuration, can the application's load be easily distributed between them?

Application-level recovery
> What applications have been tested with this configuration? If servers fail over but applications can't, you really haven't gained anything.

Intelligent monitoring
> Does a central station monitor and report on HA clusters? Are SNMP traps or any other monitoring via the system management framework supported?

Centralized management capability
> Can multiple nodes of an HA cluster or multiple HA clusters be monitored from a central location?

Application monitoring
> What sort of application monitoring is built in?

Cost
> What does it cost? All products are definitely not equal in this area.

Customer support
> The only way to accurately judge customer support is to ask for and check references.

Although they usually use different terminology, most HA packages have similar setups and configurations. Therefore, the rest of this chapter covers the general principles that make HA work.

Designing, Installing, and Maintaining an HA System

Determining how to configure the initial installation of your HA product is an important task. Your organizational needs will determine what hardware setup will accompany the HA environment. Start by asking a few questions:

- What services do you want to have highly available?

- Should some services be grouped together?

- Will one system be failed over to another with all of its applications if there is a problem, or will both systems run at the same time and share responsibilities with each other as their backups?

- Will a shared disk array be used, or is it even required to share data between a primary and secondary system?

- How many servers will you fail one system over to?

- Where are you going to install the software?

Configuring your system

Once you have installed your HA system, it is important to configure it properly. Most HA packages have a default configuration file to help you set up your fail-over environment. You will need to customize this to make the system fail over in the way that you want it to. You may first want to have the system attempt to restart an application multiple times (via the HA software) or fail over right away. Some HA vendors supply a "module" for certain common applications such as database software and firewall software. Configuring the HA product via these modules can greatly increase your availability.

Testing and monitoring your system

Once configured, test the system before putting it into a production environment. Try multiple fail-over scenarios to ensure the system will do what you expect it to and remain stable after it has failed over. Monitoring the status of the HA environment is straightforward. A GUI usually is provided (in the true sense or in an ASCII form). Systems and applications can be monitored inside the interface. A manual fail over also can be done through this interface. There are also log files that can be observed constantly for new messages, to see what is happening to the system. One common technique used to monitor systems is to use a software package such as Tivoli to trap events on the system. This is done by looking at the logs and sending notifications of significant events to a network management product such as HP OpenView, which then alerts an operations center to any problems with the system. Such a configuration could be used, with minor scripting, for monitoring an HA configuration.

The Impact of an HA Solution

With a proper HA solution in place, you will know when something goes wrong, and the system will try to react to that without human intervention. Once something does go wrong though, the purpose of the HA software is not to allow you to ignore the problem but rather to maintain stability long enough to give you a chance to diagnose the problem and fix it. Remember, an HA environment coupled with a volume management package is a complement to your normal backups, not a substitute.

What Are the Pros and Cons of HA?

HA is a great answer for mission-critical applications and environments that require close to 100 percent uptime. Properly configured and administered, an HA solution can be valuable to solve even disaster recovery situations in a timely manner.

On the negative side, a particular HA system may not provide the necessary solution for a particular application. As far as I know, there is no HA implementation that can perform application migration and duplicate an application state at failure time. If such a feature is an absolute requirement, it may be necessary to turn to fault-tolerant systems, which are briefly introduced in an earlier section.

Cost also may be a concern. HA packages are pricey and may not necessarily target a particular environment properly. Remember, HA requires a functional duplicate of your primary server, plus additional hardware and software to complete the equation. Study your options carefully and completely before making any decision.

What Does an HA Solution Cost?

Typically, a base configuration includes a one-to-one fail over with no databases or anything special (such as a module to support a third-party application) on a low-end box. If you install the software yourself, the cost runs around $10,000. A midrange configuration with vendor installation of a fairly powerful server with one or two applications (with a module) runs around $45,000. Finally, at the high end of the spectrum are high-end systems such as a clustered 64-processor system with multiple instances of a database. With multiple modules and top-of-the-line support and installation, the price is around $150,000. This may seem expensive, but the cost is worth it in the long run.

The price of a HA software package obviously varies from vendor to vendor and changes over time, but this gives you a rough estimate to work with. These numbers are valid at the time this book was printed.

How Can I Protect My Off-the-Shelf Software?

Modules are supplied by most HA vendors to take care of monitoring and failing-over popular applications. Modules have been developed to work with databases, web servers, firewalls, network monitoring applications, and certain other products. If you have an application for which there is no module, you can write your own simple script. Think about what is required to run the application: network connectivity, access to a certain port on the box, assurance that the processes are running, and on and on. You can do this yourself, or you can contact your HA vendor to see if an appropriate module is in the works or if they could write one for you.

Can I Build an HA Solution Myself?

This may sound like a good idea, but it is not a smart one. Building your own HA solution by coding it in-house can result in a poorly tested and supported product that doesn't have the advantage of regular vendor updates and certified modules. And in the end, it may not be cost effective. An alternative is to purchase a base HA product, and then tweak a module (or even write your own with scripts) to support a given application.

My HA System Is Set Up, Now What?

Setting up an HA environment has taken your organization from a reactive posture to a proactive one. Ensuring it is done properly and combining it with other building blocks will be a never-ending process. Do not turn your back on your HA system and assume that you are done, because you are not. Monitoring the system continuously (manually or automatically) is necessary. Pay attention to new technology, as there may be another building block in the near future. And, as always, *do your backups.*

Bare-Metal Backup & Recovery Methods

Part IV consists of the following five chapters which describe the process of restoring your system even when the disk containing the operating system fails:

- Chapter 7, *SunOS/Solaris*, covers bare-metal recovery in general and describes how to use Native Unix utilities to recover SunOS/Solaris systems.

- Chapter 9, *Compaq Tru64 Unix*, describes Digital's recovery system and shows how to develop a custom recovery plan using Native Unix utilities.

- Chapter 10, *HP-UX*, discusses bare-metal recovery using tools provided by Hewlett-Packard in combination with Native Unix utilities.

- Chapter 11, *IRIX*, describes bare-metal recovery using SGI's IRIX utilities.

- Chapter 12, *AIX*, describes bare-metal recovery using IBM's AIX utilities.

7
SunOS/Solaris

As mentioned previously in this book, disks will fail. Occasionally, even the disk that contains the operating system will fail. How do you protect against such a disaster? Depending on your budget and the level of availability that you need, you may explore one or more of the following options if you're running Solaris:

Solstice Disk Suite mirrored root disk

>   If you are running Solaris, you can use Solstice Disk Suite (SDS) to mirror your root disk. (Other platforms have similar products.) A mirrored disk would automatically take over if the other disk fails. SDS is bundled free with Solaris, and mirroring the root drive is relatively easy.* It's also easy to undo in case things get a little mixed up. You simply boot off a CD-ROM, mount the root filesystem from the good drive, and change the */etc/vfstab* to use the actual disk slice names instead of the SDS metadevice names. There are two downsides to this method. The first is that many people are using Veritas Volume Manager to manage the rest of their disks, and using SDS for the root disk may be confusing. The second downside is that it does not protect against root filesystem corruption. If someone accidentally overwrites */etc*, the mirroring software will only make that mistake more efficient.

 Although this chapter talks mainly about SunOS/Solaris, the principles covered here are used in the other bare-metal recovery chapters.

---

* It is beyond the scope of this book, though. There are too many products like this to cover, so I won't be covering any of them in detail.

Veritas Volume Manager encapsulated root disk

If you have purchased the Veritas Volume Manager for Solaris, you also have the option of mirroring your root drive with it. (Putting the root drive under Veritas control is called *encapsulation.*) I'm not sure what to say about this other than to say that I've heard more than one Veritas consultant or instructor tell me not to encapsulate the root disk. It creates too many potential catch-22 situations. Of course, this method also does not protect against the corruption of the root filesystem.

Standby root disk

A standby root disk is created by copying the currently running root disk to the alternate boot disk. If the system crashes, you can simply tell it to boot off the other disk. Some people even automate this to the point that the system *always* boots off the other disk when it is rebooted, unless it is told not to do so. (There is a tool on *http://www.backupcentral.com* that does just that.)

The advantage to the two previous methods is that if one of the mirrored root disks fails, the operating system will continue to function until it is rebooted. The disadvantage is that they do not protect you against a bad patch or administrator error. Anything that causes "logical" problems with the operating system will simply be duplicated on the other disk. A standby root disk is just the opposite. You will be completely protected against administrator and other errors, but it will require a reboot to boot off the new disk.

Mirrored/HA system

A high-availability (HA) system, as discussed in Chapter 6, *High Availability*, is the most expensive of these four options, but it offers the greatest level of protection against such a failure. Instead of having a mirrored or standby root disk, you have an entire system standing by ready to take over in case of failure.

What About Fire?

All of the preceding methods will allow you to recover from an operating system disk failure. None of them, however, will protect you when that server burns to the ground. Fire (and other disasters) tend to take out both sides of a mirrored disk pair or HA system. If that happens or if you didn't use any of the preceding methods prior to an operating system disk failure, you will need to recover the root disk from some type of backup.

Recovering the root disk is called a bare-metal recovery, and there are many platform-specific, bare-metal recovery utilities. The earliest example of such a utility on a Unix platform is AIX's *mksysb* command. *mksysb* is still in use today and makes a special backup tape that stores all of the root volume-group information. The administrator can replace the root disk, boot off the latest *mksysb*, and the utility automatically restores the operating system to that disk. Today, there is AIX's *mksysb*, Compaq's *btcreate,* HP's *make_recovery*, and SGI's *Backup*. Each of these utilities is covered in its own later chapter.

Without a planned bootstrap recovery system, the usual solution to the bare-metal recovery problem is as follows:

1. Replace the defective disk.

2. Reinstall the OS and its patches.

3. Reinstall the backup software.

4. Recover the current, backed-up OS on top of the old OS.

This solution is insufficient, misleading, and not very efficient. The first problem is that you actually end up laying the OS down twice. The second problem is that it doesn't work very well. Try overwriting some of the system files when a system is running from the disk to which you are trying to restore.

Homegrown Bare-Metal Recovery

There is a better way to restore the current OS configuration to a new disk, without laying down the information twice. This method is simple; here are its steps:

1. Back up all appropriate metadata (disk layout, */etc/vfstab*, etc.).

2. Take a good backup of the OS via *dump* or a similar utility.

3. Boot the system to be recovered into single-user mode using a CD-ROM.

4. Set up the recovery disk to look the same as the old root disk, and mount it.

5. Recover the OS to the mounted disk.

6. Place the boot block on the mounted disk.

7. Reboot.

What Is the Boot Block?

The key to the homegrown bare-metal recovery procedure is the recreation of the *boot block*. Without it, this procedure doesn't work. The boot block is the first few blocks of data on the root sector of the disk. ("Boot block" is actually a Sun term, but other platforms have a similar block of boot information.) Each hardware platform knows enough to look here to find the basic "boot" information. The main part of this block is the location on the disk where the kernel is stored. This block of boot information, or boot block, is stored outside, or "in front of," the root filesystem—on the raw disk itself. Without the boot block, the system will not boot off that disk.

On What Platforms Will This Procedure Work?

I originally developed this procedure for SunOS and Solaris, since Sun did not have a utility like IBM's *mksysb*; however, it is adaptable to many Unix systems. For example, all of the bare-metal recovery chapters to follow (except the AIX chapter) contain examples of how to adapt this procedure for that platform. When I describe the procedure, I use a Solaris system for the examples. A detailed Solaris bare-metal recovery example then follows the general procedure description.

Before Disaster Strikes

As is the case with most bare-metal recovery procedures, you need to do a few things up front in order to protect yourself in the event of such a disaster. The first three steps talk about backing up data that is not usually included in a filesystem-level backup. One way to back up all this information is to run *SysAudit** (or a program like it) from *cron*, and save this information in a file every day.

1. If you are going to replace the root disk with another one without reinstalling the OS, you have to partition the new disk the same way the old one was partitioned. The only way you are going to know how the old disk was partitioned is to save this partitioning information.

2. Save the *fstab* file. This file contains a list of all local filesystems and can be very useful when you're trying to rebuild a system from scratch. The names and locations of the *fstab* for various flavors of Unix are shown in Table 7-1.

Table 7-1. Locations and Names of /etc/fstab

Unix Flavor	Location of fstab File
AIX	*/etc/filesystems*
BSDI, DG-UX, FreeBSD, Next, Compaq Tru64 Unix, Irix, Ultrix, SunOS, Convex, Linux, HP-UX 10+	*/etc/fstab*
HP-UX 8.x, 9.x	*/etc/checklist*
SCO Openserver	*/etc/default/filesys*
Solaris, SVr4	*/etc/vfstab*

3. Send this information to a centralized system or more than one centralized system so you can access it if any server becomes unavailable. One of the best ways to do this is via email.

4. When you rebuild a system using a new root disk, you also need to recreate or restore the boot block. SunOS, Solaris, Compaq Tru64 Unix, IRIX, and HP-UX all have a way to recreate the boot block for you (e.g., Sun's *installboot* command). If your version of Unix has no similar command, then you also will

---

* *SysAudit* is on the CD-ROM and is available at *http://www.backupcentral.com*.

need to back up the boot block. One way to do this is to use *dd* to back up the first few blocks of data on the root slice. To use *dd*, issue a command like:

```
# dd if=/dev/dsk/device bs=10k count=10 \
of=/nfsdrive/root.systemname
```

For example:

```
# dd if=/dev/dsk/c0t0d0s0 bs=10k count=10 \
of=/elvis/bootbackups/root.apollo
```

This gives you a file called */nfsdrive/root.systemname*, which is the backup of the boot block on *systemname*.

As mentioned previously, this step is not needed in most Unix versions; it is needed only if the Unix version does not have a command to recreate the boot block. For example, Solaris uses the *installboot* command to recreate the boot block, so you do not need to perform this step on a Solaris system.

5. Back up the operating system. One way to accomplish this is to use the program *hostdump.sh*.[*] For example, suppose that the operating system is contained in the following filesystems: */*, */usr*, and */var*. To back this up with *hostdump.sh*, enter the following command:

```
# hostdump.sh 0 device logfile hostname:/ hostname:/usr hostname:/var
```

6. This creates a single tape that contains a full backup of */*, */usr*, and */var* from *hostname*. Send this backup off-site for safekeeping, but keep an on-site copy for quick restores.

The preceding example uses */*, */usr*, and */var*. Your system also may have */opt*, */usr/openwin*, or other filesystems that contain the operating system. Make sure you include all the appropriate filesystems.

After a Disaster

If you follow the previous preparatory steps you should be able to easily recover from the loss of an operating system drive using the following steps:

1. Replace the root drive with a drive that is as big as, or bigger than, the original root drive. (Past experience has shown that the closer you stay to the same drive architecture, the better chance of success you will have.)

---

[*] *hostdump.sh* is available on the CD-ROM, and on the web site *http://www.backupcentral.com*.

2. Boot the system to single-user mode or "miniroot" using the operating system CD-ROM, or a similar method. The command to do this is very platform dependent, even among the various Sun platforms.

Table 7-2 contains a list of the appropriate commands to boot the various Sun platforms into single-user mode from a CD-ROM.

Table 7-2. Various Commands to Boot a Sun from the CD-ROM

Platform	Boot Command
4/110, 4/2xx, 4/3xx, 4/4xx	*b sd(0,3,1) -s*
Sparc 1, Sparc 1+, Sparc SLC, Sparc IPC	*boot sd(0,6,2) -s*
SPARC 1E	*boot sd(0,6,5) -s*
SPARC ELC, IPX, LX, classic 2, 10, LX, 6xxMP, 1000, 2000, 4x00, 6x00, 10000 (and probably any newer architectures)	*boot cdrom -s*

3. Partition the new drive to look like the old drive. To do this on Solaris, we use the *format* command:

```
SunOS# format sd0
```

a. Choose *p* for "partition."

b. Choose *p* for "print."

c. Choose *s* for "select number."

d. Resize as appropriate.

```
Solaris# format c0t0d0
```

e. Choose *p* for "partition."

f. Choose *p* for "print."

g. Choose *s* for "select number."

h. Resize as appropriate.

4. Optionally, install and configure a volume manager.

On Solaris, it is *not* necessary to mirror the root disk via SDS or Volume Manager, even if you were using mirroring before. You can mirror it or encapsulate it later when you have time.

5. Create new filesystems on the new disk:

```
Solaris# newfs /dev/dsk/c0t0d0s0
Solaris# fsck /dev/rdsk/c0t0d0s0 # repeat for other slices
```

6. Restore the OS backup to */mnt*. If you are using something other than *hostdump.sh*, follow its procedure. If using *hostdump.sh*, follow this procedure. First, you need to get the electronic label from the tape.

The rest of this procedure assumes that you used *hostdump.sh* to back up your operating system drive. If you used another method, you will need to follow the restore procedure for that method to restore the operating system.

7. Rewind the tape. To do this, we will use the *mt* command. (See Chapter 5, *Commercial Backup Utilities*, for more information about *mt*.)

   ```
   # mt -t /dev/rmt/0 rewind
   ```

8. The *hostdump.sh* program creates a text file called */tmp/BACKUP.LABEL* that contains a list of all filesystems that will be backed up to a particular volume. It then uses *tar* to place that text file as the first file on the backup volume. Use *tar* to extract this label from the tape:

   ```
   # tar xvf /dev/rmt/0  #
   ```

9. Read */tmp/BACKUP.LABEL* to find out which file(s) on the volume contain(s) the filesystem(s) you need to restore.

10. Fast-forward to the first tape file that contains the first filesystem that you want to restore. For this example, the first *dump* file is the one we want, so it's the second file on the tape; note the use of the *n* flag to specify that the tape should not rewind when this command is complete.

    ```
    # mt -t /dev/rmt/0n fsf 1
    ```

11. Mount and restore each partition one at a time:

    a. Mount *one* of the slices of the restore disk. The first one should be mounted as */mnt*. (That will become the root filesystem.) The second disk slice (e.g., the future */var*) should be mounted as */mnt/var*:

       ```
       Solaris# mount /dev/dsk/c0t0d0s0 /mnt
       ```

       After you finish steps b and c, you will be repeating this step to mount the next operating system partition. If */var* was originally mounted on slice 1, the command to do that would be:

       ```
       Solaris# mount /dev/dsk/c0t0d0s1 /mnt/var
       ```

Steps a–c should be done one filesystem at a time. For example, mount */mnt*, then restore */* into */mnt*. Then mount */mnt/usr*, and restore */usr* into */mnt/usr*. Do not mount all of the directories at once. Restoring */* overwrites the */mnt/usr* mount point and tends to confuse things. So, mount and restore the filesystems one at a time.

b. *cd* to the filesystem you want to restore:

```
# cd /mnt
```

c. Use the appropriate command to restore that filesystem:

```
Solaris# ufsrestore rbfy 64 device_name
```

d. Repeat steps a through c until you have restored all OS filesystems.

12. Recreate the boot block image onto the root disk (e.g., *installboot, mkboot, disklabel*):

```
Solaris# installboot /usr/platform/`uname -i`/lib/fs/ufs/bootblk /dev/
rdsk/c0t0d0s0
```

13. Reboot using the new disk:

```
Solaris# reboot
```

You should now have a fully functional system. If the only disk that was damaged was the root disk, you do not even need to reinstall any applications or data.

Am I Crazy?

That looks like a lot of work, doesn't it? It is. However, you can do much of it ahead of time. You can even have a disk ready to go. This method also renders a truer copy of the original operating system much faster than any other. It's often much quicker than the method described at the beginning of this chapter that requires that you reload the operating system, since it doesn't require that you load any patches.

You also could use this procedure to standardize all your operating system disks, which would give you a chance to practice it as well. First you would need to define a partitioning standard for all your OS disks that was large enough to hold the biggest partition that you had (e.g., the biggest */usr* would have to fit this scheme). You can then partition a disk that way, restore one client's OS to it, and see if you then can install the OS on the client. If you can, you then can take that client's old OS disk and use it to make the new system's disk. By the time you're done, you could have all your OS disks set up the same way. Now *there's* a project plan . . .

Recovering a SunOS/Solaris System

Neither SunOS nor Solaris has a bare-metal recovery utility like the other operating systems covered in this book. However, the existence of *dump, restore,* and *installboot* make doing a bare-metal recovery relatively simple. The individual steps and the logic behind them were covered earlier. Following is an example of how such a recovery would look on a Solaris system. This example covers a Sparc 20. Its operating system is Solaris 2.6, and it has two filesystems, */* and */var*.

Preparing for Disaster

First, we will back up the system using *hostdump.sh*. This utility is covered in Chapter 3, *Native Backup & Recovery Utilities*, and will use *ufsdump* to back up the */* and */var* filesystems.

On the system that I used for this example, the */* and */var* filesystems contained the entire operating system. Your system may be different, so you may need to back up other filesystems such a */usr*, */opt*, */usr/openwin*, etc.

The command to do this and its results are displayed in Example 7-1.

Example 7-1. The hostdump.sh Output

```
# /usr/local/bin/hostdump.sh 0 /dev/rmt/0n /tmp/backup.log curtis:/ curtis:/var
=========================================================
Beginning level 0 backup of the following
clients: curtis:/ curtis:/var
This backup is going to curtis:/dev/rmt/0n
and is being logged to curtis:/tmp/backup.log
=========================================================


Querying clients to determine which filesystems to back up...

Including "curtis:/:ufs:sparc-sun-solaris2.6" in backup include
list.
Including "curtis:/var:ufs:sparc-sun-solaris2.6" in backup include
list.

Now checking that each filesystem is a valid directory...


Determining the appropriate backup commands...


-----------------------------------------------------
Placing label of BACKUP.LABEL as first file on /dev/rmt/0n
(and verifying that /dev/rmt/0n is set to NO-REW...)

Displaying contents of the label...


-----------------------------------------------------------------
This tape is a level 0 backup made Mon Jan  4 16:07:36 PST 1999
The following is a table of contents of this tape.
It is in the following format:
host:fs name:fs type:OS Version:dump cmmd:rdump cmmd:dump options\
:restore cmmd: rrestore cmmd:restore options:LEVEL \
:Client rsh command:Blocking factor
-----------------------------------------------------------------

curtis:/:ufs:sparc-sun-solaris2.6:/usr/sbin/ufsdump:/usr/sbin/
ufsdump:0bdsfnu~64~80000~
150000:/usr/sbin/ufsrestore:/usr/sbin/ufsrestore:tbfy~64:0:
```

Example 7-1. The hostdump.sh Output (continued)

```
/usr/bin/rsh:64
curtis:/var:ufs:sparc-sun-solaris2.6:/usr/sbin/ufsdump:/usr/sbin/
ufsdump:0bdsfnu~64~80000~150000:/usr/sbin/ufsrestore:/usr/sbin/
ufsrestore:tbfy~64:0:/usr/bin/rsh:64


------------------------------------------------------------
Also, the last file on this tape is a tar file containing a
complete flat file index of the tape. To read it, issue the
following commands:
cd /usr/tmp
/bin/mt -t /dev/rmt/0n fsf 3
tar xvf /dev/rmt/0n



============================================================
Now beginning the backups of all the systems listed above...
============================================================



===============================
Beginning /usr/sbin/ufsdump of curtis: Mon Jan  4 16:08:19 PST
1999


-------------------------------------------------
Backing up curtis:/ level 0 (Filesystem 1)
Using Command: /usr/sbin/ufsdump 0bdsfnu 64 80000 150000
/dev/rmt/0n /
  DUMP: Writing 32 Kilobyte records
  DUMP: Date of this level 0 dump: Mon Jan 04 16:08:20 1999
  DUMP: Date of last level 0 dump: the epoch
  DUMP: Dumping /dev/rdsk/c0t3d0s0 (curtis:/) to /dev/rmt/0n.
  DUMP: Mapping (Pass I) [regular files]
  DUMP: Mapping (Pass II) [directories]
  DUMP: Estimated 991718 blocks (484.24MB) on 0.01 tapes.
  DUMP: Dumping (Pass III) [directories]
  DUMP: Dumping (Pass IV) [regular files]
  DUMP: 38.81% done, finished in 0:16
  DUMP: 78.06% done, finished in 0:05
  DUMP: 991678 blocks (484.22MB) on 1 volume at 319 KB/sec
  DUMP: DUMP IS DONE
  DUMP IS DONE
  DUMP: Level 0 dump on Mon Jan 04 16:08:20 1999
/usr/sbin/ufsdump 0 Done Mon 01/04/99 16:34:21 from curtis / on curtis:/dev/rmt/0n 1


-------------------------------------------------
Backing up curtis:/var level 0 (Filesystem 2)
Using Command: /usr/sbin/ufsdump 0bdsfnu 64 80000 150000
/dev/rmt/0n /var
  DUMP: Writing 32 Kilobyte records
  DUMP: Date of this level 0 dump: Mon Jan 04 16:34:25 1999
  DUMP: Date of last level 0 dump: the epoch
  DUMP: Dumping /dev/rdsk/c0t3d0s1 (curtis:/var) to /dev/rmt/0n.
```

Example 7-1. The hostdump.sh Output (continued)

```
DUMP: Mapping (Pass I) [regular files]
DUMP: Mapping (Pass II) [directories]
DUMP: Estimated 130134 blocks (63.54MB) on 0.00 tapes.
DUMP: Dumping (Pass III) [directories]
DUMP: Dumping (Pass IV) [regular files]
DUMP: 130110 blocks (63.53MB) on 1 volume at 345 KB/sec
DUMP: DUMP IS DONE
DUMP: Level 0 dump on Mon Jan 04 16:34:25 1999
/usr/sbin/ufsdump 0 Done Mon 01/04/99 16:37:37 from curtis /var on curtis:/dev/rmt/0n 2
Backups complete... Beginning reading of tape...

Rewind complete


========================================================
 Positioning to Pt# 2 w/cmd: /bin/mt -t /dev/rmt/0n fsf 1
 Reading Filesystem curtis:/
 This was a ufs filesystem on a sparc-sun-solaris2.6 system.
 (It was backed up with ufsdump.)
  Using Command: /usr/sbin/ufsrestore tbfy 64 /dev/rmt/0n
ufsdump Pt# 2: >          2     .
ufsdump Pt# 2: >          3     ./lost+found
ufsdump Pt# 2: >       3776     ./var


.......Then it displays a whole lot of files........


========================================================
 Positioning to Pt# 3 w/cmd: /bin/mt -t /dev/rmt/0n fsf 2
 Reading Filesystem curtis:/var
 This was a ufs filesystem on a sparc-sun-solaris2.6 system.
 (It was backed up with ufsdump.)
  Using Command: /usr/sbin/ufsrestore tbfy 64 /dev/rmt/0n
ufsdump Pt# 3: >          2     .
ufsdump Pt# 3: >          3     ./lost+found


.......Then it displays a whole lot of files........


ufsdump Pt# 3: >       3776     ./sadm
ufsdump Pt# 3: >      52928     ./dt/sdtlogin
a /tmp/backup.log 4090 tape blocks
Tape read successful - ejected
```

Now that we have backed up the entire operating system, we need to save the system configuration information. The *SysAudit* program will do this for us. For this test, we will save the output to an NFS-mounted directory from another system. That way, when this system is lost, we will have its configuration information available on another system:

```
# /usr/local/bin/SysAudit >/nfsmount/SysAudit.log
```

Disaster Strikes!

Now that we've backed up the operating system and saved the configuration information, we will simulate a crash:

```
# shutdown -i0 -g0 -y

Jan  4 18:08:26 rpcbind: rpcbind terminating on signal.
Jan  4 18:08:31 snmpdx: received signal 15
syncing le systems... done
Program terminated
Type  help  for more information
```

At this point, we have simulated a disaster. The root disk has crashed, and we are at the OK prompt. In this simulation, we actually don't have a corrupted root filesystem, but we will as soon as we run the *newfs* command! (That will be done later in this demonstration.)

```
<#0> ok boot cdrom -s
Initializing Memory
Boot device: /iommu/sbus/espdma@f,400000/esp@f,800000/sd@6,0
File and args: -s
Copyright (c) 1983-1997, Sun Microsystems, Inc.

INIT: SINGLE USER MODE

Type Ctrl-d to proceed with normal startup
(or give root password for system maintenance):
Entering System Maintenance Mode
```

In Example 7-2, you see the results of the *SysAudit* command. It shows us how the operating system disk was laid out. We will use that information to rebuild this system. (You will see that we are looking at a file that is on an NFS-mounted disk. This means that either we are looking at it on another system's console, or we have enabled networking and NFS client services to be able to do this.)

Example 7-2. The Output of SysAudit

```
# cat /nfsmount/SysAudit.log


=========================================
System Configuration report for curtis
=========================================


Report data
===========
Date              :  Mon Jan  4 16:30:39 PST 1999
Version           :  $Revision: 1.12 $

Machine data
============
Uptime            :  up 12 day(s), 20:21,  3 users
Current load avg  :  0.43, 0.15, 0.11
```

Example 7-2. The Output of SysAudit (continued)

```
Machine               :  sun4m
Serial number         :  Unknown
HostID                :  72304ecb
Model                 :  SPARCstation 10MP (2 X 390Z55)
O.S. revision         :  5.6
Kernel                :  Generic_105181-07
C compiler revision   :  1.15 (bundled)
Memory                :  128 Megabytes
Swap space            :  358 Megabytes
Last login            :  oracle

Network data
============
NIS domain            :
NIS client            :  False
NIS server            :  False

NFS client            :  False
NFS server            :  False

Ethernet interfaces   :  1
IP address            :  192.168.0.5
MAC address           :  8:0:20:1a:ff:a
Netmask               :  ffffff00
Broadcast             :  192.168.0.255
Default router        :  <routed|gated running>

Disk data:
================================================================
Filesystem           kbytes    used   avail capacity Mounted on
================================================================
/dev/dsk/c0t3d0s0     592438  474356   58839   89%    /
/dev/dsk/c0t3d0s1     123231   62943   47965   57%    /var
/dev/dsk/c0t0d0s6    1854801 1268851  400470   77%    /db
/dev/dsk/c0t1d0s4      48479    1466   42166    4%    /vol2
/dev/dsk/c0t1d0s5    1767031    2923 1711098    1%    /junk
/dev/dsk/c0t1d0s3      48479    1441   42191    4%    /vol1
/dev/dsk/c0t3d0s3                            525160   swap

Solaris data
============
sar(1M) status        :  <NOT Running>
Veritas Volume Mgr    :  <NOT Running>


======================================================
111 Installed patches (from 'showrev -p')
======================================================


....    The real output would show   .....
....    a whole bunch of patches      .....
....    We've truncated this one      .....


======================================================
```

Example 7-2. The Output of SysAudit (continued)

```
0 Installed printers (from lpstat)
=================================================


=================================================
255 Installed packages (from pkginfo)
=================================================
system      SUNWypr       NIS Server for Solaris (root)
system      SUNWypu       NIS Server for Solaris (usr)
```

```
....   The real output would show    .....
....   a whole bunch of packages     .....
....   We've truncated this one      .....
```

```
#Partition table of root drive
   0       root    wm    0 - 1251    616.22MB   (1252/0/0) 1262016
   1        var    wm 1252 - 1512    128.46MB    (261/0/0)  263088
   2     backup    wm    0 - 2035   1002.09MB   (2036/0/0) 2052288
   3       swap    wu 1513 - 2033    256.43MB    (521/0/0)  525168
   4 unassigned    wm    0              0         (0/0/0)        0
   5 unassigned    wm    0              0         (0/0/0)        0
   6 unassigned    wm    0              0         (0/0/0)        0
   7 unassigned    wm    0              0         (0/0/0)        0
```

Recovering from the Disaster

In a true disaster, the root disk would be physically replaced. Once it is installed, we use the Solaris *format* command to partition the drive the same way as the original, using the *SysAudit* output as a guide. In Example 7-3, you see that we run the *format* command and select *p* for partition then *p* for print.*

Example 7-3. Getting Ready to Partition the Drive

```
# format
Searching for disks...done

AVAILABLE DISK SELECTIONS:
    0. c0t0d0 <FUJITSU-M2654S-512-010P cyl 2170 alt 2 hd 21 sec 88>

/iommu@f,e0000000/sbus@f,e0001000/espdma@f,400000/esp@f,800000/
sd@0,0
    1. c0t1d0 <HP-C2257-0BC4 cyl 2142 alt 2 hd 19 sec 96>
/iommu@f,e0000000/sbus@f,e0001000/espdma@f,400000/esp@f,800000/
sd@1,0
    2. c0t3d0 <SUN1.05 cyl 2036 alt 2 hd 14 sec 72>
/iommu@f,e0000000/sbus@f,e0001000/espdma@f,400000/esp@f,800000/
sd@3,0
Specify disk (enter its number): 2
```

---

* Yes, I know this is a fake example, and a real "blank" disk never looks like the preceding output, but I wanted to demonstrate how the partition table is built.

Example 7-3. Getting Ready to Partition the Drive (continued)

```
selecting c0t3d0
[disk formatted]

FORMAT MENU:
        disk       - select a disk
        type       - select (define) a disk type
        partition  - select (define) a partition table
        current    - describe the current disk
        format     - format and analyze the disk
        repair     - repair a defective sector
        label      - write label to the disk
        analyze    - surface analysis
        defect     - defect list management
        backup     - search for backup labels
        verify     - read and display labels
        save       - save new disk/partition definitions
        inquiry    - show vendor, product and revision
        volname    - set 8-character volume name
        !<cmd>     - execute <cmd>, then return
        quit
format> p


PARTITION MENU:
        0          - change `0' partition
        1          - change `1' partition
        2          - change `2' partition
        3          - change `3' partition
        4          - change `4' partition
        5          - change `5' partition
        6          - change `6' partition
        7          - change `7' partition
        select - select a predefined table
        modify - modify a predefined partition table
        name   - name the current table
        print  - display the current table
        label  - write partition map and label to the disk
        !<cmd> - execute <cmd>, then return
        quit
partition> p
Current partition table (original):
Total disk cylinders available: 2036 + 2 (reserved cylinders)
```

Part	Tag	Flag	Cylinders	Size	Blocks	
0	root	wm	0	0	(0/0/0)	0
1	var	wm	0	0	(0/0/0)	0
2	backup	wm	0 - 2035	1002.09MB	(2036/0/0)	2052288
3	swap	wu	0	0	(0/0/0)	0
4	unassigned	wm	0	0	(0/0/0)	0
5	unassigned	wm	0	0	(0/0/0)	0
6	unassigned	wm	0	0	(0/0/0)	0
7	unassigned	wm	0	0	(0/0/0)	0

The next step is to select the three partitions we have to resize and resize them. Example 7-4 shows how this would look. In this example you will notice that I specified the size of the partition by telling it how many blocks should be in the partition. You also may be wondering where I got that number. Remember, I am trying to make a root disk that looks exactly like the old root disk. Since I know exactly how it was partitioned, the best way to do that is to use the cylinder count method shown previously.

Example 7-4. Partitioning the Drive

```
partition> 0
Part      Tag    Flag    Cylinders   Size      Blocks
  0       root    wm       0          0        (0/0/0)              0

Enter partition id tag[unassigned]: root
Enter partition permission flags[wm]: wm
Enter new starting cyl[0]:  0
Enter partition size[0b, 0c, 0.00mb, 0b]: 1252c


partition> p


partition> 1
Part      Tag    Flag    Cylinders   Size          Blocks
  1       var     wm       0          0         (0/0/0)             0

Enter partition id tag[unassigned]: var
Enter partition permission flags[wm]: wm
Enter new starting cyl[1252]: 1252
Enter partition size[0b, 0c, 0.00mb, 0b]: 261c


partition> 3
Part       Tag    Flag    Cylinders   Size         Blocks
  3 unassigned     wm       0          0        (0/0/0)             0

Enter partition id tag[unassigned]: swap
Enter partition permission flags[wm]: wu
Enter new starting cyl[1513]: 1513
Enter partition size[0b, 0c, 0.00mb, 0.00gb]: 521c
```

Now that we've built the new partition table, we'll print it out to make sure that it looks the way we want it to look:

```
partition> p
Current partition table (unnamed):
Total disk cylinders available: 2036 + 2 (reserved cylinders)

Part       Tag    Flag   Cylinders      Size         Blocks
  0       root     wm     0 - 1251     616.22MB    (1252/0/0) 1262016
  1        var     wm    1252 - 1512   128.46MB    (261/0/0)   263088
  2      backup    wm     0 - 2035    1002.09MB    (2036/0/0) 2052288
  3       swap     wu    1513 - 2033   256.43MB    (521/0/0)   525168
  4 unassigned     wm      0             0         (0/0/0)           0
```

```
       5 unassigned    wm     0              0         (0/0/0)          0
       6 unassigned    wm     0              0         (0/0/0)          0
       7 unassigned    wm     0              0         (0/0/0)          0
```

Once we've verified that it looks correct, we need to save the partition information to disk, or it will be lost. This is done with the *l* command, for *label*:

```
partition> l
Ready to label disk, continue? Y
```

We can now quit the *format* program:

```
partition> q
```

```
FORMAT MENU:
        disk       - select a disk
        type       - select (define) a disk type
        partition  - select (define) a partition table
        current    - describe the current disk
        format     - format and analyze the disk
        repair     - repair a defective sector
        label      - write label to the disk
        analyze    - surface analysis
        defect     - defect list management
        backup     - search for backup labels
        verify     - read and display labels
        save       - save new disk/partition definitions
        inquiry    - show vendor, product and revision
        volname    - set 8-character volume name
        !<cmd>     - execute <cmd>, then return
        quit
format> q
```

Now that the disk is properly partitioned, we need to use *newfs* to lay down a fresh filesystem on each partition. After running *newfs*, I always run an *fsck* to make sure everything is fine:

```
# newfs /dev/dsk/c0t3d0s0
newfs: /dev/rdsk/c0t3d0s0
newfs: construct a new filesystem /dev/rdsk/c0t3d0s0: (y/n)? y
/dev/rdsk/c0t3d0s0:    1271328 sectors in 697 cylinders of 19
tracks, 96 sectors
        620.8MB in 44 cyl groups (16 c/g, 14.25MB/g, 6848 i/g)
super-block backups (for fsck -F ufs -o b=#) at:
 32, 29312, 58592, 87872, 117152, 146432, 175712, 204992, 234272,
263552, 292832, 322112, 351392, 380672, 409952, 439232, 468512,
497792, 527072, 556352, 585632, 614912, 644192, 673472, 702752,
732032, 761312, 790592, 819872, 849152, 878432, 907712, 933920,
963200, 992480, 1021760, 1051040, 1080320, 1109600, 1138880,
1168160, 1197440, 1226720, 1256000,

# fsck /dev/rdsk/c0t3d0s0   # Always fsck a partition after newfsing it

# newfs /dev/dsk/c0t3d0s1
```

```
newfs: construct a new filesystem /dev/rdsk/c0t3d0s1: (y/n)? y
/dev/rdsk/c0t3d0s1:     266304 sectors in 146 cylinders of 19
tracks, 96 sectors
          130.0MB in 10 cyl groups (16 c/g, 14.25MB/g, 6848 i/g)
super-block backups (for fsck -F ufs -o b=#) at:
 32, 29312, 58592, 87872, 117152, 146432, 175712, 204992, 234272,
263552,
```

 # fsck /dev/rdsk/c0t3d0s1

Now that the filesystems are there, we *mount* the / filesystem to */mnt*:

 # mount /dev/dsk/c0t3d0s0 /mnt

 # df -k /mnt
```
Filesystem            kbytes   used   avail capacity  Mounted on
/dev/dsk/c0t3d0s0     597279     10  537542     1%    /mnt
```

The / and */var* filesystems are now ready for use, and the / filesystem is mounted on */mnt*. What we need to do now is to read the label from the tape to find out where these backups are on the tape. The *hostdump.sh* utility puts a file called *BACKUP.LABEL* on the front of the tape using *tar*. Example 7-5 shows how we rewind the tape, then extract and display the label.

Example 7-5. The BACKUP.LABEL File

 # mt -t /dev/rmt/0c rewind

 # tar xvf /dev/rmt/0cb
x BACKUP.LABEL, 1050 bytes, 3 tape blocks

 # cat BACKUP.LABEL

```
------------------------------------------------------------------
This tape is a level 0 backup made Mon Jan  4 16:07:36 PST 1999
The following is a table of contents of this tape.
It is in the following format:
host:fs name:fs type:OS Version:dump cmmd:rdump cmmd:dump options\
:restore cmmd: rrestore cmmd:restore options:LEVEL \
:Client rsh command:Blocking factor
------------------------------------------------------------------

curtis:/:ufs:sparc-sun-solaris2.6:/usr/sbin/ufsdump:/usr/sbin/
ufsdump:0bdsfnu~64~80000~
150000:/usr/sbin/ufsrestore:/usr/sbin/ufsrestore:tbfy~64:0:
/usr/bin/rsh:64
curtis:/var:ufs:sparc-sun-solaris2.6:/usr/sbin/ufsdump:/usr/sbin/
ufsdump:0bdsfnu~64~80000~150000:/usr/sbin/ufsrestore:/usr/sbin/
ufsrestore:tbfy~64:0:/usr/bin/rsh:64


------------------------------------------------------------------
Also, the last file on this tape is a tar file containing a
complete flat file index of the tape. To read it, issue the
following commands:
```

Example 7-5. The BACKUP.LABEL File (continued)

```
cd /usr/tmp
/bin/mt -t /dev/rmt/0n fsf 3
tar xvf /dev/rmt/0n
```

The *BACKUP.LABEL* file said that the / filesystem is the second file on the tape, so we have to fast-forward to that file. Notice that we must use the no-rewind device, or we'll be right back where we started!

```
# mt -t /dev/rmt/0n fsf 1
```

Before we begin the restore, we must verify that we are in the correct directory. (The *ufsrestore* utility always restores relative to the current directory.)

```
# pwd
/mnt
```

Now that we've verified that, we issue the *ufsrestore* command, using the *r* option, which specifies to read the entire backup and restore it relative to the current directory. (The *v* flag is not required, but it gives extra output for the impatient.)

```
# ufsrestore rbvfy 64 /dev/rmt/0cbn
Verify volume and initialize maps
Dump    date: Mon Jan 04 16:08:20 1999
Dumped from: the epoch
Level 0 dump of / on curtis:/dev/dsk/c0t3d0s0
Label: none
Begin level 0 restore
Initialize symbol table.
Extract directories from tape
Calculate extraction list.
Warning: ./lost+found: File exists
Warning: ./var: File exists
......restore a whole bunch of files......
Make node ./usr
Make node ./usr/lib
Make node ./usr/lib/lp
Add links
Set directory mode, owner, and times.
Check the symbol table.
Check pointing the restore
```

Now that the / filesystem is restored, we can mount the /var filesystem and restore it too:

```
# mount /dev/dsk/c0t1d0s6 /mnt/var
```

```
# df -k /mnt/var
Filesystem          kbytes    used   avail capacity  Mounted on
/dev/dsk/c0t3d0s1   124415       9  111965     1%    /mnt/var
```

```
# cd /mnt/var
```

```
# pwd
/mnt/var
```

So we mounted it, *cd*ed into it, and used *pwd* to make sure we're there before we do anything else. Since we're not sure where the tape ended up after the last *restore* command,* we'll rewind and fast forward it to the third file on the tape (*fsf 2*):

```
# mt -t /dev/rmt/0cbn rewind
```

```
# mt -t /dev/rmt/0cbn fsf 2
```

We can now use *ufsrestore* to restore the */var* filesystem into */mnt/var*:

```
# ufsrestore rbvfy 64 /dev/rmt/0cbn
Verify volume and initialize maps
Dump  date: Mon Jan 04 16:34:25 1999
Dumped from: the epoch
Level 0 dump of /var on curtis:/dev/dsk/c0t3d0s1
Label: none
Begin level 0 restore
Initialize symbol table.
Extract directories from tape
Calculate extraction list.
Warning: ./lost+found: File exists
Make node ./sadm
Make node ./sadm/install
extract file ./sadm/pkg/SUNWipc/pkginfo
.....restore a whole bunch of files......
Add links
Set directory mode, owner, and times.
Check the symbol table.
Check pointing the restore
```

The / and */var* filesystems are now restored to the new root disk. The final step is to install the boot block information on the new root disk. This is done using the *installboot* command:

```
# installboot /usr/platform/`uname -i`/lib/fs/ufs/bootblk /dev/rdsk/c0t0d0s0
```

The system is now fully recovered. Just to prove it, it's time to reboot:

```
# reboot
syncing filesystems... done
rebooting...
Resetting ...
SPARCstation 10MP (2 X 390Z55), No Keyboard
ROM Rev. 2.10, 128 MB memory installed, Serial #31xx899.
Ethernet address 8:0:23:7c:fb:b, Host ID: 72xxxecb.
```

---

* This will depend on whether you use a Berkeley- or AT&T-style device. In Solaris, the Berkeley-style devices have a *b* in their name (e.g., */dev/rmt/0cbn*). When a program like *restore* closes a Berkeley-style device, the device stops right where it is. When a program closes an AT&T-style device, it automatically fast-forwards to the next partition.

```
Initializing Memory
Boot device: /iommu/sbus/espdma@f,400000/esp@f,800000/sd@3,0
File and args:
Copyright (c) 1983-1997, Sun Microsystems, Inc.
Hostname: curtis
The system is coming up. Please wait.
```

We're done!

8

Linux

Like many other things in the Linux world, the ease with which you can do a bare-metal recovery will depend on your configuration. If you are running Linux on an Intel-based system, have a parallel-port Zip drive, and can fit a compressed copy of your operating system on that Zip drive, you're in luck! That's the configuration I used to test this recovery procedure.

Chances are, of course, that your configuration is slightly different than this. If you are running Linux on an Intel-based system, this procedure will work for you without modification. If you're running Linux on a Sparc system, you will need to use a different boot floppy and *silo* instead of *lilo*. If you are using an Alpha version of Linux, your options are a bit more complicated.

How It Works

Most Linux administrators are familiar with the typical bare-metal recovery answer: install a minimal operating system and recover on top of it. However, this answer presents the same problems for Linux systems that it does for other versions of Unix—it takes too long, you could run into open-file conflicts, and it is difficult to document and recover operating system customizations.

Like the other bare-metal recovery procedures in this book, this procedure does not require a reinstallation of the operating system in order to recover it. It is based on a homegrown procedure, which breaks down into six major steps, and *will work with any Intel-based Linux distribution*:

1. Back up the important metadata.

2. Back up the operating system with a native utility.

3. Boot from alternate media.

4. Partition and format the new root disk.

5. Restore the operating system information.

6. Restore the boot block to the new root disk.

Back Up the Important Metadata

The first important piece of information that you need to save is the metadata. Metadata is the information about how the system is physically configured—specifically, how the root disk is partitioned. This information is not typically included in a normal backup.

To save this information, run the command *fdisk -l* and redirect the output to a file that will be included in the backup of the operating system. You also might want to keep a copy of the */etc/fstab* in an alternate location. If you create these files prior to running your operating system backup and place them in an easy-to-find location, you will be able to easily retrieve this data if you need it.

Back Up the Operating System with a Native Utility

If you are going to restore the operating system without reinstalling it, you will need to use a utility that is easily available. In this case, you need to use a backup and recovery utility that is available on a *rescue floppy*. (Rescue floppies are special floppies designed to help boot and rebuild a Linux box when it becomes damaged.) Both *tar* and *cpio* were available on the rescue floppy that I chose, but they were actually links to *pax*. (*pax* will emulate both *tar* and *cpio*.) I prefer *tar*'s syntax, so that is what I used to create the backup.* Since *gzip* also was available, I compressed the backup so that it would easily fit on the media.

Speaking of media, you must decide where you are going to back up your operating system. You need to back it up to something that you can access from a rescue floppy. It doesn't do any good to make a backup to a tape drive that you can't access during a recovery! If you have a tape drive and a SCSI card that is supported by one of these rescue floppies, you're set. In my case, I had a parallel-port Zip drive, and its driver was available on the rescue floppy. Since a compressed *pax* backup was only 68 MB, this was perfect for me.

If you can't figure out how to use your tape drive or other backup device from a rescue floppy, you may consider backing up to an NFS or SMB (CIFS) partition. Many of these floppies support mounting an NFS or SMB filesystem. This means that you would boot from the rescue floppy, mount the NFS or SMB filesystem to

---

* This causes *pax* to make a *tar* image instead of a *pax* image.

the system to be recovered, and then use *gzip* and *pax* to recovery the operating system.

In summary, there are three things that matter when deciding on a method of backing up the operating system:

- Make sure that the backup utility you use is available on your rescue floppy.
- Make sure that the backup utility you use is able to recover special files and named pipes, since such files will be found within the operating system. (*pax* will do this for you.)
- Make sure that the backup media you use is supported by your rescue floppy.

Boot the System from Alternate Media

In order to easily recover your operating system, you will need a "miniroot," or limited root shell where you can run *fdisk*, *mkfs*, *gzip*, and *pax/tar/cpio*, or whatever. You also will need support for whatever backup media you have chosen. This functionality is provided via rescue floppies. These floppies contain a minimal version of Linux and all of the recovery utilities listed previously. They also have several drivers for popular backup media, such as parallel-port Zip drives, SCSI tape drives, NFS, and SMB.

Intel Linux

A list of Intel rescue floppies may be found at *http://metalab.unc.edu/pub/Linux/ system/recovery*. The rescue floppy that I chose to use was *tomsrtbt* and can be found at *http://www.toms.net/rb*. Just look at all the drivers and utilities that you get on one floppy:

The 2.0.36 kernel, 3c589_cs, BusLogic, CVF, DEC_ELCP, EEXPRESS, EEXPRESS_ PRO, EL2, EL3, EXT2, FAT, FAT32, FD, IDE, IDECD, IDEFLOPPY, IDEPCMCIA, IDETAPE, ISO9660, JOLIET, LOOP, MATH_EMULATION, MINIX, MSDOS, NE2000, NFS, PROC, RAM, SD, SERIAL, SLIP, SMC, SR, TR, ULTRA, VFAT, VORTEX, WD80x3, ah152x_cs, aha152x, aha1542, aic7xxx, *ash, awk, badblocks, bdflush, bZip2, cardbus, cardmgr, cat, ce, ce.help, chattr, chgrp, chmod, chown, chroot, clear, cmp, cp, cpio, cut, date, dd, ddate, debugfs, df, dirname, dmesg, dmsdos, ds, du, dumpe2fs, dutil, e2fsck, eata, echo, egrep, elvis, emacs, extend, false, fdflush, fdformat, fdisk, fdomain, filesize, find, fmt, fsck.ext2, fsck.msdos, fstab, grep, gzip, halt, head, hexedit, hostname, i82365, ifconfig, ifport, ile, init, inittab, insmod, kill, killall5, ksyms, length, less, libc.so.5.4.13, lilo, lilo.conf, ln, loadkeys, login, losetup, ls, lsattr, mawk, memtest, mingetty, miterm, mkdir, mkdosfs, mke2fs, mkfifo, mkfs,minix, mklost+found, mknod, mkswap, mnsed, more, mount, mt, mv, nc, ncr53c8xx, nmclan_cs, ntfs, pax, pcmcia, pcmcia_core, pcnet_cs, ping, plip, ppa, printf, ps, pwd, qlogic_cs, qlogicfas, reboot, reset, rm, rmdir, rmmod, route, rsh, rshd, script, scsi_info, seagate, sed, serial_cs, setserial, sh, slattach, sleep, slip, snarf, sort, split, stty, swapoff, swapon, sync, tail, tar, tcic, tee, telnet, test, touch, tune2fs, umount, update, vi, vi.help,* and *wc.*

If the driver that you need is not available on the default floppy, Tom Oehser has compiled a huge set of drivers that you can use to build your own custom floppy and has included instructions on how to do so. He even tells me that it is possible to build a "rescue CD" that could contain all of these drivers for use anywhere, but I don't think it has been done. Needless to say, I was quite impressed with *tomsrtbt* and have included it on the CD-ROM. Tom deserves quite a bit of credit for developing such a good tool. He asked that I include this disclaimer:

```
*************************************************************************
* If you base something on it, use any of the scripts, distribute binaries or *
* libraries from it, or distribute customized versions of it: You must credit *
* tomsrtbt and include a pointer to http://www.toms.net/rb/ and tom@toms.net, *
* and include this notice verbatim. Copyright Tom Oehser 1999. This notice in *
* no way supercedes or nullifies any other protections on the component parts *
* such as the BSD and GPL copyrights which apply to practically everything!!! *
* Within these strictures you may redistribute, incorporate, copy, modify, or *
* do anything else to it or with it that you like. Tomsrtbt has no warranties *
* not even implied fitness or usefulness. If it breaks you keep both pieces. *
*************************************************************************
```

Once you boot from your rescue floppy, you can perform the rest of this procedure from a fully functional root shell.

Sparc Linux

There is a rescue floppy for UltraLinux (the new name of the Sparc Linux port) at *ftp://vger.rutgers.edu/pub/linux/Sparc/rescue*. It contains all of the necessary utilities to boot into a miniroot, partition the root drive, and restore the boot block image. To use this rescue floppy, simply insert it into the Sparc floppy drive and enter `boot floppy`. Once it prompts for the root image floppy, swap floppies and press Return. *tar, cpio, gzip,* and *silo* will all be available.

Alpha Linux

Debian Linux comes with a rescue floppy that you can use to boot into a miniroot, and you can use this floppy to recover any type of distribution. (Once you get into the miniroot, you can restore your distribution, even though you've booted from a Debian floppy.) You can find the current image at *ftp://ftp.debian.org/debian/dists/ stable/main/disks-i386/current*. How you actually boot your system with this floppy depends on which type of firmware you are using. Updated information about how to boot each type of firmware can be found in the *README* file in the preceding FTP directory. Once you have booted the system to a miniroot, you can use *tar, cpio, gzip,* or *silo* to recover your system.

Partition and Format the New Root Drive

Since you saved a copy of how the root disk was partitioned, you will be able to partition the new root drive the same way. The way to do this is with *fdisk*. Unfortunately, many people are becoming less familiar with *fdisk* and more familiar with the Disk Druid. (Disk Druid is another interface that allows you to partition your disk, and is much more user friendly than *fdisk*.) Since Disk Druid is not available on the rescue floppies, you will need to learn how *fdisk* works. An example of how to use *fdisk* is included later in this chapter.

After you have repartitioned the root drive, you'll need to use *mkfs* to recreate the root filesystem(s). Finally, you are ready to restore the data.

Restore the Operating System to the New Root Disk

First, you must have access to the backed-up data. On the system on which I tested this procedure, the *ppa* driver was already loaded, and I just needed to mount the Zip drive as a filesystem. You may have to do one of the following:

- Mount a Zip or Jaz drive as a filesystem.
- Load drivers for your SCSI card and tape drive.
- Load network and NFS drivers, configure your network interface, and mount an NFS filesystem.
- Load network and SMB drivers, configure your network interface, and mount an SMB filesystem.
- Use *pax* to spread the backup of your operating system across 200 floppies.*

My backup was made with *pax* (emulating *tar*) and *gzip*, to a Zip drive. The drivers and tools that I needed to do this were all available on *tomsrtbt*. There is an example later in this chapter that shows how to restore the operating system without reinstalling it.

Restore the Boot Block Information

The boot block is a special part of the disk that is used to load the operating system by its "bootstraps." It contains just enough executable code to locate and load the kernel. In Linux Intel situations, this boot block is referred to as the Master Boot Record (MBR), and you can restore it using the *lilo* command.

Although this restore is as simple as running *lilo*, you will not be able to use the *lilo* command provided on *tomsrtbt*; since that version probably is not the same as

---

* I remember when we were *forced* to load SVR3 like this on the AT&T 3B2s. Boy, was *that* fun!

the one on the restored root disk. If the restored operating system disk was mounted on */root*, you will need to run *chroot /root /sbin/lilo*. (If your version of *lilo* isn't in */sbin*, you will have to use the full path for your particular version.) This command performs a *chroot* to */root*, then reads */etc/lilo.conf* to determine what to put in the master boot block. It then rebuilds the boot block for you.

Once this is done, you're ready to remove the floppy and boot the restored system.

A Sample Bare-Metal Recovery

This example uses *pax* (emulating *tar*), *gzip*, *fdisk*, *lilo*, and *tomsrtbt* to back up and recover a complete Linux system on an (Intel) Toshiba Satellite Pro laptop.

Performing the Backup

As mentioned earlier, I backed up the metadata by running the command:

```
# fdisk -l >/etc/fdisk-l.txt
```

We then backed up the operating system using *pax* (emulating *tar*) to a Zip drive mounted on */backup*:

```
# cd / ; tar cf - . |gzip -c >/backup/root.tar.gz
```

Now it's time to blow it up! The following *dd* command blows away both the *lilo* boot block and the disk's partition information. Although the root filesystem is still there, we couldn't find it if we wanted to!

```
# dd if=/dev/zero of=/dev/hda bs=512 count=1
# reboot
Insert system disk in drive
Press any key when ready.
```

Perform the Recovery

As mentioned in the preceding explanation, we will need to boot the system, partition its drives, create the root filesystem, restore the system, and reinstall the boot image.

Boot the system

The first step in recovering this system is to place the *tomsrtbt* floppy into the floppy drive and press any key. Here's what it displays while it is booting:

```
Welcome to tomsrtbt-1.7.134

http://www.toms.net/rb
```

```
        #####
       #######
       ##O#O##
       #VVVVV#
     ##  VVV  ##
    #            ##
    #            ##          ~
    #            ###        . .
   QQ#          ##Q        /V\
 QQQQQQ#      #QQQQQQ     // \\
 QQQQQQQ#     #QQQQQQ    /(   )\
  QQQQQ#######QQQQ       ^`~'^
```

```
Other distributions      tomsrtbt
(15 seconds...)


boot:


Loading zImage.............
Press <RETURN> to see video modes available, <SPACE> to continue or wait 30 secs


Uncompressing Linux.............


...<extra messages deleted>...


ppa: Communication established with ID 6 using PS/2
ppa: Probing port 0278
scsi0 : Iomega parport ZIP drive
scsi : 1 host.
   Vendor: IOMEGA      Model: ZIP 100         Rev: J.03
   Type:   Direct-Access                      ANSI SCSI revision: 02
Detected scsi removable disk sda at scsi0, channel 0, id 6, lun 0
SCSI device sda: hdwr sector= 512 bytes. Sectors= 196608 [96 MB] [0.1 GB]


...<extra messages deleted>...


...Login as root.  Remove the floppy.  AltF1-AltF4 for consoles.


tty1 tomsrtbt login: root


The default "root" password is "xxxx",
edit /etc/passwd ro change it, or edit
settings.s to change it permanently


Password:


Today is Pungenday, the 19th day of Bureaucracy in the YOLD 3165
#
```

The Discordian Calendar

Notice the date displayed in the final line of *tomsrtbt*'s login message. I had to ask myself, what in the world is "Pungenday"?! As usual, the Web knows everything. Since I know that my fellow Linux users are going to want to know, here's the answer, from the *Principia Discordia*:a

> The Discordian calendar divides the year into five seasons (commonly known as Chaos, Discord, Confusion, Bureaucracy and the Aftermath) of 73 days each. Every four years, an extra day (St. Tib's Day) is inserted between Chaos 59 and Chaos 60.

> The Discordian calendar defines a week as having five days, named Sweetmorn, Boomtime, Pungenday, Prickle-Prickle, and Setting Orange (after the Five Elements). Chaos 1 is always Sweetmorn, Chaos 2 Boomtime, The Aftermath 73 Setting Orange, etc. St. Tib's Day is none of the five days of the week.

> The Discordian calendar's year 0 (notionally the time of the Original Snub) is known in the Gregorian calendar as 1166 BC; alternatively, the Gregorian year 0 (notionally the birth of the Jewish mystic Yeshua ben Yosef) is known as 1166 YOLD in the Discordian calendar. The year known in the Gregorian calendar as 1995 is known as 3161 in the Discordian calendar.

I had to ask.

---

a. The *Principia* is in the public domain.

Restore the partition information

Since we need to repartition the root disk, we need to know what it looked like. In order to do that, we need to mount the Zip drive and restore the files that contain this information. (The Zip drive shows up as */dev/sda4*.)

```
# mount /dev/sda4 /mnt

# ls -l /mnt
# ls -lt /mnt/*gz
-rw-r--r--   1 root     root      41393598 Aug 24 00:21 /mnt/root.tar.gz
# gzip -dc /mnt/root.tar.gz|tar xvf - ./etc/fstab ./etc/fdisk-1.txt
Tar: blocksize = 20
./etc/fstab
./etc/fdisk-1.txt

# cat /etc/fdisk-1.txt

Disk /dev/hda: 64 heads, 63 sectors, 658 cylinders
Units = cylinders of 4032 * 512 bytes
```

```
    Device Boot    Start    End   Blocks   Id  System
/dev/hda1    *        1     225   453568+  83  Linux native
/dev/hda2            226     658   872928    5  Extended
/dev/hda5            226     308   167296+  82  Linux swap
```

Partition the new root drive

Now that we know what the old disk looked like, we will partition the new disk. To demonstrate that the label is gone, I will display the current partition table, which is empty. Then I will add a primary partition, an extended partition, and a logical partition inside the extended partition.

```
# dd if=/dev/zero of=/dev/hda1 bs=1024 count=1

# fdisk /dev/hda

Command (m for help): p

Disk /dev/hda: 64 heads, 63 sectors, 658 cylinders
Units = cylinders of 4032 * 512 bytes

    Device Boot     Start       End   Blocks    Id  System

Command (m for help): n
Command action
   e   extended
   p   primary partition (1-4)
p
Partition number (1-4): 1
First cylinder (1-658): 1
Last cylinder or +size or +sizeM or +sizeK ([1]-658): 225

Command (m for help): n
Command action
   e   extended
   p   primary partition (1-4)
e
Partition number (1-4): 2
First cylinder (226-658): 226
Last cylinder or +size or +sizeM or +sizeK ([226]-658): 658

Command (m for help): n
Command action
   l   logical (5 or over)
   p   primary partition (1-4)
l
First cylinder (226-658): 226
Last cylinder or +size or +sizeM or +sizeK ([226]-658): 608

Command (m for help): p

Disk /dev/hda: 64 heads, 63 sectors, 658 cylinders
Units = cylinders of 4032 * 512 bytes
```

```
   Device Boot    Start     End   Blocks   Id  System
/dev/hda1             1     225   453568+  83  Linux native
/dev/hda2           226     658   872928    5  Extended
/dev/hda5           226     608   772096+  82  Linux native
```

Change the partition types

Now that we have correctly sized the partitions, there are two remaining issues. First, we must change the partition type of */dev/hda5* to "Linux Swap" (with the *t* option) and set the bootable flag on */dev/hda1* (with the *a* option):

```
Command (m for help): t
Partition number (1-5): 5
Hex code (type L to list codes): 82
Changed system type of partition 5 to 82 (Linux swap)

Command (m for help): a
Partition number (1-5): 1

Command (m for help): p

Disk /dev/hda: 64 heads, 63 sectors, 658 cylinders
Units = cylinders of 4032 * 512 bytes

   Device Boot    Start     End   Blocks   Id  System
/dev/hda1   *         1     225   453568+  83  Linux native
/dev/hda2           226     658   872928    5  Extended
/dev/hda5           226     608   772096+  82  Linux swap
```

You can see in the preceding that the bootable flag is now set, and partition five is configured as Linux Swap. Now that we have correctly sized and configured the partitions, we need to write the disk label to the disk:

```
Command (m for help): w
The partition table has been altered!

Calling ioctl() to re-read partition table.
Syncing disks.

WARNING: If you have created or modified any DOS 6.x
partitions, please see the fdisk manual page for additional
information.
```

Make a filesystem on the root drive

Now that the disk has been properly partitioned and labeled, we need to create a filesystem on it with the *mke2fs* command. When we are done, we can mount the new root filesystem.

```
# mke2fs /dev/hda1
mke2fs 1.10, 24-Apr-97 for EXT2 FS 0.5b, 95/08/09
Linux ext2 filesystem format
Filesystem label=
```

```
113792 inodes, 453568 blocks
22678 blocks (5.00%) reserved for the super user
First data block=1
Block size=1024 (log=0)
Fragment size=1024 (log=0)
56 block groups
8192 blocks per group, 8192 fragments per group
2032 inodes per group
Superblock backups stored on blocks:
        8193, 16385, 24577, 32769, 40961, 49153, 57345, 65537, 73729,
        81921, 90113, 98305, 106497, 114689, 122881, 131073, 139265, 147457,
        155649, 163841, 172033, 180225, 188417, 196609, 204801, 212993, 221185,
        229377, 237569, 245761, 253953, 262145, 270337, 278529, 286721, 294913,
        303105, 311297, 319489, 327681, 335873, 344065, 352257, 360449, 368641,
        376833, 385025, 393217, 401409, 409601, 417793, 425985, 434177, 442369,
        450561

Writing inode tables:
Writing superblocks and filesystem accounting information: done

# mkdir /root

# mount /dev/hda1 /root

# mount /dev/hda1 /root
# df -k
Filesystem          1024-blocks  Used Available Capacity Mounted on
/dev/ram0                   798   776        22      97%  /
/dev/ram1                  2546  2440       106      96%  /usr
/dev/ram3                  4049     3      4046       0%  /tmp
/dev/sda4                 95167 41094     49159      46%  /mnt
/dev/hda1                439063    13    416372       0%  /root
```

Restore the operating system

We are now ready to actually restore the operating system. We will *cd* to */root* and use *gzip* and *pax* (emulating *tar*) to restore from the backup file on the Zip disk.

```
# cd /root
# ls -lt /mnt/*gz
-rw-r--r--   1 root     root     41393598 Aug 24 00:21 /mnt/root.tar.gz
# gzip -dc /mnt/root.tar.gz|tar xf -
Tar: blocksize = 20
```

Restore the master boot record

Now that the root filesystem is restored, we need to restore the *lilo* boot block. Making this work was tricky. We cannot use the *lilo* command on *tomsrtbt*, and we cannot run the *lilo* command on the root file system directly without it complaining. It needs to run it inside an environment where it thinks */root* is actually */*. The way to do this is to run the command *chroot /root* prior to running the *lilo* command:

```
# chroot /root /sbin/lilo
Added linux *

# reboot
```

We're done! Remember, make sure that you test this procedure before you need it.

9

Compaq Tru64 Unix

This chapter explains the procedure that you would use to recover your Compaq Tru64 Unix operating system disk in case of a complete system failure—when you are left with nothing but bare metal. For suggestions on how to avoid this situation, please read the first section of Chapter 7, *SunOS/Solaris*.

Compaq Tru64 Unix, also known as Digital Unix, is a Unix-compatible operating system based on the Mach kernel and is the main survivor of the Open Software Foundation. It is different in a number of ways from Solaris, AIX, and HP-UX. During OS installs or during backup and restores, one difference shows up quickly: there are two different filesystems supported by Compaq Unix. First, there is UFS (Unix File System), which is commonly found on many other Unix flavors. Second, there is Digital's proprietary filesystem known as the AdvFS (Advanced File System). AdvFS provides a journaled filesystem, cloning, volume management, and other advanced features.

I would advise against using AdvFS on the operating system partitions. There are a number of reasons, but the first is the most compelling: during a bare-metal recovery, simplicity is a virtue. Unless you're very comfortable with AdvFS, it isn't simple. The primary advantage of AdvFS is that you are dealing with large data volumes rather than the relatively small and static OS partitions. Also, until very recently AdvF still had a number of bugs that could jeopardize the stability of a system.

Another difference is that Digital has software upgradable firmware, similar to Sun's OpenBoot PROM, which supports, depending on the hardware, booting NT, Compaq Unix, or OpenVMS. During any operating system upgrade, make sure to upgrade the firmware also. This firmware, also known as the "console," is like a minioperating system; it provides for configuration, diagnostics, and booting. During a bare-metal recovery, you need to be familiar with the firmware console.

This chapter was written by Matthew Huff, director of operations at OTA Limited Partnership. Matthew has worked as a computer professional since 1987 and specializes in complex cross-platform system architecture. He can be reached at *mhuff@ox.com*.

Compaq's btcreate Utility

Digital provides a system, similar to IBM's *mksysb*, which creates a bootable tape designed to shorten the time it takes to completely restore a system. The tape consists of a tape boot block, a specialized kernel, a stripped-down operating system, and a backup of your system partitions. Once it is created, complete restores are as simple as booting the prepared tape from the console:

```
>>> init
>>> show dev
>>> boot -fl "nc" MKA400
```

You should create such a tape after a new system has been completely configured and after any major is made. Because the facility utilizes *dump* or *vdump*, the normal caveats apply. Ideally, you should create the tape while the system is in single-user mode. This, however, restricts the ability to automate the process.

The btcreate Command

The command to create the bootable tape is */usr/sys/bin/btcreate*. If you run the command without any parameters, it prompts you for the missing information. First, it asks you for a kernel configuration file to use; make sure the kernel it creates will have the correct configuration for the devices that you need during a restore. Next, it asks whether to use a memory filesystem (ramdisk) to load the operating system during the restore. If you don't use the memory filesystem, you need to specify a partition to use (typically, the swap partition). Also, the command asks the device address of the tape drive you wish to use. Finally, it asks which partitions to dump and append to the bootable tape. Since once you have the OS completely restored, you can easily use your standard recovery tools, so it is best to specify only the OS partitions for the bootable tape.

If you don't want to use the interactive prompt, you need to specify at least the *-f*, *-k*, *-m*, *-t*, and *-s* flags:

- The *-f* flag forces *btcreate* to overwrite an existing filesystem.

- The *-k* flag specifies the name of the kernel configuration file in */usr/sys/conf*.

- The *-m* flag allows you to specify a memory filesystem or a partition to use during the restore.

- The *-t* flag specifies the device to back up to.

- The *-s* flag allows you to specify a file that contains a list of filesystems to back up.

Each line of the file must specify the device name, mount point, and type (UFS or AdvFS):

```
# /usr/sys/bin/btcreate -f -k ALAMO -m mfs -t nrmt1h -s /nfsdrive/btcreate.alamo
```

Using the Bootable Tape

Once you boot from the tape, it loads the kernel and the miniversion of Compaq Unix. It then starts */sbin/btextract* to begin the restore. It prompts whether to perform a default or advanced restore. Be careful: with a default restore you cannot choose which partitions to restore it restores every one that was specified in the file used for *btcreate*. The advanced restore prompts you for parameters including which partitions to restore.

Homegrown Bare-Metal Recovery

If you are in a heterogeneous environment with other, different Unix systems such as Sun, HP, or IBM, you might want to use a consistent method for bare-metal recovery among all your machines. This section shows how the homegrown recovery procedure described in the previous chapter can be applied, providing a complete custom bare-metal recovery plan for Compaq Unix. In addition, Digital provides a very powerful proprietary system for bare-metal recovery that has many advantages and is covered in the next section.

Before Disaster Strikes

Like most bare-metal recovery procedures, you are required to do a few things up front in order to protect yourself from such a disaster:

1. If you are going to replace the root disk with another one without reinstalling the OS, you will have to partition the new disk the same way the old one was partitioned. The only way you are going to know that is to save this partitioning information. (It also would help if all your OS disks were partitioned in the same way.) You can use *disklabel* to print the current partition information:

```
# disklabel -r raw-disk-device
```

2. Save the */etc/fstab* file. (This file is very useful when trying to rebuild a system from scratch.)

3. If you are using AdvFS, save the */etc/fdmns* directory structure:

   ```
   # tar cf /nfsdrive/fdmns.systemname.tar /etc/fdmns
   ```

4. Send this information to a centralized system, or more than one centralized system, so you can access it if any server becomes unavailable. One of the best ways to do this is via email.

 The best way to do the first four steps is to use *SysAudit** from *cron* and save this information in a file every day. This file can be printed to paper or copied to multiple locations for later reference.

---

5. Back up the OS. An easy way to accomplish this would be to use the program *hostdump.sh*. For example, suppose that the operating system is contained in the filesystems */*, */usr*, and */var*. To back up these filesystems with *hostdump.sh*, enter the following command:

   ```
   # hostdump.sh 0 device logfile hostname:/ hostname:/usr hostname:/var
   ```

If you are backing up an AdvFS filesystem, be aware that *vdump* uses a small percentage of the partition to store information. If that filesystem is very near 100%, *vdump* might not be able to dump that partition, especially if you are using the *-x* option. (The *-x* option provides tape checksums, which, while slowing normal backups somewhat, are a very good feature and should be used.)

Step 5 creates a single tape that contains a full backup of */*, */usr*, and */var* from `hostname`. Send this backup offsite for safekeeping, keeping an onsite copy for quick restores.

After Disaster

If you followed the preceding steps, you should be able to easily recover from the loss of an operating system drive:

1. Replace the root drive with a drive that is as big as, or bigger than, the original root drive. (Past experience has shown that the closer you stay to the same drive architecture, the better chance of success you will have.)

2. If your original disk was close to 100 percent utilized, you will need a larger partition than the original.

3. Determine the name of the console device.

---

* SysAudit and *hostdump.sh* are on the CD-ROM, and are available at *http://www.backupcentral.com*.

In order to boot an alphastation or alphaserver from CD-ROM, you will need the name of the console device. The console of Digital's alphastations and alphaservers has a different naming scheme than Compaq Unix. The main reasons for this is because you can run NT, Compaq Unix, or OpenVMS on the same hardware. Each operating system has, of course, its own dissimilar device names and structures.

Here is sample output from an alphastation:

```
>>>show device
```

BOOTDEV	ADDR	DEVTYPE	NUMBYTES	RM/FX	WP	DEVNAME	REV
ESA0	08-00-2B-39-78-99 , TENBT						
DKA300	A/3/0	DISK	1.05GB	FX	.	RZ26L	440C
MKA400	A/4/0	TAPE		RM		TZ87	971B
DKA600	A/6/0	RODISK	655.97MB	RM	WP	RRD43	0064
...HostID	A/7	INITR					

The device name, listed in the BOOTDEV column, is the label you use for booting, diagnostics, etc.; it is created from a combination of the device type and address. The first two characters are based on the device type (DEVTYPE column):

DK Individual SCSI disks, IDE devices masquerading as SCSI devices, or external RAID controllers

DR Internal RAID controllers

MK Individual SCSI tapes

JK Jukebox SCSI media changers

DV Floppies

ES, EW
    Ethernet

PK SCSI controllers

The third character is based on the controller, i.e., A for the first controller, B for the second, and so on. The remaining digits indicate a sequence number. For SCSI, they are based on the SCSI ID and SCSI LUN. LUNs are used mainly for large drive arrays or media changers. Normal SCSI devices also have a LUN of 00. For example, DKA300 would be a SCSI disk on controller A with a SCSI ID of 3 and a LUN of 00.

Other console variables can be listed by the *show* command at the console or by using *consvar -l* under Compaq Unix.

4. Boot the system to the "Install Unix Shell" using the operating System install CD-ROM.

```
>>> init
>>> show dev
>>> boot DKA600
```

5. Select "Unix Shell" from either the text or graphical interface.

6. If the drive was partitioned with the default layout for that particular Digital drive type, use the *-rw* option of *disklabel* to partition the drive. The *disklabel* utility requires that you specify what type of filesystem the root partition is so that it can write the correct boot block on the disk:

```
# for UFS root partitions
# disklabel -rw -t ufs device digital_drive_type
# for AdvFS root partitions
# disklabel -rw -t advfs device digital_drive_type
```

If you had a custom partition table, you will have to use *vi* to edit the partition table:

```
# for UFS root partitions
# disklabel -rz -t ufs device digital_drive_type
# for AdvFS root partitions
# disklabel -rz -t advfs device digital_drive_type
# disklabel -re device
```

7. If you have a third-party drive, there is an undocumented trick to setting up the partition table. *disklabel* can be made to use the SCSI geometry command to scan the disk and set a default partition. Instead of specifying the Digital drive type, you use the device twice. This forces *disklabel* to read the SCSI geometry:

```
# for UFS root partitions
# disklabel -rz -t ufs device device
# for AdvFS root partition
# disklabel -rz -t advfs device device
# disklabel -re device
```

8. Create a new root filesystem on the disk:

```
# for UFS partition
# newfs /dev/raw_device digital_drive_type
# for UFS partition
# fsck /dev/raw_device
# for AdvFS partition
# mkfdmn -t digital_drive_type /dev/raw_device root_domain
# for AdvFS partition
# mkfset root_domain root
```

9. Create a mount point:

```
# mkdir /var/mnt
```

10. Restore the root OS backup to */var/mnt*. If you are using something other than *hostdump.sh*, follow its procedure. If using *hostdump.sh*, follow this procedure. First you need to get the electronic label from the tape.

a. Rewind the tape:

```
# mt -t /dev/rmt0h rewind
```

b. Use *tar* to extract the label from the tape:

```
# tar xvf /dev/nrmt0h   #Remember to use the no-rewind device.
```

c. Read */tmp/BACKUP.LABEL* to find out which file(s) on the volume contain(s) the filesystem(s) you need to restore.

d. Fast-forward to the first tape file that contains the root filesystem that you want to restore. For this example, the first *dump* file is the one we want, so it's the second file on the tape.

```
#Remember to use the no-rewind device.
# mt -t /dev/nrmt0h fsf 1
```

e. Restore the root partition.

11. Mount the root partition:

```
# for UFS partition
# mount /dev/device /var/mnt
# for AdvFS partition
# mount root_domain#root /var/mnt
```

12. *cd* to the filesystem you want to restore:

```
# cd /var/mnt
```

13. Use the appropriate command to restore that filesystem:

```
# for backups that used dump
# restore -Yrf /dev/rmt0h
# for backups that used vdump
# vrestore -vxf /dev/rmt0h
```

14. *Unmount* restore root filesystem:

```
# unmount /var/mnt
```

15. Halt the system:

```
# sync; halt
```

16. Boot to single-user mode:

```
>>> init
>>> show dev
>>> boot -fl "s" DKA300
```

Restore remaining filesystems. Since the definitions of the AdvFS domains and filesets are stored on the root partitions in */etc/fdmns*, no more AdvFS configuration is necessary.

17. Prepare the */usr* partition:

```
# for UFS partition
# newfs /dev/raw_device digital_drive_type
# for UFS partition
# fsck /dev/raw_device
```

18. Rewind the tape:

    ```
    # mt -t /dev/rmt0h rewind
    ```

19. Use *tar* to extract the label from the tape:

    ```
    #Remember to use the no-rewind device.
    # tar xvf /dev/nrmt0h
    ```

20. Read */tmp/BACKUP.LABEL* to find out which file(s) on the volume contain(s) the filesystem(s) you need to restore.

21. Fast-forward to the first tape file that contains the filesystem that you want to restore:

    ```
    #Remember to use the no-rewind device.
    # mt -t /dev/nrmt0h fsf 2
    ```

22. Restore the */usr* partition.

23. Mount the partition:

    ```
    # for UFS partition
    # mount /usr
    # for UFS partition
    # mount domain#fileset /usr
    ```

24. *cd* to the filesystem you want to restore:

    ```
    # cd /usr
    ```

25. Use the appropriate command to restore that filesystem:

    ```
    # restore -Yrf /dev/rmt0h # for backups that used dump
    # vrestore -vxf /dev/rmt0h # for backups that used vdump
    ```

26. Repeat steps 17–22 for */var* if it is defined on another partition, rather than within */usr*.

27. Reboot:

    ```
    # shutdown --r now
    ```

10

HP-UX

This chapter explains the procedure that you would use to recover your HP-UX operating system disk in case of a complete system failure—when you are left with nothing but bare metal. For suggestions on how to avoid this situation, please read the first section of Chapter 7, *SunOS/Solaris*.

Bare-metal recovery under HP-UX 10 can be performed using tools provided by Hewlett-Packard with the operating system. Three primary options are provided, each suited to a particular situation.

Ignite-UX, included on the Applications CD, provides a tool called *make_recovery*. *make_recovery* can be used to build a bootable image of the system on a tape. When disaster strikes, the system can be booted from the backup media and rebuilt in the state in which it was saved. A significant advantage of *make_recovery* is that it can be run on a live system, thus minimizing the downtime imposed by bare-metal recovery planning. However, Ignite-UX imposes significant disk requirements and must be installed locally on each system that will be saved to tape. Furthermore, *make_recovery* cannot be used to recover a system that has already failed in service.

copyutil, provided on the CD-ROM, can be used to build an image of a system on tape, block by block. In the event of a disk failure, *copyutil* can be used to salvage the readable areas of the disk, since it will skip bad blocks during the backup phase. The image then can be restored to a new disk and any missing or corrupted files copied from other machines or restored from other conventional backup mechanisms. The primary drawback of *copyutil*, which prevents it from being useful as a production bare-metal recovery tool, is that the system must be taken down into the offline diagnostic environment to be used.

dump and *restore* are best suited to back up user data rather than entire systems and also may be used to back up data on live systems. Restoration of lost user data from a *dump* tape is reasonably straightforward. However, as shown later in this chapter, recovering a failed HP-UX system from *dump* tapes is a painful and complicated process, which requires significant planning and manual effort. See Chapter 3, *Native Backup & Recovery Utilities*, for more details on the use of *dump* and *restore*.

 This chapter was written by Steve Ferguson of Collective Technologies. Steve has developed system administration skills in both heterogeneous and HP-UX environments and can be reached at *stf@colltech.com*.

HP's make_recovery Utility

HP provides a tool with Ignite-UX called *make_recovery*, which can be used to create a bootable system recovery tape for an HP-UX system. In the event of a system failure, this tape can be booted from and will automatically restore the operating system to the state it was in at the time of the backup. Creating a system recovery tape requires that the appropriate Ignite-UX product (Ignite-UX 10–20 for HP-UX 10.20) be installed on the target system. This section lists the requirements for a recovery tape, raises some issues to consider when creating a system recovery tape, and details the use of the Ignite-UX utility *make_recovery* and the use of the recovery tape to restore a system. The *make_recovery* utility is similar to an older shell script of the same name provided with *BRAT*, an unsupported tool for creating bootable archive tapes, developed and distributed independently by a Hewlett-Packard engineer. The use of the unsupported *BRAT* utility is now obviated by the inclusion of the supported *make_recovery* in Ignite-UX.

make_recovery Requirements

The *make_recovery* utility requires that a DDS or 8-mm tape drive be attached locally to the system for which a recovery tape is created. The boot LIF volume can be assembled in an arbitrary location but requires 32 MB of free disk space in */var* for temporary storage during the initial phase of tape creation. The *make_recovery* utility requires that the following filesets of the Ignite-UX product be installed on the system:

- Ignite-UX.BOOT-KERNEL

- Ignite-UX.BOOT-SERVICES

- Ignite-UX.FILE-SRV-*release*

- Ignite-UX.MGMT-TOOLS

- Ignite-UX.IGNT-ENG-A-MAN.

release indicates the particular revision of HP-UX in use on the system and is represented by 10-01, 10-10, or 10-20. For HP-UX 10.x systems, the most recent patch for *pax*, which fixes problems with hard links, is also required.

Ignite-UX Issues

By default, *make_recovery* copies only the minimum core operating system to the tape. (You will see later how to include the entire root volume group.) The minimum core OS consists of the following files and directories:

/.profile	*/usr/conf*	*/usr/sam*
/.rhosts	*/usr/contrib*	*/usr/sbin*
/dev	*/usr/lbin*	*/usr/share*
/etc	*/usr/lib*	*/var/adm/cron*
/sbin	*/usr/local*	*/var/adm/sw*
/usr/bin	*/usr/newconfig*	*/var/opt/ignite/local/manifest*
/usr/ccs	*/usr/obam*	*/var/spool/cron*

The following files are considered a part of the minimum core OS if they are on the system:

> */opt/ignite/bin/print_manifest*
> */opt/ignite/share/man/man1m.Z/print_manifest.1m*
> */opt/upgrade*

If possible, the automounter should be shut down and any remote filesystems unmounted prior to the use of *make_recovery*. Otherwise, mount points will be written to tape and restored as directories. In the case of symbolic links created to point into the */tmp_mnt* directory, this will cause the automounter to fail to remount these systems after a restoration from tape. If this happens, shut down the automounter, unmount all remote filesystems, remove all NFS mount points, then restart the automounter.

The following important warnings are taken from the *make_recovery* man page:

> The *make_recovery* utility relies on the Installed Products Database (IPD) to extract files relevant to a product added to the system recovery tape via the "product" tag in the append file. It is only as reliable as the IPD. Only products installed via SD (Software Distributor) are logged into the IPD. It is also necessary that the SD commands be used to add, modify, remove these products, so that the IPD is correctly updated to reflect these changes. If there is any possibility that the product

has been manipulated without using SD, or that the product's installation/configuration scripts are not modifying the IPD reliably, then it is better to set up */var/opt/ignite/recovery/makrec.append* with all the filenames for the product as a one time effort.

On systems that support Large UID/GIDs or Large Files (>2 GB), the system recovery tape should be created for only the Minimum OS, and remaining user data recovered from normal backup media that support these features. The *make_recovery* utility does not directly support these features since *pax* (used to generate the archive) does not as yet support them.

The *make_recovery* utility does not support mirrored disks. V-class systems are not supported at first release.

Using Ignite-UX's make_recovery Command

The *make_recovery* command places only the core operating system on tape, as shown earlier. The most common option used with *make_recovery* is -A, which indicates that the entire root disk/volume group should be included in the system recovery tape. Because the core operating system does not include */var* and */opt*, most users will want to specify -A. Likewise, you can never be too careful when generating a bare-metal recovery image, so most users will want to specify -v, which causes *make_recovery* to generate verbose output. The -d option specifies the tape device, which defaults to */dev/rmt/0mn*. This should be specified as a nonrewinding tape device (which requires the use of the *n* suffix).

Because *make_recovery* generates a bootable image on the tape, it must assemble a boot LIF volume. This requires 32 MB of space and defaults to */var/tmp/uxinstlf. recovery*. However, this is in addition to the 32 MB of space required by the original boot image copied to */var*, which means that 64 MB of free space is required in */var*. The −b option may be used to specify an alternate location, indicating the filename to be used for the boot LIF volume assembly.

Including user data in the make_recovery tape

The *make_recovery* command generates the file */var/opt/ignite/recovery/arch. include*, which contains a line-by-line listing of all files to be put on the tape. It can be generated and modified prior to backup by using the -p option. Once the file has been tailored as necessary, the *make_recovery* run can be resumed using the -r option. One useful task that might be performed is to use *grep* to remove from the list any files from */tmp*, */var/tmp*, and */tmp_mnt* and any unnecessary user data, such as browser cache directories.

```
# make_recovery -A -p -v
# vi /var/opt/ignite/recovery/arch.include
# make_recovery -r -v -d /dev/rmt/0mn
```

It is also possible to configure *make_recovery* to include additional files, directories, and products with each backup. This is done by adding lines to the */var/opt/ ignite/recovery/makrec.append* file. The *file*, *dir*, and *product* keywords can be used in this file, one per line. As an example, to create a system recovery tape containing the root volume group, in addition to the */opt/home* directory, the */tmp/ foo* file, and the OmniBack-II product, edit the */var/opt/ignite/recovery/makrec. append* file to include the following lines:

```
dir /opt/home
file /tmp/foo
product OMNIBACK-II
file /opt/image/lib/libi1.1
dir /var/opt/omni/
```

The latter `file` and `dir` lines are pieces of OmniBack-II that should be backed up along with the product itself.

make_recovery output

Example 10-1 shows sample output from the *make_recovery* command. It assumes that the temporary boot image will be created in */tmp/uxinstlf.recovery* and that the tape device to be used is */dev/rmt/0mn*.

Example 10-1. Sample make_recovery Output

```
# make_recovery -A -v -b /tmp/uxinstlf.recovery -d /dev/rmt/0mn
Option -A specified. Entire Core Volume Group/disk will be backed up.
****************************************
HP-UX System Recovery
Validating append file.
     Done
File Systems on Core OS Disks/Volume Groups:
     vg name = vg00
     pv_name =  /dev/dsk/c0t3d0
vg00            /dev/vg00/lvol3/
vg00            /dev/vg00/lvol8/local
vg00            /dev/vg00/lvol4/opt
vg00            /dev/vg00/lvol1/stand
vg00            /dev/vg00/lvol5/tmp
vg00            /dev/vg00/lvol6/usr
vg00            /dev/vg00/lvol7/var
Create mount points
     /opt is a mounted directory
     It is in the Core Volume Group
     Mounted at /dev/vg00/lvol4
          /var is a mounted directory
     It is in the Core Volume Group
     Mounted at /dev/vg00/lvol7
Destination = /dev/rmt/0mn
Boot LIF location = /var/tmp/uxinstlf.recovery
****************************************
Creating the configuration file.
```

Example 10-1. Sample make_recovery Output (continued)

```
    Done
Modifying the configuration file.
    Done
Backing up vg configurations
    Volume Group vg00
    Done
Going to create the tape.
Processing tape
    Incoking instl_adm -T
    Creating boot LIF
    Done
    Writing boot LIF to tape /dev/rmt/0mn
    Done
    Creating archive - this may take about 30 minutes.
    Done
System Recovery Tape successfully created.
```

Recovery procedure

If a disaster occurs and the system recovery tape must be used to recover the system, the procedure is largely noninteractive. If the system does not have a tape drive, an external one should be connected and powered on prior to starting the recovery procedure.

Insert the system recovery tape in the tape drive and power the system on. Press the Escape key on a 700 series machine or the spacebar on an 800 series machine to halt the boot sequence and bring up the Boot Administration menu. Use the command *boot scsi.x.0* to boot the machine from the tape, substituting the SCSI target ID of the tape drive for *x*. To determine the SCSI ID of the tape drive on a 700 series machine, type *search scsi* at the boot administration prompt to locate a list of available SCSI devices. For an 800 series machine, type *iomap*. The system recovery will begin once the system starts booting from tape. When prompted, elect no intervention with Initial System Load (ISL). The remainder of the recovery process will complete unassisted.

The restore process then proceeds to re-create all logical volumes and filesystems, download a minisystem to disk to facilitate the restore, install all original software, and restore any data that was included in the backup.

The copyutil Utility

HP provides a bare-metal recovery tool on the HP-UX Support Media called *copyutil*. This utility is used to perform a block-by-block copy to tape of the contents of a hard drive. In the event of a failed system drive, *copyutil* may be used to create an image of any remaining readable blocks on tape, which can then be restored to a new drive. Any lost data should then be restored from standard backup media. *copyutil* is not the best choice for normal system backups, due to the fact that it requires that the system be taken completely offline. It can be used to preserve as much of the existing configuration as possible, rather than reinstalling a clean operating system from scratch. This section lists the requirements, issues to consider, and details of the use of *copyutil*.

copyutil Requirements

copyutil requires that the system be booted into the offline diagnostic environment (ODE). This means the machine will not be available for any other purpose during the backup and restore process. Booting into ODE requires the HP-UX Support Media and an appropriate device (the media is available on 4-mm DAT and CD-ROM). A tape drive with enough blank media to contain the entire disk contents is required to write the disk contents to tape. *copyutil* can span multiple tapes in the event that a single tape cannot store the entire contents of the disk to be dumped.

copyutil Issues

copyutil backups are based on physical devices, not logical volumes. In the event that a filesystem spans one or more physical volumes (as with striping or concatenation of drives), only that data residing on the physical device backed up to tape is saved. If a failure occurs in multiple physical devices, each one should be backed up and restored individually. In particular, it is not possible to use *copyutil* to back up and restore individual filesystems or volume groups (except where there is a one-to-one mapping between volume groups and physical volumes).

If a support tape is used instead of a CD, the tape must be left in the drive until a message is displayed stating that it is safe to remove the Support Media.

Using copyutil

Insert the Support Media in the drive and power the system on. Press the Escape key to halt the boot sequence and bring up the Boot Administration menu. Use the command *boot scsi.x.0 isl* to boot the machine from either CD or tape, substituting the SCSI target ID of the device used for *x*. To determine the SCSI ID of the device on a 700 series machine, type *search scsi* at the boot administration prompt to locate a list of available SCSI devices. For an 800 series machine, you would enter *iomap*.

At the ISL> prompt, type *ode copyutil* to begin. The system will display the *copyutil* start screen, shown in Example 10-2, and list all SCSI devices attached to the system. Each device is listed with an index number, which is used to refer to the device throughout the use of *copyutil*.

Example 10-2. Device Index Display of copyutil

```
ISL> ode copyutil
Please wait while I scan the device busses...
Ty Indx Path          Product ID                   Bus    Size    Rev
-- ---- -----------   --------------------------   ------ ------- ----
D  0    2/0/1.6.0     SEAGATEST32550N disk drive   SCSI   1.9 GB  0021
T  1    2/0/1.4.0     HPC1533A/C1530B tape drive   SCSI      N/A  HP00
Legend:
Ty            = Device type. 'D' for Disk; 'T' for tape.
Indx          = Index number used for referencing the device.
Rev       = Firmware Revision of the device.
Size          = Size of the Disk drive or 'N/A' for a Tape drive.
Note:         Due to different calculation methods used, the size
          of the device shown is only a rough approximation.
```

The *HELP* command can be used to list available commands with a brief synopsis of each. *UTILINFO* gives some additional details on the use of *copyutil*. *TAPEINFO* reads the header information from a created tape and displays data about the device, date, product string, and volume number. Each of the commands that refer to the physical devices on the system uses the device index rather than the device path. Use *BACKUP* to copy the data on a given disk block by block to tape. This can be a lengthy process. A 2-GB backup using standard SCSI-2 devices takes nearly two hours. If the nature of the data is critical, *VERIFY* should be used to validate that the tape and disk contents are identical. Once the backup is complete, *FORMAT* can be used to prepare a new disk for restoration of the data. The *RESTORE* command will cause the system to read the *copyutil* backup from tape and restore it to disk, block by block.

A sample output of the *copyutil* program is shown in Example 10-3.

Example 10-3. Sample Output of copyutil

```
COPYUTIL> backup
Enter the Disk Index ([q]/?): 0
Enter the Tape Index ([q]/?): 1
******************************************************************
*    Please Load into Tape Drive, Tape Volume 0 for Backup.
******************************************************************
If you have to, you may safely remove the SUPPORT MEDIA now.
Ready to continue ([y]/n/q/?): y
Checking for the beginning of tape: DONE.
..........10% completed
..........20% completed
..........30% completed
..........40% completed
..........50% completed
..........60% completed
..........70% completed
..........80% completed
..........90% completed
```

Example 10-3. Sample Output of copyutil (continued)

```
..........100% completed
End of BACKUP
Please wait while I rewind the tape
COPYUTIL> tapeinfo 1
******************************************************************
*   Please Load the Desired Tape into Tape Drive.
******************************************************************
If you have to, you may safely remove the SUPPORT MEDIA now.
Ready to continue ([y]/n/q/?): y
Checking for the beginning of tape:  DONE.
******************************************************************
            TAPE INFORMATION:
  Version:        3.00
VOLUME INFORMATION
  Volume #:       0
  Creation Date: 01/11/99 16:49:45 GMT (GMT)
DEVICE INFORMATION OF DATA SAVED
  Product ID:    SEAGATEST32550N disk drive
  Path:          2/0/1.6.0
  Device Rev:    0021
  Block Size:    512 (0x200)
  Max Block:     4194057 (0x3fff09)
******************************************************************
COPYUTIL> verify
Enter the Disk Index ([q]/?): 0
Enter the Tape Index ([q]/?): 1
******************************************************************
*   Please Load into Tape Drive, Tape Volume 0 (or the Desired Tape).
******************************************************************
If you have to, you may safely remove the SUPPORT MEDIA now.
Ready to continue ([y]/n/q/?): y
Checking for the beginning of tape:  DONE.
..........10% completed
..........20% completed
..........30% completed
..........40% completed
..........50% completed
..........60% completed
..........70% completed
..........80% completed
..........90% completed
..........100% completed
End of VERIFY
Please wait while I rewind the tape
COPYUTIL> format 0
WARNING!
Format is a destructive command.  All the data on the disk will be
lost after the format.
******************************************************************
*   About to format SEAGATEST32550N disk drive (2/0/1.6.0).
******************************************************************
DO YOU WANT TO FORMAT IT (y/[n])? y
```

Example 10-3. Sample Output of copyutil (continued)

```
SEAGATEST32550N disk drive was SUCCESSFULLY formatted.
COPYUTIL> restore
Enter the Tape Index ([q]/?): 1
Enter the Disk Index ([q]/?): 0
******************************************************************
*   Please Load into Tape Drive, Tape Volume 0 (or the Desired Tape).
******************************************************************
If you have to, you may safely remove the SUPPORT MEDIA now.
Ready to continue ([y]/n/q/?): y
Checking for the beginning of tape:   DONE.
..........10% completed
..........20% completed
..........30% completed
..........40% completed
..........50% completed
..........60% completed
..........70% completed
..........80% completed
..........90% completed
..........100% completed
End of RESTORE.
Please wait while I rewind the tape
```

Using dump and restore

While it is possible to use the standard *dump* and *restore* utilities as a bare-metal recovery mechanism, this method is significantly more difficult than the *make_recovery* method. However, it does allow for the use of remote backup devices, making it slightly easier to automate than *make_recovery*. It does require that you prepare some additional information before disaster strikes, though. At a minimum, the filesystem table should be recorded; a hardcopy of the */etc/fstab* file works well in this regard. If logical volumes (LVs) are used, the volume group and LV information should be recorded as well, using the *pvdisplay*, *vgdisplay*, and *lvdisplay* commands, in addition to a listing of the contents of the volume group device directory, as shown next. This information should be updated with each level-0 *dump* and stored with the archive tapes. This procedure is the most labor intensive of those covered in this chapter and should be used only if no other option is available. For detailed instructions on the use of the *dump* and *restore* commands, refer to Chapter 3.

The interesting information displayed by *pvdisplay* is the VG Name which is used for the volume group and should be kept consistent in all following commands that reference the volume group, though the */dev* prefix is not required unless explicitly specified.

```
# pvdisplay /dev/dsk/c0t6d0
--- Physical volumes ---
```

```
PV Name                     /dev/dsk/c0t3d0
VG Name                     /dev/vg00
PV Status                   available
Allocatable                 yes
VGDA                        2
Cur LV                      8
PE Size (Mbytes)            4
Total PE                    511
Free PE                     0
Allocated PE                511
Stale PE                    0
IO Timeout (Seconds)        default
```

The useful information provided by *vgdisplay* is the PE Size (MB), which will be used when re-creating the volume group. The default value is 4. The Max LV field, which specifies the maximum number of logical volumes that may be created in this volume group should be noted as well. The default is 255.

```
# vgdisplay vg00
--- Volume groups ---
VG Name                     /dev/vg00
VG Write Access             read/write
VG Status                   available
Max LV                      255
Cur LV                      8
Open LV                     8
Max PV                      16
Cur PV                      1
Act PV                      1
Max PE per PV               2000
VGDA                        2
PE Size (Mbytes)            4
Total PE                    511
Alloc PE                    511
Free PE                     0
Total PVG                   0
```

The notable fields returned by *lvdisplay* are LV Size (MB), Mirror copies, Stripes, Stripe Size (KB), Bad block, and Allocation.

```
# lvdisplay /dev/vg00/lvol1
--- Logical volumes ---
LV Name                     /dev/vg00/lvol1
VG Name                     /dev/vg00
LV Permission               read/write
LV Status                   available/syncd
Mirror copies               0
Consistency Recovery        MWC
Schedule                    parallel
LV Size (Mbytes)            48
Current LE                  12
Allocated PE                12
Stripes                     0
Stripe Size (Kbytes)        0
```

```
        Bad block              off
        Allocation             strict/contiguous
```

And finally, the contents of the volume group directory (the full VG Name path shown by *pvdisplay*) should be captured. The major and minor device numbers (64 and 0x000000 in the following example) should be recorded and used when re-creating the *group* device node (described later).

```
# ls -l /dev/vg00
total 0
crw-r-----   1 root       sys       64 0x000000 Dec 16 14:38 group
```

A CD-ROM drive, a tape drive, the original operating system installation CD-ROM, and the backup media (in addition to the system itself) are required to proceed with this procedure. If the system does not have either an internal CD-ROM drive or an internal tape drive, an external one should be connected and powered on before starting the restore procedure.

Preparing the System for Recovery

Insert the installation CD-ROM in the drive and power the system on. Press the Escape key or spacebar to halt the boot sequence and bring up the "Boot Administration" menu. Use the command *boot scsi.x.0* to boot the machine from the CD, substituting the SCSI target ID of the CD-ROM drive for *x*. To determine the SCSI ID of the CD-ROM drive on a series 700 machine, type *search scsi* to locate a list of available SCSI devices. To list the available devices on a series 800 machine, type *iomap*. The system will begin loading from CD after the *boot* command is issued.

```
    Command                                  Description
    -------                                  -----------
    Auto [boot|search] [on|off]              Display or set auto flag
    Boot [pri|alt|scsi.addr] [isl]           Boot from primary, alternate or SCSI
    Boot lan[.lan_addr] [install] [isl]      Boot from LAN
    Chassis [on|off]                         Enable chassis codes
    Diagnostic [on|off]                      Enable/disable diagnostic boot mode
    Fastboot [on|off]                        Display or set fast boot flag
    Help                                     Display the command menu
    Information                              Display system information
    LanAddress                               Display LAN station addresses
    Monitor [type]                           Select monitor type
    Path [pri|alt] [lan.id|SCSI.addr]        Change boot path
    Pim [hpmc|toc|lpmc]                      Display PIM info
    Search [ipl] [scsi|lan [install]]        Display potential boot devices
    Secure [on|off]                          Display or set security code
    -------------------------------------------------------------------
    BOOT_ADMIN> search scsi

    Searching for potential boot device.
    This may take several minutes.
```

```
To discontinue, press ESCAPE.

Device Path        Device Type
-----------        -----------
scsi.6.0           SEAGATE ST32550N
scsi.2.0           TOSHIBA CD-ROM XM-5401TA
```

Once the system has loaded, select a language at the prompt. Select a language from the list by entering the associated number. When the main installation menu appears, select "Run a Recovery Shell." Do not start up networking when prompted.

To create logical volumes, the logical volume manager (LVM) commands must be loaded from CD with the *loadfile* command:

```
# loadfile pvcreate vgcreate lvcreate lvlnboot
```

Create the volume group device nodes. The commands in this example assume that the volume group name is *vg00*, the major device number is *64*, and the minor device number is *0x000000*. This information comes from the listing of the volume group directory shown earlier in this chapter.

```
# mkdir /dev/vg00
# mknod /dev/vg00/group c 64 0x000000
```

The physical volume must be initialized and defined for the volume manager using *pvcreate*. The volume group must be created using *vgcreate*. The commands in this example assume that the system disk is set to SCSI ID 6. Change the *t6* value to match the actual target ID of the system disk. The *-f* option to *pvcreate* tells it to force the creation of a physical volume, while *-B* specifies that a bootable volume (i.e., a system disk) should be created using the named device. The first argument shown for *vgcreate* is the volume group name. This should match the volume group name used on the original system, which was captured with the *vgdisplay* command shown earlier in this chapter. The second argument is the device to be included in the volume group.

If the PE Size shown by *vgdisplay* is any value other than 4, the *-s* option should be used with *vgcreate* to specify an alternate physical extent size (i.e., *-s 8* would indicate a PE Size of 8 MB). If the **Max LV** value shown by *vgdisplay* is any value other than 255, the *-l* option should be used with *vgcreate* to specify the maximum number of logical volumes (i.e., *-l 255*).

```
# pvcreate -f -B /dev/rdsk/c0t6d0
# vgcreate vg00 /dev/dsk/c0t6d0
```

The logical volumes must be defined with *lvcreate*. The original partition table should be used as a guide to the LV sizes, though keeping the sizes the same is not strictly required. The *-L* option refers to the LV size in megabytes, noted using *lvdisplay*. The *-n* option refers to the volume name, which must match the name used on the original system. The *-C* option is used to specify a contiguous alloca-tion policy and takes *y* or *n* as a value, indicating yes or no. Contiguous alloca-tion, which tells the volume manager to keep all blocks for a given LV together on the surface of the disk, is required for the root and swap partitions; it is shown in the Allocation field of *lvdisplay* as *contiguous*. The *-r* option sets the bad block relocation policy, which must be set to *n* (no bad block relocation) for the root partition. Bad block relocation is shown by *lvdisplay* using the Bad Block field and is set to either *on* or *off.* The final argument is the name of the volume group that was just created, in this case *vg00*. If a non-0 number of Mirror Copies was shown by *lvdisplay*, the *-m* option should be used to indicate mirroring for the logical volume. Note that mirroring with a strict allocation policy cannot be configured with a single hard disk. The value is the number of mirror copies, which may be 0, 1, or 2; 0 is the default value. Similarly, the *Stripes* and *Stripe Size (KB)* fields can be carried over from *lvdisplay* and specified using the *-i* and *-I* options respec-tively.

```
# lvcreate -L 64 -n lvol1 -C y -r n vg00      ( / )
# lvcreate -L 128 -n lvol2 -C y vg00          ( swap )
# lvcreate -L 288 -n lvol3 vg00               ( /opt )
# lvcreate -L 512 -n lvol4 vg00               ( /usr )
```

The *lvlnboot* command must be used to identify the boot, root, swap, and dump partitions to the system. Invoke the *lvlnboot* command with each of the *-b, -r, -s,* and *-d* options, respectively, followed by the name of the applicable logical vol-ume. In the following example, we set the root partition with the boot and root flags and the swap partition with the swap and dump flags. This is appropriate for most configurations.

```
# lvlnboot -b /dev/vg00/lvol1      ( / )
# lvlnboot -r /dev/vg00/lvol1      ( / )
# lvlnboot -s /dev/vg00/lvol2      ( swap )
# lvlnboot -d /dev/vg00/lvol2      ( swap )
```

Before proceeding, the LVM commands must be removed from the RAM disk to make room for the filesystem creation commands.

```
# rm /sbin/pvcreate /sbin/vgcreate /sbin/lvcreate /sbin/lvlnboot
# loadfile fs_wrapper /sbin/newfs /sbin/mkfs /sbin/fs/hfs/newfs \
  /sbin/fs/hfs/mkfs /sbin/mount /sbin/fs/hfs/mount /sbin/lib/mfsconfig.d
```

Any logical volumes that will be mounted as filesystems must be initialized. Use the *newfs* command to create filesystems on all of the volumes except for swap, which is accessed randomly by the system and need not be formatted. The *-F* option is used to indicate the type of filesystem to be created. In this case, an *hfs* filesystem will be created, though *vxfs* also may be specified. The *-L* option indi-cates that the filesystem should support long filenames. The final argument to *newfs* is the raw device, in this case, a logical volume, to be formatted.

```
# newfs -F hfs -L /dev/vg00/rlvol1
# newfs -F hfs -L /dev/vg00/rlvol3
# newfs -F hfs -L /dev/vg00/rlvol4
```

Create mount points for any filesystems that will be restored from tape. The *mkdir* command should be used to do this; note that the *-p* option is not available on the command loaded into the RAM disk.

```
# mkdir /a
# mkdir /a/root
# mkdir /a/opt
# mkdir /a/usr
```

Mount the logical volumes using the block devices on the newly created mount points using the *mount* command.

```
# mount /dev/vg00/lvol1 /a/root
# mount /dev/vg00/lvol3 /a/opt
# mount /dev/vg00/lvol4 /a/usr
```

The commands used to create filesystems must now be removed to make room for the commands used to restore data from the *dump* tape. The *rm* command available on the RAM disk supports *-r* for removing only directories, not files. The *-f* option will mask any problems if it is used here, so avoid it.

```
# rm /sbin/fs_wrapper /sbin/newfs /sbin/mkfs /sbin/fs/hfs/newfs \
  /sbin/fs/hfs/mkfs /sbin/mount /sbin/fs/hfs/mount
# rm -r /sbin/lib/mfsconfig.d
```

Recovering the System

Load the remaining commands from CD:

```
# loadfile restore mkboot /usr/lib/uxbootlf
```

Now the actual filesystem data may be restored, one filesystem at a time. When *restore* is run, it will complain that the *lost+found* directory already exists. This directory is created by *newfs*; the error may be ignored. Data should be restored into the proper directory by using *cd* to change into the correct logical volume prior to performing the restore for each filesystem.

In the *restore* commands shown next, the actual tape device number may differ depending upon the SCSI ID of the tape drive (though 0 is not the SCSI ID in this case). To display the nodes created for all tape devices detected by the system at boot time, use *ls /dev/rmt**. The following commands assume that the */opt*, and */usr* partitions were backed up in order and will be restored in the same order.

The *r* option tells *restore* to select all files and place them into the current directory. The *f* option is used to specify the tape device; the letter *n* at the end of the name tells the tape drive to use nonrewinding mode. For further information about the use of the *restore* command, refer to Chapter 3.

```
# cd /a/root
# restore rf /dev/rmt/0mn
# cd /a/opt
# restore rf /dev/rmt/0mn
# cd /a/usr
# restore rf /dev/rmt/0m
```

The boot block must be installed at the beginning of the system drive. The SCSI target ID used here is the same as the one that was used to create the volume group with the *vgcreate* command earlier.

```
# mkboot -l /dev/dsk/c0t6d0
```

Finally, flush the I/O buffers using *sync* to ensure that all changes to the filesystems are committed. The system may then be rebooted.

```
# sync; sync
# reboot
```

Postinstallation recovery tasks

If the system configuration needs to be modified prior to a full multiuser network boot, it is possible to bring it up in single-user mode to make necessary changes at this time. Press the Escape key or spacebar to halt the boot sequence and boot into Initial System Load (ISL) mode. Type *boot scsi.x.0 isl* at the "Boot Administration" menu prompt. The system drive SCSI ID should be substituted for *x*. Then tell the system to boot into single-user mode from the primary disk using *hpux -iS disk(;0)/stand/vmunix*. This command tells the system to load the kernel, located on the default disk device at */stand/vmunix*, to boot to *init* level *S* (single-user mode) from the primary system disk.

```
BOOT_ADMIN> boot scsi.6.0 isl

Booting
ISL Revision A.00.30 OCT 26, 1994
ISL> hpux -iS disk(;0)/stand/vmunix

Boot
: disk(2/0/1.6.0.0.0.0.0;0)/stand/vmunix
```

The */usr* partition should be mounted using *mount /usr* to enable access to the *vi* command if its use is required. The */var* partition also should be mounted if it is separate from the root partition. At this point, any system files may be modified as necessary. When all required configuration changes have been completed, *sync* the disks and *reboot* as before using *sync, sync, reboot*.

11

IRIX

This chapter explains the procedure that you would use to recover your SGI IRIX operating system disk in case of a complete system failure—when you are left with nothing but bare metal. For suggestions on how to avoid this situation, please read the first section of Chapter 7, *SunOS/Solaris*.

Before discussing bare-metal recovery of an IRIX system, it is important to discuss the layout of an IRIX system, since it is a little different from most other flavors of Unix that use Berkeley (BSD) style partitioning. At a minimum, an IRIX system disk contains four partitions. The first partition that contains data is partition 0, the *root* partition, and partition 1 is the first *swap* partition. Partition 10, the *volume*, is the whole disk, overlapping all the other partitions. The very first partition physically on a system disk is partition 8, the *volume header*. It starts at block 0 and contains the system disk parameters, partition table, and volume directory as well as any programs that are necessary for booting, such as *sash*, the standalone shell. *sash* is required to be in the volume header of the system disk; we talk more about *sash* later in this section. Some system disks will have an additional partition for */usr*, which is partition 6. System disks that have XFS filesystems with external XLV log partitions also have an additional partition, number 15, called the *xfslog* partition. This could be used with a separate */usr* partition since the root partition cannot have an external XLV log.

When you install IRIX or are going to be performing a bare-metal recovery, it is important to note that the *miniroot*, which contains the installation tools, is copied to partition 1 (*swap*) of the system disk; any data that the miniroot contains will be trashed. It is therefore advantageous to follow the IRIX standard partitioning scheme described in the preceding paragraph. Any nonstandard partitioning and disk schemes aren't discussed here; if you've done any customization like that, it is hoped that you know what you're doing already.

All of the bare-metal recoveries discussed in this chapter assume that the boot PROM has not been corrupted or changed from a default IRIX installation. In other words, the boot device and boot filename have not been changed or customized.

This chapter describes two backup/recovery tools: the one that SGI provides for the IRIX operating system and the IRIX version of the homegrown procedure introduced in Chapter 7.

This chapter was written by Blayne Puklich of Collective Technologies. Blayne works on as many Unix platforms as he can get his hands on. He likes to mountain bike and listen to extremely loud music in his spare time. He may be reached at *blayne@colltech.com*.

SGI's Backup and Restore Utilities

SGI's IRIX operating system has two built-in bare-metal recovery commands, surprisingly enough called *Backup* and *Restore*. *Backup* is a shell script that performs full and incremental system backups. The *Backup* commands under IRIX 5.3, 6.1, and 6.2 all use the *Bru* command, IRIX 6.3 and 6.4 use *tar*, and IRIX 6.5 uses *cpio*. Only a full *Backup* can be read by the Recover System Maintenance Menu choice; no other backup method is supported. A full *Backup* contains *sash* as well as the contents of every local filesystem on the system.

Restore is also a shell script that can recover files from a *Backup* tape. (*sash* cannot be recovered this way.) The command is backward compatible; the *Restore* command from IRIX 6.5 can read *cpio*, *tar*, and *Bru* backups. *Restore* is not used for bare-metal recovery. The Recover System Maintenance Menu choice is used for that.

The value provided by IRIX's built-in bare-metal recovery tools is significantly reduced once you deviate from the standard disk-partitioning scheme.

Standard Backup Commands

SGI recommends unmounting and running *fsck* against each filesystem that you want to back up. It is probably sufficient, however, just to make sure the system is fairly quiet. You also can perform a backup while in single-user mode for some added security.

You can run *Backup* either graphically, using the *Toolchest*, or from the command line; both methods will create a tape that can be used by the *Recover* command.

Make sure that you do not have any CD-ROMs mounted, because *Backup* will happily back them up for you.

To use the graphical version, choose the System Manager menu choice from the System Toolchest. From the menu on the left side of the System Manager, choose Files & Data, and then choose either Backup Files or the Backup and Restore Manager. Starting the backup from either choice is straightforward; just perform a full system backup to an attached tape drive or to a drive attached to another SGI system that you have permission to use.

To create a recoverable system backup from the command line, place a blank tape in the tape drive and invoke the *Backup* command, specifying that you want to back up from root:

```
# Backup /
```

The default tape drive to write to is */dev/nrtape*. If this is not the tape drive you wish to use, you must specify a different tape drive. The full command with options, from the *Backup* manpage, is the following:

```
# Backup [-h hostname] [-i] [-t tapedevice] [directory_name | file_name]
```

To back up your system to the tape drive */dev/rmt/tps0d3nr* (a tape drive set to SCSI ID 3 attached to SCSI controller 0), you would use this command:

```
# Backup -t /dev/rmt/tps0d3nr /
```

An example command for backing your system up to a tape drive attached to another SGI system is:

```
# Backup -h tapehost -t /dev/rmt/tps0d3nr /
```

This would back up your system to the tape drive */dev/rmt/tps0d3nr* attached to the system called *tapehost*, assuming you have permission to do so. All that is required is that root on the system you are going to back up can start a remote shell as the user *guest* on *tapehost*.

Keep in mind that only a full *Backup* can be restored from the Recover System System Maintenance Menu choice, so you cannot specify *-i* to the *Backup* command if you expect to be able to use that tape for bare-metal recovery.

You can use the *List_tape* command to list the contents of a *Backup* tape that was previously created:

```
# List_tape
```

This command also defaults to the tape drive */dev/nrtape*. The options for *List_tape* are quite like *Backup*; listing the contents of a *Backup* tape in the tape drive */dev/rmt/tps0d3* can be accomplished by using this command:

```
# List_tape -t /dev/rmt/tps0d3nr
```

To list the contents of a tape in the tape drive */dev/rmt/tps0d3nr* attached to *tapehost*, we would just add the *-h* option:

```
# List_tape -h tapehost -t /dev/rmt/tps0d3nr
```

To do this, you also need the correct permission to use the tape drive on *tapehost*. You can read more about *List_tape* in its manpage.

Making Bootable Tapes

In order to make bootable tapes, you need your original IRIX installation media, which can be either a tape or a CD-ROM, and a blank tape. These tapes are useful if you prefer not to use your original installation media for recovery purposes or do not always have bootable installation media available. Bootable tapes are supported only by IRIX 5.3 and 6.1. None of the newer versions of IRIX can boot from tape; they must be booted from CD-ROM.

You can copy an installation tape and make a bootable tape if you have two tape drives or one tape drive and sufficient disk space. Creating a bootable tape from a CD-ROM requires a CD-ROM drive, a tape drive, and a blank tape. Bootable tapes are just tapes that have the *sa* (standalone) image as well as possibly an IRIX installation image on them. These tapes are created using the *distcp* command; refer to the *distcp* manpage for more information.

Two tape drives

If you have two tape drives and your installation media is also a tape, you can make a bootable tape from your installation tape and also make a complete copy of the installation tape at the same time. Write-protect and insert your installation tape into one of your tape drives and the blank tape into the other, and issue a command like the following:

```
# distcp device1 device2
```

Replace *device1* with the name of the tape drive containing the installation tape, and *device2* with the name of the tape drive that has the blank tape. You must specify a no-rewind tape drive name for the source drive *device1*, such as */dev/nrtape*.

One tape drive

To copy from tape to tape with only one tape drive, follow these steps. Note that you must have sufficient disk space in order to copy your entire installation tape.

1. Insert your IRIX installation tape into your tape drive. Issue these commands:

```
# mkdir /usr/tmp/dist
# distcp /dev/nrtape /usr/tmp/dist
# mt -f /dev/nrtape rewind
```

2. Eject the IRIX installation tape and insert the blank tape for copying.

   Use either of the following two versions of the *distcp* command. This first version copies just the standalone image to the blank tape to make it bootable:

   ```
   # distcp /usr/tmp/dist/sa /dev/tape
   ```

   This second version makes a copy of the entire distribution, as well as the standalone image:

   ```
   # distcp /usr/tmp/dist/* /dev/tape
   ```

3. Finally, rewind and clean up any temporary files:

   ```
   # mt -f /dev/tape rewind
   # rm -rf /usr/tmp/dist
   ```

4. Eject the new bootable tape. Make sure to write-protect and label the tape!

CD-ROM and tape drive

You can make a bootable tape from an installation CD-ROM by just copying the standalone image to a blank tape. Put your installation CD-ROM into the CD-ROM drive and the blank tape into your tape drive, and issue this command:

```
# distcp CD-ROMhost:/CD-ROM/dist/sa /dev/tape
```

In this example, we have specified that we want to use a CD-ROM drive attached to the SGI system called *CD-ROMhost*; as with *Backup* and *List_tape*, you need the correct guest permissions in order for this to succeed.

System Recovery with Backup Tape

Bare-metal recovery on an SGI system can be performed by the Recover System Maintenance Menu choice as long as you have a full backup tape made with the *Backup* command. When an SGI system boots, you are given a chance to stop the boot process by pressing the Escape key, which will present the System Maintenance Menu. If the SGI system has a graphics capability, you can either press Escape or click on the Stop for Maintenance button. Note that some SGI systems are configured to always stop at the System Maintenance Menu, so this step may not be necessary (the menu just appears).

```
Starting up the system...

To perform system maintenance instead, press Esc
```

Your system should stop and print out the following System Maintenance Menu, or display it graphically.

```
System Maintenance Menu
   (1) Start System
   (2) Install System Software
```

```
(3) Run Diagnostics
(4) Recover System
(5) Enter Command Monitor
```

To start bare-metal recovery, you first should boot the standalone version of *fx* to ensure that the system disk partition table is intact. You can do this from either a local CD-ROM drive or a remote directory. To boot the standalone *fx* from a local CD-ROM drive, first choose option *5*, enter *Command Monitor*. At the command monitor, you first should make sure that all the hardware you expect to be available is shown by the *hinv* command:

```
>> hinv
                 System: IP22
              Processor: 250 Mhz R4400, with FPU
    Primary I-cache size: 16 Kbytes
    Primary D-cache size: 16 Kbytes
    Secondary cache size: 2048 Kbytes
            Memory size: 256 Mbytes
               Graphics: GR3-XZ
              SCSI Disk: scsi(0)disk(1)
            SCSI CD-ROM: scsi(1)CD-ROM(3)
              SCSI Tape: scsi(1)tape(4)
                  Audio: Iris Audio Processor: version A2 revision 0.1.0
```

Next, boot the standalone *fx* program. The filenames of the *sash* and *fx* programs for the various SGI processor types are included in Table 11-1.

Table 11-1. sash and fx Programs for Different Architectures

CPU Architecture	sash	fx
IP17	*sashIP17*	*fx.IP17*
IP19, IP20, IP22, IP32	*sashARCS*	*fx.ARCS*
IP21, IP25, IP26, IP27, IP30	*sash64*	*fx.64*

To boot from a local CD-ROM drive, use a command like this:

```
>> boot -f dksc(1,3,8)sashARCS dksc(1,3,7)stand/fx.ARCS --x
```

Replace *dksc(1,3,8)* and *dksc(1,3,7)* with the appropriate CD-ROM drive from the *hinv* output of the system being recovered, and *sashARCS* and *fx.ARCS* with the appropriate standalone program names from the table. Some of the *sash* and *fx* filenames have the processor type as a suffix, such as *sashIP17* and *fx.IP17*. To boot *fx* from a remote machine, check to make sure the boot PROM variable *netaddr* is set to the system's IP address, then issue the *boot* command:

```
>> printenv netaddr
netaddr=192.0.2.1
>> boot -f bootp()remote:/CD-ROM/stand/fx.ARCS -x
```

The *fx* program will prompt you for the device name of the disk, the controller number, and the drive number; the default values are what most systems would use:

```
fx: "device-name" = (dksc)
fx: ctrl# = (0)
fx: drive# = (1)
```

You should check for any existing partition information using the */show/label/partition* command. If the partition information appears to be correct, you can exit *fx* to return to the System Maintenance Menu; if not, you have to correct the partition information. Most standard SGI system disks use either the *rootdrive* or *usrrootdrive* partition template, which can be found in the repartition submenu of *fx*. Make sure to use the */label/sync* command to ensure that the system disk partition table is written out, and then use the *exit* command to leave *fx* and return to the System Maintenance Menu.

Now we can start the system recovery by choosing menu option 4, Recover System. The system may display the following, or an equivalent if graphics are available:

```
System Recovery...

             Press Esc to return to the menu.
```

From this point on, the prompts and your responses will differ depending on the age of the system.

Older SGI Systems

Some older SGI systems present you with the following prompt after a short time:

```
Insert the installation tape, then press <enter>:
```

At this point you would make sure that either a bootable tape (your IRIX installation tape will work) is loaded into a local tape drive or that an IRIX installation CD-ROM is in a local CD-ROM drive. You then would press Enter to start loading the miniroot onto partition 1 of the system disk. Note that this procedure requires that the installation device be physically attached; booting from a remote system is described later. After a few minutes, the system prompts you for the type of restore:

```
CRASH RECOVERY
      You may type sh to get a shell prompt at most questions.
      Remote or local restore: ([r]emote, [l]ocal): [l]
```

Choose the appropriate type of restore, either *remote* or *local.* If you choose *remote,* the system prompts you for the name of the remote host and the tape drive name on the remote host. Make sure that your *Backup* tape is in the remote tape drive, and enter the IP address for the remote host as well as the name of the tape drive. If you choose to perform a *local* restore, the system prompts you only for the name of the local tape drive. Make sure that the *Backup* tape is in your local tape drive, and enter the full name of the tape drive rather than */dev/tape*. As an example, if you want to use a tape drive that is set to SCSI ID 3 and is attached to SCSI controller 0, you would use */dev/rmt/tps0d3nr*.

If you do not have a tape or CD-ROM locally attached to the system you are recovering, you will need to enable *tftp* on a remote system and configure the boot PROM to enable booting across the network. On the remote system, edit the file */usr/etc/inetd.conf*. Find the line that contains *tftp* and change it to be the following:

```
tftp dgram udp wait guest /usr/etc/tftpd tftpd
```

This allows *tftp* full access to the filesystems on the remote system; make sure to either change this line back to what it was before or comment it out completely once the recovery is completed. Also, make sure that you use Tabs for the whitespace separating the individual words. Next, signal *inetd* on the remote system by sending it a HUP signal. On some older versions of IRIX, *inetd* is broken, requiring you to issue a *killall -9 inetd* and restart it by hand.

Now you need to configure the system you are recovering to boot from the remote system. Rather than choosing menu item 4 from the System Maintenance Menu, choose item 5, Enter Command Monitor. Issue the following PROM commands:

```
>> setenv netaddr ip-address
>> init
>> exit
```

Replace *ip-address* with the IP address of the system you are recovering, not the remote system. When the system returns to the System Maintenance Menu, choose item 4, Recover System, and follow the preceding steps for recovering.

Newer SGI systems

Newer systems will present you with this short menu, or something much like it if graphics are available, for specifying where the installation media is:

```
1) Remote Tape  2) Remote Directory  3) Local CD-ROM  4) Local Tape

    Enter 1-4 to select source type, Esc to quit,
    or Enter to start:
```

Choices 1 (Remote Tape) and 4 (Local Tape) are not supported as bootable as of IRIX 6.2. To start recovery using a local CD-ROM, put your installation CD-ROM into the CD-ROM drive and choose item 3. Choose item 2 for either a remote CD-ROM or a remote software distribution directory. The system prompts you for the local system's IP address, if not set by the boot PROM, and the remote hostname and directory. The format should be *remotehost:/directory/dist*, where *remotehost* is the name of the remote host, and *directory* the name of the

remote directory. If you want to use a remote CD-ROM drive, the remote host
name might look much like:

```
remotehost:/CD-ROM/dist
```

When using a remote software distribution directory, the remote hostname contains just the full pathname to the directory, like:

```
remotehost:/directory/dist/6.3
```

The system returns to the Source Type menu; press Enter to begin reading the
installation tools to partition 1 of the system disk. After a few minutes, the following is displayed:

```
    ************************************************************
    *                                                          *
    *                  CRASH      RECOVERY                      *
    *                                                          *
    ************************************************************

    You may type  sh  to get a shell prompt at most questions

    Please enter your hostname (system name)  : muddy
    Please enter the IP address for muddy's
       Integral Ethernet interface (ec0): 172.16.0.1

Starting networking with primary hostname muddy

    Checking for tape devices
```

If the system you are recovering has a locally attached tape drive, you will see the
following:

```
    Restore will be from /dev/tape.  OK? ([y]es, [n]o): [y]
```

If this is correct, press Enter. If not (and you answer no to the prompt) or if a local
tape drive cannot be found, then the following is displayed:

```
    Remote or local restore ([r]emote, [l]ocal): [l]
```

At this point, choosing *[l]ocal* allows you to specify a different local tape drive if
the previous message was incorrect. Choosing *[r]emote* asks you for the remote
hostname and the remote tape drive name. The system then prints out tape drive
status information and prompts you for the first tape:

```
        Insert the first Backup tape in the drive, then
        press (<enter>, [q]uit (from recovery) ,[r]estart):
```

Insert the first full *Backup* tape and press Enter. After a few minutes, messages like
the following will be shown:

```
    Backup is a cpio archive
    label: Full system backup from /
    Thu Feb 25 17:25:47 PST 1999
```

```
user: root
group: sys
IRIX muddy 6.5 05190003 IP22
IRIX 6.5:1274627333 built 4/29/98 at zebub:/xlv55/kudzu-apr12/root $
options: /sbin/cpio -KWovO /dev/tape
    Do you want to proceed ([y]es, [r]etry, [q]uit): [y]
```

If this is the correct tape information, press Enter and the system configuration files will be read. Next, you will have the opportunity to re-create the filesystems on the system disk:

```
Erase all old filesystems and make new ones (y, n, sh): [n]
```

Choosing *y* will destroy any data remaining on your system, while choosing *n* will allow you to preserve the old filesystems. You also can choose *sh* for a shell, which will let you use the miniroot commands to poke around your old filesystems to see if anything can be salvaged.

If you choose *y*, the system asks you for confirmation when rebuilding each filesystem. If you choose *n*, or when you finish rebuilding the filesystems, a table of the currently mounted filesystems will be displayed. If everything is there, press Enter to start recovery from the *Backup* tape. Once that has completed, it will ask if you want to read any incremental *Backup* tapes, at which point you can choose to do so. The very last step allows you to read the first *Backup* tape again, start over from the beginning, or reboot the recovered system:

```
Reboot, start over, or first tape again? ([r]eboot, [s]tart, [f]irst) [r]
```

If you haven't made any mistakes, you should choose to reboot. Congratulations! Your SGI system should be in the same state that it was when the *Backup* tape used for recovery was created.

Homegrown Bare-Metal Recovery

This procedure for recovering a failed SGI IRIX system takes a few shortcuts from what SGI would have you do. Their recommendation is to perform an IRIX installation, followed by the use of *restore* (or *xfsrestore* for restoring XFS dumps). We will bypass the IRIX installation and instead use the miniroot to perform the bare-metal recovery.

In order to perform this type of bare-metal recovery you will need the correct IRIX installation tape or CD-ROM or a bootable IRIX tape (only for IRIX 5.3 and 6.1). You also will need your current *dump* volumes, along with a listing of which partitions are on what volumes and in what order, and printed copies of the output of the *hinv* command, the system's partition and volume header information, and the */etc/fstab* file. You might guess that it is a little difficult to keep track of how many tape files a dump is made up of and much easier to recover a system during a panic situation if you keep your *dump* volumes simple.

The installation media and configuration information needs to be gathered before disaster strikes. You should periodically print out all of the system configuration information. It is very difficult, if not impossible, to return a failed system to its original state without these things.

Finding the partition information for each drive can be accomplished using the *prtvtoc* command. You would run the command once for each disk drive attached to the system and print the results:

```
# prtvtoc /dev/rdsk/dks0d1vh
```

This command would print the volume table of contents, or partition information, for the SCSI drive on controller 0 with SCSI ID 1, which is typically the system disk. Another way to gather this information is by using *fx*:

```
# echo "/label/show/partition" | fx 'dksc(0,1)'
```

This shows the same information for the SCSI drive on controller 0 with SCSI ID 1 but in a format that might be easier to use, since we will be using *fx* during system recovery.

You can use the *dvhtool* command to list the contents of the system disk volume header:

```
# dvhtool -v list /dev/rvh
```

We need this list to know what standalone files to put into the volume header if the header becomes damaged. Usually, the only standalone files that might have to be reinstalled are *sash* and possibly *ide*.

If the system has any LV logical volumes, you will need a printed copy of */etc/lvtab*. Note that the system's actual root and swap partitions cannot be LV volumes, but if */usr* is separate, it is conceivable that it may have been grown by making it into an LV volume and adding an additional partition; recovering this case is beyond the scope of this book.

You also will need a printed copy of the XLV configuration if it is using any XLV volumes, as well as a printed listing of the contents of the */dev/dsk/xlv* directory. The root filesystem can be an XLV mirror (also called a *plex*), and */usr* may have also been grown on the fly by making it an XLV volume and adding an additional partition. Recovering a */usr* filesystem that has been changed in this way is beyond the scope of this book.

To create a file that contains a script that will duplicate your XLV configuration, you can use the *xlv_mgr* command. This is the same way that the IRIX *Backup* script extracts the configuration:

```
# echo "script all\nquit\n" | xlv_mgr > /tmp/xlv_config_script
```

To begin a bare-metal recovery, we will start out as if we are performing recovery with a *Backup* tape. We need to get the SGI system to the System Maintenance Menu. If your system prints messages like the following, either press Escape or click on the Stop for Maintenance button, if available:

```
Starting up the system...

To perform system maintenance instead, press Esc
```

Your system should then stop and print out the System Maintenance Menu:

```
System Maintenance Menu
     (1) Start System
     (2) Install System Software
     (3) Run Diagnostics
     (4) Recover System
     (5) Enter Command Monitor
```

This is where we deviate from the steps for bare-metal recovery using a *Backup* tape. Our methods will now be more down and dirty.

First, we enter the Command Monitor to make sure all of our hardware is visible. Use the *hinv* command, paying special attention to the type of processor the system has and the SCSI disk, CD-ROM, and tape drives. We also will set the PROM variable *AutoLoad*:

```
Command Monitor. Type "exit" to return to the menu.
>> hinv
System  SGI-IP27
2 180 MHz IP27 Processors
Main memory size: 640 Mbytes
Integral SCSI controller 0
Integral SCSI controller 1
Integral Fast Ethernet
IOC3 serial port
Integral SCSI controller 2
Integral SCSI controller 3
     Disk drive: unit 1 on SCSI Controller 0, (dksc(0,1,0))
     Disk drive: unit 4 on SCSI Controller 0, (dksc(0,4,0))
     Disk drive: unit 6 on SCSI Controller 0, (dksc(0,6,0))
     CD-ROM: unit 6 on SCSI Controller 1, (CD-ROM(1,6,7))
     Tape drive: unit 3 on SCSI Controller 2
>> setenv AutoLoad No
```

Write down the processor type, the disk drive names *(dksc(0,1,0))*, the CD-ROM drive names *(CD-ROM(1,6,7))*, and the tape drive information *(controller 2, SCSI ID 3)*. (This information may already be in the printed *hinv* output gathered while the system was alive.) Setting *AutoLoad* prevents the system from booting, stopping it at the System Maintenance Menu. If the system does not have an ARCS PROM, the older *bootmode* variable has to be set instead:

```
>> setenv bootmode m
```

(You will know if the system has an ARCS PROM based on the name of the *sash* and *fx* programs from the previous table.)

The next step is to boot the standalone *fx* program from the Command Monitor prompt to repair the system disk partitioning. You can boot either from a locally attached CD-ROM drive or from a CD-ROM drive on a remote system. The filenames of the *sash* and *fx* programs for the various SGI processor types are included in the previous table.

To boot *fx* from a local CD-ROM drive, use a command like this:

```
>> boot -f dksc(1,6,8)sashARCS dksc(1,6,7)stand/fx.ARCS --x
```

Replace *dksc(1,6,8)* and *dksc(1,6,7)* with the appropriate CD-ROM drive from the *hinv* output of the system being recovered, and *sashARCS* and *fx.ARCS* with the appropriate standalone program names from the table. To boot *fx* from a remote machine, check to make sure the boot PROM variable *netaddr* is set to the system's IP address, then issue the boot command:

```
>> printenv netaddr
netaddr=172.16.0.1
>> boot -f bootp()remote:/CD-ROM/stand/fx.ARCS -x
```

The *fx* program will prompt you for the device name of the disk, the controller number, and drive number; the default values are what most systems would use:

```
fx: "device-name" = (dksc)
fx: ctrl# = (0)
fx: drive# = (1)
```

Before making any changes, it may be valuable to check for any existing partition information using the */show/label/partition* command. If the partition information appears to be correct, you can exit *fx* to return to the System Maintenance Menu; if it is not correct, you will have to duplicate the partition information previously gathered. Most system disks have either the *rootdrive* or *usrrootdrive* partition scheme. If the partitioning is not standard, it may speed things up to start with a *rootdrive* template and modify it. Make sure to use the */label/sync* command to make sure that any changes to the partitioning are written to the volume header.

Once we have partitioned our system drive, we will boot the miniroot as if we were going to perform an IRIX installation. Choose menu item number 2, Install System Software. The system will then ask you for the source of the installation media. Select either the locally attached CD-ROM or a remote tape or directory.

To boot from a remote system, you will need to perform some of the same steps that were necessary for recovery using a *Backup* tape. You need to enable *tftp* on the remote system by editing the file */usr/etc/inetd.conf* and changing the *tftp* line to the following:

```
tftp dgram udp wait guest /usr/etc/tftpd tftpd
```

This allows full access to the filesystems on the remote system. You should change this back to its previous value when you are finished with the recovery. Then, signal *inetd* by sending it a HUP signal.

Back on the system you are recovering, it will ask you for the local system's IP address (if not set by the boot PROM), the remote system name, and the path to the installation directory. On older SGI systems, you may have to set the boot PROM variable *netaddr* to the local system's IP address.

Once you tell the system where to install from, the system begins to load the installation tools to the swap partition. It prints out some messages and possibly shows a status bar as the installation tools are copied and the IRIX kernel boots. If the filesystems were completely destroyed, the system will ask you to make new ones as necessary. When creating a new XFS filesystem, it may ask you for a block size; just use 4096 unless there are some special requirements. There also may be partitions that the system is able to mount but that are, in fact, very corrupted. If this happens, the system will print out messages to that effect, then stop and prompt you with:

```
Press Enter to invoke C shell csh:
```

You should choose to launch the shell at this time. From the shell, you can use the *mount* command to see what mounted. You can run *mkfs* for each filesystem from the shell, but the quickest way to correct any corrupted filesystems may be to *umount* all of the system disk filesystems, exit the shell, and run the *inst* command *admin mkfs*. This will prompt you to rebuild each filesystem, and remount everything once it's complete. To do this, launch the shell, and immediately exit. The system will attempt to mount the remaining partitions, fail and launch the *inst* program. Sometimes you will need to run *admin mkfs* twice because of problems with unmounting filesystems.

If all of the system disk partitions are mounted and correct, the system just loads the *inst* program. After *inst* loads, you should check and reset the system date if necessary:

```
Inst> admin date
Sat Jan 16 21:36:01 CST 1999
Inst> admin date mmddhhmm[cc]yy
```

Once you have checked the system date, you can launch a shell using the *inst* command *admin sh* and begin to recover the system disk filesystems. You should first unmount all of the disk filesystems except for */root*:

```
# mount
/dev/miniroot on / type xfs (rw)
/proc on /proc type proc (rw)
/hw on /hw type hwgfs (rw)
/dev/dsk/dks0d1s0 on /root type xfs (rw)
/hw on /root/hw type hwgfs (rw)
/dev/dsk/dks0d1s6 on /root/usr type xfs (rw)
# umount /root/usr
```

If the root filesystem was an XLV plex, you should force the plex to be re-created from the restored root filesystem by using the *xlv_set_primary* command:

```
# xlv_set_primary /dev/dsk/dks0d1s0
# rm -rf /dev/dsk/xlv /dev/rdsk/xlv
# xlv_assemble -Pq -h muddy
```

Replace */dev/dsk/dks0d1s0* with the name of the root partition on the system disk, and *muddy* with the system's hostname. You then may want to compare the contents on */dev/dsk/xlv* with the printed copy you made while the system was alive, and repair anything that is missing using commands from the script created by running the *xlv_mgr script all* command.

If your system was dumped using *xfsdump*, recovering the root filesystem can be done with a command like the following, after you place the level-0 *dump* tape for root into the tape drive:

```
# xfsrestore -r -f /dev/nrtape /root
```

You should replace */dev/nrtape* with the appropriate tape drive name, derived from the output of *hinv*, if */dev/nrtape* is not the correct tape drive. Using the *-r* flag tells *xfsrestore* that you will potentially be restoring not only a level-0 *xfsdump*, but some higher incremental levels as well. If you used *dump* to back up your filesystems, you could recover your root filesystem with commands like this:

```
# cd /root
# restore rf /dev/nrtape
```

If necessary, recover the */usr* filesystem by mounting it on */root/usr*, putting the correct *dump* tape into the tape drive, and using either *xfsrestore* or *restore*:

```
# For xfsdump
# mount /root/usr
# xfsrestore -r -f /dev/nrtape /root/usr
# For dump
# mount /root/usr
# cd /root/usr
# restore rf /dev/nrtape
```

Use the same procedure for recovering any additional filesystems as required and for recovering any higher-level dumps for the system disk filesystems.

Once you have recovered all of the filesystems on the system disk, you need to use *dvhtool* to copy *sash* and any other necessary files from the installation CD-ROM to the volume header to make the system disk bootable. Mount the CD-ROM if it's not already mounted, run *dvhtool*, and create the volume header files:

```
# mkdir /CD-ROM
# mount -t efs -o ro /dev/dsk/dks1d3s7 /CD-ROM
# cd /CD-ROM/stand
# dvhtool /dev/rdsk/dks0d1vh

Command? (read, vd, write, or quit): vd
(d FILE, a UNIX_FILE FILE, c UNIX_FILE FILE, g FILE UNIX_FILE or l)?
      l

Current contents:
        File name      Length      Block #
        sgilabel          512            2

(d FILE, a UNIX_FILE FILE, c UNIX_FILE FILE, g FILE UNIX_FILE or l)?
      c sashARCS ide
(d FILE, a UNIX_FILE FILE, c UNIX_FILE FILE, g FILE UNIX_FILE or l)?
      c sashARCS sash
(d FILE, a UNIX_FILE FILE, c UNIX_FILE FILE, g FILE UNIX_FILE or l)?
      l

Current contents:
        File name      Length      Block #
        sgilabel          512            2
        ide            316416            3
        sash           316416          621

(d FILE, a UNIX_FILE FILE, c UNIX_FILE FILE, g FILE UNIX_FILE or l)? <Return>

Command? (read, vd, write, or quit): write

Command? (read, vd, write, or quit): quit
```

Replace */dev/dsk/dks1d3s7* with the correct CD-ROM device name and */dev/rdsk/dks0d1vh* with the name of the volume header for the system disk.

You now should have a bootable system disk with everything restored. Exit from the shell and issue the *inst* the *exit* commands; do not use the *quit* command because *inst* will try to rebuild the kernel, and that can cause problems. The system then will prompt you for rebooting:

```
Ready to restart the system.  Restart? { (y)es, (n)o, (sh)ell, (h)elp) }:
```

Restarting the system will bring it up into multiuser state, which you probably should not do until you check the rest of the filesystems. You can force the system to halt by launching a shell from the prompt and using the *uadmin* command:

```
# uadmin 2 0
```

Then you can reboot to single-user mode by going to the command monitor from the System Maintenance Menu and typing *single* at the command monitor prompt. When the system is up, recover the remaining drives and rebuild any LV or XLV volumes as necessary. Check the partition tables using *fx -x*, build filesystems using *mkfs*, mount and restore the filesystems using either *xfsrestore* or *restore* depending on the type of *dump* used. If only the system disk was lost, more than likely the rest of the data on the system is still intact, so you may not need to do any of these steps.

At this point, you should have a fully recovered system. You now can check and reset the *AutoLoad* PROM variable back to *Yes* and halt the system:

```
# nvram AutoLoad
N
# nvram AutoLoad Y
# halt
```

Finally, you can remove the *xfsrestorehousekeepingdir* directories from any filesystems that you recovered using *xfsrestore*. You now should be able to boot your system into multiuser mode.

12

AIX

This chapter explains the procedure that you would use to recover your IBM AIX operating system disk in case of a complete system failure—when you are left with nothing but bare metal. For suggestions on how to avoid this situation, please read the first section of Chapter 7, *SunOS/Solaris*.

IBM was the first Unix vendor to deliver a true bare-metal recovery tool. The following are the tools and products that are available to perform a bare-metal recovery of an AIX system:

- The *mksysb* command makes a complete "bootable" backup of the root volume group (*rootvg*) only.

- *Sysback* is a combination of scripts written by IBM that expands the functionality of *mksysb*. *Sysback* allows backups of multiple volume groups (VGs) on one tape. It also allows backup on remote tapes to a *Sysback* backup server.

The homegrown bare-metal recovery method discussed in Chapter 7 does not work for AIX, since there is no AIX equivalent to *installboot*.

 This chapter was written by Charles Gagnon and Brian Jensen of Collective Technologies. Charles specializes in installing, configuring, and maintaining heterogeneous environments. Brian has been administering both AIX and heterogeneous environments for several years. Charles may be reached at *charlesg@colltech.com*, and Brian may be reached at *bjensen@colltech.com*.

IBM's mksysb Utility

The basis for a bare-metal recovery of an AIX system is the *mksysb* utility, which is included in most versions of AIX. It will copy all the files in the root volume group (*rootvg*).

mksysb is useful in many situations but has limitations that may prevent it from becoming your only backup solution. Some of these limitations are:

- Cannot back up filesystems on something other than *rootvg* (see *savevg*)

- Cannot back up raw logical devices

- Limited or no ability to preserve logical volume layout (version dependent)

- Problems restoring across multiple RS/6000 architectures (see "System Cloning," near the end of this chapter)

- Cannot track backups or perform incremental backups

- Not intended to perform remote tape backups

There are also significant differences in the *mksysb* program among different versions of AIX. If you know the features and limitations of the version of *mksysb* you are using, it can be a useful part of your overall disaster recovery plan. *mksysb* will back up any filesystems in the root volume group. More recent versions even have the ability to preserve logical volume characteristics and paging space size. *mksysb* will not back up raw logical volumes. It cannot back up anything other than the root volume group unless it is invoked as *savevg*.

mksysb also can be a good solution if you need to make occasional tape backups of your system in case of disk failure. It also can make an excellent companion to other backup programs that will handle your application and user data and provide things that *mksysb* cannot, such as incremental backups and remote restores. *mksysb* is not a good solution for environments that are using raw logical volumes, have data outside *rootvg*, or need to be able to do incremental backups, flexible restores, and backups across the network.

IBM has an additional program called *Sysback/6000* that overcomes some of the limitations of *mksysb*, including the ability to back up non-*rootvg* volume groups and raw logical volumes, as well as greater flexibility. There is also a utility included with the versions 4.x of AIX called *savevg*, which is actually a link to the *mksysb* command. When invoked this way, you can back up any volume group on your system, but the other *mksysb* constraints still apply.

How mksysb Works

mksysb works by creating several files on the tape. The first few are to boot the kernel, and the last contains the files to be restored in *tar* format for AIX 3.2.x, or *backup* format for AIX 4.x. (The AIX *backup* format is essentially the same as *dump*.) Figure 12-1 contains a logical representation of such a tape:

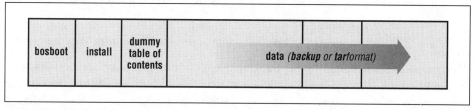

Figure 12-1. A logical representation of a mksysb tape

The tape block size for the first three files is 512 bytes, while the block size for the image data is variable, based on the settings of the tape drive at the time of the backup. If you choose 0 as the block size for that device, systems will, when possible, back up with 1024 bytes.

Using mksysb

The simplest and most common scenario is to back up all filesystems in *rootvg* with a locally attached tape drive. In this situation, you would issue the following command from a root prompt:

```
# mksysb -i /dev/rmt0
```

This also can be achieved through the *smit* menus, of course, and the following fast path will bring you directly to the correct screen:

```
# smit mksysb
```

You should be able to use any 4-mm or 8-mm SCSI tape drive supported by AIX.

Getting ready

The first thing that you must decide is whether you should log off all users and/or shut down your applications for the duration of the backup. The answer depends on your system configuration. The backup will likely take at least an hour, and any changes to files during the backup may lead to an inconsistent image on tape. There should not be any problems backing up files that are currently open, although any pending writes to the file at the time it is backed up will obviously not make it to the tape archive. If you have most or all of your user data off *rootvg*, and your system files are not constantly changing, then you should have no problem doing *mksysb* backups on a "live" system.

If you will be using this *mksysb* image to build other systems, you may want to prepare the *rootvg* even further. For example, you may want to do the following:

- Clear out */tmp*.

- Disable the network (comment out from *inittab*, *rc.net*, *rc.tcpip*, *rc.nfs*, anything that will hang the computer if it has no network).

- Remove the root password, or set it to a well-known password in your environment.

- Clear the error report using *errclear*, clear */var/spool*, */var/adm*, */var/logs*, etc.

Next, decide what needs to be backed up. You can prevent specific files from being backed up to the archive by creating a file called */etc/exclude.rootvg* and using the *-e* flag to *mksysb* (or *savevg*). Entries in this file can be simple lists of files, such as:

```
/etc/passwd
```

If you use the *-e* flag, *mksysb* filters out the files in your */etc/exclude.rootvg* using *egrep*, so in effect it supports *egrep*'s syntax. This allows complex entries such as:

```
.*/core$
^/tmp/
.*\.o$
```

The */image.data* file contains information about how disks, filesystems, logical volumes, and paging space will be rebuilt when the tape is restored. In general, the entries in *image.data* correlate to flags in the *mklv* and *crfs* commands (commands used to create logical volumes and filesystems). Running the *mkszfile* command before the *mksysb* creates the *image.data* file itself. You also can start *mksysb* with the *-i* option, which calls *mkszfile* to generate the *image.data* file automatically. Running *mkszfile* independently gives you the option of editing *image.data* and changing what is backed up, the size of the filesystems, and various other variables. You also can edit *bosinst.data* to customize what will be run after the image is restored. If you run *mkszfile* and edit *image.data*, make sure you run *mksysb* without the *-i* option, or your modifications will be overwritten.

If you specify the *-m* option to *mkszfile*, a map file will be created for each logical volume in the archive. Each map describes where on the disk the logical volume should be created at restore time. This is similar to the options available to the *mklv* command (exact layout ability). The map file for a given logical volume contains one line for each physical partition (PP) it occupies, along with the hard disk (hdisk) it is on. Note that this is useful only if the target system has the exact disk layout as the source system.

Here are some examples of what the *image.data* file contains. The AIX documentation gives a more complete description of all the options contained in the *image.data* file.

[SHRINK = yes]
> Shrinks the filesystems on restore.

[VG_SOURCE_DISK_LIST = hdisk0]
> Changes the target disk for the restore.

Once on tape, these files cannot be edited. You can, however, create a customized diskette containing an *image.data* and/or *bosinst.data* file. The diskette could be used at restore time instead of the files located on the tape. To create a customized diskette, follow this simple procedure:

Edit *image.data* and/or *bosinst.data* extracted from a tape (see the instructions for extracting a single file from a *mksysb* tape), place a diskette in the drive, and issue the following command:

```
# ls ./bosinst.data ./image.data | backup -ivqf /dev/rfd0
```

Starting mksysb

Once you have the system prepared for the backup, decide where the *mksysb* image should be saved. The most common choice is a local tape drive:

```
# mksysb device
```

The difference between the various ways to access a tape device on AIX systems is illustrated in Table 12-1 and explained in detail in the manpages.

Table 12-1. AIX Device-Naming Conventions

Device Name	Density	Rewind on Close	Retention on Open
/dev/rmt*	Setting #1	Yes	No
/dev/rmt*.1	Setting #1	No	No
/dev/rmt*.2	Setting #1	Yes	Yes
/dev/rmt*.3	Setting #1	No	Yes
/dev/rmt*.4	Setting #2	Yes	No
/dev/rmt*.5	Setting #2	No	No
/dev/rmt*.6	Setting #2	Yes	Yes
/dev/rmt*.7	Setting #2	No	Yes

You also can direct a *mksysb* image to a file, which can be installed via the Network Install Manager (NIM) or be used to build a *mksysb* tape at a later date.

Make sure the file is not in the root volume group, or the backup could be caught in a loop. Often, *mksysb* files/images are stored on an NFS-mounted partition:

```
# mksysb /some_NFS_filesystem/mksysb_filename
```

From this disk image, you can build a *mksysb* tape, if needed, using the following procedure:

1. Change the tape device block size and make sure the tape in the drive is rewound properly:

   ```
   # chdev -a block_size=512 device
   # mt -f device rewind
   ```

2. Install the boot block on the tape device. Make sure you use the no-rewind tape device (*/dev/rmt/*.[1,3,5,7]*), or everything will be overwritten later:

   ```
   # bosboot -d no-rewind-device -a
   ```

3. Make the installation tape. This part of the tape will contain the files that control the boot restore menus and start the restore itself. Continue to use a non-rewinding tape device:

   ```
   # mkinsttape no-rewind-device
   ```

4. Place a dummy table of contents on the tape:

   ```
   # echo "Dummy tape TOC" \
     | dd of=no-rewind-device bs=512 conv=sync
   ```

5. Change the block size back to the original block size:

   ```
   # chdev -a block_size=1024 device
   ```

6. Finally, *dd* the *mksysb* file made earlier:

   ```
   # dd if=/some_NFS_filesystem/mksysb_filename \
     of=device bs=1024
   ```

On older 3.2.x systems, all these steps can be performed on a completely different machine since the boot block and the installation files are compatible from one system to another. For AIX 4.x systems, you may need to install the files to support all possible devices before doing so. If not all device types are supported, a tape made on one machine will not boot properly on a different architecture. See "System Cloning" near the end of this chapter for more information on this topic.

mksysb to a remote tape drive

You can perform a *mksysb* directly to a remote tape by following this procedure. For the purpose of this example, we will consider two machines:

tapeserver
   The machine with the local tape drive

client

The machine to be backed up

First, make sure the */.rhosts* or */etc/hosts.equiv* file is set up properly on both machines to allow *rsh* from the client to the tapeserver. On the tapeserver, start the procedure to manually create a *mksysb* image shown in the previous section:

```
tapeserver# chdev -a block_size=512 device
tapeserver# mt -f device rewind
tapeserver# bosboot -d no-rewind-device -a
tapeserver# mkinsttape no-rewind-device
tapeserver# echo "Dummy tape TOC" | dd of=no-rewind-device bs=512 conv=sync
tapeserver# chdev -a block_size=1024 device
```

Now that we have the bootable part of the tape (i.e., the boot block), the installation files, and the dummy table of contents, we need to transfer the data. On the client, run *mkszfile*, and create a file */etc/exclude.vg* that contains only */tmp/mksysb.pipe*. Then, direct the *mksysb* to a named pipe. Finally, *cat* the contents of the pipe to the tapeserver's tape drive:

```
client# mknod p /tmp/mksysb.pipe
client# cat /tmp/mksysb.pipe \
        | rsh tapeserver "dd of=device obs=100b bs=1024 > /dev/null 2>&1" &
client# mksysb -e /tmp/mksysb.pipe
```

Checking and restoring data from a mksysb image

Now that you have the tape, you may want to verify the contents of the archive. The most thorough test of a *mksysb* tape is to actually do a restore, but you can get an idea of the integrity of the tape by listing the contents of the archive. First make sure the tape is at the beginning and then use the *restore* command to list the contens of the tape:

```
# mt -f device rewind
```

For AIX 4.x:

```
# restore -s4  -Tvf no-rewind-device
```

For AIX 3.2.x:

```
# mt -f no-rewind-device fsf 3
# tar -tvf device
```

You can use a variation of those commands to extract one or more files from the tape.

For AIX 4.x:

```
# restore -s4 -Xvf [ ./file | ./directory | ./file1 ./file2 ]
```

For AIX 3.2.x:

```
# mt -f no-rewind-device fsf 3
# tar -xvf no-rewind-device [ ./file | ./directory | ./file1 ./file2 ]
```

Files in the *tar* archive will have relative pathnames.

IBM's Sysback/6000 Utility

IBM offers another solution for bare-metal recovery on AIX 3.2.x and 4.x systems called *Sysback/6000*, usually referred to as *Sysback*. This product is not included with the AIX operating system and must be purchased separately from IBM. Contact your IBM sales representative for more information on the *Sysback* solution.

This section presents a short overview of *Sysback*. Anyone serious about using *Sysback* should read the *AIX System Backup and Recovery/6000 User and Reference Manual*, published by IBM.

Features

Sysback is a series of scripts written by IBM that complement a good disaster recovery plan. Among other things, *Sysback* allows:

* Backups and restores of various types (full system dumps, volume groups, filesystems, logical volumes, or specific files and directories)

* Backups and restores to a remote host configured as a *Sysback* server

* Complete set of *smit* menus and fast paths to configure and perform backups

Installing Sysback

Sysback has the following prerequisites:

* The AIX Base Operating System (BOS). Make sure that the version of *Sysback* that you buy is compatible with your OS level.

* The *bos.sysmgt.sysbr* fileset.

* The *bos.rte.net* and *bos.net.tcp.client* are required for the remote services functions.

* The *bos.net.nfs.client* is required to perform network boots and installations.

* The *bos.rte.bosinst*, *bos.rte.archive*, and *bos.rte.libnetsvc* are installed by default with the AIX distribution and must not be removed if *Sysback* is to function properly.

Once all the prerequisite software has been installed, log in as root and install the *Sysback* software using *installp*:

```
# installp -acgNqX -d /dev/cd0 all
```

AIX 4.2 users also can use the *smit install_latest* fast path.

Select the appropriate device for the source media:

/dev/cd0
> To install from a CD-ROM

/dev/fd0
> To install from a diskette

/some_directory
> If the installation files were copied to a filesystem

Overview of Sysback Menu Options

To access the *Sysback* menu with SMIT, type:

> # **smit sysback**

This menu contains the main *Sysback* options. The specifics of these menus vary, depending on the operating system level installed and the version of *Sysback* available.

Backup & Recovery Options
> Lists further options for backing up, restoring, listing, or verifying information for various types of backups

Configuration Options
> Gives the user access to various configuration options for local access, remote services, etc.

Tape Drives
> Allows for further configuration of tape devices

Utilities
> Lists extra utilities (create boot tape, display configuration, etc.)

Backing Up Your System

There are several options available within the *Sysback* menus.

To perform a backup of your system, run the following command:

> # **smit sysback**
> *Then choose:* Backup & Recovery Options
> *Then choose:* Backup Options

The backup menu then presents the following options:

Backup the System (Installation Image)
> Makes a bootable image of the entire system. Includes the *rootvg* and any other VGs desired.

Backup Volume Groups

    Makes a backup of a specific VG.

Backup Filesystems

    Backs up a specific JFS filesystem.

Backup Logical Volumes

    Backs up a specific LV. Use only for raw partitions; regular JFS filesystems and LVs should be backed up with the previous option.

Backup Files or Directories

    Backs up a specific file or a specific directory on the system.

Choosing the backup type

If you want to make a full dump of the system, choose:

```
Backup the System (Installation Image)
```

Sysback then asks if any VG, besides *rootvg*, should be backed up. The *rootvg* is backed up by default, so entering None at this point would mean backing up only the *rootvg*.

Once you have selected what to back up, *Sysback* asks where the image should be stored. If there are tape drives available, it displays a list of those tape drives:

```
Tape      /dev/rmt0    5.0 GB 8mm Tape Drive
Dir       /usr/lpp/sysback/images/local
server1   /dev/rmt0    5.0 GB 8mm Tape Drive
server1   /usr/lpp/sysback/images/all
```

If a machine has no local tape drive and no remote hosts are defined, only the local file option is offered:

```
Dir       /usr/lpp/sysback/images/local
```

Backing up to a file

When backing up to a file (local or remote), the filename for each backup follows this format:

```
/usr/lpp/sysback/images/[all|local]/
type.hostname.uniqueID.extension
```

The variables in the preceding string are described here:

type

    Represents the type of backup:

    SB System Backup

    VG Volume Group

    LV Logical Volume

FS   Filesystem

FD   File or Directory

`hostname`

The normal hostname of the system being backed up.

`uniqueID`

Unique identification number for the image. By default, *Sysback* uses the date and time of the backup (*MMDDhhmm*). Take note the default string does not contain any year digit, which could be a problem for a long-term disaster recovery plan. You can define the unique ID as you please, but I strongly recommend following some sort of recipe to generate them. It makes finding the right image file that much easier when recovery time comes.

`extension`

This is an extension automatically added by *Sysback* on each file. Each system backup could contain more than one file. These files will be differentiated by their extensions:

TOC

Table of contents

hd1

The *hd1* logical volume

hd9var

The *hd9var* logical volume

Deciding on other backup options

Once the destination of the backup is decided, you will be presented with various backup options:

Hostname of Server

Do not modify this option. When a network backup is chosen, the name of the remote host will appear here.

Device Name

Name of the device where the backup will be saved (i.e., */dev/rmt0*).

Images Directory

This option appears only when a backup to a file was chosen. You should never modify this value since the target directory has been decided previously.

Create a Power Backup? (Yes/No)

A power backup backs up all filesystems as raw partitions. Power backups normally give better backup and restore performance but have less flexibility. When this option is turned on, it is impossible to restore single files. Only restores on complete filesystems (other than */*, */usr*, and */var*) will be available. It won't be possible to restore */*, */var*, and */usr* since restores of raw partitions require the LVs to be inactive, and those three are always active. Since all filesystems are backed up as raw LVs, the entire LV is backed up even if only a quarter of the filesystem is used. Although the resulting backup may contain more raw data than a non-power backup, backing up and recovering data using this feature usually is faster. When the power-backup option is turned on, it is impossible to change any filesystem attributes, logical volume name, logical volume size, or the volume group for a specific LV.

Backup File ID

You can input the name of the file used for the backup. This option is available only for backups to files and not to tapes or diskettes.

Report Output Type

Decide what kind of output is desired: progress indicator, file list, or errors only.

Platform/Kernel Type for Tape Boot Image

Choose the kernel type of the boot image on the tape:

chrp

Common Hardware Reference Platform

chrp/MP

Multiprocessor chrp

rs6k RISC

System/6000

rs6k/MP

Multiprocessor rs6k

rspc

PCI-based RISC System/6000

rspc/MP

Multiprocessor rs6k

(AIX 4.2 users can use the *bootinfo -T* command to see what kernel type the machine booted with.)

Network Install Support to Include

Choose the network type of the adapter that will be used to access the remote host in the event of a Network Install:

ent

Ethernet interface

tok

Tokenring interface

fddi
FDDI interface

Include Non-JFS Logical Volumes? (Yes/No)
Choose whether to include nonjournaled (non-JFS or raw) filesystems in the backup.

Rewind Tape Before Starting Backup? (Yes/No)
This option appears only in the event of a backup to a tape device; it prevents the tape from being rewound before the backup is started. This option is useful mainly when more than one backup image is stored on the same tape.

Compress Data Before Writing to Media? (Yes/No)
Compressing usually reduces by 25–40 percent the amount of space required for the backup. The compression also will be a lot more intensive on the CPU. Compression defaults to No for tapes and to Yes for images on file.

User Description
This can be used to add a short description of the backup, which can be up to 60 characters long. The description will appear when the content of a backup is listed. This option can be used to keep track of certain special backup images; here is an example:

```
Description: "Backup of system1 before the upgrade to AIX 4.3".
```

Host Read Permission
This option applies only to backups of files. It sets the host permissions for the image file. This option lists the hosts that will have read access to the backup file; this may be a list of hostnames or specific keywords like "all."

User Read Permission
This option applies only to backups of files. It sets the user permissions for the image file. This option lists the users who will have read access to the backup file; this may be a list of usernames or specific keywords like "all."

Buffer Size (in Kbytes)
This represents the amount of data written to the output in a single I/O operation. This option will vary depending on the backup media. When writing to the media, the data first is buffered and then written out in "chunks." This option allows you to specify the size of the chunks used.

Preserve Physical Partition Mapping? (Yes/No)
A volume re-created with the option set to Yes is recreated on the same physical partition as the original volume. Note that saying Yes to this option also will preserve fragmentation that develops on logical volumes as they are incrementally expanded during normal use.

Device Name for Remote Volume Prompt

> This permits you to specify the device name where the volume prompt (tape change) message will be sent instead of the current *smit* screen (i.e., */dev/tty0*, */dev/lft0* or */dev/pts/5*).

Non-rootvg Volume Groups to Include

> To list the extra VGs to be backed up. If you decided on earlier screens to back up nonroot VGs, you are now asked to select which ones to back up.

In addition to all those options, pre- and postbackup scripts can be added to the system. *Sysback* will automatically use:

/usr/lpp/sysback/scripts/install.pre

> As a preinstall script

/usr/lpp/sysback/scripts/install.post

> As a postinstall script

These scripts are stored on the tape image and run at restore time. Here is one example:

/usr/lpp/sysback/scripts/install.post_rmnet

> Removes all network configuration and host ID.

Verifying and Listing Backup Content

Two functions are provided with *Sysback* to verify or list the content of a backup. Use:

    # smit sb_verify

Select the appropriate device as well as the data to be verified. *Sysback* will run an integrity test on the data. You also can use:

    # smit sb_list

Select the appropriate device to list the full content of a backup tape or file.

Restoring Data

Sysback offers two options when it comes to restoring data:

Recreate Volume Groups, Logical Volumes & Filesystems

> Allows you to recreate any VGs, LVs, or filesystems in the event of a hardware failure. Recreating these "containers" allows you to restore the data in them later.

Restore Data from a Backup

> Allows you to restore actual data contained on a *Sysback* backup file or tape.

System Cloning

Cloning a system is the action of restoring the complete image of one system onto a completely different system. The "restored" system is then a perfect image of the original one. This could be useful in the case of a fire or a similar catastrophe in which the hardware is completely lost. In such a case, you could use an offsite *mksysb* or *Sysback* to recover the old system onto new hardware.

AIX 3.2.x Operating System

To perform system cloning of an AIX 3.2.x system, follow the same procedure explained for *mksysb* restores and *Sysback* restores. The new system will become an image of the system backed up on tape. No special procedure must be followed since AIX 3.2.x supports only the channel architecture.

AIX 4.x Operating System

The newer version of AIX requires special attention since not all the drivers are installed with the BOS. In this case, you are left with two choices:

- Install all device drivers for all available architectures before taking the *mksysb* or *Sysback* backup of the system. That allows the tape to be booted from and restored onto any IBM RS/6000 and is the only viable option for *Sysback*.

- If device drivers were not installed, you can simply boot the new machine from the CD- ROM containing the AIX 4.x operating system. After the boot, choose the "Restore from tape backup" option, insert the *mksysb* tape, and start the restore. This last method is the one recommended by IBM in its documentation; this option works only for *mksysb* tapes and is not available with *Sysback*.

Database Backup & Recovery

Part V consists of the following four chapters which discuss database backups and detail the steps to back up and recover each of these widely used databases:

- Chapter 13, *Backing Up Databases*, provides an overview of database backup, concepts, terminology, and procedures.
- Chapter 14, *Informix Backup & Recovery*, discusses backup and recovery facilities and provides step-by-step recovery instructions.
- Chapter 15, *Oracle Backup & Recovery*, discusses Oracle's backup and recovery facilities and provides step-by-step recovery instructions.
- Chapter 16, *Sybase Backup & Recovery*, discusses Sybase's backup and recovery facilities and provides step-by-step recovery instructions.

13

Backing Up Databases

Performing regular database backups is one of the hardest tasks that lies before today's system administrator. The primary reason is that databases are infinitely larger and more complex than simple filesystem files. In order to properly back up a database, you first need to:

- Understand the internal structure of your database

- Understand the available utilities

- Have an excellent working relationship between system administrators and database administrators

Once you've accomplished all of that, you'll need to choose among your various options:

- Buy an expensive commercial utility

- Find or write your own utility

- Perform cold backups without a utility

Almost anyone who reads this list will find at least one of these steps daunting. Many people work with databases that operate 24 hours, seven days a week. They can't shut them down for hours at a time to back them up. Even if they could, if a database uses raw devices it can't be backed up with a regular *dump*. Of course *dd* would work, but that would mean doing one thing for filesystems and a different thing for databases. A common theme throughout this book is that different is bad. Every special case is a chance for failure. It's something else you have to code for, something else you have to watch—something else to break. The result is that database backups are not easy.

Part of the problem is the design process of the actual database engine itself. Historically, the need for bigger storage and faster queries drove the design of a product much more than its ability to back itself up. (This goes for filesystems too. Most Unix vendors have added support for a multiple-terabyte filesystem that break the 2-GB file-size barrier, but at least one man page for *dump* says "WARNING: *dump* will not back up a filesystem containing large files.") Over the last few years, databases have grown from a gigabyte or so to an average size that is daily growing closer to a terabyte. This growth in size and performance happened because the customer base screamed for it. Unfortunately, they weren't simultaneously screaming for a backup utility to support those huge databases.

The Nature of the Beast

About five years ago, I had a conversation with a developer at Informix, in which I was complaining that they were selling us a 150-GB database without a decent utility to back it up. (We were using onarchive. See Chapter 14, *Informix Backup & Recovery*, for details.) His response was, "Good backup utilities don't sell databases. Good databases do. Developers have to have their priorities." *Wonderful.* You can't really hold this against Informix, though. All the database companies did about the same thing at the same time. They are all finally starting to come out with utilities that are much more functional. Informix is now the easiest database to back up and recover; *onbar* is *so* much easier than *rman.* And yet, Informix still doesn't have Oracle's market share. I guess the Informix developer was right.

Can It Be Done?

Think about database backups from a big-picture perspective, comparing them to filesystem backups. There are a number of good backup utilities on the market now. Why aren't there just as many for database backups? There is certainly a demand for it.

One of the reasons is the complexity of the task. In order to release a database backup product, a company would need to consider several factors:

Multiple moving targets
> How do you get a database to hold still? Have you ever tried to take a picture of 100 people? Designing a backup utility for a database is very hard, since you have to "take a picture" of hundreds of files all at once.

Interrelationship between the files
> A database backup program needs to understand all of the database elements and how they relate.

Necessity to work with the database engine

This is essential. If the database understands that you are running a backup, it can help you. If you don't interface with the database, you'll be backing up blind.

The size of the job

How do you get one terabyte of data to a backup drive in one hour? That's what some of the backup requirements are! The only answer to that is a multi-threaded backup program. (See "Simultaneous Backup of One Client to Many Drives" in Chapter 5, *Commercial Backup Utilities*, for more details.)

Recoverability versus cost

You need all of the preceding, but you don't want to mortgage your house to get it.

Differing levels of automation

Different customers want different levels of automation. Some want everything managed by the library, while others would rather do it themselves.

With these kinds of requirements, is there any hope of getting commercial utilities that are up to the challenge? The answer is "Yes!" Database companies have finally recognized that backup utilities do have an effect on the overall sales of a database engine. They have finally started producing good utilities that interface with other commercial backup products. Vendors have even taken an active lead in making sure that customers use a utility that works properly on both the backup and the restore sides. Now that there are decent backup utilities, though, you have another problem—confusion.

Confusion: The Mysteries of Database Architecture

Any system administrator who has been in the business for any length of time can probably tell you how to back up the home directories on any system. Start asking about backing up databases, though, and even the most seasoned veterans may start to squirm. To many administrators, the architecture of a database is a mystery. Unfortunately, you really need to understand how the database works to properly recover from a disaster. They know how to back up a filesystem, but ask them to find the backups for data space A in database B in instance C, and they look at you with fear in their eyes! They just don't have any experience in database design—nor do they have time to get that experience. If they work in a heterogeneous shop with more than one database, it gets even harder. Their only hope is that the database administrators (DBAs) know what they are doing.

DBAs spend much of their time normalizing databases, designing user forms, and making sure the database performs adequately. They know how to back up their database disk, maybe even to a standalone backup drive, but they don't have any experience with commercial backup software or large, automated libraries. If the database is too big to back up to disk and they don't have a standalone backup drive to back up to, they have to work with the system administrators (SAs) to get the backup done. Their only hope is that the SAs know what they are doing.

Database products also differ from one another. Try to get an Informix DBA and an Oracle DBA to agree on what a tablespace is!* One of the reasons this is difficult is that different products use the same term for different logical elements. What Informix calls a tablespace, Oracle calls a segment. Don't confuse that, however, with a Sybase segment, which is closer to what Oracle calls a tablespace. Are you confused yet? Don't worry.

The Muck Stops Here: Databases in Plain English

This chapter explains everything you need to know in order to learn more about database backup and recovery. You then will be prepared to read and understand the vendor-specific database chapters in this book, as well as any of the appropriate sections of your favorite DBA book or manual. This chapter assumes no prior knowledge, beginning with some of the very basic elements such as tables and rows, so that even the most junior person can understand everything. However, that does not mean that a seasoned SA or DBA should not read this chapter. It took several experienced DBAs of a number of different types of databases to come up with the information you see here, so almost any DBA should be able to learn something from this chapter.

This chapter includes an extremely useful table that lists all of the elements of database storage for each of three big databases:† Oracle, Informix, and Sybase. If you're not a DBA, the information here will allow you to discuss backup matters intelligently with your DBA. If you are a DBA for one product, this will help you to discuss backup and storage strategies with DBAs for other products—without confusing one another! The desired result for your organization is that you can all agree on why and how to protect your database data. What a beautiful world that will be!

---

* I know. It took weeks to compile the comparison table in this chapter. It would be easier to get Unix administrators to agree on which editor is the best!

† DB2 and Ingres are not included in this edition. The reason for this is lack of research material. If I can find some good books to read and DBAs to work with, they might be included in a later revision of this book. If I do, the updated table will be put on the web page for your enjoyment.

What's the Big Deal?

Why, all of a sudden, are we hearing so much about database backups? Why are they so hard? Why don't utilities currently exist to do all this? Can't I just shut down the database and back up the whole system? These are all questions that may be going through your head. If you already know the answers, feel free to skip to the next section.

Why, all of a sudden, are we hearing so much about database backups?

The demand for Relational Database Management Systems (RDBMSs) has grown exponentially in the last few years. Not only are there more databases, they are faster, larger, and more complex than ever before. Companies are relying increasingly on bigger and bigger databases to store their information—information that, if lost, would be irreplaceable. Customers have started to recognize the importance of safeguarding their data, and the demand for better backup and recovery utilities has followed. Database companies and backup product companies have finally responded with utilities that are up to the task at hand.

Why is backing up a database so hard?

Actually, backing up a database isn't that hard. It's restoring the database that has caused many people to go insane! Seriously, though, the reason it is so difficult is that you need a good SA and a good DBA to design a good backup plan. Most people know only one side well. If you or your people know both sides, then consider yourself very lucky. In some companies, it's tough to get both sides to work together.

Why aren't there utilities already available to do all this?

Much to the chagrin of a certain backup book author, backups aren't sexy. Historically, customers have asked for faster databases, or easier-to-program databases. Therefore, the existence of a good backup utility was not even considered until well after a product was purchased, installed, and quite often in production. Many times it even took a disaster to get some people to realize that backup and recovery is an essential part of any database system.

This finally has changed. Maybe it was because customers finally realized that they needed to ask about backup and recovery when they were evaluating a database product. Maybe the database companies' support departments beat up the developers because they were spending all their time on down system calls. (Hell hath no fury like a customer who has suffered data loss that could have been prevented by a better backup utility.)

One of the most important tasks that customers needed was the ability to integrate their database backups into their commercial backup utility. Remember, though, that these products haven't been on the market for that long. Until a few years ago, if you asked your database vendor if its database worked with product X, they were likely to say, "Who are they and why should we?" It's not clear who broke the barrier first, but all three big vendors did the same thing within a year or two of one another—they cooperated with commercial backup companies to develop and release their own utility that was designed specifically to work with third-party backup products.

Can't I just shut down the database and back up the whole system?

In a small numbers of cases, yes. There are a number of considerations that might prevent you from doing this, including your database platform, whether you are using raw or filesystem files and whether you need point-in-time recovery. Those details are covered in appropriate chapters in this book.

Database Structure

There are many terms thrown around when one is discussing RDBMSs. The good news is that you don't need to know all of them to properly back up and recover databases. You do need to know some of them, though—about 20 individual terms. It's helpful to know:

- What all the different storage elements are and what they are called
- How these elements are logically organized within the RDBMS
- What facilities are in place to protect and back up the data

This information can be complex, because it depends a lot on how you look at the data. This chapter presents this information from first a power user's, then a DBA's, point of view. The various building blocks of a database are defined, although we may have to go up and down the building a bit before we're done!

The Power User's View: Logical Elements of a Database

Before looking at how databases are stored on disk, let's look at the "user's" view of a database. This is necessary since some of these terms are used in the definition of the storage elements. It might be more appropriate to call this a "power user's view," since many users will have little or no knowledge of any of these terms. But unless they want to start doing the DBA's job of putting a database together, these terms may be all that they would ever need. The terms are presented in no particular order, since it is very difficult to define one term without using another one. Therefore, it may help some readers to read this section more than once.

This view also could be called the "logical" view, since many of the elements described in this view don't exist in a physical sense. That fact is one of the many things that differentiate an RDBMS from a simple spreadsheet. A spreadsheet has one table that resides in one physical file. An RDBMS table, on the other hand, gives the appearance that its data is all sitting in one place, but it may be spread out all over the system.

Instance

Term	Informix	Oracle	Sybase
Instance	Instance	Instance	Server

Instance is probably the most difficult term to explain because it means different things to different people—and to different database platforms. The simplest definition is that an instance is a process (or set of processes) on one machine, through which the databases on that machine* communicate with shared memory. There often can be multiple databases within an instance, and a database also can be distributed across multiple instances on the same machine or on separate machines within a cluster. (In order to distribute a database across multiple instances, you must use a parallel database product such as Informix Extended Parallel Option (XPO) or Oracle's Cluster Server (OCS).) Therefore, an instance and a database are two entirely different concepts.

The Sybase term "server" stems from the original intent that each *machine/server* would have one Sybase *instance/server* on it, although it is now quite common to have more than one instance on each machine. Informix occasionally uses the term in this manner, and it can be rather confusing. They tend to use *server* when speaking about the software and *instance* when speaking about a running engine environment and especially when discussing running multiple instantiations of the server.

If an instance needs to be shut down and restarted for any reason, all databases within that instance are unavailable during the shutdown.† Perhaps this helps to understand the original definition, since all of the databases within an instance have a single connection to shared memory, which is provided by the instance. If the instance is shut down, that connection is no longer available. (See Figure 13-1 for a graphical representation of an instance.)

---

* An instance can actually be spread across multiple machines.

† That is why it is not correct to say that you are going to stop/start a database. You are actually stopping/starting an *instance* that *contains* the database.

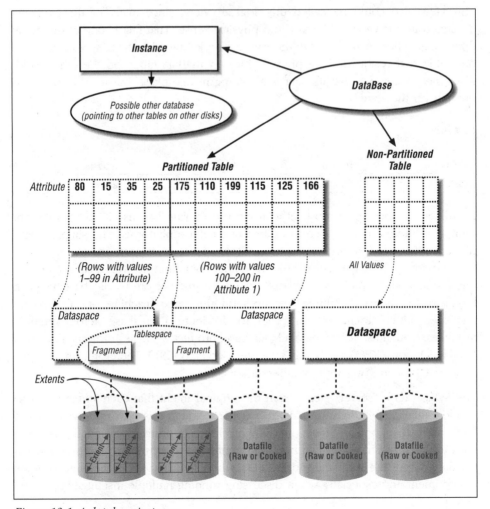

Figure 13-1. A database instance

 Most database backup utilities are able to back up only an entire instance, although they may be able to restore a single database within that instance.

Database

Term	Informix	Oracle	Sybase
Database	Database	Database	Database

A *database* is a collection of database objects. It may be a very simple database with one table and no indexes, or it could contain many tables, indexes, and other database objects. (All database products have the ability to have more than one database object and more than one type of database object.) For example, the "customer" database may contain a table that has customer addresses and an index for that table. It also may contain a Binary Large OBject (BLOB) table that contains a scanned-in image of the customer's contract, a regular table that contains the data from that contract, and an index for that table. Then there might be another database that keeps track of all the widgets that your company sells. (See Figure 13-2 for a graphical representation of a database.)

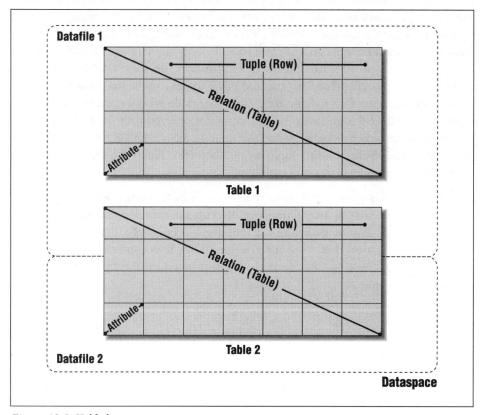

Figure 13-2. Table layout

One element of database architecture that is slightly related to the database is the *schema*. Although the parallel is not exactly the same, comparing a database to a Unix box may help to explain the difference between a database and a schema. If you think of the database as a Unix server and database objects as filesystems, the schema could be the password file and set of Unix permissions that grant a user access to that machine and to the various filesystems and files within that machine. Some database products allow multiple schemas per databases; others do not.*

Table

Term	Informix	Oracle	Sybase
Table	Table	Table	Table

A *table* is a grouping of related information. (That is why it is called a *relation* in formal database terminology.) Information is grouped in such a way that data is not replicated between tables except when necessary. In the previous example, the customer database could contain the "customer information" table, and each customer is given a unique account number. Then the BLOB table that stores the customer's signed contract would need to store only the customer's account number to be able to tie the two pieces of information together. (BLOB data is discussed later in this chapter.) That method takes up less space than storing the customer's whole name with the contract. The order table would contain that account number as well, and it might list what a customer ordered only by part number. If you wanted to see the details about that part number, the instance could reference the "parts" database using that part number. (See Figure 13-2 and Figure 13-3 for graphical representations of a table.)

A related term is a *view*, which usually refers to a *virtual* table. For example, you may put together a view that references the customer, order, and parts tables to present a united view of information about a given customer. Data often is replicated in a virtual view, but since it's a *virtual* table, it doesn't take up extra storage space on the disk; A view normally is constructed on the fly from the results of a *SELECT* statement.

---

* I don't believe that it is necessary to understand schemas in order to properly back up and recover databases. One of my technical reviewers made me put it in.

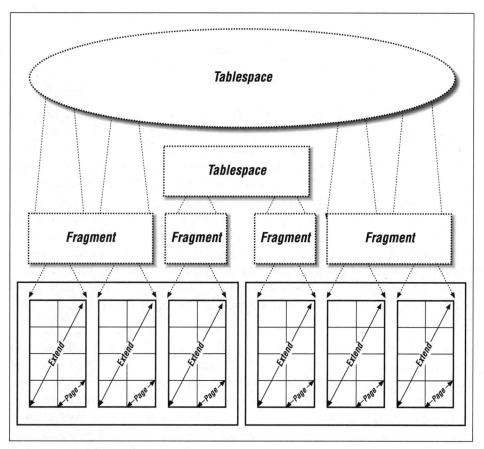

Figure 13-3. Tablespace layout

Index

Term	Informix	Oracle	Sybase
Index	Index	Index	Index

An *index* is a special-purpose table that allows for quicker lookups of a normal table. A table is indexed by the value that you usually would use to look up a record (row). For example, the customer database might be indexed by last name if customers frequently call in and do not know their account number. It has a unique ability when recovering a database, since you can always recreate an index from an existing table instead of recovering it.

BLOB space

Term	Informix	Oracle	Sybase
BLOB space	BLOBspace, Smart BLOBspace	BLOB, CLOB, BFILE data types	Image data type

BLOB data has grown in popularity within the last few years. It refers to anything that does not fit into a "normal" table. This may range from a large piece of text data to a scanned-in image. Most databases use the term "BLOB" to refer to both types, but Oracle8 differentiates between Character LOB (text) and Binary LOB (graphics and the like) data. Oracle and Sybase store BLOB data inside a normal table by using a special data type. Oracle8 also allows you to store BLOB data in the regular filesystem and have it referenced in the database by using the BFILE data type. (I have seen custom data types that do this in other databases as well.) Informix, the first to offer this type of storage, has a special dataspace—called a BLOBspace—reserved just for BLOB data. (Dataspaces are defined later.) Informix Universal Data Option also has what it calls a "Smart BLOBspace," which allows BLOB data to contain nonstandard information that can be used to manage the BLOB data in a "smart" way.

If the BLOB data is stored inside the database, it presents no unique backup requirements. However, the use of the BFILE data type and custom data types that allow the storage of the BLOB data outside the database (i.e., in the filesystem) are a different story. While they may provide many performance enhancements, they do present a unique backup challenge. The BLOB data needs to be backed up in sync with the database data. That is because the database is keeping track of what files are where. Suppose a piece of BLOB data was inserted at 11:00. If you back up the filesystem at 10:00 and the database at 12:00, the database will know about a file that exists out on the filesystem, but that file will not be found on your filesystem backup. Even more confusion may be added if the filesystem backup spans the time of the database backup. In other words, it begins at 10:00 and ends at 4:00, although the database backup begins at 12:00 and is done by 2:00.

There are only two ways to resolve this conflict. The easiest way is to shut down the database or put it in read-only mode during the entire time of your filesystem backup. This may be impractical for many environments. The second way is to use the *snapshot* concept. This allows you to take a "snapshot" of the entire filesystem in just a few seconds and then take all night to back it up. This provides a consistent picture of the filesystem at a certain point in time. (See "Using Snapshots to Back Up a Volatile Filesystem" in Chapter 19, *Miscellanea*.)

Object

Term	Informix	Oracle	Sybase
Object	Object	Object	Object

This generic term refers to any type of table within a database. All database objects are tables by its strictest definition, but the term *table* usually refers to a simple table, as discussed earlier. So we use the term *object* to describe any type of table that may be in a database. This includes, but is not limited to, simple tables, indexes, BLOB tables, stored procedures, and triggers.

Row

Term	Informix	Oracle	Sybase
Row	Tuple	Tuple	Tuple

A row (called a *tuple* in formal database terminology) is a collection of related attributes. For example, there may be a row that contains all the basic information about a customer such as her name, address, account number, and phone number (this is also similar to a row in a spreadsheet). Each row has at least one unique attribute, such as the account number, to distinguish it from other rows. A row is also sometimes called a "record." (See Figure 13-1 for a graphical representation of a row.)

Attribute

Term	Informix	Oracle	Sybase
Attribute	Attribute	Attribute	Attribute

An *attribute* is the basic element of data within a table. It is a single value, such as a customer's name or Zip Code. An attribute may be very small, such as a Zip Code, or very large, such as a BLOB. An attribute is the value that a database user changes when performing a "transaction." (Transactions are covered later in this chapter.) (See Figure 13-1 for a graphical representation of an attribute.)

The DBA's View: Physical Elements of a Database Environment

The DBA has to know quite a bit more about the database than even the most sophisticated power user, since the DBA must create databases, tune them, back them up, and recover them in the case of failure. DBAs also know a programming language called SQL that allows them to construct precise types of queries to increase the usability of the database. Good DBAs also need to know quite a bit about operating system technology, so that they can efficiently use the storage capabilities of their operating environment.

The good news is that, unless you're a DBA, you won't need to know all of that to properly back up and recover databases. This section describes the physical elements of database storage and how they are combined with the logical elements discussed earlier.

The bad news is that, unlike the terms in the user's view, the elements in the database view are called something different in almost every product. Often, the same term presented in the previous section is used to describe different types of elements in different products. This took quite a bit of work to be able to discuss them all in a single chapter. It often was very difficult to find a generic term that would apply to all of them without confusing things. Therefore, the "Term" column often contains a word that was coined just for that purpose. This generic term is used throughout this chapter when discussing the different types of storage elements and how they fit together. The product-specific terms are used only when referring to the products themselves. It should be noted that some of the coined terms that follow may be useful only when discussing things with someone else that has read this chapter. If you are discussing storage elements with a particular DBA who has not read this chapter, be sure to use the appropriate terms for the product that DBA knows.

Page

Term	Informix	Oracle	Sybase
Page	Page	Block	Page

The *page*, also called a *block*, is the basic building block of every database. It is the smallest amount of data that is moved in an I/O operation. It is similar to, although not exactly the same as, a filesystem block. (You can have a 2-K block inside a database that sits on a filesystem that has an 8-K block size.*) It is usually 2 K or 4 K in size, but some database products allow you to specify a custom page size for your environment. Whatever size the page is, it is the smallest atomic entity within a database. When one modifies a table within a database, it eventually will modify one or more pages stored somewhere on disk. (See Figure 13-2 and Figure 13-3 for graphical representations of a page.)

---

* That is why I prefer the term "page" over the Oracle term, "block." It helps to differentiate between filesystem blocks and database blocks, or pages. I have seen DBAs and SAs confuse each other talking about what block size a given Oracle database should have.

Datafile

Term	Informix	Oracle	Sybase
Datafile	Chunk	Data File	Device

A *datafile* is where the data is stored. This may be a *raw** device (e.g., */dev/rdsk/c0t0d0s3*), a *cooked device* (e.g., */dev/dsk/c0t0d0s3*), or a *cooked file* (e.g., */oracle/data/dbs01.dbf*). Some products require the use of raw partitions, while others merely suggest it. Some products allow a mixture of raw and cooked files. The only real difference to the DBA is how they are initially created and how they are backed up. Other than that, they look the same within the database. (See Figure 13-2 and Figure 13-3 for graphical representations of a page.)

Extents

Term	Informix	Oracle	Sybase
Extent	Extent	Extent	Extent

An *extent* is a number of pages that are logically grouped together and are considered "logically contiguous." They may or may not be physically contiguous. (If the pages in an extent are physically contiguous, that means that they are physically next to each other.) Informix extents are physically contiguous, while others may or may not be, depending on when and how they were created. All extents are considered *logically* contiguous, since they are treated as a single block of storage that is allocated to a table. Extents do not span more than one datafile, but a datafile may contain any number of extents. The actual size of an extent is determined by the database platform. (See Figure 13-2 and Figure 13-3 for graphical representations of an extent.)

Fragment

Term	Informix	Oracle	Sybase
Fragment	Tblspace	N/A	Allocation unit

A *fragment* is a collection of logically contiguous extents that may or may not be physically contiguous. Informix calls this a "tblspace." This is *not* to be confused with what Oracle calls a "tablespace"! (See the sidebar about these terms.) In Sybase, an *allocation unit* is the smallest block of storage that is given to a database, and it is 32 extents.

---

* "Raw" refers to an unbuffered disk device. Typically these are in */dev/rdsk*, or named */dev/rxxx*. The term "cooked" seems a little silly, but it is simply the opposite of "raw."

Tablespace

Term	Informix	Oracle	Sybase
Tablespace	Tblspace	Segment	Disk fragment

Again, this is where more of the confusion comes in. A *tablespace* (in this context) is defined as "the space that a table occupies," not to be confused with a *dataspace*, which is "the space that a table goes *in*." When one creates a table, it usually is created on or in a dataspace (defined next), which may contain that table and many others. The quantity of physical storage *space* that this *table* takes up is referred to as its "tablespace." Informix calls this a "tblspace" as well but also uses the term for the fragments that make up a tblspace (see the sidebar "Tablespace or Tblspace?"). (See Figure 13-2 and Figure 13-3 for a graphical depiction of a tablespace.)

Tablespace or Tblspace?

The term "tablespace" is thrown around enough to make things confusing. Informix confuses the issue even more by using it for two different things. A "tablespace" as defined here is "the space that a table goes in." That also is called a "tablespace" in Informix. But, as shown in Figure 13-1 and Figure 13-2, a tablespace can consist of extents that are in different datafiles. As defined here, when a tablespace spans datafiles, each block of extents within a datafile is called a "fragment." Informix also calls this a "tblspace!"

Dataspace

Term	Informix	Oracle	Sybase
Dataspace	Dbspace	Tablespace	Segment

A *dataspace* is a much larger storage element that may contain one or more tablespaces (as defined previously; not to be confused with what Oracle calls a "tablespace") and consists of one or more datafiles. (See Figure 13-2 and Figure 13-3 for a graphical depiction of a dataspace.) A table is created in a dataspace (e.g., *create table in dataspace alpha*). Both Informix and Oracle require you to create dataspaces before you can create a database. Informix and Oracle also create a dataspace prior to creating a new instance. When creating an instance, you specify which datafile will be the main (or system) dataspace. Informix and Oracle then create this dataspace for you automatically.

A DBA simply tells Sybase to "create a database on these devices." When you do this, Sybase creates the *default* tablespace or *segment*. Sybase allows you to then create a table within a database, and it gets stored on the same dataspace as the rest of the tables in the database. If you do not define a custom user segment, all tables will be created in the default segment. However, you can create a segment that consists of one or more datafiles and then create a table on that segment. Therefore, when you use segments in Sybase, they serve the same function as dbspaces in Informix and tablespaces in Oracle. However, since many Sybase DBAs do not define custom user segments, they do not think of segments as dataspaces.

Partition

Term	Informix	Oracle	Sybase
Partition	Fragment	Partition	N/A

One of the biggest advancements in RDBMS technology is the ability to *partition* a table across multiple dataspaces. Typically, a table had to be contained within a dataspace, as described before. Now you can specify that a table is partitioned across multiple tablespaces based on the values of certain attributes. For example, you could create a table that is partitioned across dataspaces A and B. You could specify that all records with value 1–100 in attribute A go to dataspace A, and all records with value 101–200 in attribute A go to dataspace B. (See Figure 13-3 for a graphical depiction of a partitioned table.) A partitioned table does not present any unique backup requirements. Informix says that a table is *partitioned* into multiple *fragments*.

Master database

Term	Informix	Oracle	Sybase
Master database	Sysmaster, onconfig file, rootdb	Control file	Master database

Each instance has some way of keeping track of all the storage elements that it has at its disposal. This *master database* keeps track of all the devices and their status. It keeps track of any information that all the databases need to have access to. If multiple databases are allowed, it needs to keep track of them as well. Sybase has a special database to do this, and Oracle has what it calls a *control file*, which keeps track of this information. Informix also has a special database, called the *Sysmaster*, that keeps track of the status of every object within an instance. However, some information is tracked by the *onconfig* file and reserved pages within the *rootdb*.

Transaction

Term	Informix	Oracle	Sybase
Transaction	Transaction	Transaction	Transaction

A *transaction* is an activity within a database that changes one or more attributes within one or more tables. If a user changes a customer's address, that is a transaction. There are two types of transactions, a simple transaction and a complex transaction. A simple transaction is done in one statement (e.g., *update attribute X in table Y to 100*). A complex transaction may be much longer, and opens with a *begin transaction* statement and closes with an *end transaction* statement. There may be a number of simple statements in between the open and close statements, or there may be a complicated SQL program that updates hundreds of values based on certain parameters. For example, a number of new area codes have been created in several large cities. A complex transaction could be designed that would scan all customer phone numbers and change their area code based on their three-digit exchange. A complex transaction is treated as an "atomic" event—it's all or nothing. Both the start transaction and end transaction statements are recorded in the transaction log (defined later), and if anything happens before the end transaction statement is recorded, all changes that were made by that transaction are *rolled back*, or undone. Things that could cause that to happen are the user logging out in the middle, the database being shut down, the system crashing, or even the user changing his mind.

Rollback log

Term	Informix	Oracle	Sybase
Rollback log	Physical log	Rollback segment	Transaction log

From a data integrity standpoint, it is important to realize what a transaction does. While to a user's eyes a transaction changes a record in the database, it actually changes one or many pages. It is on the page level that transaction recovery is done. If a given transaction modifies 100 pages and then the transaction does not complete, those 100 pages must be returned to what they looked like before the transaction occurred. This is referred to as *rolling back* the page to its *before image*. (The before image is what the page looked like *before* it was changed.) The following elements describe the facilities that databases have to ensure that this (and other data integrity activities) occurs properly.

The *rollback log* is the place where the database stores this before image. Informix and Oracle have a dedicated log just for this purpose. The before image of each changed page is stored in this log until the transaction is complete, or *committed*. Sybase records both the before image and the transaction data in the *trans-*

action log. It is important to note that this before image must be physically written to disk before any pages are to be physically changed. That ensures that the before image is available if the system crashes. How this before image is actually used varies widely between database products.

Transaction log

Term	Informix	Oracle	Sybase
Transaction log	Logical log	Redolog	Transaction log

Suppose that a system were to crash in such a way that it needed to be recovered from your latest database backup. If there were no way to redo the transactions that have occurred since the last backup, all such transactions would be lost. A *transaction log* records each transaction and what pages it changed. This information is used in case of a system crash that requires reentering those transactions. The master database knows what state each datafile is in, and it looks at each of them upon starting up. If it detects any that are corrupt, you have to restore those datafiles from your backup. The master database then looks at the datafile and realizes that it was restored from an earlier point in time. It then goes to the transaction log to "redo" all the transactions that have been recorded since that time. Uncommitted transactions are then rolled back. The actual order of this process differs from product to product. However, the main purpose remains the same. The rollback and transaction logs work together to ensure that all pages are returned to their proper state after a crash or reboot.

Many people have difficulty understanding the difference between the rollback log and the transaction log. Informix's terminology helps in this case, because their terms *physical* and *logical* log illustrate exactly what the logs contain. The physical log contains a physical "image" of a page prior to it being changed by a transaction. It doesn't know or care how the page was changed; it just knows what it looked like before it was changed. The logical log, on the other hand, keeps track of *how* the page was changed, so that the database can recreate this change after a recovery.

Checkpoint

Term	Informix	Oracle	Sybase
Checkpoint	Checkpoint	Checkpoint	Checkpoint

In order to increase performance, databases keep a lot of data in memory: recently changed pages, commonly accessed pages, before images of modified pages, and the transactions themselves. This means that if the system crashes at some point, some data will be lost, since RAM is volatile. The database needs some way to go back to a time that it knows everything was on disk and nothing was in memory. This point in time is called the *checkpoint*.

At certain intervals, defined by user-configurable parameters, the database flushes everything to disk. All datafiles and log files are therefore in a consistent state. If the system were to crash without damaging the datafiles, the database would revert to this checkpoint, then replay any completed transactions that have been recorded since that checkpoint, and finally roll back any incomplete transactions. This ensures that the database can always be backed up in a consistent state.

An Overview of a Page Change

We ask a lot of RDBMSs. We want them to be big and fast but to always ensure that the data is in a consistent state. To accomplish the speed requirement, they've got to keep lots of things in memory. But to ensure the integrity requirement, they've got to be very careful. It's difficult to juggle knives without cutting off a finger or two.

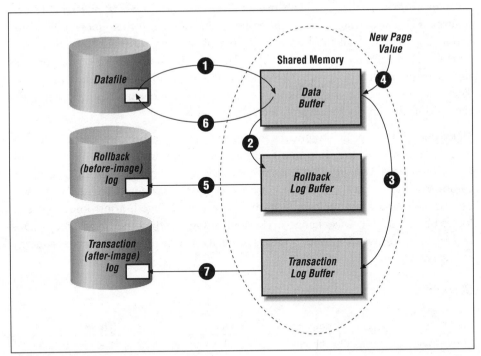

Figure 13-4. Anatomy of a page change

Please refer to Figure 13-4 throughout this section. That figure shows that there are four main storage areas of an RDBMS. There is the datafile itself, the rollback log, the transaction log, and shared memory. Shared memory is further divided into the data buffer, the rollback log buffer, and the transaction log buffer. Not all RDBMSs work exactly this way, but they are all similar. What happens when a user enters a transaction? Before anything happens, the beginning of the transaction is recorded in the transaction log. Then, for each page that needs to be changed, the following steps are taken:

1. The RDBMS reads the page that is to be modified and loads it into the data buffer. Until proper safeguards have been put in place, this is where the page stays for a while.

2. The transaction then wants to change the page, but first it saves a copy of what it looked like prior to changing it. This before image is placed in the rollback log buffer.

3. The after image of the page is recorded in the transaction log buffer.

4. The transaction can now change the actual page that it wants to change. This change is made only to the copy of the page that is stored in the data buffer. Recording the change in the transaction log buffer before actually making the change is a safety measure.

5. Notice that up to this point no changes have been made to disk. If the system were to crash right now, the disks would have no record of this transaction. Before the system can make any changes on disk, it needs to make sure the before image is safe. This is because it will need that before image to roll back this change if it doesn't complete due to a canceled transaction or a rebooted system. To ensure that the before image will be available, it flushes the rollback log buffer to the *physical* rollback log (the log on disk).

6. Now that the system has safely preserved the before image of the page to be changed, it can flush the changed page to disk.

7. The after image of the page is now flushed to the physical transaction log. This image will be necessary if the transaction needs to be redone.

At some point, the transaction is committed. This fact is immediately recorded in the transaction log. That way, the system knows that the entire transaction completed and should redo it in case of a system crash. This process ensures that no matter what time the system crashes (and it *will* crash), the system will remain in a consistent state.

What Can Happen to an RDBMS?

A lot of things can happen to interfere with the normal operation of a database. What you need to do to get the database running again will depend on what broke it in the first place. The following is a list of some of the things that can happen to an RDBMS:

Device ownership change

Someone can accidentally change the ownership of the raw devices or files that the database is using for datafiles. Since the database can no longer write to the files, it will cease to function. You will need to return the device to its proper ownership and possibly restore data.

Device permissions change

This is similar to an ownership change, since the database engine can no longer write to the file. The fix is the same as the previous one.

Removing device symbolic link

In Unix, you are well advised not to use the actual raw device when setting up a database. You should make a symbolic link to a name that makes sense (e.g., *ln -s /dev/rdsk/c0t0d0s0 /dev/informix/chunk1*). This allows for much greater flexibility if that device goes bad. However, you need to document what device the database is pointing to so that you can remake the link in case someone deletes it. (You also can restore this information from backup, but it would be much faster to remake it if you knew what to link it to.)

Disk goes bad

The only real protection against a bad disk is mirroring and backups.

Controller goes bad

If you are mirroring some of your devices, you should set up the mirroring so that a device on one SCSI controller is mirrored to a device on another SCSI controller. This ensures that if a SCSI controller does go bad it won't take out both mirrors at once.

Assign a database raw device as a swap or filesystem

This one's a bad one. This is where proper documentation comes in handy. It also helps if your administrators are trained to look at the ownership of a device before they use it. If it is owned by someone other than root, then don't use it. To recover from this, you need to undo the change and restore from backup.

Another application using the raw device as mirror

This is similar to the preceding scenario; an administrator tries to use one of the database disks for something other than the database. Again, you will have to undo the change and restore from backup.

Raw Devices Versus Cooked Files

This is an often-debated topic in DBA circles. Many DBAs want to use raw devices because that is faster than using filesystem files. (This actually is less true every day with the advent of some of the modern filesystems. Veritas's *vxfs*, for example, claims superior performance than that of a raw device—with none of the drawbacks.) Some DBAs prefer to use filesystem (cooked) files due to their ease of administration.

The historical reason for using raw partitions is increased data integrity. A database spends a lot of time trying to ensure all the data is in its proper state. It logs every changed page and knows the exact condition of every page at any point in time. It assumes that when it tells the OS to write a page to the data file, it does so. However, many filesystems cache writes to increase performance. This means that the database thinks that a page has been modified on disk when it really hasn't. This is a bad thing. (Veritas's Database Edition for Oracle does not have this problem.)

Modern databases resolve this problem by opening a cooked file in *O_SYNC* mode, which automatically flushes any changes from the OS buffer to the disk. This means that this historical argument is no longer true with most databases. Therefore, the only remaining reason for using raw partitions as datafiles is performance. Many claim 5–15 percent performance increase over filesystem files. Your mileage may vary; these tests were performed on a closed track with a professional driver; *please do* try this at home. Find out what works best for you.

Backing Up an RDBMS

Protecting an RDBMS is very complex. There are several storage elements, including datafiles, rollback logs, transaction logs, and the master database. How you get all of the data to a secondary storage medium if it's changing all the time?

Physical and Logical Backups

There are two primary methods of backing up an RDBMS: physical backups and logical backups. A *physical backup* physically backs up the data *files*. This also is referred to as a database backup. There are also two types of physical backups, a *cold* backup and a *hot* backup. A *cold backup* is done by quiescing, or shutting down, the database prior to doing the backup. This is often the simplest way to do a database backup, especially if your database's data files reside in the filesystem. All you have to do is shut down the database and run your normal filesystem backup utility. Unfortunately, this method may require your database to be shut down for a long time. That is why more and more environments are performing *hot backups*, which are done while the database is online. This, of course, requires a lot more work behind the scenes, since you are trying to copy the data files while the database is writing to them. This requires a backup utility that understands the internal structure of the database. The purpose of this utility is to log the changes to a particular datafile while it is being copied to the backup media. This allows for a consistent backup image.

A *logical backup* copies, or *exports*, data *objects* (usually tables) but does not record the data's location. A logical backup can be used to restore a deleted table without having to restore all of the datafiles in which it resides. It also can be used to move a table from one database to another. These options are made possible by the definition of a logical backup: it backs up the data and not the data's location. Therefore, it can be restored into any location. Logical backups, however, do not have the ability to do a point-in-time recovery. They also can introduce referential integrity problems, since you could load a table that requires information from another table that is not present. The biggest problem with exports, though, is that they almost always need to be done with the database offline.

There are several methods of doing physical backups:

- If you are using Oracle or Sybase, and your datafiles are cooked files, you can simply shut down the database and do a full system backup. Since everything exists as a regular filesystem file, you will get everything backed up. If you need to restore, you can then restore the entire database from this backup. You then would need to replay the transaction logs against the old database files. This is why you cannot do this with Informix; Informix has no way of playing the transaction logs without restoring from a backup that was made with its backup utility.

- If you are using Oracle or Sybase, and your datafiles are raw partitions, you still can shut down the database and back them up if you have a utility or script to do so. For example, in Unix you would use *dd*. This is quite a bit more complex than the first method, though, because you need to know which devices to run *dd* against.

- The next method of backing up a database is to back it up live to disk or tape, using a utility provided for that purpose. Informix provides the *ontape* utility and Sybase provides the *dump* utility. Oracle does not have such a utility,* but it does provide the ability for you to write your own. (Oracle's *alter database*

---

* Oracle7 has *EBU*, and Oracle8 has *rman*. Both are utilities that can back up the database to a commercial backup product. Oracle8 also comes bundled with a stripped-down version of Legato NetWorker, which can be used in conjuction with *rman* to back up to disk. However, this is not the same as Informix's *ontape* or Sybase's Backup Server, both of which can back up directly to a tape or disk file without the intervention of a third-party product.

begin/end backup commands allow you to back up an Oracle database in a number of ways.) This provides a lot of flexibility but also a lot of hassle if you're not really good at scripting. However, Chapter 15, *Oracle Backup & Recovery*, describes *oraback.sh*, a public domain utility that you should be able to use with no problem.

- The newest method of backing up databases is to use a utility that sends one or more streams of data to a commercial storage manager (i.e., backup software). This is the cleanest method if you can afford it (it costs several thousand dollars per system). Each of the three major database vendors provides a utility to send data to third-party storage managers: Informix provides Online Backup and Recovery (*onbar*), Sybase provides *dump*, Oracle7 provides the Enterprise Backup Utility (*EBU*), and Oracle8 provides Recovery Manager (*rman*).

- A few commercial utilities provide functionality that is different from that of the previously listed options. The most popular of these is *SQL Backtrack*, which is now sold by BMC software. These utilities wrap around some of the native utilities and do not always use the vendor-supplied API. They also provide the ability to send a data stream to commercial backup products, and some products have interfaces to the utilities. Still other options include interfaces to products that do not use the newer interfaces. For example, many vendors prefer not to use Oracle's *EBU* and have written commercial interfaces that use the same native commands that *oraback.sh* uses. The vendors claim more reliability and/or faster performance. The validity of backup and recovery programs that do not use the vendor-supplied API is left as a decision for the reader.

Logical backups are actually much simpler than physical backups. Each of the databases has an export utility that creates a logical backup of one or more database objects to a file. Some of the commercial utilities also allow you to integrate logical and physical backups into your backup system.

Get Every Instance

Chapter 2, *Backing It All Up*, includes a section called "Are You Backing Up What You Think You're Backing Up?" It talks about how your backup programs should be written in such a way that everything in your system is automatically discovered and backed up. If you add a new filesystem, you should not then have to edit your backup scripts to get it backed up. This goes double for databases, because they often are added and deleted much more frequently than filesystems.

You need some way to ensure that every database instance on every server is being backed up. In Chapter 4, *Free Backup Utilities*, there is a program called *hostdump.sh. hostdump.sh* makes sure that it backs up all the filesystems on the box by starting at the *fstab* file, which lists all filesystems. Wouldn't it be nice if you had such a file for databases? Oracle and Sybase already do. Sybase has the *interfaces* file that lists every server on each system. If an instance is not listed in this file, users cannot connect to it. Oracle has the *oratab* file that accomplishes the same task, but its use is not mandatory, as Sybase's *interfaces* file is. For example, some sites don't use the *oratab* file because they have only one instance. The best way to enforce the use of the *oratab* file is to write startup scripts that start up only databases that are in that file.

Informix has no file that stores all of the Informix instances on a server. This is disappointing since there are many companies that run more than one instance of Informix on a server. The good news is that you can make your own. You can create an *inftab* file that looks a lot like the *oratab* file and accomplishes the same thing. Again, the way to enforce its use is to write startup programs that start up only instances that are in that file.

Since the files described here are not always used and yet should be, I'd like to emphasize what I just said: you need a centralized file that lists all of the instances on the server. You then should start with that file to determine what instances are on a given server—instances that need to be backed up. Sybase already has the *interfaces* file and enforces its use. Oracle has the *oratab* file, but its use is optional. You can create an *inftab* file for Informix, but its use also would be optional. Enforce the use of the *oratab* and *inftab* files by writing startup scripts* that start up only instances that are listed in those files. A wayward (or busy) DBA still can create an instance without putting it in this file and can even get it running. But if you reboot the box enough times, the DBA will be sure to put it in the startup file so she doesn't have to manually start it every time!

Transaction Log Dumps Are Not Incremental Backups

This important topic often is misunderstood. The confusion comes from Sybase documentation that often refers to a transaction log dump as an incremental backup. They are not the same thing!

What is the difference between the two? An *incremental backup* is a special backup that contains only the changed pages (blocks) since the last full (or higher level incremental) backup. A *transaction log dump* is a backup of all the *transactions* that have occurred since the last transaction log dump. They may sound simi-

---

* This often can be done by making slight modifications to the default startup scripts that come with the database.

lar, but they're not. The latter is much more difficult to manage and much slower to read.

Perhaps the best way to illustrate this would be to discuss Informix's *ontape* program, which has both incremental and transaction log backups. Suppose that you created a level-0 (full) backup on Friday. During the week, you did not perform any full backups and ran only continuous (transaction log) backups. Now suppose that it is Thursday, and you need to restore your database. You would have your full backup from Friday and your continuous (transaction log) backups from each day. To restore, you would need to read your full backup and then read each of the continuous backup volumes in order. Assuming you made one backup volume per day, you would need seven volumes.

Now assume the same scenario as the preceding, except that you also ran an incremental (level-1) backup every night. If you needed to restore the database on Thursday, you would need the full backup from Friday, the latest incremental backup volume (presumably Wednesday's), and the continuous backup volume for Thursday. That is three volumes instead of seven. That is because the level-1 incremental backup contains all changes since the level-0 backup.

Besides the difference in complexity, reading an incremental backup also is much quicker than reading a transaction log backup. Ask anyone who has rolled through several days' worth of transaction logs. In one benchmark that I performed, reading two weeks of transaction logs took 36 hours. Reading an incremental backup covering the same time period took only one hour. The reason for this is simple. A given page may be changed several times. Replaying the transaction log also would change it several times. Loading a true incremental backup would change it only once, to its last value.

Sybase's *Backup Server* and Oracle7's *EBU* have no concept of this type of incremental backup. Informix's *ontape* and *onbar* do. (Oracle8's *rman* does have an incremental backup capability.)

Do-It-Yourself: Creating Your Own Backup Utility

You don't have to use a high-priced commercial utility to back up your databases. Doing so certainly can make your backups more automated or centrally controlled, but since most of them run $3,000–$8,000 per system, many people are using homegrown systems.

Intermediary disk

This is one of the most popular ways to do homegrown database backups. It's fast, clean, and easy. The basic idea uses a script that backs up the database to disk. That backup then is treated as a regular file and backed up by the nightly filesystem backup. You can even save the amount of disk space needed by compressing the file after it's backed up. If you're really pressed for space, and you're running Unix, you can use named pipes to compress the backup *as* it's being written. In that case, you would need a backup disk that is only one-third to one-half the size of your original database disk (depending on the compression rate you get). Unless you have a very large database, this probably is cheaper than buying a commercial utility to perform this task. Each of the vendor-specific database backup chapters in this book contains a script that is able to do this.

Dedicated backup drive

You can use homegrown backup scripts to back up to a dedicated backup drive. This is a little more complicated and requires somewhat more work on your part. Depending on the size of your database, this may be more or less expensive than backing up to disk, but it definitely will be slower. It is also more complex, since you must keep track of each volume and label it in such a way that you know which database was backed up to it. (If you back up to disk, this can be done by naming the backup file the same name as the database.)

Shell scripts

I assume that you are doing the preceding backups by using some sort of shell script. Shell scripts are much better than having a simple *cron* or *at* entry that says "*back up databaseA to deviceB*." Shell scripts can do lots of error checking and can be told to do things such as notify the DBA if something is wrong.

Calling a Professional

This is one of the biggest growth markets within the backup product industry. Most commercial filesystem backup products now have interfaces to automatically back up your database to volumes that are managed by their product. It's really a beautiful thing, but it does come at a price! Some of these products also have an interface to a third-party program (e.g., SQL Backtrack) that accomplishes the same task.

The Big Three

Each of the three biggest Unix database vendors—Informix, Oracle, and Sybase— has a backup utility that can interface with commercial backup products, also referred to as *storage managers*. On a high level, these backup utilities all work in essentially the same way. The database vendor's utility generates one or more backup streams via an API that storage managers can talk to. The companies that produce the storage managers then can write a utility that talks to their storage manager on one side, and the database backup utility's API on the other side.

Although the database backup utilities come bundled with the database products, the commercial backup products' utilities cost several thousand dollars.

Of the three main database vendors, only Sybase's backup utility can perform backups without interfacing with a commercial storage manager. Oracle's *rman* and Informix's *onbar* both have advanced capabilities, but without a storage manager to talk to, the products are essentially useless. Since Oracle and Informix didn't want to force their customers to buy a storage manager or the interface to their backup utility, they came up with a compromise. Both of these vendors now bundle a free, stripped-down version of Legato NetWorker and its Business Suite Module with their product. This "OEM" version of NetWorker has significantly less functionality than the full-featured version, but it gives you enough functionality to be able to use *rman* and *onbar* to do backups. Figure 13-5 uses Oracle and this bundled version of Legato NetWorker to illustrate the different pieces of the backup puzzle. Oracle uses *rman* to interface with the database on one side and the storage manager on the other side. NetWorker communicates with the backup media on one side and its Business Suite Module on the other side. NetWorker then uses the Business Suite module to interface between NetWorker and *rman*. The backup data flows from the Oracle database, through *rman*, through the Business Suite Module, through NetWorker, and to the backup media. Restores obviously flow in the opposite direction.

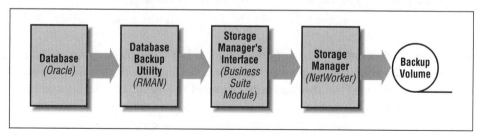

Figure 13-5. A typical commercial database backup utility setup

Each of the three big databases's utilities has its own backup and recovery history.

Informix

Informix has always been the easiest database to back up and recover. They have always had *tbtape* (now called *ontape*), which is a standalone backup command designed to back up to tape. *ontape* is simple, has incremental capabilities, also can back up to disk, and backs up the database live. Some of these features, which always were assumed by Informix users to be present in other database systems, are just now appearing in other products. (Informix also has a product called *onarchive*, which is not recommended; *onarchive* and other Informix utilities are covered in Chapter 14.) Informix now also has *onbar*, which is designed specifically to send a stream of backup data to a commercial product. Some backup vendors have ported to the earlier *ontape* command, while others waited for *onbar*. Whichever command you use, you can recover individual dbspaces.

Oracle

Historically, Oracle did not have a true backup utility, but it did have commands that allowed you to write your own—even allowing you to do live backups. (The *oraback.sh* script in Chapter 15 uses these commands.) Now Oracle7 has the Enterprise Backup Utility, or *EBU*, and Oracle8 has Recovery Manager, or *rman*. Both are designed to give streams of backup data to a commercial backup utility. Both of these utilities require a storage manager to be able to do backups, but Oracle8 now comes bundled with a stripped-down storage manager that you can use. Some storage manager vendors have stayed away from *EBU* and *rman* interfaces, citing reasons such as performance or flexibility. BMC's SQL Backtrack is probably the best known among these products. SQL Backtrack can do a true incremental backup, as discussed earlier. (The ability to do incremental backups is now provided by Oracle8's *rman*, but as of this writing there are still hundreds of thousands of Oracle7 databases out there. The only way to do a true incremental backup of an Oracle7 database is to use a product like SQL Backtrack.) Whichever utility you use, you can recover individual files or tablespaces.

Sybase

Sybase has come a long way in the backup arena, but they still have a long way to go. The *dump* command used to be very slow, and its speed severely impacted database performance, but that problem was fixed in System 10. The fix was done by separating the *dump* processes from the database engine and creating the Backup Server. The Backup Server also now has a nice ability to stream data to multiple backup devices simultaneously; its main problem now is that it is an all-or-nothing utility. You cannot recover an individual dataspace or device; you must restore the entire database or nothing at all. This means that if you have a 500-GB Sybase database and you lose one 4-GB disk, you have to restore the entire 500 GB. (This lack of functionality is what originally created the market for BMC's SQL Backtrack.)

Restoring an RDBMS

The process of restoring an RDBMS varies according to the backup methods that you used, of course. How you proceed to restore is based on the status of your nondata and data disks and whether you are able to do partial restores online.

Loss of Any Nondata Disk

A "data" disk is defined as any disk that contains a database object. (A database object and other terms are defined earlier in this chapter.) If you keep your database objects intact, you actually don't need to restore the database, you've just got to restore all of the parts that make it work! This can range from a restore of a single database setup file to a complete restore of everything on another system.

Executables

Your database can't work if its executables aren't there. This part of the recovery is much simpler if you have all your executables located in a special filesystem.

Setup files

In a pinch, you can restore the executables by copying them from a known good system, but that won't work for your database setup files. Each instance often has an initialization file that sets up certain variables like the instance name and the location of the master database. These setup files usually can be recreated if you have good logs that tell you how you made them the first time, but it is probably easier to recover them from backup.

Customized OS files

Databases often require you to edit system configuration files such as /etc/system. Changes to these files might include things like customizing shared memory or changing the TCP port over which software will communicate. If you are restoring onto a brand new install or onto another system, these changes will need to be repeated, and often changes to your OS files are forgotten or poorly documented. Unless you properly prepared for this situation, it's probably easier to just follow the installation instructions for a standard installation. If you're reading this in advance of such an outage, now is the time to find out what these changes are and document them. If you know what files are typically changed, you can even write a program that automatically documents them for you.

License setup files

Database products have not typically used heavy licensing enforcement systems, but this will probably change over time. If yours does use such a system (e.g., FlexLM), you need to restore these files before your database will function properly.

Loss of a Data Disk

The complexity and difficulty of your restore can vary greatly depending on which data disk you lost and how well you prepared in advance for such a loss.

Master database

The complete loss of a Sybase master database, Informix *rootdbs*, or Oracle control file is very difficult to recover from—so much so that you need to ensure that it never happens. (You'll be sorry if you don't!) Mirror your Sybase master database. Mirror your Informix root dbspace. Mirror your Oracle control files. Just do it. Even if you can't afford enough disk to mirror anything else, mirror this. It doesn't take up that much extra disk space, and the time and frustration you will save yourself are immense. This is the easiest thing you can do to save huge amounts of time in a major restore.

Losing the Master Database

Recovering the master database is full of catch-22s, because a lot of configuration and status information is stored inside that database. This information can be recreated if you lose it, but it must be recreated manually. You must have a complete history of the instance, how it was put together, where the database file and log files are, and what status they are in. Then you have to tell the master database all the things that it should know already. This won't be too hard if you saved all this information in an easy-to-find location up front. If not, you're in for a long, painful recovery.

Other databases

Unless you are using Oracle (which has a one-to-one database-to-instance relationship), you may have multiple databases within an instance. If you lose only one device within a database (other than the master database), recovering from this is not too bad. You also probably can leave the rest of the instance and any other databases online while you are doing the restore. The best thing you can do to automate restoring single databases is to properly document where they are and what devices they consist of.

Backups

One of the most popular methods of backing up a database is to save it to disk and then allow the filesystem backup program to put it onto a backup volume. This is a very efficient method for many reasons. However, it does have one downside. Suppose you lost a data disk and the disk on which you store the backups. You first must restore the disk backup file from the backup volume, then restore the database from the disk file. If this two-step procedure is required, it will take longer than recovering straight from a backup volume.

Transaction log backups

The same rule applies to the backups of your transaction logs. This includes the results of a *dump tran* in Sybase, an *ontape -c* in Informix, or the archived redo logs in Oracle. You will need every one of these that were made since the last full or incremental database backup. Before you start a large restore, check the time that the backup was made and make sure that you have all the transaction log backups since then. If you don't, you can start restoring them before you actually need them.

If you do database backups infrequently, you may need quite a few transaction log backups to complete the restore. While restoring them, you must be careful that you have enough space to do so. You may have to restore them into an alternate location or compress them. You then can move (or uncompress) them a few at a time as the *restore* program asks for them.

Online transaction logs

This is where you can suffer data loss. Even if you have a good backup and all the transaction logs since the last backup, you can be in trouble if you lose the data with the online logs in it. This would be the disk with Informix's logical log or Oracle's online redologs. (Sybase stores the online transaction log in the master database.) One of the ways of preventing this tragedy is to mirror this log.

Online Partial Restores

Some databases allow you to bring part of the database online while leaving one dataspace or datafile offline. This partial availability may allow you more time to complete a difficult restore or reduce the overall impact to your user community. This is especially true if the portion of the database that you are restoring contains a table that is not accessed frequently. Before considering such a restore, though, consider these factors:

Interdependency of data within the database

If the table contains data that is not accessed frequently, this may be a perfect candidate for a partial restore. You also might consider such a restore if the rest of the database can function normally (or in a slightly diminished capacity) without this table. However, suppose the database is the sales database, and this table contains all of the actual sales transactions. The rest of the database is fine (e.g., names, phone numbers, addresses), but the sole purpose of this database is to track these sales. Without this table of transaction data, the database is useless. Since doing a partial restore increases the overall restore time, doing a partial restore would be a bad idea in this case.

Physical relationship between tables and dataspaces

Most database backup products do not allow you to restore on the table level. They sometimes allow you to restore on the dataspace level, however. Suppose you have lost one disk. You need to recover the dataspace that this disk resides in, right? Suppose that you had a partitioned table that resides on multiple dataspaces. That would mean that the entire table would be unavailable. If this table is not needed for normal operation, as described before, you might consider a partial restore. Again, however, remember that a partial restore increases your overall restore time.

Time requirement for a complete restore

Some environments don't want to hear about partially functioning databases. "Tell when it's up. Don't say it's almost up or partially up, just tell me when you're done!" These environments are more concerned with overall downtime and should be treated thusly. You need to restore the database in the fastest way possible. That probably would be to shut down the database and restore the affected dataspace.

Documentation and Testing

Restoring an RDBMS is the most complex procedure that you will ever do, and there is usually very little time in which to do it. The users want the database up now and don't really care that you've never done this before. You need to document and test your database backup procedures often to make sure that they work. The following guidelines may help:

1. Set up a standalone machine that does not have any other databases on it. This machine doesn't have to be large or even dedicated to this purpose, but it would be good if you could reinstall the OS for a new test. This often can be done when you buy a new machine. Before you put it to work for real, do some test database restores on it.

2. When you test your restores, test the worst-case scenario. Make sure that you know how to install the product onto a new system and that you know all of the files that you need to edit to make it work. This is why you should be doing this on a virgin operating system. That way, you will always have to edit */etc/system*, for example, instead of forgetting it without penalty because it's already been edited.

3. You can set up a test instance and then back up and restore that. However, the best thing to do is to take a normal database backup from one of your production systems and try to restore it to the test system.

4. Make the procedure detailed enough that anyone with good SA or DBA skills should be able to follow it. If possible, do not have the person who wrote the procedure perform the test. This is the perfect task to hire a consultant for. See if someone who knows what they are doing but doesn't know your environment can follow the procedure.

5. Have all your DBAs participate, whether they've got time or not! The worst thing that can happen is that one or two people know how to restore the databases. Then when a database crashes, one of them is sick and the other one just quit or is on vacation in the Bahamas. (I once saw a restore go on for hours because the DBA didn't know he had to press Return! He called me saying, "Man, this thing is taking forever!") Make sure every DBA knows how to restore your databases!

Unique Database Requirements

The unique backup and recovery requirements of Informix, Oracle, and Sybase could generate an entire book for each product. What, then, is the purpose of these chapters? That's simple—to break down, once and for all, the "Berlin Wall" that exists between DBAs and SAs. Until now, if you wanted to learn about how to back up Informix, you had to buy an Informix book. The same was true for Sybase and Oracle. One of the problems with these books is that they assume you are a DBA! The authors assume that you understand tablespaces and transaction logs and rollbacks. The result is that you get only half the story. This book, on the other hand, assumes only that you have read this chapter and Chapter 3, *Native Backup & Recovery Utilities*, of this book.

Another problem with many backup books is that they provide "example" scripts to back up your database. These scripts are not to be used in actual production environments. Instead, they are examples of what your scripts should look like. Most of the scripts that you find in this book have been published previously and are being run by hundreds of companies around the world. They run on many different platforms and should run on yours with very little customization.[*]

---

[*] The lawyers, of course, would have me remind you that these programs come with no guarantee or warranty. They are distributed with the GNU public license, allowing you to use and distribute them as much as you want. But as with any public domain software, there is no guarantee that it will work for *you*!

14

Informix Backup & Recovery

Informix is one of the easiest databases to back up and recover. Although it is a highly complex, very advanced relational database, it has the least complex recovery of all three database products covered in this book. Informix also was the first among the three products to come out with a live, multilevel backup and restore program. *tbtape*, as it was called in the early days, was simple enough to understand and use, yet smart enough to handle the job. (The complete documentation set for *tbtape* was only 14 pages.)

The large number of utilities available to back up Informix databases can be quite confusing, but each is actually made for a separate application. *ontape* (as *tbtape* is now called) is Informix's oldest physical backup utility and is used primarily in environments without a storage manager. *onbar* is Informix's newest physical backup utility and is designed only for environments with a storage manager. *onunload* is a logical backup utility, and *onarchive* is deprecated and should not be used for new backup systems.

This chapter covers the three basic ways to back up and recover an Informix database:

- Physical backups without a storage manager, using *ontape*
- Physical backups with a storage manager, using *onbar*
- Logical backups, using *onunload*

This chapter also makes recommendations on how to increase the data integrity of your Informix instance, as well as how to recover the instance when necessary.

Informix Architecture

Let's begin with a discussion of Informix's architecture. This chapter uses only Informix-specific terms. To see how a particular term relates to one used in Oracle or Sybase, consult Chapter 13, *Backing Up Databases.*

Power User's View

Power users typically understand these elements of Informix architecture. They may use them when conversing with database administrators and system administrators.

Instance

Similar to the other database products, an Informix *instance* is a single connection to shared memory. It is represented by one or more *oninit* processes. When Informix is started or stopped, these processes appear and disappear. Informix used to use the term "server" when referring to an instance, hence the environment variable *DBSERVERNAME.* This created a problem, though. System administrators would think that they were speaking about a Unix server, and database administrators would think they were talking about an Informix server. Although some of these variables are still around, Informix documentation now typically uses the term "server" when referring to the database installation and software and "instance" when referring to the connection to shared memory. To keep from confusing any DBAs who may be reading this chapter, I use the term "host" or "machine" when referring to the machine on which the Informix instance resides.

 Some Informix backup utilities back up on the instance level, although they are able to restore at the dbspace level. (dbspaces are covered later.) That is, they back up one instance at a time. The utilities also back up the entire instance, although they will allow you to recover a single dbspace from such a backup. (*onbar* can back up a single space.)

Database

An Informix database's architecture is not that much different from any other product's database,* except that multiple databases may be found inside a single instance. Informix cannot recover a single database inside an instance. However, a

---

* Informix would, of course, dispute this! I am merely saying that the term *database* refers to the same general structure in Informix that it does in other databases.

DBA who isolated a database by putting it into a separate dbspace then could recover that database by recovering that dbspace. This is a very common practice.

Table or index

An Informix table or index is functionally the same as any RDBMS table or index. (They work differently internally, but that is not important to understand for backup and recovery purposes.) Informix cannot back up or recover on the table or index level, except via the export/import facilities. (Again, a DBA who isolated a table in a separate dbspace could recover that table by itself by recovering that dbspace.)

DBA's View

Typically, only a DBA needs to understand the terms covered in this section. An SA who also understands them will be better equipped to communicate with the DBA about backup issues.

BLOB space

All Informix Binary Large Object (BLOB) data is kept inside the database, but there is a special dbspace for BLOB data.

Chunk

A *chunk* is a physical portion of disk on which Informix stores its data. A chunk can be either a raw partition or a filesystem file. Informix suggests that a chunk's name be a symbolic link to the actual chunk. For example, if you are using */dev/ rdsk/c6t0d0s1* as a chunk, you could create a symbolic link named */dev/informix/ chunk1* that points to */dev/rdsk/c6t0d0s1*. That way, if there are ever any problems with that disk, you could replace the disk with another one and just change the symbolic link.

Page

An Informix page is a physically contiguous portion of a chunk. A page can be either 2 KB or 4 KB, depending on the operating system.

Extent

An *extent* is a logical grouping of at least four physically contiguous pages. When you create a table in Informix, you specify the amount of space in kilobytes. Informix then will allocate as many contiguous pages as possible to satisfy this request. If it cannot allocate enough space in one contiguous section, other extents will be created as necessary. As a table grows, the existing extents that a table is using are used up, and Informix will allocate additional pages for that table. It will try to allocate physically contiguous pages if it can. If not, it again will allocate another extent.

Other database products' extents may not be physically contiguous, depending on when and how they were created.

tblspace

An Informix *tblspace* is a logical grouping of all extents allocated to a table—possibly spanning multiple chunks. It is what most Informix DBAs are referring to when they say something that sounds like "tablespace," but the proper Informix spelling is "tblspace."

Tablespace

Informix documentation also uses the spelling "tablespace," and it is defined as the space that a table occupies within a chunk. That is, it is a logical grouping of the extents within a chunk that are allocated to a table. They may or may not be physically contiguous. A tablespace does not span a chunk. This term "tablespace" (as opposed to "tblspace") is rarely used in Informix and is defined here only because you may encounter it in Informix documentation. An Informix chunk can contain several tablespaces for many tables.

 To Oracle DBAs: Do not confuse either of these with what Oracle calls a "tablespace," since an Oracle tablespace is simply a logical collection of datafiles. The closest Informix equivalent to an Oracle tablespace would be a *dbspace*, which is defined below.

---

dbspace

A dbspace is a storage element that consists of one or more chunks. A dbspace contains one or more tblspaces, as defined earlier. Although Informix backups usually are done on the instance level, restores can be done on the dbspace level. That is, you can restore a single dbspace.

Fragment

When a table is partitioned across multiple dbspaces, the portion of the table that resides in a single dbspace is called a *fragment*. It does not present any unique backup requirements.

sysmaster database

The *sysmaster* database is the database of databases. That is, it is the master data-base within an Informix instance that keeps track of all databases within that instance. Remember, though, there may be multiple Informix instances on a sin-gle host, and there is no master database of all master databases.

Transaction

Informix *transactions* are the same as those in any other RDBMS. A transaction is a single atomic event that must complete successfully. Any partially completed (committed) transactions are rolled back if the instance crashes.

LRU queue

The least recently used (LRU) queues and their associated buffers are the part of shared memory that stores data that is about to be used (and may be changed) by transactions. Before a page is modified, it is read into one of the LRU queues, which are filled up in a random fashion. Informix then monitors these queues based on the LRU_MAX_DIRTY and LRU_MIN_DIRTY parameters that are set to a percentage from 0 to 100 in the *onconfig* file. The LRU_MAX_DIRTY parameter specifies what percentage of buffers in a single LRU queue must be dirty before the page cleaners start flushing and freeing queues, and the LRU_MIN_DIRTY para-meter specifies the percentage of dirty buffers at which the page cleaners can stop.

The cleaning works as follows: Once Informix determines that the LRU queues are dirty enough (as specified by the LRU_MAX_DIRTY parameter), it starts flushing buffers starting with the least recently used buffers first. Once a buffer's dirty pages are flushed to disk, they are available for reuse. The page cleaners continue flush-ing queues to disk until they reach the value specified by LRU_MIN_DIRTY. Informix then continues to monitor the queues again until they reach the value specified by LRU_MAX_DIRTY, and the cleaning process starts again. As explained in "I'm Confused by All the Logging!" later in this section, higher LRU_MIN_DIRTY and LRU_MAX_DIRTY values result in higher data integrity. However, having a higher LRU_MAX_DIRTY value will result in more dirty pages being flushed during checkpoints. This means that your checkpoints will take longer.

Physical log

Informix's physical log stores the before-images of any pages that have changed since the last checkpoint. That is, prior to modifying a page, Informix saves its before-image in the physical log. It does this only once per page; if the page is modified many times since the last checkpoint, it needs only to store the before-image once. It is simply a record of what the page looked like at the time the last checkpoint was taken. When a checkpoint occurs, all buffers are flushed to disk, and the physical log is cleared of all pages. Since a checkpoint occurs as part of a normal Informix shutdown, the physical log should be empty when an instance is started.

The physical log is then read during *fast recovery*, a special mode that an Informix instance goes into during initialization. During fast recovery, Informix looks in the physical log to see if it contains any before-images. If it does, it knows that the instance was not shut down properly, since a proper shutdown would have performed a checkpoint and emptied the physical log. By writing these before-images back to their original location, Informix returns the instance to what it looked like at the time the last checkpoint was taken. This is referred to as a known point of *physical consistency*. The logical logs then can be used to return the database to a point of *logical consistency*.

To the Oracle DBA: At first, this may sound exactly like Oracle's roll-back segments, but it's slightly different. The first difference is that Oracle keeps the before-images associated with a particular transaction in its rollback segment until that transaction is committed. Informix clears the entire physical log after a checkpoint. Oracle also uses the rollback log during recovery to roll back, or "undo," a partially committed transaction. Informix uses the logical log (defined next) for this purpose.

Architecturally, the *physical log* is composed of two physical log buffers (in shared memory) and one actual physical log (on disk). For performance reasons, before-images actually are written to the physical log buffer during normal activity. Informix then flushes the physical log buffer to disk under any of three circumstances:

- During a checkpoint
- When a physical log buffer is full
- When an LRU queue must be flushed

The first circumstance under which the physical log buffer is flushed to disk is during any checkpoint. Once the checkpoint is complete, the physical log is cleared.

The second circumstance under which Informix flushes the physical log buffer to disk is when one of the two physical log buffers is full. In that case, Informix begins writing to the second buffer and flushes the first buffer to disk.

The final circumstance under which the physical log buffer is flushed to disk is when a page cleaner needs to flush an LRU queue. Recall that flushing an LRU queue involves writing to disk some or all of the modified pages managed by that queue. If there are before-images in the physical log buffer that have not yet been flushed to disk, the flushing of the LRU queue will wait until the before-images are flushed to disk. Since forcing the page cleaners to wait can significantly decrease your performance, you should take steps to ensure that this doesn't happen very often. See "I'm Confused by All the Logging!" later in this section for more information.

Logical log

Informix's logical log is similar to the transaction logs of other RDBMSs. The logical log is used to redo, or roll forward, transactions in case of recovery, or an explicit *ROLLBACK WORK* statement. It also stores the before-images of the records that each transaction will change, so it can be used to roll back any transactions that have not committed. It is called a *logical log* because it contains a log of how the database was changed logically. That is, it contains a record of which *rows* were changed and how, rather than which physical pages contained those rows.

If you needed to recover the database from an older backup, the logical log would be used to roll forward any transactions that have occurred since your last backup. It also is used when a database instance goes into fast recovery mode. During either operation, it eventually reaches the end of the log. Once it has done so, it looks to see if it has attempted to roll forward any transactions that have not been committed. If so, it then rolls those transactions back using the row-level before-image information that also is stored in the logical log.

Logical logs are actually tables within Informix. By default, there are six logical logs in the root dbspace. It also is quite common to create a separate dbspace that contains only logical logs. Similar to the physical log, the logical log is composed of three logical log buffers (in shared memory) and several logical logs (on disk). Transaction logs are always written to the logical log buffer first and then flushed to disk at different times. How often the log buffers are flushed to disk depends on the type of *logging mode* that is used. There are three logging modes:

No logging

Very little information is written to the logical log. Some of the things it does log include the creation of dbspaces, tables, and indexes. Normal transaction-redo information is not recorded. Nonlogging databases are useful only in databases that are modified using batch loads. Transactions cannot be redone in case of recovery from backup or an instance that crashes and goes into fast recovery mode.

Buffered logging

A database operating in buffered-logging mode flushes a logical log buffer to disk only when that logical log buffer is full. This results in efficient use of disk and memory, as well as higher performance. The trade-off is that if the instance crashes, all transactions that have not been flushed to disk are lost.

Unbuffered logging

When a database operates in unbuffered-logging mode, the logical log buffer is flushed to disk every time a transaction is committed. Remember that during buffered logging, Informix writes one large block of data to disk when the logical log buffer is full. In contrast, unbuffered logging writes small blocks of data more or less constantly. Since it always is more efficient to write larger blocks of data less often, an unbuffered database is always a little slower than a buffered database. Another downside to unbuffered logging is that flushing is done in page increments. A page that is partially filled by a transaction must be completely flushed to disk. Therefore, unbuffered logging also causes more information to be written to the logical logs.

Despite its slight performance cost, *unbuffered logging offers the greatest level of data integrity.* All transactions are flushed to the logical log on disk as soon as they are committed. Therefore, whenever an instance crashes, Informix is able to redo all committed transactions. Only uncommitted transactions would be lost in a host crash. This is why almost all DBAs running a transaction-based database run their Informix databases in unbuffered-logging mode.

Informix requires that the instance be in quiescent mode in order to change logging modes. It also requires you to perform a backup when moving from nonlogging mode to either of the logging modes, because the only reason for switching to logging mode is for better data integrity. What kind of data integrity do you have if you haven't made a backup? Informix support or documentation sometimes suggests that you simply perform a quick backup to */dev/null.* I've never understood this practice; there is a reason that you're being forced to make a backup—logging is worthless without it. Sending the backup to */dev/null* makes Informix *think* that you have made a backup, when you really haven't. Think twice before using this common procedure.

Since the logical logs reside on disk, they must be backed up. If they are not backed up, they will not be available for use during a recovery from backup. Informix provides two methods of backing up the logical logs: automatic and continuous. The "automatic" method is not automatic at all, and I've never understood why Informix calls it that. It consists of a command that does a one-time backup of the current logical logs to the storage media. Continuous backups, as their name implies, run continuously while the instance is online. When continuous backups are running, and a logical log fills up, it is backed up automatically to the storage device specified. Each logical log is appended to the storage device until it is full. The actual command to perform either automatic or continuous backups depends on whether you are using *onbar* or *ontape*. (Both commands are discussed later.) The storage media for logical log backups has historically been tape. This chapter also discusses backing up logical logs to disk.

Whether you choose to use automatic or continuous backups is entirely up to you. Many sites are now performing automatic backups using the ALARMPROGRAM parameter in the *onconfig* file that runs a shell script for you when a log becomes full or is manually closed (*ontape -l*). A sample shell script, *log_full.sh*, which backs up the logical logs using *onbar*, is included with Informix. The shell script included with this book uses continuous backups.

Checkpoint

A checkpoint flushes all pages in shared memory to disk. This means that physical log buffers are flushed to the physical log, and logical log buffers are flushed to the logical log. It provides a point in time during which all data is on disk. This is a point in time to which Informix can be rolled back, if necessary. Once the checkpoint has completed, all pages in the physical log can be removed.

During a checkpoint, the three different buffer areas are flushed in a particular order. The physical log is flushed first, followed by the logical log. Once the logs have been flushed, all pages that have been changed by committed transactions can be flushed.

Fast recovery

Fast recovery is a process through which the different elements of the architecture cooperate to bring the database into a consistent state after a crash. When an instance is brought online, it goes into fast recovery mode and in this state checks the physical log to see if it contains any before-images. The presence of any before-images in the physical log indicates that the system crashed, so any before-images that are in the physical log are written back to their original location. Informix then uses the logical log to redo any transactions that began after the last checkpoint. Eventually it will reach the end of the log. Once it does that, it rolls back any transactions that were not committed. (It works through the log in a serial fashion, so it begins a transaction as soon it sees a *begin transaction* statement. If it reaches the end of all transaction logs and does not see a corresponding *end transaction* statement, it rolls that transaction back. This is how the checkpoint, physical log, and logical log are used to bring the database to a consistent point in time after an instance crash.

I'm Confused by All the Logging!

Let's review. The LRU queues contain all disk pages that have been read into memory, including pages that were changed by a transaction. These queues are flushed periodically to disk by page cleaners at a rate determined by the number and size of the queues, as well as the values that you specify for LRU_MIN_DIRTY and LRU_MAX_DIRTY. This flushing writes to disk some or all of the modified pages in a particular queue, changing the status of these dirty pages to "clean."

The physical log contains the before-images of the physical pages that have been changed since the last checkpoint. This log really consists of two physical log buffers that are flushed to disk when one is full and cleared when a checkpoint occurs—and a checkpoint always occurs during a normal shutdown. These before-images are read only during fast recovery. If there are pages in the physical log when an Informix instance starts up, it means the instance did not shut down properly.

The logical log contains a record of which rows have been changed and how they were changed. The logical log actually consists of logical log buffers that are occasionally flushed to disk; how often they are flushed depends on your logging mode. If you are running in buffered-logging mode, a logical log buffer is flushed to disk only when it becomes full. If you are running in unbuffered-logging mode, the portion of the logical log buffer that pertains to a given transaction is flushed to disk as soon as that transaction is completed.

How bad (and good) things happen

Suppose for a moment that you were operating in buffered-logging mode. Now suppose that the current physical and logical log buffers are not full, the LRU queues are beginning to approach the value specified by LRU_MAX_DIRTY, and Art has just committed a large transaction while Greg begins another large transaction. Informix sees that the LRU queues have too many dirty pages and begins flushing the LRU queues to disk to make room for Greg's transaction.

We are operating in buffered-logging mode, which means that the logical log buffer will flush to disk only when it is full. This means that all roll-forward and rollback information pertaining to Art's and Greg's transactions are only in memory. However, the page cleaners need to flush the LRU queues that contain Art's transaction to disk. Before they are allowed to do so, however, the physical log will need to be flushed to disk. This ensures that the before-images are available to return the instance to a known point of physical consistency. One of two bad things could now happen.

The first thing that could happen is that the system crashes before the physical log buffer finishes flushing to disk, and all the information in both the physical and logical log buffers is lost. Since the physical log buffer was partially flushed to disk, Informix will realize that something went wrong when it restarts the instance and goes into fast recovery mode. It then rewrites the before-images back to their original locations, although the pages that it is overwriting have not actually been changed, since the LRU queues were never flushed because they were waiting for the physical log to continue flushing to disk.

The second thing that could happen is that the physical log buffer finishes flushing to disk, the LRU queues begin flushing to disk, and *then* the system crashes. The result is essentially the same. When Informix restarts the instance, it will see that there are pages in the physical log, which means it did not do a proper shutdown. It then rewrites the before-images to the original locations, overwriting any pages that were changed by the LRU queue being flushed.

Regardless of when the system crashes, the before-images of any pages to be changed will always be available. Once Informix has rewritten these images to their original locations, it can use the logical log to roll forward any committed transactions and roll back any uncommitted transactions.

Could this be better?

There are two problems with the preceding scenario described. The first problem is that the log of Art's transaction should have been flushed to disk as soon as the transaction was committed. Changing the instance to unbuffered logging fixes this problem. With the previous buffered logging example, Art's transaction would be lost. However, if it were flushed as soon as it was committed, the chances of the transaction being lost would be greatly reduced.

To be honest, I can't find a good reason to run an instance in buffered-logging mode anymore. Buffered logging used to provide a performance gain, but in Informix 7.x, the performance difference between unbuffered and buffered logging is minimal. (In fact, many DBAs tell me the gain was never that great.) This performance gain was the only reason for using unbuffered logging, and I believe the risk of database corruption is just too great.

Some have suggested that you could run a data warehouse in buffered-logging mode. Why would you? Buffered-logging mode is meant to make transactions that modify pages faster, and such a database should have very few transactions of this type. Therefore the performance increase would not even be noticeable.

The second problem was that there weren't enough buffers. The idea behind flushing least recently used transactions is to allow the logical log to flush to disk before transactions that are in that log are flushed to disk. If your buffers are numerous enough, the logical log containing a given transaction should flush to disk well before the LRU queues reach the value specified by LRU_MAX_DIRTY, resulting in the queue that contains that transaction's pages being flushed to disk. Another potential problem could be that the value for LRU_MAX_DIRTY was set too low. Informix DBAs set this value low to cause pages to be flushed more often, resulting in faster checkpoints, since the checkpoint does not have to flush very many dirty pages to disk. However, it increases the chance of data loss.

In summary, Informix will do the right thing and ensure that your database will not get corrupted if the system crashes. However, operating in unbuffered-logging mode and having enough buffers significantly decreases the chance of data loss.

Automating Informix Startup: The dbstart.informix.sh Script

Not having a global configuration file makes a lot of things more difficult, one of them being backups. When writing a shell script to back up all Informix instances on a given machine, how do you know what instances to back up? You can't ask Informix, which definitely does not know about the other instances. I would like to suggest a different method of starting Informix that also would make backups easier. Let's start with the basics.

In order for an Informix database to be started up after a system reboot, a startup script must be placed somewhere in */etc*. Startup scripts are run by root and, therefore, should be owned by root and placed in a directory that root controls. A startup script in */etc* should not be calling a startup script in Informix's home directory. However, this creates an extra task for both the SAs and DBAs. The DBA must find an SA every time he wants to add a new instance to the startup script. The SAs would rather not have to do this, but they don't want root running shell scripts found in Informix's home directory. The SAs also are normally in charge of backups, and this is one way to find out that there is a new instance to back up.

How does Oracle accomplish this task? It's as simple as the *oratab* file. The startup scripts are in a directory owned by root, and the *oratab* file is in a directory owned by the oracle ID. The startup script starts up any instances in the *oratab* file that have a Y in the third field. All a DBA needs to do to have a new instance started is add the instance to the *oratab* file. This also gives backup scripts a great place to start. For example, the *oraback.sh* utility automatically backs up any instances that it finds in the *oratab* file.

Sure, it's possible for a DBA to create and start up a new instance that does not get put into the *oratab* file. However, if the *oratab* file is being used to both start up and back up Oracle, DBAs will get into the habit of putting new instances there. Otherwise, they will continually have to start the instances manually, and the instances also will never get backed up.

With a little practice, Informix DBAs can be shown to do the same thing that Oracle DBAs do with the *oratab* file . . . I present the *inftab* file, an Informix version of Oracle's *oratab* file.

The inftab File

This *inftab* file in Example 14-1 has several comments but only one actual configuration line. This line tells the startup scripts that there is an Informix instance called *crash*, that its *$INFORMIXDIR* is */informix*, and that it should be restarted after a reboot. Its logical logs should go to */informix/logical*. (The logical backup destination variable will be used for the backup scripts that are covered later in this chapter.)

Example 14-1. A Sample inftab File

```
#  This file is used by the startup, shutdown, and backup scripts.
#  Provided in "Unix Backup & Recovery," O'Reilly & Assoc., Inc.
#
#  Author: W. Curtis Preston
#
#  Use a colon, ':', as the field terminator.
#  Lines that begin with an octothorpe, or pound sign (#), are comments.
#
#  Entries should follow this form:
#      $ONCONFIG:$INFORMIXDIR:<N|Y>:
#
#  The first field is the Informix server name.
#  The second field is the INFORMIXDIR variable that the Informix server uses.
#  A Y in the third field indicates if this instance should be started
#  automatically after a system reboot.
#  The fourth field is where logical logs will go.  If you want to go
#  to disk, put a directory name.  If you want to go to tape, put the
#  device file of the tape drive here.
#
#  Multiple lines with the same $ONCONFIG variable are not allowed.
#
crash:/informix:Y:/informix/logical
```

The *dbstart.informix.sh* script in Example 14-2 acts very much like Oracle's *dbstart* script (see Chapter 15, *Oracle Backup & Recovery*). It starts by reading the *inftab* file to determine the names of all instances. Then it either starts or stops each of the instances that have a Y specified in the third field. It also calls *rclogs.sh* for each of those instances. *rclogs.sh*, discussed later, automatically starts continuous backups in the background.

Example 14-2. The dbstart.informix.sh Script

```
#!/bin/sh
#
```

Example 14-2. The dbstart.informix.sh Script (continued)

```
INFTAB=/informix/etc/inftab

Usage()
{
 echo "Usage: [dbshut|dbstart] [start|stop]"
 echo "\n(Either this script must be called with the name of dbshut or dbstart,"
 echo "or it must be called with a start or stop argument.)"
 echo "\nIf called by the name dbstart, or with the argment of 'start,'"
 echo "it will start all Informix instances listed in $INFTAB"
 echo "\nIf called by the name dbshut, or with the argument of 'stop,'"
 echo "it will STOP all Informix instances listed in $INFTAB."
}

#This script starts up all instance on this box specified in $INFTAB.
#It is of the form:
#$ONCONFIG:$INFORMIXDIR:<Y|N>

SCRIPT=`basename $0`

if [ $SCRIPT != dbstart -a "$1" != start ] ; then
 if [ $SCRIPT != dbshut -a "$1" != stop ] ; then
  Usage
  exit
 fi
fi

WHO=`id | awk -F'(' '{print $2}' | awk -F')' '{print $1}' `

if [ "$WHO" = root ] ; then
   su informix -c $0 $*
   exit $?
fi

grep -v '^#' $INFTAB \
|while read LINE
do

  STARTUP=`echo $LINE|cut -d: -f3`
  TBCONFIG=`echo $LINE|cut -d: -f1`
  ONCONFIG=`echo $LINE|cut -d: -f1`
  INFORMIXDIR=`echo $LINE|cut -d: -f2`
  #INFORMIXSERVER and ONCONFIG can be different, so get it from the onconfig file.
  INFORMIXSERVER=`grep DBSERVERNAME $INFORMIXDIR/etc/$ONCONFIG|awk '{print $2}'`

  BINDIR=$INFORMIXDIR/local/bin
  PATH=$INFORMIXDIR/bin:$BINDIR:$PATH
  export TBCONFIG ONCONFIG INFORMIXSERVER INFORMIXDIR PATH BINDIR

  if [ `basename $0` = dbstart -o "$1" = start ] ; then
   if [ "$STARTUP" = "Y" ] ; then
    echo "Starting Informix Instance $ONCONFIG"
    oninit
```

Example 14-2. The dbstart.informix.sh Script (continued)

```
  [ -f $BINDIR/rclogs.sh ] && rclogs.sh start
 else
  echo "NOT Starting Informix Instance $ONCONFIG.  (No 'Y' in $INFTAB.)"
 fi
else
 echo "Stopping Informix Instance $ONCONFIG"
 [ -f $BINDIR/rclogs.sh ] && rclogs.sh stop
 onmode -ky
fi

done
```

An *inftab* file provides a single point for all global Informix activities. The difficult part is getting in the habit of using one. However, if all startup, backup, and monitoring scripts base their actions on the *inftab* file, it will get used soon enough. The DBAs will be happy because they can change a single file that they own, and Informix will automatically start up, back up, and monitor a new instance. The SAs will be happy because they won't have to worry about changing a root-owned shell script every time a new instance is created.

Installing the dbstart.informix.sh Script

If you'd like to begin using *dbstart.informix.sh* to start up your Informix instances automatically, follow the upcoming steps to install and customize it for your environment.

Install the files

Copy the *dbstart.informix.sh, dbstart*, and *dbstop* programs into the same directory (e.g., *$INFORMIXDIR/local/bin*) and make sure that they are executable. If you have only *dbstart.informix.sh*, *dbstart* and *dbstop* are merely hard links to that file. You can make those links yourself by entering:

```
$ ln dbstart.informix.sh dbstart
$ ln dbstart.informix.sh dbstop
```

Copy *inftab* into a directory that the `informix` user ID can write to (e.g., *$INFORMIXDIR/etc*). (They can be placed in the same directory as the other files but do not need to be.)

If you plan to use *rclogs.sh* with *dbstart.informix.sh*, you need to read about it later in this chapter and to configure it as well.

Edit the inftab file

If you have not already done so, edit the file *$INFORMIXDIR/etc/inftab*. This works basically like Oracle's *oratab* file. Each Informix instance should be listed in this file, in the following format:

```
onconfig_file:$INFORMIXDIR:Y|N:log_destination
```

`onconfig_file`
> The first field should be the relative name of the *onconfig* file for that instance (e.g., *prod*, not *$INFORMIXDIR/etc/prod*).

`$INFORMIXDIR`
> The second field should contain the value for the *$INFORMIXDIR* variable for that instance.

`Y|N`
> If you also are using *dbstart.informix.sh*, placing a Y in the third field causes *dbstart* to automatically start this instance after a reboot. (Please note that the Y is case-sensitive.)
>
> Some DBAs prefer to start their Informix instances manually. If you wish to use *dbstart.informix.sh* but do not want the instances to start automatically, simply set this field to N.

`log_destination`
> If you are using *rclogs.sh*, the fourth field should contain the value that you want to use for the archive log destination. This can be a directory or device name. (If it is a directory, make sure that it is writable by `informix`.)

Edit the dbstart.informix.sh script

The main thing that you need to do is to make sure that the location specified for the *inftab* file is correct. This is done by changing the *$INFTAB* variable at the top of the script. If you are not going to use *rclogs.sh*, you also want to delete the lines that refer to it.

Change the startup files

Check your system documentation for the proper location of startup and shutdown scripts and place *dbstart.informix.sh* there. On a SVr4-style Unix, you are looking for a file in one of the *rc* directories. For example, on Solaris, there is probably a file in */etc/init.d*, with links to it in other directories. If the file is called *informix*, simply copy *dbstart* to *informix*. This will cause the links to it to run it with the appropriate stop and start arguments. On a BSD-style Unix, you are looking for a command somewhere in */etc/rc* or */etc/rc.local*.

Make a Fake oninit Command

There is one other change in the area of Informix startup that can help increase
your data integrity. One of the most frequent causes of data corruption is an acci-
dental *oninit -i* command. This causes Informix to completely reinitialize the
instance, overwriting the rootdbs. (I don't know how many times I've seen this in
comp.databases.informix.) Once begun, the only way out is a cold restore of the
critical dbspaces.

The best way to protect yourself from this mistake is to replace *oninit* with a script
that calls the real *oninit.* For example, move *oninit* to *oninit.cmd.* Then replace
oninit with the following script:

```
#!/bin/sh
CMD=${0}.cmd
if [ "$1" = "-i" ] ; then
        echo "
   WARNING!  oninit -i will completely erase this instance!"
   If that's what you REALLY want to do, then re-run this command
   using a capital '-I' instead.  (e.g. $0 -I )."
fi
[ "$1" = "-I" ] && $CMD -i || $CMD $*
```

Don't forget to make the script executable!

```
$ chmod 555 oninit
```

Protect the Physical Log, Logical Log, and sysmaster

These three elements of an Informix database are completely interrelated, and the
loss of any one of them will require a physical restore of all of them. Depending
on which of them is damaged, it also could mean a restore of the entire database.
That is why you should seriously consider the following recommendations for any
production Informix database. The first set of recommendations has to do with
moving the physical and logical logs to their own dbspaces. Since all three objects
are interrelated, this doesn't actually decrease the chance that you'll need to do a
restore; what it does is make it easier on Informix by distributing the load among
three separate dbspaces. Distributing the load in this way makes it easier on Informix once you follow the second set of recommendations and mirror these
dbspaces.

Recommendation: Put the Physical Log in Its Own dbspace

Moving the physical log into its own dbspace does not increase your data integrity, since the physical log, logical log, and sysmaster database are interdependent. It simply moves the physical log's I/O operations to a separate dbspace. The following paragraphs show an example of moving the physical log (for an instance called *crash*) to a separate dbspace called *plogdbs*.

The first thing we need to do is to create a separate, mirrored dbspace called *plogdbs*, as shown in Example 14-3. (How to mirror an existing dbspace is covered later.)

Example 14-3. Creating a New dbspace

```
curtis$ onspaces -c -d plogdbs -p /informix/physlog.dbf -o 0 -s 10000 -m /informix/
physlog_mirror.dbf 0
Verifying physical disk space, please wait ...
Verifying physical disk space, please wait ...
DBspace/BLOBspace successfully added.
```

As shown in Example 14-4, we then must take the instance into quiescent mode, tell it to use the new dbspace for the physical log, and then bring it online again.

Example 14-4. Adding a New Physical Log

```
curtis$ onmode -sy

curtis$ onstat -l|grep Version
INFORMIX-OnLine Version 7.23.UC4    -- Quiescent -- Up 00:15:40 -- 8976 Kbytes

curtis$ onparams -p -s 5000 -d plogdbs -y
Shutting down, please wait ...
Initializing, please wait ...
Recovering, please wait ...

curtis$ onmode -m

curtis$ onstat -l|grep Version
INFORMIX-OnLine Version 7.23.UC4    -- On-Line -- Up 00:02:00 -- 8976 Kbytes
```

The physical log is now in its own dbspace. You now can proceed to put the logical log in its own dbspace. Again, this is for performance reasons, not data integrity reasons.

Recommendation: Put the Logical Log in Its Own dbspace

Putting the logical log into its own dbspace is a bit more complicated. The first step, shown in Example 14-5, is obviously the same: we create a separate, mirrored dbspace that will eventually contain the logical logs.

Example 14-5. Creating a New dbspace

```
curtis$ onspaces -c -d llogdbs -p /informix/logiclog.dbf -o 0 -s 10000 -m /informix/
logiclog_mirror.dbf 0
Verifying physical disk space, please wait ...
Verifying physical disk space, please wait ...
DBspace/BLOBspace successfully added.
```

Next, we perform a log switch and checkpoint, then use *onstat -l* to verify that all but the current log have been backed up (flag B). (See Example 14-6 for examples of these commands.) Otherwise, we will not be able to drop the logs in the next step. If the output shows that the logs were not backed up, we would need to use *ontape* or *onbar* to get them backed up before continuing with this procedure. (See "Physical Backups Without a Storage Manager: ontape," later in this chapter, for more information about *ontape*.)

Example 14-6. Performing a Log Switch

```
curtis$ onmode -l; onmode -c
curtis$ onstat -l    #(output abbreviated)
address  number  flags    uniqid  begin    size   used   %used
a04b424  1       U-B----  25      100233   250    5      2.00
a04b440  2       U-B----  26      10032d   250    5      2.00
a04b45c  3       U-B----  27      100427   250    5      2.00
a04b478  4       U-B----  28      100521   250    5      2.00
a04b494  5       U---C-L  29      10061b   250    13     5.20
a04b4b0  6       U-B----  24      100715   250    20     8.00
```

The next step is to take the database to quiescent mode and drop all but three of the logs, as shown in Example 14-7. (Three is the minimum number of logs that Informix recommends.)

Example 14-7. Dropping All but Three of the Logical Logs

```
curtis$ onmode -sy
curtis$ onstat -l    #(output abbreviated)
address  number  flags    uniqid  begin    size   used   %used
a04b424  1       U-B----  46      300611   250    3      1.20
a04b440  2       U-B----  47      30070b   250    3      1.20
a04b45c  3       U-B----  48      300805   250    3      1.20
a04b478  4       U---C-L  49      300035   250    3      1.20
a04b494  5       U-B----  44      30012f   250    3      1.20
a04b4b0  6       U-B----  45      300229   250    3      1.20
```

Example 14-7. Dropping All but Three of the Logical Logs (continued)

```
curtis$ onparams -d -l 6
WARNING: Dropping a logical log file.
Do you really want to continue? (y/n)y
Logical log 6 successfully dropped.

curtis$ onparams -d -l 4
WARNING: Dropping a logical log file.
Do you really want to continue? (y/n)y
Logical log 4 successfully dropped.

curtis$ onparams -d -l 5
WARNING: Dropping a logical log file.
Do you really want to continue? (y/n)y
Logical log 5 successfully dropped.

curtis$ onstat -l   #(output abbreviated)
address  number  flags    uniqid  begin     size    used   %used
a04b424  1       U-B----  34      100233    250     1      0.40
a04b440  2       U---C-L  35      10032d    250     4      1.60
a04b45c  3       F------  0       100427    250     0      0.00
```

The maximum number of logs must now be modified to be the original maximum plus 3. (That is because we are going to add the same number of logs to the new *llogdbs* dbspace while the original three logs still exist.) This change is made by running *onmonitor* and entering P (for Parameters) and S (for Shared-Memory). You then should get a screen that looks like the one in Example 14-8.

Example 14-8. The onmonitor Utility

```
SHARED MEMORY: Make desired changes and press ESC to record changes.
    Press Interrupt to abort changes.   Press F2 or CTRL-F for field-level help.
                        SHARED MEMORY PARAMETERS
Server Number                 [    0]     Server Name [crash           ]
Server Aliases [                                                       ]
Dbspace Temp    [                                                      ]
Deadlock Timeout              [  60] Secs Number of Page Cleaners   [   1]
Forced Residency              [N]         Stack Size (K)            [  32]
Non Res. SegSize (K)      [   8000]       Optical Cache Size (K) [     0]

                                          Dbspace Down Option          [2]
                                          Preserve Log For Log Backup  [N]
Heterogeneous Commit          [N]         Transaction Timeout       [ 300]
Physical Log Buffer Size  [   32] K       Long TX HWM               [  50]
Logical Log Buffer Size   [   32] K       Long TX HWM Exclusive     [  60]
Max # of Logical Logs       [  6]         Index Page Fill Factor    [  90]
Max # of Locks            [ 2000]         Add SegSize (K)         [ 8192]
Max # of Buffers          [  200]         Total Memory (K)        [    0]

Resident Shared Memory size [      880] Kbytes      Page Size [   2] Kbytes

Enter the maximum # of logical logs that INFORMIX-OnLine can use
```

By looking at the *Max # of Logical Logs* field in Example 14-8, we can see that the current maximum number of logical logs for this instance is set to 6. Since we are going to add six logs to the new dbspace, we would need to change this maximum to 9. To make the change, use your arrow keys to move the cursor to the appropriate field and change its value. Once you make the change, enter Esc, Y. (Yes to save changes), Y (Yes to shutdown), then Enter. Once that is done, the instance should be offline. You then need to return it to a quiescent state with *oninit -s*, and add the logical logs to the new dbspace, as shown in Example 14-9.

Example 14-9. Adding the New Logical Logs

```
curtis$ oninit -s
curtis$ for I in 1 2 3 4 5 6 ; do
> onparams -a -d llogdbs
> done
Logical log successfully added.
Logical log successfully added.
Logical log successfully added.
Logical log successfully added.
Logical log successfully added.
Logical log successfully added.
```

You now must perform a level-0 archive to make these logs available for use. (An example level-0 archive is shown in Example 14-10.)

Example 14-10. A Level-0 Archive

```
curtis$ ontape -s
Please enter the level of archive to be performed (0, 1, or 2) 0

Please mount tape 1 on /informix/logical/crash/crash.level.0 and press Return to
continue ...
100 percent done.

Please label this tape as number 1 in the arc tape sequence.
This tape contains the following logical logs:

35

Program over.
```

As shown in Example 14-11, we now switch logs three times, which will cause the current log to be one of the new logs on the separate dbspace. Then we will force a checkpoint and perform a logical log backup. This will free the logs that are on the old dbspace, so that we may drop them.

Example 14-11. Performing a Log Switch and Starting Continuous Backups

```
curtis$ onmode -1 ; onmode -1 ; onmode -1
curtis$ onmode -c
curtis$ ontape -c
```

Example 14-11. Performing a Log Switch and Starting Continuous Backups (continued)

```
Performing continuous backup of logical logs.

Please mount tape 1 on /informix/logical/crash.log and press Return to continue
...
```

In another window, we run an *onstat -l* that shows us that the logical log backup is done. We now can stop the *ontape -c* with a Ctrl-C. We also can drop the original three logical logs. See Example 14-12 for an example of these steps.

Example 14-12. Example onstat Output and onparams Command

```
curtis$ onstat -l  #(output abbreviated)
address  number  flags    uniqid  begin    size   used   %used
a04b424  1       U-B----  34      100233   250    1      0.40
a04b440  2       U-B----  35      10032d   250    15     6.00
a04b45c  3       U-B----  36      100427   250    0      0.00
a04b478  4       U---C-L  0       300035   250    0      0.00
a04b494  5       F------  0       30012f   250    0      0.00
a04b4b0  6       F------  0       300229   250    0      0.00
a04b4cc  7       F------  0       300323   250    0      0.00
a04b4e8  8       F------  0       30041d   250    0      0.00
a04b504  9       F------  0       300517   250    0      0.00

curtis$ onparams -d -l 1
WARNING: Dropping a logical log file.
Do you really want to continue? (y/n)y
Logical log 1 successfully dropped.

curtis$ onparams -d -l 2
WARNING: Dropping a logical log file.
Do you really want to continue? (y/n)y
Logical log 2 successfully dropped.

curtis$ onparams -d -l 3
WARNING: Dropping a logical log file.
Do you really want to continue? (y/n)y
Logical log 3 successfully dropped.
curtis$ onstat -l  #(output abbreviated)
address  number  flags    uniqid  begin    size   used   %used
a04b478  4       U---C-L  37      300035   250    7      2.80
a04b494  5       F------  0       30012f   250    0      0.00
a04b4b0  6       F------  0       300229   250    0      0.00
a04b4cc  7       F------  0       300323   250    0      0.00
a04b4e8  8       F------  0       30041d   250    0      0.00
a04b504  9       F------  0       300517   250    0      0.00
```

At this point, we have successfully moved all logical logs into the new dbspace. The following steps are purely a matter of personal preference. I like my logs to be numbered starting with one. In order to do that, I have to add three more and drop the last three, as demonstrated in Example 14-13. The new logs will be given log numbers 1–3. Then we drop logs 7–9 in reverse order. (It's less confusing to delete them in reverse order.)

Example 14-13. Dropping and Adding Logical Logs

```
curtis$ onparams -a -d llogdbs
Logical log successfully added.
curtis$ onparams -a -d llogdbs
Logical log successfully added.
curtis$ onparams -a -d llogdbs
Logical log successfully added.
curtis$ onparams -d -l 9
WARNING: Dropping a logical log file.
Do you really want to continue? (y/n)y
Logical log 9 successfully dropped.

curtis$ onparams -d -l 8
WARNING: Dropping a logical log file.
Do you really want to continue? (y/n)y
Logical log 8 successfully dropped.

curtis$ onparams -d -l 7
WARNING: Dropping a logical log file.
Do you really want to continue? (y/n)y
Logical log 7 successfully dropped.
```

```
curtis$ onstat -l   #(output abbreviated)
address  number  flags    uniqid  begin    size    used   %used
a04b424  1       A------   0       300611   250     0      0.00
a04b440  2       A------   0       30070b   250     0      0.00
a04b45c  3       A------   0       300805   250     0      0.00
a04b478  4       U---C-L   37      300035   250     16     6.40
a04b494  5       F------   0       30012f   250     0      0.00
a04b4b0  6       F------   0       300229   250     0      0.00
```

Recommendation: Mirror Essential dbspaces

If you have the space, it is best to mirror the entire database. However, many places do not have that luxury. It doesn't take up much disk space to mirror the *essential* dbspaces, though. The essential dbspaces are those that contain the sysmaster database and the physical and logical logs. Of these, the *most* essential dbspace would be the one that contains the logical logs. That is because all other dbspaces can be recovered up to the point of failure—*if the logical logs are intact.*

When creating dbspaces, they can be set up as mirrored dbspaces. (This is demonstrated in the previous example about moving your logs to dedicated dbspaces.) However, it also can be done after the dbspace is created. Since we've already covered creating a mirrored dbspace, this section covers turning on mirroring for an existing dbspace. Assume for this example that we have a dbspace called *plogdbs*, and that we wish to mirror it to */informix/physlog_mirror.dbf*. We would run the commands shown in Example 14-14.

Example 14-14. Adding Mirroring to an Existing dbspace

```
$ onspaces -m plogdbs -f /informix/physlog_mirror.dbf -y
$ onstat -d  # (output abbreviated)
a12a728 3       2       3       1       M       informix plogdbs
    (The M flag above says that the plogdbs is mirrored.)
address chk/dbs offset  size    free    bpages  flags pathname
    (It lists two chunks below.  One is primary and the other secondary.)
a12a358 2   2   0       5000    2447            PO-   /informix/physlog.dbf
a12a508 2   2   0       5000    0               MO-   /informix/physlog_mirror.dbf
```

Recommendation: Leave Room for the Logs

Remember that the logical logs are absolutely essential for maintaining the integrity of your database. A common problem with many installations is that the logs become full. This is caused by either not backing up the logs or a long transaction that keeps too many logs open.

Back up your logical logs

Informix instances must have their logical logs backed up. If you do not back them up, all logical logs eventually become full. Once this happens, all activity on the instance stops, and you are forced to do a logical log backup. The problem is that backing up the logical logs requires creating more logical log entries. If all logs are full, you can't back up the logs.

The only option that remains is a special tool that can be run only by Informix support. They have to be able to dial or telnet into your system. They then transfer the file to your system, run it, and remove it. They do not allow you to keep the tool, and there is no way for you to get it without Informix accessing your system. In short, this is not a situation you want to be in.

Informix recently introduced a new parameter that prevents logical log entries from becoming full. Unfortunately, it is turned off by default.* The `LBU_PRESERVE` parameter (found in the *onconfig* file) needs to be set to 1 to reserve the last logical log for administrative activity, such as logical log backups.

Long transactions

Another "log full" problem is caused by a *long transaction*. A long transaction occurs when a user or application starts a transaction and does not commit it

---

* I really don't understand this one. This is such a bad situation to get into, I can't imagine anyone who wouldn't want to turn on this new feature.

within a reasonable time. The problem with this is that a log cannot be freed if it contains an uncommitted transaction. Suppose there are 10 logical logs, and a long transaction is started in the first log. Once the first log is full, Informix moves on to the next log, but it cannot free the first log for reuse until the long transaction is completed and that log file has been backed up. If the transaction were allowed to remain open until the 10th log was full, there would be no more free logs. One transaction has managed to span the entire set of logical logs. This is why it is called a long transaction. One might think that the transaction could be rolled back. However, rolling back a transaction requires creating *more* logical log entries. No more logical log entries can be created because there are no more free logical logs. Does that sound familiar?

The long-transaction problem is why they introduced the high-water-mark parameters that are found in the *onconfig* file. The first is the long-transaction high-water mark (LTXHWM), and its default value is 50. Once the percentage of full logical logs reaches this value, the transaction is automatically aborted and rolled back. However, since other transactions are allowed to continue, the logical logs are still in danger of filling up. The second parameter, the long-transaction exclusive-access high-water mark (LTXEHWM), is designed to protect the instance from this; its default value is 60. If the percentage of full logs reaches this value, most database activity is suspended and the transaction is given "exclusive access" to the remaining logical logs so that it can complete its rollback. The values of 50 and 60 are the new default values for these parameters, and *oninit* complains if you attempt to initialize an instance with values higher than these.

In summary, leave the LTXHWM and LTXEHWM values where they are and turn on LBU_PRESERVE by changing its value to 1 in the *onconfig* file. For more details about these values, consult the *IDS Administration Guide*.

Which Backup Utility Should I Use?

Before examining how to perform Informix backups, we need to understand the various backup options that are available to an Informix DBA. There are three backup utilities available with Informix: *onbar*, *onarchive*, and *ontape*.

A Quick History of onarchive, onbar, and ontape

Around 1993 and 1994, very large Informix databases started to appear. (Back then, "large" meant anything greater than 100 GB.) The only utility that Informix customers had was *ontape. ontape*'s one big flaw is that it is single-threaded. How do you back up 100 GB to a single device, especially when the devices available could back up only at rates ranging from 500 KB/s to 3 MB/s? Informix customers started screaming for a multithreaded backup system. (I was one of them.)

Informix, in an attempt to meet these demands, purchased the rights to a third-party program that became known as *onarchive*. Its syntax was arcane, complex, and completely unlike any other command on Unix. (It wasn't as complex as *sendmail*, but it was close!) The forward-slash method of passing options to a command seemed bizarre to most Unix system administrators, and it came with a manual that is almost the size of this book.

I was there

By the time in my career that I met *onarchive*, I had learned dozens of products just by browsing the manuals. I read the *onarchive* manual cover to cover four times *and* attended the Informix *onarchive* class. I was still confused. The most disconcerting part of the class was how the instructor kept talking about this thing called *onbar* that would soon replace *onarchive*.

I remember having 15 open bug reports for *onarchive* at one time. I remember calling support and getting the feeling that they didn't want to support the product any more than I wanted to use it. I remember spending months configuring and testing our *onarchive* setup. Informix came and saw what we did and thought it was one of the most impressive *onarchive* installations they had ever seen.

Then we tested the restore. It didn't work. No matter what we did, we couldn't restore the instance that we had backed up with *onarchive*. It just wouldn't work. Suddenly we received approval to buy a much faster tape drive and go back to *ontape*.

As a result of the input that they received from the field, Informix began work on a replacement for *onarchive* almost immediately. *onbar* was released with Version 7.21. Unfortunately, this created a problem. Users who need the multithreaded capabilities of *onbar* were required to purchase an interface to their storage manager—at a cost of more than $5000 per system. To avoid that cost, people who needed a multithreaded backup product were still being driven toward *onarchive*; this product, despite its incredible complexity and horrible reputation, remained the only choice available for some customers.

Informix wanted to fix this problem, so they negotiated an arrangement with Legato Systems that allowed them to bundle a scaled-down version of Legato Net-Worker with IDS 7.3. This product is known as Informix Storage Manager, or ISM. It allows you to send up to four data streams simultaneously to four storage devices (i.e., one data stream per drive). This is enough parallelism to back up a relatively large instance. Assuming that each data stream can "stream" each of four DLT 7000s, that is a total potential throughput of 40 MB/s, 144 GB/hr, or 1.1 TB in an eight-hour period. (Unfortunately, on many systems, you'll need more than one thread to stream a device; this reduces the overall effective throughput of an *ISM/onbar* combination, but it is still going to be faster than *ontape*.)

Don't use onarchive

If you downloaded both the *Archive and Backup Guide* and the *Backup and Restore Guide* from *http://www.informix.com/answers*, you might get the impression that there are three viable options for backing up Informix databases: *ontape*, *onbar*, and *onarchive*. The manuals do explain that *onbar* is designed to work with storage managers, and *ontape* and *onarchive* are not. What the documentation does not explain is why two products (*ontape* and *onarchive*) that appear to perform the same function exist. Further, you might get the impression after reading the manual that *onarchive* is the way to go. *It's not.*

The release of ISM means that there remains no valid reason for configuring a new backup system using *onarchive*. If you can live without multithreaded backup and recovery, use *ontape* and *infback.sh* (or something similar). If you need multithreaded capability or want some other advanced feature, use *onbar* and ISM. If you can afford an Informix server that needs more than four backup threads, you can afford a full-featured storage manager and its interface to *onbar*. If you're having trouble convincing your management to spend that money, show them this chapter.

Informix plans to phase out *onarchive* over time. You can already see references that say things like "*onbar* is the preferred solution for 7.3," and "*ontape* and *onarchive* are supported for now." The only reason that they don't drop *onarchive* today is there are still people using it. I wouldn't be surprised if a future release of Informix configures *onarchive* in such a way that you would no longer be able to make backups with it. The restore functionality will be left for those who still have *onarchive* backup tapes. (I doubt that Informix will drop *ontape*, though, because it's so easy to use and support. They aren't adding any new features to it, but that could be considered a feature in itself.)

Some people reading this section may disagree with my assessment of *onarchive*'s value. They like the flexibility that such a complex product offers them. They don't care that they need to read almost 500 pages of documentation just to figure out how to back up their Informix database. They've figured it out now—and they don't want to have to figure out another product. If that is how you feel, please know that you are in the minority. The whole reason that *onbar* exists is that the Informix user community was in an uproar about *onarchive*. Remember also that a product that is difficult to use is difficult to support. Informix is probably doing everything it can to put this utility behind them. If you're using *onarchive* today, you should seriously consider looking at *onbar* as soon as possible or going back to *ontape* if you can. Trust me: *onbar* is as easy as it gets.

Pick a Utility, but Not Any Utility

Here is a quick summary of the three utilities available for Informix backups:

onbar

> *onbar* is the latest in Informix backup technology and is used only for interfacing with storage managers like the Informix Storage Manager (ISM). (*onbar* is covered in "Physical Backups with a Storage Manager: onbar.") If you are running Informix 7.3 or greater, *onbar* offers enhanced functionality and flexibility.

onarchive

> *onarchive* was Informix's first attempt at an enhanced product, but its incredible complexity caused it to be just a stopgap measure until *onbar* was available. *onarchive* will not be supported in the future and therefore should not be used as the basis for any new backup system. (See "Don't use onarchive," earlier in this chapter, for more information.)

ontape

> *ontape* is Informix's oldest backup utility, but it's still going strong. It does not interface with storage managers, therefore it is the easiest and best way to perform physical backups without a storage manager.

In summary, if you do not have a storage manager, you really should be using *ontape* if you can. If your database is really large, and you need the multithreaded capabilities of *onbar*, you should either purchase a third-party storage manager or upgrade to a recent version of Informix that includes a free (albeit scaled-down) storage manager. Once you have done that, you can use the advanced functionality of *onbar*. I would not advise designing any new backup systems around *onarchive*. It is too difficult to learn, and it is being phased out.

Physical Backups Without a Storage Manager: ontape

If you do not have access to a storage manager, *ontape* might be the perfect tool for you. This section covers *ontape*'s basic usage, then shows you how to automate it using shell scripts. Many environments without storage managers use *ontape* to automate their backups.

Despite its age, many people continue to use *ontape* for several reasons:

Informix version

> *ontape* does not require a storage manager. If you are not running Informix 7.3 or greater, you do not have ISM. That means that you will need to purchase a

storage manager and its interface to *onbar*. If you are running a version older than Informix 7.21, you don't even have access to *onbar*.

Cost

> *ontape* is free. Although *onbar* itself is free, it will cost as much as $7000 *per host*[*] to purchase the interface to *onbar*, even if you already have one of the commercial storage management applications (e.g., those discussed in Chapter 5, *Commercial Backup Utilities*).

Ease of use

> *ontape* is a breeze to learn. It has four required options, *-s* for archive,[†] *-c* for continuous backups, *-a* for automatic backups, and *-r* for restore. That's it. In contrast, *onarchive* is a nightmare of complexity. Its manual spans 436 pages, compared to *ontape*'s 49 pages or *onbar*'s 125 pages. *onbar* is much simpler to use than *onarchive*, but adding a storage manager into the picture still makes it more complicated than *ontape*. (The slight increase in complexity does come with greatly increased functionality, though.)

ontape is easy to use. Even more importantly, *ontape* recoveries work! *ontape* was developed many years ago, before the advent of backup automation in the Unix world. It was ahead of its time with multilevel backups, but it does have one design flaw: it was designed to be run by an operator on a console. It prompts the operator for information even during normal operations. It was not designed for automated backups, but that doesn't mean you can't use it that way. Many scripts have been written that answer its prompts, providing a level of functionality never envisioned by the original programmers. Before looking at how to automate the use of *ontape*, though, we cover its basic usage.

Configuring ontape

Prior to running *ontape*, you must configure some parameters using the *onmonitor* utility. This utility changes these parameters in the file *$INFORMIXDIR/etc/ $ONCONFIG*, where *$INFORMIXDIR* is a required environment variable specifying the Informix directory, and *$ONCONFIG* is a required environment variable specifying the name of the Informix configuration file. It is an editable text file, but not all changes will go into effect until you restart the instance if you edit it manually. Specifically, the LTAPE parameters must be changed using *onmonitor* if you want them to go into effect immediately. To configure *ontape*, run the *onmonitor* utility, choosing menu option A (for Archive) and T (for Tape Parameters). (An

---

[*] Every commercial backup application charges per host for its interface to the database backup applications. In a large Informix environment, this can therefore reach $100,000 very quickly. It does provide significantly better functionality, but it is difficult to justify such an expense for a little 1-GB instance.

[†] I finally figured out why archive is *-s*! It stands for "save"!

ontape backup of an instance is referred to as an *archive*.) This takes you into a screen that looks like Figure 14-1.

```
Press ESC to change tape parameters.
  Press Interrupt to return to Archive menu.
  Press F2 or CTRL-F for field level help.


                     MODIFYING TAPE PARAMETERS


      Tape Device [/dev/rmt/0c                                  ]

        Block Size [        32] Kbytes      Tape Size [      102400] Kbytes

  Log Tape Device [/dev/rmt/0c                                  ]

        Block Size [        32] Kbytes      Tape Size [       10240] Kbytes

```

Figure 14-1. onmonitor tape parameters menu

The values in Figure 14-1 should be changed to ones appropriate for your environment. The appropriate values are also listed in Table 14-1.

Table 14-1. Tape Configuration Values

Variable in the $ONCONFIG file	Value in onmonitor Screen	Purpose
TAPEDEV	Tape Device	Device to which archives (backups) are sent
TAPEBLK	Block Size	Block size of tape device in kilobytes
TAPESIZE	Tape Size	Size of tape in kilobytes
LTAPEDEV	Log Tape Device	Device to which logical log backups are sent
LTAPEBLK	Block Size	Block size of log device in kilobytes
LTAPESIZE	Tape Size	Specifies the tape device for logical log backups.

These values usually are set once and should be changed only if your configuration changes. One of the best ways to do this is to make the device name to which you are backing up a symbolic link to the real device. For example, you can specify that the tape device is */informix/tapedev* and make that a symbolic link to */dev/rmt/0cn*. That would allow you to change the actual tape device without accessing *onmonitor*. Although optimum block size settings are determined by your tape drive manufacturer, a value of 64 or 128 is quite common. You should experiment with different values to see how they affect backup performance.*

---

* It is usually true that the bigger the block size, the better the backup performance. However, in recent tests I found that a block size of 64 KB was actually faster than a block size of 128 KB. Your mileage may vary.

I like to set the TAPESIZE parameter to something slightly larger than the instance size but less than the actual tape size. For example, suppose you have a 16-GB tape but a 4-GB instance. One option would be to set the tape size to 15 GB and not worry about changing it again for a long time. You also could set it at 5 GB, and then watch the logs to make sure that backups complete. Once backups start failing because the tape is filling up, change the TAPESIZE parameter to 8 GB. This method lets you to see how big the instance is growing over time, allowing you to document when the instance is going to exceed the size of your 16-GB tape drive so you can purchase a *bigger* tape drive long before it ever becomes a problem. Setting the TAPESIZE to 15 GB would result in successful archives for a long time, followed by a failure once the database got bigger than 15 GB. Unfortunately, though, you would have no idea when it is going to reach 16 GB and have *very* little time to purchase a bigger tape drive.

Some DBAs prefer to set the TAPESIZE parameter to the size of the tape and then chart the growth of the instance with *sysdbspaces*. You should do whatever works best for you!

 It should be noted that Informix backups can span tapes. It will prompt the operator for a second tape if the first one fills up. However, if you are automating your backups with shell scripts, the prompt probably will not get answered, and the backup will fail.

Tape or Disk?

Informix assumes that the devices that you specify for TAPEDEV and LTAPEDEV are tape drives, as evidenced by the variable names. It is common, however, to use files on disk instead. To back up to disk, Informix needs an empty disk file to which it can write. This usually is done with the *touch* command. For example, the previous example window shows the Log Tape Device set to */informix/logical/crash.log*. This is a disk file created by issuing the following command:

```
$ touch /informix/logical/crash.log
```

What's wrong with tape?

One of the most difficult things about *ontape*'s continuous backups is that they are designed to back up the logical logs to a single tape. Once the tape fills up, the logical log backups stop, and the logical logs begin to fill up. If all logical logs fill up during this time, all activity on the instance is suspended. This means that the DBA must constantly watch several tape drives, swapping tapes throughout the day. Nor can he tell how full a tape is getting. (A DBA could write a separate script to monitor how many logs have been written to a device and use that to estimate how full the tape is getting. However, different compression ratios may cause this estimate to be way off.) It doesn't help that Informix requires a separate tape device for each instance. What does a DBA do with a machine that has several Informix instances on it?

 If you are archiving to tape, make sure that your scripts rewind the tape before starting an archive. Failure to do so may result in unexpected results!

Backing up to disk can help

The alternative is to back up the logical logs to disk. All of the logical log backups on a single host can share a single */logical* filesystem. For each Informix instance, you'll need a script that:

1. Stops continuous backups for a moment

2. Moves the current logical log backup file to a date/timestamped file

3. Creates another logical log backup file

4. Starts continuous backups again

Once this has been done, the only management required is monitoring the available space in the filesystems where you're sending your logical logs and deleting old logical log files that have been backed up.

Is it OK to back up to disk?

Some DBAs feel that the logical logs are extremely important and that backing them up to disk places them at risk. Disks can fail. If the disk drive that contains your logical logs fails at the same time as the disk drive that contains your database, you are out of luck. They feel it is safer to get the backups out to tape.

There are strong arguments *for* backing up to disk. Proponents say the value added by backing up to disk far outweighs the added risk. They also say that backing up to tape has risks as well. Their reasoning is as follows:

- Backing up to disk allows complete automation. No one has to remember to swap tapes, no one needs to be available to swap tapes, continuous backups just happen. It's always a good thing to automate backups. Why have operators swapping tapes when a simple shell script will do the job—day in and day out?

- The slowest part of an Informix database restore is the reading of the logical logs. Placing the logical logs on disk significantly increases the speed of this critical path of a restore.

- The all-your-eggs-in-one-basket problem is solved by using remote devices. For example, *elvis* logical logs can back up to a filesystem on *apollo*—all you need to do is specify *apollo:/logical/servername/logfile* as the logical tape device. This significantly reduces the chance that both the logical tape device and the database instance will be damaged at the same time.

- The proponents of logical log backups to tape also would contend that backing up to disk would not protect the data from a fire that destroys both systems. Don't forget that a fire also would destroy any tapes that are in the drives.

- Tape is safer than disk, right? The quicker the logical logs get to tape, the safer they are. Performing logical log backups to disk actually makes this easier. Why is that? If the logical logs are being backed up to disk, logging can be stopped and started throughout the day, creating multiple log files. These log files can be immediately backed up using a homegrown or commercial backup system. They can even be backed up or copied multiple times. This is something that is impossible with tape backups. As long as the tape device is open by Informix, it can't be accessed. Talk about putting all your eggs in one basket! Instead, you could easily have multiple copies of the disk backup, as well as tape copies that can be sent off-site without disturbing Informix.

Doesn't Informix try to rewind the tape?

A common misconception is that Informix rewinds the tape before and/or after a backup or restore. This is what is commonly used as an argument against disk backups. It also is commonly used to explain why you are not supposed to put more than one archive on a tape device.

Informix does not rewind the tape at any time. It expects the tape to be rewound already. This allows you to back up to disk or to put multiple archives on a single tape by using the no-rewind device. Recent changes to the Informix FAQ and discussions in the *comp.databases.informix* newsgroup have confirmed this.

If you *do* back up to disk, all "tape" management is up to you. *ontape* will not know that the backup really went to disk. It is up to you to track that information and to manipulate disk devices during a restore so that the "tape" is always where *ontape* expects it to be.

However, if you do put multiple archives or log backups on a tape by using the no-rewind device, a restore from those backups will not work. This is because Informix opens and closes the tape several times during a restore, expecting it to rewind. If you have multiple backups on a tape, you must copy each backup to a separate tape in order to do a restore.

The two-gigabyte file size limit

There is one downside to backing up to disk. Informix still has a 2-GB file-size limit, so you will not be able to create a disk archive of a database that results in a file larger than 2 GB. There are two options that you can explore to get around the 2-GB file-size limitation:

- Use *expect* (or the *expect* module of *perl*) to respond to the prompts from *ontape*.

- Don't use *ontape*; use *onbar*.

Use expect to swap tapes. The first option is to use *expect* or *perl* to respond to the multiple prompts from *ontape*. You then could set the TAPESIZE parameter to something just short of 2 GB. Once *ontape* reaches this size, it will prompt you for a second tape. You then could use *expect* to move the first file from its original location, create another file, and respond to *ontape*'s prompt for a second tape. This method will allow you to make an archive as large as the available space on the filesystem.

Use a storage manager and onbar. The second option, and one you should seriously consider, is to use Informix Storage Manager (or some other storage manager) and *onbar*. This combination would work around the 2-GB limit, still allow you to back up to disk if you wish, while providing you with the features that are available only in *onbar*.

Backing Up the Instance

The Informix term for a backup of an instance is an *archive*. First, you must configure TAPEDEV as explained in "Configuring ontape," earlier in this chapter. Then to perform an archive, run one of the following commands:

```
$ ontape -s            # on a 5.x instance
$ ontape -s <-Llevel>  # on a 6.x and higher instance
```

You may specify a 0, 1, or 2 for *level*. Specifying a 0 performs a full archive. Specifying a 1 causes Informix to back up anything that has changed since the last

---

I'll Use Disk for Continuous Backups. . .

I remember once managing five or six Informix instances and having to run down the hall into the server room to swap tapes because a logical log tape was full, causing our production Informix instance to hang. (We used TK70s for this.) I had to open five or six windows every time we rebooted an instance, just so we could start continuous backups to tape. Then I remember the day that we wrote *rclogs.sh*. Suddenly, we had a program that would start logical logging for us. We could reboot a host, and continuous backups would just magically turn on. We went from a few instances to well over 50 and never had to swap a tape again. (We also never had to explain to an angry manager why her Informix database was temporarily unavailable during the busiest time of her day.) *I can't imagine going back to the old way.*

---

level 0. Specifying a 2 causes Informix to back up anything that has changed since the last level 1 or 0. If you do not specify the level using the *-L* option, *ontape* prompts for it. *ontape* also prompts you to hit Enter once you have mounted the tape.

If *ontape* detects that it has reached the end of a volume, it prompts for another tape. *ontape* supports three levels and multivolume archives but cannot use more than one device at a time; you must use the same device throughout the archive. Once the volume on that device is full, you must swap that volume and answer *ontape*'s prompts for the next tape. If you are backing up to disk, this means that you have to move the original backup file to another location.

Backing Up the Logical Logs

Recovering an Informix instance from an archive recovers the database to the point in time that the archive was taken. In order to redo any transactions that have occurred since then, you also must restore the logical logs. In order for the logs to be available during a restore, you must back them up. You can:

Back up the logs continuously
> *ontape* offers a particular type of logical log backup, referred to as "continuous backups," by using the *-c* option of *ontape*. *ontape* runs continuously in the foreground, appending logical logs to the storage media as it becomes full.

Back up the logs manually
> A "manual backup" is a one-time backup performed by the *-a* option of *ontape*. It overwrites the storage media with all full logical logs and the current logical log.

Back up the logs with a script and the ALARMPROGRAM parameter

As of 7.xx, there is a new way to back up your logs. You can use the ALARMPROGRAM parameter to automatically run a shell script for you when a log is full or is manually closed.

Elect not to back up the logs

You could decide not to back up the logical logs. This is done by setting the backup device to */dev/null.*

Backing up logical logs continuously

The historically preferred way to back up your logical logs is to use the continuous backup option of *ontape*. When continuous backups are running, logical logs are automatically backed up to the specified device as soon as they are full. The logs are appended to the backup device, which is held open by Informix as long as continuous backups are running.

To perform a continuous backup of the logical logs, run the following command:

```
$ ontape -c
```

This command prompts you to hit Enter once you have mounted the tape; from then on, it performs a continuous backup of the logical logs to the storage media until you enter Ctrl-C or kill the process. It continues to append logical log backups to a particular piece of media until the media is full. A tape is "full" when *ontape* can longer write to it, or the amount of data that has been written to it exceeds the value specifid by the TAPESIZE parameter in the *onconfig* file.

Backing up logical logs manually

Another method of backing up logical logs is to perform a manual backup only when required. This method differs from continuous backups in two ways. First, it is a onetime backup that backs up full logs, along with the current logical log. It opens the device once, writes these logs to it, and closes the device. Second, and perhaps more important, a manual backup overwrites any backups found on the storage media. To perform a manual backup of the logical logs, run the following command:

```
$ ontape -a
```

There are some environments that have written automation scripts around this command. They monitor the logs to see how many are full. Once a certain percentage of them are full, they run the *ontape -a* command to back up the logs. A script that operates in this way is simulating the continuous backup operation of *ontape -c*. It requires more tape or disk space than the continuous backup method, because it backs up the current log whether it is full or not, whereas continuous backups back up logs only when they are full.

There is nothing wrong with simulating continuous backups using scripts and *ontape -a*, and it is slightly easier to automate than *ontape -c*. This is exactly what the ALARMPROGRAM is for. You specify the script that Informix should run whenever a log is full.

Electing no backup of logical logs

The least preferred method of backing up the logical logs is to not back them up at all. You do this by setting the LTAPEDEV value to */dev/null*, which causes Informix to mark the logs as backed up as soon as they become full. (See the earlier explanation under "Configuring ontape" for details on how to do this.) Since no actual backup occurs, this is not an option to use if you will need point-in-time recovery. Using this option allows you to recover only from your latest archive. You will not be able to redo any transactions since the time of that archive. This option typically is used only for development instances or instances in which data is loaded only via batch loads. If you are considering using this option for a batch-load instance, you should experiment with this option and with the continuous backup option. Find out the impact of both on your environment, including performance during loads and recovery speed.

To Oracle DBAs: This is the Informix equivalent to running an Oracle database in NOARCHIVELOG mode.

Automating Archives with ontape: the infback.sh Utility

infback.sh is a shell script that automates performing archives with *ontape*. Before examining how *infback.sh* works, we explain why automating *ontape* backups is difficult.

Why automating ontape is difficult

The *ontape* utility is simple and flexible, but automating it has always been somewhat difficult, because it is a little picky about how it receives the answers to its questions. For example, some versions of *ontape* do not accept a typical "here document,"* as shown in Example 14-15.

---

* A here document is a Unix trick that allows a script to answer prompts from a command. It starts with <<*STRING* and ends with *STRING*.

Example 14-15. Calling ontape with a Here Document

```
LEVEL=0
ontape -s <<EOF >/tmp/logfile
$LEVEL

EOF
```

ontape now accepts the use of a *-L level* argument, but it still requires you to respond to a prompt after executing the command. *ontape* can still give you difficulties if you use the syntax in Example 14-15.

The method shown in Example 14-15 is often mentioned in FAQs and other books, but it does not work on every version of Informix. The method that does always seem to work is shown in Example 14-16.

Example 14-16. A More Reliable Way to Call ontape

```
LEVEL=0
echo "$LEVEL

"| ontape -s | head -100 > /tmp/logfile
```

There are two differences between the methods shown in Example 14-15 and Example 14-16. The first difference is the way in which the answers are passed to *ontape*; the second method seems to be a little more robust. The second difference between the two methods is the addition of the *head* command in the second one. The *head* command is not required but is a good precaution in case the backup device becomes full. Here's why: once *ontape* detects that the backup device is full, it prompts for a second tape. It is not very easy to provide a second tape and answer this prompt without using a program such as *expect*.[*] (There is a way to answer prompts like this by redirecting `stdin` and `stdout` to named pipes, but that can be really tricky with *ontape*. *ontape* prompts repeatedly for the second tape and things get pretty ugly very quickly.) The *head* command keeps this repeated prompting from happening, since it truncates the output to 100 lines, but once the 100 lines have been reached, *ontape* aborts.

How infback.sh works

infback.sh is a shell script that automates performing archives with *ontape*. (As discussed earlier, its one limitation is that it cannot handle multivolume archives.)

---

[*] *expect* is a public domain utility designed to answer a program's prompts for information. It is sophisticated enough to be able to give different answers for different conditions, such as a full tape. A typical shell script and here document can provide only one set of answers to a program. While using *expect* would probably increase the functionality of the script, I have tried very hard not to require the installation of other packages to make mine work.

infback.sh consists of several files:

infback.sh
>   This is the main backup program that looks at the configuration files to decide how and what to back up.

rclogs.sh
>   This program is another main program that automates continuous backups of the logical logs using *ontape -c.*

infback.conf
>   This file is used by *infback.sh* to specify how, when, and what to back up.

inftab
>   This file lists all Informix instances on a machine. It is used by *dbstart. informix.sh*, *rclogs.sh*, and *infback.sh* to determine what instances are on the machine.

localpath.sh, rempath.sh, config.guess
>   These files accompany these other programs and assist them in determining what commands to run on various Unix platforms.

infback.sh is based on the same logic as Oracle's *oraback.sh* and Sybase's *syback.sh.* *infback.sh*:

-   Uses a global tabulation file (*inftab*) to list all Informix instances
-   Uses a global configuration file (*infback.conf5*) to configure backups
-   Automatically performs full or incremental backups of all instances found in *inftab*
-   Optionally performs full or incremental backups of any instances listed on the command line
-   Can write archives to disk or tape
-   Sends email, notifying of the success or failure of the backup
-   Backs up databases that reside on raw partitions or filesystems

infback.sh can be called in one of three ways:

With no arguments
>   If you call *infback.sh* with no arguments, it decides what to back up and what device to use by looking at *infback.conf.*

With arguments specifying backup parameters
>   You can tell *infback.sh* which device and level to use by giving them as arguments. If you do this without giving it a list of instances to back up, it will back up any instances it finds in *inftab*. If you specify instances to back up, it will back up only the instances that you specify.

With at as the first argument, with or without backup parameter arguments
  Specifying *at* as the first argument causes *infback.sh* to look at *infback.conf* to
  determine what time to back up. It then schedules an *at* job using the same
  arguments given after the *at* argument. (That means that the scheduled
  backup will figure out what and how to back up via either *infback.conf* or the
  arguments that were given.)

When infback.sh runs

One of the first things that *infback.sh* does is to check if the word "skip" is in field
2 of *infback.conf*. If so, it skips the backup once and removes the word "skip"
from *infback.conf*. (This allows a DBA to manually skip tonight's backup, but does
not allow the DBA to accidentally disable backups forever.)

If *infback.sh* determines that it is not supposed to skip the backup, it then needs
to determine what instances to back up (*$INSTANCE_LIST*), what level backup to
run (*$LEVEL*), and what device to use (*$DEVICE*). How *infback.sh* does this
depends on which arguments (if any) it receives.

If infback.sh is called with no arguments

If called with no arguments, like this:

```
$ infback.sh
```

infback.sh looks at the third field in *infback.conf* to determine what level of
backup to run. That field specifies the full backup day. If today is the full backup
day, then it performs a level-0 archive. If it is not today, it performs a level-1
archive. *infback.sh* then looks at fields 6 and 7 of *infback.conf* to get the name of
the device server and device to which it should back up. Finally, it looks at *inftab*
for a list of instances to back up.

If infback.sh is called with arguments specifying backup parameters

If *infback.sh* is called with arguments as follows:

```
$ infback.sh level [device|host:device] [instancea instanceb ...]
```

it will determine its level and device from the arguments. If it also receives a list of
instances to back up, it will use that as the list of instances. If not, it determines
the list of instances to back up by listing each instance list in *inftab*. The arguments and their possible values are as follows:

`level`
  This should be a valid level for an Informix archive (0, 1, or 2).

device | host:device
> This should be a valid device name or directory name. It also can be *hostname:device* (e.g., *apollo:/dev/rmt/0cbn*).

[instancea instanceb ...]
> These arguments are optional. You may specify one or more Informix instances to back up. Specifying no instances causes *infback.sh* to back up all instances listed in *inftab*.

If infback.sh is called with at as the first argument

If *infback.sh* is called with *at* as the first argument (as it would be called in *cron* or *at*):

> ```
> $ infback.sh at
> ```

infback.sh sets the *$TIME* variable so that the backups take place at a specified time. If it is a level-0 backup, *infback.sh* sets the *$TIME* variable to the value in field 4. If it is a level-1 backup, it sets the *$TIME* variable to the value in field 5. *infback.sh* then schedules an *at* job that will perform the backup at the time specified by *$TIME*. If there were other arguments given after the *at* argument, those arguments are passed to the scheduled run of *infback.sh*. When the *at* job runs *infback.sh*, it will then determine what and how to back up based on the arguments (if any) that it was given.

The backup begins

Once the actual backup is supposed to run, *infback.sh* checks to see if the database is up. If it is not, *infback.sh* complains and exits. If it is up, *infback.sh* checks to see if there is enough space to make a change to the *onconfig* file.* What it does next depends on whether you specified that compression should be used.

If there is a value specified in *infback.conf* for *$COMPRESS*, *infback.sh* creates a named pipe called *$INFORMIXDIR/$INSTANCE.level.$LEVEL.fifo*, and changes **TAPEDEV** to that filename. It does this using *onmonitor*, so the change will be effective immediately. After creating the named pipe and telling *ontape* to use it, it calls *compress* and tells it to read from the named pipe, compress the data, and write it to the location specified as the original device. *infback.sh* then calls either *ontape* or *tbtape*, depending on the version of Informix you are running,† passing

---

* This part is to get around an old problem that may have been fixed in newer versions of Informix. If you attempted to change the *config* file, and the filesystem was full, you would end up with an empty *config* file!

† Believe it or not, this script works just fine with Informix 5! It might even work with Informix 4, but I haven't seen one of those in ages.

it the appropriate level. It checks the status of the backup command and, if backing up to disk, compresses the backup file.

If there is no value specified for *$COMPRESS*, *infback.sh* sets TAPEDEV to *$DEVICE_SERVER:$DEVICE_FILE* using *onmonitor*. It then calls *ontape* to perform the archive to the specified device.

Installing infback.sh and its configuration files

If you'd like to use *infback.sh*, you'll need to install the files in the appropriate directory, configure *inftab* and *infback.conf*, and customize *infback.sh* to your environment.

Copy *infback.sh*, *localpath.sh*, *rempath.sh*, and *config.guess* into the same directory (e.g., *$INFORMIXDIR/local/bin*) and make sure that they are executable. Copy *inftab* and *infback.conf* into a directory to which Informix can write (e.g., *$INFORMIXDIR/etc*). *infback.sh* needs to be able to write to this directory for the "skip" feature to work. *inftab* and *infback.conf* can be placed in the same directory as the other files, but they do not need to be.

Editing the infback.sh configuration files

If you have not already done so, you should configure *inftab* for use on this system. For details on how to do that, see "Edit the inftab file" earlier in this chapter.

Editing infback.conf. infback.conf is the configuration file for *infback.sh* and *rclogs.sh*. It should contain one line for each machine in the following format:

```
hostname.master::full_day:full_time:inc_time:device_server:archive_dest:allow_
ids:compress:mail_ids
```

hostname.master

> Replace *hostname* with the base hostname. For example, if the hostname is *apollo.domain.com*, this field should contain apollo.master.

full_day

> This is the day of the week that full backups should run. (All other days of the week will receive level-1 backups.)

full_time

> If using the *at* argument, this is the time that the program should schedule level-0 backups. Suppose that it says 1900, and the full backup day is Mon. At 1500 on Monday, there is a *cron* job that runs *infback.sh at*. That will see that Monday is a full backup day and schedule an *at* job to run at 1900.

inc_time

> If using the *at* argument, this is the time that the program should schedule level-1 backups.

device_server

> Set this to the hostname of the server that contains the backup device. If it is the same as this host, enter the base hostname only (just like in the first field). For all other hosts, use the Fully Qualified Domain Name (FQDN) if it is appropriate.

archive_dest

> This should be set to a device or directory that will contain all archives. If it is a directory, make sure that it is writable by Informix. Also, if it is a directory, *infback.sh* will create a subdirectory for each instance inside this directory.

allow_ids

> This is a |-separated list of user IDs that are allowed to run *infback.sh*. This is usually only Informix.

mail_ids

> This is a comma-separated list of user IDs that should receive mail about the success of *infback.sh*.

Editing infback.sh. There are a few minor changes that you need to make to the *infback.sh* file itself. Locate the following variable and function declarations in the top of the script, and set them to the appropriate value for your environment:

DEBUG=

> Set this to Y if you want to see debug information for all functions (i.e., turns on *set -x*).

BINDIR=

> Set this to the directory where you copied the backup programs (e.g., *$INFORMIXDIR/local/bin*).

LOGDIR=

> Set this to the directory where you want *infback.sh* to log its information (e.g., *$INFORMIXDIR/log*).

LOG=

> Set this to the full path of the name of the log file you want it to use (e.g., *$LOGDIR/infback.log*).

INFCONF=

> Set this to the full path of *infback.conf* (e.g., *$INFORMIXDIR/etc/infback. conf*).

INFORMIX=

> Set this to the user that owns the Informix instance (usually *informix*).

INFTAB=

> Set this to the full path of *inftab* (e.g., *$INFORMIXDIR/etc/inftab*).

TMP=

Set this to the directory you want *infback.sh* to use for temporary files.

Preback

Anything that is put inside this function will be executed prior to running the backup.

Postback

Anything that is put inside this function will be executed when the backups are finished.

Centralized configuration

Just like *oraback.sh*, the configuration file *infback.conf* can be shared via NFS. If multiple servers share the same configuration file, and you are using the *at* argument, you could make changes to all Informix backups by changing one file. Suppose that Informix backups currently are set up to run a full backup on Sunday at 1900. However, you know that the network will be down this Sunday. With most homegrown backup scripts, you would need to log into several servers and change multiple cron entries. With a centralized *infback.conf* file, you need only to change field 3 for each server from "Sun" to "Mon." If you know that there will be some intensive processing this evening, you also could skip all *infback.sh* backups by putting the word "skip" in field 2.

Scheduling backups

To use all scheduling features of *infback.sh*, create a cron entry that calls *infback. sh* at a time earlier than the earliest time specified in fields 4 and 5 in *infback.conf*. Since most backups are run after 6:00 P.M., a common entry would be like the following:

```
0 17 * * * /informix/local/bin/infback.sh at
```

This says to run the script with the *at* argument at 5:00 P.M. This causes *infback.sh* to look at the *infback.conf* file to determine what level of backup to run and what time to run it. It then will schedule an *at* job for the appropriate time.

The reason for keeping the entry as late as possible is to allow the DBAs to make changes to *infback.conf*. Since *infback.sh* does not look at the file until 5:00 P.M., they can change tonight's backup time or skip tonight's backups by changing the file any time before then.

Why Automating Continuous Backups Is Difficult

The original design of *ontape -c* continuous backups was that they would be run from an operator's console. They also would be monitored by that operator; when the system prompted for another tape, the operator would respond by changing tapes.

Automating a program that was designed to run and be monitored by a human around the clock is a challenge. It's even more difficult than automating an archive. *ontape* is designed to continue logging to a tape until the tape is full. Although you can write a program that will monitor the tape and let you know when it is full, how does the program notify you so you can replace the tape? The program can send you an email, but if you're not reading your email or the email gets lost in transit, the tape does not get swapped. Then, processing is eventually halted on that instance once all the logical logs become full and are not backed up. The secret to complete automation is to back up to disk instead. Backing up to disk does remove the need to swap tapes, but it's slightly more involved than simply changing the `LTAPEDEV` field to a disk.

Any automated system designed to automate continuous backups needs to manage many things. The program must emulate the human that *ontape* was originally designed to interact with. Here are the tasks that must be handled:

Put a tape in drive

>   *ontape* expects a device it can write to. Historically this has been a tape drive with a tape in it. The way to emulate that on disk is to use the *touch* command to create a file that Informix can write to. The file needs to be owned by the Informix user ID and writable to both the Informix user and Informix group.

Watch for a full tape

>   Historically this was done by watching the terminal for a prompt. When backing up to tape, there are a couple of ways to do this. One way is to write a program that watches how many logs are backed up and checks that number against the number of logs you have determined will fit on a tape. This is somewhat complicated but is preferred over the second method. The second method would be to use the *onstat -l* command to watch for logs that get filled but are not backed up. This means that the tape device is already full, since no more logs are being backed up. (The problem with this method is that you may need to swap tapes very quickly, and you do not get notified right away.) When backing up to disk, the "tape" becomes full when the filesystem is full. Therefore, you simply need to monitor the filesystem where you are sending the logical logs. You then need to compress or remove files to make room for more continuous backups. You can start doing this once a filesystem reaches a certain threshold, such as 75 percent.

Remember that Informix depends on the `TAPESIZE` parameter to tell it how much data will fit on a "tape." It considers the tape full once it has put that much data on a tape, and it will request another tape. If it encounters a file-system or tape that is actually full (as evidenced by a failed attempt to write more data) prior to reaching this value, the archive will actually abort.

Swap tapes

When backing up to tape, you must swap tapes manually. A program that is running continuous backups for you will need to notify you in some way that this needs to happen. If backing up to disk, this is done by moving the "tape" file to another location and re-creating a file in the same location using the *touch* and *chown* commands.

Tell ontape there is another tape

When using continuous backups, this is the difficult part to automate. As mentioned previously, *ontape* has a tendency to immediately send hundreds of prompts to a program trying to talk to it, so it's somewhat impractical to actually try to answer these prompts. It works just as well to *stop* continuous backups, then restart them once you've swapped the "tape." A good way to stop them is to use the *onmode -z* command. If you can keep track of the session ID that is associated with your *ontape* process, you simply pass this value to the *onmode -z* command, and it will close the session gracefully. If that doesn't work, you can always kill the process ID.

 If you are using Informix 5.x, never kill an *ontape* process of any kind with the -9 option. The instance will need to be restarted to recover from this. (Informix 7.x recovers from this condition gracefully.)

Move the backup tape or disk to another location

It doesn't do any good to back up your logical logs to a tape or disk and then leave that backup sitting right on the server. You need to move the backup to another location. When backing up to tape, this must be done manually of course. When backing up to disk, this can be automated by copying the file to an NFS-mounted filesystem or running another backup program to back it up to a tape somewhere else. Do something other than just leave the one file or tape all by itself on the server, *especially if you are backing up to disk.* Copying it to another location on disk is so simple. *Not* copying it leaves you open to an electrical surge that takes out both the backup disk and the disk(s) that contained the instance.

The *rclogs.sh* program was written to automate all of the preceding tasks.

Automating Continuous Backups: the rclogs.sh Utility

The *rclogs.sh* program can back up to either tape or disk, but it works best if backing up to disk because it can automate the "swap tapes" step by automatically moving and creating files as needed. The first step that *rclogs.sh* performs is to check that the Informix instance is online. It performs a *while* loop until the instance reports "On-line" or "Read-only." If it stays in this loop for 60 seconds, it exits with an error. Without this feature, a malfunctioning instance would prevent other instances from starting when this program is called from *dbstart*.

The next thing that *rclogs.sh* does is check to see if there are any *ontape -c* backups running for this instance. If so, it stops them. If *rclogs.sh* was called with the *stop* argument, it then exits. If it was called with the *start* argument, it then needs to "swap tapes." If backing up to disk, *rclogs.sh* moves the continuous backup file to a date/timestamped file and creates an empty file for the next *ontape -c* session. If backing up to tape, this program cannot be run from *cron*; it must be run manually from a terminal because once it stops the *ontape -c* session, it can only notify the operator running the program to swap the tape and wait for notification that this has been done. Once *rclogs.sh* knows that the tape has been swapped, it will start a new *ontape -c* session in the background. It then queries Informix to verify that continuous backups are running and sends notification of success or failure.

Installing rclogs.sh and its configuration files

Install the files *rclogs.sh*, *localpath.sh*, *rempath.sh*, and *config.guess* in the same directory (e.g., $INFORMIXDIR/local/bin) and make sure that they are all executable. Install *inftab* and *infback.conf* in a directory writable by informix (e.g., $INFORMXDIR/etc). (These two files do not have to be in the same directory as the executables, but they can be.)

Editing rclogs.sh and its configuration files

Make sure you have already configured the *inftab* and *infback.conf* files for use on this system; details on how to do this can be found in the previous section, "Editing the infback.sh configuration files." (The only field that *rclogs.sh* uses from *infback.conf* file is the mail IDs field.)

Check the site-specific section at the top of *rclogs.sh* and make sure that all the values are appropriate for your environment. The following values are found there:

DEBUG=

Set this to Y if you wish to see debug information (*set -x*).

INFTAB=
> Set this to the full path of your *inftab* file.

COMPRESS=
> Set this to the compression command that you wish to use (e.g., *gzip*).

COMPSUFF=
> If you change the compression command from the default value of "compress," then you need to change this value. It is the suffix that your compression command uses (e.g., use *gz* for *gzip*).

BINDIR=
> Set this to the location of *infback.sh* and the other programs (e.g., $INFORMIXDIR/local/bin).

THRESHHOLD=
> This should be set to a percentage between 50 and 100 if you are backing up to disk. Once the filesystem specified by $ARCHIVEDEST is this full, it does some extra cleanup and notifies you.

TMP=
> Set this to the directory that you wish to use for temporary files.

INFORMIXDIR=
> This normally can be left alone, since it is determined from *inftab*.

ONCONFIGFILE=
> This also can normally be left alone, but if you have a unique location for your *onconfig* files, specify it here.

ARCHIVE_DEST=
> This also is determined by looking at *inftab*.

INFORMIXSERVER=
> This is automatically determined by looking at the *onconfig* file.

LOGDIR=
> Set this to a directory that you want to use for logs (e.g., $INFORMIXDIR/ logs).

LOG_FILE=
> Set this to the name of the log file that you wish to use.

PATH=
> You normally should not need to change this.

DBAS=
> If you've already specified the use of *infback.conf*, the value of this field is determined from there. If not, you can specify a list of mail IDs to mail to. (Enclose them within quotes if there are more than one.)

Testing the rclogs.sh program

Before adding the *rclogs.sh* script to *cron*, you might want to run it a few times to make sure that it works in your environment. Run *rclogs.sh*:

- With the *stop* argument to make sure that it stops the appropriate logs
- With the *start* argument to make sure it creates the file and starts the *ontape -c* process
- Multiple times with the *start* argument to make sure that it stops and starts the appropriate logs

Scheduling backups

Once you are sure the program works for you, you have a few options for how it is used. If you have installed *dbstart.informix.sh*, it automatically calls *rclogs.sh* when the system shuts down or starts up. This means that continuous backups are started automatically when the instance is started using *dbstart.informix.sh*.

If you are backing up to disk, you can greatly increase your recoverability options by running *rclogs.sh* every hour or half hour. This is especially true if you have added some commands to the *Backup_the_backup* function. Instead of having one large log for each day, you will have many small logs that get backed up throughout the day. Doing this ensures you'll never lose more than 30 minutes worth of data. The following *cron* entry runs *rclogs.sh* every half hour:

```
00,30 * * * * /informix/local/bin/rclogs.sh start
```

Using the Scripts Together

The scripts discussed in the previous sections all work together. *dbstart*, *rclogs.sh*, and *infback.sh* all use the *inftab* file. *rclogs.sh* and *infback.sh* both use the *infback.conf* file. *dbstart* automatically calls *rclogs.sh*. Running *rclogs.sh* on an hourly or half-hourly basis will provide you with multiple logical log backups that you can use at recovery time. Running a weekly full and daily incremental backup using *infback.sh* will reduce the amount of time spent doing backups and still requires only three tapes for a restore (the third tape is the logical log backup).

Physical Backups with a Storage Manager: onbar

ontape is a program that has been around for years, and its greatest single feature is simplicity. It does have limitations, though, that were addressed with the release of *onbar*. *onbar* has the following features that *ontape* does not have:

XBSA interface

The XBSA interface is what separates *onbar* from *ontape* or *onarchive*. This interface is designed specifically for use with third-party storage management (TPSM) applications, such as those discussed in Chapter 5. XBSA allows you to use *onbar* to back up Informix data directly to the TPSM's tapes. Whereas *ontape* requires you to keep track of all the archive tapes, *onbar* and the TPSM will do that for you. When you need to restore a database, you simply tell *onbar* to do so; *onbar* and the TPSM figure out which tapes they need. If you have a jukebox, they even automatically put the necessary tapes in the drives.

Restartable restore

This is a new feature in Informix 7.3. With earlier versions, if you are restoring a large database and the restore fails at 90 percent complete, you have to redo the entire restore. The restartable restore feature allows the restore to pick up where it left off.

Restore of online storage spaces

"Storage space" is a new term in Informix documentation that refers to any storage element, such as a dbspace, a blobspace, or a chunk. (It used to be necessary to take a storage space offline prior to restoring it.)

External backup and restore

External backup and restore is an interesting feature, also new in 7.3, which allows you to copy disks containing storage spaces to another location and restore them with *onbar*.

Storage-space-level backup and recovery

ontape allowed you to recover a single dbspace, but you still needed to back up the entire instance at one time. With *onbar*, you can back up or restore any storage space within an Informix instance.

Multiple backup streams

This is a feature that *ontape* never had and what most people went to *onarchive* to get. This feature allows the TPSM to accept or request multiple backup streams (or threads) at the same time. This means that the TPSM may back up 50 or more dbspaces at a time! (In case you are wondering, it can also read multiple streams simultaneously during a restore.)

Simplicity of ontape with the flexibility of onarchive

This is how *onbar* was always billed, and it really is true. It really does give you the flexibility that Informix users have always needed, without the incredible complexity of *onarchive*.

Since *onbar* and ISM are well documented and easy to use, there is not much sense in covering *onbar* in detail in this chapter. It is especially difficult to discuss the configuration of *onbar* without discussing a particular storage manager. This section of this chapter, then, serves only as an overview of what lies before you if you choose to use *onbar.*

Configuring onbar

The first thing that you need to do is make sure that you have recent releases and patches of both *onbar* and your storage manager. Then, look for the following values in your *onconfig* file:

```
# Backup/Restore variables
BAR_ACT_LOG      /tmp/bar_act.log
BAR_MAX_BACKUP  0
BAR_RETRY       1
BAR_NB_XPORT_COUNT 10
BAR_XFER_BUF_SIZE 31
```

BAR_ACT_LOG

This should be set to the full path of a filename that *onbar* can use for its own logs.

BAR_MAX_BACKUP

This is the maximum number of threads (as defined previously) that *onbar* is allowed to start simultaneously.

BAR_RETRY

If there is an error when *onbar* tries to back up a storage space, you can specify what it should do next. If BAR_RETRY is set to a number (e.g., 10), it retries that storage space in 10 seconds. Setting it to BAR_CONT means that *onbar* should continue to the next storage space. A value of BAR_ABORT means that *onbar* should abort the entire operation if it encounters any errors. Typically, this value is set to BAR_CONT.

BAR_NB_XPORT_COUNT

This is the number of buffers that *onbar* is allowed to use when passing data to the TPSM.

BAR_XFER_BUF_SIZE

This specifies how large the *onbar* buffers should be. The default value depends on the OS page size. Exercise extreme caution when modifying either BAR_XFER_BUF_SIZE or BAR_NB_XPORT_COUNT, as bad values can adversely affect the performance of both *onbar* and the Informix instance.

You also should know that *onbar* will create a file called *$INFORMIXDIR/etc/ixbar. servernum.* This is called the "emergency boot file" and contains the information that *onbar* needs to perform a cold restore of an instance.

Configuring the Storage Manager

Most of the work in getting *onbar* to do its job is on the storage manager side. It is here that you have to define tape pools, backup definitions, and schedules. If your storage manager is worth its salt, all these steps should be properly documented. It also may include a shell script that automates basic configuration.

Once properly configured, you should be able to back up your Informix database from either side of the system. That is, you should be able to run a backup from your storage manager and have it automatically activate *onbar*, causing it to begin sending an Informix backup to the storage manager. You also should be able to execute *onbar* commands from the Informix command line and have it automatically activate the storage manager, causing it to load tapes and begin accepting data from *onbar*. (The same is true for restores.)

Performing Backups

There are three types of backups available in *onbar*. You may back up:

- The whole instance
- Part of the instance
- The logical logs

When backing up all or part of the instance, you also may specify three backup levels. When backing up the logical logs, you may back up the current log or all full logs or salvage any logs that are not backed up. There isn't actually a continuous backup feature, but there is a shell script that emulates it.

Backing up the whole instance

To back up the whole instance, run the following command. Specifying the level is optional and can be 0, 1, or 2. If you do not specify a level, it defaults to a level 0. This is the *onbar* equivalent of the *ontape -s* command.

```
$ onbar -b [ -L level ]
```

You also can add a *-w* option to the command, which causes it to do a "whole system" backup, which backs up all storage spaces serially.

```
$ onbar -b -w [ -L level ]
```

Backing up part of the instance

To back up part of the instance, drop the *-w* and list one or more dbspaces after the *onbar* command:

```
$ onbar -b [ -L level ] dbspace1 dbspace2 [...]
```

This functionality is not available with *ontape.*

Backing up the logical logs

The following command is somewhat equivalent to the *ontape -a* command, since it backs up all full logs. However, unlike the *ontape -a* command, it is the preferred command to back up the logical logs with *onbar.* In fact, the following *log_full.sh* script uses this option to do continuous backups. One main difference is that it does not also back up the current log; it backs up only logs that are marked as full.

```
$ onbar -l
```

The following command backs up the current log and switches the instance to the next log:

```
$ onbar -l -c
```

An *onbar* recovery automatically performs a log salvage prior to overwriting the logical log, but this command is for the paranoid administrator who would rather do that *before* beginning a restore:

```
$ onbar -l -s
```

As mentioned previously, *onbar* doesn't have continuous backups in the same sense that *ontape* did. That is, it does not have an option that keeps a backup device open continuously. The reason for this is that there is no need to dedicate a single device to a process that may happen only a few times a day. However, since you probably do want to back up logical logs as soon as they are full, Informix has provided a program called *log_full.sh* that you will find in the *$INFORMIXDIR/etc* directory. To use this program, change the following line in your *onconfig* file:

```
ALARMPROGRAM    $INFORMIXDIR/etc/log_full.sh    # Alarm program path
```

Recovering Informix

Recovering Informix is much easier than recovering other databases. One reason is that the commands to actually perform the recovery are simple—there is only one argument for *ontape* and only two arguments for *onbar.* This section covers just about any recovery scenario that you might find yourself in, yet it has fewer than 20 main steps.

Another reason that Informix recoveries are simple is that the sysmaster database, physical log, and logical log are considered critical. In order to recover one of them, you have to recover all of them. In Oracle, for instance, there are four or five different recovery tactics that you can use, depending on which one of these objects is damaged. With Informix, there is only one recovery tactic.

The Informix recovery procedure does not assume that you know why your database went down. It does assume that you have been making backups via *ontape* or *onbar*. It also assumes that if you are using *ontape*, you know which tapes or files contain the latest level-0 and/or level-1 backups, as well as the location of all logical log backups since your last physical backup. If you are using *onbar*, this procedure assumes you know how to use your storage manager well enough that you know how to respond to its prompts for any media that may not be in an autochanger. In short, all media management is up to you.

The following examples use *ontape*. The example hostname is *curtis*, and the instance name is **crash**. The archives are being sent to disk files named */informix/ logical/crash/crash.level.level.Z*, and continuous backups are being sent to a disk file named */informix/logical/crash.log*.

The flowchart shown in Figure 14-2 is meant to be used in conjunction with the following procedure. Each element in the flowchart corresponds to a step in the procedure. You should start with Step 1.

Step 1: Does oninit Work?

The obvious first step in determining if an instance is in need of recovery is to try and start the instance. Do this by issuing the *oninit* command with no options. If it works, it just returns the prompt to you. You also could see one of two errors.

```
curtis $ oninit
WARNING: Cannot access configuration file $INFORMIXDIR/etc/$ONCONFIG.
```

This error is pretty obvious. If you see it, you are missing your configuration file and should proceed to Step 2.

If any of your critical dbspaces has damaged or missing chunks, you may see an error like this one.

```
oninit: Cannot open chunk '/informix/rootdbs.dbf'. errno = 2
oninit: Cannot open chunk '/informix/rootdbs_mirror.dbf'. errno = 2
oninit: Fatal error in shared memory initialization
```

If all critical dbspaces are mirrored, and only one-half of the mirror is damaged, you do not see this error. It also does not appear if a noncritical dbspace is damaged. This error appears only if *all* chunks in a *critical* dbspace are damaged.

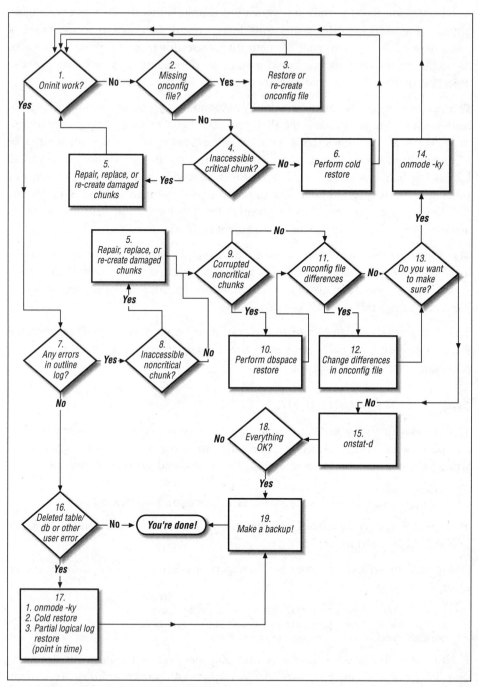

Figure 14-2. Informix recovery flowchart

If you see an error like the previous one, proceed to Step 2. If you don't see either error, proceed to Step 7.

Step 2: Is the onconfig File Missing?

The *oninit* utility uses the *onconfig* file to determine the basic information needed to start the instance. This includes, but is not limited to, the following instance-specific information:

- The location of the root dbspace
- The location of the physical log
- The SERVERNUM value
- The base address of shared memory
- Sqlhosts information

 If the *onconfig* file is missing or corrupted, proceed to Step 3. If this is not the reason the instance would not start, proceed to Step 4.

Step 3: Restore or Re-create the onconfig File

If you are running *onbar*, it can automatically re-create the *onconfig* file. However, if this file is the only one damaged, there's no need to do a full restore just to restore this file. Restoring or re-creating it is easy enough.

If you are running *infback.sh*, it makes a backup copy of the *onconfig* file before it changes it. DBAs and other scripts often do the same. Look first to see if you have such a backup copy. If not, try to restore the file from the nightly filesystem backups. If you cannot find a backup copy and cannot restore one from backup, you will need to re-create it. If any of the following objects is available, it will be easy:

- The chunk (or its mirror) that contains the root dbspace
- A level-0 or -1 archive created by *ontape* on disk
- A level-0 or -1 archive created by *ontape* on tape

To re-create the *onconfig* file from the root dbspace chunk or an *ontape* archive on disk, run the following command, where filename is the name of the chunk or archive on disk:

```
$ strings filename |grep '^[A-Z][A-Z_]*' >$INFORMIX/etc/$ONCONFIG
```

If you have only an archive available on tape, the command is similar:

```
$ dd if=$TAPEDEV bs=$TAPEBLK | strings |grep '^[A-Z][A-Z_]*' \
> $INFORMIX/etc/$ONCONFIG
```

This creates an editable text file that contains all the parameters and their current values. The *grep* command does not completely remove extraneous lines, so you should edit it and remove any lines that do not look like the following:

```
PARAMETER value
```

If you do not have one of these objects available, you need to manually re-create the file. Copy the *onconfig.std* file in *$INFORMIXDIR/etc* to the name of the *onconfig* file. The values that you must change are ROOTNAME, ROOTPATH, DBSERVERNAME, SERVERNUM, and SHMBASE. These values will allow you to restore the instance.

"Jagged Little Pill"[a]

During one attempt to restore the database that I used for this chapter, *ontape* kept asking me for a second tape that I knew did not exist. I grew very frustrated and eventually had to leave for a doctor's appointment. On the way to the appointment I figured out what happened. During some earlier tests, I had changed the value of tape size to a very small number to get it to use more than one tape. There was no second tape, but the tape size value told *ontape* that it had reached the end of the tape. If you do have to re-create your *onconfig* on the fly, or restore one from backup, make sure that you don't repeat my stupid mistake.

---

a. As I was searching my brain for a title to this sidebar, this Alanis Morissette song came on the radio. It's the one with the phrase ". . . You live, you learn . . ." Somehow it seemed appropriate!

Step 4: Is There an Inaccessible or Critical Chunk?

If an Informix instance will not start, the most common cause is a missing or corrupt critical chunk. (If a noncritical chunk is damaged, the instance starts and records the problem to the online log file.) The error that you receive may look something like the following:

```
oninit: Cannot open chunk '/informix/rootdbs.dbf'. errno = 2
```

According to *errno.h*, an Error 2 means "No such file or directory." This means that the chunk or the symbolic link that Informix uses to refer to that chunk is missing. Another common error is 13, which means "Permission denied." This means that someone other than Informix owns the device. Any error other than those usually means that the physical file is all right, but the data within it is corrupted.

If the file is missing or its permissions are wrong, proceed to Step 5. If not, proceed to Step 6.

Step 5: Repair or Replace the Missing Chunk

This step is necessary only if the physical file is somehow damaged. If it were a filesystem file, it might be deleted or its permissions changed. If it were a raw device, the disk drive could be damaged or missing or its permissions could be wrong. Another problem could be that you are using a symbolic link to the real chunk, and the symbolic link was deleted accidentally.

If the missing file is a symbolic link, you simply need to restore or re-create the file in its original location. The only difficult part is that Informix doesn't tell you which file it was symbolically linked to. Restoring the symbolic link from your regular filesystem backups is probably the easiest answer. Another method would be to consult any documentation that you may have about how you put the instance together. (Restoring from backup obviously is much easier.)

If it is not a symbolic link, the damaged file may be a filesystem file or raw device. If it is a filesystem file and the filesystem itself is intact, simply re-create a new file with the *touch* command. After doing so, make sure that the file is read/write for the `informix` user and `informix` group. If the filesystem is not intact, you need to relocate the file. Hopefully, you followed the common practice of using symbolic links to point to the actual chunks. If you did, you can re-create the chunk file anywhere on the system and just change the symbolic link to point to the new location. If you did not, you need to make a symbolic link in the original location to point to the new file.

For example, assume that the filesystem */data1* is destroyed, and it contained chunk */data1/rootdbs.dbf.* However, you set up the Informix instance to point directly to */data1/rootdbs.dbf*, instead of to a symbolic link to that chunk. You create a new file called *rootdbs.dbf* in */data2*, but you have to tell *oninit* to use the new file. You need to *unmount /data1* (although it probably is already) and create a symbolic link in the old location with the following command:

```
$ ln -s /data2/rootdbs.dbf /data1/rootdbs.dbf
```

This is, of course, a very bad solution since repairing and remounting */data1* will overwrite the symbolic link. If you have to do this, consult your IDS Administration Manual about permanently relocating the file. (Use a symbolic link this time.)

Before continuing, you may wish to verify that all chunks are all right. If you don't have a complete list of filenames, you can obtain them by running the *strings* command on a root dbspace chunk or an *ontape* archive:

```
$ zcat /informix/logical/crash/crash.level.1.Z | strings | grep '^/'
```

Make sure that you have checked both of the following conditions:

Permissions

Ensure that someone didn't accidentally change the ownership or permissions of any chunks. If you are using symbolic links to point to the actual chunks, the only permissions that matter are those for the final file to which the symbolic link is pointing. For example, suppose that you have a symbolic link called */informix/chunk1* that points to */dev/dsk/c0t0d0s5*. If you are running Solaris, and if you run an *ls -l* on */dev/dsk/c0t0d0s5*, you will find this:

```
lrwxrwxrwx   1 root      other        84 Nov  5 02:29 /dev/dsk/c0t0d0s5 -> ../..
/devices/iommu@f,e0000000/sbus@f,e0001000/espdma@f,400000/esp@f,800000/sd@0,0:f
```

It is the permissions of *sd@0,0:f* that matter, not the symbolic link */dev/dsk/c0t0d0s5*. To verify its permissions, run the following command:

```
$ Ls -lL /dev/dsk/c0t0d0s5
```

Adding the *-L* option causes it to display the ownership and permissions of the source file, not of the link. Make sure that both the owner and the group are informix, and that the file is read/write for both the owner and the group.

Symbolic link

This problem usually happens when the DBA is trying to "clean house." If you're using symbolic links to point to the actual chunks, and someone deletes the symbolic link, you obviously have a problem. If you are using symbolic links, make sure that you remake the symbolic link instead of creating a chunk in its place.

If the instance is currently down because a critical dbspace could not be opened, return to Step 1 and run *oninit* again. If the instance is already up and you were sent here by Step 8, proceed to Step 9. If you have repaired or replaced any missing chunks and the instance still won't start, proceed to Step 6.

Step 6: Performing a Cold Restore

You should perform this step only if directed to do so by Step 5.

Make sure you need this step

This is not a step to be taken lightly. Depending on the size of your instance, a cold restore may take a considerable amount of time. Please take a moment to verify that you really do need to perform a restore; if you do, follow the appropriate section below.

Both *ontape* and *onbar* allow you to specify a list of dbspaces to restore. This even works with critical dbspaces. However, if you restore just the critical dbspaces, the restore leaves all other chunks in an "inconsistent" state, as specified by the *I* flag that they display after the restore is done. Informix support does have a tool that will change this flag to consistent, but your mileage will vary on this one. If you are restoring a critical dbspace, you really should restore the whole thing.

Restoring with ontape

After removing the current logical log tape or file from its current location, place the latest level-0 archive in the device specified by $TAPEDEV. If you are backing up to disk, this may require uncompressing and moving a file to the appropriate location. If you're backing up to tape, it involves placing the latest level-0 archive in the tape drive. After doing so, execute the following command:

```
$ ontape -r
```

ontape prompts you for everything that it needs. You need to know if you have a level-1 or -2 backup, since it will ask you that. You'll also need to know the location of all logical log backups since the latest archive was taken.

Make sure to remove the current logical log "tape" prior to beginning a physical restore. If you're backing up to disk, this means moving the file to a different location. If you're backing up to tape, this means physically removing the current logical log tape. When performing a physical restore with *ontape*, it asks you if you want to back up the current log, and you should *always say yes*. However, this performs an *ontape -a* backup, not an *ontape -c* backup. Remember that the primary difference between these two options is that *ontape -a overwrites* the "tape" currently in the drive. *If it contains any logs other than the current log, they will disappear forever.*

The following example was done with an instance that is archiving to disk using *infback.sh. infback.sh* now uses named pipes, so the value for TAPEDEV will be a named pipe (e.g., */informix/logical/crash.level.1.fifo*) that reflects the last level that was performed. Since *infback.sh* will re-create the named pipe when it needs to, we will overwrite it with symbolic links. The instance also used *rclogs.sh* to continuously back up the logical logs to disk. The value for LTAPEDEV is */informix/logical/crash.log*, and when it switches logs, it copies them to */informix/logical/$ONCONFIG.year.month.day.hour.minute.second.*

Informix asks you if you want to back up the logs. *Always say yes,* but make sure that you are giving it a fresh tape or file to back up to, since *it will overwrite it—not append to it.*

An *ontape* restore with archives on disk always requires more than one window, and this section needs to show both of the windows described later to fully demonstrate the example. To reduce confusion, it uses a regular paragraph like this one when switching windows. Since it still needs to explain the reasoning behind certain commands or answers within a window, it uses *this font* to do that. There is also a heading on each body of computer output specifying either Restore Window or Alternate Window. The Restore Window is the window in which the *ontape -r* command is being run, and the Alternate Window will be the window in which we perform other commands. We will start with Example 14-17, the Restore Window.

Putting All the Logs on One Tape

If you are backing up your logical logs to disk, this trick may save you some time. If you concatenate all necessary logs (in chronological order) to one big log, Informix can read all the logs that it needs in one shot.

If you are using *rclogs.sh*, this is easy. The names of the files that it uses are made in such a way that a *ls* of the files will list them in chronological order. Again, assume the latest archive was taken at midnight on January 20, and the database was damaged at 3:00 P.M. If you have been running *rclogs.sh* on an hourly basis, you might see something like this:

```
curtis$ ls crash.log.1999.01.21*   #Today is the 21st of January
crash.log.1999.01.21.00.01.00.Z   crash.log.1999.01.21.01.01.00.Z
crash.log.1999.01.21.02.01.00.Z   crash.log.1999.01.21.03.01.00.Z
crash.log.1999.01.21.04.01.00.Z   crash.log.1999.01.21.05.01.00.Z
crash.log.1999.01.21.06.01.00.Z   crash.log.1999.01.21.07.01.00.Z
crash.log.1999.01.21.08.01.00.Z   crash.log.1999.01.21.09.01.00.Z
crash.log.1999.01.21.10.01.00.Z   crash.log.1999.01.21.11.01.00.Z
crash.log.1999.01.21.12.01.00.Z   crash.log.1999.01.21.13.01.00.Z
crash.log.1999.01.21.14.01.00.Z   crash.log.1999.01.21.15.01.00.Z
```

You can even concatenate them into another filesystem if you don't have room in the current one. In this example, we will concatenate them into */home1*. To concatenate all logs that Informix will need in chronological order, run the following command:

```
curtis$ zcat crash.log.1999.01.21* >/home1/big.log
```

After you answer yes to the "Back up the current log?" question, you can then concatenate *that* log onto the end of *this* one:

```
curtis$ zcat /informix/logical/crash.log >> /home1/big.log
```

After making a copy of the current log, you can then move the "big log" where Informix expects to find it. The easiest way to do that is to use a symbolic link:

```
curtis$ cp /informix/logical/crash.log /informix/logical/crash.log.1999.01.
21.15.05.00.Z
curtis$ ln -s /home1/big.log /informix/logical/crash.log
```

Example 14-17. Starting an ontape Restore

```
[Restore Window]

#The first thing that we need to do is
#uncompress the archive files.
curtis$ uncompress /informix/logical/crash/crash.level.*.Z
curtis$ ls /informix/logical/crash
crash.level.0  crash.level.1

# Now we need to remove the named pipe and replace it with a
```

Example 14-17. Starting an ontape Restore (continued)

```
# symbolic link to the actual backup file.
curtis$ rm /informix/crash.level.0.fifo
curtis$ ln -s /informix/logical/crash/crash.level.0 /informix/crash.level.0.fifo

#Now we can begin the restore.
curtis$ ontape -r

Please mount tape 1 on /informix/logical/crash/crash.level.0 and press Return to
continue ...

Archive Tape Information


Tape type:      Archive Backup Tape
Online version: INFORMIX-OnLine Version 7.23.UC4
Archive date:   Thu Jan 21 00:57:14 1999
User id:        informix
Terminal id:    ?
Archive level:  0
Tape device:    /informix/crash.level.0.fifo
Tape blocksize (in k): 16
Tape size (in k): 1024000
Tape number in series: 1


Spaces to restore:
1 [rootdbs         ]
2 [plogdbs         ]
3 [llogdbs         ]
4 [testdbs         ]

Archive Information

INFORMIX-OnLine Copyright(C) 1986-1995  Informix Software, Inc.
Initialization Time       03/04/98 20:08:25
System Page Size          2048
Version                   4
Archive CheckPoint Time   01/21/99 00:57:17

Dbspaces
number  flags    fchunk  nchunks  flags   owner     name
1       2        1       1        M       informix  rootdbs
2       2        2       1        M       informix  plogdbs
3       2        3       1        M       informix  llogdbs
4       1        4       1        N       informix  testdbs


Chunks
chk/dbs offset   size    free     bpages  flags pathname
1  1   0         10000   9051             PO-   /informix/rootdbs.dbf
1  1   0         10000   0                MO-   /informix/rootdbs_mirror.dbf
2  2   0         5000    2447             PO-   /informix/physlog.dbf
2  2   0         5000    0                MO-   /informix/physlog_mirror.dbf
3  3   0         5000    3447             PO-   /informix/logiclog.dbf
```

Example 14-17. Starting an ontape Restore (continued)

```
3   3   0       5000    0               MO-   /informix/logiclog_mirror.dbf
4   4   0       500     191             PO-   /informix/testdbs.dbf


# Ontape displays all this information to you so that you know
# that this is the right tape to restore the right instance.
# It doesn't actually do anything until you respond "y" to the next question.
Continue restore? (y/n)y

# Always say "YES" to this next question.
Do you want to back up the logs? (y/n)y

Please mount tape 1 on /informix/logical/crash.log and press Return to continue ...
Would you like to back up any of logs 65 - 67? (y/n) y
```

This next section is from another window. We need to move the old logical log "tape" out of the way so that the salvaging of the current log does not overwrite it. In Example 14-18, we will use the same naming convention as the other files.

Example 14-18. Preparing Disk-Based Logical Log Backups

[Alternate Window]

```
curtis$ cp crash.log crash.log.1999.01.21.17.04.00
curtis$ compress crash.log.1999.01.21.15.05.16
curtis$ ls -1 crash.log.1999.01.21*
total 2424
-rw-rw----   1 informix informix    73961 Jan 21 01:12 crash.log.1999.01.21.01.13.02.Z
-rw-rw----   1 informix informix     1949 Jan 21 01:13 crash.log.1999.01.21.01.14.08.Z
-rw-rw----   1 informix informix   557056 Jan 22 17:04 crash.log.1999.01.22.17:04:00.Z
```

Once we've copied the "tape" to another location, it is safe to tell Informix to salvage the current logical log. Note in Example 14-19 that when asked for the oldest log that we would like to back up, we reply with the oldest number available. (It never hurts to have too many logical log backups. If we were to answer "66," what would happen if the restore needed log 65 and it had not been backed up, or its backup had been damaged? We would be out of luck, that's what.

Example 14-19. Backing Up the Current Logical Logs

[Restore Window]

```
Logical logs 65 - 67 may be backed up.
Enter the id of the oldest log that you would like to backup? 65

Please label this tape as number 1 in the log tape sequence.

This tape contains the following logical logs:
    1 - 67
Log salvage is complete, continuing restore of archive.
```

Example 14-19. Backing Up the Current Logical Logs (continued)

```
# We do have a level-1 archive, so when it asks if we have one,
# we will answer "yes."
Restore a level 1 archive (y/n) y
Ready for level 1 tape
```

You may recall that prior to beginning the restore, we created a symbolic link from the level-0 archive on disk to the location that Informix expects the archive to be. Now that we are "swapping tapes," we need to remove that link and create another one that points to the level-1 backup. (The commands in Example 14-20 are obviously being done in another window.)

Example 14-20. Simulating a Tape Swap

```
[Alternate Window]
```

```
curtis$ rm /informix/crash.level.0.fifo
curtis$ ln -s /informix/logical/crash/crash.level.1 /informix/crash.level.0.fifo
```

Now that we have swapped tapes, we can respond to the prompt shown in Example 14-21.

Example 14-21. Responding to ontape's Prompts

```
[Restore Window]
```

```
Please mount tape 1 on /informix/logical/crash/crash.level.0 and press Return to
continue ...

Archive Tape Information

Tape type:       Archive Backup Tape
Online version:  INFORMIX-OnLine Version 7.23.UC4
Archive date:    Thu Jan 21 01:10:13 1999
User id:         informix
Terminal id:     ?
Archive level:   1
Tape device:     /informix/crash.level.1.fifo
Tape blocksize (in k): 16
Tape size (in k): 1024000
Tape number in series: 1

# We do not have a level-2 archive, so we will answer no to
# following prompt.
Restore a level 2 archive (y/n) n

# We do want to restore log tapes, though...
Do you want to restore log tapes? (y/n)y

Roll forward should start with log number 65
```

Again, we must move over to the other window and prepare the logical log "tape."
First, we move the salvage logs to an appropriately named file and compress it.
Then we use the log concatenation method discussed in the previous sidebar.
Since the logs are compressed, in Example 14-22 we create a single concatenated
log using *zcat.*

Example 14-22. Creating One Large Logical Log Backup

```
[Alternate Window]

curtis$ mv crash.log crash.log.1999.01.21.18.00.00
curtis$ compress crash.log.1999.01.21.18.00.00
curtis$ ls -l crash.log.1999.01.2*
total 2424
-rw-rw----   1 informix informix   73961 Jan 21 01:12 crash.log.1999.01.21.01.13.02.Z
-rw-rw----   1 informix informix    1949 Jan 21 01:13 crash.log.1999.01.21.01.14.08.Z
-rw-rw----   1 informix informix  557056 Jan 22 17:04 crash.log.1999.01.22.17:04:00.Z
-rw-rw----   1 informix informix  557056 Jan 22 18:00 crash.log.1999.01.22.18.00.00.Z
curtis$ zcat *1999* >crash.log
curtis$ chmod 664 * crash.log
```

Now that we have created the single log, we can respond to the prompt in
Example 14-23.

Example 14-23. Completing the Restore and Starting the Instance

```
[Restore Window]

Please mount tape 1 on /informix/logical/crash.log and press Return to continue ...

# Since we put all logs into this single log, there are no
# more logs to restore.
Do you want to restore another log tape? (y/n)n

Program over.

# The next step is very important.  You must bring the
# instance online when you are done, or you will
# need to do the restore all over again.

curtis$ onmode -m
```

Make sure that you use *onmode -m* to bring the instance online after
doing a cold restore. If you do not, you will need to completely redo
the restore if you stop and start the instance before doing so.

Restoring with onbar

The first and simplest recovery with *onbar* is to enter *onbar -r*. This specifies to do a complete restore of any offline dbspaces. It automatically performs the following three steps for you:

1. *onbar -l -s*

   Salvages the logical log

2. *onbar -r -p* [*-w*]

   Completes *physical restore*, which reads the archive only

3. *onbar -r -l*

   Completes *logical restore*, which reads all available logical logs

You also may add an optional *-w* flag (*onbar -r -w*) that specifies using the latest whole backup when performing the restore. If you have not been performing *-w* backups, then you cannot use *-w* on the restore. If you have been using *-w* on your backups, then you can use the same option on the restore. You also have the option of not using the *-w* option on the restore, even if you did use it to back up.

Unlike with *ontape*, you do not even need to move files around or swap tapes if you have an autochanger. *onbar* automatically retrieves the appropriate volumes that it needs to write to or read from. Even if you do not have an autochanger, it prompts you for the appropriate tapes by name.

You also have the option of performing the three steps by yourself. This allows you to use a number of flags to do different kinds of restores based on your needs of the moment. The first thing you need to do, though, is issue the *onbar -l -s* command to salvage any logical logs that have not been backed up.

After doing that, you have a number of options when performing the physical and logical restores. As started earlier, a physical restore is one that just reads the archive tape. It does not apply any logical logs. Applying the logical logs is called the *logical restore*. The following *onbar* command represents your options when beginning the physical restore. Please note the grouping of the options. The *-p*, *-n*, and *-t* options are mutually exclusive, and so are the *-w*, `dbspace_list` and `noflags` options.

```
$ onbar -r \
   [ -p | -n xxx | -t time ] [ -w | dbspace_list | noflags ]
```

Here is a listing of the various options and how they affect the restore:

-p Adding the *-p* option to the *onbar -r* command tells it to perform *only the physical restore*. If you use this option, you need to run the *onbar -r -l* com-

mand to perform the logical restore. If you do not specify this option, *onbar* performs both a physical and a logical restore.

-n xxx or -t `time`

If you do not specify *-p*, you also can use these flags to decide how the logical restore is performed. For details on these flags, see "Restoring from a Logical Backup," near the end of this chapter.

-w

This specifies to *use the latest whole backup* when restoring the database. Although using this flag will perform a restore of the whole database, this flag actually is telling *onbar which backup to use*, not what kind of restore to do. The reason this flag is here is that if you do restore from a whole backup, you have the option of *not* doing a logical restore, since you have restored the database to a consistent point in time. (This option is not available to you if you have not been making backups with the *-w* option.)

`dbspace_list`

If you do not use the *-w* option, you can optionally list the dbspaces that *onbar* should recover, separated by whitespace.

`noflags`

This is actually just a placeholder to demonstrate what would happen if you used no other flags at all.[*] If you enter *onbar -r* or *onbar -p without* specifying *-w* or a list of dbspaces to recover, it automatically detects and recovers any dbspaces that are offline. The noflags option, as described here, is meant to reiterate the fact that you do not have to specify the *-w* flag to get a complete restore. The *-w* flag specifies the restore's *source*, not its *destination*.

If you specified just a physical restore, you may now perform the logical restore. When doing so, you have three options:

onbar -r -l

This is the default method and performs a logical restore using all logical logs that were created since the latest archive.

onbar -r -l -n `lognumber`

If you know the last log that you wish to use, you may use this option. You may specify the last log that *onbar* should read using *-n `lognumber`*.

onbar -r -l -t `time`

You've been waiting for this one. You know that you accidentally deleted a major table at 14:02. You would like to replay all transactions *except that one*. You may tell *onbar* to do this using the new *-t `time`* option. (In the previous deleted-table example, you probably would enter *onbar -r -l 14:00*.)

---

[*] I found the available documentation on these different flags confusing. I hope that documenting the flags in this way will help reduce the confusion and not add to it!

Make sure that you use *onmode -m* to bring the instance online after doing a cold restore. If you do not bring the instance online with *onmode -m* before the next time you stop and start the instance, you will need to completely redo the restore.

In summary, an *onbar* restore offers you the same simplicity as an *ontape* restore, since both have the all-encompassing *-r* option that means to do a complete physical and logical restore. However, if you need extra options like point-in-time or point-in-log restores, they are available. It also has the added benefit of working with your storage manager so that you no longer have to worry about what tape has what backup. If you have not begun to look at *onbar*, perhaps now is the time to start.

Nine out of every 10 restores will end right here. To make sure that everything is okay, return to Step 1 and restart the instance *after first bringing it online with onmode -m.*

Step 7: Are There Errors in the Online Log?

Perhaps the instance started on your first try. Perhaps you needed to do a cold restore in order to get it started. The next thing to do would be to check the online log for any errors. Examples of the types of errors you may see are shown in Example 14-24.

Example 14-24. Example Errors in the Online Log

```
23:27:34  Assert Failed: WARNING! pthdrpage:ptalloc:bad bfget
23:27:34    Who: Session(7, informix@curtis, 0, 169149316)
                Thread(13, fast_rec, a12ccd8, 1)
23:27:34    Results: Cannot use TBLSpace page for TBLSpace 4194305
23:27:34    Action: Run 'oncheck -pt 4194305'
23:27:34    See Also: /tmp/af.d79e5
23:27:34  Cannot Open DBspace 4.
```

If you see any errors like this, you should run an *onstat -d* to see which chunk is having a problem:

```
Chunks
address  chk/dbs offset    size    free    bpages  flags pathname
# Output abbreviated...
a12a508  4  4    0        500     191             PD-   /informix/testdbs.dbf
```

The preceding flags show you that the */informix/testdbs.dbf* chunk is down. What you need to find out now is why it is down.

If you start the instance and there are no errors in the online log, then proceed to Step 16. If there are errors in the log, proceed to Step 8.

Step 8: Is There an Inaccessible Noncritical Chunk?

If *oninit* is able to access all critical chunks, it brings the instance online. If any noncritical chunks are inaccessible, it just logs the problem in the online log. If, after checking the online log and running an *onstat -d*, you have verified that a noncritical chunk is inaccessible to Informix, you need to repair or replace it.

If a noncritical chunk is inaccessible, return to Step 5. If you have verified that the problem chunk is now accessible and has the correct permissions, proceed to Step 9.

Step 9: Is There a Corrupted Noncritical Chunk?

You should be performing this step only if directed to do so by Step 5 or 8.

You might not need a restore

The best way to find out if your noncritical chunks are corrupted is to try to bring them online. In order to be able to do that, the following conditions must be true:

- You were sent to this step because the instance started, but there were errors in the online log.
- One or more chunks is currently marked down.
- The reason it was marked down was that *oninit* couldn't access it.
- The access problem was due to bad permissions or a deleted symbolic link.
- Its permissions are now OK, or the symbolic link was re-created.

If all these conditions are true, you probably can save yourself a restore by bringing the dbspaces online using *onspaces*. Run the following command for each chunk that was marked down:

```
$ onspaces -s dbspacename -p chunkname -o offset -O
Warning:  Bringing chunk back online.
 Do you really want to continue? (y/n)y
Verifying physical disk space, please wait ...
Chunk status successfully changed.
```

If you see successful messages like this one, you won't even need to do a restore. If it complains that the chunk is inconsistent, you have to do a restore to bring it to a consistent state.

 If you were able to bring all down dbspaces online, proceed to Step 11. If not, proceed to Step 10 to restore them.

Step 10: Perform a dbspace Restore

There isn't much that can be said in this step that wasn't already covered in Step 6. However, there are a few differences between the restore discussed in Step 6 and this one:

- The instance may be left online.

- Only the affected dbspaces need to be taken offline, and the recovery program will do that for you.

- You will be listing specific dbspaces to recover.

- You will not be asked to back up the logical logs.

Read Step 6 in detail, then run one of the following commands:

```
$ ontape -r -D dbspace dbspace     # Will recover any dbspaces
$ onbar -r                         # Will recover all down dbspaces
$ onbar -r dbspace                 # Will recover any dbspaces listed
```

Both *onbar* and *ontape* prompt you with the same standard questions. The main differences are that you may be warned that the affected dbspaces will be taken offline, and you will not be asked the "Do you want to back up the logs?" question. A sample output from an *ontape* restore can be found in Example 14-25.

Example 14-25. Sample ontape Output

```
curtis$ onstat -d|grep testdbs.dbf
a12a508  4  4  0      500      191           PD-   /informix/testdbs.dbf
curtis$ ontape -r -D testdbs
```

Example 14-25. Sample ontape Output (continued)

```
DBspace 'testdbs' is online; restoring 'testdbs' will bring all chunks
comprising the DBspace OFFLINE and will terminate all active
transactions and queries accessing the DBspace.

OK to continue?y

Please mount tape 1 on /informix/logical/crash/crash.level.0 and press Return to
continue ...

Archive Tape Information

Tape type:        Archive Backup Tape
Online version: INFORMIX-OnLine Version 7.23.UC4
Archive date:   Thu Jan 21 00:57:14 1999
User id:          informix
Terminal id:    ?
Archive level:  0
Tape device:     /informix/crash.level.0.fifo
Tape blocksize (in k): 16
Tape size (in k): 1024000
Tape number in series: 1
Continue restore? (y/n)y

Spaces to restore:1 [testdbs              ]
Restore a level 1 archive (y/n) n
Do you want to restore log tapes? (y/n)y

Roll forward should start with log number 65

Please mount tape 1 on /informix/logical/crash.log and press Return to continue ...
Do you want to restore another log tape? (y/n)n

Program over.
curtis$ onstat -d|grep testdbs.dbf
a12a508  4   4   0       500     191                 PO-   /informix/testdbs.dbf
```

Once the restore of all down dbspaces is complete, they will be
brought online. Proceed to Step 11.

Step 11: Are There Wrong Values in the onconfig File?

If you were forced to use an old *onconfig* file backup or to create one from
scratch, you may have some wrong values. Depending on which values are
wrong, they may prevent the instance from operating properly. If so, *oninit* logs
them in the online log.

```
02:13:58  Onconfig parameter LTAPEBLK modified from 32 to 16.
02:14:46  Onconfig parameter MIRROROFFSET modified from 1 to 0
```

 If you see any errors like this, proceed to Step 12. If not, then proceed to Step 13.

Step 12: Change the Bad Values in the onconfig File

This one is about as easy as they come. Change any bad values in the *onconfig* file back to their original values. For example, if you saw the errors displayed in Step 11, you need to change **LTAPEBLK** to 32 and **MIRROROFFSET** to 1. Unfortunately, most of these values are read only at startup.

 Once you have changed any incorrect values, proceed to Step 13.

Step 13: Ensuring That the Instance Will Restart

If you changed any values in Step 12, you need to restart the instance to have *oninit* read the new values. Also, if you had to follow a lot of steps to get to this step, you may want to make sure that everything will start correctly the *next* time. The only way to be sure of that is to restart the instance now.

 If you wish to restart the instance, proceed to Step 14. If not, proceed to Step 15.

Step 14: Taking the Instance Offline

If you had to do any restores to get to this step, make sure that you bring the instance online before you take it offline again. To make sure that it is online, run the following command:

```
$ oninit -
INFORMIX-OnLine Version 7.23.UC4   -- On-Line -- Up 00:00:29 -- 8976 Kbytes
```

If you see the preceding output, then the instance was brought online. If you see the following output, you need to bring the instance online by running the command *onmode -m*.

```
INFORMIX-OnLine Version 7.23.UC4   -- Quiescent -- Up 00:01:17 -- 8976 Kbytes
```

Once you are sure that the instance is online, you can take it offline:

```
$ onmode -ky
```

 Once you have done so, return to Step 1.

Step 15: Confirming That dbspaces and Chunks Are Online

If you don't restart the database, you should make doubly sure that all dbspaces and chunks are online. To do so, run the command *onstat -d*, as shown in Example 14-26.

Example 14-26. A Sample onstat Output

```
curtis$ onstat -d

INFORMIX-OnLine Version 7.23.UC4   -- On-Line -- Up 00:06:45 -- 8976 Kbytes

Dbspaces
address  number  flags  fchunk  nchunks  flags  owner     name
a12a100  1       2      1       1        M      informix  rootdbs
a12a790  2       2      2       1        M      informix  plogdbs
a12a800  3       2      3       1        M      informix  llogdbs
a12a870  4       1      4       1        N      informix  testdbs
 4 active, 2047 maximum

Chunks
address  chk/dbs  offset  size   free  bpages  flags  pathname
a12a170  1   1    0       10000  9307         PO-    /informix/rootdbs.dbf
a12a248  1   1    0       10000  0            MO-    /informix/rootdbs_mirror.dbf
a12a358  2   2    0       5000   2447         PO-    /informix/physlog.dbf
a12a5e0  2   2    0       5000   0            MO-    /informix/physlog_mirror.dbf
a12a430  3   3    0       5000   3447         PO-    /informix/logiclog.dbf
a12a6b8  3   3    0       5000   0            MO-    /informix/logiclog_mirror.dbf
a12a508  4   4    0       500    191          PO-    /informix/testdbs.dbf
 4 active, 2047 maximum
```

Check the flags column in the Dbspaces section for flags P, L, or R. Also check the flags column of the Chunks section for flags D or I. The meanings of these flags are:

P   The dbspace has been physically recovered and is awaiting logical recovery.

L   The dbspace is being logically recovered.

R   The dbspace is being physically recovered.

D   The chunk is down.

I   The chunk is in an inconsistent state.

Once you know if there are any of these flags, proceed to Step 18.

Step 16: Recovering a Deleted Table or Database

Perhaps the instance started OK, but there is a different problem. If a DBA accidentally deleted a dbspace, or a user accidentally deleted an important table, there is really only one way to recovery that—a point-in-time restore.*

If you need a point-in-time restore, proceed to Step 17. If not, proceed to Step 18.

Step 17: Performing a Point-in-Time Restore

In order to do a point-in-time restore, you need to do a cold restore of the entire database. (Details on how to do that are in Step 6.)

If you are using *ontape*, you will need to apply all logical logs until you reach the one during which the user/DBA error occurred. Do not apply that logical log.

If you are using *onbar*, you can use the *-n xxx* or *-t time* features of *onbar -r* to recover up to a point in time just prior to the user/DBA error.

---

* Yes, I realize you cannot restore just a table from backup, unless you use the famous *arcunload* utility. (See Informix support for details.) However, you could restore the whole instance and stop the restore before the point in time when the table was deleted.

Once you have done this, proceed to Step 19.

Step 18: Is Everything OK?

If you saw any of the flags mentioned in Step 15, return to Step 8. If not, proceed to Step 19.

Step 19: Making a Backup

Every restore should be followed immediately by a full backup. Of course, Informix allows you do so online. Don't consider the restore finished until you have completed this backup.

Logical Backups

Informix has two logical backup commands: *onunload* and *dbexport. onunload* is much faster than *dbexport*, but it has many more constraints placed on it than *dbexport* has. There are advantages and disadvantages to each utility.

onunload exports, or *unloads*, a database or table into a binary output file, consisting of a logical backup of a database or table. The resulting file can be used to import data into another database using the *onload* utility. *onunload* is faster because it copies the data in page mode, instead of having to convert the data to ASCII format as *dbexport* does. However, since the files are binary, only the same version of *onload* can read an *onunload* backup. This utility typically is used for moving data between computers but cannot be used for moving data between databases that are not the same version. *onunload* locks the database in shared mode while it is running. An error is returned if it cannot obtain a shared lock.

dbexport unloads a database into text files and creates a schema file. The resulting files can be used to import data into another database using the *dbimport* utility. Since the files are ASCII format, they can be moved between databases running different versions of Informix. The *dbexport* command is not part of OnLine XPS and Informix Dynamic Server with Advanced Decision Support and Extended Parallel Options, but *onunload* is. It is much slower than *onunload* since it has to convert the data to ASCII format. It also can back up only a database, whereas *onunload* can back up a database or table. *dbexport* locks the database in exclusive mode while it is running. An error is returned if it cannot obtain an exclusive lock.

 I cover only *onunload* and *onload* in this chapter for three reasons: One is that these programs require only a shared lock, where *dbexport* requires an exclusive lock. Another is that *onunload* feels more like a backup and recovery tool, whereas *dbexport*'s emphasis seems to be moving data between different databases. The final reason is that I can't cover everything in a book of this size. *onunload* and *dbexport* use the same method of determining what device to use, as well as its block size and tape size, so that portion of this section may be useful to you if you plan on using *dbexport*.

The Constraints for onunload

Since the export created by *onunload* is actually a binary file, there are constraints on how that file may be used:

- The Informix instance receiving the data must use the same page size and the same representation of numeric data as the instance that performed the *onunload*.

- The Informix instance must be running the same version of the *onunload/onload* utilities.

- When unloading and loading a *table*, *onunload* does not preserve access privilege, synonyms, views, constraints, triggers, or default values. You must use *dbschema* to transfer this information. (This information is preserved if you unload and load an entire database.)

- You must have DBA privileges or be user informix to unload a database.

- You must be the owner of a table, have DBA privileges, or be user `informix` to unload a table.

- The logging mode of the database is not preserved.

Making an Export: onunload Syntax

The *onunload* utility can write the exported data to a file on a hard drive or to a tape device. It can unload an entire database or just a table within that database. The syntax of the command is as follows:

```
$ onunload [-l | -b blocksize -s tapesize -t device ] database[[:owner].table]
```

Specifying the device parameters

There are two methods of specifying the device parameters for *onunload*. The first is to use the *-l* option, which specifies that *onunload* should read the *device*, *tapesize*, and *blocksize* values from the *onconfig* file. It will use LTAPEDEV, LTAPESIZE, and LTAPEBLK values, respectively.

 Please note that LTAPEDEV is the same device that you are using for your logical log backups. That means that if you do not specify a tape device, you could accidentally overwrite your logical backup tape! It is therefore safer to specify another device if you can. If you cannot, make sure you take your logical backup tape out of the drive before running this command.

The second method for specifying device parameters is to specify each of them individually using the *-b blocksize*, *-s tapesize*, and *-t device* options.

Specifying the database and table to unload

At a minimum, you must specify the name of the database to unload. To do this, simply name the database as the last argument of the *onunload* command. Optionally, you can specify a name of a table and the owner of that table. To do this, add the name of the table and its owner after the name of the database using this format:

```
database:owner.table
```

Restoring from a Logical Backup

onload is *onunload*'s counterpart and will read the logical backup created by *onunload*. It will create a database or table in the specified dbspace and load the data from the logical backup into that database or table. If you do not specify a dbspace to load the database or table into, it will be loaded into the root dbspace.

Specifying the device parameters

As with *onunload*, you can specify the device parameters for *onload* by using the *-b blocksize*, *-s tapesize*, and *-t device* options. You also can use the *-l* option, which tells *onload* to read the device parameter information from the *onconfig* file.

Specifying the database and/or table to unload

You specify the name of the database or table to load the same way you do with the *onunload* utility. Specify the database by listing it as the last option. To specify the owner and table to load, list them after the database name in the following format:

```
database:owner.table
```

Specifying the create options

Now that you have specified the device to use and the database or table to load, there are options that determine how the database or table is created:

Target dbspace
> Specify the dbspace where the database or table will be stored using the *-d dbspace* option.

New index name
> You can rename an index during an *onload* restore using the *-i oldindex newindex* option. This is done to avoid conflict with existing index names.

Relocated data fragment
> The *-fd olddbspace newdbspace* option can be used to move a data fragment from one dbspace to another.

Relocated index fragment
> The *-fi indexname olddbspace newdbspace* option can be used to move an index from one dbspace to another.

15

Oracle Backup & Recovery

Historically, Oracle did not have a standalone backup utility like Informix's *ontape* or Sybase's *dump*, opting instead for commands that allow the DBA to use any backup utility. Oracle7 introduced the EBU, or Enterprise Backup Utility, but it is designed to work only with other commercial backup utilities.* Oracle8 introduced the Recovery Manager (*rman*), which also is designed to work with commercial backup utilities, and added a lot more functionality. Environments without a commercial utility must use backup scripts of some kind. This method is certainly the least user-friendly and most difficult to learn if one is new to Oracle and scripting, but its design also allows for the greatest flexibility during both backup and restore. This complexity, of course, requires a bit more explanation, which is what this chapter is about.

 This chapter will use the Oracle8 command *svrmgr* for interfacing with Oracle databases. If you are running Oracle7, the command is *sqldba*.

Oracle Architecture

As mentioned in Chapter 13, *Backing Up Databases*, it is important to understand the design of the database that is being backed up. Therefore, this chapter starts with a discussion of Oracle architecture. Similar information is provided in Chapter 13, but this chapter concentrates on information specific to Oracle. Just as

---

* Oracle8 now comes bundled with an OEM version of Legato Networker, which means that you do have another free option now, but this setup is still not as easy to use as *ontape* or *dump*.

in Chapter 13, we start with the power user's view of the database, then continue with that of the database administrator. This chapter uses Oracle-specific terms. To see how a particular term relates to one used in Sybase or Informix, consult Chapter 13. As much as possible, these architectural elements are presented in a "building block" order. Elements that are used to explain other elements will be presented first. For example, we explain what a *segment* is before explaining what the *rollback segment* is.

Power User's View

Unless a power user wants to start doing the DBA's job of putting a database together, the following terms should be all they need to know. This view also could be called the "logical" view, since many of the elements described in this view don't exist in a physical sense.

Instance

An instance is a set of processes through which the Oracle database talks to shared memory. Often, there is more than one instance on a single system. On a Unix system, an instance can be identified by a set of processes with the pattern ora_*ORACLE_SID*_, where *ORACLE_SID* is the instance name. When an Oracle instance is started, the database within it becomes available. On a Unix system, an instance is started with the *dbstart* command and shut down with the *dbshut* command.

Database

The database is what most people think about when they are using Oracle. That's because it is the database that contains the data! It contains all the tables, indexes, and other important database objects. In Oracle, there is a one-to-one relationship between instances and databases. A database resides in only one instance, and there is only one database within an instance. That is why an Oracle DBA or user may use the two terms interchangeably.[*] Technically, though, the *instance* is a set of processes through which the database talks to shared memory, whereas the *database* is the collection of data itself.

Table

A table is a collection of related rows that all have the same attributes. In Oracle, a table can be "partitioned," or spread across multiple tablespaces. Other than that, Oracle tables are the same as any other RDBMSs.

---

[*] You will find the terms used interchangeably in this chapter as well. The term "instance" actually is used rather sparingly, since the term "database" is more widely known.

Index

A database index is analogous to an index in a book: it allows Oracle to find data quickly. Again, an Oracle index is the same as anyone else's index, and it presents no unique backup requirements. An index is a *derived* table. It is created based on the attributes in another table, so it could be re-created during a restore. However, it almost always is going to be quicker to restore it than to re-create it.

BLOB datatypes

Oracle8 has special datatypes called *BLOB*, *CLOB*, and *BFILE* for storing large objects such as text or graphics. The Binary Large OBject (*BLOB*) and Character Large OBject (*CLOB*) datatypes present no special backup requirements since they are stored within the database itself. (A *BLOB* typically contains image files, and a *CLOB* normally contains text data.) However, the *BFILE* datatype stores only a pointer inside the database to a file that actually resides somewhere in the filesystem. This does require some special attention during backups. See the note in the overview chapter about this.

Object

An *object* is any type of database object, such as a table or an index. This is really a generic term rather than an Oracle-specific term. Unfortunately, Oracle also uses the term "object" to refer to reusable components created by object-oriented SQL programming.* Here, it is used simply as a generic way to refer to any type of table or index.

Row

A *row* is a collection of related attributes, such as all the information about a specific customer. Oracle also may refer to this as a "record."

Attribute

An *attribute* is any specific value (also known as a "column" or "field") within a row.

DBA's View

Now that we have covered the logical structure of an Oracle database, we will concentrate on the physical structure. Since only the DBA should need to know this information, we will call it the "DBA's view."

---

* This really depends on which book you buy. Different Oracle authors use different terms. For example, some use the term "data file" (with a space), while others prefer to use "datafile"; at least one book uses the term "objects" as a generic term and to refer to object-oriented components.

Blocks

A *block* is the smallest piece of data that can be moved within the database. Oracle allows a custom block size for each instance; the size can range from 1024 to 8096 bytes. A block is what is referred to as a *page* in other RDBMSs.

Extents

An *extent* is a collection of Oracle blocks that are treated as one unit. The size of each extent is determined by the DBA.

Segment

A *segment* is the collection of extents dedicated to a database object (table). Depending on the type of table, extents may be allocated or taken away to meet the storage needs of a given table. A perfect example is the rollback segment, described later, which would be all the extents on which the rollback logs are stored. The size of the rollback segment may increase or decrease depending on how many uncommitted transactions are currently open. Oracle adds extents to (or subtract extents from) the rollback segment as it needs them.

Datafile

An Oracle datafile can be either a raw (disk device) or cooked (filesystem) file. Once they are created, the syntax to work with raw and cooked datafiles is the same. However, backup scripts do have to take the type of datafile into account. If the backup script is going to support datafiles on raw partitions, it will need to use *dd* or some other command that can back up a raw partition. Using *cp* or *tar* will not work, since they support only filesystem files.

Each Oracle datafile contains a special header block that holds that datafile's System Change Number (SCN). This SCN is updated every time a change is made to the datafile, and the control file keeps track of the current SCN. When an instance is started, the current SCN is checked against the SCN markers in each datafile. (See the definition of *control file* later in this chapter.)

 Please see an important explanation of the role that the SCN plays during hot backup in the section "Inside a Hot Backup," later in this chapter.

Tablespace

This is the virtual area onto which a DBA creates tables. It consists of several datafiles and is created by the *create tablespace* `tablespace_name` *on* `devicea`, `deviceb`, `devicec` command. A tablespace may contain several tables. The space that each table occupies within that tablespace is a segment (see the earlier definition of segment).

Every Oracle instance has at least one tablespace, the *system* tablespace. The files that make up the *system* tablespace must be specified when creating a new Oracle instance. The *system* tablespace stores the data dictionary, PL/SQL programs, view definitions, the *system* rollback segment, and other types of instancewide information. When it comes to backup and recovery, the main difference between the *system* tablespace and the rest of the tablespaces is that it must be recovered offline. That is because the instance cannot be brought online without the *system* tablespace. Other tablespaces can be recovered after the instance has been brought online.

Partition

A table can be spread out across multiple tablespaces. When this is done, each tablespace is referred to as a *partition*.

Control file

The *control file* is a database (of sorts) that keeps track of the status of all the objects within the database. It knows about all tablespaces, datafiles, and redologs within the database. It also knows the current state of each of these objects by tracking each object's SCN. Every time it makes a change to a file, the SCN gets incremented both in the control file and in the actual datafile. (See the definition of *datafile* earlier in the chapter.) That way, when the system reboots and the instance is starting up, the control file has a record of what SCN the file should be at, and it checks that against the SCN that the file has. This is how it "notices" that a file is older than the control file and is in need of media recovery. Also, if an older control file is put in place, Oracle will see that the SCN of the datafiles are higher than those that it has recorded in the control file. That's when Oracle displays the "datafile is more recent than the control file" error.

Control files can be backed up using the *backup control file to* `filename` command in *svrmgr*, but restoring control files is a bit tricky. The mechanics of this recovery are covered later in the chapter. It is best to avoid having to recover or rebuild a control file. Oracle7 provided a way to do this with the mirrored control file feature in which there can be multiple copies of the control file, each of which is updated simultaneously by Oracle. Make sure that this feature is being used. Mirrored control files take up almost no space, and provide an incredible amount of recovery flexibility.

Transaction

A *transaction* is any activity by a user or a DBA that changes one or more attributes in an Oracle database. (If a set of commands is contained between a *begin transaction* and *end transaction* statement, the entire set of commands is treated as one transaction.) Logically, a transaction modifies one or more attributes, but what actually occurs physically is a modification to one or more blocks within the Oracle database.

Rollback segment

Remember that a segment is all the extents allocated to a database object. A *rollback segment*, then, is all the extents allocated to a rollback log. Before a page is physically changed on disk, the *before* image (its image before it was changed) needs to be recorded in case the transaction must be "rolled back." This before image is stored in a rollback log, which is contained within a rollback segment. (There can be several rollback segments within a given instance, and a transaction may even be told which rollback segment to use.) Oracle writes to only one extent within the rollback segment at one time. It also writes to these extents in a cyclical fashion, filling each extent one by one until all the extents are full, then returning to the "first" extent and overwriting it. However, it cannot start writing to an extent if there is an uncommitted transaction whose before images are found in that extent, because the before images must be preserved until the transaction is committed. Oracle then must assign *additional* extents so that additional before images may be saved. (This typically happens with a long transaction whose before images will span several extents within the rollback segment.) Once all transactions that need the before images in a particular extent are committed, that extent then is available for use by the rollback segment. If the number of extents needed by the rollback segment decreases, Oracle can release extents as necessary to shrink the rollback segment.

There is always at least one rollback segment created, the *system* rollback segment, which is stored in the *system* tablespace. Neither this rollback segment nor the tablespace in which it is stored is sufficient for a normal production database. Therefore, the DBA will create additional rollback segments in other tablespaces and take the *system* rollback segment offline. A common practice is to create a tablespace that will contain nothing but rollback segments. Oracle assigns rollback segments to transactions on a round-robin basis or to a specific rollback segment specified manually by the transaction. Taking the *system* rollback segment offline makes sure that no transactions will be assigned to it. This allows the *system* tablespace to concentrate on other matters, without being slowed down to record rollback information. The main reason to understand rollback segments (and where they go) is their unique roll in a database recovery. Remember that the rollback segments store the before images of all changed blocks. After a crash or recovery, these pages are essential to return the database to a consistent state. They are needed in order to roll back any uncommitted transactions and return the necessary blocks to their before-transaction status. (This is the entire purpose of the rollback segment.)

The result of this restriction is that, while a rollback segment can be recovered online, a normal tablespace cannot be brought online until the rollback segment that it uses is completely restored. Therefore, Oracle does not allow the instance to be brought online unless all defined rollback segments are available. If you try to open the database without any of them, Oracle gives the error "rollback segment '*segment_name*' specified not available." This is covered in more detail later.

Checkpoint

A *checkpoint* is the point at which all data that is kept in memory is flushed to disk. In Oracle, a DBA can force a checkpoint with the *alter system checkpoint* command, but a checkpoint also is done automatically every time the database switches redolog files.

Redolog

If the rollback segment contains a rollback log, the redolog could be called a "roll-forward" log. Every time that Oracle needs to change a block on disk, it records the change vector in the redolog; that is, it records how it changed the block, not the value it changed it to. A mathematical explanation may be helpful here. Suppose that you had a variable with a value of 100 and added 1 to it. To record the change vector, you would record +1; to record the changed value, you would record 101. This is how Oracle records information to the redologs *during normal operation.* As explained in the later section "Inside a Hot Backup," it switches to recording the changed *value* when a tablespace is in hot-backup mode.

In times of recovery, the redolog is used to "redo" transactions that have occurred since the last checkpoint or since the backup that is being used for a restore. Oracle has both online redologs and offline (archived) redologs.

 The online and archived redologs are essential to recovering from a crash or disk failure. Learn everything you can about how they work and protect them as if they were gold!

Originally, the online redologs were three* or more files to which Oracle wrote the logs of each transaction. The problem with this approach is that the log to which Oracle was currently writing always contained the only copy of the most recent transaction logs. If the disk that this log was stored on were to crash, Oracle would not be able to recover up to the point of failure. Oracle7 introduced the concept of log groups. A *log group* is a set of two or more files that are written to simultaneously by Oracle—essentially a mirror for the redologs. A set of log files is called a "log group," and the separate files within that log group are referred to as members. Each log group is treated as a single log file, and all transaction records are simultaneously written to all disks within the currently active log group.

Now, instead of three or more separate files, any one of which could render the database useless if damaged, there are three or more separate log groups of mirrored files. If each log group is assigned more than one member, every transaction is being recorded in more than one place. After a crash, Oracle can read any one of these members to perform crash recovery.

Oracle writes to the log groups in a cyclical fashion. It writes to one log group until that log group is full. It then performs a log switch and starts writing to the next log group. As soon as this happens, the log group that was just filled is then copied to an archived redolog file, *if automatic archiving is enabled.* If automatic archiving is not enabled, this file is not copied and is simply overwritten the next time that Oracle needs to write to that log.

Each of the online redologs is copied to the filename pattern specified by the `LOG_ARCHIVE_DEST` parameter in the *initORACLE_SID.ora* file, followed by an incremented string specified by the `LOG_ARCHIVE_FORMAT` parameter in the *initORACLE_SID.ora* file. For example, assume that `LOG_ARCHIVE_DEST` was set to */archivelogs/arch* and `LOG_ARCHIVE_FORMAT` is set to `%s`.*log*, where `%s` is Oracle's variable for the current sequence number. If the current sequence number is 293, a listing of the *archivelogs* directory might show the following:

```
# cd /archivelogs
# ls -l arch*
arch291.log
arch292.log
arch293.log
```

Depending on how much activity a database has, there may be hundreds of files in the archive log destination directory over time. Nothing is done by Oracle to manage this area, so a *cron* job must be set up to clean up this directory. As long as these files are being backed up to some kind of backup media, they can be

---

* Oracle requires only two logs, but the typical practice is to have three or more. That allows one log to be active, one to be completely inactive, and one to be in the process of being archived.

removed after a few days. However, the more logs there are on disk, the better off the database will be. That is because it sometimes may be necessary to restore from a backup that is not the most current one. (For example, this could happen if the current backup volume is damaged.) If all the archive logs since the time that old backup was taken are online, it's a breeze. If they aren't, they have to be restored as well. That can create an available-space problem. This is why I recommend having enough space to store enough archive logs to span two backup cycles. For example, if the system does a full database backup once a night, there should be enough space to have at least two days' worth of redologs online. If it backs up once a week, then there should be enough storage for two weeks' worth of transaction logs. (This is yet another reason for backing up every night.)

In summary, the online redologs are usually three or more log groups[*] that Oracle cycles through to write the current transaction log data. A log group is a set of one or more logs that Oracle treats as one redolog. Log groups should have more than one member, since that almost completely removes the chance for data corruption in the case of disk failure. Once Oracle fills up one online redolog group, it copies that redolog to the archive log destination as a separate file with a sequence number contained in the filename. It makes this copy only if automatic archiving is enabled.

The following sections cover physical and logical backups. If you are unfamiliar with these terms, please consult Chapter 13.

Physical Backups Without a Storage Manager

Storage managers can be very expensive, so they are not always available for every application. Even if you have a storage manager, you may not want to spend several thousand dollars per server for the Oracle interface. This section discusses methods that can be used to safely back up Oracle without using a storage manager. You can back up to disk and then back that disk up using your normal backup procedures, or you can back up directly to tape.

Like most RDBMSs, Oracle databases can reside on cooked filesystem files or raw disk devices. Unlike Sybase and Informix DBAs, though, Oracle DBAs typically have put their databases on cooked files. There is a very good reason for this: if all

---

[*] Oracle always uses the term "log groups," even if a log group has only one member.

of the database files are accessible via the filesystem, backing up is very simple. That is because copying the data can be done by any standard copy (*cp*) utility or backup (*dump, cpio*) utility.

Backups can be done offline (a *cold* backup) or online (a *hot* backup).

Cold Backup

A cold backup of an Oracle database that is based on filesystem files is the easiest of all database backups. This is because most companies already have some system that backs up their filesystem files. It could be a homegrown program that runs *dump*, or it could be a commercial backup product. To perform a cold backup of an Oracle database, simply shut down Oracle before running the normal backup. Oracle will do a checkpoint, flushing any data stored in memory to disk, and then stop all processes that allow access to the database. This puts all Oracle files into a clean, consistent, quiescent state.

This assumes, of course, the use of filesystem files. An Oracle database also could be sitting on raw devices. A cold backup of such a database requires a little more effort, since one needs to understand the structure of the database. The procedure would start out the same, by shutting down the database. A filesystem backup at this point, though, would get only the executables and any database objects that reside in the filesystem, such as the control file. The database itself would require extra effort. The first thing to figure out is where all the database files are. A script can "ask" Oracle this question, but that script would have to be written. (The script *oraback.sh*, covered later in this chapter, does this automatically.) Once the locations of all files are known, *dd* can back them up to a file somewhere in the filesystem or send them directly to a backup volume. If they are backed up to a file in the filesystem, it must be done before the normally scheduled filesystem backup. That way, the files are automatically backed up to a backup volume.

Therefore, backing up an Oracle database that uses raw partitions is harder than backing one up that is based on filesystem files. This is one of the reasons why Oracle DBAs have historically used the filesystem to store their database files, even though raw partitions yield slightly better performance. (There is a new option available now, with Veritas's Database Edition for Oracle. It gives you the flexibility of a filesystem database, with performance that's apparently better than raw partitions.)

Hot Backup

If an Oracle database is providing the data for the customer service web page or any other application that requires 24-hour uptime, a cold backup is not acceptable because it requires that the database be shut down on a regular basis. Even if this is done late at night, customers accessing the web page may do so at any time. A company will have a much better web image if it is able to leave the web page up all the time. What is needed, then, is a hot backup.

A hot backup requires quite a bit more work than a cold backup, even more when the cold backup is of a database using raw devices. The following steps must be taken every time a hot backup is performed:

1. Ask Oracle for a list of all tablespaces and datafiles.

2. Ask Oracle for the location of the archived redologs.

3. Ask Oracle for the location of the control files (optional).

4. Put each tablespace into backup mode, using the command *alter tablespace* `tablespace_name` *begin backup.*

5. Copy each tablespace's datafiles to an alternate location such as disk or tape.

6. Take each tablespace out of backup mode, using the command *alter tablespace* `tablespace_name` *end backup.*

7. Switch the redolog file.

8. Back up the control file using the command *backup control file.*

9. Manually copy the control file (optional).

10. Manually copy the online redologs.

11. Ensure that all archived redologs that span the time of the backup are preserved.

This is obviously a lot of work. A good knowledge of scripting is required, as well as a good knowledge of the commands necessary to accomplish these tasks.* To explain the whole process, let's break it down by section:

Determine structure

Steps 1–3 have to do with figuring out where everything is. Many DBAs do this step only once or only when they change the structure of the database. This results in a static script that backs up only the tablespaces that were discovered the last time these steps were done. This is too open to human error and not recommended. It is much better to automate these steps and do them each time an instance is backed up. That ensures that the configuration data is always current—and that the backups never miss a thing.

---

* As the author of the *oraback.sh* script, I should know! The script represents years of coding, testing, and improvement. It incorporates almost every advanced Bourne shell programming feature I know.

Put files into backup mode and copy them

Copying the database files while the database is running can be done only by placing a tablespace in backup mode. The datafiles that are in that tablespace then can be copied or backed up at will. Since the files are still being written to as you are backing them up, Oracle refers to this as a "fuzzy" backup, but don't worry: Oracle will be able to "focus" the files just fine if you restore them.

 Please see the upcoming section, "Inside a Hot Backup," for a debunking of the common misconception that datafiles are not being written to when they are in hot backup mode.

Back up related files

The datafiles are just one of the many sections of Oracle that need to be backed up. Also back up the control file, the archived redologs, the configuration files, and the online redologs. (It is unlikely that the online redologs will ever be useful during a restore, but it doesn't hurt to save them.) If it is a cold backup, though, copying the online redologs creates a complete copy of the database at that point in time.

Inside a Hot Backup

What happens during a hot backup is widely misunderstood. Many people[*] believe that while a tablespace is in backup mode, the datafiles within that tablespace are not written to. They believe that all changes to these files are kept in the redologs until the tablespace is taken out of backup mode, at which point all changes are applied to the datafiles just as they are during a media recovery. (The concept of media recovery is covered in the recovery section later in this chapter.) Although this explanation is easier to understand (and swallow) than how things really work, it is *absolutely not* how hot backups work in Oracle.

A common reaction to this statement is a very loud "What?" followed by crossed arms and a really stern look. (I reacted the same way the first time I heard it.) "How could I safely back up these files if they are changing as I'm backing them up?" Don't worry, Oracle has it all under control. Remember that every Oracle datafile has an SCN that is changed every time an update is made to the file. Also remember that every time Oracle makes a change to a datafile, it records the vector of that change in the redolog. Both of these behaviors change during hot back-

---

[*] "Many people" used to include me and includes the authors of some books. A huge thanks goes to the DBA who pointed this out to me and who proved it when I didn't believe him.

ups. When a tablespace is put into backup mode, the following three things happen:

1. Oracle checkpoints the tablespace, flushing all changes from shared memory to disk.

2. The SCN markers for each datafile in that tablespace are "frozen" at their current values. Even though further updates will be sent to the datafiles, the SCN markers will not be updated until the tablespace is taken out of backup mode.

3. Oracle switches to logging full images of changed database blocks to the redologs. Instead of recording how it changed a particular block (the change vector), it will log the entire image of the block after the change. This is why the redologs grow at a much faster rate while hot backups are going on.

After this happens, your backup program works happily through this datafile, backing it up block by block. Since the file is being updated as you are reading it, it may read blocks just before they're changed, after they're changed, or even while they're changing! Suppose that your filesystem block size is 4 KB, and Oracle's block size is 8 KB. Your backup program will be reading in increments of 4 KB. It could back up the first 4 KB of an 8-KB Oracle data block before a change is made to that block, then back up the last 4 KB of that file after a change has been made. This results in what Oracle calls a "split block." However, when your backup program reaches the point of the datafile that contains the SCN, it will back up that block the way it looked when the backup began, since that block is frozen. Once you take the tablespace out of backup mode, the SCN marker is advanced to the current value, and Oracle switches back to logging change vectors instead of full images of changed blocks.

How does Oracle straighten this out during media recovery? It's actually very simple. You use your backup program to restore the datafile. When you attempt to start the instance, Oracle looks at the datafile and sees an old SCN value. Actually, it sees the value that the SCN marker had *before* the hot backup began. When you enter *recover datafile*, it begins to apply redo against this datafile. Since the redologs contain a complete image of every block that changed during your backup, it can rebuild this file to a consistent state, regardless of when you backed up a particular block of data. Isn't that wonderful?

If you're like me, you won't believe this the first time that you read it. So I'll prove it to you. Let's create a table called *tapes* in the tablespace *test*, insert the value "DLT" into it, and force a checkpoint:

```
SQL> create table tapes (name varchar2(32)) tablespace test;
Table created.
SQL> insert into tapes values ('DLT');
1 row created
SQL> commit;
```

```
Commit complete.
SQL> alter system checkpoint;
System altered.
```

Now we ask Oracle what block number contains the new value:

```
SQL> select dbms_rowid.rowid_block_number(rowid) blk, name from tapes;
    BLK NAME
------- ----------------
      3 DLT
```

The value "DLT" is recorded in the third data block. Allowing nine blocks for the datafile headers, we can read the third block of data with *dd* and run *strings* on it to actually see that the value is there:

```
$ dd if=/db/Oracle/a/oradata/crash/test01.dbf ibs=8192 skip=11 count=1|strings
1+0 records in
16+0 records out
DLT
```

Now we place the tablespace in hot-backup mode:

```
SQL> alter tablespace test begin backup ;
Tablespace altered.
```

Now we update the table, commit the update, and force a global checkpoint on the database:

```
SQL> update tapes set name = 'AIT';
1 row updated
SQL> commit;
Commit complete.
SQL> alter system checkpoint;
System altered.
```

Now we extract the same block of data to show the new value was actually written to disk:

```
$ dd if=/db/Oracle/a/oradata/crash/test01.dbf ibs=8192 skip=11 count=1|strings
1+0 records in
16+0 records out
DLT,
AIT
```

We now can take the tablespace out of backup mode:

```
SQL> alter tablespace test end backup;
```

This test proves that datafiles are indeed being written to during hot backups!

Automating Backups: The oraback.sh Script

There is a program that performs cold and hot backups of Oracle, and it currently is being used by hundreds of companies around the world. *oraback.sh* is written in the Bourne shell, which is compatible with every Unix system. By using GNU's *config.guess* script, the list of Unix platforms that it runs on is perhaps limitless. The only thing that *oraback.sh* assumes is that the *oratab* file is properly configured; by default, *oraback.sh* automatically backs up every instance listed there. *oraback.sh* supports these features:

- Backing up to disk or tape

- Automatic detection of database configuration

- Backing up of databases on filesystems or raw partitions

- Multitasking, which can reduce backup time by up to 75 percent

- Mail-based success and error notification

- Backing up from one or more of the instances in *oratab*. To back up all instances, run it with no arguments:

  $ **oraback.sh**

  To back up one or more instances, run it with those *ORACLE_SID*s as arguments:

  $ **oraback.sh ORACLE_SID1 ORACLE_SIDn**

To schedule a backup for the time specified in *oraback.conf* (described later in this section), run it with the *at* argument:

  $ **oraback.sh at**

You also may combine these arguments:

  $ **oraback.sh at** *ORACLE_SID1 ORACLE_SIDn*

to specify both a backup time and the instances to be backed up.

Installing oraback.sh

To install *oraback.sh*, first put *oraback.sh*, *config.guess*, and *localpath.sh* in one directory, then check the following values in the site-specific section at the top of the script. They must be changed to fit the environment.

BINDIR
> Should be set to where *oraback.sh* is installed.

ORATAB
> Should be set to the name and location of Oracle's *oratab* file.

ORACONF
> Should be set to the name and location of the *oraback.conf* file (it must be located in a directory that Oracle can write to)

Review and confirm all other preference variables in the site-specific section, including ORADIR, TMP, LOG, and PATH. Also verify:

- Which instances are using archiving

- That Oracle can create directories in the filesystem that is being used for backups (specified in the *oratab* file)

Configuring and customizing oraback.sh

oraback.conf is the main configuration file for *oraback.sh*. A normal *oraback.conf* file contains a *hostname. master* line that specifies several options such as which users are authorized to perform the backup, what backup device should be used, and on what days/times cold/hot backup should be performed. If you specify *oraback.sh* with the *at* argument, it is the *hostname. master* line that *oraback.sh* uses to find the dates and times to run the backups. The *hostname. master* line is described here:

```
hostname.master:[skip]:Cold Day:Cold Time:Hot Time:[tape device]:users:
Parallelism:Backup Dir:Y::user ids:
```

The preceding fields are described as follows:

Field 1: hostname.master
This system's hostname generated by *uname -n* or *hostname*, minus its domain name. (e.g., *apollo.domain.com* becomes *apollo*).

Field 2: [skip]
If you want all backups skipped on this host tonight, put **skip** here.

Field 3: Cold Day
The day on which *oraback.sh* should do cold backups. This can be a day of the week (**Fri**) or month (**03**).

 If there is a blank in this field, cold backups will never be performed.

Field 4: Cold Time
The time of the day (using a 24-hour clock) to do cold backups (e.g., 1830).

Field 5: Hot Time
The time of the day (using a 24-hour clock) to do hot backups (e.g., 1830).

Field 6: [Tape Device]
No-rewind tape device, to back up to tape. (Blank for disk-only backup.)

Field 7: [Users]

> A "|"-separated list of usernames permitted to run *svrmgr* and this script, such as `oracle|dba`. (Blank allows only Oracle.)

Field 8: [Parallelism]

> The number of simultaneous datafile copies to run. (Blank=1.)

Field 9: Backup dir

> Must be set to a directory or filesystem that has enough room for a compressed copy of all database files. If backing up to tape, this doesn't need to be that much, but it still needs some space on disk. This is because it still uses this directory to back up the control files and redologs.

Field 10:[Y]

> A `Y` means to compress the files before they are written to tape or disk.

Field 11: mail ids

> Set this to a comma-delimited list of mail IDs to mail success or failure to (e.g., `dba@herworkstation.com, root`).

In addition, there are four predefined functions, unused by default, which are listed in the site-specific section of *oraback.sh*. These are listed as follows, with their respective usage times:

Preback

> The *Preback* function runs before entire backup starts.

Preshut

> The *Preshut* function runs before shutdown of each instance.

Poststart

> The *Poststart* function runs after startup of each instance.

Postback

> The *Postback* function runs after entire backup finishes.

Using these functions is very simple. For example, to restart *orasrv* after an instance is restarted (with a script called *rc.orasrv.sh*), change the *Poststart* function to read:

```
Poststart(){
rc.orasrv.sh
}
```

Deciding what or if to back up

Before actually running the backup, *oraback.sh* checks *oraback.conf* to determine:

- Whether the user running the backup is oracle, or is a valid user (listed in Field 7 of *oraback.conf*). If the user ID running the backup is not a valid user, the script will not continue.

- If it is a valid user, *oraback.sh* then looks to see whether the word `skip` is in Field 2. If so, it skips the backup once and removes the word `skip` from *oraback.conf.* (This allows a DBA to manually skip tonight's backup but does not allow the DBA to accidentally disable backups forever.)

- The script then does one of the following, depending on which arguments (if any) it receives:

  — It backs up everything.

    If given no arguments, it performs a backup of all instances listed in Oracle's *oratab* file.

    ```
    $ oraback.sh
    ```

  — It backs up selected instances.

    If given one or more instance names (ORACLE_SIDs, or SIDs for short) as arguments, the script performs a backup of each of them.

    ```
    $ oraback.sh ORACLE_SID1 ORACLE_SIDn
    ```

  — It schedules a backup for later.

    If called with *at* as an argument (this is what would be in *cron*), the script checks *oraback.conf* to see whether the day in Field 3 (the cold backup day field) is today. If so, it sets the variable $TIME to the time in Field 4. If not, it sets $TIME to the time in Field 5. The script then schedules an *at* job that will run *oraback.sh* at the time specified by $TIME.

    ```
    $ oraback.sh at
    ```

Deciding where and how to back up

oraback.sh then checks the `hostname.master` line in *oraback.conf* to find out if: (a) there is a tape device in Field 6 (If so, it labels the tape, making sure the no-rewind device is being used.) and (b) there is a number in Field 8. If so, it will perform that many simultaneous copies of database files.

Next, *oraback.sh* asks Oracle questions that will determine how (or if) the SID will be backed up. It asks if:

- The instance is online. If so, *oraback.sh* makes a set of configuration files needed later.

- Archiving is running.

- The instance is excluded from hot backup.

- This is a cold backup. If so, it shuts down the instance.

The script assumes that all instances want hot backups (though you may specify cold backups), which requires automatic archiving of redologs. *oraback.sh* warns if any instances do not have automatic archiving turned on. It continues to complain until this situation is corrected or *oraback.conf* is customized for that instance. (You do this by editing *oraback.conf*.)

If it's a hot backup

If the instance is online, logs are on, and the instance is not excluded from hot backups. Then the script:

1. Puts each tablespace into backup mode by using the *svrmgrl* command *begin backup*

2. Copies that tablespace's files to the backup device

3. Takes the tablespace out of backup mode with the *svrmgrl* command *end backup*

These three steps are the core of the hot backup. While the tablespace is in backup mode, the files can be safely backed up.

 See the earlier section "Inside a Hot Backup" for important information explaining why it is safe to copy the files.

The script supports simultaneous copying of individual datafiles to dramatically increase the speed of the backup. Depending on how many files there are per tablespace, there may be one or more tablespaces in backup mode at once. This is done in order to perform the number of concurrent file copies (using *dd*) that are specified in Field 8 of *oraback.conf*, if you are using this feature.

After all datafiles are backed up

Next, the script forces a checkpoint and archive log switch, which causes the online redolog to be sent to an archived redolog. It should be noted that it forces a log switch using the command *alter sytem archive log current*, instead of the older *alter system switch logfile*. The reason for this is that switching log files does just that, switches the log file and immediately returns the *svrmgr* prompt. The *archive log current* command waits until the copy of the old redolog to its archived location is done before it returns the prompt. This is because the next thing the script is going to do is copy this archived redolog to the backup location for safekeeping. If we used the old command, we might by copying it from the archived log location while it is being created. That way we are assured that the file we are copying is stable.

The script then backs up the control files to disk using both *svrmgr* and a manual copy. The manual copy is just for the paranoid; it's not a supported method of backing up the control file.* Finally, the script makes copies of the essential redologs and compresses them. (Essential logs are those that span the time of the backup.) If the backup device is a tape, it then backs up all files that were sent to disk to the tape device.

If it's a cold backup

If the instance is offline, *oraback.sh* only needs to copy the datafiles to the backup device. The script then backs up the control files and redologs the same way it does during a hot backup. This is perhaps the only time that manually copying the control files and online redologs does any good. That's because one could use these files to do a restore of the database to this point, without it ever knowing what happened. To do that, all the control files and online redologs would be needed.

Special cases

If the instance is online, but archiving is off, *oraback.sh* checks *oraback.conf* for a line that reads:

    HOST:ORACLE_SID:NOARCHIVELOG:[offline|nohotbackups]

If that line is not found, *oraback.sh* complains and sends you mail. That is because archiving must be on in order to do hot backups. If the line is found, it looks for the word `offline` on that same line. This tells *oraback.sh* that this instance is not supposed to have archive logs running, and it always should do an offline, or cold, backup of this instance. If it sees the word `offline`, *oraback.sh* shuts down the instance, performs a cold backup, and then restarts the instance. (This is one of the ways to customize *oraback.sh* for different instances.)

If the instance is online, *oraback.sh* also looks for a line in *oraback.conf* that reads:

    HOST:ORACLE_SID:::nohotbackup

This tells *oraback.sh* that although *ORACLE_SID* qualifies for a hot backup (it has archiving on), *oraback.sh* should not do hot backups of this instance. This is best suited for a development database, where the weekly cold backup is sufficient. If this line is found, the script skips this instance when performing a hot backup.

---

* This was a feature requested by the users of the program, who apparently are even more paranoid than I am!

Customizing backups of an instance

If there is an instance that will not run archiving or hot backups, put a line in *oraback.conf* that starts with:

```
HOST:ORACLE_SID::::
```

- Put NOARCHIVELOG in Field 3 if the instance does not use archiving.
- Put offline in Field 4 if the instance does not use archiving, and *oraback.sh* should do a cold backup every time.
- Put nohotbackups in Field 5 to skip hot backups for this instance. (It will be backed up only when cold backups run.)

Testing oraback.sh

For testing, select a small instance and run the following command as *Oracle*:

```
$ /usr/local/bin/oraback.sh <instance>
```

Be aware that if the word *offline* is in *oraback.conf* or if the day that is specified for cold backups is today, the instance will be shut down!

If this test functions properly, put an entry in Oracle's *cron* or in the *at* system. Add a *cron* entry that contains the command */usr/local/bin/oraback.sh at*, scheduled to run at around 12:00. It checks the *oraback.conf* and schedules an *at* job that will perform the backup.

Using oraback.sh

The best way to use this program is to have one single *oraback.conf* file that is NFS-mounted or shared to all Oracle systems. That way, all *cron* or *at* entries can run at 15:00, and backup configuration changes (system-wide or otherwise) can be made by editing one file. For example, to cause all Oracle backups to be skipped tonight, instead of having to edit a number of *cron* or *at* entries, you can edit this one file before 15:00. That way, it will see the word "skip" in there and not run backups that evening. (It will, however, take this word out so backups will run tomorrow night.)

Set the SUCCESSMAIL flag to Y, to be mailed every time *oraback.sh* backup runs, successful or otherwise. That allows a quick email check in the morning to see that all backups ran successfully. Simply check the subject line, since it will say ERROR if *oraback.sh* had any kind of errors.

Physical Backups with a Storage Manager

A commercial backup utility, like those covered in Chapter 5, *Commercial Backup Utilities*, can actually deliver a completely integrated backup solution for all Oracle databases. That is, there is no need to first back up to an intermediate storage area such as a disk. The commercial utilities can back up to any storage media, then inventory these backups just as they do regular filesystem backups, allowing a "point-and-click" restore. Commercial utilities back up Oracle in one of two ways.

Vendor-Supplied Storage Managers

The first, and less common, method is to use the same basic Oracle commands that *oraback.sh* uses. Products that do this have simply written their own backup utility. Although most of these were developed before Oracle's EBU and Recovery Manager (*rman*) became widely available, some vendors continue to develop these products because they claim they are faster or more reliable than EBU or *rman*. One such product is BMC's SQL Backtrack. Originally designed for Sybase, this product has been ported to both Oracle and Informix. As of this writing, it is a standalone product, since SQL Backtrack does not do volume management. It can, however, interface with other commercial storage managers, allowing them to provide volume management.

Oracle Storage Managers

The second commercial method of backing up Oracle is to use Oracle7's EBU or Oracle8's *rman*. EBU/*rman* are Oracle internal products that are designed to give a backup utility a stream (or many streams) of backup data from the database. The command that is run is called *obackup* or *rman*. After a onetime setup, the commercial backup software can communicate with Oracle at any time to initiate a backup. It tells Oracle that it wants to back up instance ORACLE_SID, and it is able to receive *n* threads of data. (See "Commercial Backup Utilities" in Chapter 5 for an explanation of how backup threads work.) EBU/*rman* then does all the internal communication that it needs to do to supply the backup utility with *n* threads of data. Both the utility and EBU/*rman* record the time of the backup for future reference. After things have been set up, it is also possible for a DBA to run the *obackup* or *rman* command from the command line. This command then calls the appropriate programs to connect with the backup utility. The commercial backup utility then responds to this as to any other backup request, loading volumes as necessary.

Since EBU is no longer supported in Oracle8, we do not cover it here. Recovery Manager is supported in Oracle8 and has a number of advantages over EBU. One of the main advantages is that it understands the structure of the database a lot better. It can be told, for example, to *restore* a tablespace. It knows what files are in that tablespace and then restores the most recent backup of those files. Once that is accomplished, it then can be told to *recover* that tablespace or apply media recovery to it. This is far better than having to find out what files to restore. *rman* is too complex to be covered in detail in a chapter of this size; consult Oracle's *Backup and Recovery Guide* for an explanation of how *rman* works.

What I would like to include in this chapter, however, is what is not included in the documentation—how to use *rman* to completely automate the process of backing up all Oracle instances on a server *rman*. To completely automate such a process, you must start at the top, with the *oratab* file (the *oratab* file contains a list of all Oracle instances). A script should read the *oratab* file, then generate backup requests for *rman* based on that file. These backup requests could be used to back up both the databases and the archive logs. Such a script has to use *rman* scripts as well to be able to give *rman* all the commands that it needs. I have used *rman* and have written such scripts (they are included here for example only). Unlike *oraback.sh*, these scripts have not been extensively tested on multiple platforms, but they are short, and their principles can be used to automate the backups of any Unix database server.

Sample rman scripts

The three sample scripts are *rman.sh*, *database.rman*, and *archivelog.rman*. *rman.sh* is the "parent" script. It is called from *cron* with one required argument: *database* or *archivelog*. This tells *rman.sh* what it is supposed to do.

```
$ rman.sh [ database.full.rman | database.inc.rman ]
```

If called in this manner, *rman.sh* tells *rman* to use the command file *database. level.rman*. This command file tells *rman* to back up the entire database and switch log files when it is done. The level of the backup is determined by which *rman* script is called. (*database.full* does a level-0 backup, and *database.inc* does a level-1 backup.) If the PARALLELISM parameter at the top of the script is set to a number higher than 1, it backs up multiple instances at one time.

```
$ rman.sh [ archivelog.full.rman | archivelog.inc.rman ]
```

If called in this manner, *rman.sh* tells *rman* to use the command file *archivelog. level.rman*. This command file tells *rman* to back up all archive logs it finds but not to delete them when it is done. (There is an *rman* option to do this, but I believe it is better to leave the files around for a few days before they are deleted.) Again, the level is determined by which script is called.

The rman.sh Script

Here is the *rman.sh* script:

```
#!/bin/sh
#
####################################################
##Site-specific section (change as appopriate)

PATH=/usr/bin:/usr/sbin:/usr/ucb:/oracle/app/oracle/product/8.0.4/bin:/oracle/opt/
bin:/oracle/opt/rcs:/oracle/app/oracle/olap/olap/bin:/oracle/backupbin
ORACLE_BASE=/oracle/app/oracle
DEBUG=Y                   # Set this to "Y" to turn on set -x for all functions
BINDIR=/oracle/backupbin  # Location of this and related programs
ORACLE=oracle             # ID that script will run as
DBAGROUP=dba              # GROUP that should own backup directory
ORATAB=/var/opt/oracle/oratab
ORACLE_HOME=`grep -v '^#' $ORATAB|awk -F':' '{print $2}' |tail -1`
TMP=/var/tmp              # Where temporary and permanent logs are kept
PATH=$PATH:/usr/bin:/usr/sbin:/sbin:/usr/5bin:/bin:$BINDIR
GLOBAL_LOGIN_PASSWD=internal/manager
RMAN_LOGIN_PASSWD=rman/rman
RMAN_SID=admin
ORIG_PATH=$PATH

SID_PARALLELISM=2         # The number of instances to back up simultaneously.

LOGDIR=/oracle/backupbin

Preback() {               #Run prior to backup.
[ "$DEBUG" = Y ] && set -x
}

Postback() {              #Run after entire backup finishes.
[ "$DEBUG" = Y ] && set -x
}

export BINDIR ORATAB ORACONF TMP PATH ORIG_PATH

##End site-specific configuration section
####################################################

Usage()
{
echo "Usage: $0: cmdfile
(Substitute 'cmdfile' with an rman cmdfile script (located in $BINDIR)
that will be run by $0. ... e.g. database.rman)"
exit 1
}

[ "$DEBUG" = Y ] && set -x

ORACLE_SIDS=`grep -v '^#' $ORATAB|awk -F':' '{print $1}'|grep -v '\*'`
```

```
[ $# -eq 1 ] || Usage

CMDFILE=$1

PSID=sodfwer98w7uo2krwer987wer

for ORACLE_SID in $ORACLE_SIDS ; do

  CT=`ps -ef|grep -c 'rman.target'`
  while [ $CT -gt $SID_PARALLELISM ] ; do
    # Give the last command a little time to get going and/or fail.
    sleep 15

    if [ `ps -ef|grep -c " $PSID "` -gt 1 ] ; then
      # If the command that we just backgrounded is now running, add it to the CT.
      CT=`ps -ef|grep -c 'rman.target'`
      sleep 30
    else
      # If not, break out of this loop cause we'll be here forever.
      break
    fi
  done

  rman cmdfile "${BINDIR}/$CMDFILE" > $LOGDIR/rman.$ORACLE_SID.$CMDFILE.log 2>&1 &
  PSID=$!

done
```

The database.full.rman command file (level-0 backup)

Here is the *rman* command file used to perform a level-0 backup:

```
Run {
target passwd@oracle_sid;
rcvcat passwd@rman_sid;

allocate channel t1 type 'sbt_tape';
allocate channel t2 type 'sbt_tape';
allocate channel t3 type 'sbt_tape';
allocate channel t4 type 'sbt_tape';
backup incremental level 0 format 'backup_test_%t_%s_%p' database ;
sql 'alter system archive log current';}
```

The archivelog.full.rman command file (level-0 archive logs)

Here is the *rman* command file used to back up all level-0 archive logs:

```
Run {
target passwd@oracle_sid;
rcvcat passwd@rman_sid;
allocate channel t1 type 'sbt_tape';
allocate channel t2 type 'sbt_tape';
allocate channel t3 type 'sbt_tape';
allocate channel t4 type 'sbt_tape';
```

```
backup incremental level 0 format 'backup_test_%t_%s_%p' archivelog all ;
sql 'alter system archive log current';}
```

The database.inc.rman command file (level-1 backups)

Here is the *rman* command file used to perform a level-1 backup:

```
Run {
target passwd@oracle_sid;
rcvcat passwd@rman_sid;
allocate channel t1 type 'sbt_tape';
allocate channel t2 type 'sbt_tape';
allocate channel t3 type 'sbt_tape';
allocate channel t4 type 'sbt_tape';
backup incremental level 1 format 'backup_test_%t_%s_%p' database ;
sql 'alter system archive log current';}
```

The archivelog.inc.rman command file (level-1 archive logs)

Here is the *rman* command file used to back up all level-1 archive logs:

```
Run {
target passwd@oracle_sid;
rcvcat passwd@rman_sid;
aenteringchannel t1 type 'sbt_tape';
allocate channel t2 type 'sbt_tape';
allocate channel t3 type 'sbt_tape';
allocate channel t4 type 'sbt_tape';
backup incremental level 1 format 'backup_test_%t_%s_%p' archivelog all ;
sql 'alter system archive log current';}
```

Difficulties with rman

Oracle has come a long way since *alter tablespace begin backup. rman* is a powerful, flexible tool, but it's also a complex one with a large command set that must
be learned in order to use it properly. (I wish they didn't make it so hard.) The
default documentation also tells you to enter the *rman* password on the command line. This makes it available to anyone who can enter *ps -ef.* (The preceding
scripts do not do this, but you can see that it was done by manually entering the
passwords into the script.) The Oracle Enterprise Manager is designed to make
rman and other Oracle products easy to use. A DBA learning *rman* for the first
time would do well to experiment with this tool.

Managing the Archived Redologs

How common is the question, "Should I have archiving turned on?" Yes, yes, a
thousand times *yes*! When in doubt, archive it out! Here's what is possible only if
archiving is enabled:

- Recover up to the point of failure.

- Recover from a backup that is a month or more old—if all the archived redologs since then are available.

- Perform a complete backup of the database without even shutting it down.

The existence of archive logs does all this without adding significant overhead to the entire process. The only difference between having archiving on or off is whether or not Oracle copies the current redolog out to disk when it "switches" from one redolog to the next. That's because even with archiving off, it still logs every transaction in the online redologs. That means that the only overhead associated with archiving is the overhead associated with copying the online file to the archive location, which is why there may be only a 1–3 percent performance hit in an environment with many transactions—if there is one at all. Feel free to experiment, but it is very difficult to justify turning off archiving on any production database.

Archiving Saves the Day

I know of one company that had a 250-GB database that did not use archiving at all. The biggest downside to this was that they could not do hot backups, and a cold backup took too long. The result was that they didn't do any backups! The DBAs didn't want to turn on archiving because they said that it would make the batch loads take too long. They also believed that having archiving turned on would somehow cause database corruption. This is just not possible. Again, the only difference between running and not running archiving is whether the old redolog is copied to the archive destination. The rest of the database works exactly the same.

I tried to convince them to turn on archiving. I even bet them that turning on archiving would not add more than a 3 percent overhead to their load times. In other words, a five-hour load would take only five hours and nine minutes. I lost the bet because it took five hours and ten minutes. The DBAs agreed to turn on archiving, and the database received its first backup ever in five years. *Two weeks later that database lost five disks—believe it or not.* We were able to recover the database overnight with no downtime to the users.

In my opinion, there are only two environments in which turning off archiving is acceptable. The first is an environment in which the data does not matter. What type of environment would that be? The only one is a true test environment that is using fake data or data restored from production volumes. No structure changes are being made to this database, and any changes made to the data will be discarded. This database does not need archiving and probably doesn't even need to be backed up at all.* It should be mentioned, though, that if you're doing any type of benchmarking of a database that will go into production, backup and archiving should be running.† The test will be more realistic—even if all the archive logs are deleted as soon as they are made.

Development databases do not fall into this category. That's because, although the data in a development database may be unimportant, the structure of the database often is highly important. If archiving is off, a DBA cannot restore any development work that he has done since the last backup. That creates the opportunity to lose hours' or even days' worth of work, just so a development database can be 1–3 percent faster. That is a big risk for such a small gain.

The second type of database that doesn't need archive logs is a *completely* read-only database or a "partially read-only" database *where an archive log restore would be slower than a reload of the original data.* The emergence of the data-warehouse has created this scenario. There are now some databases that have completely read-only tablespaces and never have data loaded into them. This type of database can be backed up once and then left alone until it changes again.

A partially read-only database is one that stays read only for long periods of time and is updated by a batch process that runs nightly, weekly, or even as needed. The idea is that, instead of saving hundreds of redologs, the database would be restored from a backup that was taken before the load. The DBA then could redo the load. There are two choices in this scenario. The first is to turn off archiving, making sure that there is a good *cold* backup after each database load. If the load aborted or a disk crashed after the load but before the next backup, you could simply load the older backup and then redo the load. The cold backup will cost some downtime, but having archiving off will speed up the loads somewhat. The other option would be to turn on archiving. That allows taking a hot backup anytime and creates the option of using the redologs to reload the data instead of doing an actual data reload. This method allows for greater backup flexibility. However, depending on the database and the type of data, an archive log restore could take longer than a reload of the original data—especially if it is a multi-threaded load. It is a tradeoff of performance for recoverability. Test both ways to see which one works best for you.

---

* Did I just say that?

† I say this because I remember being told to turn off archiving and not run backups because the DBAs were running a "load test" to see how well the database would perform. I always argued that such a test was worthless, since you didn't test it under real conditions.

Recovering Oracle

Since an Oracle database consists of several interrelated parts, recovering such a database is done through a process of elimination. Identify which pieces work, then recover the pieces that don't work. The following recovery guide follows that logic and works regardless of the chosen backup method. It consists of a flow-chart (Figure 15-1) and a procedure whose numbered steps correspond to the elements in the flowchart.

Using This Recovery Guide

The following process for recovering an Oracle database assumes nothing. Specifically, it does not assume that the cause of the database failure is known. By following these steps you'll work through a series of tasks that determine which part(s) of the database is/are no longer functional. You then can bring the database up as soon as possible, while allowing recovery of the pieces that are damaged. ("Damaged" may mean that a file is either missing or corrupted.)

Start with Step 1. If it succeeds, it directs you to Step 10. If the "startup mount" fails, it directs you to Step 2. Each of the steps follows a similar pattern, directing you to the appropriate step following the failure or success of the current step. The flowchart follows the same pattern as the printed steps. Once you are familiar with the details of each step, you may find the flowchart easier to follow than the printed instructions. If you are following the flowchart and get to a step that is unfamiliar to you, simply refer to the printed steps.

The electronic version of this procedure* contains a flowchart that is an HTML image map. Each decision or action box in the flowchart is a hyperlink to the appropriate section of the printed procedure. For more detailed information about individual steps, please consult Oracle's documentation, especially the *Oracle8 Backup and Recovery Manual.*

Restore or recover?

In this chapter, the words "restore" and "recover" have different meanings: "Restore" means to use the backup and restore system to restore that particular file or files. For example, if it says to restore a database file that was backed up to disk, simply copy the backup copy of that file from the backup directory on disk to its original location. If a commercial backup utility is being used, it means to restore that file using that product's interface. The term "recover," on the other hand, refers to doing something within Oracle to synchronize the various pieces of

---

* It is available on the CD that comes with this book and at *http://www.backupcentral.com.*

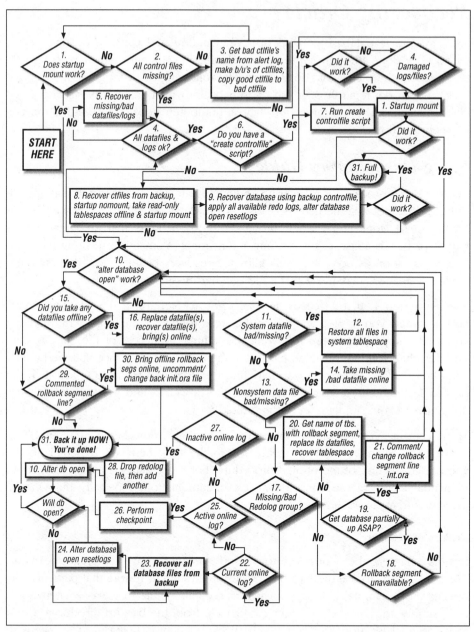

Figure 15-1. Oracle recovery flowchart

the database. For example, *recover database* rolls through all the redologs and applies any applicable changes to the datafiles associated with that database.

Step 1: Try Startup Mount

The first step in verifying the condition of an Oracle database is to attempt to mount it. This works because mounting a database (without opening it) reads the control files but does not open the datafiles. If the control files are mirrored,* Oracle attempts to open each of the control files that are listed in the *initORACLE_SID. ora* file. If any of them is damaged, the mount fails.

To mount a database, simply run *svrmgrl*, connect to the database, and enter *startup mount*:

```
$ svrmgrl
SVRMGR > connect internal;
Connected.
SVRMGR > startup mount;
Statement processed.
```

If it succeeds, the output looks something like this:

```
SVRMGR > startup mount;
ORACLE instance started.
Total System Global Area   5130648 bytes
Fixed Size                              44924 bytes
Variable Size                         4151836 bytes
Database Buffers                       409600 bytes
Redo Buffers                          524288 bytes
Database mounted.
```

If the attempt to mount the database fails, the output looks something like this:

```
SVRMGR > startup mount;
Total System Global Area                5130648 bytes
Fixed Size                                44924 bytes
Variable Size                           4151836 bytes
Database Buffer to s                      409600 bytes
Redo Buffers                             524288 bytes
ORACLE instance started.
ORA-00205: error in identifying controlfile, check alert log for more info
```

 If the attempt to mount the database succeeds, proceed to Step 10. If it database fails, proceed to Step 2.

---

* Which they'd better be! If you learn anything from this procedure, it should be that you really don't want to lose all of the control files and/or all of the current online redologs. Oracle will mirror them for you if you just tell it to do so. So do it!

Step 2: Are All Control Files Missing?

Don't panic if the attempt to mount the database fails. Control files are easily restored if they were mirrored and can even be rebuilt from scratch if necessary. The first important piece of information is that one or more control files are missing.

Unfortunately, since Oracle aborts the mount at the first failure it encounters, it could be missing one, two, or all of the control files, but so far you know only about the first missing file. So, before embarking on a course of action, determine the severity of the problem. In order to do that, do a little research.

First, determine the names of all of the control files. Do that by looking at the *configORACLE_SID.ora* file next to the term `control_files`. It looks something like this:

```
control_files          = (/db/Oracle/a/oradata/crash/control01.ctl,
                          /db/Oracle/b/oradata/crash/control02.ctl,
                          /db/Oracle/c/oradata/crash/control03.ctl)
```

It's also important to get the name of the control file that Oracle is complaining about. Find this by looking for the phrase `control_files:` in the alert log. (The alert log can be found in the location specified by the `background_dump_dest` value in the *configinstance.ora* file. (Typically, it is in the *ORACLE_BASE/ ORACLE_SID/admin/bdump* directory.) In that directory, there should be a file called *alert_ORACLE_SID.log*. In that file, there should be an error that looks something like this:

```
Sat Feb 21 13:46:19 1998
alter database  mount exclusive
Sat Feb 21 13:46:20 1998
ORA-00202: controlfile: '/db/a/oradata/crash/control01.ctl'
ORA-27037: unable to obtain file status
SVR4 Error: 2: No such file or directory
```

Some of the following procedures may say to override a potentially corrupted control file. Since one never knows which file may be needed, always make backup copies of all of the control files before doing any of this. That offers an "undo" option that isn't possible otherwise. (Also make copies of the online redologs as well.)

With the names of all of the control files and the name of the damaged file, it's easy to determine the severity of the problem. Do this by listing each of the control files and comparing their size and modification time. (Remember the game "One of these is not like the others" on *Sesame Street?*) The following scenarios assume that the control files were mirrored to three locations, which is a very common practice. The possible scenarios are:

The damaged file is missing, and at least one other file is present

If the file that Oracle is complaining about is just missing, that's an easy thing to fix.

If this is the case, proceed to Step 3.

The damaged file is not missing; it is corrupted

However, if all the online redologs are present, it's probably easier at this point to just run the *create controlfile* script discussed in Steps 6 and 7. This rebuilds the control file to all locations automatically. (Before that, though, follow Steps 4 and 5 to verify if all the datafiles and log files are present.)

This is probably the most confusing one, since it's hard to tell if a file is corrupted. What to do in this situation is a personal choice. Before going any farther, make backup copies of all control files. Once you do that, try a "shell game" with the different control files. The shell game consists of taking one of the three control files and copying it to the other two files' locations. Then attempt to mount the database again. The "shell game" is covered in Step 3.

All of the control files are missing, or they are all different sizes and/or times.

If all of the control files are corrupt or missing, they must be rebuilt or the entire database must be restored. Hopefully your backup system has been running the *backup control file to trace* command on a regular basis. (The output of this command is a SQL script that rebuilds the control files automatically.)

To rebuild the control file using the *create controlfile* script, proceed to Steps 4 through 7.

If the *backup control file to trace* command has been running, proceed to Steps 4 through 7. If not, proceed to Step 8.

Step 3: Replace Missing Control File

If the file that Oracle is complaining about is either missing or appears to have a different date and time than the other control files, this will be easy. Simply copy another one of the mirrored copies of the control file to the damaged control file's name and location. (The details of this procedure follow.) Once this is done, just attempt to mount the database again.

Be sure to make backup copies of all of the control files before over-writing them!

The first thing to do is to get the name of the damaged control file. Again, this is relatively easy. Look in the alert log for a section like this one:

```
Sat Feb 21 13:46:19 1998
alter database  mount exclusive
Sat Feb 21 13:46:20 1998
ORA-00202: controlfile: '/db/a/oradata/crash/control01.ctl'
ORA-27037: unable to obtain file status
SVR4 Error: 2: No such file or directory
```

Always make backups of all the control files before copying any of them on top of one another. The next step would be to copy a known good control file to the damaged control file's location.

Once that is done, return to Step 1 and try the startup mount again.

"But I don't have a good control file!"

It's possible that there may be no known good control file, which is what would happen if the remaining control files have different dates and/or sizes. If this is the case, it's probably best to use the *create controlfile* script.

To use the *create controlfile* script, proceed to Steps 4 through 7.

If that's not possible or probable, try the following procedure: First, make back-ups of all of the control files. Then, one at a time, try copying every version of each control file to all the other locations—excluding, the one that Oracle has already complained about, since it's obviously damaged.

 Each time a new control file is copied to multiple locations, return to Step 1.

For example, assume there are three control files: */a/control1.ctl*, */b/control2.ctl*, and */c/control3.ctl*. The alert log says that the */c/control3.ctl* is damaged, and since */a/control1.ctl* and */b/control2.ctl* have different modification times, there's no way to know which one is good. Try the following steps:

First, make backup copies of all the files:

```
$ cp /a/control1.ctl /a/control1.ctl.sav
$ cp /b/control2.ctl /b/control2.ctl.sav
$ cp /c/control3.ctl /c/control3.ctl.sav
```

Second, try copying one file to all locations. Skip *control3.ctl*, since it's obviously damaged. Try starting with *control1.ctl*:

```
$ cp /a/control1.ctl /b/control2.ctl
$ cp /a/control1.ctl /c/control3.ctl
```

Now attempt a startup mount:

```
$ svrmgrl
SVRMGR > connect internal;
Connected.
SVRMGR > startup mount
Sat Feb 21 15:43:21 1998
alter database  mount exclusive
Sat Feb 21 15:43:22 1998
ORA-00202: controlfile: '/a/control3.ctl'
ORA-27037: unable to obtain file status
```

This error says that the file that was copied to all locations is also damaged. Now try the second file, *control2.ctl*:

```
$ cp /b/control2.ctl /a/control1.ctl
$ cp /b/control2.ctl /a/control3.ctl
```

Now attempt to do a startup mount:

```
SVRMGR > startup mount;
ORACLE instance started.
Total System Global Area  5130648 bytes
```

```
Fixed Size                              44924 bytes
Variable Size                         4151836 bytes
Database Buffers                       409600 bytes
Redo Buffers                           524288 bytes
Database mounted.
```

It appears that *control2.ctl* was a good copy of the control file.

Once the attempt to mount the database is successful, proceed to Step 10.

Step 4: Are All Datafiles and Redologs OK?

Steps 4 and 5 are required only prior to performing Step 6.

The *create controlfile* script described in Step 7 works only if all the datafiles and online redologs are in place. The datafiles can be older versions that were restored from backup, since they will be rolled forward by the media recovery. However, the online redologs must be current and intact for the *create controlfile* script to work.

The reason that this is the case is that the rebuild process looks at each datafile as it is rebuilding the control file. Each datafile contains a System Change Number (SCN) that corresponds to a certain online redolog. If a datafile shows that it has an SCN that is more recent than the online redologs that are available, the control file rebuild process will abort.

If it's likely that one or more of the datafiles or online redologs is damaged, go to Step 5. If it's more likely that they are all intact, go to Step 6.

Step 5: Recover Damaged Datafiles or Redologs

If one or more of the datafiles or online redologs are definitely damaged,* follow all the instructions given here to see if there are any other damaged files. (A little extra effort now will save a lot of frustration later.) If it's possible that all the datafiles and online redologs are OK, another option would be to skip this step and try to re-create the control file now. (An unsuccessful attempt at this will not cause any harm.) If it fails, return to this step. If there is plenty of time, go ahead and perform this step first.

> To try to re-create the control files now, proceed to Step 6.

The first thing to find out is where all of the datafiles and redologs are. To determine this, run the following command on the mounted, closed database:

```
SVRMGR > connect internal;
Connected.
SVRMGR > select name from v$datafile;
(Example output below)
SVRMGR > select group#, member from v$logfile;
(Example output below)
```

Example 15-1 contains sample output from these commands.

Example 15-1. Sample v$datafile and v$logfile Output

```
SVRMGR > select name from v$datafile;
NAME
--------------------------------------------------------------------------------
/db/Oracle/a/oradata/crash/system01.dbf
/db/Oracle/a/oradata/crash/rbs01.dbf
/db/Oracle/a/oradata/crash/temp01.dbf
/db/Oracle/a/oradata/crash/tools01.dbf
/db/Oracle/a/oradata/crash/users01.dbf
/db/Oracle/a/oradata/crash/test01.dbf
6 rows selected.
SVRMGR > select group#, member from v$logfile;
MEMBER
--------------------------------------------------------------------------------
1 /db/Oracle/a/oradata/crash/redocrash01.log
3 /db/Oracle/c/oradata/crash/redocrash03.log
2 /db/Oracle/b/oradata/crash/redocrash02.log
```

---

* For example, you might be performing this step after a failed run of the *create controlfile* script. If so, that script would have told you which file is missing or corrupted. You also might know this if you know which filesystems were damaged.

Example 15-1. Sample v$datafile and v$logfile Output (continued)

```
1 /db/Oracle/b/oradata/crash/redocrash01.log
2 /db/Oracle/a/oradata/crash/redocrash03.log
3 /db/Oracle/c/oradata/crash/redocrash02.log
6 rows selected.
SVRMGR >
```

Look at each of the files shown by the preceding command. First, look at the datafiles. Each of the datafiles probably has the same modification time, or there might be a group of them with one modification time and another group with a different modification time. The main thing to look for is a missing file or a zero-length file. Something else to look for is one or more files that have a modification time that is newer than the newest online redolog file. If a datafile meets any one of these conditions, it must be restored from backup.

Redolog files, however, are a little different. Each redolog file within a log group should have the same modification time. For example, the output of the preceding example command shows that */db/Oracle/a/oradata/crash/redocrash01.log* and */db/Oracle/a/oradata/crash/redocrash01.log* are in log group 1. They should have the same modification time and size. The same should be true for groups 2 and 3. There are a couple of possible scenarios:

One or more log groups has at least one good and one damaged log

> This is why redologs are mirrored! Copy the good redolog to the damaged redolog's location. For example, if */db/Oracle/a/oradata/crash/redocrash01.log* was missing, but */db/Oracle/a/oradata/crash/redocrash01.log* was intact, issue the following command:

> ```
> $ cp /db/Oracle/a/oradata/crash/redocrash01.log \
>      /db/Oracle/a/oradata/crash/redocrash01.log.
> ```

All redologs in at least one log group are damaged

> This is a bad place to be. The "create controlfile" script in Step 6 requires that all online redologs be present. If even one log group is completely damaged, it will not be able to rebuild the control file. This means that the only option available now is to proceed to Steps 23 and 24—a complete recovery of the entire database followed by an *alter database open resetlogs*.

Mirror, Mirror, Mirror!

Losing all members of any log group is the only scenario under which data loss is assured. There is also a good chance of referential integrity corruption. Therefore, protect against it at all costs. Make sure the online redologs are mirrored!

Making it happen is easy. First, determine where the mirrored redologs are going to reside. Remember that if the redolog is mirrored three times, it means Oracle will have to write every change to all three logs. That means that all three mirrors should be on the fastest disks available. Make sure that the different mirrors also are located on different disks!

For this example, assume that there are three log groups with one member each. Here is the output of a *select group#, member from v$logfile*:

```
1 /logs1redolog01.log
2 /logs1redolog02.log
3 /logs1redolog03.log
```

For this example, we will mirror these three logs to */logs2* and */logs3*. I prefer to keep the filenames of the members of a log group the same. Therefore, in this example, *redolog01.log* will be mirrored to */logs1*, */logs2*, and */logs3*. To do this, we issue the following commands:

```
SVRMGR > alter database add logfile member
         '/logs2redolog01.log' to group 1;
Selection processed
SVRMGR > alter database add logfile member
         '/logs3redolog01.log' to group 1;
Selection processed
SVRMGR > alter database add logfile member
         '/logs2redolog02.log' to group 2;
Selection processed
SVRMGR > alter database add logfile member
         '/logs3redolog02.log' to group 2;
Selection processed
SVRMGR > alter database add logfile member
         '/logs2redolog03.log' to group 3;
Selection processed
SVRMGR > alter database add logfile member
         '/logs3redolog03.log' to group 3;
Selection processed
```

These commands will create three mirrors for each log group. This significantly decreases the chance that all members of a single log group could be damaged.

This is a drastic step! Make sure that *all* members of at least one log group are missing. (In the previous example, if both */db/Oracle/a/ oradata/crash/redocrash01.log* and */db/Oracle/a/oradata/crash/ redocrash01.log* were damaged, this database would require a complete recovery.)

If all the redologs in at least one group are damaged, and all the control files are damaged, proceed to Steps 23 and 24.

If the redologs are all right, but all the control files are missing, proceed to Step 6.

If the database will not open for some other reason, proceed to Step 10

Step 6: Is There a create controlfile Script?

 Steps 4 and 5 must be completed prior to this step.

The *svrmgr* command *alter database backup control file to trace* creates a trace file that contains a *create controlfile* script. This command should be run from *cron* on a regular basis. To find out if there is such a script available, follow these instructions. The first thing to find out is the destination of the trace files. This is specified by the user_dump_dest value in the *configinstance.ora* file, usually located in *$ORACLE_HOME/dbs*. (Typically, it is *$ORACLE_BASE/$ORACLE_SID/admin/ udump*.) First *cd* to that directory, then *grep* for the phrase CREATE CONTROLFILE, as shown in Example 15-2.

Example 15-2. Locating the Most Recent create controlfile Script

```
$ cd $ORACLE_HOME/dbs; grep user_dump_dest configcrash.ora
user_dump_dest                = /db/Oracle/admin/crash/udump
$ cd /db/Oracle/admin/crash/udump ; grep 'CREATE CONTROLFILE' * \
  |awk -F: '{print $1}'|xargs ls -ltr
-rw-r-----  1 Oracle   dba          3399 Oct 26 11:25 crash_ora_617.trc
-rw-r-----  1 Oracle   dba          3399 Oct 26 11:25 crash_ora_617.trc
-rw-r-----  1 Oracle   dba          1179 Oct 26 11:29 crash_ora_661.trc
```

In Example 15-2, *crash_ora_661.trc* is the most recent file to contain the "create controlfile" script.

If there is a *create controlfile* script, proceed to Step 7. If there is not a *create controlfile* script, and all the control files are missing, proceed to Step 8.

Step 7: Run the create controlfile Script

First, find the trace file that contains the script. The instructions on how to do that are in Step 6. Once you find it, copy it to another filename, such as *rebuild.sql.* Edit the file, deleting everything above the phrase # The following commands will create, and anything after the last SQL command. The file then should look something like the one in Example 15-3.

Example 15-3. Example create controlfile Script

```
# The following commands will create a new control file and use it
# to open the database.
# Data used by the recovery manager will be lost. Additional logs may
# be required for media recovery of offline datafiles. Use this
# only if the current version of all online logs are available.
STARTUP NOMOUNT
CREATE CONTROLFILE REUSE DATABASE "CRASH" NORESETLOGS ARCHIVELOG
    MAXLOGFILES 32
    MAXLOGMEMBERS 2
    MAXDATAFILES 30
    MAXINSTANCES 8
    MAXLOGHISTORY 843
LOGFILE
  GROUP 1 '/db/a/oradata/crash/redocrash01.log'  SIZE 500K,
  GROUP 2 '/db/b/oradata/crash/redocrash02.log'  SIZE 500K,
  GROUP 3 '/db/c/oradata/crash/redocrash03.log'  SIZE 500K
DATAFILE
  '/db/a/oradata/crash/system01.dbf',
  '/db/a/oradata/crash/rbs01.dbf',
  '/db/a/oradata/crash/temp01.dbf',
  '/db/a/oradata/crash/tools01.dbf',
  '/db/a/oradata/crash/users01.dbf'
;
# Recovery is required if any of the datafiles are restored backups
# or if the last shutdown was not normal or immediate.
RECOVER DATABASE
# All logs need archiving and a log switch is needed.
ALTER SYSTEM ARCHIVE LOG ALL;
# Database can now be opened normally.
ALTER DATABASE OPEN;
# Files in read-only tablespaces are now named.
ALTER DATABASE RENAME FILE 'MISSING00006'
  TO '/db/a/oradata/crash/test01.dbf';
# Online the files in read-only tablespaces.
ALTER TABLESPACE "TEST" ONLINE;
```

Once the file looks like Example 15-3, add the following line just above the STARTUP NOMOUNT line:

```
connect internal;
```

After you add this line, run the following command on the mounted, closed database, substituting *rebuild.sql* with the appropriate name:

```
$ svrmgrl < rebuild.sql
```

If all of the datafiles and online redolog files are in place, this will work without intervention and completely rebuild the control files.

 If any of this instance's datafiles are missing, return to Step 4. However, if any of this instance's online redologs are damaged or missing, *this option will not work*; proceed to Step 8.

Step 8: Restore Control Files and Prepare the Database for Recovery

 This step is required only if Steps 2 through 7 have failed.

If the precautions mentioned elsewhere in this chapter were followed, there is really only one scenario that would result in this position—loss of the entire system due to a cataclysmic event. Loss of a disk drive (or even multiple disk drives) is easily handled if the control files are mirrored. Even if all control files are lost, they can be rebuilt using the trace file created by running the *backup control file to trace* command. The only barrier to using that script is if all members of an online log group are missing. The only way that you could lose all mirrored control files and all members of a mirrored log group would be a complete system failure, such as a fire or other natural disaster. And if that is the case, then a complete database recovery would be more appropriate.

But I didn't mirror my control files or my online redologs

Follow the next steps, starting with restoring the control files from backup. Chances are that the database files will need to be restored as well. This is because one cannot use a control file that is older than the most recent database file. (Oracle will complain and abort if this happens.) To find out if the control file

---

Stay Away From This Step!

Hopefully, this section is for learning purposes only, because it's not a situation to be in. Recovering from the loss of all control files (without the use of the *create controlfile* script) requires opening the database with the *resetlogs* option. When forced to do this, there are two negative ramifications.

The first is that the referential integrity of the database is in question. "Referential integrity" refers to maintaining the integrity of the relationships between different tuples (or rows) within a given database. For example, suppose the customer table says that Joe Smith is to receive the items on invoice number 2004. If invoice number 2004 is deleted from the invoices table, that is referred to as a referential integrity problem. The chances of this can be reduced with proper SQL coding. As long as all related transactions are contained within a single *begin transaction* and *end transaction* statement, referential integrity theoretically should not be a problem. In the preceding example, this would mean that the creation of invoice 2004 in the invoices table and the update to choose Smith's record would be contained within a single transaction. That way, a rollback of either update would force a rollback of the other update.

The second negative ramification of opening the database with the *resetlogs* option is that Oracle cannot use redologs to roll through this action. Consider this drawing:

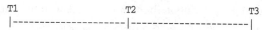

Suppose that a backup was made at time T1 and an *open database resetlogs* performed at time T2. Also suppose that a backup was not taken immediately after the recovery, and it is now time T3. You might think that you could take the backup from time T1 and use the redologs to roll forward to time T3, but that is not possible if an *alter database open resetlogs* was performed at time T2. That is why you *must* perform an immediate backup after opening the database with the *resetlogs* option.

---

is newer than the datafiles, try the following steps without overwriting the database files and see what happens:

Restore control files from backup

The very first step in this process is to find and restore the most recent backup of the control file. This would be the results of a *backup control file to* `filename` command. This is the only supported method of backing up the control file. Some people (*oraback.sh* included) also copy the control file manually. If there is a manual copy of the control file that is more recent than an "official" copy, try to use it first. However, if it doesn't work, use a backup

copy created by the *backup control file to* `filename` command. Whatever
backup control file is used, copy it to all of the locations and filenames listed
in the *configORACLE_SID.ora* file after the phrase `control_files`:

```
control_files          = (/db/Oracle/a/oradata/crash/control01.ctl,
                          /db/Oracle/b/oradata/crash/control02.ctl,
                          /db/Oracle/c/oradata/crash/control03.ctl)
```

Again, this backup control file must be more recent than the most recent database file in the instance. If this isn't the case, Oracle will complain.

Startup mount

To find out if the control file is valid and has been copied to all of the correct
locations, attempt to start up the database with the *mount* option. (This is the
same command from Step 1.) To do this, run the following command on the
mounted, closed database:

```
$ svrmgrl
SVRMGR > connect internal;
Connected.
SVRMGR > startup mount;
Statement processed.
SVRMGR > quit
```

Take read-only tablespaces offline

Oracle does not allow read-only datafiles to be online during a *recover
database using backup control file* action. Therefore, if there are any read-only
datafiles, take them offline. To find out if there are any read-only datafiles,
issue the following command on the mounted, closed database:

```
$ svrmgrl
SVRMGR > connect internal;
Connected.
SVRMGR > select enabled, name from v$data file;
Statement processed.
SVRMGR > quit
```

For each read-only datafile, issue the following command on a mounted,
closed database:

```
$ svrmgrl
SVRMGR > connect internal;
Connected.
SVRMGR > alter database data file 'filename' offline;
Statement processed.
SVRMGR > quit
```

Once this step has been completed, proceed to Step 9.

Step 9: Recover the Database

 This step is required only if Steps 2 through 7 have failed.

Once the control file is restored with a backup copy, attempt to recover the database using the backup control file.

Attempt to recover database normally

Since recovering the database with a backup control file requires the *alter database open resetlogs* option, it never hurts to try recovering the database normally first:

```
$ svrmgrl
SVRMGR > connect internal;
Connected.
SVRMGR > recover database;
```

If the backup control file option is required, Oracle will complain:

```
SVRMGR > recover database
ORA-00283: Recover session cancelled due to errors
...
ORA-01207: file is more recent than controlfile - old controlfile
```

 If the recover database command works, proceed to Step 10. If it doesn't, then attempt to recover the database using the backup control file, as described below.

Attempt to recover database using backup control file

Attempt to recover the database using the following command on the mounted, closed database:

```
$ svrmgrl
SVRMGR > connect internal;
Connected.
SVRMGR > recover database using backup controlfile
```

If it works, the output will look something like Example 15-4.

Example 15-4. Sample Output of recover database Command

```
ORA-00279: change 38666 generated at 03/14/98 21:19:05 needed for thread 1
ORA-00289: suggestion : /db/Oracle/admin/crash/arch/arch.log1_494.dbf
ORA-00280: change 38666 for thread 1 is in sequence #494
```

If Oracle complains, there are probably some missing or corrupted datafiles. If so, return to Steps 4 and 5. Once any missing or corrupted datafiles are restored, return to this step and attempt to recover the database again.

Sometimes you can be trapped in a catch-22 when recovering databases and Oracle is complaining about datafiles being newer than the control file. The only way to get around this is to use a backup version of the datafiles that is older than the backup version of the control file. Media recovery will roll forward any changes that this older file is missing.

Apply all archived redologs

Oracle will request all archived redologs since the time of the oldest restored datafile. For example, if the backup that was used to restore the datafiles was from three days ago, Oracle will need all archived redologs created since then. Also, the first log file that it asks for is the oldest log file that it wants.

The most efficient way to roll through the archived redologs is to have all of them sitting uncompressed in the directory that it suggests as the location of the first file. If this is the case, simply enter *auto* at the prompt. Otherwise, specify alternate locations or press enter as it asks for each one, giving time to compress or remove the files that it no longer needs.

Apply online redologs if they are available

If it is able to do so, Oracle will automatically roll through all the archived redologs and the online redolog. Then it says, `Media recovery complete`.

However, once Oracle rolls through all the archived redologs, it may prompt for the online redolog. It does this by prompting for an archived redolog with a number that is higher than the most recent archived redolog available. This means that it is looking for the online redolog. Try answering its prompt with the names of the online redolog files that you have. Unfortunately, as soon as you give it a name it doesn't like, it will make you start the *recover database using backup controlfile* command again.

For example, suppose that you have the following three online redologs:

```
/oracle/data/redolog01.dbf
/oracle/data/redolog02.dbf
/oracle/data/redolog03.dbf
```

When you are prompting for an archived redolog that has a higher number than the highest numbered archived redolog that you have, answer the prompt with one of these files (e.g., */oracle/data/redolog01.dbf*). If the file that you give it does not contain the recovery thread it is looking for, you will see a message like the following:

```
ORA-00310: archived log contains sequence 2; sequence 3 required
ORA-00334: archive log: '/oracle/data/redolog01.dbf'
```

Oracle will cancel the recovery database, requiring you to start it over. Once you get to the same prompt again, respond with a different filename, such as */oracle/data/redolog02.dbf*. If it contains the recovery thread it is looking for, it will respond with a message like the following:

```
Log applied.
Media recovery complete.
```

If, after trying all the online redologs, it is still asking for a log that you do not have, simply enter CANCEL.

Alter database open resetlogs

Once the media recovery is complete, the next step is to open the database. As mentioned earlier, when recovering the database using a backup control file, it must be opened with the *resetlogs* option. Do this by entering:

```
$ svrmgrl
SVRMGR > connect internal;
Connected.
SVRMGR > alter database open resetlogs;
SVRMGR > quit
```

Take a backup immediately after recovering the database with the resetlogs option! It is best if it is a cold backup after shutting down the database. Perform a hot backup if absolutely necessary, but realize that there is a risk that:

- The entire recovery might need to be performed again.

- All changes made after using the *resetlogs* option will be lost.

If the database did not open successfully, return to Step 1 and start over.

If the database did open successfully, perform a backup of the entire database immediately—preferably a cold one. Congratulations! You're done!

Step 10: Does "alter database open" Work?

If the *startup mount* worked, this is actually only the second step that you will perform. Mounting the database only checks the presence and consistency of the control files. If that works, opening the database is the next step. Doing so will check the presence and consistency of all datafiles, online redolog files, and any rollback segments. To open the database, run the following command on the mounted, closed database:

```
$ svrmgrl
SVRMGR > connect internal;
Connected.
SVRMGR > alter database open;
SVRMGR > quit
```

If the attempt to open the database worked, Oracle will simply say, "Statement processed." If this is the first attempt to open the database, and no datafiles or rollback segments were taken offline, you're done!

 If directed to this step by Steps 26 or 28 (damaged log groups) and the attempt to open the database failed, return to Step 23 to recover the entire database.

If the database did open, proceed to Step 15.

If the attempt to open the database did *not* work, the output will vary depending on the condition. Here is a listing of what those conditions may be, accompanied by what the error might look like when that condition occurs:

Missing datafile

```
ORA-01157: cannot identify data file 1 - file not found
ORA-01110: data file 1: '/db/Oracle/a/oradata/crash/system01.dbf'
```

Corrupted datafile

A corrupted datafile can generate a number of different errors. For instance, it may mimic a missing datafile:

```
ORA-01157: cannot identify data file 1 - file not found
ORA-01110: data file 1: '/db/Oracle/a/oradata/crash/system01.dbf'
```

It also may completely confuse Oracle:

```
ORA-00600: internal error code, arguments: [kfhcfh1_01], [0], [], [], [],
```

A corrupted datafile also may cause a "failed verification check" error:

```
ORA-01122: database file 1 failed verification check
ORA-01110: data file 1: '/db/Oracle/a/oradata/crash/system01.dbf'
ORA-01200: actual file size of 1279 is smaller than correct size of 40960
blocks
```

These are just a few examples of the types of errors that Oracle may give if a datafile is corrupted.

Missing member of any online log group

If the redologs are mirrored and one or more of the mirrored copies are lost but at least one good copy of each online redolog remains, Oracle will open the database without any errors displayed to the terminal.* The only error will be a message like the following one in the alert log:

```
Errors in file /db/Oracle/admin/crash/bdump/crash_lgwr_10302.trc:
ORA-00313: open failed for members of log group 2 of thread 1
```

All members of any online log group are corrupted

However, if all members of any online log group are corrupted, Oracle *will* complain and the database will not open. The error might look something like this:

```
ORA-00327: log 2 of thread 1, physical size  less than needed
ORA-00312: online log 2 thread 1: '/db/Oracle/b/oradata/crash/
redocrash02.log'
ORA-00312: online log 2 thread 1: '/db/Oracle/a/oradata/crash/
redocrash03.log'
```

Missing all members of any online log group

A similar problem is if all members of an online log group are missing. Oracle will complain and the database will not open. The error looks something like this:

```
ORA-00313: open failed for members of log group 2 of thread 1
ORA-00312: online log 2 thread 1: '/db/Oracle/b/oradata/crash/
redocrash02.log'
ORA-00312: online log 2 thread 1: '/db/Oracle/a/oradata/crash/
redocrash03.log'
```

Damaged rollback segment

If a rollback segment is damaged, the error will be like the following one:

```
ORA-01545: rollback segment 'USERS_RS' specified not available

Cannot open database if all rollback segments are not available.
```

Damaged datafile

A damaged datafile actually is very easy to recover from. This is a good thing, because this will occur more often than any other problem. Remember that there is only one copy of each datafile, unlike online redologs and control files that can be mirrored. So, statistically speaking, it's easier to lose one datafile than to lose all mirrored copies of a log group or all mirrored copies of the control file.

---

* I'm sure they consider this a feature, but it sure would be nice if it would at least complain. It's great that it opens the database. I just wish that this potentially dangerous situation was a little more visible.

Oracle also has the ability to recover parts of the database while other parts of the database are brought online. Unfortunately, this helps only if a partially functioning database is of any use to the users in your environment. Therefore, a database that is completely worthless unless all tables are available will not benefit from the partial online restore feature. However, if the users can use one part of the database while the damaged files are being recovered, this feature may help to save face by allowing at least partial functionality during an outage.*

There are three types of datafiles as far as recovery is concerned:

The first is a datafile that is not a part of the *system* tablespace and does not contain any rollback segments. Recovering this file (with the database online or offline) is very easy.

The second type of datafile is also a nonsystem datafile but one that happens to contain a rollback segment. Since rollback segments are needed to open the database, recovering such a file with the database online is difficult.

The final type of datafile is a file contained within the *system* tablespace. This datafile cannot be recovered with the database online, because the database cannot be brought online without it.

Damaged log group

If all members of a log group are damaged, there is a great potential for data loss. The entire database may have to be restored, depending on the status of the log group that was damaged and the results of some attempts at fixing it. This may seem like a broken record, but this is why mirroring the log groups is so important.

If the error refers to a damaged log group, one option is to proceed directly to Step 17. However, to verify that nothing else is wrong, read the rest of this step and proceed to the next one.

Damaged rollback segment

Since Oracle has to open the datafiles that contain this rollback segment before it can verify that the rollback segment is available, this error will not occur unless a datafile has been taken offline. If Oracle encounters a damaged datafile (whether or not it contains a rollback segment), it will complain about that datafile and abort the attempt to open the database.

---

* Since doing an online (partial) restore actually makes more work for you, you should seriously investigate whether this option will help if you use it—before you actually have to use it. That way, when you need to do a large restore, that question will already be answered.

Remember that a *rollback segment* is a special part of a tablespace that stores *rollback* information. Rollback information is needed in order to undo (or roll back) an uncommitted transaction. Since a crashed database will almost always contain uncommitted transactions, recovering a database with a damaged rollback segment is a little tricky. As previously mentioned, a damaged datafile may be taken offline, but Oracle will not open the database without the rollback segment.

The strategy for dealing with this is to make Oracle believe that the rollback segment doesn't exist. That will allow the database to be brought online. However, there will be transactions that need to be rolled back that require this rollback segment. Since Oracle believes this rollback segment is no longer available, these rollbacks cannot occur. This means that the database may be online, but portions of it will not be available.

For example, suppose that we create a table called *data1* inside tablespace *USERS*. Tablespace *USERS* contains the datafile */db/oracle/a/oradata/crash/users01.dbf*. Unfortunately, the database crashed before this transaction was committed, and the datafile that contains the rollback segment for this transaction was destroyed. In the process of recovering this database, we took that datafile offline, convinced Oracle that the rollback segment it contained was not needed, and opened the database. If we run the command *select * from data1*, we will receive the error shown in Example 15-5.

Example 15-5. Sample Datafile Error

```
$ svrmgrl
SVRMGR > connect internal;
Connected.
SVRMGR > select * from data1;
C1
------------
ORA-00376: file 7 cannot be read at this time
ORA-01110: datafile 7: '/db/oracle/a/oradata/crash/users01.dbf'
```

This is because Oracle does not know if the uncommitted transactions in the datafile */db/oracle/a/oradata/crash/users01.dbf* have been rolled back or not. In order to make this database fully functional, the damaged datafile must be recovered and the rollback segment brought online.

Be aware, therefore, that if you bring a database online without all of its rollback segments, the database may be online—but it probably will not be fully functional.

If the error indicates that there is a damaged rollback segment, proceed to Step 18.

Before going any farther . . .

Remember that Oracle will stop attempting to open the database as soon as it encounters an error with one file. This means, of course, that there could be other files that are damaged. If there is at least one damaged datafile, now is a good time to check and see if there are other files that are damaged. Detailed instructions on how to do that are provided in Step 5.

Once you know the names of all the damaged files, you may recover them as described below.

How media recovery works

If any datafiles are restored from backup, the *svrmgr recover* command will be needed. This command uses the archived and online redologs to redo any transactions that have occurred since the time that the backup of a datafile was taken. You can recover a complete database, a tablespace, or a datafile by issuing the commands *recover database, recover tablespace tablespace_name* and *recover datafile data_file_name*, respectively. These commands are issued inside a *svrmgr* shell. For example:

```
$ svrmgrl
SVRMGR > connect internal
SVRMGR > startup mount
SVRMGR > recover datafile '/db/Oracle/a/oradata/crash/datafile01.dbf'
```

These commands allow the restore of an older version of a datafile and use redo to roll it forward to the point of failure. For example, if we took a backup of a datafile on Wednesday night, and that datafile was damaged on Thursday evening, we would restore that datafile from Wednesday night's backup. Of course many transactions would have occurred since Wednesday night, making changes to the datafiles that we restored. Running the command *recover* [*database* | *tablespace* | *data file*] would reapply those transactions to the restored datafile, rolling them forward to Thursday evening.

This recovery can work in a number of ways. After receiving the *recover* command, Oracle prompts for the name and location of the first archived redolog that it needs. If that log and all logs that have been made since that log are online, uncompressed, and in their original location, enter the word *AUTO*. This tells Oracle to assume that all files that it needs are online. It therefore can automatically roll through each log that it needs.

In order to do this, all files that Oracle will need must be online. First, get the name of the oldest file, since that is the first file it will need. That filename is displayed immediately after issuing the *recover* command:

```
ORA-00279: change 18499 generated at 02/21/98 11:49:56 needed for thread 1
ORA-00289: suggestion : /db/Oracle/admin/crash/arch/arch.log1_481.dbf
ORA-00280: change 18499 for thread 1 is in sequence #481
Specify log: {<RET>=suggested | filename | AUTO | CANCEL}
```

In the preceding example, the first file that Oracle needs is */db/Oracle/admin/ crash/arch/arch.log1_481.dbf*. Make sure that this file is online and not compressed or deleted. If it is deleted, restore it from backup. If it is compressed, uncompress it and any archived redolog files in that directory that are newer than it. That is because Oracle may need all of them to complete the media recovery. It might be necessary to delete some of the older archived redologs to make enough room for the files that need to be uncompressed. Once all archived redologs that are newer than the one requested by Oracle have been restored and uncompressed, enter AUTO at the "Specify log" prompt.

If there isn't enough space for all of the archived redologs to be uncompressed, a little creativity may be required. Uncompress as many as possible, and then press Enter each time it suggests the next file. (Pressing Enter tells Oracle that the file that it is suggesting is available. If it finds that it is *not* available, it prompts for the same file again.) Once it has finished with one archive log, compress that log, and uncompress a newer log, since it will be needed it shortly. (Obviously, a second window is required, and a third window wouldn't hurt!)

At some point, it may ask for an archived redolog that is not available. This could mean some of the archived redologs or online redologs are damaged. If the file cannot be located or restored, enter CANCEL.

More detail on media recovery is available in Oracle's documentation.

 If any of the damaged datafiles is a member of the *system* tablespace, proceed to Step 12. If none of them is a member of the *system* tablespace, proceed to Step 13.

Step 11: Damaged System File?

If the damaged file is part of the *system* tablespace, an offline recovery is required. All other missing datafiles can be recovered with the database online. Unfortu-

---

Can You Run svrmgrl Commands Against a Down Database?

The next few steps require running several different *svrmgrl* commands to find out the status of certain parts of the database. All of the commands require that the database be mounted, but not open. When the database is in this state, queries can only be run against *fixed tables* (or *views*). Examples of such views are: *V$DATAFILE*, *V$LOGFILE*, *V$TABLESPACE*, and *V$LOG*.

For a complete list of fixed tables that are available when the database is mounted, run the following command on the mounted, closed database:

```
$ svrmgrl
SVRMGR > connect internal;
Connected.
SVRMGR > select * from V$FIXED_TABLE ;
```

---

nately, Oracle complains only that the datafile is missing—without saying what *kind* of datafile it is. Fortunately, even if Oracle is down, there is an easy way to determine which files belong to the *system* tablespace. (Finding out if the datafile contains a rollback segment is a little more difficult, but it is still possible.) To find out which datafiles are in the *system* tablespace, run the following command on the mounted, closed database:

```
$ svrmgrl
SVRMGR > connect internal;
Connected.
SVRMGR > select name from v$datafile where status = 'SYSTEM' ;
NAME
--------------------------------------------------------------------------------
/db/oracle/a/oradata/crash/system01.dbf
1 row selected.
```

This example report shows that the only file that is a member of the *system* tablespace is */db/Oracle/a/oradata/crash/system01.dbf*. In your configuration, however, there may be multiple datafiles in the *system* tablespace.

 If any of the damaged datafiles is a member of the *system* tablespace, proceed to Step 12. If none of them is a member of the *system* tablespace, proceed to Step 13.

Step 12: Restore All Datafiles in the SYSTEM Tablespace

Unlike other tablespaces, the *system* tablespace must be available in order to open the database. Therefore, if any members of the *system* tablespace are damaged, they must be restored now. Before doing this, make sure that the database is not open. (It is OK if it is mounted.) To make sure, run the following command on the mounted, closed database:

```
$ svrmgrl
SVRMGR > connect internal;
Connected.
SVRMGR > select status from v$instance;
STATUS
-------
MOUNTED
1 row selected.
```

(The preceding example shows that this instance is mounted, not open.)

If the database is not open, restore the damaged files from the most recent backup available. Once all damaged files in the *system* tablespace are restored, run the following command on the mounted, closed database:

```
$ svrmgrl
SVRMGR > connect internal;
Connected.
SVRMGR > recover tablespace system;
SVRMGR > media recovery complete
```

Once this command has completed, the *systems* tablespace will be recovered to the time of failure.

> If it does complete successfully, and no other datafiles are damaged, return to Step 10. For more information about the *recover tablespace* command, read the earlier section "How media recovery works" at the end of Step 10. If there are other datafiles to recover, proceed to Step 13.

Step 13: Damaged Nonsystem Datafile?

So far, we have mounted the database, which proves that the control files are okay. It may have taken some effort if one or more of the control files were damaged, but it succeeded. We also have verified that the *system* tablespace is intact, even if it required a restore and recovery. Most of the rest of this procedure concentrates on disabling damaged parts of the database so that it may be brought online as soon as possible. The process of elimination will identify all damaged datafiles once the database is opened successfully. They then can be easily restored.

    If there are damaged datafiles that are not part of the SYSTEM tablespace, proceed to Step 14. If there are no more damaged data-files, proceed to Step 17.

Step 14: Take Damaged Datafile Offline

To open a database with a damaged, nonsystem datafile, take the datafile offline. (If the file that is taken offline is part of a tablespace that contains rollback segments, there will be one other step, but we'll cross that bridge when we come to it.)

If this instance is operating in *ARCHIVELOG* mode, just take the datafile offline. It can be restored and recovered later, after the instance has been brought online. The command to do this is:

```
$ svrmgrl
SVRMGR > connect internal;
Connected.
SVRMGR > alter database datafile 'filename' offline;
```

If the instance is operating in *NOARCHIVELOG* mode, that's a different problem. Oracle does not allow the datafile to be taken offline, because it knows it can't be brought back online without media recovery. Without *ARCHIVELOG* mode, there is no media recovery. The only thing Oracle does allow is to drop the datafile entirely. This means, of course, that the tablespace that contains this file will have to be rebuilt from scratch. This is but one of the many reasons why a production instance should not be operating in *NOARCHIVELOG* mode. The command to do this is:

```
$ svrmgrl
SVRMGR > connect internal;
Connected.
SVRMGR > alter database datafile 'filename' offline drop;
```

    Once any damaged files are taken offline, return to Step 10 and attempt to open the database again.

Step 15: Were Any Datafiles Taken Offline?

 Perform this step only if the database has been opened.

This step is really a very simple question: If the database were opened without taking any datafiles offline, proceed to Step 29. If some datafiles were taken offline to open the database, proceed to Step 16. If unsure, proceed to Step 16.

Step 16: Bring Datafile(s) Back Online

First find out which datafiles were taken offline. To do this, run the following command:

```
$ svrmgrl
SVRMGR > connect internal;
Connected.
SVRMGR > select name from v$datafile where status = 'OFFLINE' ;
NAME
------------------
/db/oracle/a/oradata/crash/temp01.dbf
/db/oracle/a/oradata/crash/tools01.dbf
/db/oracle/a/oradata/crash/users01.dbf
```

Restore the damaged datafiles

Once the names of the datafiles that need to be restored are determined, restore them from the latest available backup. Once they are restored, recovery within Oracle can be accomplished in three different ways. These ways vary greatly in complexity and flexibility. Examine the following three media recovery methods and choose whichever one is best for you.

Datafile recovery

If there are a small number of datafiles to recover, this may be the easiest option. As each file is restored, issue the *recover datafile* command against it and then bring it online:

```
$ svrmgrl
SVRMGR > connect internal;
Connected.
SVRMGR > recover datafile 'datafile_name' ;
Statement processed.
SVRMGR > alter database datafile 'datafile_name' online ;
Statement processed.
```

The downside to this method is that media recovery may take a while for each datafile. If recovering multiple datafiles within a single tablespace, this is probably wasting time.

Tablespace recovery

This is the hardest of the methods, but it may work faster than the previous method if there are several damaged datafiles within a tablespace. If forced to leave the partially functional database open while recovering the damaged datafiles, and there are several of them to recover, this is probably the best option.[*]

First find out the names of all datafiles and the tablespace to which they belong. Since the database is now open, this can be done in one step, as demonstrated in Example 15-6.

Example 15-6. Listing of dba_data_files

```
$ svrmgrl
SVRMGR > connect internal;
Connected.
SVRMGR > select file_name, tablespace_name from dba_data_files;
Statement processed.
FILE_NAME
 TABLESPACE_NAME
-----------------------------------------------------------------------------
 -----------------------------
/db/oracle/a/oradata/crash/users01.dbf
 USERS
/db/oracle/a/oradata/crash/tools01.dbf
 TOOLS
/db/oracle/a/oradata/crash/temp01.dbf
 TEMP
/db/oracle/a/oradata/crash/rbs01.dbf
 RBS
/db/oracle/a/oradata/crash/system01.dbf
 SYSTEM
/db/oracle/a/oradata/crash/test01.dbf
 TEST
```

The only problem with this output is that it's not very easy to read and could be impossible to read if there are hundreds of datafiles. One way to make it easier to read is to modify the command, as shown in Example 15-7.

Example 15-7. Readable Listing of Datafiles

```
$ svrmgrl <<EOF |sed 's/  */        /' |sort >/tmp/files.txt
connect internal;
select file_name, tablespace_name from dba_data_files;
```

---

[*] Hopefully you can take the time to investigate these different options before disaster strikes and get to know which one works best for you.

Example 15-7. Readable Listing of Datafiles (continued)

```
quit;
EOF
$ grep '^/' /tmp/files.txt
/db/oracle/a/oradata/crash/rbs01.dbf      RBS
/db/oracle/a/oradata/crash/system01.dbf   SYSTEM
/db/oracle/a/oradata/crash/temp01.dbf     TEMP
/db/oracle/a/oradata/crash/test01.dbf     TEST
/db/oracle/a/oradata/crash/tools01.dbf    TOOLS
/db/oracle/a/oradata/crash/users01.dbf    USERS
```

This way, the files are sorted in alphanumeric order, making it easy to find the necessary file(s).

Once all of the datafiles are restored and the names of all the tablespaces that contain these datafiles have been determined, issue the *recover tablespace* command against each of those tablespaces. Before doing so, however, each of those tablespaces must be taken offline, as shown in Example 15-8.

Example 15-8. Tablespace-Based Recovery

```
$ svrmgrl
SVRMGR > connect internal;
Connected.
SVRMGR > alter tablespace tablespace_name1 offline;
Statement processed.
SVRMGR > recover tablespace tablespace_name1 ;
ORA-00279: change 18499 generated at 02/21/98 11:49:56 needed for thread 1
ORA-00289: suggestion : /db/Oracle/admin/crash/arch/arch.log1_481.dbf
ORA-00280: change 18499 for thread 1 is in sequence #481
Specify log: {<RET>=suggested | filename | AUTO | CANCEL}
Auto
Log applied
Media Recovery Complete
SVRMGR > alter tablespace tablespace_name1 online;
Statement processed.
SVRMGR > alter tablespace tablespace_name2 offline;
Statement processed.
SVRMGR > recover tablespace tablespace_name2 ;
ORA-00279: change 18499 generated at 02/21/98 11:49:56 needed for thread 1
ORA-00289: suggestion : /db/Oracle/admin/crash/arch/arch.log1_481.dbf
ORA-00280: change 18499 for thread 1 is in sequence #481
Specify log: {<RET>=suggested | filename | AUTO | CANCEL}
Auto
Log applied
Media Recovery Complete
SVRMGR > alter tablespace tablespace_name2 online;
Statement processed.
```

It's obvious that this method is quite involved! It's not pretty and it's not easy, but it allows recovery of multiple tablespaces while the instance continues to operate.

If a partially functioning database is of any value to the users, this method may be their best friend.

Database recovery

This is actually the easiest method, but it requires that the database be shut down to perform it. After restoring all the database files that were taken offline, close the database and issue the *recover database* command.

Once all the database files are restored, issued commands shown in Example 15-9.

Example 15-9. Normal Database Recovery

```
$ svrmgrl
SVRMGR > connect internal;
Connected.
SVRMGR > alter database close ;
Statement processed.
SVRMGR > recover database ;
ORA-00279: change 18499 generated at 02/21/98 11:49:56 needed for thread 1
ORA-00289: suggestion : /db/Oracle/admin/crash/arch/arch.log1_481.dbf
ORA-00280: change 18499 for thread 1 is in sequence #481
Specify log: {<RET>=suggested | filename | AUTO | CANCEL}
Auto
Log applied
Media Recovery Complete
SVRMGR > alter database open
Statement processed.
```

To make sure that all tablespaces and datafiles have been returned to their proper status, run the commands shown in Example 15-10.

Example 15-10. Obtaining the Names of all Datafiles, Control Files, and Log Files

```
$ svrmgrl
SVRMGR > connect internal;
Connected.
SVRMGR > select name, status from v$datafile
NAME
 STATUS
---------------------------------------------------------------------------------
 -------
/db/oracle/a/oradata/crash/system01.dbf
 SYSTEM
/db/oracle/a/oradata/crash/rbs01.dbf
 ONLINE
/db/oracle/a/oradata/crash/temp01.dbf
 ONLINE
/db/oracle/a/oradata/crash/tools01.dbf
 ONLINE
/db/oracle/a/oradata/crash/users01.dbf
 ONLINE
/db/oracle/a/oradata/crash/test01.dbf
```

Example 15-10. Obtaining the Names of all Datafiles, Control Files, and Log Files (continued)

```
ONLINE
6 rows selected.
SVRMGR > select member, status from v$logfile
NAME
 STATUS
------------------------------------------------------------------------
 -------
/db/oracle/a/oradata/crash/system01.dbf
 SYSTEM
/db/oracle/a/oradata/crash/rbs01.dbf
 ONLINE
/db/oracle/a/oradata/crash/temp01.dbf
 ONLINE
/db/oracle/a/oradata/crash/tools01.dbf
 ONLINE
/db/oracle/a/oradata/crash/users01.dbf
 ONLINE
/db/oracle/a/oradata/crash/test01.dbf
 ONLINE
6 rows selected.
SVRMGR> select * from v$controlfile;
STATUS   NAME

-------  ----------------------------------------------------------------
--------
        /db/oracle/a/oradata/crash/control01.ctl

        /db/oracle/b/oradata/crash/control02.ctl

        /db/oracle/c/oradata/crash/control03.ctl

3 rows selected.
```

Example 15-10 shows that all datafiles, control files, and log files are in good condition. (In the case of the log files and control files, no status is good status.)

> Once any datafiles that were taken offline have been restored and recovered, proceed to Step 29.

Step 17: Is There a Damaged Log Group?

When we refer to a "damaged log group," we mean that all members of a log group are damaged. If at least one member of a mirrored log group is intact, Oracle opens the database and simply puts an error message in the alert log. How-

ever, if all members of a log group are damaged, the database will not open, and
the error will look something like this:

```
ORA-00313: open failed for members of log group 2 of thread 1
ORA-00312: online log 2 thread 1: '/db/Oracle/b/oradata/crash/redocrash02.log'
ORA-00312: online log 2 thread 1: '/db/Oracle/a/oradata/crash/redocrash03.log'
```

If there is no error like this, there is no damaged log group. Proceed
to Step 18.

The first thing that must be determined is the status of the damaged log group.
The three possibilities are current, active, and inactive. To determine the status of
the damaged log group, run the following command on the mounted, closed database:

```
$ svrmgrl
SVRMGR > connect internal;
Connected.
SVRMGR > select group#, status from v$log;
```

The output looks something like this:

```
GROUP#      STATUS
----------  ----------------
         1  INACTIVE
         2  CURRENT
         3  ACTIVE
3 rows selected.
```

The preceding example shows that log group 1 is inactive, group 2 is current, and
group 3 is active. What follows is an explanation of the different statuses and how
each affects the recovery:

Current

> The current log group is the one to which Oracle was writing when the fail-
> ure occurred. It will still be listed as active until the server is brought online
> and a log switch occurs.

Active

> An active log group is usually the log group that Oracle just finished writing
> to. However, until a checkpoint occurs, this group is still needed for media
> recovery. Since a log switch always forces a checkpoint, a status of active is
> actually very rare. In fact, the only way to see this (before the system crashed)
> is to run the preceding command while a checkpoint is in progress. (In a
> properly tuned database, this is a very short period of time.)

Inactive

An inactive log group is one that is not being used by Oracle in any way.

To determine what action to take next, first give the number of the log group whose log files are damaged. In the preceding example error, it reads `open failed for members of log group` 2. Reference this number against the log groups listed by the *select * from v$log* command. In the previous example, log group 2 was current at the time the database crashed.

If the damaged log group was current, proceed to Step 22. If it was active, proceed to Step 25. If it was inactive, proceed to Step 27.

Step 18: Are Any Rollback Segments Unavailable?

If a rollback segment is damaged, Oracle will complain when attempting to open the database. The error looks like the following:

```
ORA-01545: rollback segment 'USERS_RS' specified not available

Cannot open database if all rollback segments are not available.
```

If you haven't already read the tip about damaged rollback segments in Step 10, do so now.

If the preceding error is displayed when attempting to open the database, proceed to Step 19. If not, return to Step 10.

Step 19: Does the Database Need to Be at Least Partially Up ASAP?

Because of the unique nature of damaged rollback segments, there are two choices for recovery. The first is to get the database open sooner, but that may leave it only partially functional for a longer period of time. The second choice takes a little longer to open the database, but once it is open it will not have datafiles that are needed for this rollback segment. Which is more important: getting even a partially functional database open as soon as possible or not opening the database until all rollback segments are available? The latter is more prudent, but the former may be more appropriate to the environment.

If the database needs to be partially open ASAP, proceed to Step 21. If it's more important to make sure all rollback segments are available prior to opening the database, proceed to Step 20.

Step 20: Recover Tablespace Containing Unavailable Rollback Segment

Perform this step only if directed to do so by Step 19.

The first thing that must be determined is which tablespace the damaged rollback segment is in. Unfortunately, there is no fixed view that contains this information. That means that it will have to be discovered through common sense and deduction. First, remember that this error is not displayed unless a datafile has been taken offline. To get a complete list of files that were taken offline, run the following command on a mounted, closed database:

```
$ svrmgrl
SVRMGR > connect internal;
Connected.
SVRMGR > select TS#, name from v$datafile where status = 'OFFLINE' ;
NAME
--------------------------------------------------------------------------
5  /db/oracle/a/oradata/crash/test01.dbf
1 row selected.
```

Then find out the name of the tablespace that contains this datafile:

```
$ svrmgrl
SVRMGR > connect internal;
Connected.
SVRMGR > select name from v$tablespace where TS# = '5' ;
NAME
--------------------------------------------------------------------------
TEST
1 row selected.
```

That was too easy!

Admittedly, the previous example was easy. There was only one datafile that was offline, which made finding its tablespace pretty easy. What if there were multiple datafiles that were contained within multiple tablespaces? How do we know which one contains the rollback segment? Unfortunately, there is no way to be sure while the database is closed. That is why it is very helpful to put the rollback segments in dedicated tablespaces that have names that easily identify them as such. It's even more helpful if the datafiles are named something helpful as well. For example, create a separate tablespace called *ROLLBACK_DATA*, and call its datafiles *rollback01.dbf, rollback02.dbf,* and so on. That way, anyone who lands in this scenario will know exactly which datafiles contain rollback data.

The rest of this step is simple. Restore any files that were taken offline, and use either the *recover datafile* or *recover tablespace* commands to roll them forward in time. If there are only one or two damaged datafiles, it's probably quicker to use the *recover datafile* command. If there are several damaged datafiles, especially if they are all in one tablespace, the *recover tablespace* command is probably easiest. Either way will work.

 Once any datafiles that contain rollback segments have been restored and recovered, return to Step 10 and attempt to open the database again.

Step 21: Comment Out Rollback Segment Line(s) in the init.ora File

---

 Perform this step only if directed to do so by Step 19.

There is a quicker way to open the database with damaged rollback segments. In order for Oracle to know what rollback segments to look for, the following line is inserted into the *initORACLE_SID.ora* file:

```
rollback_segments        = (r01,r02,r03,r04,users_rs)
```

(The *initORACLE_SID.ora* file usually is found in *$ORACLE_HOME/dbs*.) Since the preceding example error says that it is the *USERS_RS* rollback segment that is unavailable, simply delete that part of the line. It is wise, of course, to comment out and copy the original line.* First, shut down Oracle completely (this includes

---

* After you have opened the database, you are going to restore this tablespace and return this line to normal. Obviously, the easiest way to do that is to just uncomment the original line and delete the modified one.

un-mounting it as well). Then copy and comment the rollback segment line in the
initORACLE_SID.ora file:

```
#rollback_segments        = (r01,r02,r03,r04,users_rs)
rollback_segments         = (r01,r02,r03,r04)
```

> Once this change has been made in the *initORACLE_SID.ora* file,
> return to Step 10 to open the database.

Step 22: Is the Current Online Log Damaged?

> Perform this step only if instructed to do so by Step 17. Otherwise,
> return to Step 17 now.

If the current online log group is damaged, there would be a message like the following when attempting to open the database:

```
ORA-00313: open failed for members of log group 2 of thread 1
ORA-00312: online log 2 thread 1: '/db/Oracle/b/oradata/crash/redocrash02.log'
ORA-00312: online log 2 thread 1: '/db/Oracle/a/oradata/crash/redocrash03.log'
```

In the preceding example, a *select group#, status from v$log* command also would
have shown that log group 2 was *CURRENT* at the time of failure.

This is the worst kind of failure to have because there definitely will be data loss.
That is because the current online log is required to restart even a fully functioning database. The current control file knows about the current online log and will
attempt to use it. The only way around that is to restore an older version of the
control file. Unfortunately, you can't restore only the control file because the datafiles then would be more recent than the control file. The only remaining option is
to restore the entire database.

> If the current online redo log is damaged, proceed to Step 23. If not,
> proceed to Step 25.

Step 23: Recover All Database Files from Backup

There are only two reasons to perform this step. The first is if instructed to do so by Step 22. The other is if there were an unsuccessful attempt to open the database after performing either Steps 26 or 28. This step is the most drastic method of recovery and should not be performed unless absolutely necessary.

Perform this step only after verifying (or rebuilding or restoring) the control files, and verifying that all members of the current online log group are damaged. This procedure is relatively easy. Simply determine the names and locations of all of the datafiles and restore them from their latest backup.

Restore only the datafiles, not the control files. Do not restore or overwrite the control files unless instructed to do so by Step 9!

To determine the names of all the datafiles, run the following command on the mounted, closed database:

```
$ svrmgrl
SVRMGR > connect internal;
Connected.
SVRMGR > select name from v$datafile ;
```

Once all datafiles are restored, proceed to Step 24.

Step 24: alter database open resetlogs

Perform this step only if instructed to do so by Step 23. This is another drastic step that should be performed only if necessary!

This command causes Oracle to open the database after clearing all contents of the online redolog files. Since there is no way to undo this step, it is a good idea to make copies of the online redolog files now. To find out all their names, run the following command on a mounted, closed database:

```
$ svrmgrl
SVRMGR > connect internal;
Connected.
SVRMGR > select member from v$logfile ;
```

To create an "undo" option, copy each of these files to *filename.bak.*

After making a backup of the online redolog files, run the following command on a mounted, closed database:

```
$ svrmgrl
SVRMGR > connect internal;
Connected.
SVRMGR > alter database open resetlogs ;
Statement processed.
```

If the database opens, congratulations!

Make a backup of this database *immediately*, preferably with the database shut down. That is because Oracle cannot roll through this point in time using the redologs. Oracle *must* have a full backup taken after using the *open resetlogs* command in order to restore this database using any logs that are made after the *open resetlogs* was performed.

Once that backup is completed, you're done!

Step 25: Is an Active Online Redolog Damaged?

Perform this step only if instructed to do so by Step 17. If not, return to Step 17 now.

If an *ACTIVE* online log group is damaged, there will be a message like the following when attempting to open the database:

```
ORA-00313: open failed for members of log group 2 of thread 1
ORA-00312: online log 2 thread 1: '/db/Oracle/b/oradata/crash/redocrash02.log'
ORA-00312: online log 2 thread 1: '/db/Oracle/a/oradata/crash/redocrash03.log'
```

In the preceding example, a *select group#, status from v$log* command also would have shown that log group 2 was *ACTIVE* at the time of failure.

Remember that an *ACTIVE* log is one that is still needed for recovery. The reason that it is still needed is because a checkpoint has not flushed all changes from shared memory to disk. Once that happens, this log will no longer be needed.

> To perform a checkpoint, proceed to Step 26. If there are no damaged active online redologs, proceed to Step 27.

Step 26: Perform a Checkpoint

The way to attempt to recover from the scenario in Step 25 is to perform a checkpoint. If it is successful, the database should open successfully. To perform a checkpoint, issue the following command on the mounted, closed database:

```
$ svrmgrl
SVRMGR > connect internal;
Connected.
SVRMGR > alter system checkpoint local ;
Statement processed.
```

Be patient. The reason that there is an *ACTIVE* log group is that the checkpoint took a long time in the first place. Wait for Oracle to say that the checkpoint succeeded or failed. If it succeeded, Oracle will simply say, `Statement processed.` If it fails, there could be any number of Oracle errors.

> After issuing the checkpoint, even if it were unsuccessful, return to Step 10 and attempt to open the database. If this attempt fails, return to Step 23 and recover the entire database.

Step 27: Is an Inactive Online Redolog Damaged?

> Perform this step only if instructed to do so by Step 17. Otherwise, return to Step 17 now.

If an *INACTIVE* online log group is damaged, there would be a message like this when attempting to open the database:

```
ORA-00313: open failed for members of log group 2 of thread 1
ORA-00312: online log 2 thread 1: '/db/Oracle/b/oradata/crash/redocrash02.log'
ORA-00312: online log 2 thread 1: '/db/Oracle/a/oradata/crash/redocrash03.log'
```

In the preceding example, a *select group#, status from v$log* command also would have shown that log group 2 was *INACTIVE* at the time of failure.

In comparison, this one should be a breeze. An *INACTIVE* log is not needed by Oracle. If it is not needed, simply drop it and add another in its place.

To drop and add an *INACTIVE* log group, proceed to Step 28.

Step 28: Drop/Add a Damaged, INACTIVE Log Group

Perform this step only if instructed to do so by Step 27.

In all the previous examples, the damaged log group was group 2. Before we drop that group, we should make sure that we can add it back easily. Ensure that all the original redolog locations are still valid. To do this, get the names of all of the members of that log group:

```
$ svrmgrl
SVRMGR > connect internal;
Connected.
SVRMGR > select member from v$logfile where GROUP# = '2 ;
```

For this example, Oracle returned the values:

```
/logs1redolog01.dbf
/logs2redolog01.dbf
/logs3redolog01.dbf
```

Verify that the locations of all these files are still valid. For this example, assume that */logs3* is completely destroyed, and we are relocating all its contents to */logs4*. Therefore, the members of log group 2 will be */logs1redolog01.dbf, /logs2redolog01.db*, and */logs4redolog01.dbf.*

To drop log group 2, issue the following command on a mounted, closed database:

```
$ svrmgrl
SVRMGR > connect internal;
Connected.
SVRMGR > alter database drop logfile group 2 ;
Statement processed.
```

Once that command completes successfully, add the log group back to the database. To do this, issue the following command (Remember that we have replaced */logs3redolog01.dbf* with */logs4redolog01.dbf*):

```
$ svrmgrl
SVRMGR > connect internal;
Connected.
SVRMGR > alter database add logfile group 2 ('/logs1redolog01.dbf', '/
logs2redolog01.dbf', '/logs4redolog01.dbf') size 500K ;
Statement processed.
```

Once this command completes successfully, return to Step 10 and attempt to open the database.

Step 29: Were Any Rollback Segment Lines Changed in init.ora?

There was an option in Step 21 to comment out rollback segments from the *initORACLE_SID.ora* file. If that option were taken, there should be a line in that file that looks like the following:

```
#rollback_segments       = (r01,r02,r03,r04,users_rs)
rollback_segments        = (r01,r02,r03,r04)
```

If any rollback segments were taken offline, proceed to Step 30. If there were not, back up the database now. You're done! If you did comment out any rollback segments, proceed to Step 30.

Step 30: Return Offline Rollback Segments to Normal Condition

To check which rollback segments are offline, run the following command:

```
SVRMGR> select segment_name from dba_rollback_segs where status = 'OFFLINE' ;
SEGMENT_NAME
-------------------------------
USERS_RS
1 rows selected.
```

Since all datafiles and redolog files should be recovered by now, just return the offline rollback segments to an online status:

```
$ svrmgrl
SVRMGR > connect internal;
```

```
Connected.
SVRMGR > alter rollback segment users_rs online ;
Statement processed.
```

Once this has been completed, make sure that any commented lines in the *initORACLE_SID.ora* file are put back to their original condition. The example in Step 29 used the suggested method of commenting out the original line and changing a copy of it. Return the line in *initORACLE_SID.ora* to its original condition:

```
rollback_segments       = (r01,r02,r03,r04,users_rs)
```

This step ensures that the next time this database is opened, the *USERS_RS* rollback segment will be used.

You're Done!

If you've made it this far, you're done! All datafiles, control files, and log files should be online. Take a backup of the entire database immediately, preferably a cold one with the database down. If that can't be done, then perform a hot backup.

Logical Backups

Physical backups protect you from physical damage, such as a damaged disk drive. A logical backup protects you from logical damage, such as when your DBA accidentally deletes an important table. Logical backups are done by Oracle's *exp* utility (short for *export*), which stores the data in a binary file that is useful only to Oracle. Before deciding whether to implement logical backups for Oracle, though, consider carefully their advantages and disadvantages:

Locates data block corruption

This is probably the biggest advantage to logical backups. They actually examine the logical structure of the database as the export is being performed. Therefore, every data block is examined for consistency. Since this is not done with physical backups, this is the only way to know that there is no corruption of any data blocks anywhere in the database. (Of course, a user attempting to read a bad block would complain as well, but a logical backup reveals this problem *before* that user needs the block!)

Ability to import a single table

This may or may not be a benefit to everyone, depending on the structure of a given database. If there is a one-to-one relationship of tables to tablespaces, restoring the datafile probably is quicker than restoring from an export. If tables are partitioned across multiple tablespaces, it also is faster to use a physical recovery. However, if there are large tablespaces with multiple tables in them, then it might be much quicker to restore the table than to restore the entire tablespace. The only way to do this is with an export.

Multiple export levels

Oracle's export utility allows a complete (full), incremental, or cumulative export. The cumulative export exports only tables that have changed since the last cumulative or complete export. The incremental export exports only tables that have changed since the last incremental, cumulative, or complete. Although incremental and cumulative exports sound the same, they are not. Suppose exports were taken in the following order: a complete, a cumulative, an incremental, a second cumulative, then a second incremental. The second cumulative would export all tables since the first cumulative, but the second incremental would export only those tables that have changed since the second cumulative. Note that cumulative and incremental backups do not export changed *records*; they export changed *tables*. That means that if a single attribute is changed in a table, the entire table is exported.

Portable to other Oracle databases

Unlike backups of datafiles, exports can be imported into another Oracle database on the same machine or even on another machine. Physical backups can be used to restore an entire database to another machine, and then that restored database can be used to transfer the tables. However, this obviously takes longer than just loading an export.

No transaction recovery

It is very important to note that exports are a picture of the database at some point in time, and they can be used to recover that table only to that point in time. There is no way to apply transaction logs (redologs) on top of an imported table to bring it up to date. So although it might be quicker to restore a table using an import, it might be better just to restore the entire tablespace. The *recover until time* option can be used to redo all transactions except for the one that deleted the table.

Longer than physical backups

Exports take longer than physical backups since there is a lot of checking going on during the process. Depending on the speed of the system, this may be a little bit longer or quite a bit longer!

No intertable consistency

A snapshot is taken of a table just before exporting, so the data within that export is considered consistent. However, there is no guarantee of consistency between tables if the data is being changed while the export is going on. This also is known as a "lack of referential integrity." That is because a full (every table) export is still performed one table at a time.

Full export requires RESTRICT mode

Here is the biggest drawback of exports. Since Oracle cannot guarantee the referential integrity of an export taken while the database is operating normally, the database must be shut down and then opened in *RESTRICT* mode. That way no one can make changes to the database while the export is running. (Of course, this means that no one can access it either.)

Performing a Logical Backup

The type of export covered here is an export of the entire database, also known as a "full export." To do this, put the database in *RESTRICT* mode. Then perform the export and take it out of *RESTRICT* mode. The commands to do that are found in Example 15-11. Substitute the appropriate *username* and *password*, as well as the appropriate `level` (*complete*, *cumulative*, or *incremental*). (The username and password need to have the appropriate permissions to do an export.)

Example 15-11. Sample Database Export

```
$ export ORACLE_SID=ORACLE_SID
$ svrmgrl
svrmgr > connect internal;
svrmgr > shutdown immediate;
svrmgr > startup restrict open;
svrmgr > exit;

$ exp userid=username/passwd full=Y inctype=level constraints=Y file=file_name

$ svrmgrl
svrmgr > connect internal;
svrmgr > alter database disable restricted session;
svrmgr > exit;
```

This performs a full (every table), level `level` export of *ORACLE_SID* to *file_name*. For more information on the *exp* command, consult the *Oracle Utilities User's Guide*.

Recovering with a Logical Backup

If you made any logical backups, or exports, using Oracle's *exp* utility, they may be imported using Oracle's *imp* utility. In order to use the following command, you must substitute the appropriate *username*, *passwd*, and *file_name*. For level, you need to use *system* or *restore*. (When to use these levels is covered next.)

```
$ imp username/passwd inctype=level full=Y file=file_name
```

You actually can use exports to rebuild a deleted database. It will create the appropriate tables that it needs as it imports the data. Of course, if your intent is to re-create the same database, you need to create the same tablespaces that you had in the old database. Then you need to import the data in the following order:

1. Import the *most recent* export file (complete, cumulative, or incremental) with *inctype=system*. This restores the database definitions.

2. Bring all rollback segments online.

3. Import the most recent *complete* export file with *inctype=restore*.

4. Import, in chronological order, all *cumulative* exports since the most recent *complete* export, using *inctype=restore*.

5. Import, in chronological order, all *incremental* exports since the most recent *cumulative* export, using *inctype=restore*.

You also can import individual tables by using the *tables=`table_list`* option to the *imp* command. For more information on exports, consult the *Oracle Utilities User's Guide*.

A Broken Record

There are some common threads that appear throughout this chapter. Here they are once again:

Mirror the redologs

If all members (or the only member) of an *ACTIVE* or *CURRENT* log group are lost, there will be data loss. If the redologs are not mirrored, the chances of this happening are much greater than if the redologs are mirrored. If the redologs are mirrored, the chance that all members of a log group would be damaged is incredibly small. A little research and a little effort up-front will significantly reduce the chances of data loss.

Watch the alert log

Even if the redologs are mirrored, one or more members of a log group may be damaged while the database is operating. The only notification will be an entry in the alert log. Automate the checking of the alert logs for error messages. Otherwise, there may be only one functioning member of a log group, and you may not even know it.

Mirror the control files

A significant portion of this recovery procedure is dedicated to recovering from the loss of all control files. If they are not mirrored, they should be— another example that Prior Proper Planning Purges the Person from the Performance of Painful Procedures.

Use ARCHIVELOG mode

Without *ARCHIVELOG* mode, Steps 23 and 24 could replace the entire recovery procedure. If one datafile is lost, restore all of them and open the database with the *resetlogs* option. All changes since the last cold backup will be lost, and a cold backup is the only kind of backup possible, since hot backups require *ARCHIVELOG* mode.

16

Sybase Backup &
Recovery

Sybase has provided two utilities, *dump* and *bcp*, to facilitate the backup and recovery processes. But like Informix and Oracle, these utilities provide only a basic backup ability. At this point in time, using these utilities, it takes more than just running one simple command to make sure the data server can be restored from any calamity. Because running the various commands by hand could lead to errors (and lack of sleep for the operators), environments without a commercial utility must use backup scripts of some kind to automate the process and provide consistency. This chapter provides a solid foundation in Sybase backup and recovery techniques, so in case your server suffers an unexpected problem, the data server can be fully restored.

 This chapter was written by Bryn Smith, a senior consultant with Collective Technologies. Bryn started his career in computers back in sixth grade because of the encouragement and dedication of an exceptional teacher and friend, Dorothy Edwards at North Cow Creek School. Thank you Mrs. E! Bryn has come a long way since then, is now experienced at both system and database administration, and can be reached at *bryn@colltech.com*.

Sybase Architecture

As in the Oracle and Informix chapters, it is important to understand the design of the database that is being backed up. Therefore, this chapter starts with a discussion of Sybase architecture. This is similar to the information provided in Chapter 13, *Backing Up Databases*, but contains some specific information about Sybase. Just as in the overview chapter, we start with the power user's view of the database, then continue with that of the database administrator. This chapter uses only the Sybase-specific terms; to see how a term relates to Oracle or Informix, consult Chapter 13.

 All Transact-SQL (T-SQL) commands used in this chapter assume the user knows to enter the command *go* on a separate line to have Sybase begin processing it.

The Power User's View

Power users of your database know enough to call you and ask questions about the terms in this section. They probably won't know anything more than these terms, though.

Server

A *server* is a set of processes through which the Sybase database talks to shared memory. On a Unix system, the primary process that identifies a server is the *dataserver*. One of the command-line options used with this process is the *SERVER_ID*. When a Sybase server is started, all the databases within it become available. On a Unix system, a server is started with the *startserver –f RUN_FILE* command, where the *RUN_FILE* filename usually follows the pattern *RUN_SERVER_ ID*. Though the term "server" might make you think there is only one server allowed per machine, actually, you can have as many servers as your system's resources can support. In fact, for availability reasons, it might make sense to have multiple servers running per machine. Then if something goes wrong with one server, the other servers might not be affected unless it is a systemwide problem.

Database

The *database* is what most people think about when they are using an RDBMS product, because it contains all the data. It contains all the tables, all the indexes, and all other important database objects. A server can contain more than one database, but the opposite is not true; a database can reside on only one server. Like Oracle, technically a *server* is a set of processes through which the database talks to shared memory, processes user queries, and returns output. The *database* is the organized collection of the data itself.

Table

A *table* is a collection of related rows that all have the same attributes. In Sybase 11.5 and higher, a table can be *partitioned*, or spread across multiple page chains.

This should not be confused with operating system disk partitioning. This partitioning is used to provide a better degree of parallelism during queries and *bcp*s. (The *bcp* utility will be covered under "Logical Backups," later in this chapter.) Other than that, Sybase tables are the same as any other RDBMSs.

Index

A database *index* is analogous to an index in a book—it allows Sybase to find data quickly. Again, a Sybase index is the same as anyone else's index, and it presents no unique backup requirements. Because an index is *derived* from data in a table, it can be re-created during a restore. However, it is almost always going to be quicker to restore it than to re-create it.

Object

An *object* is any type of database object, such as a table or an index.

Row

A *row* is a collection of related attributes, such as all the information about a specific customer. Sybase also may refer to this as a *record*.

Attribute

An *attribute* is any specific value (also known as a column or field) within a row.

The DBA's View

The Sybase-specific terms that follow are those that are of interest to a database administrator. A power user should not need to know them.

Page

A *page* is the smallest piece of data that can be moved within the database. Sybase's page size is 2048 bytes and cannot be changed. Certain Sybase commands, such as *disk_init*, require a size in terms of blocks instead of bytes.

Extent

An *extent* is a collection of eight 2-K pages that Sybase treats as one unit. Whenever a table or index requires space, Sybase allocates another extent to the object.

Segment

A *segment* is a named collection of database devices available to a particular database. This is equivalent to Oracle's tablespaces and can be used to place database objects on specific devices. When a database is created, the segments *system*, *default*, and *logsegment* are created automatically. In addition to these segments, additional segments can be added using the *sp_addsegment* stored procedure. A database may contain several segments, which in turn can contain many objects, such as tables, indexes, and stored procedures.

Datafile

A Sybase *datafile* can be either a raw (disk device) or cooked (filesystem) file. Once created, the syntax to work with raw and cooked datafiles is the same. However, when doing a cold backup on raw devices, backup scripts should use a tool such as *dd*, since it can read data directly from the raw device.

Sybase recommends the use of raw devices whenever possible. By using raw devices, Sybase controls all input and output to the device rather than relying on the operating system to manage it. Most operating systems improve input/output performance by caching disk operations in memory and periodically writing them out to the physical disk. The problem with this is Sybase assumes the I/O has already been written to disk when the I/O completes. If the operating system stops while there are still items to write to disk, the disks will not match what Sybase thinks is out there, which can lead to corruption of the databases.

Partition

A *partition* is a chain of pages. A table can be partitioned into multiple partitions to allow a great degree of input/output parallelism.

Configuration file

The *configuration file* is new to Sybase 11. Before Version 11, a DBA who wanted to change a configuration option on a server would run *sp_configure* `configoption configvalue`, then *reconfigure*. The *sp_configure* command changes the configuration option `configoption` to the `configvalue` value, and `reconfigure` checks the new values to make sure they are reasonable and correct and then writes them to memory. But some of the value changes require a restart of the server. Unfortunately, those same changes might not allow the server to come up correctly. To fix one of these problems was a real pain. First, the DBA had to reset all the configuration values back to the default values using *buildmaster -r*. Then, each of the values that had been changed had to be restored by hand. Version 11 cleans up this problem by writing out a file containing all configuration options each time a reconfigure is run and by saving all previous versions of the file. The *dataserver* program also was modified to accept a *-c* `configfile` option. So, when some configuration change causes the server not to restart, the DBA now just has to rename the previous saved configuration file to the current configuration filename and restart. Also, a configuration option can now be changed just by editing the configuration file at the operating system level. This is not recommended, because reconfigure does not have a chance to validate the changes or ensure that the previous configuration file is saved.

Transaction

A *transaction* is any activity by a user or DBA that changes an attribute in a Sybase database. Logically, a transaction modifies an attribute, but what actually occurs physically is a modification to one or more blocks within the Sybase database.

Transaction log

A *transaction log* is a special system table (*syslogs*) in which all changes to the database are recorded. Transaction logging cannot be turned on or off for Sybase databases, but it can be thwarted in its primary duty—maximum recoverability—by setting database options like *truncate log on checkpoint.*

The transaction log is both a memory object and a disk object. When a transaction is going to change data, data first is read into memory cache, a page at a time. As each data page is changed in cache, a transaction log entry is written to its cache in memory. When no more data pages can be read into memory, the oldest data page is written out to disk along with its transaction log entry. When a transaction completes, all data pages are written to disk along with their transaction log entries.

Now, if the transaction changes more pages than can fit into memory, and the transaction takes a long time, there is a window of vulnerability when some of the changes are on disk but some changes are only in memory. If the server were to die at this point, when it came back up, the data on disk would be inconsistent. This is why there is a transaction log.

When the server restarts, it first reviews the transaction log on disk for all transactions that have not been committed and written fully to disk. It then uses the uncommitted entries to reverse the changes to the database. Once the database has been reverted to a fully committed version, it then is brought online with fully consistent data. If the database's transaction log was lost, the server could not bring up the database because it could not be sure of the consistency of the data.

The transaction log also is important in backups; it is used by Sybase to provide a way to recover a database to any point in time. It's also used to speed up the backup process. A full database backup can take a very long time and a lot of backup media, so many sites cannot afford to run a full backup every time.

Fortunately, since only the changes to the database are recorded in the transaction log, backing it up can take much less time than backing up the full database. Often a large site will do a full backup of the database maybe once a week and then back up the transaction logs every night. Recovery takes the step of first applying the last full database backup, then each of the backed-up transaction logs. Each dumped transaction log can be restored only in sequential order, oldest to newest. Sybase will complain if you try to restore a log out of order.

As an added feature as of Sybase 11.92, a database now can be restored to a specific point in time. Before this change, you could restore the database only up to the last transaction log backup. So, if someone added important data at 12:00 P.M. and then someone else deleted this data by accident at 2:00 P.M., before Version 11.92, you would have had no way to get this data back. Now, you can use the transaction logs to restore the database prior to the 2:00 P.M. deletion. Data is back, and the users are happy.

Stored procedure

A *stored procedure* is a collection of T-SQL statements and optional control-of-flow statements stored under a name. Sybase recommends using provided system-stored procedures to manipulate database objects rather than changing system tables by hand. In this chapter, we use only Sybase stored procedures whenever possible.

Checkpoint

A *checkpoint* is the time at which all data that is kept in memory is flushed to disk. In Sybase, a DBA can force a checkpoint with the *checkpoint* command. A checkpoint also is done periodically, with the time interval between checkpoints being configurable with various options. The time between checkpoints significantly impacts your recovery time. The more often you do a checkpoint, the quicker your database will be able to start up, since the number of transaction logs that it must review is very small. However, a high frequency of checkpoints also can negatively impact the speed of your database. Experiment with different checkpoint time values to find one that works best for you.

Interface(s) file

The *interface file* (also called the *interfaces file*) contains information used by Sybase processes to connect to other Sybase processes on the same machine and others. The DBA must use the *sybinit* program to add entries to this file. Using *sybinit* adds some encoded information to the entry that is required by Sybase.

However, once a server entry is in the interface file, a text editor can be used to delete it or copy it into another interface file. There must be an entry in the interface file for each data server the system needs to connect to, including itself.

Backup server

Versions of Sybase data server before 10 suffered significant performance problems during hot backups of the data. The problem was that the system was fighting with itself, trying to both back up the server in a consistent method and provide full database access. To fix this problem, Sybase decided to separate the backup processing to a separate backup server process. This allowed each process to concentrate on its primary task. Also, because the backup server runs independently of the data server, backups now could be run on any server and backed up to any other backup server reachable via the network.

The backup server has the ability to stripe the backup across a maximum total of 32 media devices and do multitape or multifile backups. The backup server can do two types of backups—full database dumps and incremental transactions dumps. When the backup server does a full backup, all the database pages that contain data are backed up along with the current transaction log. Using this backup, a full restore of the database can be accomplished and will contain all the changes up to the end of the backup.

The transaction log backup backs up the incremental changes since the last full database backup or transaction log backup. By first applying the full backup and then the transaction log backups, the database can be restored to a specific point in time.

If the database system and transaction logs are stored on separate physical devices, a transaction dump still can be accomplished even if the database system devices are damaged. You use the log segment to put the transaction log on a separate device. This allows the system to have up-to-the-minute recoverability. (See your Sybase documentation for information about how to do this.)

Dump device

Sybase provides two forms of dump devices, logical and physical. The logical dump devices are entries in the *sysdevices* table that point to physical devices like disk files and tape drives. The physical dump devices are the full pathnames to either hardware devices or disk files.

You might ask why Sybase provides these logical devices. One reason is to allow an easy way to unify backup scripts. For example, if one system had a tape drive called */dev/rmt5*, but another system used */dev/rmt0*, the script would have to be changed for each system. By creating a logical device, say *tapedump1*, on both systems, which points to their respective physical devices, the same script could refer to *tapedump1* and be used on each system.

To create a logical backup device, use the following T-SQL command:

```
sp_addumpdevice {"tape" | "disk"}, logicalname, physicalname [, tapesize]
```

If you are creating a dump device that points to a file or nontape device, use *disk* in your command. If you are creating one that points to a tape device, use *tape*. The `logicalname` is any name you want to call the new dump device. The `physicalname` is a sufficient pathname that points to the device, such as */dev/ rmt0* or */usr/backups/myback.dmp*. The `tapesize` refers to the maximum number of bytes the tape device can hold.

Protecting Your Database

When working with any database, the old maxim "an ounce of prevention is worth a pound of cure" holds true. Before covering how to perform a hot backup of your Sybase database, there are a few maintenance tasks performed using the *dbcc* utility that are part of Sybase's "ounce of prevention." In addition to these *dbcc* tasks, there are transaction log administrative tasks required to keep the data server healthy. If you follow these tasks, you will help maintain the database, keeping it running smoothly and ready for proper backups.

About transaction logs

As transactions are run on a database, entries are stored in the transaction log. If a large transaction is run, or many transactions are running at the same time, the transaction log space for that database could become full. When this happens, all processing on that database is halted and a warning message to all active users appears, explaining that space needs to be found for the transaction log.

There are two things an SA can do at this point:

- Add additional space to the transaction space by using the *alter database on log* command.

- Dump the transaction log and reset the pointer in it, freeing up space. If the transaction log is always filling up, then the log probably is undersized, and additional space should be added. If this is the first time the log has filled up, perform a *dump transaction with truncate_only* to free up space in the log.

Sometimes, though, the log gets so full that truncating it does not help. This sounds as if there is something wrong with the *dump transaction with truncate_only* command, but there is not. To understand what really happens in a transaction log, consider that there are two pointers in the transaction log. The first one points to the last transaction in the log; the second one points to the last committed transaction in the log. When a *dump transaction with truncate_only* is run, it resets the point of the committed transactions to the point of the last uncommitted transaction, freeing the space formerly occupied by committed transactions. But, if the log is completely full of uncommitted transactions, then there will be no space freed up.

When this happens, there are only two things to be done. The safest is to just add additional space to the transaction log. The second—dumping the log *with nolog option*—is much more risky. Dumping the log this way clears out all the space in the transaction log, allowing transactions to continue their processing. This method is risky compared to a regular transaction dump, because all the transactions in the log are lost, and logging is disabled from that point on. If you use this command, be sure to run a full database backup as soon as it is feasible. Otherwise, you are risking the loss of the database up to the point of your last full backup and all subsequent transaction log backups.

Database consistency checker: the dbcc utility

Even though Sybase's data server products are very robust, and much effort has gone into making them fault tolerant, problems can occur. For very large tables, some of these problems might not show until very specific queries are run. This is one of the reasons there is the database consistency checker, *dbcc*. This utility can review all the database page allocations, linkages, and data pointers, finding the problems and, in many cases, fixing them before they become insurmountable.

Along with running *dbcc* periodically as a preventive measure, *dbcc* also should be run (if possible) before backing up a database, thereby adding an additional level of reliability to the backups. If a database is corrupt when it is backed up, the backup also will contain the corruption.

 Running *dbcc* will reduce the amount of time that you have available for backups.

There are different types of checks *dbcc* can run on a database, and they differ in terms of runtime length, locking levels used, and completeness of the check. Some of the checks check only data pages of the data, while others check the index consistency and sort order. Which check should be run depends on the database size, the database access requirements, and the thoroughness required.

In its most thorough check and when it is repairing the database, *dbcc* requires complete control of the database, so no access is allowed except for *dbcc*. A number of the less thorough checks do not have this restriction. *dbcc* is invoked using various keywords that specify the type of check that *dbcc* should perform. There are access restrictions on the different keywords, and they are listed along with what they accomplish in Table 16-1.

Table 16-1. dbcc Keyword Definitions

Keyword	Purpose	Access Restrictions
checkalloc	Checks page allocations for all tables and indexes. Can fix some problems if allowed. Reports errors and the amount of space used. Very slow to run—lots of I/O, but very little locking.	Database owner only
checkcatalog	Checks the consistency of system tables between themselves in a database—very quick check. Outputs report on segments defined for database.	Database owner only
checktable	Runs various consistency checks on a per-table basis. Fixes minor sort order and updates row count in first Object Allocation Map (OAM) page. Prints out a report of its findings and any major errors.	Table owner only
checkdb	Runs the same checks as *checktable*, but for all tables in a database.	Database owner only
dbrepair	Used to drop databases too corrupt to drop using the *drop database* command.	SA only
fix_text	Updates text data when switching to a multibyte character set.	Table owner only
indexalloc	Checks page allocations for indexes. Can fix some problems if allowed. Reports errors and the amount of space used. Share-level locking, lots of I/O.	Database owner only
reindex	Rebuilds indexes when sort order is changed. Runs a quick version of *checktable*.	Table owner only
tablealloc	Checks page allocations for tables. Can fix some problems if allowed. Reports errors and the amount of space used. Share-level locking, lots of I/O.	Database owner only

Checks for backups

It is not required that any checks be performed before doing a backup, but without them, there is a chance that hidden problems could be stored in your backup. Of the checks listed in Table 16-1, *checkcatalog*, *checkalloc*, *indexalloc*, and *tablealloc* are the ones that should be run before doing a backup. Because they can potentially take a substantial amount of time and resources, not all of them should be scheduled to run before every backup. Only *checkcatalog* should be run with every backup, because it very quickly makes sure the system tables are consistent in the database.

If and when the rest of the *dbcc* checks should be run depend on how important the data is, how much data there is (the larger the size, the more time *dbcc* will take), and the frequency with which the data changes. If there is a large amount of data but it does not change often, it should be sufficient to run *checkalloc* every once in a while. If there are only a few tables that have important data that change often, then running *tablealloc* and *indexalloc* more often on them while running the overall *checkalloc* less often would be appropriate. If the database is small, or all of it changes often, run *checkalloc* frequently.

Here is the syntax for these checks:

```
$ dbcc indexalloc ( { table_name | table_id }, index_id
[, {full | optimized | fast | null} [, fix | nofix]])

$ dbcc tablealloc ({ table_name | table_id}
[, {full | optimized | fast | null} [, fix | nofix]])

$ dbcc checkalloc [( database_name)] [, fix | nofix]])

$ dbcc checkcatalog [( database_name )]
```

A *table_id* is Sybase's internal object ID number for the table to be checked. This can be obtained by using the T-SQL function *object_id* like this:

```
select object_id("table_name")
```

To get the index ID for an index, use a T-SQL *select* command on the *sysindexes* system table like the following:

```
select name as table_name,id as table_id,indid as index_id from sysindexes where
name like '%table_name%'.
```

The *fix* and *nofix* options control whether *dbcc* should repair the problems it encounters. The default is to not fix the problem. If the *fix* option is used, one of the report options—*full, optimized, fast,* or *null*—also must be used.

The report options (*full, optimized, fast,* and *null*) refer to what type of report *dbcc* should generate after it completes.

- The *full* option reports on all allocation errors.

- When the *optimized* option is used, a report on the allocation pages used is produced, but the checks or fixes on unallocated extents are not run.

- When the *fast* option is used, a report on the pages that are referenced but not allocated in an extent is produced.

- The *null* option tells *dbcc* to use the default report of *optimized.*

For more information on how to read the various reports, please see the *Sybase System Administration* manual.

In the *indexalloc* command, either the table name or table ID is required along with the index ID. The *tablealloc* command requires either the table ID or table name. The *checkalloc* and *checkcatalog* commands require the database name.

If any of the tables, indexes, or databases are system owned, then the database containing them must be set to single-user mode with this T-SQL command:

```
sp_dboption baddbname, "single user", true
```

This command requires that no one can be accessing the database when it is run. Once it is run, only the user who ran it can access the database. Because this prevents other users from accessing the database, the preceding check commands should be run first with the *nofix* option, and then when errors are detected, the *dbcc checkindex* and *checktable* commands should be run with the *fix* option.

Physical Backups Without a Storage Manager

 The following section covers physical backups. If you are unfamiliar with these terms, please consult Chapter 13.

There are a number of third-party backup utilities that can aid in the backup of Sybase databases, but because of their expense, not every site can afford them for all data servers. Even if you have a backup application, you may not want to spend several thousand dollars per server for the Sybase interface. Because Sybase was developed before many of these utilities, there are methods that can be used to back up a Sybase server at a fraction of the cost and with a fair amount of stability and uniformity. These methods include backups directly to both disk and tape.

Sybase databases can reside on both cooked filesystem files and raw disk devices. Sybase recommends not using the filesystem because of the delay caused by the I/O caching. When Sybase writes out data to disk, it assumes the data is written to disk immediately. When using a filesystem-based database, the operating system first writes the data to a memory cache and then at a later point the data is written to disk. Because Sybase writes out changed data pages to disk along with a transaction log entry during transaction processing, if there is a delay in writing out the pages and a problem occurs, not all the data and transaction pages would be written out. This could leave the database with changed pages, no record in the transaction log, and a partially completed transaction. In other words, the database would be corrupted.

There are situations in which a database based upon a filesystem is OK, but the database should be small and should hardly change. This way backups can be done quickly to disk, and the changes can all be loaded into memory and all written out to disk quickly. Sybase recommends not using a filesystem database for any of the system databases.

When it comes to a filesystem database, data could be copied with any standard copy (*cp*) utility or backup (*dump, cpio*) utility. If the database is based upon raw disks, only raw disk access commands (*dd*) can be used.

Backups can be done offline (a cold backup) or online (a hot backup). They are discussed in the next two sections.

Performing a Cold Backup

The biggest difference between doing a cold backup and a hot backup is that in a cold backup the database is completely shut down. By shutting down the database, we are assured that the database remains unchanged and consistent during the whole backup. This is important, because otherwise the utilities being used cannot back up the underlying database files or disks quickly enough to get all changes for all transactions. Imagine the database file being a large deck of cards. The utility starts backing up the cards at the beginning of the deck, but the data server could be changing cards toward the end of the deck. When the utility gets to those changed cards and backs them up, the data server might be changing cards at the front of the deck. If all these changed cards represent one transaction, this backup would not contain all the changes; it would have caught only the changes at the end of the deck. With the data server shut down, this problem does not exist, because no changes are occurring.

The best way to shut down the data server is through the T-SQL command *shutdown.* When this command is run, the database disables all logins except the login for the SA, performs a checkpoint on each database, and waits for all currently running statements or procedures to complete. If there are user connections that have not completed their transactions, the shutdown will hang. If you do not want to wait for these transactions to complete, you can try shutting down using *nowait* in another T-SQL session. The *nowait* option will stop all transactions immediately and continue with the shutdown, but because there could be uncommitted transactions in progress, recovery time will be increased. It is highly recommended that the user community be consulted before doing this. (Otherwise, there might be one less DBA in the world when the users track down the person responsible for pulling the rug out from under them.) Here are example outputs of the T-SQL *shutdown* command:

```
1>shutdown
Server SHUTDOWN by request.
```

```
The SQL Server is terminating this process.
DB-LIBRARY error:
        Unexpected EOF from SQL Server.
```

Once the database is shut down, a standard operating system backup of the database files and devices can occur. To make sure the database can be restored in any situation, these items must be included in the backup:

- The installation directory for Sybase

- All scripts dealing with starting, stopping, backing up, and restoring the Sybase server

- Any related documentation files that describe the data server system (I have seen too many times where there is a wonderful recovery procedure, but because no one knew how to run it, hours were lost trying to piece it together)

- Any scripts that were used to create the server and could be used to re-create the database

- The hardcopy backups and *bcp* files of the five important system tables in the master database: *sysdevices, syslogins, sysloginroles, sysdatabase*, and *sysusages*

- All filesystems or raw disks that comprise the datafiles of the data server

Performing a Hot Backup

A hot backup is run while the database is up and active. In Sybase, this is accomplished by running *dump database* and *dump transaction* commands to create a physical backup and by running *bcp* to create logical backups. A logical backup is one in which the data from a table is copied out to a file. This data then can be selectively restored and altered. A physical backup is the byte-by-byte copy of the database structure and its data. In this case, all of the structure and data must be restored together. The benefit of doing a hot backup is that the database can remain active throughout.

The Sybase hot backup should include the first five items in the list in the previous section in order to re-create the surrounding infrastructure of the database, but there is no need to back up the datafiles or raw disks during a hot backup. Instead of backing these up using operating system commands, the data inside these items will be backed up using the *dump* and *bcp* commands.

As part of a good backup scheme, one that saves all the data most efficiently, both full and incremental backups need to be performed. In a Sybase database, these equate to doing a full database backup and then regularly scheduled and system-generated incremental transaction log backups. The system-generated ones are created when a user-defined threshold, such as the transaction log becoming 90 percent full, is met on a database. At this point, an automatic transaction dump is performed by a user-defined stored procedure. For more information on this type of threshold, please see a good Sybase DBA manual or the Sybase documentation.

There are a few things that must be set up before doing a full database backup. The first of these is making sure the backup server and data server are up and running. On a Unix system, this can be done by making sure their processes exist on their respective systems. Sybase provides a shell script file called *$SYBASE/install/showserver*. If for some reason this script does not work, the Unix *ps* command also will list all running processes. It is easy from this command's output to see if there are processes called *backupserver* and *dataserver* running.

Example 16-1 shows both commands and their outputs from a Linux system.

Example 16-1. Sample ps and showserver Outputs

```
# ps ax
  191  ?  S    0:00 in.telnetd
   94  ?  S    0:00 /usr/sbin/portmap
  114  ?  S    0:00 /usr/sbin/atd
  120  ?  S    0:00 /usr/sbin/httpd -f /etc/httpd/httpd.conf
  121  ?  S    0:00 /usr/sbin/httpd -f /etc/httpd/httpd.conf
  122  ?  S    0:00 /usr/sbin/httpd -f /etc/httpd/httpd.conf
  123  ?  S    0:00 /usr/sbin/httpd -f /etc/httpd/httpd.conf
  124  ?  S    0:00 /usr/sbin/httpd -f /etc/httpd/httpd.conf
  157  ?  S    0:00 sh /opt/sybase/install/RUN_SYB_BACKUP
  160  ?  S    0:00 sh /opt/sybase/install/RUN_SYB_TITANIA
  164  ?  S    0:00 /opt/sybase/bin/dataserver -d/sybdata/master.dbf
                         -sSYB_MYDB
  168  ?  S    0:00 /opt/sybase/bin/backupserver -SSYB_BACKUP -e/opt/sybas
e/logs

# $SYBASE/install/showserver
sybase    164  0.1 10.4 16224  6592 ?  S    22:18   0:00
  /opt/sybase/bin/dataserver  d/sybdata/master.dbf -sSYB_MYDB
  -e/opt/sybase/logs/SYB_MYDB.errorlog -i/opt/sybase
sybase    168  0.0  6.4  6660  4092 ?  S    22:18   0:00
  /opt/sybase/bin/backupserver
  -SSYB_BACKUP -e/opt/sybase/logs/SYB_BACKUP.errorlog -I/opt/sybase/interf
aces
  -M/opt/sybase/bin/sybmultbuf -Lus_english -Jiso_1  -c/opt/sybase/backup
_tape
```

An additional check can be run using the *isql* program. The *isql* program is a simple command-line interface in which T-SQL commands can be run against a Sybase server. Just by using this command and connecting to the server, the status of the server can be verified. Here is an example of this process, connecting to a data server *SYB_MYDB* and to a backup server *SYB_BACKUP*:

```
# isql -S SYB_MYDB -U sa -P passwd
1> quit
```

```
# isql -S SYB_BACKUP -U sa -P passwd
1> quit
```

If either of these processes is not up, an error message like the following will appear:

```
isql -S SYB_MYDB -U sa -P passwd
Operating-system error:
        Connection refused
DB-LIBRARY error:
        Unable to connect: SQL Server is unavailable or does not exist.
```

If the *backupserver* or *dataserver* processes are not up and running, follow the appropriate operating system commands to start them.

Once both servers are up, the next step requires the use of the T-SQL *dump* command. The *dump* command has many different options, but they can be broken down into three categories—what to back up, where to back it up to, and how to back it up.

What to back up

Start constructing the command by first deciding if a full database backup or a transaction log backup needs to be performed. A full database backup starts like this:

```
> dump database somedb
```

A transaction log backup starts like this:

```
> dump transaction somedb
```

Where to write the backup

A backup can be sent to a tape device, a disk file, or a device defined in Sybase using the stored procedure *sp_adddumpdevice*. The *sp_adddumpdevice* command creates a logical name for a physical tape device or disk file. This is handy when a single script file is used to back up multiple servers. The script file can use a single logical name that can be defined differently for each server.

A feature of the *dump* command is the ability to split the backup among multiple tape devices; this is called *striping*. The tape devices do not have to be on the same machine, just accessible by a backup server. In this way, Sybase has maximized the backup performance by having more than one backup device and more than one machine doing the work. Here are some examples of these different backups:

Dump the database *somedb* to the Unix tape device *device*:

```
> dump database somedb to "device"
```

Dump the transaction log for the database *somedb*, striping the backup to the Unix tape device *device1* on the current machine and to the tape *device2* on *somemachine*:

```
> dump transaction somedb to "device1" \
  stripe on "device2" at somemachine
```

Dump the database *somedb* to the file */home/sybase/backups/filename*:

```
> dump database somedb to "/home/sybase/backups/filename"
```

Dump the database *somedb* to the logical dump device *mydumpdevice*:

```
> dump database somedb to mydumpdevice
```

How to back up

The *how* part of the command can be grouped into two sets of optional arguments. The first set of arguments changes the default behavior of a particular backup device. The second set of arguments changes some other default behaviors of *dump*, such as whether or not it will truncate the transaction log when it completes.

The following optional arguments change the default behavior of a particular backup device:

Blocksize
: A multiple of the 2048-byte page size

Capacity
: Number of kilobytes a single tape can hold

dumpvolume
: The dump volume name

filename
: The filename to use on the tape

If more than one modifier is used, they must be separated by commas. For example, a *dump database* command to the tape device */dev/nrmt0*, with a 20-GB tape capacity and a block size of 4096, is shown here:

```
1> dump database somedb to "/dev/nrmt0"
2> capacity=20000000, blocksize=4096
```

Other default behaviors of *dump* also can be changed with other optional arguments:

[nounload | unload]
: Should the tape be rewound after the backup completes?

retaindays

> (Unix only) The number of days the tape should be retained before it will be overwritten.

[noinit | init]

> Should the tape be initialized before use, or should the backup be appended?

no_truncate

> Part of the transaction dumping command. See the Sybase Reference manual or "Recovering Sybase," later in this chapter, for more information.

notify = {client | operator_console}

> On Unix, tape mounting messages can be routed to the process that is running the backup command (*client*) or to the one running the backup server process (*operator_console*).

A sample dump command

With all three parts of the *dump* command put together, you can accomplish any type of Sybase hot backup to any supported device on any backup server. Example 16-2 shows a sample run of both a full database backup and its transaction log backup.

Example 16-2. Sample dump Commands

```
1> dump database mydb to '/sybase/backups/mydb.990312.bck'
2> go
Backup Server session id is:  20.  Use this value when executing the
'sp_volchanged' system stored procedure after fulfilling any volume change
request from the Backup Server.
Backup Server: 4.41.1.1: Creating new disk file /sybase/backups/mydb.990312
.bck.
Backup Server: 6.28.1.1: Dumpfile name 'mydb9909106EF4   ' section number 0001
mounted on disk file '/sybase/backups/mydb.990312.bck'
Backup Server: 4.58.1.1: Database mydb: 338 kilobytes DUMPed.
Backup Server: 4.58.1.1: Database mydb: 344 kilobytes DUMPed.
Backup Server: 3.43.1.1: Dump phase number 1 completed.
Backup Server: 3.43.1.1: Dump phase number 2 completed.
Backup Server: 3.43.1.1: Dump phase number 3 completed.
Backup Server: 4.58.1.1: Database mydb: 352 kilobytes DUMPed.
Backup Server: 3.42.1.1: DUMP is complete (database mydb).

1> dump transaction mydb to '/sybase/backups/mydb.tlogdmp'
2> go
Backup Server session id is:  23.  Use this value when executing the
'sp_volchanged' system stored procedure after fulfilling any volume change
request from the Backup Server.
Backup Server: 6.28.1.1: Dumpfile name 'mydb9909106F49   ' section number 0001
mounted on disk file '/sybase/backups/mydb.tlogdmp'
Backup Server: 4.58.1.1: Database mydb: 16 kilobytes DUMPed.
Backup Server: 4.58.1.1: Database mydb: 20 kilobytes DUMPed.
Backup Server: 3.43.1.1: Dump phase number 3 completed.
```

Example 16-2. Sample dump Commands (continued)

```
Backup Server: 4.58.1.1: Database mydb: 24 kilobytes DUMPed.
Backup Server: 3.42.1.1: DUMP is complete (database mydb).
```

Some of the output will change depending upon the size of the database being backed up, the devices being backed up to, and even how the backup is being done. In all cases, if you are unsure about the specific use of a command, please refer to the Sybase System Administration manuals for additional guidance. The good thing is there is very little chance of damaging the database by doing a backup. In fact, the only way to accomplish this is by accidentally overwriting one of the data server files or devices with the dump.

Automating Hot Backups: the syback.sh Script

The free script *syback.sh* can automate the process of doing hot backups of Sybase. It is written in the Bourne shell, which is compatible with most Unix systems. By using GNU's *config.guess* script, the list of Unix platforms on which it runs is perhaps limitless. By setting various configuration options in a config file, *syback.conf*, a wide range of hot backups can be accomplished. *syback.sh* supports these features:

- Backs up to disk or tape
- Backs up databases on filesystems or raw partitions
- Mail-based success and error notification

 The *syback.sh* script was written by R. Neill Carter of Collective Technologies. Neill specializes in large database projects, prefers working with interesting and slightly freaky people, and goes by the name Bongo. He can be reached at *cartern@colltech.com.*

How syback.sh works

Starting off, *syback.sh* sets up all the variables and paths it needs to run the backup. It uses *config.guess* to find out which flavor of Unix it is running on and then sets what is appropriate for that system. After this, it then opens up its configuration file *syback.conf.* It locates this file in the directory where it was first started.

syback.sh reads each line of its configuration file, loading them into its memory. There are three different entry classes it can read—backup class entry, disk device entry, or tape device entry. The backup class entry defines what to back up, where to back it up to, when to back it up, who to back it up as, and certain required Sybase environmental variables. The tape and disk entries define which backup server to use and what device or directory to use on that server.

Once all the entries are read in, *syback.sh* sequentially runs through each entry, and depending on the current time and the times specified in the backup class entry, it tries to run a backup. When it finds an entry that meets the time criteria, it outputs the entry. Next, it checks the entry and makes sure all the items in it are valid. The last of these checks uses the username and password entered to connect to the data server to be backed up. If any checks fail, a failure email is sent to the ADMIN entry defined in *syback.conf.*

When the entry passes all checks, *syback.sh* creates a T-SQL *dump* command to back up of the databases selected to the appropriate backup server and devices.

Installing syback.sh

Put the files *syback.sh, syback.conf, config.guess, localpath.sh*, and *rempath.sh* into the same directory, then check the CONFIG_FILE value in the user-defined variables section at the top of the script. Set this to the full pathname of the *syback. conf* configuration file.

Configuring and customizing syback.sh

Edit *syback.conf* in your favorite text file editor. You will need to edit this file and add backup class entries and tape/disk device entries in order to configure your backup. The *syback.conf* file contains three type of entries, along with comments. The comment lines begin with the # character. First, change the following parameters to the appropriate value for your environment:

BINDIR
Set this to the directory where you installed *syback.sh*.

ADMIN
Set this to the user ID that will run *syback.sh*.

SUCCESSMAIL
Set this to **yes** if you want to receive mail when *syback.sh* runs successfully.

FAILMAIL
Set this to **yes** if you want to receive mail when *syback.sh* fails.

You now need to edit the backup class, tape class, and disk class definitions.

The backup class lines define what type of backup should be run and when, along with any parameters required to run the backup. Here is the definition of a backup class line along with an explanation of each parameter. Review the comments in the *syback.conf* file to see examples of this entry.

```
-c MM:HH:DOM:MN:DOW:SERVER_NAME:DUMP_TYPE:USER:PASSWORD:SYBASE:INTERFACES:
LOG:DATABASE(S)_TO_INCLUDE:DATABASE(S)_TO_EXCLUDE:DEVICE_TYPE:
DUMP_DEVICE(S):UNLOAD:RETAINDAYS:INIT
```

The MM, HH, DOM, MN, and DOW parameters specify when this particular *dump* should run. These parameters are not yet used in this version of *syback.sh*. The appropriate value for each parameter is listed here:

MM
> Minute (0–59)

HH
> Hour (0–23)

DOM
> Day(s) of Month (1–31)

MN
> Month (1–12)

DOW
> Day of Week (0–6 with 0=Sunday)

Now we will specify which server this line is for and how it should perform its dump:

SERVER_NAME
> Sybase server name.

DUMP_TYPE
> Type of backup—full (FULL) or transaction (TRAN).

USER
> Sybase user with backup ability.

PASSWORD
> Sybase user password.

SYBASE
> Full path of Sybase product directory.

INTERFACES
> Full path of Sybase interfaces file.

LOG
> Log file for backup.

DATABASE(S)_TO_INCLUDE
> List of databases to include in backup. If left blank, all databases except those in the DATABASE_TO_EXCLUDE list will be backed up.

DATABASE(S)_TO_EXCLUDE
> List of databases to exclude from backup.

DEVICE_TYPE

> If TAPE, the DUMP_DEVICE entries are of tape device class defined in a "-t" line. If DISK, the DUMP_DEVICE entries are of disk device class defined in a "-d" line.

DUMP_DEVICE(S)

> The list of disk or tape devices to which to back up. These must be defined in a "-t" or a "-d" line in the configuration file.

UNLOAD

> Causes tape(s) to be unloaded after backup. This has no effect on a disk device.

RETAINDAYS

> Specifies number of days backups are protected from overwriting.

INIT

> Causes tape(s) to be initialized and overwritten.

Now that you have defined what type of backups should be performed, the following tape class definition line:

```
-t LOGICAL_NAME:SQL_SERVER:BACKUP_SERVER:DUMP_DEVICE:BLOCKSIZE:CAPACITY
```

defines the output tape device where the backup can be placed. It contains fields that relate to the backup server that contains the tape device and parameters that define more about the tape device's abilities. Again, review *syback.conf* for sample entries. The fields are:

LOGICAL_NAME

> Logical name assigned to this tape.

SQL_SERVER

> Sybase server associated with the named backup server. If not specified, value is taken from environmental variable *DSQUERY*.

BACKUP_SERVER

> Sybase backup server associated with this tape. If not specified, backup_ server is assumed to be associated with sqlserver taken from environmental variable *DSQUERY*.

DUMP_DEVICE

> Physical name for this tape.

BLOCKSIZE

> Overrides the default block size for a device.

CAPACITY

> Maximum amount of data that the device can write to a single volume.

The final type of entry in the *syback.conf* file is the disk class. These entries define disk files on backup servers. Examples of this entry also can be found in the *syback.conf* file.

```
-d LOGICAL_NAME:SQL_SERVER:BACKUP_SERVER:DIRECTORY_NAME
```

LOGICAL_NAME

Logical name assigned to this file.

SQL_SERVER

Sybase server associated with the named backup server. If not specified, value is taken from *$DSQUERY.*

BACKUP_SERVER

Sybase backup server associated with this tape. If not specified, backup_ server is assumed to be associated with sqlserver taken from *$DSQUERY.*

DIRECTORY_NAME

Directory that will hold backup files.

Finally, with *syback.conf* file edited with the proper definitions, *syback.sh* is ready to run its first backup. To invoke *syback.sh*, run it from a shell prompt. It requires no command-line options and just needs to be invoked while the default directory is set to the location of the *syback.conf* file.

syback.sh will generate various messages as it runs. What you first will see is information about all the parameters that are set using the backup, tape, and disk classes. Next, the output of each backup as it occurs will be displayed. Finally, when all the backups have been processed, if the backup was successful and a success email was selected in the backup class entry, a success email containing the backup log will be sent to the administrator email address. If the backup was unsuccessful and failure email was selected, then a failure email containing the backup log will be sent to the administrator email address.

crontab entries

syback.sh works slightly differently than *oraback.sh*; *syback.sh* does not schedule itself to run. Instead, the user must either invoke *syback.sh* interactively or set it up to run noninteractively with *cron*. *syback.sh* tries to match the current time to a time entry in *syback.conf*. It then does the backup that is defined for that time.

Here is an example of an entry using *crontab*:

```
0 2 * * * /opt/syback/syback.sh 2>&1 > /var/adm/syback/syback.last
```

This entry says run *syback.sh* at 2:00 A.M. every day and put all output into the file *syback.last*. Refer to your operating system's manuals to find out how to schedule the automatic running of *syback.sh*.

Physical Backups with a Storage Manager

Many commercial backup utilities, like those covered in Chapter 5, *Commercial Backup Utilities*, actually can have a completely integrated backup solution for all Sybase databases. They will have an interface that communicates directly with Sybase's backup server. This interface provides additional functionality by having some way of creating, scheduling, and executing the backups via a graphical user interface (GUI). This lets the backups and restores be run by just a few clicks with a mouse.

Sometimes, these utilities are on the same system as the data server; at other times, only a client part of the application will be on the data server system, and a separate backup application will be on a networked system. No matter how it is set up, these applications will provide an easier and reliable backup solution.

In addition to providing support for physical backups, these utilities described in Chapter 5 also can provide support for logical backups. They add additional functionality to *bcp*, such as easy scheduling, a GUI frontend, and allowing the logical backups to be stored on remote backup devices. (The *bcp* utility is covered in "Logical Backups," later in this chapter.)

Because of the strong integration with Sybase's backup system, sometimes the only change seen on the Sybase side might be to the destination or source device used. This allows easy merging of the new product with existing backup procedures. For example, where the physical tape device had been */dev/nrmt0* in a script, the new device might have the form of:

```
"3rdPartybackup::'99.3.10.04.00.master.full' "
```

The *3rdPartybackup* phrase tells the Sybase backup server that the backup should go to the third-party utility. The *99.3.10.04.00.master.full* phrase represents the time, database, and what type of backup is being done. In this way, information about the backup can be sent to the backup utility so it knows how to record and store the backup. This value would be used both in the backup and recovery commands in Sybase.

Recovering Sybase

Once you have backups of the database, you need to know how to apply them so that you can recover the database in the case of problems. This section discusses how to recover using both cold backups and warm backups and presents a step-by-step recovery procedure. The procedure takes you from trying to start the data server through diagnosing why it did not start, to fixing the problems preventing it from starting. With these procedures and good backups, you should be able to recover from any Sybase problem.

Restoring from a Cold Backup

When restoring a system using a cold backup, nearly everything that was originally backed up needs to be restored. As in the cold backup, the data server must be shut down during the whole restore procedure. Depending upon the circumstances requiring the backup, one or more items might not need be restored. Run through these points to determine which items need to be restored:

- Was one of the raw disks or filesystems replaced?

  Even if only one of them was replaced, all of them will have to be restored because there is no way to restore only part of a cold backup of the datafiles or raw disks.

- Hardcopies of five system tables in the master database (*sysusages*, *syslogins*, *sysdatabases*, *sysdevices*, *sysloginroles*) will be needed for the recovery to confirm the recovery was complete. These can be gotten by either *bcp*ing the tables into text files using the *-c* option and then printing out the files or by using the T-SQL *select* command and printing out the results.

  At the end of a number of the recoveries, double-checking the five system tables will help make sure the recovery was successful. Always make sure these hardcopies are updated after any system change.

- If something is wrong with the system backups of the datafiles or raw disks, the database might need to be re-created.

  Copies of the creation scripts will save a lot of time, so restore these from backup.

- Have all the documentation available for reference.

  Because most complex data centers have more than one data server and database, having clear documentation will help prevent mistakes, as configurations can be confused. Also, as SAs come and go at large sites, not all system information will be known by all SAs.

- Was the filesystem that contained the starting/stopping/backups replaced?

  If the data server does not have all these scripts, a lot of time and effort will be needed to re-create all your hard work.

- Is a Sybase installation directory available?

  Even though the Sybase installation directories can be re-created from the installation materials, there are a number of customized files, such as configuration files and interface files, that reside in these directories in a standard setup. Also, if additional EBFs (Sybase patches) or upgrades were installed, they will have to be reapplied. It is much quicker to restore from a single backup of these directories.

Restoring from a Hot Backup

Sybase reduces the time it takes to perform a hot backup by saving only the pages that contain data. It also saves them exactly as they are on the devices and in the order they are found in the database. Because of this, the recovery requires that the database be re-created with exactly the same layout it had before the recovery. In other words, if the database was created with a 40-MB default segment and a 10-MB log segment, and at a later point, an additional 40-MB was added to the default segment, then the database needs to be re-created with a 40-MB default segment and 10-MB log segment and then altered to add the last 40-MB. Otherwise, when the load of the hot backup occurs, Sybase will do unpredictable things with the allocation.

In the previous example, these commands would be:

```
create database mydb on mydefseg = 40, mydefseg = 40
log on mylogseg = 10
alter database mydb on mydefseg = 40
```

Once the database creation is complete, the full dump of the database needs to be applied using the *load* command. The *load* command has all of the same parameters as the *dump* command. It needs to know what to restore, from where to get it, and how to get it from there. To restore from a tape, use exactly the same parameters as were used to create the tapes.

First, restore the full database backup to the database. This will give you a base point against which to restore all the transaction logs. Example 16-3 contains a sample load of a full database dump.

Example 16-3. Sample load database Command

```
1> load database mydb from '/sybase/backups/mydb.990312.bck'
2> go
Backup Server session id is:  26.  Use this value when executing the
'sp_volchanged' system stored procedure after fulfilling any volume change
request from the Backup Server.
Backup Server: 6.28.1.1: Dumpfile name 'mydb9909106EF4   ' section number
0001
mounted on disk file '/sybase/backups/mydb.990312.bck'
Backup Server: 4.58.1.1: Database mydb: 17926 kilobytes LOADed.
Backup Server: 4.58.1.1: Database mydb: 19462 kilobytes LOADed.
Backup Server: 4.58.1.1: Database mydb: 19470 kilobytes LOADed.
Backup Server: 3.42.1.1: LOAD is complete (database mydb).
Use the ONLINE DATABASE command to bring this database online; SQL Server
will not bring it online automatically.
```

If there are no transaction logs for this database, then as the command output says, this database could be brought online. Enter the *online database baddbname* command to have Sybase bring it up and make it available for use.

If there are transaction logs, they will need to be applied to bring the database up to the most current point possible. Use the load transaction command to apply a transaction log to the database. To restore the transaction logs for the database *mydb* in the preceding dump example, enter the command shown in Example 16-4.

Example 16-4. Sample load transaction Command

```
1> load transaction mydb from '/sybase/backups/mydb.tlogdmp'
2> go
Backup Server session id is:  28.  Use this value when executing the
'sp_volchanged' system stored procedure after fulfilling any volume change
request from the Backup Server.
Backup Server: 6.28.1.1: Dumpfile name 'mydb9909106F49   ' section number
0001 mounted on disk file '/sybase/backups/mydb.tlogdmp'
Backup Server: 4.58.1.1: Database mydb: 24 kilobytes LOADed.
Backup Server: 3.42.1.1: LOAD is complete (database mydb).
Use the ONLINE DATABASE command to bring this database online; SQL Server
will not bring it online automatically.
```

Repeat the transaction logs loads until there are no more transaction logs to apply. When they are done, the database has been restored completely and should be brought online using the *online database baddbname* command.

Because of a quirk in some versions of Sybase on some platforms, the preceding loads might not work for using the physical devices. To get by this "feature," you can use logical devices instead. The only differences in the examples would be changing the physical device to a logical device after the logical dump device is created. For more information on how to create logical dump devices, see the definition of dump devices under "The DBA's View," near the beginning of this chapter.

As of Sybase Version 11.92, a database can now be restored up to a specific point in time as long as it is covered by a transaction log dump. To specify the time to which the database should be restored, use the new *until_time* parameter. This parameter takes a single value of a time and date in the default format for the data server. For example, to restore a database up to April 1, 1999, at 12:34:32:650 A.M., first apply the full database dump, then apply all transaction log dumps up to the one that contains the stop time. With this dump, add *until_time*, like this:

```
load transaction mydb
from '/sybase/backups/mydb.tlogdmp'
with until_time = 'April 1, 1999 at 12:34:32:650AM'
```

Once the database has been restored and brought online, it is important to check all the major objects in the system and validate the data. Run a number of queries on the database tables to make sure the data is as it should be and then check the consistency of the database structure using the *dbcc checkalloc.*

When all of these checks have been passed, do a full database dump to make sure a consistent recent backup is on hand in case additional problems arise. Also, it will save time because none of the transaction logs restored earlier will need to be restored again.

Using the Recovery Procedure

Recovering from a database problem starts with diagnosing exactly what is wrong with the database. Maybe *isql* will not connect to the data server, maybe the database is marked suspect, or maybe an error message in the error log occurs when the data server is started. In all of these cases and others, something has gone wrong where it had gone right before. Fortunately, with the proper backups, many of these problems can be fixed and the database restored to full working order.

Sybase has many parts that are interrelated, but like Sherlock Holmes investigating a mystery, if we eliminate from consideration the items that are working correctly, only the error-causing parts will remain. This section provides step-by-step directions to diagnosing and repairing all of these error-causing parts, and when completed, will leave a fully functional data server.

A flowchart that appears at the beginning of these steps (Figure 16-1) should help you in the recovery process. Each item in the chart is numbered the same as the steps and procedures that follow. The electronic version of this procedure* contains a flowchart that is an HTML image map. Each decision or action box in the flowchart is a hyperlink to the appropriate section of the printed procedure. For more detailed information about individual steps, please consult Sybase's System Administration documentation, especially the "Backup and Recovery" chapter.

To begin the investigation, start the data server as it is normally started. If problems show up in the Sybase error log file or the data server does not come up, start with Step 1 to begin the recovery/diagnosis procedure.

Step 1: Runfile OK?

Sybase starts up by using the *startserver* program. This program takes an additional parameter *-f runfilename* that is the file containing the server startup command and parameters. If this file is missing or the path given for the runfile is

---

* It is available at *http://www.backupcentral.com* and on the CD that comes with this book.

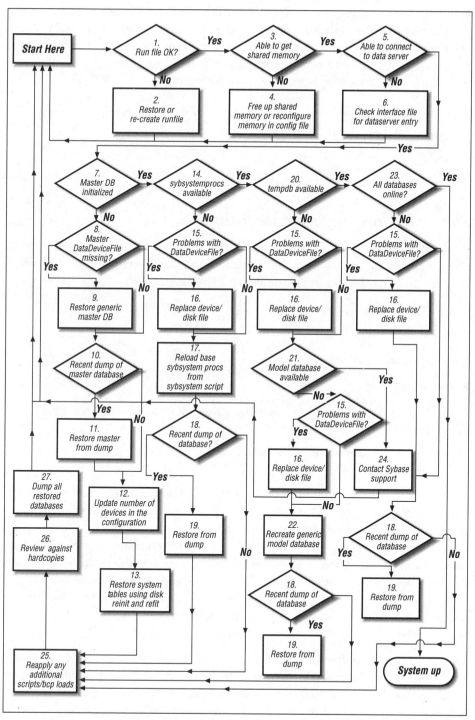

Figure 16-1. A Sybase recovery flowchart

incorrect, the *startserver* command will return an error `Cannot execute file` *runfilename*. If the path is incorrect for the file, correct it and start again. If you are unsure of the path being used, change your directory to the location of the runfile, then run the command, but specify only the runfile name. Sybase then will try looking in your current default directory for the file.

 If the runfile is OK, proceed to Step 3. If not, go to Step 2.

Step 2: Restore or Re-create Runfile

If the file is missing, it can be re-created fairly easily. There is nothing magical about this text file. It contains the command and parameters to start the server. Example 16-5 contains a sample runfile for a Unix system.

Example 16-5. Sample Runfile

```
#!/bin/sh
#
# SQL Server Information:
#  Name:                  SYB_TITANIA
#  Master device:         /sybdata/master.dbf
#  Master device size:    10752
#  Errorlog:              /opt/sybase/logs/SYB_MYDB.errorlog
#  Interfaces:            /opt/sybase
#
/opt/sybase/bin/dataserver -d/sybdata/master.dbf -sSYB_MYDB \
-e/opt/sybase/logs/SYB_MYDB.errorlog -i/opt/sybase
```

As seen in the comment lines, *dataserver* takes a number of different parameters. Again, check Sybase's documentation for your OS for more details. The most important parameter shown is the master device. The master device is the primary device used by the master database, and the master database is one of the key-stones of a Sybase server. The master database contains a majority of the information about all the other databases, devices, and other data server objects, including the location of the master device. The *-s dataservername* is how the data server knows what name to call itself. If this is omitted, Sybase assumes a data server of the name *SYBASE* is being started.

The *-e errorlog* points to the full filename and pathname of the data server's error log. During an install, Sybase defaults to the *$SYBASE/install* directory. Because this directory contains a number of important files other than the error log, it is recommended that this be changed to point to another directory, maybe

$SYBASE/logs/. Also, if there is more than one data server on the system, the *errorlog* filename should be changed. Appending the *.errorlog* suffix to each data server name provides each server with its individual *errorlog* file, making tracking down errors much simpler.

The next parameter to look at is the interface parameter, *-i interfacedir*. This is the directory where Sybase can find the interface file. In some systems, there might be two interface files—one or more for the users to use and one for the Sybase system to use. The different interface files could contain different selections of server entries, preventing the users or the data server from accessing all the Sybase servers available. If this parameter is omitted, Sybase will look in the directory pointed to by *$SYBASE* environmental variable.

One parameter that is not shown here is the configuration file parameter *-c configfile*. As of Version 11, Sybase can be started using a configuration file. This file contains the text of all the configuration options on the data server and their values. When no *-c* parameter is specified, Sybase defaults to the file *servername. cfg* found in the directory where the data server is started.

The Origins of the Configuration File

Before Version 11, all configuration parameters were kept only in tables in the master database. When a configuration option was changed and required a restart of the data server, the data server might not come up because of this change. Because the server was not up, there was no way to reset the option except by running a command to reset all the options to their default values. They then had to be reset to their values before the final incorrect option change. In other words, a real pain in the you-know-what. Now, the configuration file contains all these options in an easily edited file. To revert a value back, a text editor can be used to change the value in the file. When the data server is next restarted with the reverted values, the data server will restart cleanly.

Two additional parameters can be used with the *dataserver* program—the version parameter *-v* and the single-user mode parameter *-m*. The version number parameter is handy to use when you need to see the current version of the database program, and do not want to search for it in the error log.

The single-user, or maintenance, mode *-m* is used to bring the data server up so only the *sa* account can access the data server. This is required when doing certain recovery procedures and, in general, when there is a need to prevent user access while maintenance is being done.

It is easy to re-create this file by using a text editor to create a script like the preceding one, but with the values of your data server. Once the file is created and the account that starts the data server has access to it, run the *startserver -f* `runfile` command.

 Once you've replaced the runfile, return to Step 1.

Step 3: Able to Get Shared Memory?

Like most database products, Sybase uses shared memory to communicate between data server processes, process queries, and store sections of the database for quick access. If Sybase is prevented from acquiring the minimum shared memory it needs, it will fail to come up and instead will error out with a message like the following:

```
00:1999/03/21 23:39:02.78 kernel  os_create_region: can't allocate 2147479552
                                   bytes
00:1999/03/21 23:39:02.80 kernel  kbcreate: couldn't create kernel region.
00:1999/03/21 23:39:02.80 kernel  kistartup: could not create shared memory
```

 If you are able to get to shared memory, proceed to Step 5. If not, proceed to Step 4.

Step 4: Free Up Shared Memory or Reconfigure Memory in Configuration File

As mentioned earlier, changes in configuration parameters can cause the Sybase server to need additional memory. This in turn can require the Sybase server to request a larger shared memory segment from the OS. There are two things that can prevent this from happening:

1. The maximum shared memory segment size is undersized.

2. There is not enough shared memory on the system to allow this to run.

In the first case, the solution is to increase the maximum shared memory segment value appropriately for the OS. Because Sybase is supported on many different

OSs, how to change this is not shown here. Please refer to the appropriate operating system Sybase installation manual for further information on setting this value.

In the second case, either shared memory needs to be added to the system, or shared memory needs to be freed up from other processes. Please contact a system administrator for help in accomplishing either of these.

You can view the shared memory being used by using the *ipcs* command. Check the manpages for the correct usage of the command, but the output should look something like this:

```
------ Shared Memory Segments --------
shmid     owner     perms     bytes       nattch    status
129       sybase    600       11964416    1
2         sybase    666       1024        3
56        curtis    606       33334342    3
```

Here, the **curtis** process has also taken some of the shared memory for itself. By stopping this process, the shared memory should be freed up. If stopping the process does not free up the memory, it can be freed using the Unix command *ipcrm*. Again, check the Unix manpages for more information on this command on your operating system.

If none of these solutions helps the problem, the changes in the configuration options will need to be reverted to allow the data server to come up correctly.

If possible, make one change to the configuration options at a time. Sybase configuration options interact, some causing the system to need more memory, others less. By making one change at a time, the configuration option that prevents the system from restarting is known and can be adjusted accordingly.

Once you have corrected these problems, return to Step 1.

Step 5: Able to Connect to Data Server?

When Sybase starts, it needs the interface file so it can set up all the interprocess and network communication parameters. This interfaces file is usually named *interfaces, interface,* or *sql.ini,* depending on the operating system.

If you are able to connect, proceed to Step 7. If you are unable to connect, go to Step 6.

Step 6: Check Interface File

If Sybase cannot find the file or there is something wrong with it, Sybase will error out during startup with a message like one of the following:

```
00:1999/03/22 00:17:46.54 kernel  Could not open interface file
          '/opt/sybase/interfaces'

00:1999/03/22 00:22:16.15 kernel  Could not find name 'SYB_MYDB' in the
          interfaces file /opt/sybase/interfaces
```

To correct the first error, make sure the interface file is located where the runfile says it should be located. If the interface file is in a different directory, either adjust the runfile to point to the correct directory or move the interface file to the directory specified in the runfile.

The second entry means the lines for the data server being started (in this case *SYB_MYDB*) cannot be found in the interface file. To fix this problem, add an entry using the appropriate method for your operating system. Please see the Sybase OS-specific documentation for more information.

Once the entry is in the correct interface file, rerun the *startserver* command to see if this has fixed the problem.

Once you have corrected any problems with the interface file, return to Step 1.

Step 7: Master Database Initialized?

The master database is the most important database in the system: not only does it contain all the information about all the other databases but also it is the repository of all information regarding logins, roles, devices, usage of those devices, and configuration options on the system. It is imperative that this database comes up correctly. Otherwise, the rest of the data server would not work at all.

If the master database did initialize, proceed to Step 14. If it did not, go to Step 8.

Step 8: Master Device/File Missing?

The first information that something is wrong with the master database would most likely be the following error messages displayed during startup:

```
00:1999/03/22 00:53:48.44 kernel  kdconfig: unable to read primary master
device
00:1999/03/22 00:53:48.44 kernel  kiconfig: read of config block failed
```

These lines are preceded by a line that will tell you why the system could not read the primary master device.

 To fix these problems, go to Step 15. If none of the solutions in that section corrects the problem, you must restore the master database (go to Step 9).

If there are no problems accessing the master data device, then the problem might be the master database has been corrupted. This type of problem could show a number of strange symptoms if the data server was already running. For example, *isql* will crash with program errors when trying to connect, or currently running queries will crash.

If strange things like these start happening, the best thing to do is to try to restart the data server. However, in situations like this, almost all access to the data server will be blocked, so the *isql* command *shutdown* cannot be used normally. Instead, the *dataserver* process must be stopped at the operating system level. In Unix, this can be done using the *kill* command. This should be used only during extreme situations such as when the data server is consuming all the processing of the system. Use *kill* only if nothing else will help, because it could cause corruption of the databases in the data server.

Once the data server is down, check to make sure memory used by Sybase has been freed. See Steps 3 and 4 for more information on shared memory. When the shared memory has been freed, try starting the data server using normal starting procedures.

If the data server fails to start, see if there are errors on the master device in the data server error log. Go to Step 15 and make sure there are no problems there. If there are, correct the problem with the device, and try restarting again.

If there are no problems with the physical devices, the master database will need to be completely recovered from backup.

If there are any problems with the physical devices, proceed to Step 9. Otherwise, proceed to Step 10.

Step 9: Restoring Generic Master Database

Follow these steps to restore the generic master database:

1. Backup server up?

   Make sure your backup server is up and running. It will be used later to restore any backups of the master database and to back up the restored database when the recovery is finished.

2. Create data device.

   Since the master device was corrupted, it must be created anew. Open up the runfile used to start the Sybase server in a text editor. Note the master device path and the size of the master device; they will be used in the *buildmaster* command to re-create the master device.

   To re-create the master device, enter the following *buildmaster* command or the OS equivalent needed by the downed server:

   ```
   buildmaster -d /sybdata/master.dbf -s 8704
   ```

   The *-d* option is the master device path and the *-s* option is the size in pages. For this example, the master device being created is 17 MB (8704 2-K pages) on */sybdata/master.dbf.*

3. Startup in master recovery mode.

   To start the data server in master recovery mode, first make a copy of the current runfile. Edit this file, and add the *-m* master recovery mode parameter. When the change is done, use this file to start the *dataserver* process with the *startserver -f master_runfile* command. This mode will allow the master database's system tables to be updated and prevent users from accessing the system.

4. Re-create master's entries in usages.

   Before anything more can be done to restore the data into the master database, the master device needs to be restored to the same usage as it was when the last backup of the master database was performed. Using hardcopies of the system tables *sysusages*, *sysdevices*, and *sysdatabases*, the entries in *sysusages* can be re-created with the *alter database* and *create database* commands.

To decide if anything needs to be done at this point, examine the *dbid* column in *sysusages*. If more than one entry for *dbid* equals 1 (see *sysdatabases*, *dbid* = 1 = master db), additional space will need to be added into the master database to make the *sysusages* in the server match the one on paper. If there is only one entry, the *sysusages* entry does not need any work and you can move on to Step 5, "Add backup server entry into sysservers."

Example 16-6 through Example 16-8 contain example outputs of the three tables needed for this restore. The T-SQL statement to extract this information is provided above the table output.

Example 16-6. sysdatabases

```
select name,dbid from sysdatabases order by dbid
name                           dbid
------------------------------ ------
  master                         1
  tempdb                         2
  model                          3
  sybsystemprocs                 4
  sybsyntax                      5
  mydb                           6
```

Example 16-7. sysusages

```
select * from sysusages order by vstart
dbid    segmap      lstart      size        vstart      pad    unreservedpgs
------  ----------- ----------- ----------- ----------- ------ -------------
     1           7           0        1536           4  NULL             112
     3           7           0        1024        1540  NULL             608
     2           7           0        1024        2564  NULL             608
     1           7        1536        1024        3588  NULL             920
     5           7           0        1024        4612  NULL             272
     1           7        2560        2048        5636  NULL            2048
     4           7           0        8192    16777216  NULL             864
     6           3           0        5120    67108864  NULL            4720
     6           4        5120        2560    83886080  NULL            2552
```

Example 16-8. sysdevices

```
select * from sysdevices
low        high        status cntrltype name          phyname
--------   ----------- ------ --------- ------------  -------------------------
       0         10751      3         0 master        d_master
67108864      67113983      2         0 mydbdev       /sybdata/mydbdev.dbf
83886080      83888639      2         0 mydblogdev    /sybdata/mydblogdev.dbf
16777216      16785407      2         0 sysprocsdev   /sybdata/sybprocs.dbf
       0          1280     16         3 tapedump1     /dev/st0
       0         20000     16         4 tapedump2     /dev/st1
```

Since this is a recovery of the master database, we only have to restore up to the last master database entry in *sysusages*. These would be those where *dbid*

= 1, and the *vstart* is less than or equal to the *high* value from the master device, *master*, in *sysdevices*. Notice that there are entries between the first and last master db entries on the master device. When restoring the master database, these entries also must be duplicated. In this example,

Fortunately, *buildmaster* has already done part of the work by re-creating the first three entries that correspond with the *master, tempdb*, and *model* databases. In this example, there are only three entries to restore.

Now that the entries to be restored are known, the work of restoring them with the *alter database* and *create database* commands can begin. Use the *dbid* value in *sysusages* to find out which database entry needs to be added next. In this example, the master database was extended for an additional 1024 blocks. This equates to 2 MB of space on the master device. Because the master database already exists, this *alter database* command must be used:

```
alter database master on master = 2
```

The next entry has a *dbid* that corresponds to the *sybsyntax* database. Its segment size is also 1024, so it size is 2MB. Since this database has not been created yet, the following create database command must be used:

```
create database sybsyntax on master = 2
```

Continuing to the final entry, the *dbid* signifies that it is another entry for the master database. The size in this case is 2048 blocks that equal 4 MB (2048/512). The next command to run therefore would be:

```
alter database master on master = 4
```

Now that all the entries for the master database are finished, a load can be performed of the backup, but only after the data server knows about the backup server.

5. Add backup server entry into *sysservers*.

    To be able to do the recovery, the data server needs to know the name of the backup server. If it is not *SYB_BACKUP*, an entry will need to be added to *sysservers*.

    Use the following T-SQL command to update an entry into *sysservers*:

    ```
    begin transaction

    update sysservers
    set srvnetname = "BIG_BACKUP"
    where srvname = "SYB_BACKUP"
    go

    /* Make sure the change is correct */
    select srvnetname,srvname from sysservers
    where srvname = "SYB_BACKUP"
    ```

```
/* If the change is correct  */
commit transaction

/* If the change is not correct */
rollback transaction
```

Proceed to Step 10.

Step 10: Recent Dump of Master Database?

If there is a recent dump of the master database, proceed to Step 11.
If one does not exist, go to Step 13.

Step 11: Restore Master from Dump

Use the following T-SQL command to load the backup of the master database into the system. You might have to change the "from" section of the command to match what is needed for your operating system and environment. Review the section "Restoring from a Hot Backup" for more information. When the backup finishes, the data server will shut itself down automatically.

```
load database master from "/dev/nrmt0"
```

Proceed to Step 12.

Step 12: Update Number of Devices in the Configuration

When a *buildmaster* is performed, the configuration options of the system start at their default values. This can cause problems when the system next comes up because the number of devices is one of those values. This value needs to be set to the value it was when the backup was done, or not all the original devices will come up.

If the Sybase version of the data server is older than Version 11, follow the procedures in the Sybase System Administration manual to set the value of "Number of Devices" to the value it was before the recovery began.

If the version is 11 and later, edit the data server's configuration file and make sure the number of devices is set correctly. Next, edit the runfile created earlier, adding or modifying the *-c* configuration file parameter to point to the proper configuration file.

At this point, the recovery is nearly done, but before the users are allowed back onto the system, it is best to double-check all the changes made during the recovery. Also, if additional device or database changes were made since the time of the master database backup, these changes will all need to be made.

To prevent the users from accessing the system and to allow the system tables to be updated, again start the data server in master recovery mode. Use the runfile edited in Step 2 in a start server command appropriate for your operating system.

 Proceed to Step 13.

Step 13: Restore System Tables Using *disk reinit* and *disk refit*

Once the system comes up, check the system tables *sysusages*, *sysdevices*, and *sysdatabases* against the backup hardcopies. If there are devices on your hardcopy that are not listed in the system, then an additional device was added since the master backup was performed. In this case, a *disk reinit* will update the *sysdevices* table from information on the device. If the *alter database* or *create database* commands were run since the last backup, *disk refit* must be run to resync the data server with the additional devices and databases available on the system.

disk reinit

The command to resync devices is *disk reinit*, and it will add a device back into the *sysdevices* table without initializing the device itself. To run this command correctly, you will need the parameters used when the device was first being created with the *disk reinit* command. The command syntax is in Example 16-9.

Example 16-9. Syntax of disk reinit

```
begin transaction

disk reinit
name = " device_name",
physname = "physical_name",
vdevno = virtual_device_number,
size = number_of_blocks
[, vstart = virtual_address,
cntrltype = controller_number]
go

/* Review the sysdevices table to make sure it matches with
   what is in hard copy  */

select * from sysdevices
go

/* If everything matches */
commit transaction

/* If there are differences */
rollback transaction
```

As you can see, the syntax is exactly like the *disk init* command except for the word *reinit*. Make sure to run this only for devices that do not already appear in the *sysdevices* table.

disk refit

Once all devices that had been added to the system after the backup have been redefined in *sysdevices*, all database additions and changes after the backup can be resynced. The command to do this is called *disk refit*. What it does is visit every disk defined on the system and use system information stored in it to reset the *sysusages* and *sysdatabases* tables to what they should be. The command syntax is in Example 16-10.

Example 16-10. Syntax of disk refit

```
disk reinit
```

There are two restrictions on this command. First, it must be run as *sa*, and second, the system must be started in single-user mode, or the command will not be allowed. Once the command finishes running, the system will automatically shut down.

Once either or both of these commands have been run, compare the values in *sysusages* and *sysdatabases* to make sure they match the hardcopy of these tables. If they do not, the system could come up without all devices and databases being online.

For more information on how to run *disk refit* and *disk reinit*, see the *Sybase System Administration Guide.*

Review sysusages/sysdatabases/sysdevices/syslogins/sysloginroles

Because the master database contains information about all the other databases, it is important to make sure everything is in working order. Follow these checks to help confirm the fitness of your newly restored master database:

1. Check the *sysdevices, sysusages,* and *sysdatabases* system tables.

2. Review each database, checking all the major tables. Run common selects on these tables verifying the data inside.

3. Run the *dbcc checkalloc* command on all databases. For information on how to run this command, see the section "Database consistency checker: the dbcc utility," earlier in this chapter.

4. Double-check the ownership and permissions of all databases. If user logins have been added or deleted since the backup of the master database, these changes will need to be run against the system again in the same order they were added to the system originally. If these changes are done out of order, the *suid*s of the logins added will be different than when they were first added to the system. This will cause a mismatch between the *suid* controlling the ownership and permissions in a database and those in the system logins. Because of this, there could be problems with access to the databases and objects in the data server.

   To make sure the *suid*s are the same, compare the hardcopy of the *syslogin* system table and the online version of the table. If they do not match, there could be problems. Refer to Sybase's Security Information Guide for more information on re-creating changes to logins if the original scripts cannot be found.

   Another art of Sybase's security is login roles. The *sysloginroles* system table contains information regarding these roles. It is important that this table also is checked to make sure all roles are the same as before the problem started, otherwise users might not have the same abilities as before. To make sure they are the same, compare the hardcopy of *sysloginroles* system table and the online version of the table. Refer to Sybase's Security Information Guide to help re-create changes to the system roles if they do not match.

   Proceed to Step 25.

Step 14: sybsystemprocs Available?

The *sybsystemprocs* database is where Sybase locates all the system stored procedures. When a stored procedure is created here, it is available from any database in the data server. Therefore, when this database is unavailable, many important system stored procedures will be unavailable, such as *sp_help*, *sp_helpdb*, and *sp_helpdevices*. The rest of the data server databases will come up as long as they do not have problems, but the functionality of the data server will be severely degraded.

 If sybsystemprocs is available, go to Step 20. Otherwise, go to Step 15.

Step 15: Problem with Data Devices?

If the data server's error log file shows there are problems initializing a data device, then follow these procedures to check OS device problems, fix them, and maybe replace them:

1. Check ownership and permissions on devices.

   Use the OS commands to check permissions and make sure the process running the Sybase *dataserver* program has permissions to read and write to these devices. If they do not, either change the permissions on the devices or change the user that is running the *dataserver* program to one that does have the correct permissions

2. Is the device functioning correctly or does the device even exist?

   Sometimes, because of a change in the system, the operating system might no longer "see" the device. Also, there might be hardware failures or configuration errors that could cause the device to not appear. Use the appropriate OS procedure to check the device's status and review all error logs.

3. Is the OS unable to detect device at startup?

   Sometimes, when an OS cannot detect a device when a Sybase server is started, the device will be unavailable, and Sybase will not be able to recover the database. In this case, the database will be marked "suspect." This flag on the database tells Sybase not to waste any time trying to recover this database the next time the data server restarts. This is efficient, but if the device's problems are fixed with the data intact, the database should be able to come up the next time the system starts.

To get around this problem, the "suspect" flag must be cleared from the database. Unfortunately, there is no easy stored procedure to run to do this. If you are sure the database will come up OK on a restart, run the T-SQL commands in Example 16-11, replacing *yourdbname* with the name of the database the server needs to recover.

Example 16-11. Removing the Suspect Flag

```
use master

/* Tell dataserver to allow changes to system tables */

sp_configure "allow updates", 1
reconfigure with override
go

/* Change the suspect status bit */
begin transaction
update sysdatdabases        /* Only make change */
set status = status - 256   /* Turn the suspect flag (2^8 bit set) off   */
where dbname = 'yourdbname'    /* only on this database */
and status & 256 = 256                  /* and only if flag is set */
go
commit transaction
/* Tell dataserver to not allow changes to system tables */

sp_configure "allow updates", 0
reconfigure
```

Restart the server at this point. If the database still does not come back on, then something else must be wrong with the database. Review the data server error log for more information and possibly contact Sybase support.

If there are still problems with the device files, repeat Step 15, then proceed to Step 16. If the device files are fine, proceed to Step 17.

Step 16: Replace Device/Disk File

If a drive goes bad, but another one of the same size is available, the new one can be used in the place of the old in the Sybase database. This is because Sybase uses logical devices that point to the actual devices.

All databases that were using this device will need to be restored. To find out which databases these are, run the T-SQL command shown in Example 16-12.

Example 16-12. Locating Databases That Use a Particular Device

```
select sysdevices.name as DevName,
sysdatabases.name as DBName,
sysusages.size/512 as Size
from sysdatabases, sysusages, sysdevices
where
sysdevices.name="BadDeviceName" and
sysdevices.low <= sysusages.vstart  and
sysdevices.high >= sysusages.vstart and
sysusages.dbid = sysdatabases.dbid
```

Example Output:

DevName	DBName	Size
BusDev1	BillingDB	3
BusDev1	ClientDB	2

 This command will work only if the master database at least comes up.

With this information, the original device must be deleted from the system before the new device can be added. Before this, all databases that were using this device first must be dropped from the system. Use the *drop database* or the *dbcc repairdb(dropdb,dbname)* command to drop the databases. Once they are all gone, then the device can be dropped by using the *sp_dropdevice* stored procedure.

Once the device is dropped, the new device can be added back into its place. Use the same *disk init* command that was used to create the bad device, but replace the physical name of the bad device with the name of the good device and use a different *vdevno*. For example, if the original disk's physical name was */dev/rdsk/ c0t2d1s0* with a *disk init* command of:

```
disk init
name="BusDev1",
physname="/dev/dsk/c0t2d1s0",
vdevno=6,
size=2048
```

the new command using the replacement device */dev/dsk/c1t3d0s1* would be:

```
disk init
name="BusDev1",
physname="/dev/dsk/c1t3d0s1",
vdevno=10,
size=2048
```

Once the device has been restored, then all the databases that were using that device need to be restored.

   Proceed to Step 17.

Step 17: Restore Base sybsystemprocs from sybsystemprocs Script

When the *sybsystemprocs* database needs to be restored, follow these directions:

1. Find out which devices *sybsystemprocs* was installed on.

   First, try the command *sp_helpdb sybsystemprocs* to find out how large and on what device it was created. Most likely this will not work. In that case, run the T-SQL command in Example 16-13 instead.

   Example 16-13. Finding Out Size of Device

   ```
   select sysdevices.name, sysusages.size/512
   from sysdatabases, sysusages, sysdevices
   where
   sysdatabases.name = "sybsystemprocs" and
   sysusages.dbid = sysdatabases.dbid and
   sysdevices.low <= sysusages.vstart  and
   sysdevices.high >= sysusages.vstart
   Example output:

   name
   ----------------------------- -----------
   sysprocsdev                            16
   ```

2. Drop the *sybsystemprocs* database.

   In case the *sybsystemprocs* database is corrupt, it is best to drop it and re-create it fresh. First try the T-SQL command *drop database sybsystemprocs*. But, if it is not allowed by the system, use *dbcc dbrepair (sybsystemprocs,dropdb)* to drop the database.

3. Re-create the *sybsystemprocs* database on the device shown in the preceding command:

   ```
   1> create database sybsystemprocs on sysprocsdev= 16MB
   ```

4. Run *installmaster* or restore from backup.

If there is a current backup of the *sybsystemprocs* database, then it can be used to restore the database with the *load* command like this:

```
load database sybsystemprocs from "device"
```

Use the appropriate OS command for the data server environment.

If there is no backup of the *sybsystemprocs* database, it will need to be re-created using the T-SQL script *installmaster*. This script can be run safely without worry that it will affect other databases. To run the script, provide it as input to the *isql* program like this:

```
isql -U sa -S SYB_MYDB -P mypasswd \
 -i $SYBASE/scripts/installmaster
```

or:

```
isql -U sa -S SYB_MYDB -P mypasswd \
 < $SYBASE/scripts/installmaster
```

There will be a lot of output from this command, but it can be safely ignored until the script ends with the message "Loading of the master database is complete."

5. Add any additional stored procedures/changes.

   If additional stored procedures have been added to the system since the backup or since the initial install, re-create them now using the scripts used to originally create them or by entering the commands interactively.

6. Check stored procedures.

   As with all the other recoveries, it is important to check out the recovery. The following command will show if the *sybsystemprocs* database is restored correctly:

   ```
   sp_helpdb sybsystemprocs
   ```

   If output describing the *sybsystemprocs* database is displayed when this is run, then system stored procedures have been restored correctly. Run any user-defined stored procedures to confirm they run correctly.

7. Dump the *sybsystemprocs* database.

   Once the database has been restored, make a complete backup of it with the *dump* command.

Proceed to Step 18.

Step 18: Recent Dump of Database?

 If there is no dump of the database to restore, go to Step 25 to reapply any creation/alteration scripts and load any *bcps* from the database. If there is a recent dump, continue to Step 19.

Step 19: Restore from Dump

If the database is still offline at this point, then something is wrong with it internally, and it should be restored from a backup. Before anything else is done, retrieve information about the database to use in the re-creation. Enter the command in Example 16-14 to find out about the allocations used by this database.

Example 16-14. Database Allocations

```
select sysdevices.name,
size as Blocks,
size/512 as Mbytes
from sysusages, sysdevices, sysdatabases
where sysdatabases.name = "baddbname" and
sysusages.dbid = sysdatabases.dbid and
sysdevices.low <= sysusages.vstart  and
sysdevices.high >= sysusages.vstart and
sysdevices.cntrltype = 0
order by vstart
```

```
Example Output:
```

name	Blocks	Mbytes
device1	1536	3
logdev1	1024	2
device3	2048	4

Take the following steps to do the restore:

1. Drop the database.

   First, try to drop the database using this T-SQL command:

   drop database *baddbname*

   If this command fails, use this *dbcc* command to drop the database:

   dbcc repairdb(dropdb, *baddbname*)

   To verify the database has been dropped, run the stored procedure *sp_helpdb*. If the database is shown in the output, something went wrong with the *drop database* command.

2. Re-create the database.

Using the database allocations determined above, re-create the database using the same allocations it had. Here is an example based upon the preceding example output:

```
create database baddbname
on device1 = 3
log on logdev1 = 2
alter database baddbname
on device3 = 4
```

3. Bring the database online.

At this point, the database has been re-created, but the system will not bring it online until it is told to. The reason the system does this is it has no way of knowing if there are any more transaction logs to process. Tell Sybase the database should be brought up by running the *online database baddbname* command.

4. Load the database from dumps.

Now reload the database using the most recent database and transaction dumps. First, apply the full database backup. For our example database, here is an example Unix *load* command using the tape device */dev/nrmt0*:

```
load database baddbname from '/dev/nrmt0'
```

After this completes, apply each transaction log starting with the oldest and finishing with the newest. The system will not allow load of the transaction logs to occur out of order. In fact, if any of the logs are missing or corrupt, the rest of the logs cannot be applied. To load the transaction logs for our preceding example, enter the following command, repeating it for each transaction dump:

```
load transaction baddbname from '/dev/nrmt0'
```

For more information on how to load dumps and transaction logs, please refer to "Restoring from a Hot Backup," earlier in this chapter.

5. Dump the database.

Whenever a database is restored, run a full backup on the database, and back up the master database, too. The reason for the backup of the master database is because there was a removal and creation of a database. Whenever there are major changes to the data server, back up the master database. Continuing our example, the *dump* command would be:

```
dump database baddbname to '/dev/nrmt0'
```

Proceed to Step 25.

Step 20: Is tempdb Available?

Is the tempdb online and available? To see this, review the messages generated when trying to start the database. There will be error messages complaining about tempdb not being available. The system will not be able to come up at this point.

If there are error messages, proceed to Step 15 to make sure tempdb's devices are all available. If tempdb is available, continue to Step 23 to begin checking all the user-defined databases.

Step 21: Model Database Available?

If the model database is online and available, proceed to Step 24. If it is not, return to Steps 14 and 16. Then proceed to Step 22.

Step 22: Re-create Generic Model Database

The model database is used by the data server when creating all other databases. If a specific attribute (larger size, tables, permissions, stored procedures) is required in all databases, make the change first in the model database. Then, from that point on, every database created will contain this change.

If you have a backup of the model database and you can use the *isql use* command, then the database can be restored directly from backup using the *load* command. If not, then the database must be restored from scratch. Use the following commands to accomplish this:

1. Run *buildmaster*.

   If there is no backup of the model database available, the *buildmaster* command can be used to restore the model database to the same state as when the data server was first installed. Here is a Unix example:

   ```
   buildmaster -d/syback/master.dbf -x
   ```

In this example, the *-d* parameter is the master database file path, and the *-x* parameter tells *buildmaster* to restore the model database. Be sure to use the appropriate *buildmaster* command for your OS. This can be found in the Sybase Utilities manual.

2. If a backup of the model database is available, use it in a *load* command to restore it from the backup:

```
load database model from "/sybackups/model.dmp"
```

3. If additional changes were made since the last backup, apply them at this point.

4. Back up the model database using the *dump* command.

    Return to Step 18.

Step 23: All Databases Online?

If when the data server is coming up, and an error occurs with any of the devices associated with that database or something has corrupted the database, the non-system database could be prevented from coming and will be marked "suspect."

To see if all the databases after the system databases are online, review the messages generated when trying to start the database. There will be error messages complaining about any databases not being available. Fortunately, because all the system databases are available, the Sybase server will come up. If this happens, go to Step 15 to make sure all the user database devices are all available. If all the database are available, then the system is up and no recovery is required.

    If all the databases are online, you are done. If not, return to Step 15.

Step 24: Contact Sybase Support

If you have reached this step, then some problem that might be specific to the OS, version of Sybase, or other factors is occurring. Please refer to the Sybase System Administration guides for your OS or contact Sybase support for additional help.

Return to Step 1.

Step 25: Reapply Any Additional Scripts or bcps

If any additional scripts had been run on the database since the last dump, then these scripts need to be run again. Since they are user created, you will need to refer to the user's instructions on how to run these.

On top of additional scripts, there might be *bcp* files of data from these databases. Follow the steps needed to restore these datafiles to the originating database tables. Please refer to "Logical Backups," the next major section, for information on loading data into the system.

 Proceed to Step 26.

Step 26: Review Against Hardcopies

Using hardcopies of the system tables and any important user tables, compare the current data with the data captured in the hardcopies. If there are discrepancies, then there could be additional problems with the data server. Refer to the Sybase Administration manuals to find out if the differences need to be repaired or are OK. Double-check all permissions on the database if any changes were made in the syslogin or sysrole tables. If there are, correct them before turning the system over to the user population.

 Proceed to Step 27.

Step 27: Dump all Restored Databases

Now that the database has been restored, dump the database to a new dump file. This way a current dump of the database, including all scripts and data changes, will be saved. This will help facilitate recovery in case of future problems.

Return to Step 1.

Logical Backups

The *dump* command is a very powerful backup tool, but there are limitations to its abilities. For one thing, it can only back up all of the database objects together. If a backup of a single table in the system is needed, this command cannot be used. Also, the *dump* backups cannot be used to copy a database between servers running different operating systems; this is because the backups are copies of the data disk blocks, and these disk blocks are dependent on the operating system. The need to back up only parts of a database and make them useful on all types of operating systems is why Sybase created the logical backup utility *bcp*. This utility also provides the final piece to make sure all the information needed to restore the data server is collected.

bcp provides another key feature. Because it refers to the internal structure of the database, it is an excellent tool to confirm whether there is corruption, while also backing up the data. The *bcp* command will error out if it has any problems reading the data out of the system.

The two drawbacks to *bcp* are that:

- It takes much longer to use it to back up the whole database than it takes with the *dump* command.

- Every single object in the database would have to be backed up separately, and any stored procedures, triggers, or other nondata objects would have to be output using a different method.

The *bcp* command is run at the operating system level like *isql*, and it too takes a number of different parameters. This discussion addresses only the few parameters needed as part of a good backup procedure. Again, please check the Sybase literature for more information on all Sybase parameters.

```
bcp [[database_name.]owner.]table_name {in | out} datafile -c
-S servername -U username -P password
```

The first parameter *bcp* takes is the table to be copied. This parameter is in ANSI standard format, but the minimum needed is the *table_name*. The other two parts, if left out, will default to the default database and the username of the data server login used to run the command.

The *bcp* utility is used to copy the data in and out of the database table. Choose *in* to copy the data from a file into a table. Choose *out* to copy the data from a table to a datafile. The `datafile` is the path of a file in which to place the data or from which to get the data. The last parameter, *-c*, is optional. It directs the *bcp* command to output the datafile in a compatible text mode that can be used interchangeably between any operating system. If this is not used, the output defaults to a system-specific format and cannot be guaranteed to be interchangeable.

Performing a Logical Backup

The *bcp* utility has one major caveat when it comes to importing data into a table. If the table does not have indexes or triggers, *bcp* uses a fast mode of inserting the data. This mode is faster because none of the changes is logged into the transaction log. In fact, when this is done, a transaction log dump is not allowed until a full database dump is done. This should be used when a large amount of data is being inserted into a table. Just remember to run a full database dump when the *bcp* completes; otherwise, the database will be running from that point on without the safety net of the transaction log.

 To be sure to have all the data needed for recovery, it is recommended to *bcp* out these five system tables in the master database: *sysdatabases*, *syslogins*, *sysroles*, *sysusages*, and *syssegments*. Use the *-c* option to be able to view the data in the datafiles even if the data server is down.

If an index or trigger exists on the table, the slower, logged mode of *bcp* is used. Be careful when inserting large amounts of data. The transaction log can get very big very quickly and potentially could fill up, stopping processing on the database. If this happens, be sure to dump the transaction log, emptying it out. Here is sample output from a *bcp* command run on the system table *master.dbo.sysusages*. The output is in character format into a file in */sybackups/sysusages.bcp*:

```
# bcp master.dbo.sysusages out /sybackups/sysusages.bcp -c -S SYB_MYDB -U \
        sa -P mypassword
Starting copy...

9 rows copied.
Clock Time (ms.): total = 1000   Avg = 111    (9.00 rows per sec.)
```

Performing a Logical Restore

One prerequisite before using *bcp* to restore data into a table is to make sure the table exists beforehand. *bcp* does not create objects; it just transfers data in and out of the database. *bcp* also is handy when you need to import data from a delimited data source such as a comma-separated set of values (CSV file). The latter topic is beyond the scope of this book, but more information can be found in the Sybase Utilities manual. Here, we will discuss how to store table data in a file and how to restore it back into a database.

The only big syntax difference between *bcp*ing data into a table rather than out of a table is changing the word "out" to "in." (Isn't that exciting!) All other parameters are exactly the same. A few important factors that do not come into play when *bcp*ing data out are *-e errorfile* and *-m maxerrors*. The *-m* option specifies the maximum nonfatal errors *bcp* will allow before quitting. The *-e* option specifies the error file where the data rows from the *bcp* file that caused the nonfatal errors are stored for later review. (In both cases, any error messages display at the terminal.) These parameters are used to allow the *bcp* command to continue after encountering nonfatal errors and to record the records that error for later correction.

Here is an example:

```
# bcp mydb.dbo.zyx in /sybackups/zyx.bcp -c -S SYB_MYDB -U sa
              -P mypassword
Starting copy...

192 rows copied.
Clock Time (ms.): total = 1000    Avg = 5     (192.00 rows per sec.)
```

When the *bcp* file is created using the *-c* option, the records are stored in a character-based, transportable record format. This is very handy when adjustments need to be made to the data before *bcp*ing them back into a database. This format allows the use of a simple text editor to make the changes. For example, if the third column in the *bcp* file represents department names, and one of the names has been changed, use an editor to open the file and do a replacement of the old name with the new name. Also, if a number of records are erroring out and they are preventing the *bcp*-in from continuing, edit the file, deleting the problem lines.

This trick is particularly handy when using *bcp* to restore system tables. When the master database is re-created, certain default entries—such as the *syslogins* entry *sa*—are always created in the system tables. When trying to restore using a *bcp* of this table, the *bcp* will fail because of the unique index on this table. To get around this, copy the syslogins *bcp* file and remove the entries from the copy that is already in the **syslogins** table. Once these are gone, *bcp*ing this altered copy of the file will succeed.

An Ounce of Prevention . . .

One common thread throughout this chapter and the other database recovery chapters is that recovering without the proper backups is, at the least, very difficult, and, at the worst, impossible. If you employ the following tips, you will have a better chance at keeping your system healthy and in a state from which it can be easily recovered.

Starting Out

- Run a full cold backup of the data server. Make sure to have both online *bcp*s of the system tables and hardcopy outputs.

- Run a full hot backup. Store a copy onsite and a copy offsite.

- Document all backup and recovery procedures.

- Make sure all databases have transaction logging enabled and running. A quick way to check this is to dump the transaction log. If it does not work, check the *dboptions* of the database making sure *select into/bcp* is not enabled.

- Mirror the system databases. This way more than one physical device will be covering the system databases. If one of the devices has problems, it can be taken out of the set automatically, and the system keeps functioning smoothly. If you can afford the disk space, mirroring other databases also will provide added security.

Day to Day

- Run a regularly scheduled automated backup procedure.

- Check the system error logs regularly. Take appropriate action as soon as possible when any error shows up.

- Run *dbcc* checks periodically to make sure the internal structures of your databases are OK.

After Major Changes

- Run a full backup of the system tables whenever you add devices, add databases, change configurations, or make substantial object changes. That not only will speed up recovery time but also will provide an added level of reliability.

- Run a full backup if any nonlogged events such as *bcp*ing large amounts of data or performing a *select into* occurs. If either of these happens, this system will stop logging changes in the transaction logs until a full backup is performed.

If in doubt, make as full a backup as possible. Also, if you can, run through a full backup using your procedures. Then use the procedures to restore from these backups. I have seen more than one site have backups that, when they needed them, were completely useless.

VI

Backup & Recovery Potpourri

Part VI consists of the following three chapters:

- Chapter 17, *ClearCase Backup & Recovery*, describes backup and recovery of ClearCase, a software configuration management tool.
- Chapter 18, *Backup Hardware*, provides information on the characteristics of, and trade-offs among, various hardware architectures.
- Chapter 19, *Miscellanea*, discusses other backup topics, such as volatile filesystems, gigabyte Ethernet, and disk recovery companies.

17

ClearCase Backup & Recovery

ClearCase is a software configuration management tool developed and marketed by Rational, Inc. ClearCase is most commonly used in software projects involving at least several developers but often in environments with hundreds of developers in many groups. Like many other chapters in this book, this chapter is here due to ClearCase's popularity. Since I've been asked hundreds of times about how to back up and recover ClearCase, I thought it would make a great addition to this book.

The following description can be found on the ClearCase web site (*http://www. rational.com/products/ClearCase*):

> ClearCase provides comprehensive configuration management, including version control, workspace management, build management, and process control—without forcing you to change your existing environment, your tools, or the way you work.

As with almost any DBMS, ClearCase must be quiescent before backups can be performed. Hence, the general strategy is to lock or make unavailable the items(s) being backed up, do the backup, and then reactivate the ClearCase access to those items. This may seem like a simplistic approach, but it is the most reliable. In the following sections, you will see this paradigm used extensively.

 This chapter was written by Bob Fulwiler, who lives outside Seattle, Washington, and specializes in Unix system administration and software configuration management. Bob may be reached at *bobf@oz.net*.

ClearCase Architecture

I'll begin with a discussion of ClearCase architecture, since many of the terms that are used to describe ClearCase may be unfamiliar.

VOBs and Views

ClearCase has a "multilevel" architecture:

- The first, or base, layer is the Unix filesystem with all the usual components and restrictions.

- The second layer is Rational's proprietary Multi-Version File System (MVFS); it is this layer which acts very much like a DBMS and allows the multiversion functionality of ClearCase.

- The third layer is the *Versioned Object Base* (*VOB*); the VOB is the basic data container for items under control of ClearCase. A ClearCase installation typically has several VOBs at any given time. Each VOB is owned and used by a particular group or groups in order to do their work.

- The fourth, and last, layer is a ClearCase *view*. Just as a database view selectively accesses particular database items, so does a ClearCase view determine which items a worker can access at any given time. Views also have their own data storage containers that hold temporary items such as program files that are currently being modified. The mechanics of how these containers are accessed is not germane to this discussion, but if you're interested, you can find more information on the Rational ClearCase web site.

  A view is similar to a VOB in that it has its own storage directory, but is accessed through a *view tag*. A VOB tag is a full pathname because it is a mount point. However, a view tag is a simple name because it is accessed as part of a directory pathname. Like a VOB, a view must be explicitly activated; usually with the *setview* command. Views are discussed in greater detail later.

A distinction needs to be made between what ClearCase considers *public* and *private*; these concepts can apply to both VOBs and views. Public items are essentially community property to which access is controlled by the owning group, but which several people may be accessing (of course, not the same item) simultaneously. Anyone with the appropriate group permissions may access the VOBs/views in a manner very similar to the use of Unix filesystem ACLs. Private VOBs/views typically are owned and administered by one individual and are usually for her personal use in development or testing. An owner may allow access to others, but private items usually are not considered "public" property. For this reason, many sites do not back up private VOBs/views as they do public ones but instead leave that activity to the VOB/view owner. However, I show how to back up private as well as public items.

Registry

The ClearCase *Registry* is the "glue" that binds all of the ClearCase items and functions together. It contains pointers and records to each ClearCase item, including characteristics of the item, modifications, ownership, and permissions. Each time a ClearCase action is taken on a ClearCase object, the Registry is updated to reflect that action. As a result, when backups are done on VOBs and/or views, the Registry also should be backed up. It also should be restored at the same time as a VOB/view restore in order to keep all the parts of a ClearCase environment synchronized.

License Server

The ClearCase license server, like any license server, controls how many users may access ClearCase at any given time. While it usually isn't necessary to back up the license file as frequently as VOBs/views, I would suggest that, at a minimum, you keep a copy of the license file outside the ClearCase environment or print a hardcopy in the few instances in which a manual restore or fix is required.

Useful Terms

These parts of ClearCase should be considered when implementing backups:

Versioned Object Base (VOB)
> A repository that stores versions of file elements, directory elements, derived objects, and metadata associated with these objects. With MultiSite (see "MultiSite backup," later in this chapter), a VOB can be replicated at multiple sites.

VOB server
> A machine that physically stores the VOB files and runs a process called *vob_server* that clients communicate with in order to access VOB data.

Registry server
> A registry server is the host on which all ClearCase data storage areas (all VOBs and views) in a local area network are centrally registered. ClearCase supports a primary and backup registry server host. The backup host is used if the primary host becomes unavailable.

License server
> A license server is a host whose *albd_server* process controls access to the licenses defined in its license database file. Any ClearCase client must be able

to communicate with a license server in order to access any ClearCase-related data.

View

A view is a ClearCase component that provides a work area for one or more users—to edit source versions, compile them into object modules, format them into documents, and so on. Users in different views can work with the same files without interfering with one another. For each element in a VOB, a view's configuration specification selects one version from the element's version tree. Each view also can store view-private files and view-private directories, which do not appear in other views.

MVFS

An MVFS is a directory tree that, when activated (mounted as a filesystem of type MVFS), implements a ClearCase VOB. To standard operating system commands, a VOB appears to contain a directory hierarchy. ClearCase commands also can access the VOB's metadata. Also, "MVFS filesystem" refers to a filesystem extension to the operating system, which provides access to VOB data.

MultiSite replica

An instance of a VOB, located at a particular site; refers to the VOB's database and all of the VOB's data containers.

View-private file

A file that exists only in a particular view. A private file is not version controlled, except insofar as it is separate from private files in other views.

Registry Backup and Recovery Procedures

All VOBs and views are "registered" in the ClearCase storage Registry. Someone first setting up ClearCase designates a *registry server host*. The Registry itself is contained in the directory */usr/adm/atria/rgy* (on some platforms, */var/adm/atria/rgy*). This directory contains at least six files: *vob_tag*, *vob_object*, *view_tag*, *view_object*, *regions*, and *site_config*. In order to adequately back up the Registry, all six files must be included in the backup. The *albd_server* process services the Registry.

Registry backups

The simplest way to ensure good registry backups is to designate one or more machines as *backup registry server host(s)*. A backup registry host takes periodic snapshots of the primary registry host's registry files (see the *rgy_backup* command in the ClearCase manuals) and client list and stores these snapshot files in the directory */usr/adm/atria/rgy/backup* (on some platforms, */var/adm/atria/rgy/backup*). In the event of primary registry server failure, an administrator can run *rgy_switchover* to activate a backup registry server and reset all client hosts accordingly.

Here is the procedure for making a backup registry host after ClearCase is installed (for ClearCase Versions 3.0–3.2).* On the primary registry host:

1. Edit the *rgy_hosts.conf* file to identify the primary and backup registry servers. The first line of this file should contain the name of the primary registry host; the second line should have the name(s) of one or more hosts to be backup registry servers, that is:

   ```
   primary_registry_host
   first_backup_host,second_backup_host
   ```

2. Copy the *~gy.hosts.conf* file to the */usr/adm/atria/rgy* directory on every client host (including the backup registry host(s)).

3. Usually, the *rgy_backup* program runs automatically once a day on each backup registry host. However, if you feel the need to do a manual backup, log on to the backup registry host as "root" and execute the command *$CCHOME/bin/rgy_backup*.

If you are using one host for all ClearCase server functions, the Registry still should have periodic backups. This is done by shutting down the *albd_server*, backing up the Registry directory, and then restarting the *albd_server*. Since these are just flat files, any available backup method may be used for this backup. The script in Example 17-1 demonstrates the steps to perform a flat-file backup.

Example 17-1. Registry Backup Script: regback.sh

```
#!/bin/sh
#

# This script should be run as "root"

#######################################################
##Site-specific section (change as appopriate)

PATH=/usr/bin:/usr/sbin:/usr/ucb:$CC
CC=$CC/cleartool              # ClearCase executable
# Uncomment one of the following to set the media to be used to
# hold the registry backup.  Be sure to make the same change
# on the restore script.
# dev="/dev/rmt/0"           # default tape drive
# dev="/usr/adm/backup"      # disk

# Step 1:  Shut down the albd_server
```

---

* For the sake of brevity, the variable $CCHOME will be used to represent the ClearCase executable directory in use at your site. It may be */usr/atria/*, */opt/atria/v32*, or the executables directory at your site.

Example 17-1. Registry Backup Script: regback.sh (continued)

```
$CC/atria_start stop

# Step 2: Back up the registry
#
# Insert your usual backup method here.
#
# If you do not have commercial or homegrown backup facilities,
# please see the Native Backup Utilities: Unix chapter for
# suggestions and sample scipts.
# Example command to back up the registry to a local
# 8-mm tape drive on a Solaris system (assuming that the 8 mm is
# the default drive):

#  dump 0fuv /dev/rmt/0 /usr/adm/atria/rgy

# Step 3: Restart the aldb_server

$CC/atria_start start


####################################################
echo "ClearCase Registry Backup complete."
####################################################
```

Registry recovery

The restore process follows the same sequence of events: shut down the *albd_server*, restore the files, and restart the *albd_server*. The actual restore can be done using the same tools that were used to create the backup.

1. On the secondary server (**first_backup_host**), execute the following command:

   ```
   $ rgy_switchover -backup "second_backup_host primary_registry_host"
   primary_registry_host first_backup_host
   ```

2. For any client that was down or for some reason unreachable by the network (record their name in the previous step), do the following after the client is available once again:

   a. Log in to the client.

   b. Stop ClearCase (shut down the *albd_server*) by executing the command *$CCHOME/etc/atria_start stop*.

   c. Change the *rgy_hosts.conf* so that the first line is **first_backup_host**.

   d. Restart ClearCase (start the *albd_server* process) by executing the command *$CCHOME/etc/atria_start start*.

The script in Example 17-2 demonstrates the steps required to perform this type of restoration.

Example 17-2. Registry Restore Script: regrest.sh

```
#!/bin/sh
#
# This script should be run as "root"


#####################################################
##Site-specific section (change as appopriate)

PATH=/usr/bin:/usr/sbin:/usr/ucb:$CC
CC=$CC/cleartool              # ClearCase executable
# Uncomment one of the following to set the media to be used to
# hold the registry backup.  Be sure to make the same change
# on the restore script.
# dev="/dev/rmt/0"           # default tape drive
# dev="/usr/adm/backup"      # disk


# Step 1:  Shut down the albd_server

$CC/atria_start stop


# Step 2: Restore the registry
#
# Insert your usual restore method here.
#
# If you do not have commercial or homegrown restore facilities,
# please see the Native Backup Utilities: Unix chapter for
# suggestions and sample scipts.
# Example command to restore the registry from a local
# 8-mm tape drive on a Solaris sytem:

#  ufsrestore rxfv /dev/rmt/0 /usr/adm/atria/rgy

# Step 3: Restart the aldb_server

$CC/atria_start start

#################################################
echo "ClearCase Registry Restoration complete."
#################################################
```

When the primary server host is once again available, follow the same procedure to make it the actual primary registry server host again. Make sure that the two servers are synchronized by backing up the original primary before switching back to the original configuration.

VOB Backup and Recovery Procedures

A VOB (Versioned Object Base) is a data repository for a directory tree. A VOB is implemented as a standard directory tree, whose top-level directory is termed the *VOB storage directory*. The directory contains files and subdirectories. The VOB storage area is recognizable by its *vbs* suffix.

The VOB must be activated on the host by mounting it as a filesystem of type MVFS (ClearCase multiversion filesystem type). See the ClearCase *mount* reference page for more information. As mentioned earlier, most sites leave the backup/restore of private VOBs to the individual owner, but if the site wants to include private VOBs in their normal backup, the following procedures can apply to private VOBs as well.

VOB Backup Strategies

The general VOB backup strategy is to follow a three-step process:

1. Make the VOB quiescent.

2. Back up the storage directory.

3. Reactivate the VOB.

This section discusses the various ways in which this can be done.

Common strategies for doing a VOB backup include (but are not limited to): standard and snapshot (the two most common), disk backup, and the use of mirrors. Since the main thrust is the backing up of the physical storage directory, there are many ways this can be accomplished, including the use of commercial tools.

Standard strategy

The standard backup procedure is to "lock" the VOB, thereby ensuring that it is unavailable to other processes during the backup. It is extremely important that the VOB remain locked during the backup process; otherwise, incomplete and unpredictable results will occur. It also should be noted that backup utilities that reset *atime* should be avoided, because it prevents other parts of ClearCase from functioning properly.

Example 17-3 provides an example of this type of VOB backup script.

Example 17-3. Standard VOB Backup Script: vob_standard.s

```
#!/bin/sh

# Export the correct path so that all the required binaries
#can be found

case $0 in
```

Example 17-3. Standard VOB Backup Script: vob_standard.s (continued)

```
/* ) PATH=/usr/atria/bin:/bin:/usr/bin:`/bin/dirname $0`
     c=`/bin/basename $0`
;;
* ) PATH=/usr/atria/bin:/bin:/usr/bin:/usr/sbin
     c=$0
;;
esac
export PATH

if [ $# -ne 1 ] ; then
  echo "
Usage: $0 <lock|unlock>
       (Will lock or unlock all clearcase vobs on this server...)"
exit 1
fi

HOST=`hostname|awk -F. '{print $1}'`

#Get a list of all vobs on this server
VOBS=`cleartool lsvob -host $HOST|sed 's/*//' |awk '{print $1}'`

case $1 in

lock )

  for VOB in $VOBS ; do
   # (Lock VOBS)
   cleartool lock -c 'VOB backups in progress' -vob $VOB \
   > /tmp/voblock.log 2>&1
  done

 ;;

unlock )

  for VOB in $VOBS ; do
   # (Unlock VOBS)
   cleartool unlock -vob $VOB > /tmp/vobunlock.log 2>&1
  done

 ;;

* )
   echo "
 Usage: $0 <lock|unlock>
     (Will lock or unlock all clearcase vobs on this server...)"
 exit 1
 ;;

esac
```

Snapshot strategy

The ClearCase term for this strategy is *semilive*. To enable database snapshots, execute the ClearCase command *vob_snapshot_setup* on a VOB (see the ClearCase Reference manual for details). This approach has costs and benefits that need to be considered:

- This is the *least hands-on* strategy, as the system automatically takes snapshots of the current VOB contents.

- This strategy has the benefit of reducing the amount of time a VOB needs to be locked.

- Since the snapshot is stored on disk, it increases disk space usage.

- The restore procedures are more complex, and if the restored pools are older than those currently in the VOB, some data may be lost.

Use the following procedure to configure VOBs to use the snapshot utility. For more detail, see the ClearCase Reference Manual. Use the command *vob_snapshot lsvob* to determine which VOBs are set up for snapshotting. If the VOB you wish to snapshot is not already set up, use the *vob_snapshot_setup* utility to configure it for snapshotting. Consider the following command:

```
$ vob_snapshot_setup modparam -snap_to /snapshots/src /vobs/src
```

This would cause the VOB */vobs/src* to be snapshot to */snapshots/src* whenever the *vob_snapshot* utility is run (typically from *cron*, but not necessarily right before backups). In order to execute the snapshot utility on a regular basis, put an entry into the root *crontab*:

```
0 22 * * * /bin/sh /usr/atria/config/cron/vob_snapshot.sh
```

It is important that you back up both the snapshot directory and the VOB storage directory.

See Example 17-4 for this type of VOB backup script.

Example 17-4. Snapshot VOB Backup Script: vob_snap.sh

```
#!/bin/sh

case $0 in
/* ) PATH=/bin:/usr/bin:/usr/sbin:/sbin:`/bin/dirname $0`
;;
* )  PATH=/bin:/usr/bin:/usr/sbin:/sbin
;;
esac

export PATH

Lockvobs()
```

Example 17-4. Snapshot VOB Backup Script: vob_snap.sh (continued)

```
{
/nsr/bin/vobs.sh lock
}

Unlockvobs()
{
/nsr/bin/vobs.sh unlock
}

X=$$
VXCONFIG=/etc/vxfs_lock.list
VFSTAB=/etc/vfstab

#vxconfig file is in the format:
#vxfs_device:snapsize:snapshot_device:snapshot_mount_point

Snap()
{

#Make a startup file that will clean this up if the system
#reboots in the middle of it

echo "#!/bin/sh
X=\$\$

  for LINE in \`cat $VXCONFIG\`
  do

  VXFS_DEVICE=\`echo \$LINE|awk -F: '{print \$1}'\`
  SNAPSHOT_DEVICE=\`echo \$LINE|awk -F: '{print \$3}'\`
  SNAPSHOT_RAW_DEVICE=\`echo \$SNAPSHOT_DEVICE\
    |sed 's-/dsk/-/rdsk/-'\`
  SNAPSHOT_MOUNT_POINT=\`echo \$LINE|awk -F: '{print \$4}'\`

  grep -v \"\$SNAPSHOT_DEVICE\$SNAPSHOT_RAW_DEVICE\$SNAPSHOT_MOUNT_POINT\" $VFSTAB
|sed 's/^#SNAPPED#//' > /tmp/\$X.vfstab.tmp
  mv /tmp/\$X.vfstab.tmp /tmp/\$X.vfstab
  done

  mv /tmp/\$X.vfstab $VFSTAB

  rm /etc/rc0.d/S10cleanupvxfs "\
  >/etc/rc0.d/S10cleanupvxfs

cp $VFSTAB /tmp/$X.vfstab

cat $VXCONFIG|while read LINE ; do

  VXFS_DEVICE=`echo $LINE|awk -F: '{print $1}'`
  SNAPSIZE=`echo $LINE|awk -F: '{print $2}'`
  SNAPSHOT_DEVICE=`echo $LINE|awk -F: '{print $3}'`
  SNAPSHOT_RAW_DEVICE=`echo $SNAPSHOT_DEVICE|sed 's-/dsk/-/rdsk/-'`
```

Example 17-4. Snapshot VOB Backup Script: vob_snap.sh (continued)

```
SNAPSHOT_MOUNT_POINT=`echo $LINE|awk -F: '{print $4}'`

[ -d $SNAPSHOT_MOUNT_POINT ] || mkdir -p $SNAPSHOT_MOUNT_POINT

mount -F vxfs -o snapof=$VXFS_DEVICE,snapsize=$SNAPSIZE \
  $SNAPSHOT_DEVICE $SNAPSHOT_MOUNT_POINT

sed "s-.*${VXFS_DEVICE}.*-#SNAPPED#&-" /tmp/$X.vfstab \
  >/tmp/$X.vfstab.tmp

echo "$SNAPSHOT_DEVICE$SNAPSHOT_RAW_DEVICE
  $SNAPSHOT_MOUNT_POINTvxfs9  yes -" >> /tmp/$X.vfstab.tmp

mv /tmp/$X.vfstab.tmp /tmp/$X.vfstab

done

cp $VFSTAB $VFSTAB.sav.1
mv /tmp/$X.vfstab $VFSTAB

}

Unsnap()
{

cp $VFSTAB /tmp/$X.vfstab

cat $VXCONFIG|while read LINE ; do

  SNAPSHOT_DEVICE=`echo $LINE|awk -F: '{print $3}'`
  SNAPSHOT_RAW_DEVICE=`echo $SNAPSHOT_DEVICE|sed 's-/dsk/-/rdsk/-'`
  SNAPSHOT_MOUNT_POINT=`echo $LINE|awk -F: '{print $4}'`

  umount $SNAPSHOT_MOUNT_POINT
  grep -v "$SNAPSHOT_DEVICE\
    $SNAPSHOT_RAW_DEVICE$SNAPSHOT_MOUNT_POINT" \
$VFSTAB |sed 's/^#SNAPPED#//' > /tmp/$X.vfstab.tmp
  mv /tmp/$X.vfstab.tmp /tmp/$X.vfstab

done

cp $VFSTAB $VFSTAB.sav.2
mv /tmp/$X.vfstab $VFSTAB

rm /etc/rc0.d/S10cleanupvxfs

}

case `basename $0` in
snap.sh )
        Lockvobs
        Snap
```

Example 17-4. Snapshot VOB Backup Script: vob_snap.sh (continued)

```
        Unlockvobs
;;

unsnap.sh )

#####Take these three lines OUT if you use 5.1 & savepnpc
#####instead of cron!!
while [ `ps -ef|grep -c save` -gt 1 ] ; do
  sleep 900
done
#####Take these three lines OUT if you use 5.1 & savepnpc
#####instead of cron!!

        Unsnap
;;
esac
```

Other strategies

The preceding two strategies do not represent an exhaustive list of possibilities but are the two most common methods. Other methods include disk backup, mirrors, and many other possibilities; the number is limited only by the reader's imagination. The main thing to remember, no matter how you do the backup, is the lock-backup-unlock sequence.

Disk backup. If you have enough free disk space, you could just back up the VOB(s) to disk. The VOB would need to be locked only during the time the disk backup was being accomplished. At that point, you could unlock the VOB and back up the copy to tape or whatever media you choose.

Mirrors. Many sites use mirroring as a fault-tolerance mechanism. This methodology also can be used to back up/restore VOBs. There are too many different mirroring tools to discuss them in depth here. However, the use of good mirroring procedures along with good backup strategies can be combined to perform the required functions. One of the advantages of mirroring is that the VOB needs to be locked for only as long as it takes to break the mirror and again for only as long as it takes to reestablish the mirror. The following generic procedure is fairly simple in concept but may be more problematic in implementation:

1. Lock the VOB.

2. Break the mirror.

3. Unlock the VOB.

4. Back up the mirror using your normal backup procedures.

5. Lock the VOB.

6. Reestablish the mirror.

7. Manually resynchronize the mirrors, if necessary.

8. Unlock the VOB.

Other VOB Backup Issues

Once you have decided what method you will use to back up your VOBs, there are a few other issues that you will need to address.

Remote storage pools

Occasionally, you will come across VOBs that have one or more of their storage pools located remotely, i.e., not in the local VOB storage directory. These must be backed up at the same time as their owning VOB, using the same method, to ensure that all of the parts are synchronized. A good method of determining whether a VOB has any remote pools is to execute the command:

```
$ cleartool lspool -invob vob:vob_tag
```

This command lists all storage pools for the requested VOB. Any remote storage pools are annotated with a system-created comment similar to the following: *remote cleartext storage pool for* **vob_tag** *VOB*. This step should allow remote storage pools to be identified and processed accordingly.

Incremental backup

Many people commonly use an incremental backup strategy as part of their general data and application backups. An incremental strategy also may be used to back up ClearCase VOB storage areas. However, this method has some noteworthy problems:

- When ClearCase updates its data (for example, when an element is checked in), it uses a *delta* format. At update time, ClearCase creates a new version of the delta file, stores it at a new location, changes the Registry to reflect the new location, and deletes the old delta file. Hence, incremental backups may capture several instances of the delta file because they have slightly different pathnames.

- In order to restore a VOB with incremental backups, it is necessary to restore *all* the different versions as the incremental tapes are used. This may lead to disk space problems if disk space is clear and will result in many different versions of the delta file being placed in the storage area even though only one is needed.

- The "extra" items can be eliminated by executing the *checkvob* command. Be aware that executing the *checkvob* command will result in many error/warning messages as it cleans up the unnecessary files.

Due to these problems, Rational recommends that only a "few" incremental backups be taken for any given VOB. However, given that restoration is easier when all the required data is in one place, it is recommended that all VOB backups be complete (level 0) in order to save on time and complexity when a restore is required.

MultiSite backup

According to Rational's web site:

> ClearCase MultiSite is a ClearCase product option that enables parallel development across geographically distributed project teams. Available on Windows NT and Unix, ClearCase MultiSite extends ClearCase's reach to team members down the street or across the world, delivering automated, error-free replication of project databases and transparent access to all software elements.

The basic thrust is that one can have replicated VOBs/views anywhere on the network. For backups, the replica can be subject to backup separate from the primary VOB. The replica would be handled using the basic paradigm and be resynced after the backup is done. However, the "best" backup solution is to synchronize the replicas frequently. This may increase network traffic somewhat but has dividends in case restoration is needed (see "MultiSite recovery," later in this chapter).

One of the more interesting notions is that one could have a MultiSite replica on the VOB server as well as in the usual VOB storage. This allows the replica to be offline for backups while the primary VOB server is still active for use. For this type of backup, all you would need to do is:

1. Resync the replica (to make sure it matches the primary VOB).
2. Lock the replica.
3. Perform a backup using your preferred procedure.
4. Unlock the replica.
5. Resync to capture any changes made during the backup.

MultiSite has the advantage of being able to establish replicas nearly anywhere on the network where the basic requirements for MultiSite are met. If you have, or acquire, MultiSite, this is a good solution for backups.

VOB Recovery

VOB recovery or restoration can get to be a complicated process. Rather than try to give all-inclusive directions or scripts here, we refer you to the *ClearCase Administrator's Manual (UNIX)* for details. However, the following is offered as an example of VOB restoration.

General approach

Just as VOB backup has a generic process, so does VOB restoration. The Clear-Case *restore_vob* command is one method, but a "standard" process also can be described as follows:

1. Unmount the VOB. (This makes the VOB quiescent.)

2. Unregister the VOB and remove the *vob_tag*. (Removes storage from Clear-Case control.)

3. Copy in the backup. (Recovers the desired data.)

4. Register the VOB and make a new VOB tag. (Puts storage under ClearCase control once again.)

5. Remount the VOB. (Makes the VOB available to users.)

Restore using the "standard" or mirror backup scenarios

In the first backup example above, I used a simple lock-backup-unlock methodology for performing a VOB backup. The following will restore a VOB when using that backup procedure. Moreover, since a backup of a mirrored set is basically the same type of backup as the "standard" backup, the same general paradigm may be used. The main difference is the use of metadevices to perform the actual restore.

1. Unmount the VOB in order to make it both quiescent and unavailable to update:

   ```
   $ cleartool umount vob_tag
   ```

2. Remove the VOB tag entry in the Registry and unregister the VOB using the physical storage area since the *vob_tag* has been removed:

   ```
   $ cleartool rmtag -vob vob_tag
   $ cleartool unregister -vob /export/vobstore/vob_name.vbs
   ```

3. Restore the physical VOB storage area. Use whichever restore command is relevant to the method of backup. If the VOB has remote storage pools, be sure to restore them as well.

4. Reregister the VOB and make a new *vob_tag*:

   ```
   $ cleartool register -vob  /export/vobstore/vob_name.vbs
   $ cleartool mktag -vob -tag vob_tag [...] /export/vobstore/vob_name.vbs
   ```

5. Mount the VOB so that it is once again accessible:

```
$ cleartool mount [...] vob_tag
```

This is the basic scenario for VOB restores. Other options such as mirrors, Multi-Site replicas, disk backups, or any other strategy will use either this paradigm or the *vob_restore* command illustrated in the next section.

Restore using the "snapshot" backup scenario

If you need to recover a VOB that was "snapshot," follow these steps:

1. Lock the VOB:

```
$ cleartool lock -c "recovering src vob" vob:/vobs/src
```

2. Restore the snapshot directory if necessary; it may still be on disk from the previous day. However, please note that *$RESTORE* refers to whichever method was used to do the physical backup. The primary notion is that the contents of */snapshots/src* are available to the restore process.

```
$ $RESTORE /snapshots/src
```

3. Run *vob_restore*, and it will prompt you for each necessary step, including restoring the VOB storage from your backup media. Note that the *vob_restore* command will unregister the VOB.

```
$ vob_restore /vobs/src
```

4. Run *checkvob* to ensure that the database is not corrupt:

```
$ checkvob
```

5. Restart ClearCase on the VOB server:

```
$ $CCHOME/etc/atria_start stop; $CCHOME/etc/atria_start start
```

6. Reregister the VOB, because *vob_restore* unregisters it:

```
$ cleartool mktag -vob -tag /vobs/src /vobstore/src.vbs
$ cleartool register -vob /vobstore/src.vbs
```

MultiSite recovery

If you have been backing up replicated VOBs, restoration is fairly straightforward, albeit a bit complicated. If you lose the storage directory of a replicated VOB, most work may be recoverable. If the actions have been sent to replicas, they can be retrieved and used to bring the VOB up-to-date. However, please note that the restore VOB and all replicated VOBs *must be consistent*. If they are not consistent, irreparable damage can occur. As was mentioned in "Other VOB Backup Issues," frequent synchronization between the local VOB and its replicas can be extremely helpful in restoration. Step 6 in the following list is where the benefits are clearest.

Here is the process of restoring a VOB using MultiSite (all activities must be performed as root):

1. Unmount the VOB on all ClearCase hosts.

2. Recover the VOB storage directory from backup.

3. Execute the command: *multitool restorereplica -vob* `vob_tag`.

4. Ensure that all previous MultiSite updates have been processed by the replica hosts.

5. Create new synchronization packets for all replica hosts.

6. Wait for all the replicas to send the local host synchronization/update packets.

7. Process the incoming packets with the command *syncreplica -import*.

8. Unlock the VOB.

Conclusion

The ability to back up and restore VOBs is as crucial to the administration of ClearCase as any software application data is to that application. As you can see, there are several ways to handle those tasks. It is beyond the scope of this book to determine which method(s) should be used at your particular site. However, ClearCase commands, in conjunction with standard Unix utilities, should make the process as painless as possible as long as you remember that, for changes outside ClearCase, the VOB needs to be quiescent during the backup or recovery of the physical data containers within the VOB.

View Backup and Recovery Procedures

The ClearCase view is the developer's window into the data stored in the VOBs. It is a short-term storage area for data created in the development process. A view holds both checked-out versions of files stored in the VOBs and view-private files that have no VOB counterpart. Like VOBs, views are implemented as a view storage directory. View storage directories can be recognized by their *vws* suffix. A developer activates a view by running the *cleartool setview* command.

The *public* versus *private* debate is intensified here because there will most likely be more private views than private VOBs. In addition, there is some debate on whether views need to be backed up at all. The crux of this argument is that, views being so volatile, it is not necessary to back up the contents, as they can always be derived from existing resources. For private views, this is probably true. For public views that are used by multiple developers, it is usually wise to have a good backup, as some things may be hard to recreate, such as a build with a particular error that is being investigated.

View Backup Strategies

It is not a requirement that individual views be backed up in order to preserve the integrity of the ClearCase data. However, individual developer data may be contained in the views, and backing them up will preserve that data. Backing up views is, in most cases, simpler than backing up VOBs. Unlike a VOB, a view can have only a single storage pool, either local or remote. It is necessary to back up this storage pool with the main view storage directory.

The main problem, however, is that you cannot lock a view, so you are left with two basic approaches. First, pick a time of day (or night) when the traffic is low and warn developers not to access the view. Second, you can temporarily rename the view storage area during the backup.

The following procedure should work well for both public and private views:

1. Generate a list of views for backup.

2. Determine the location of the storage directory for a given view. This can be done using the *lsview* command, which will list the local and remote access paths. You can use the *view server access path* if the backup runs locally but will have to use the *global path* if the backup is being done over the network.

   ```
   $ cleartool lsview -long view_tag
   ```

3. If you cannot get the developers to refrain from using the view at a given time, the following procedure will make the view quiescent:

   a. Stop the view server process:

   ```
   $ cleartool endview -server view_tag
   ```

   b. Rename the view storage directory; save the name for use at the end of the process.

   ```
   $ mv /export/viewstore/view_tag.vws /export/viewstore/tmp-view_tag.vws
   ```

4. Determine whether the view storage directory is local or remote:

   ```
   $ cd Global_path
   $ ls -ld .s
   ```

5. If this is a link, then you have a remote storage pool.

6. Perform the actual backup. If the view has a remote storage pool, remember to back that up as well. You may need to use two different tapes, depending upon your network organization. The following command is for demonstration purposes only and should be replaced by your favorite backup command:

   ```
   $ dump 0fuv /dev/rmt/0 view_storage_directory
   ```

7. If you renamed the view storage directory in Step 3, change the temporary directory back to its original name. You do not have to restart the view server

process, as that will happen automatically when someone tries to use *setview* or a similar command:

```
$ mv /export/viewstore/tmp-view_tag.vws
     /export/viewstore/view_tag.vws
```

Example 17-5 presents a sample view backup script.

Example 17-5. Simple View Backup Script: viewback.sh

```
#!/bin/sh

##############################################################
# This script will back up all views on its host.  The script
# requires a parameter (s or m).  "s" will do a simple backup,
# and "m" will do a backup where the view storage area is copied
# to a different location and the backup done on the new location.
##############################################################
# Export the correct path so that all the required binaries can
# be found

PATH=/opt/atria/bin:/bin:/usr/bin:/usr/sbin
export PATH

CC="/usr/bin/atria/cleartool"
TEMPDIR="/tmp/ccbkup"
LOGDIR="/var/adm/atria/logs"
LOGFILE=$LOGDIR/$DATE.data

date=`date '+%m/%d/%y%n'`
DATE=`echo $date |  sed s:\/::g`
DEVICE="/dev/rmt/0n"

case $1 in
    s)  BUTYPE=999
        ;;
    m)  BUTYPE=0
        ;;
    *)  echo "Usage $0 [s|m]"
esac

HOST=`hostname|awk -F. '{print $1}'`

#Get a list of all vobs on this server
VIEWS=`cleartool lsview -host $HOST | sed 's/*//' \
 | awk '{print $1}'`

# Loop thru the views
for view in $VIEWS; do
    # Get the physical storage directory location
    VWS_PATH=`cleartool lsview -l $VIEW_TAG | grep -i Global \
     | awk -F": " '{ print $2 }'`
    BUDIR=$VWS_PATH                        # reset the variable

    if [ ! -d $TEMPDIR }; then
```

Example 17-5. Simple View Backup Script: viewback.sh (continued)

```
        mkdir -p -m777 $TEMPDIR
    fi
    if [ $BUTYPE ]; then
        # stop the view server
        $CC endview $VIEW
        #copy the view to the new area
        cp $VWS_PATH $TEMPDIR
        BUDIR=$TEMPDIR/$VIEW.vws
    fi
    # Back up the view
    # dump 0fuv $DEVICE $BUDIR

    # Write the log record
    echo "$VWS_PATH" >> $LOGFILE
done
#######################################################
echo "View backups completed."
#######################################################
```

View Recovery

The procedure to restore a view is quite simple. The view can be restored to the same location as the original view or to a new location. Here is the process:

1. Stop the view server process:

   ```
   $ cleartool endview -server view_tag
   ```

2. Rename the view storage directory so that it is moved aside:

   ```
   $ mv /export/viewstore/xxx.vws \
        /export/viewstore/xxx.vws.OLD
   ```

3. Restore the physical storage directory using a *restore* command relevant to the backup command used to create the backup. This example assumes that the *dump* command was used to create the backup. A gotcha at this point is remote storage. If the storage was in a remote directory, be sure to restore that directory as well.

   ```
   $ restore rv /dev/rmt/0 /export/viewstore/xxx.vws
   ```

4. Restore the actual view by executing:

   ```
   $ cleartool recoverview -tag view_tag
   ```

5. If you restored the view storage directory to a new location, it is necessary to reregister the view so that the new physical location is correct in the Registry. It also a good idea to remake the view tag to be sure everything is consistent:

   ```
   $ cleartool register -view -replace \
        /export/viewstore/xxx.vws
   $ cleartool mktag -view -tag view_tag -replace /export/viewstore/xxx.vws
   ```

If you did not restore the view to a different location, the view should now be ready for use. It is not necessary to start the view server process, as the next attempt to access the view will start its server process. Example 17-6 presents a view restoration script that is paired with the script in Example 17-5 and uses common data.

Example 17-6. Simple View Restoration Script: viewrest.sh

```sh
#!/bin/sh


#
################################################################
# This script will restore a view storage area. It has two
# parameters: date (mmddyy format) and the view tag.  It looks
# up in that day's log file what was actually backed up (real or
# temp area).  It then calculates the position of the backup file
# on a tape, restores the area, and if it isn't the original view
# storage directory, moves it there and cleans up the registry.
################################################################
# Export the correct path so that all the required binaries can
# be found

PATH=/opt/atria/bin:/bin:/usr/bin:/usr/sbin
export PATH

DEVICE="/dev/rmt/0"
CC="/usr/bin/atria/cleartool"
LOGDIR="/var/adm/atria/logs"

VIEWTAG=$1
DATE=$2
LOGFILE=$LOGDIR/$DATE.data
if [ ! -f $LOGFILE ]; then
    echo "Backup file entry for '$DATE' not found."
    exit(1)
fi
LINE=`cat $LOGFILE | grep $VIEWTAG`
if [ $? ne 0 ]; then
    echo "View tag backup reference not found."
    exit (1)
fi


# OK, passed the initial edits, let's get to it.
# Which file position on the tape?
FILECNT=`fgrep -n $VWS_PATH | awk -F: '{ print $1 }'`

# Get the full view storage path
VWS_PATH=`cleartool lsview -l $VIEW_TAG | grep -i Global \
| awk -F": " '{ print $2 }'`

# Get the file position on the tape
FILECNT=`fgrep -n $VWS_PATH $LOGFILE | awk -F: '{ print $1 }'`
```

Example 17-6. Simple View Restoration Script: viewrest.sh (continued)

```
# Stop the view server
$CC endview -server $VIEWTAG

#Move the old stuff aside
mv $VWS_PATH $VWS_PATH.OLD

# Position the tape
mt fsf $FILECNT

# Do the restore using your favorite procedure
restore rv $DEVICE $VWS_PATH

# Update registry info
$CC register -view -replace $VWS_PATH
$CC mktag -view -tag $VIEWTAG -replace $VWS_PATH
######################################################
echo "View restore completed."
######################################################
```

If you restored the view to a different physical location, the view and any VOBs with associated items must be resynchronized just as if you had moved the physical location of the view storage. The following steps will accomplish the "resynchronization":

1. Generate a list of VOBs that may need to be synchronized.

2. Determine if an individual VOB has a reference to the view.

3. If so, do a checkout and then an uncheckout on some element to resync the VOB and view storages.

See Example 17-7 and Example 17-8 for a pair of scripts that will resync the VOBs. Example 17-7 is a general VOB resync script and Example 17-8 is a script that checks for VOBs that need to be resynced due to the existence of derived objects in the VOB that are linked to the view.

Example 17-7. VOB Resynchronization Script #1

```
#!/bin/sh

# This script resynchs the VOBs.
# This script should be run as "root" or "ccadm"

###################################################
##Site-specific section (change as appropriate)

PATH=/usr/bin:/usr/sbin:/usr/ucb
CC=/usr/atria/bin/cleartool              # ClearCase executable

VIEW_TAG=$1
# resynch the vobs
```

Example 17-7. VOB Resynchronization Script #1 (continued)

```
$CC setview -exec "./resynch.sh" $VIEW_TAG | tee /var/adm/atria/log/mvview.log
```

resynch.sh

Example 17-8. VOB Resynchronization Script #2

```
#!/bin/sh

# This script should be run as "root" or "ccadm"

#####################################################
##Site-specific section (change as appopriate)

PATH=/usr/bin:/usr/sbin:/usr/ucb
CC=/usr/atria/bin/cleartool                 # ClearCase executable

VIEW_TAG=`cleartool pwv | grep Set | awk -F": " '{ print $2 }'`
echo ""
# Inform user of what we are doing
echo "Checking for VOBs that need to be resynched due to existence
of do's in the vob linked to the view.\n\nPlease be patient as
this may take a while."

# Gen a list of vobs to be checked
COMPLETEVOBLIST=`cleartool lsvob | awk '{print $2 }'`

# Find and process effected vobs
for i in $COMPLETEVOBLIST
do
    echo ".\c"
    cleartool describe -l -vob $i 2>/dev/null | grep $VIEW_TAG > /dev/null
    if [ "$?" = "0" ]; then
        # get an element.  This algorithm should return the first element
ELEMENT=`cleartool ls -l $i | awk -F/ '{ print $4 }' \
 | awk -F@ '{ print $1 }' | sed 1q`

    # Need full element path since we have not physically cd'ed
    # to the vob directory
        FULL_ELEMENT_PATH="$i/$ELEMENT"

        # co + unco resynchs the vob to the new view storage

        cleartool co -nc $FULL_ELEMENT_PATH
        cleartool unco -rm $FULL_ELEMENT_PATH
        echo "\n$i processed\n"
    fi
done
```

Summary

Backup and recovery is an important part of ClearCase administration. While you can always devise these methods after ClearCase is operational, it is best to make these considerations part of the ClearCase architecture and planning process. Registry and view backup are fairly straightforward, but VOB backup and recovery can become quite complex. Create and dry run some backup/restore scenarios during the ClearCase implementation planning phase. This might take a bit more time at the beginning but will bear many fruits after the product is implemented and developers actually are using the product.

View backups are appropriate for some environments in which files might not be checked in on a regular basis or a large amount of view-private data exists and needs some level of protection. The procedures for view backup and recovery are fairly simple and straightforward. However you choose to implement a backup/restore strategy, rest assured that it will be necessary at some time in the future. Take your time, plan well, and then rest easy knowing that loss of data will be minimal at worst, and nonexistent at best.

18

Backup Hardware

How does one decide which backup drive to purchase? There are big drives, small drives, fast drives, slow drives, quick-acting drives, slow-acting drives, tape drives, and optical drives ranging from a few hundred dollars to around $100,000 apiece. This decision actually is much easier to make than you might think. It's certainly much easier than deciding on a commercial backup product. There are only five critical factors in the decision: reliability, transfer speed, time-to-data, capacity, and cost. (Compare this to the backup software RFI that has more than 300 questions.) This chapter covers each of these factors in detail and provides as much market data as possible to help you decide which backup drive is appropriate for you. Specific manufacturers' offerings are presented briefly, but due to the changeable nature of this information, updated data will be available on *http://www. backupcentral.com*.

This chapter also discusses common questions about backup hardware, such as compression, density, cleaning, and tape usage. Hopefully it will answer your questions in this area and assist you in getting the most out of your backup hardware.

Choosing on a Backup Drive

As you decide which type of drive to buy, see how the following five decision factors relate to your environment:

Reliability
Transfer speed
Time-to-data
Capacity
Cost

Most importantly, you should prioritize these factors based on that environment. For example, an environment with a six-terabyte database probably cares about reliability first, transfer speed second, and cost last. On the other hand, an environment that is going to use some type of Hierarchical Storage Management (HSM) system will be concerned about reliability first, time-to-data second, and transfer speed last.

Reliability

Any electronic repair shop will tell you that moving parts fail. If a mechanism to be repaired contains 25 circuit boards and one spinning wheel, they always check the spinning wheel first. The bad news is that backup drives have more moving parts than any other part of your computer system. This means that, statistically speaking, a backup drive has a much greater chance of mechanical failure than a CPU or even a disk drive.

The good news is that drive failures normally do not cause data loss. A malfunctioning backup drive will be temporarily unable to read volumes, but other drives can read those volumes just fine. (Of course, cheap media can certainly cause data loss. Don't buy cheap media!) Drives that fail on a regular basis affect your system availability, since replacing some drives requires shutting down the system. Unfortunately, what usually happens is that the replacement of malfunctioning drives is very low on the priority list. A bad drive may wait several days or even weeks to be replaced. This means that if drives fail too often, their failure can significantly affect the overall integrity of the backup system. That is, drives could fail so often that a large backup or restore would not have enough drives available to complete within a reasonable time frame. This is why drive reliability is a very important factor in deciding what backup drive to get.

Drive manufacturers use the Mean-Time-Between-Failure (MTBF) value to represent the reliability of their drives. Unfortunately, these numbers usually are derived from artificial environments that attempt to simulate thousands of hours of use. (How else would a drive that has been on the market for only six months be able to advertise a 30,000-hour MTBF? That's almost 3.5 years.) The best source of information about the reliability of different drives is the Internet. Use several search engines to locate discussions about the backup drive in question. Probably the most useful search engine for this type of research is *http://www.deja.com.* Search its complete archive for different phrases that might locate discussions about the drive you are considering (e.g., DLT, DLT7000, "DLT 7000," Quantum, and so on). If you don't find any, post your own message and see who replies. (The most useful Usenet group for this topic is *comp.arch.storage.*)

Transfer Speed

When comparing different drives, always compare native transfer speeds, not compressed ones. (Compression usually is offered only on tape drives.) This often is difficult to do, since many drives quote only the compressed numbers. They will, however, usually attach a footnote to that number that says something like, "This number assumes a 2-to-1 compression ratio. The actual transfer speed will vary based on the compressibility of the data." The reason for this is that different manufacturers make different claims regarding compression ratios. Some vendors have claimed a typical compression ratio of as much as 5 to 1. While it is true that different compression algorithms do yield different results, it is very difficult to verify a particular vendor's claims of better compression. To make sure that you are comparing apples to apples, always compare the native transfer speeds.

Some vendors do not use the term "native" transfer rate. They might use the term "head-to-tape" transfer rate, which refers to how fast the recording head can write the data on the tape. This rate does not change with compression. If the data is compressed prior to being sent to the recording head, the drive's effective throughput is increased, but the head-to-tape speed will not change.

When looking at drive specifications, try to locate the word "sustained," because comparing sustained transfer rates allows for fairest comparison between drives. Some drives quote "burst" rates and "synchronous" rates, but these are both temporary, best-case scenarios. (Based on your application, you may wish to compare burst and synchronous transfer rates as well; just make sure you know that's what you're doing.)

Another commonly overlooked decision factor is your system's ability to stream the drive that you're buying at its optimum speed. Suppose that you have a dedicated network backup server with a 100-Mb connection. The most data that you can push through that network connection is 10 MB/s. Do you really need a four-drive DLT 7000 library capable of writing at 40 MB/s? Consider your backup system's capability when deciding on how many drives to purchase.

The drives that excel in this area are usually the large, streaming tape drives. By the time this book is on the shelf, tape drives with transfer speeds of 100 MB/s will be just over the horizon. These drives typically take longer to load, position, stop, and start, but once they get going, they are much faster than other drives. In an environment in which transfer rate is the most important factor, it also helps to have large capacity volumes, since smaller volumes would require more loading and unloading, thus slowing down the overall transfer rate.

Time-to-Data

Transfer speed is not always the most important deciding factor. Obviously, having a faster drive makes backing up and restoring large amounts of data easier. However, many restore requests are for a single file or a small group of files. Depending on your environment, this may account for 99 percent of your restores. What counts most in a small restore is *time-to-data*: how long does it take to load a volume, seek to the appropriate place on the volume, and start reading data? I mentioned earlier that streaming tape drives usually are "slower on the draw" and therefore have a much longer time-to-data. The winners in the time-to-data category are the optical drives. The worst time-to-data value for an optical drive is typically around 12 seconds, allowing 5 seconds for a robotic exchange. If the file being restored is on a platter that is already loaded, time-to-data is less than a second.

Hierarchical Storage Management (HSM) applications place the highest importance on the time-to-data value. This is because of how HSM works. An unused file is automatically migrated from disk to a less expensive storage medium. The user does not realize this and may eventually attempt to access the file. The HSM system detects that the file is needed and automatically retrieves it from the backup medium. All the user sees is a delay in accessing the file. If the delay is 12 seconds or less, the user may not even notice. However, suppose that the file is placed on a DLT 7000 tape whose time-to-data is almost two minutes. A typical user is either going to call the help desk or reboot by that time. That is why HSM environments should use either optical media or one of the newer tape drives that have been designed with very low time-to-data values.

In extremely high volume HSM environments, it also matters how long it takes to rewind and eject the volume. The time-to-data is added to the data transfer time and rewind and eject time to create something called *cycle time.* If the cycle time of a particular tape drive is two minutes, the HSM system can service 30 file migration requests per hour per drive. An eight-drive autoloader would increase that to 240 files per hour. In comparison, an average optical platter has a cycle time of less than 30 seconds. This means an eight-drive autoloader using optical platters can service up to 1,000 migration requests per hour. Consider carefully how important the time-to-data value is in your environment.

Capacity

Capacity used to be the most important factor and still is in nonautomated environments. If a full backup of your entire system could fit on one volume, you do not have to worry about swapping volumes in the middle of the night. However, using an autoloader significantly reduces the importance of volume capacity. In fact, having your data on multiple smaller volumes actually may make a restore go faster with today's backup software.

Having a drive of insufficient capacity will affect your overall transfer rate, though. Suppose that you are backing up to a 10-GB volume with a transfer rate of 10 MB/s and a cycle time of four minutes. At 10 MB/s, you can fill the entire volume in just over 16 minutes. You would would need to swap volumes, which would take four minutes. That means that it actually took 20 minutes to back up the 10-GB, reducing your overall effective throughput to 8 MB/s—not 10. Suppose that there was a bank of eight of these drives in an autoloader; the overall throughput for an eight-hour period would be reduced from 2.9 TB to 2.3 TB—a 600-GB difference. If your volume had a capacity of 50 GB, though, the amount of transferred data lost due to volume swaps is reduced to around 100 GB.

Also remember that larger capacity usually means a longer time-to-data—especially in tape drives. (Obviously it takes longer to get halfway through a 2000-foot tape than it does to get halfway through a 1000-foot tape.)

Another capacity consideration is the intended use of the drive. Are you planning to use backup software that writes continuously to each volume until it is full, or will you be making lots of small backups to a single volume? For example, suppose that you regularly make database exports to tape and send them to a partner who imports that data into his database. Do you really need a 50-GB tape to export a 500-MB database? Every export will require an expensive 50-GB tape. It would be more cost effective to use a cheap, small DDS drive for such a purpose.

Cost

What can I say? Drives that are more reliable, store more data at a faster rate, and have a smaller time-to-data value usually cost more. The only time when you may get a price break on a reliable, quick drive is if a manufacturer is trying to break into a market that is dominated by another manufacturer. Of course, then you bear the risk of the drive being taken off the market. (Consider, for example, the quick disappearance of the Shark drive in the PC market. It was a great drive that did not get market acceptance and disappeared in about a year. Now it's almost impossible to get media for it.)

Another cost factor to consider is reusability of media. There are several Write-Once-Read-Many (WORM) technologies that do not allow you to reuse media. These drives have a definite purpose, such as making bootable CDs, but you definitely should consider whether you are allowed to reuse the media when calculating total cost of ownership.

Summary

While there are several drives that fit into the middle-of-the-road category, most drives excel in one or more of our five critical factors. IBM's 34x0 line has the most proven reliability track record, and the tapes themselves are rock solid, but they're not the fastest things in the world. Metrum drives win in the transfer rate category but are quite expensive and work with only a few types of libraries. Optical media obviously provides the quickest time-to-data, but they definitely have smaller capacity and yet cost more than their tape counterparts. DDS drives probably win in the cost category but are extremely slow compared to today's tape drives, and the DDS media is quite fragile. You must decide which factors are most important in your decision.

Using Backup Hardware

There are a number of questions that repeatedly show up on Usenet. Hopefully this section will help to answer them.

Hardware Data Compression

To save space, data can be compressed before being written to the drive. There are two methods of compression: software and hardware. Software compression is performed by compressing the data using *compress* or *gzip* prior to sending it to the drive. When using hardware compression, uncompressed data is sent to the drive and a specialized chip on the drive does the compression. Figure 18-1 tries to show the paths that the two different types of compression take.

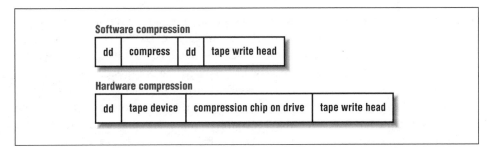

Figure 18-1. Data paths of software and hardware compression

Software compression obviously requires more usage of the host CPU than does hardware compression. Sending a data stream through *compress -c* or *gzip -c* makes things take longer but allows for more data to fit on the volume. Hardware compression, on the other hand, actually makes things go faster. The specialized compression chip can compress data at line speed. That is, if you have a tape drive that can write at 5 MB/s, and the incoming data is allowing for a 2-to-1 compression ratio, the drive can accept data at 10 MB/s. It compresses the incoming 10-MB/s stream and generates a 5-MB/s output that is then written to the actual tape drive. If the incoming data could be compressed 3-to-1, the drive could accept data at 15 MB/s and generate the same 5-MB/s output for the tape drive.

Therefore, you can see that the actual throughput of the drive is highly dependent on the compression ratio of the data. Certain kinds of data compress better than others. Text data, for example, compresses very well. Certain kinds of image formats (e.g., TIFF) are already compressed and cannot be compressed further. If you are backing up the filesystem containing nothing but TIFF files, you'll probably achieve no more than the native speed of the drive. However, if you are backing up the filesystem containing nothing but log files, you may get transfer rates that are well in excess of the published rates of the drive, since most of them are based on a 2-to-1 compression ratio.

Density Versus Compression

Density and compression often are confused. As I mentioned earlier, hardware compression actually uses compression algorithms to compress the data prior to sending it to the actual recording head. The way that the recording head writes the data to the drive actually doesn't change. Density, on the other hand, refers to how densely the data is physically written on the tape. Density is represented by a bits-per-inch, or bpi, value. This is how later generations of tape drives achieve higher throughput and capacity even with the same physical tape. If a drive moves the tape at the same speed but can write bits closer together on the tape, the drive can write the data faster and can fit more on the tape.

Sometimes drive manufacturers will come out with a new drive model that also has a new media associated with it. For example, the DDS-2 drive uses 120-m tapes, instead of the 90-m tapes that went with the DDS-1 drive. If you insert a 120-m tape into a DDS-2 drive, it records in a density that is unreadable by a DDS-1 drive. If you stick the 120-m tape into a DDS-1 drive, the Media Recognition System (MRS) will simply eject it, since it knows it can't read it. However, if you insert a 90-m tape into a DDS-2 drive, it will recognize it as a DDS-1 tape and record in a lower density that can be read by the DDS-1 drive.

Changing Compression and Densities

You do have some control over compression algorithms and density settings, although this is highly dependent on the type of OS and drive. Some tape drives allow you to specify whether to use compression on the command line. For example, in Solaris, compression is specified by the addition of the *c* or *u* flag in the device filename. Some drives also allow you to specify the *density* on the command line, usually with the use of the *l*, *m*, and *h* flags in the device filename. (Which flag causes a particular drive to write in a particular density or compression setting depends on the type of drive, media, and OS that you're using.)

Suppose that you are using an Exabyte 8500c. In Solaris, you can specify the densities and compression settings by using special device files:

Density/Format	Appropriate Device File
Default format	*/dev/rmt/0*
8200	*/dev/rmt/0l*
8500	*/dev/rmt/0m*
8200c	*/dev/rmt/0h*
8500c	*/dev/rmt/0c*

Another way to set density or compression settings is via a button or LCD interface on a standalone tape drive. Such a button or interface forces the drive to use a particular compression or density setting regardless of what the OS tells it to do. This also can be done via dip switches on internal drives. Consult your drive's documentation for the settings that work for you.

How Often Should I Change My Media?

Media life is described by manufacturers in terms of number of passes. A pass is any time that the medium passes by the recording head. This means every time a tape is written to or read from, as well as any time the tape is retensioned. Most manufacturers of data-grade media specify that a given piece of media can survive several thousand passes. Under normal use of one backup and one restore per week, it would take almost 20 years to reach 2000 passes. Reusing your media for 10 years would be one extreme.

At the other are those who feel that media should be used only 10 times before it is discarded. They often cite personal examples of tapes becoming unusable after just a few passes. These experiences are usually very rare and quite specific to a given environment, such as an extremely dirty industrial environment.

I could not in good conscience recommend that you throw away media after only a few uses. I also could not recommend that you never replace your media. I believe that you adopt a wait-and-see approach to replacing media. You should perform regular backup and restore tests on your media. Pull volumes out at random and attempt to restore files from them. Replace a volume if it gives the slightest indication of trouble. If you see a trend of a particular bad batch of tapes, you should perhaps do more testing to see if the problem is widespread. If you watch your backup logs, you also may occasionally see I/O errors when writing to a particular tape. That tape also should be replaced.

Cartridge Care

Today's backup media is much more resilient than it used to be. (I remember accidentally dropping a nine-track tape on the floor and watching it unravel all over the place.) You still need to treat media with care, though. Tapes should be stored with the spline up and the axis of the tape spool parallel to the ground. (If this were a cassette tape, and you stuck a pencil through the tension wheel, the pencil would be pointing straight out—not straight up.) This prevents gravity from causing the tape to settle around the spool.

If you accidentally drop a tape, pick it up and shake it. If you hear noise, do not use the tape. This is especially true of single-spool tapes such as the DLT cartridge. There are delicate mechanisms inside that allow the tape to be brought back into the cartridge. Dropping a DLT tape can cause one of the springs to pop off its pedestal. If you then put that tape into a drive, the tape will be spooled into the drive and will not be able to be pulled out. The only way to repair it is to disassemble the drive.

Drive Care

Clean your drive according to the manufacturer's recommendations. So many problems can be prevented by this simple maintenance step. Read the manual for your particular model of drive, and follow the directions that you read there. What else can I say? Also remember that many manufacturers are extremely hard to deal with when repairs come up if you have not religiously followed the maintenance schedule.

Please note that some drive manufacturers want you to clean their drives only when the drives request to be cleaned. Chief among these are the DLT and AIT drives. These drives are built to be self-cleaning and should get dirty only under adverse circumstances. These drives are made to notify you when they need to be cleaned, and cleaning them more often than they request to be cleaned can actually shorten the life of the drive.

Nearline and Offline Storage

Two terms that you may see when considering the purchase of backup hardware are *nearline* and *offline*. Offline is what you typically think of when you're thinking about backups. It is a second copy of the data that is online. It is not intended to be the primary copy of the information, unless of course it is needed for a restore. A nearline copy, though, is completely different. "Nearline" implies that a file is "close to being online." That is, it is stored in an automated library on a less expensive storage device. It may take several seconds, or even a minute, to get the data, but it can be automatically retrieved. An HSM implementation requires nearline storage.

Tape Drives

Before listing the various tape drive technologies, we will discuss the two main technological differences between different types of tape drives.

- The method that is used to record the data on the tape—*helical scan* or *linear*
- The method used to spool the tape itself—*cartridge* or *cassette*

Linear Versus Helical Scan

One of the best ways to illustrate the difference between helical scan and linear recording technologies is to look at a typical VCR, since it actually incorporates both technologies and illustrates an important point. Have you ever recorded and watched a movie on a non-hi-fi* VCR using the Extended Play (EP) setting? When you play that tape, it sounds horrible. Yet if you were to record the same movie on the same setting with a hi-fi VCR, the audio sounds fine. Have you ever wondered why?

Look at Figure 18-2. A VCR's tape is brought out of the cartridge and wrapped around a rotating drum. As you can see in Figure 18-3, the drum is angled slightly and has recording heads on its side. (The rectangle sitting at an angle in Figure 18-3 represents the angled drum with its rotating recording heads.) As the tape is pulled slowly around the drum, the diagonally positioned recording heads write "stripes" of video data diagonally across the tape, as can be seen in the bottom of Figure 18-3. Although the tape is moving very slowly around the drum, the drum is spinning very fast. This means that the recording heads on the edge of the drum actually are moving across the tape very quickly, *resulting in a good quality video signal.*

The drum spins at 1800 RPM, or 30 revolutions per second, with one head on each side of the drum. This means that the recording heads are writing a stripe of data 60 times each second. Each one of these stripes contains half of an interlaced

---

* This analogy worked much better 5–10 years ago when all VCRs were not of the hi-fi variety. If you've never had a non-hi-fi VCR, you'll just have to trust me. Recording a movie on EP sounds like garbage!

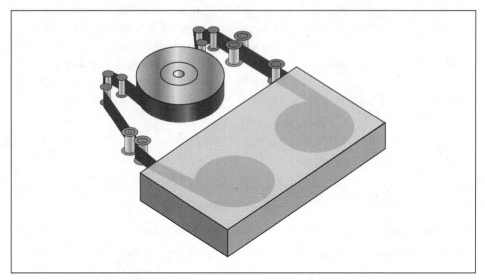

Figure 18-2. VCR tape path

video frame. A synchronization signal also is written along the edge of the tape
that keeps the tape in sync with the spinning recording heads. The VCR interlaces
these images into what you see as full-motion video.

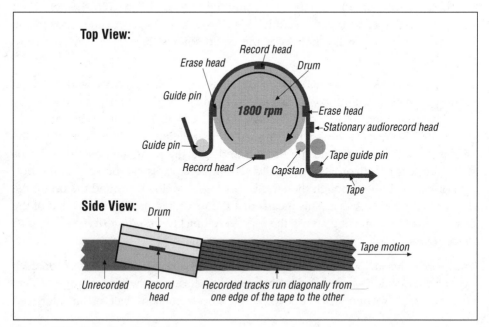

Figure 18-3. Helical scan recording

In a VCR, the tape also passes by a *stationary* audio head that records a linear audio signal along the edge of the tape; this is very similar to how an audiocassette player works. You can see the stationary audio recording head in Figure 18-3. A hi-fi VCR has this same stationary head for backward compatibility reasons, but it also has *audio* heads on the spinning drum. This means that it records audio tracks as diagonal stripes alongside the video data, as can be seen in Figure 18-4. The audio recording heads in a hi-fi VCR are moving across the tape at a high speed, whether you are recording in Extended Play (EP) or Standard Play (SP) mode. This is why a hi-fi VCR can record a good audio signal regardless of the speed at which the tape is moving around the drum.

The result is a videotape that looks like the one in Figure 18-4. The video tracks are recorded in diagonal stripes across the tape. In a non-hi-fi VCR, the audio track is recorded slowly, in a linear fashion, along the bottom of the tape as the tape passes by the stationary recording head. A hi-fi VCR also records the audio this way but also records it in quick, diagonal stripes parallel to the video tracks.

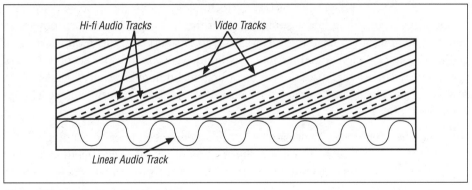

Figure 18-4. A section of videotape

Remember that in a non-hi-fi VCR, the video heads move very quickly across the tape, but the audio heads do not. The result is a good-quality video signal, but a poor-quality audio signal. However, when a hi-fi VCR records audio, it records it just like it records the video—in rapid diagonal stripes across the tape. This results in high-quality audio and video signals. This shows how, in order to record a high-quality signal to tape, the recording head must be moved across the media very quickly. This is important, because in a data drive the quality of the signal is everything.

This in-depth explanation of how VCRs work also explains the difference between helical scan and linear recording technologies. Helical scan drives record data just like a VCR records video, by wrapping the tape around a spinning drum with recording heads attached to it. Linear tape drives move the tape quickly across a stationary recording head. Let us look at these two types of drives in more detail.

Helical scan

As seen in Figure 18-3, a helical drive pulls the tape out of the drive and wraps it around a spinning drum that is turned on a slight angle. On the side of the spinning drum are recording heads that write diagonal stripes across the tape. This allows the tape to move very slowly around the spinning drum, while the recording heads can move across the tape's surface very quickly. This is exactly the same way a VCR records the video signal.

The downside of such a device is that the tape must be wrapped all the way around this spinning drum. Advocates of linear recording technology say that this puts undue stress on the tape. Helical scan manufacturers say that they have changed the way the tape is pulled around the drive in a way that reduces the stress on the tape. Helical scan technology is used in several drives, such as 8-mm, DDS, Redwood, Ampex DTS, and Sony DTF.

Linear

A tape drive that uses linear recording technology pulls the tape very quickly across a fixed recording head. Remember that the recording head must move very quickly past the tape. Since the recording head is stationary, this requires moving the tape at a very high speed, as much as hundreds of inches per second. One of the popular drives that uses linear recording technology is Digital Linear Tape (DLT); its tape path is illustrated in Figure 18-5. (A DLT 7000 moves at 150 ips while recording.)

Most modern tape drives, including DLT, use an enhanced linear technology called linear serpentine. A drive using the linear serpentine recording method records several stripes of data across the tape from one end to the other. Then the head moves slightly up or down and writes another several stripes of data in the reverse direction. Depending on the model of the drive, it may do this several times before it uses up the entire recording surface.

How important is it to keep a tape drive streaming?

Tape drives must keep the tape moving at a constant rate in order to write a good signal. Helical scan tape drives must move at a predictable rate in order to keep in sync with the synchronization signal being written along the edge of the tape. Linear tape drives can record only when the tape is moving very quickly past the recording head. If the drive is expecting 5 MB/s, and the application supplies it with less than that, the drive will attempt to compensate by the use of a RAM buffer. However, at some point, the buffer will be empty and there will be no more data coming into the drive. When this happens, the drive is no longer streaming and will begin repositioning itself to keep up with the incoming data

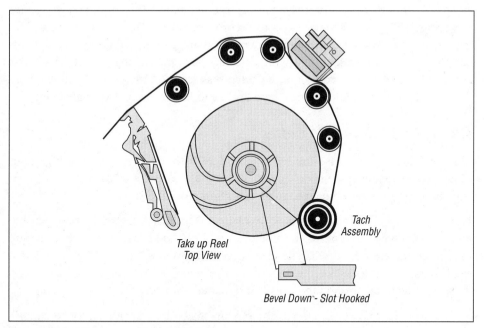

Figure 18-5. Linear recording technology

rate. How it does this depends on whether it uses helical scan or linear recording technology.

If the drive is a helical scan drive, it will "notice" that there is a "gap" in the data. It will stop moving the tape forward at that point. It then will *rewind* the tape and attempt to find the point in the synchronization signal where it left off. As it attempts to sync up with that signal, it may move the tape back and forth several times. Once it is synchronized, it can wait indefinitely for more data. (The tape just sits still while the rotating drum continues to spin.) This attempt to resync with the synchronization signal takes time, as much as a second or more.

A drive using linear recording technology has a slightly different problem. Once the drive notices that there is a gap in the data, it also must stop and rewind the tape. Since the tape is moving at as much as 150 inches per second, a significant amount of tape will pass by the recording head before the tape actually stops moving forward. The drive then needs to rewind past all that extra tape, while watching for the point in the tape where it stopped recording. The speed at which the tape is moving will even cause the drive to go past that point, then stop. Then it moves forward again to where it left off. This resynchronization process also takes time, as much as a second or more.

This means that whatever type of tape drive you are using, if you are not supplying it with the data rate that it is expecting, you will not be streaming it. This means that the drive will be resyncing itself continually. The more time it spends resyncing itself, the less time it has to record your data. Things could get so bad that your drive spends more time resyncing than it does recording data. If this happens, the drive actually will write at a rate slower than the rate at which you are supplying it. Since every time the drive resyncs itself the tape is pulled across the recording head multiple times, tape and head life are decreased significantly.

Cartridges Versus Cassettes

Although many people use the term "cartridge" to refer to any type of tape, cartridges are actually single-spool tapes, such as a 3480 or a DLT. A cassette contains two spools within the tape, such as an 8-mm or DDS drive.

The reason for discussing this is to explain one primary difference between the way the two types of tape work. A single-spool cartridge does not have a take-up reel inside the cartridge itself. The take-up reel is inside the drive. That means that single-spool cartridges like the DLT have the entire tape pulled out of the cartridge and wrapped around the drive's internal take-up reel.

A cassette's tape, however, effectively remains inside the cartridge. Most technologies pull a certain amount of the tape outside of the cassette at a time, but the bulk of the tape remains inside the cassette. There are a few technologies, such as IBM's Magstar MP, that can use a cassette without pulling any of the tape outside of the cassette.

Tape Drive Technologies

This section briefly covers the tape drives that are available on the market today and a few that are about to become available. The information is very general and often historical and is offered mainly to assist you in differentiating among the different types of drives. This should be an exhaustive list of every unique tape drive available today, and I have listed the manufacturer when appropriate. The drives are listed in alphabetical order, so as not to show any preference for any particular drive. Some of the drives covered here are either brand new to the market or not even released as of this writing. Others are specialty drives that I don't have much data on, since I've never worked anywhere that could afford them. (I will keep *http://www.backupcentral.com* updated as I receive more information.)

3480/3490/3490E drives

Although today these drives are made by a number of different manufacturers, they originally were created for the IBM mainframes. These drives, therefore, have the longest history of stability and reliability of any drive currently being sold in the Unix market today. They are rather slow and small in capacity, but they have a relatively quick load and access time.

8-mm drives

This family of drives was originally made only by Exabyte, although other manufacturers now make them. (It does not include the AIT or the Mammoth, which are covered separately.) The first drive in this family was the 8200, which could store 2.3 GB and wrote a pitifully slow 275 KB/s. Capacity and speed gradually improved with the introduction of the 8500 and then the 8505. These drives have a poor reliability history. Insiders will tell you that is because the mechanisms that go into these drives are the same mechanisms that go into Sony 8-mm camcorders. They actually are made on the same assembly line. Tear-down analysis of failed drives has shown drive failure is almost always caused by these consumer-grade components. However, upgrading a single component in the mechanism would require changing all mechanisms on the assembly line or a completely separate line just for data-grade drives. The number of 8-mm backup drives sold per year pales in comparison to the number of 8-mm camcorders. It is what economists refer to as a "perfectly competitive" industry, where a change in process of just a few dollars would mean that consumers would buy another camera.

AIT drive

The AIT drive is Sony's attempt to take the 8-mm drive into the new millennium. The first generation of these drives, released just a few years ago, had a native capacity of 25 GB and a native transfer rate of 3 MB/s in a 3.5-inch half-height form factor. Sony invented a new type of media just for the drive. It is called Advanced Metal Evaporative (AME), and consists of an evaporated metal recording layer covered by a protective layer and lubricant. This new media type reportedly has superior recording and magnetic retention capabilities over the standard magnetic particle tape. The tape also contains an EEPROM called Memory In Cassette (MIC). This EEPROM contains historical information about the tape, and potentially could be used to partition the tape into multiple logical volumes. The AIT drive cannot read traditional 8-mm tapes.

The drive does deliver on its promise of capacity and throughput. The cartridges also seem to be more resilient than the original 8-mm cartridges. It does all this at a relatively low price point and attempts to compete with the DLT market. I have personally heard nothing but good experiences from actual AIT users.

Ampex DST drive

If you need a drive that can store hundreds of gigabytes on a single tape and do it fast, this is a drive for you—if you've got the money. This drive has a native transfer speed of 20 MB/s and can store as much as 330 GB on a single tape. Ampex originally invented helical scan technology and has now taken it to a new level. The only problem is the drive's list price.

DDS drive

Originally put out by HP, the Digital Data Storage (DDS) drive borrowed the format from the DAT market. (Just for the record, it is not proper to call a DDS drive a DAT drive, since DAT refers to digital audio tape.) Many people still call DDS drives DAT drives, even though it's about the same as calling an 8-mm drive a camcorder. Very few people will notice or care if you make this common mistake. (It probably would be easier to get people to stop saying "PIN number.") DDS drives are the least expensive and slowest drives in the Unix market. Even the newest DDS drive, the DDS-3, has a native speed of 1.6 MB/s, roughly one-third that of a DLT. They work, they're inexpensive, and they're pretty reliable—but they are slow.

The DLT drive

Easily the most popular tape format on the market today is the Digital Linear Tape, or DLT. They were originally developed by Digital Corp., based on their original TK-50 and TK-70 lines. They kept the same basic media format and redesigned the drive that it went into. (The first generation of DLTs were actually able to read the old TK tapes.) Two years later they improved the design with what would come to be known as the DLT 2000, with twice the capacity and 60 percent greater throughput than its nearest competitor. The only problem was that no one outside Digital's installed base was buying the drives. In 1994, they decided to sell the technology to a hard-drive manufacturer, Quantum Technology. The rest, as they say, is history. DLT drives now dominate the midrange storage market.

DLT drives have a relatively fast transfer rate of 5 MB/s and an extremely good reliability history. The only downside to a DLT is its time-to-data value, which is more than two minutes. For most backup applications, this is not a problem. However, some environments are beginning to employ them in nearline applications such as HSM. This is an inappropriate use of this excellent technology and almost guarantees that the HSM implementation will be extremely unpopular.

Exabyte Mammoth drive

The Mammoth drive is Exabyte's attempt to go on their own. They listened to the complaints from their customers about the original 8-mm line but were unwilling to completely reject the format. They believed that the failure of the original line was due to the consumer-grade components produced on the camcorder assembly line. They decided, therefore, to go on their own and produce their own mechanism. They increased the form factor so that the parts wouldn't be so cramped, and they upgraded several key parts of the design. This was a complete redesign, including everything from metal thickness to a different kind of material for the capstan rollers.

Unfortunately, the first generation of Mammoth drives was not very reliable. Exabyte then released a second generation with modifications made from lessons learned in the first generation. Exabyte now claims that this generation of drives has a failure rate of less than 1 percent.

AIT or Mammoth?

There are benchmarks on both sides that show that one drive is better than the other. They cost about the same, they're about the same speed and capacity, and they take about the same amount of time to load and gain access to a file. I'm afraid this one's going to have to be a matter of personal preference. Do you choose the Sony drive whose core mechanism is still made alongside that of camcorders? Or do you choose the Exabyte drive, although this is their first attempt at making their own mechanism? There is a potential reliability concern either way. Any data I have was gathered in a very unscientific manner, so I can't publish it in good conscience. The best advice I can offer you is to research both devices using *http://www.deja.com* and hear from people who have used both drives.

The Mammoth tapes also use the new AME media developed by Sony, but do not have a MIC (Memory in Cassette) like the AIT drive does. The Mammoth tapes have a capacity of 20 GB and a native transfer speed of 3 MB/s. Unlike the Sony AIT, they are also read-compatible with the older 8-mm tapes. However, older tapes should be read only on a limited basis, since the drive must be cleaned immediately after it reads an older magnetic particle tape. It is unclear whether future generations of Mammoths also will be able to read the older 8-mm tapes.

IBM Magstar MP (3570) drive

The Magstar MP is the most unusual looking tape cartridge to come on the market. It's sort of a trapezoidal shape that allows for some unique features. The tape mounts midpoint and never leaves the cartridge. (In the tradition of borrowing old technologies, this one reminds me of an old cassette tape. You remember how pinchers were inserted into the tape, and the rollers pulled the tape along without removing it from the cartridge? This mechanism is reminiscent of that.) The Magstar MP loads in under seven seconds and can reach a file anywhere on tape in less than 20 seconds. The tape has a relatively slow transfer rate of 2.2 MB/s, but transfer rate is not the most important factor in the market that this tape is aimed at. It is a potential nearline solution, since it has a total time-to-data of less than 30 seconds, only twice that of optical drives. It is one of the quickest acting tapes on the market.

IBM Magstar 3590 drive

The 3590 is the great-grandchild of the 3480 and continues in its great tradition of stability and reliability. The 3590 is a fast tape drive, with a native transfer speed of 9 MB/s and a capacity of 10 GB. The cartridges are rock solid just like all the other cartridges in this family, so the drive itself has a very good reputation for reliability. The only concern for both the 3590 and the 3570 described is limited support outside of AIX. If you're using AIX systems, though, this may be a perfect match.

LTO drive

Welcome to the vaporware category. This drive's linear tape open (LTO) format is a result of a joint agreement between HP, IBM, Seagate, and Fujitsu. As of this writing, there are no LTO drives available, but there may be by the time you are reading this. The LTO specification describes two tape formats that are based on the 3570 and 3590 media formats. The idea it is that all four companies will release drives that are compatible with one another. This is similar to the way that the original DVD format was created. See *http://www.lto.org* for details and updates.

Metrum line of drives

Do you want speed? Metrum makes the fastest drives available on the market, with a native transfer speed of 64 MB/s. Metrum drives have been around a long time, and they also work inside the large EMass libraries. Just bring your checkbook.

Plasmon LMS NCTP drive

Phillips LMS originally made this drive, but Phillips LMS was sold to Plasmon. The Laser Magnetic Storage (LMS) NCTP drive can read or write to 3480 and 3490E cartridges. It has a native transfer speed of 10 MB/s and a capacity of 18 GB per cartridge.

Sony DTF drive

This is Sony's entrance into the high-capacity, high-speed market, with a native capacity of 42 GB and a native transfer rate of 12 MB/s.

The Storagetek 9840 (Eagle) drive

Imagine a tape drive that is twice as fast as a DLT 7000 and loads and searches almost as fast as an optical platter, and you've got Storagetek's new Eagle drive. Storagetek has been talking about the 9840 for some time, and it is finally here.

The 9840 has a native 10 MB/s transfer rate and a 20-GB capacity. But its biggest advantage is that it loads the tape in eight seconds, and its average search time to a file is also only eight seconds! This combination makes it the quickest, fastest, biggest drive on the market today.

The Storagetek Redwood SD-3 drive

The Redwood drive is Storagetek's first drive based on helical scan technology and has been out for a while with widespread acceptance. It is a very fast drive with a large storage capacity. It uses a 3490E cartridge but has a capacity of 50 GB and a transfer rate of 11 MB/s.

The Tandberg MLR 1-3 drive

Just as the DLT drive was a modified TK 70, the MLR drives are a completely new drive based on QIC media. With a capacity of 25 GB and a native transfer rate of 2 MB/s, it hasn't broken any new ground but may give you another reasonably fast choice for less money than its competitors.

Optical Drives

Optical drives of various types are finally beginning to gain acceptance. They have always been popular with a small crowd because of their very short time-to-data values. Once mounted, some of them are as fast as disk when randomly accessing files. This is not something you can say for tapes. There are two reasons that optical drives are now gaining more acceptance. Their cost is dropping relative to tape technology, and their capacities and transfer speeds have dramatically increased in the last few years.

This section is divided into four main subsections: optical recording methods, CD recording formats, DVD recording formats, and magneto-optical recording Formats. Throughout, a recording *method* refers to how the data is physically represented on disk, and a recording *format* refers to what type of drive may use these recording formats. For example, the most common recording method is the phase change method. There are several formats that use this, such as CD-RW, DVD-RW, DVD-RAM, and DVD+RW.

Optical Recording Methods

Optical recording methods can be divided into two categories, recordable and rewritable. Recordable technologies produce read-only disks, while rewritable technologies allow a disk to be overwritten many times. Within each of these categories, there are several different competing recording methods.

Most people understand that traditional disk drives record digital (binary) data by polarizing sections of the disk. With most optical recording methods, *pits* (or holes) in the *land* (or surface) of the disk represent the binary data. Historically, the land was the flat surface of the disk, and the pits were actual holes burned into the land. When the laser reads the disk, pits don't reflect as much light as the land, and this is translated into binary data. Many newer recording technologies do not produce *actual* pits. The land is composed of material that is sensitive to high-powered lasers. When a laser is applied to a certain area, it changes the reflective properties of that area so that it *appears* to be a pit in the land. (Although they aren't actually pits, they still are referred to as such.) The magneto-optical recording method is a hybrid of magnetic and optical technologies, thus its name. Binary data still is represented by realigned magnetic particles, as with a traditional disk or tape drive. A laser is used during the recording process, and a laser is used when reading the drive as well. (More on this later.)

WORM recording methods

These Write-Once-Read-Many (WORM) recording methods are used to create "one-off," or "read-only," disks, and are used in CD-R and DVD-R recorders. There are a number of different WORM recording methods that produce similar results, including ablative, phase transition, bubble formation, alloy formation, and texture change. The most popular technology is ablative, which uses a tellurium alloy as a recording layer. This alloy has a low enough melting point that the high-power laser actually does make physical pits in it. The other technologies are similar to the rewritable technologies, except that they cannot be erased.

Magneto-optical recording method

The original and most popular rewritable optical recording method is magneto-optical (M-O). The recording layer is heated by a laser, which makes it easier to polarize. The data then is recorded using traditional magnetic recording techniques, although the heated nature of the recording surface allows precise control over the magnetized areas. Once the recording layer cools, it is less susceptible to magnetic degradation. M-O drives range in size from a few hundred megabytes to several gigabytes. This is the least expensive and most popular rewritable optical recording method. M-O media traditionally has been permanently contained within a cartridge that looks similar to a very big 3.5-inch floppy, but there is now a CD-MO format that is not made this way.

Phase change recording method

Disks recorded with this method contain a special recording layer that changes between a crystalline and amorphous state when heated by a laser, which is why it is called "phase change." The amorphous state has different reflective properties than the crystalline state, and sections of the disk that are in the amorphous state appear as pits when the disk is read. A higher-powered laser returns the entire disk to the crystalline state, thus erasing the data. This is the second most popular method, but it is the most popular *truly* optical recording method. It is used in CD-RW, DVD-RAM, and DVD+RW.

Dye polymer recording method

This recording method has been adopted by a few manufacturers and uses a special die that bubbles when heated. The bubbled areas have different reflective properties than the nonbubbled areas, and appear as a pits when read by the laser. Again, a higher-powered laser resets the dye to its original state, thus erasing the data. This is the least popular recording method, but it does not have any apparent limitations compared to the phase change method.

CD Recording Formats

CD-R recorders

CD-R recorders use one of the WORM recording methods to create read-only CDs that can be read in any normal CD-ROM or audio CD player. CD-R media has a very small capacity (680 MB) and a relatively slow transfer rate. However, since the disks produced in a CD-R recorder can be read in any CD player, this is a very popular format. CD-R recorders usually are used to create permanent archives or bootable CDs.

CD-RW recorders

CD-RW recorders use the phase change recording method to produce CDs that can be overwritten if desired. Unfortunately, CD-RW CDs are not readable in a normal CD-ROM drive. They are readable in "multiread" CD-ROMs and some CD-R recorders. Most CD-RW drives also can produce CD-R CDs that can be read in normal CD-ROM drives. They have the same 680-MB capacity as any CD, but the biggest disadvantage to this format is that it is extremely slow. CD-RW drives can write at only 300 KB/s when creating a CD-RW disk.

Read compatibility

Table 18-1 lists CD recording devices across the top and recording formats down the left. It shows which formats can be read in which drives. For example, you can see that a CD-RW disk cannot be read in a normal CD-ROM, but it can be read in a multiread CD-ROM.

Table 18-1. CD-RW/CD-R/DVD Compatibility Chart

Disk Type	CD-ROM or Audio CD Player	Multiread CD-ROM	CD-R Recorder	CD-RW Recorder
CD-RW	No	Yes	Depends on manufacturer	Yes
CD-R	Yes	Yes	Yes	Yes
DVD (any)	No	No	No	No

DVD Recording Formats

Digital Versatile Disk (DVD) is a relatively new format, but it promises to bring a lot to the table. The different recordable formats can fit between 2.6 GB and 4.6 GB per side. That's 9.2 GB per disk. The transfer rate is still very slow compared to modern tape drives, but two of the recordable DVD formats support random access, so they are going to have a very quick time-to-data. Once the recordable DVD format wars are over, it might just replace M-O as the most cost effective (and most popular) solution.

After reading this section, you might wonder how many recordable DVD formats there possibly could be. As you can see, there is one read-only format and three rewritable formats. It is likely that all three rewritable formats will continue for some time, but a clear popularity winner probably will emerge during the next year or two. DVD-RAM disks usually are not readable in other drives, and DVD-RW drives are sequential access and are supposed to cost around $5000. Combine CD-RW's projected $500–$700 price with its proposed backward compatibility and random-access capabilities, and I think we've got a winner. The funny thing is that it's the only format that is not endorsed by the official DVD forum. Time may prove me wrong. (It's happened before.) Regardless of which format wins the war, this DVD section will help you wade through the remaining choices of drives.

DVD-RAM format

DVD Random-Access Memory (DVD-RAM) is the first readily accessible, affordable, rewritable DVD format. It uses a phase change recording method like CD-RW to record up to 2.6 GB per side of each disk. Although it is endorsed by the DVD forum, DVD-RAM disks are not readable in normal DVD drives. (Apparently, Panasonic drives can read the disks, and other drives could read them with a $10–15 modification.) Currently, these drives are selling for around $500.

DVD-R format

DVD-Recordable (DVD-R) is the only DVD format to use the dye polymer recording method. Although this is a rewritable recording method, the DVD-R drives are WORM drives that produce read-only drives. DVD-R's big plus is that the disks that

DVD-R drives produce can be read easily in any other DVD drive. That is because they appear identical to a "normal" DVD disk. It also holds more data than DVD-RAM, at 3.9 GB per side. One difficulty is that the parts that go into this drive aren't used anywhere else. Couple that with an incredible demand, and you've got the classic "supply-and-demand" relationship. That's why they currently cost $17,000.

DVD-RW format

DVD-Rewritable is the second rewritable format to be endorsed by the DVD forum, and it will use the phase change recording method. It proposes to fit more on a DVD disk than any other format, at 4.7 GB per side. It also will be readable in most DVD-ROM and drives and should be readable in all of them with a firmware upgrade. It is supposed to cost around $3000–$5000, which is significantly less than the DVD-R drive. It is significantly more expensive than DVD-RAM, but it does not have DVD-RAM's drawbacks. The first DVD-RW drives should be hitting the shelves right along with this book.

DVD+RW format

DVDReWritable (DVD+RW) is the newest rewritable DVD format, and it was proposed by Sony, HP, Ricoh, Yamaha, and Phillips. Note the slight change in capitalization between DVD-Rewritable (DVD-RW) and DVD-ReWritable (DVD+RW). As of this writing, this format has not been endorsed by the DVD forum. It will use the phase change recording method and will be able to create either a sequential or random access disk. DVD+RW will initially support writing 3 GB per side, but 4.7 GB is expected by the year 2000. It may be the most versatile format if it lives up to its claims. The drives are expected to be on the shelves around the same time as this book and should cost around $500–$700. The CD+RW format is the only one that will have the same look-and-feel of a "normal" CD or DVD without requiring a cartridge.

DVD read compatibility

Table 18-2 shows which CD/DVD formats can be read in which kind of drive. For example, it shows that DVD-ROM disks are readable in any kind of drive, but only DVD-RAM recorders can read DVD-RAM disks without modification.

Table 18-2. DVD Read Compatibility Guide

Disk Type	DVD-ROM or Video DVD Player	DVD-R Recorder	DVD-RAM Recorder	DVD-RW Recorder	DVD+RW Recorder
CD-RW	No	No	Yes	No	Possible[a]
CD/CD-R	Yes	Yes	Yes	No	Yes
DVD-ROM	Yes	Yes	Yes	Yes	Yes

Table 18-2. DVD Read Compatibility Guide (continued)

Disk Type	DVD-ROM or Video DVD Player	DVD-R Recorder	DVD-RAM Recorder	DVD-RW Recorder	DVD+RW Recorder
DVD-R	Yesb	Yes	Yes	Yes	Yes
DVD-RAM	With modification	No	Yes	No	Possible
DVD+RW	Yes	No	No	No	Yes

a Alledgedly, when DVD+RW drives are released, they should have full backward compatibility to other formats. Early reports were that DVD+RW could not read CD-RW and DVD-RAM.

b Older DVD players may be less forgiving, but the word is that a firmware upgrade takes care of this problem.

A Rewritable DVD comparison

Table 18-3 is reprinted with permission from Dana Parker's article "Writable DVD: A Guide for the Perplexed." The text of the entire article is available online. The information is valid as of this writing.

Table 18-3. Rewritable DVD Comparison Table

Format	DVD-R	DVD-RW	DVD-RAM	DVD+RW
Availability	Now	Q2 1999	Now	Q2 1999
Recording Layer	Dye	Phase change	Phase change	Phase change
Capacity/Side (Current)	3.9 GB	4.7 GB	2.6 GB	3 GB
4.7 GB Expected	Q1 1999	Q2 1999	Q4 1999	2000
Number of Rewrites	None	1,000	100,000	100,000
Read/Write	Sequential	Sequential	Random	Either
Readable in DVD-ROM/V?	Yes	Most	Panasonic only	Sony only
Cost of Compatibility?	None	None	$10–$35	Under $1
DVD Formats Not Read	RAM and +RW	RAM and +RW	DVD+RW	DVD-RAM
Non-DVD Formats Read	CD-ROM/R	CD-ROM/R	CD-ROM/R, PD	CD-ROM/R
Formats Re/Written	DVD-R	DVD-R, DVD-RW	DVD-RAM, PD	DVD+RW
Write Method	Wobbled groove	Wobbled groove	Wobbled land/ groove	Wobbled groove
Cartridge	Not required	Not required	Optional (single-side)	Not required
Drive Price	$17,000	$3,000–$5,000	$500–$700	$500–$700
Media Price	$45	$45	$25	$25

Magneto-Optical Recording Formats

Magneto-optical (M-O) is the most popular optical recording format for a lot of reasons:

- The media is inexpensive and easily available from a number of vendors.
- Per-disk capacities have grown from 100 MB to 6.4 GB.
- The drives themselves are inexpensive.
- The media retains data longer than many competing formats.

M-O drives use the M-O recording method and are readily available from a number of vendors. There is also a big line of automated libraries that support M-O drives and media. This level of automation, combined with its low cost, make M-O an excellent choice for nearline environments.

The format isn't perfect, though. Overwriting an M-O cartridge requires multiple passes. However, there is a proposed technology, called Advanced Storage Magneto-Optical (ASMO), that promises to solve this problem. ASMO promises a high-speed, direct overwrite-rewritable optical system capable of reading both CD-ROM and DVD-ROM disks. It is supposed to have faster transfer rates than any of the DVD technologies, a capacity of 6 GB, and an infinite number of rewrites. Compare this to DVD-RW's 4.7 GB and 1,000 rewrites, DVD-RAM's 2.6 GB and 100,000 rewrites, and DVD+RW's 3 GB and 100,000 rewrites. The reason that the number of rewrites is important is that one of the intended markets is as a permanent secondary storage device for desktop users. If it can achieve a transfer rate of 2 MB/s, a user could create a full backup of a 6-GB hard drive in under an hour. Making this backup would be as easy as a drag and drop, and the resulting disk could be removed to a safe location. The best part, though, is that the restore is also a simple drag and drop, and accessing the file would take seconds, not minutes.

For More Information

This entire optical section could not have been written without the folks at *http://www.cdpage.com*, especially Dana Parker. They were the only available source for a lot of this information. They are keeping close tabs on this highly volatile industry, especially the CD and DVD part of it. Make sure you check their web site for updated information.

Automated Backup Hardware

So far this chapter covers only the tape and optical drives themselves. However, today's environments are demanding more and more automation as databases, filesystems, and servers become larger and more complex. Spending a few thousand dollars on some type of automated volume management system can reduce the need for manual intervention, drastically increasing the integrity of a backup system. It reduces administrator frustration by handling the most common (and most boring) task associated with backups—swapping a volume.

There are essentially three types of automated backup hardware. Some people may use these three terms interchangeably. For the purposes of this chapter, these terms are used as they are defined here:

Stacker

> This is how many people enter the automation market. A stacker gets its name from the way they were originally designed. Tapes appeared to be "stacked" on top of one another in early models, although many of today's stackers have the tapes sitting side by side. A stacker is traditionally a sequential access device, meaning that when you eject tape 1, it automatically puts in tape 2. If it contains 10 tapes, and you eject tape 10, it puts in tape 1. You cannot tell a true stacker to "put in tape 5." (This capability is referred to as *random access*.) It is up to you to know which tape is currently in the drive and to calculate the number of ejects required to get to tape 5. Stackers typically have between 4 and 12 slots and one or two drives.

> Many products that are advertised as stackers support random access, so the line is slightly blurred. However, in order to be classified as a stacker, a product must support sequential-access operation. This allows an administrator to easily use shell scripts to control the stacker. Once you purchase a commercial backup product, you have the option of putting the stacker into random-access mode and allowing the backup product to control it. (Control of automated backup hardware is almost always an extra-cost option.)

Library

> This category of automated backup hardware is called many things, but the most common terms are "library," "autoloader," and "jukebox." Each of these terms connotes an addressable group of volumes that can be automatically loaded via unique volume addresses. This means that each slot and drive within a library is given a location address. For example, the first lot may be location 0000, and the first drive may be location 1000. When the backup software controlling the library tells it to put the tape from slot 1 into drive 1, it actually is saying "move the volume in location 0000 to location 1000."

> The primary difference between a library and a stacker is that a library can operate only in random-access mode. Today's libraries are starting to borrow advanced features that used to be found only in silos, such as import/export ports, bar code readers, visual displays, and Ethernet ports for SNMP monitoring. Libraries may range from 12 slots to 500 or more slots. The largest librar-

ies have even started to offer pass-through ports, which allows one library to pass tapes to another library. (This is usually a standard feature in silos.)

Silo

Since many libraries now offer features that used to be found only in silos, the distinction between the two is getting very blurred. The main distinction between a silo and a library today is whether or not it allows multiple hosts to connect to the same silo. If multiple hosts can connect to a silo, they can all share the same drives and volumes. However, with the advent of Storage Area Networks and SCSI switches, libraries now offer this feature too. Silos typically contain at least 500 volumes.

Vendors

I would like to make a distinction between Independent Hardware Vendors (IHVs) and Value Added Resellers (VARs). The IHVs actually manufacturer the stackers, libraries, and silos. A VAR may bundle that piece of hardware with additional software and support as a complete package, often relabeling the original hardware with their logo and/or color scheme. There is a definite need for VARs. They can provide you with a single point of contact for all issues related to your backup system. You can call them for support on your library, RAID system, and the software that controls it all—even if they came from three different vendors. VARs sometimes offer added functionality to a product.

 The following should not be considered an exhaustive list of IHVs. These are simply the ones that I know about. Inclusion in this list should not be considered an endorsement, and exclusion from this list means nothing. I am sure that there are other IHVs that offer their own unique set of features.

Since there are far too many VARs to list here, we will only be listing IHVs.

Stackers and Autoloaders

ADIC (http://www.adic.com)

ADIC makes stackers and libraries of all shapes and sizes for all budgets. After establishing a solid position in this market, they decided to expand. They recently acquired EMASS, one of the premier silo vendors, and now sell the largest silos in the world.

ATL (http://www.atlp.com)

> ATL makes some of the best-known DLT stackers and libraries on the market. Many VARs relabel and resell ATL's libraries.

Breece Hill (http://www.breecehill.com)

> Breece Hill is another well-known DLT stacker and library manufacturer. Their new Saguaro line expands their capacity to more than 200 volumes per library.

Exabyte (http://www.exabyte.com)

> At one time, all 8-mm stackers and libraries came from Exabyte. Although this is no longer the case, they still have a very big line of stackers and libraries of all shapes and sizes.

Mountain Gate (http://www.mountaingate.com)

> Mountain Gate has been making large-scale storage systems for a while and has applied their technology today to the DLT and 3590 libraries. These libraries offer capacities of up to 134 TB.

Overland Data (http://www.overlanddata.com)

> Overland Data offers small DLT libraries with a unique feature—scalability. They sell an enclosure that can fit several of the small libraries, allowing them to exchange volumes between them. This allows those on a budget to start small while accommodating growth as it occurs.

Qualstar (http://www.qualstar.com)

> Qualstar's product line offers some interesting features not typically found in 8-mm libraries. (They also now make DLT libraries.) Their design reduced the number of moving parts and added redundant, hot-swappable power supplies. Another interesting feature is an infrared beam that detects when a hand is inserted into the library.

Quantum

> Quantum, the makers of DLT tape drives, has a line of small stackers and libraries. They are now sold exclusively through ATL.

Seagate (http://www.seagate.com)

> Seagate has a small line of DDS stackers.

Sony (http://www.sony.com.)

> Sony also has a small line of DDS stackers.

Spectralogic (http://www.spectralogic.com)

> Spectralogic's have a very easy to use LCD touch screen, and almost all parts are Field Replaceable Units (FRUs). The power supplies, tape drives, motherboards, and slot system can all be replaced with a simple turn of a thumbscrew.

Large Libraries and Silos

ADIC (http://www.adic.com)

ADIC/Emass is the only library manufacturer that allows you to mix drive and media types within a single library. This allows you to upgrade your drives to the current technology while keeping the library. ADIC has the largest silos available, expandable to up to 60,000 pieces of media for a total storage capacity of over 4 petabytes.

IBM (http://www.ibm.com)

IBM makes a line of expandable libraries for their 3490E and 3590 tape drives that can fit up to 6240 cartridges for a total storage capacity of 187 terabytes.

Storagetek (http://www.storagetek.com)

Storagetek also offers a line of very large, expandable table libraries. Most of their libraries can accept any of the Storagetek drives or DLT drives. The libraries have a capacity of up to 6000 tapes and 300 TB per library storage module. Almost all of their libraries can be interconnected to provide an infinite storage capacity.

Optical jukeboxes

HP Optical (http://www.hp-optical.com)

Hewlett-Packard is the leader in the optical jukebox field, providing magneto-optical jukeboxes of sizes up to 1.3 TB in capacity.

Maxoptix Optical (http://www.maxoptix.com)

Maxoptics specializes in M-O jukeboxes and also offers them in a number of sizes ranging to 1.3 TB.

Plasmon Optical (http://www.plasmon.com)

Plasmon makes the biggest M-O jukebox currently available, with a capacity of 500 slots and 2.6 TB. They also have a line of CD jukeboxes available.

Hardware Comparison

Table 18-4 summarizes the information in this chapter. It contains an exhaustive list of the types of Unix-compatible storage devices available to you. Some drives, like the 4-mm, 8-mm, CD-R, and M-O drives, are made by a number of manufacturers. The specifications listed for these drives therefore should be considered approximations. Check the actual manufacturer of the drive you intend to purchase for specific information.

Table 18-4. Backup Hardware Comparison

Model Name or Generic Name	Vendor	Media Type, Comments, (Expected release date)	H/L	Capacity (Giga-bytes)	MB/s	Avg Load Time (sec)	Avg Seek Time (sec)
DST 312	Ampex	DST	H	50–330	15/20		
8205XL	Exabyte et al.	8-mm	H	3.5	275 K		
8505XL	Exabyte et al.	8-mm	H	7	500 K		
8900— Mammoth	Exabyte et al.	AME 8-mm	H	20	3	20	
DDS-1	Various	Very rare	H	1.3	250 K		
DDS-2	Various	DDS	H	4	510 K		20
DDS-3	Various	DDS	H	12	1.6		
DDS-DC	Various	DDS	H	2	250 K		
3570— Magstar MP	IBM	Midpoint load		5	2.2		
3590	IBM	3590		10	9		
3480	Various	3480	L	200 MB	3	13	
3490	Various	3490	L	600 MB	3	13	
3490E	Various	3490E	L	800 MB	3	13	
DTR-48	Metrum	M-II		36	48		
Model 64	Metrum	Super VHS		27.5	64		
LMS NCTP	Plasmon	3480 3490E		18	10	30	81
DLT 2000XT	Quantum	Very rare	H	15	1.25	45	45
DLT4000	Quantum	DLT	L	20	1.5	45	68
DLT7000	Quantum	DLT	L	35	5	40	60
Super DLT	Quantum	(Release date unknown)		100–500	10–40		
DTF	Sony	DTF		42	12		
DTF-2	Sony	DTF Will have fiber channel interface (1999)	H	100	24	7	
DTF-3	Sony	DTF (2000)	H	200	24		

Table 18-4. Backup Hardware Comparison (continued)

Model Name or Generic Name	Vendor	Media Type, Comments, (Expected release date)	H/L	Capacity (Giga-bytes)	MB/s	Avg Load Time (sec)	Avg Seek Time (sec)
DTF-4	Sony	DTF (200x)	H	400	48		
AIT-1	Sony/Seagate	AIT/AME	H	25	3	7	27
AIT-2	Sony/Seagate	AIT/AME	H	50	6	7	27
AIT-3	Sony/Seagate	AIT/AME (1999)	H	100	12		
AIT-4	Sony/Seagate	AIT/AME (2000)	H	200	24		
4490	Storagetek						
9490—Timberline	Storagetek	3480 or EETape			6	4.3–5.0	10.4
9840	Storagetek	3840/3490E Media Stays in Cartridge	L	20	10	4	11
SD-3—Redwood	Storagetek	3490E	H	10–50	11.1	17	21–53
MLR-1	Tandberg	QIC MLR-1	L	16	1.5	30	55
MLR-3	Tandberg	QIC MLR-3	L	25	2	30	55
MO 640	Fujitsu	M-O		128 MB–643 MB	1-4	7	28 ms
MO 540	Sony	M-O		2.6			
MO 551	Sony	M-O		5.2	5		25 ms
MO 5200ex	HP	M-O		5.2	Write 2.3 Read 4.6	5.5	35 ms
CD-R Spressa 9488	Sony	CD-R		680 MB	Write 600 KB Read 1.2 MB		220 m
CD-RW 8100i	HP, JVC, Mitsumi, NEC, Phillips, Panasonic, Ricoh, Sony, Teac, Plextor, Yamaha	CD-RW CD-R		680 MB	CD-R & RW Read 3.6 MB	7	200 m

Table 18-4. Backup Hardware Comparison (continued)

Model Name or Generic Name	Vendor	Media Type, Comments, (Expected release date)	H/L	Capacity (Giga-bytes)	MB/s	Avg Load Time (sec)	Avg Seek Time (sec)
					CD-R Write 600 KB		
					CD-RW Write 300 KB		
DVD-R	Pioneer	DVD-R		4	1.3		
DVD-RAM	Matsushita, Toshiba, Hitachi	DVD-RAM		2.6	1.35		120 m
DVD-RW				4.7			
DVD +RW	Sony, Phillips, HP, Ricoh, Yamaha, Mitsubishi	DVD+RW		3			

19
Miscellanea

No matter how we organized this book, there would be subjects that wouldn't fit anywhere else. This chapter covers these subjects, including such important information as backing up volatile filesystems and handling the difficulties inherent in gigabit Ethernet.

Volatile Filesystems

A volatile filesystem is one that changes heavily while it is being backed up. Backing up a very volatile filesystem could result in a number of negative side effects. The degree to which a backup will be affected is directly proportional to the volatility of the filesystem and highly dependent on the backup utility that you are using. Some files could be missing or corrupted within the backup, or the wrong versions of files may be found within the backup. The worst possible problem, of course, is that the backup itself could become corrupted, although this could happen only under the most extreme circumstances. (See "Demystifying dump" for details on what can happen when performing a *dump* backup of a volatile filesystem.)

Missing or Corrupted Files

Files that are changing during the backup do not always make it to the backup correctly. This is especially true if the filename or inode changes during the backup. The extent to which your backup is affected by this problem depends on what type of utility you're using and how volatile the filesystem is.

For example, suppose that the utility performs the equivalent of a *find* command at the beginning of the backup, based solely on the names of the files. This utility then begins backing up those files based on the list that it created at the beginning of the backup. If a filename changes during a backup, the backup utility will receive an error when it attempts to back up the old filename. The file, with its new name, will simply be overlooked.

Another scenario would be if the filename does not change, but the file's contents do change. The backup utility begins backing up the file, and the file changes while being backed up. This is probably most common with a large database file. The backup of this file would be essentially worthless, since different parts of it were created at different times. (This is actually what happens when backing up Oracle database files in hot-backup mode. Without Oracle's ability to rebuild the file, the backup of these files would be worthless.)

Referential Integrity Problems

This is similar to the corrupted files problem but on a filesystem level. Backing up a particular filesystem may take several hours. This means that different files within the backup will be backed up at different times. If these files are unrelated, this creates no problem. However, suppose that two different files are related in such a way that if one is changed, the other is changed. An application needs these two files to be related to each other. This means that if you restore one, you must restore the other. It also means that if you restore one file to 11:00 P.M. yesterday, you should restore the other file to 11:00 P.M. yesterday. (This scenario is most commonly found in databases but can be found in other applications that use multiple, interrelated files.)

Suppose that last night's backup began at 10:00 P.M. Because of the name or inode order of the files, one is backed up at 10:15 P.M. and the other at 11:05 P.M. However, the two files were changed together at 11:00 P.M., between their separate backup times. Under this scenario, you would be unable to restore the two files to the way they looked at any single point in time. You could restore the first file to how it looked at 10:15, and the second file to how it looked at 11:05. However, they need to be restored together. If you think of files within a filesystem as records within a database, this would be referred to as a referential integrity problem.

Corrupted or Unreadable Backup

If the filesystem changes significantly while it is being backed up, some utilities may actually create a backup that they cannot read. This is obviously one of the most dangerous things that can happen to a backup, and it would happen only under the most extreme circumstances.

Torture-Testing Backup Programs

In 1991, Elizabeth Zwicky did a paper for the LISA[*] conference called "Torture-testing Backup and Archive Programs: Things You Ought to Know But Probably Would Rather Not." Although this paper and its information are somewhat dated now, people still refer to this paper when talking about this subject. Elizabeth graciously consented to allow us to include some excerpts in this book:

> Many people use *tar, cpio,* or some variant to back up their filesystems. There are a certain number of problems with these programs documented in the manual pages, and there are others that people hear of on the street, or find out the hard way. Rumors abound as to what does and does not work, and what programs are best. I have gotten fed up, and set out to find Truth with only *Perl* (and a number of helpers with different machines) to help me.

> As everyone expects, there are many more problems than are discussed in the manual pages. The rest of the results are startling. For instance, on Suns running SunOS 4.1, the manual pages for both *tar* and *cpio* claim bugs that the programs don't actually have any more. Other "known" bugs in these programs are also mysteriously missing. On the other hand, new and exciting bugs—bugs with symptoms like confusions between file contents and their names—appear in interesting places.

Elizabeth performed two different types of tests. The first type were static tests that tried to see which types of programs could handle strangely named files, files with extra long names, named pipes, and so on. Since at this point we are talking only about volatile filesystems, I will not include her static tests here. Her active tests included:

- A file that becomes a directory
- A directory that becomes a file
- A file that is deleted
- A file that is created
- A file that shrinks
- Two files that grow at different rates

Elizabeth explains how the degree to which a utility would be affected by these problems depends on how that utility works:

> Programs that do not go through the filesystem, like *dump*, write out the directory structure of a filesystem and the contents of files separately. A file that becomes a directory or a directory that becomes a file will create nasty problems, since the

---

[*] Large Installation System Administration Conference, sponsored by Usenix and Sage (*http://www.usenix.org*).

content of the inode is not what it is supposed to be. Restoring the backup will create a file with the original type and the new contents.

Similarly, if the directory information is written out and then the contents of the files, a file that is deleted during the run will still appear on the volume, with indeterminate contents, depending on whether or not the blocks were also reused during the run.

All of the above cases are particular problems for *dump* and its relatives; programs that go through the filesystem are less sensitive to them. On the other hand, files that shrink or grow while a backup is running are more severe problems for *tar*, and other filesystem based programs. *dump* will write the blocks it intends to, regardless of what happens to the file. If the block has been shortened by a block or more, this will add garbage to the end of it. If it has lengthened, it will truncate it. These are annoying but nonfatal occurrences. Programs that go through the filesystem write a file header, which includes the length, and then the data. Unless the programmer has thought to compare the original length with the amount of data written, these may disagree. Reading the resulting archive, particularly attempting to read individual files, may have unfortunate results.

Theoretically, programs in this situation will either truncate or pad the data to the correct length. Many of them will notify you that the length has changed, as well. Unfortunately, many programs do not actually do truncation or padding; some programs even provide the notification anyway. (The "*cpio* out of phase: get help!" message springs to mind.) In many cases, the side reading the archive will compensate, making this hard to catch. SunOS 4.1 *tar*, for instance, will warn you that a file has changed size, and will read an archive with a changed size in it without complaints. Only the fact that the test program, which runs until the archiver exits, got ahead of *tar*, which was reading until the file ended, demonstrated the problem. (Eventually the disk filled up, breaking the deadlock.)

Other warnings

Most of the things that people told me were problems with specific programs weren't; on the other hand, several people (including me) confidently predicted correct behavior in cases where it didn't happen. Most of this was due to people assuming that all versions of a program were identical, but the name of a program isn't a very good predictor of its behavior. Beware of statements about what *tar* does, since most of them are either statements about what it ought to do, or what some particular version of it once did. . . . Don't trust programs to tell you when they get things wrong either. Many of the cases in which things disappeared, got renamed, or ended up linked to fascinating places involved no error messages at all.

Conclusions

These results are in most cases stunningly appalling. *dump* comes out ahead, which is no great surprise. The fact that it fails the name length tests is a nasty surprise, since theoretically it doesn't care what the full name of a file is; on the other hand, it fails late enough that it does not seem to be an immediate problem. Everything else fails in some crucial area. For copying portions of filesystems, *afio* appears to be about as good as it gets, if you have long filenames. If you know that all of the files will fit within the path limitations, GNU *tar* is probably better, since it handles large numbers of links and permission problems better.

There is one comforting statement in Elizabeth's paper: "It's worth remembering that most people who use these programs don't encounter these problems." Thank goodness!

Using Snapshots to Back Up a Volatile Filesystem

What if you could back up a very large filesystem in such a way that its volatility was irrelevant? A recovery of that filesystem would restore all files to the way they looked when the entire backup began, right? A new technology called the *snapshot* allows you to do just that. A snapshot provides a *static view* of an active filesystem. If your backup utility is viewing a filesystem via its snapshot, it could take all night long to back up that filesystem—yet it would be able to restore that filesystem to exactly the way it looked when the entire backup began.

How do snapshots work?

When you create a snapshot, the software records the time at which the snapshot was taken. Once the snapshot is taken, it gives you and your backup utility another name through which you may view the filesystem. For example, when a Network Appliance creates a snapshot of */home*, the snapshot may be viewed via */home/.snapshot*. Creating the snapshot doesn't actually copy data from */home* to */home/.snapshot*, but it appears as if that's exactly what happened. If you look inside */home/.snapshot*, you'll see the entire filesystem as it looked at the moment when */home/.snapshot* was created.

Actually creating the snapshot takes only a few seconds. Sometimes people have a hard time grasping how the software could create a separate view of the filesystem without copying it. This is why it is called a snapshot. It didn't actually copy the data, it merely took a "picture" of it.

Once the snapshot has been created, the software monitors the filesystem for activity. When it sees that a block of data is going to change, it records the before image of that block in a special logging area (often called the *snapshot device*). Even if a particular block changes several times, it needs to record the way it looked only before the first change occurred. That is because that is a way the block looked when the snapshot was taken.

When you view the filesystem via the snapshot directory, it watches what you're looking for. If you request a block of data that has not changed since the snapshot was taken, it will retrieve that block from the actual filesystem. However, if you request a block of data that has changed since the snapshot was taken, it will retrieve that block from the snapshot device. This, of course, is completely invisible to the user or application accessing the data. The user or application simply views the filesystem via the snapshot, and where the blocks come from is managed by the snapshot software.

Available snapshot software

There are two software products that allow you to perform snapshots on Unix filesystem data and a hardware platform that supports snapshots:

CrosStor Snapshot (http://www.crosstor.com)
> CrosStor, formerly Programmed Logic, has several storage management products. Their CrosStor FS and Snapshot products work together to offer snapshot capabilities on Unix.

Veritas's VXFS (http://www.veritas.com)
> Veritas is the leader in the enterprise storage management space, and they offer a number of volume and filesystem management products. The Veritas Filesystem, or VXFS, offers several main advantages over traditional Unix filesystems. The ability to create snapshots is one of them.

Network Appliance (http://www.netapp.com)
> Network Appliance makes a plug-and-play NFS server that also offers snapshot capabilities on its filesystems.

What I'd like to see

Right now, snapshot software is not integrated with backup software. You can tell your backup software to create a snapshot, but getting it to automatically back up that snapshot instead of the live filesystem still requires custom scripts on your part. There was one backup product that intelligently created a snapshot of every filesystem as it backed up. Unfortunately, the company that distributed that product was recently acquired, and its product will be off the market by the time this book hits the shelves. Hopefully, the company that acquired this product will look into this feature and incorporate it into their software.

Demystifying dump

cpio and *tar* are filesystem-based utilities, meaning that they access files through the Unix filesystem. If a backup file is changed, deleted, or added during a backup, usually the worst thing that can happen is that the contents of the individual file that changed will be corrupt. Unfortunately, there is one huge disadvantage to backing up files through the filesystem: the backup affects inode times (*atime* or *ctime*).

dump, on the other hand, does *not* access files though the Unix filesystem, so it doesn't have this limitation. It backs up files by accessing the data through the raw device driver. Exactly how *dump* does this is generally a mystery to most system administrators. The *dump* manpage doesn't help matters either, since it creates FUD (Fear, Uncertainty, & Doubt). For example, Sun's *ufsdump* man page says:

> When running *ufsdump*, the filesystem must be inactive; otherwise, the output of *ufsdump* may be inconsistent and restoring files correctly may be impossible. A filesystem is inactive when it is unmounted [sic] or the system is in single user mode.

From this warning, it is not very clear the extent of the problem if the advice is not heeded. Is it individual files in the dump that may be corrupted? Is it entire directories? Is it everything beyond a certain point in the dump? Is it the entire dump? Do we *really* have to dismount the filesystem to get a consistent dump?

Questions like these raise a common concern when performing backups with *dump.* Will we learn (after it's too late) that a backup is corrupt just because we dumped a mounted filesystem, even though it was essentially idle at the time? If we are going to answer these questions, we need to understand exactly how *dump* works.

 "Demystifying dump" was written by David Young, a principal consultant with Collective Technologies. David has been administering Unix systems while reading and writing code for many years. He can be reached at *davidy@colltech.com*.

Dumpster Diving

The *dump* utility is very filesystem specific, so there may be slight variations in how it works on various Unix platforms. For the most part, however, the following description should cover how it works, since most versions of dump are generally derived from the same code base. Let's first look at the output from a real dump. We're going to look at an incremental backup, since it has more interesting messages than a level-0 backup:

```
# /usr/sbin/ufsdump 9bdsfnu 64 80000 150000 /dev/null /
DUMP: Writing 32 Kilobyte records
DUMP: Date of this level 9 dump: Mon Feb 15 22:41:57 1999
DUMP: Date of last level 0 dump: Sat Aug 15 23:18:45 1998
DUMP: Dumping /dev/rdsk/c0t3d0s0 (sun:/) to /dev/null.
DUMP: Mapping (Pass I) [regular files]
DUMP: Mapping (Pass II) [directories]
DUMP: Mapping (Pass II) [directories]
DUMP: Mapping (Pass II) [directories]
```

```
DUMP: Estimated 56728 blocks (27.70MB) on 0.00 tapes.
DUMP: Dumping (Pass III) [directories]
DUMP: Dumping (Pass IV) [regular files]
DUMP: 56638 blocks (27.66MB) on 1 volume at 719 KB/sec
DUMP: DUMP IS DONE
DUMP: Level 9 dump on Mon Feb 15 22:41:57 1999
```

In this example, *ufsdump* makes four main passes to back up a filesystem. We also see that Pass II was performed three times. What is *dump* doing during each of these passes?

Pass I

Based on the entries in */etc/dumpdates* and the *dump* level specified on the command line, an internal variable named DUMP_SINCE is calculated. Any file modified after the DUMP_SINCE time is a candidate for the current dump. *dump* then scans the disk and looks at all inodes in the filesystem. Note that *dump* "understands" the layout of the Unix filesystem and reads all of its data through the raw disk device driver.

Unallocated inodes are skipped. The modification times of allocated inodes are compared to DUMP_SINCE. Modification times of files greater than or equal to DUMP_SINCE are candidates for backup; the rest are skipped. While looking at the inodes, *dump* builds:

- A list of *file* inodes to back up

- A list of *directory* inodes seen

- A list of *used* (allocated) inodes

Pass IIa

dump rescans all the inodes and specifically looks at directory inodes that were found in Pass I to determine whether they contain any of the files targeted for backup. If not, the directory's inode is dropped from the list of directories that need to be backed up.

Pass IIb

By deleting in Pass IIa directories that do not need to be backed up, the parent directory may now qualify for the same treatment on this or a later pass, using this algorithm. This pass is a rescan of all directories to see if the remaining directories in the directory inode list now qualify for removal.

Pass IIc

Directories were dropped in Pass IIb. Perform another scan to check for additional directory removals. This ends up being the final Pass II scan, since no more directories can be dropped from the directory inode list. (If additional directories had been found that could be dropped, another Pass II scan would have occurred.)

Pre-Pass III

This is when *dump* actually starts to write data. Just before Pass III officially starts, *dump* writes information about the backup. *dump* writes all data in a very structured manner. Typically, *dump* writes a header to describe the data that is about to follow, and then the data is written. Another header is written and then more data. During the Pre-Pass III phase, *dump* writes a dump header and two inode maps. Logically, the information would be written sequentially, like this:

header
> TS_TAPE-dump header

header
> TS_CLRI

usedinomap
> A map of inodes deleted since the last dump

header
> TS_BITS

dumpinomap
> A map of inodes in the dump

The map *usedinomap* is a list of inodes that have been deleted since the last dump. *restore* would use this map to delete files before doing a restore of files in this dump. The map *dumpinomap* is a list of all inodes contained in this dump. Each header contains quite a bit of information:

> Record type
> Dump date
> Volume number
> Logical block of record
> Inode number
> Magic number
> Record checksum
> Inode
> Number of records to follow
> Dump label
> Dump level
> Name of dumped filesystem
> Name of dumped device
> Name of dumped host
> First record on volume

The record type field describes the type of information that follows the header. There are six basic record types:

TS_TAPE
> *dump* header

TS_CLRI
> Map of inodes deleted since last dump

TS_BITS
> Map of inodes in dump

TS_INODE
> Beginning of file record

TS_ADDR
> Continuation of file record

TS_END
> End of volume marker

It should be noted that when *dump* writes the header, it includes a copy of the inode for the file or directory that immediately follows the header. Since inode data structures have changed over the years, and different filesystems use slightly different inode data structures for their respective filesystems, this would create a portability problem. So *dump* normalizes its output by converting the current filesystem's inode data structure into the old BSD inode data structure. It is this BSD data structure that is written to the backup volume.

As long as all *dump* programs do this, then you should be able to restore the data on any Unix system that expects the inode data structure to be in the old BSD format. It is for this reason that you can interchange a *dump* volume written on Solaris, HP-UX, and AIX systems.

Pass III

This is when real disk data starts to get dumped. During Pass III, *dump* writes only those directories that contain files that have been marked for backup. As in the Pre-Pass III phase, during Pass III *dump* will logically write data something like this:

> Header (TS_INODE)
> Disk blocks (directory block[s])
> Header (TS_ADDR)
> Disk blocks (more directory block[s])
> .
> .
> .

Header (TS_ADDR)
Disk blocks (more directory block[s])
Repeat the previous four steps for each directory in the list of directory inodes
to back up

Pass IV

Finally, file data is dumped. During Pass IV, *dump* writes only those files that were
marked for backup. *dump* will logically write data during this pass as it did in Pass
III for directory data:

Header (TS_INODE)
Disk blocks (file block[s])
Header (TS_ADDR)
Disk blocks (more file block[s])

.

.

.

Header (TS_ADDR)
Disk blocks (more file block[s])
Repeat the previous four steps for each file in the list of file inodes to back up.

Post-Pass IV

To mark the end of the backup, *dump* writes a final header using the TS_END
record type. This header officially marks the end of the dump.

Summary of dump steps

The following is a summary of each of *dump*'s steps:

Pass I
   dump builds a list of the files it is going to back up.

Pass II
   dump scans the disk multiple times to determine a list of the directories it
   needs to back up.

Pre-Pass III
   dump writes a dump header and two inode maps.

Pass III
   dump writes a header (which includes the directory inode) and the directory
   data blocks for each directory in the directory backup list.

Pass IV
   dump writes a header (which includes the file inode) and the file data blocks
   for each file in the file backup list.

Post-Pass IV
> *dump* writes a final header to mark the end of the dump.

Answers to Our Questions

Let's review the issues raised earlier in this section.

Question 1

Q: *If we dump an active filesystem, will data corruption affect individual directories/files in the dump?*

A: Yes.

The following is a list of scenarios that can occur if your filesystem is changing during a dump.

A file is deleted before Pass I
> The file is not included in the backup list, since it doesn't exist when Pass I occurs.

A file is deleted after Pass I but before Pass IV
> The file may be included in the backup list, but during Pass IV *dump* checks to make sure the file still exists and is a file. If either condition is false, *dump* skips backing it up. However the inode map written in Pre-Pass III will be incorrect. This inconsistency will not affect the dump, but *restore* will be unable to recover the file even though it is in the restore list.

The contents of a file marked for backup changes (inode number stays the same); there are really two scenarios here
> Changing the file at a time when *dump* is *not* backing it up does not affect the backup of the file. *dump* keeps a list of the inode numbers, so changing the file may affect the contents of the inode but not the inode number itself.
>
> Changing the file when *dump* is backing up the file probably will corrupt the data dumped for the current file. *dump* reads the inode and follows the disk block pointers to read and then write the file blocks. If the address or contents of just one block changes, the file dumped will be corrupt.

The inode number of a file changes
> If the inode number of a file changes after it was put on the backup list (inode changes after Pass I, but before Pass IV), then when the time comes to back up the file, one of three scenarios occurs:
>
> — The inode is not being used by the filesystem, so *dump* will skip the backing up of this file. The inode map written in Pre-Pass III will be incorrect. This inconsistency will not affect the dump but will confuse you during a restore (a file is listed but can't be restored).

— The inode is reallocated by the filesystem and is now a directory, pipe, or
    socket. *dump* will see that the inode is not a regular file and ignore the
    backing up of the inode. Again, the inode map written in Pre-Pass III will
    be inconsistent.

— The inode is reallocated by the filesystem and now is used by another file;
    dump will back up the new file. Even worse, the name of the file dumped
    in Pass III for that inode number is incorrect. The file actually may be of a
    file somewhere else in the filesystem. It's like *dump* trying to back up */etc/
    hosts* but really getting */bin/ls*. Although the file is not corrupt in the true
    sense of the word, if this file were restored, it would not be the correct
    file.

A file is moved in the filesystem; again, there are a few scenarios:

The file is renamed before the directory is dumped in Pass III. When the directory is dumped in Pass III, the new name of the file will be dumped. The
backup would proceed as if the file was never renamed.

The file is renamed after the directory is dumped in Pass III. The inode doesn't
change, so *dump* will back up the file. However, the name of the file dumped
in Pass III will not be the current filename in the filesystem. Should be harm-
less.

The file is moved to another directory in the same filesystem before the directory was dumped in Pass III. If the inode didn't change, then this is the same
as the first scenario.

The file is moved to another directory in the same filesystem after the directory was dumped in Pass III. If the inode didn't change, then the file will be
backed up, but during a restore it would be seen in the old directory with the
old name.

The file's inode changes. The file would not be backed up, or another file may
be backed up in its place. (If another file has assumed this file's old inode.)

Question 2

Q: If we dump an active filesystem, will data corruption affect directories?

A: Possibly.

Most of the details outlined for files also apply to directories. The one exception is
that directories are dumped in Pass III instead of Pass IV, so the time frames for
changes to directories will change.

This also implies that changes to directories are less susceptible to corruption,
since the time that elapses between the generation of the directory list and the

dump of that list is less. However, changes to files that normally would cause corresponding changes to the directory information still will create inconsistencies in the dump.

Question 3

Q: If we dump an active filesystem, will data corruption affect the entire dump or everything beyond a certain point in the dump?

A: No.

Even though *dump* backs up files through the raw device driver, it is in effect backing up data inode by inode. This is still going through the filesystem and doing it file by file. Corrupting one file will not affect other files in the dump.

Question 4

Q: Do we REALLY have to dismount the filesystem to get a consistent dump?

A: No,

There is a high likelihood that dumps of an idle, mounted filesystem will be fine. The more active the filesystem, the higher the risk that corrupt files will be dumped. The risk that files are corrupt is about the same for a utility that accesses files using the filesystem.

Question 5

Q: Will we learn (after it's too late) that dumping a mounted filesystem that is essentially idle was found to be corrupt?

A: No.

It's possible that individual files in that dump are corrupt, but highly unlikely that the entire dump is corrupt. Since dumps back up data inode by inode, this is similar to backing up through the filesystem file by file.

A Final Analysis of dump

As described earlier, using *dump* to back up a mounted filesystem can dump files that are found to be corrupt when restored. The likelihood of that occurring rises as the activity of the filesystem increases. There are also situations that can occur where data is backed up safely, but the information in the dump is inconsistent. For these inconsistencies to occur, certain events have to occur at the right time during the dump. And it is possible that the wrong file is dumped during the backup; if that file is restored, the administrator will wonder how that happened!

The potential for data corruption to occur is pretty low but still a possibility. For most people, dumping live filesystems that are fairly idle produces a good backup. Generally, you will have similar success or failure performing a backup with *dump* as you will with *tar* or *cpio.**

Gigabit Ethernet

As the amount of data that needed to be backed up grew exponentially, backup software became more and more efficient. Advanced features like dynamic parallelism and software compression made backing up such large amounts of data possible. However, the amount of data on a single server became so large that it could not be backed up over a normal LAN connection. Even if the LAN were based on ATM, only so many bits can be sent over such a wire. (This is why I believe that 2000 will be the year of the SAN. For more information on SANs, read Chapter 5, *Commercial Backup Utilities.*)

Gigabit Ethernet was supposed to save the backup world. Ten times faster than its closest cousin (Fast Ethernet), surely it would solve the bandwidth problem. Many people, including me, designed large backup systems with gigabit Ethernet in mind. Unfortunately, we were often disappointed. While a gigabit Ethernet connection could support 1000 Mb/s between switches, maintaining such a speed between a backup client and backup server was impossible. The number of interrupts required to support gigabit Ethernet consumed all available resources on the servers involved.† Even after all available CPU and memory had been exhausted, the best you could hope for was 300 Mb/s. While transferring data at this speed, the systems could do nothing else. This meant that under normal conditions, the best you would get was around 200 Mb/s.

One company believes it has the solution for this problem. Alteon Networks (*http://www.alteon.com*) believes that the problem is the frame size. The maximum frame size in Ethernet is 1500 bytes. Alteon believes that if you were to use large frames (9000 bytes), that gigabit Ethernet would perform faster. They have developed NICs and switches that use these jumbo frames, and claim that they get a 300% performance increase with a 50% reduction in CPU load. Support for jumbo frames

---

* One difference, of course, is that *dump* writes the table of contents at the beginning of the archive, whereas *cpio* and *tar* write it as the archive is being created. Therefore, the chance that a file will be listed in the table of contents but not contained within the archive is higher with *dump* than with *cpio* or *tar.*

† For one test, we had a Sun E-10000 with eight CPUs and eight GB RAM for the client and a Sun E-450 with four CPUs and four GB RAM for the server. Even with this amount of horsepower, the best we got during backup operations was a little over 200 Mb/s. The details on these tests are available in a paper on the book's web site, *http://www.backupcentral.com.*

is starting to show up in several operating systems, and they hope to make them standard soon.

Please note that gigabit Ethernet is still an emerging technology. I wouldn't be surprised if various vendors come out with better performance numbers by the time this book hits the shelves.

Disk Recovery Companies

It seems fitting that the last section in this book should be dedicated to disk recovery companies. When all else fails, these are the guys who might be able to help you. Every once in a while, a disk drive that doesn't have a backup dies. A disk recovery company actually disassembles this drive to recover its data. This service can cost several thousand dollars, and you pay their fee regardless of the success of the operation. Although they may be expensive, and they may not get all the data back, they may be the only way to recover your data. There are several such companies, and they can be found by a web search for "disk recovery."

Here's hoping that you never need to use them…

Yesterday

When this little parody* of a John Lennon song started getting passed around the Internet, it got sent to me about a hundred times! What better place to put it than here?

> Yesterday,
> All those backups seemed a waste of pay.
> Now my database has gone away.
> Oh I believe in yesterday.
>
> Suddenly,
> There's not half the files there used to be,
> And there's a milestone hanging over me
> The system crashed so suddenly.
>
> I pushed something wrong
> What it was I could not say.
> Now all my data's gone
> and I long for yesterday-ay-ay-ay.
>
> Yesterday,
> The need for backups seemed so far away.

---

* The original author is unknown.

I knew my data was all here to stay,
Now I believe in yesterday.

Trust Me About the Backups

Here's a little more backup humor that has been passed around the Internet a few times. This is another parody based on the song "Use Sunscreen," by Mary Schmich, which was a rewrite of a speech attributed to Kurt Vonnegut. (He never actually wrote or gave the speech.) Oh, never mind. Just read it!

Back up your hard drive.

If I could offer you only one tip for the future, backing up would be it.

The necessity of regular backups is shown by the fact that your hard drive has a MTBF printed on it, whereas the rest of my advice has no basis more reliable than my own meandering experience.

I will dispense this advice now.

Enjoy the freedom and innocence of your newbieness.

Oh, never mind. You will not understand the freedom and innocence of newbieness until they have been overtaken by weary cynicism.

But trust me, in three months, you'll look back on www.deja.com at posts you wrote and recall in a way you can't grasp now how much possibility lay before you and how witty you really were.

You are not as bitter as you imagine.

Write one thing every day that is on topic.

Chat.

Don't be trollish in other peoples newsgroups.

Don't put up with people who are trollish in yours.

Update your virus software.

Sometimes you're ahead, sometimes you're behind.

The race is long and, in the end, it's only with yourself.

Remember the praise you receive.

Forget the flames.

If you succeed in doing this, tell me how.

Get a good monitor.

Be kind to your eyesight.

You'll miss it when it's gone.

Maybe you'll lurk, maybe you won't.

Maybe you'll meet F2F, maybe you won't.

Whatever you do, don't congratulate yourself too much, or berate yourself either.

Your choices are half chance.

So are everybody else's.

Enjoy your Internet access.

Use it every way you can.

Don't be afraid of it or of what other people think of it.

It's a privilege, not a right.

Read the readme.txt, even if you don't follow it.

Do not read Unix manpages.

They will only make you feel stupid.

Get to know your fellow newsgroup posters.

You never know when they'll be gone for good.

Understand that friends come and go, but with a precious few you should hold on.

Post in r.a.sf.w.r-j, but leave before it makes you hard.

Post in a.f.e but leave before it makes you soft.

Browse.

Accept certain inalienable truths: Spam will rise. Newsgroups will flamewar. You too will become an oldbie.

And when you do, you'll fantasize that when you were a newbie, spam was rare, newsgroups were harmonious, and people read the FAQs.

Read the FAQs.

Be careful whose advice you buy, but be patient with those that supply it.

Advice is a form of nostalgia.

Dispensing it is a way of fishing the past from the logs, reformatting it, and recycling it for more than it's worth.

But trust me on the backups.

Index

About the Author

W. Curtis Preston has specialized in designing backup and recovery systems for more than six years, and has designed such systems for many environments, both large and small. The first environment that Curtis was responsible for went from seven small servers to 250 large servers in just over two years, running Oracle, Informix, and Sybase databases and five versions of Unix. He started managing this environment with homegrown utilities and eventually installed the first of many commercial backup utilities. His passion for backup and recovery began with managing the data growth of this 24x7, mission-critical environment.

Having designed backup systems for environments with small budgets, Curtis has developed a number of freely available tools, including ones that perform live backups of Oracle, Informix, and Sybase. He has ported these tools to a number of environments, including Linux, and they are running at companies around the world. Curtis is now a principal consultant for Collective Technologies, where they have developed a proven system for choosing a commercial backup utility when the environment and budget allow one to be purchased. This system has been used to select commercial backup systems for some of the world's largest environments, including a six-terabyte Oracle database and one site with a total storage capacity of five petabytes. Once software and hardware selection is completed, Collective Technologies designs and implements a complete system based on the customer's requirements.

Curtis states that he could have never written the book without the use of the Collective Intellect™, or the C.I., as he calls it. Collective Technologies' 400 consultants have administered every major operating system, and they support each other by freely sharing their "collective" experiences, referred to as the Collective Intellect. While writing the book, Curtis asked the C.I. hundreds of questions that would have taken him years to research on his own. In a few cases, entire chapters were written by people who demonstrated expertise in a certain area. Curtis believes that the C.I. has made this a far better book than he ever envisioned, which is why it is listed as a coauthor.

Colophon

Our look is the result of reader comments, our own experimentation, and feedback from distribution channels. Distinctive covers complement our distinctive approach to technical topics, breathing personality and life into potentially dry subjects.

The animal on the cover of *Unix Backup & Recovery* is an Indian gharial (sometimes spelled gavial), a resident of deep, fast-moving rivers in India and neighboring countries. Growing six to seven meters long, the gharial is one of the largest members of the crocodilian family. It is most notable for its extremely long, narrow snout. This snout, which is lined with razor-sharp teeth, is perfectly suited for catching and eating fish, the gharial's principal food. The narrow shape results in little water resistance, making rapid side-to-side snatched easy. The many sharp teeth are well-suited for holding onto struggling, slippery fish. The gharial's short, poorly muscled legs make it a very awkward mover on land, and thus it only emerges from the water for nesting and basking in the sun. Like other crocodiles, the gharial has often been accused of being a man eater. However, this animals is as poorly suited for eating humans as it is well-suited for eating fish. Findings of human remains and jewelry in gharial stomachs has perpetuated this belief, but since Hindi burial rituals in the gharial's habitat involve setting the cremated body afloat in the river, this is probably where these items come from.

Gharials are highly endangered, and came close to extinction in 1970s. Thanks to conservation efforts there has been some recovery of the gharial population. They have been protected since the 1970s, but males are still sometimes hunted for their snouts, which are said to have aphrodisiac properties. Gharials can also become caught in fishing nets, resulting in their death.

In summary, in the words of this book's author: "Let's see . . . huge, intimidating, ugly creature that's not actually harmful to humans . . . That sounds like backups to me!"

Clairemarie Fisher O'Leary was the production editor and Norma Emory was the copyeditor for *Unix Backup & Recovery*. Nancy Wolfe Kotary was the production manager. Ellie Fountain Maden and Melanie Wang provided quality control. Mike Sierra provided FrameMaker technical support. Ellen Troutman wrote the index.

Edie Freedman designed the cover of this book, using a 19th-century engraving from the Dover Pictorial Archive. The cover layout was produced with QuarkXPress 3.32 using the ITC Garamond font. Whenever possible, our books use RepKover™, a durable and flexible lay-flat binding. If the page count exceeds RepKover's limit, perfect binding is used.

The inside layout was designed by Edie Freedman and implemented in FrameMaker 5.5 by Mike Sierra. The text and heading fonts are ITC Garamond Light and Garamond Book. The illustrations that appear in the book were produced by Robert Romano and Rhon Porter using Macromedia FreeHand 8 and Adobe Photoshop 5. This colophon was written by Clairemarie Fisher O'Leary.

How to stay in touch with O'Reilly

1. Visit Our Award-Winning Web Site

http://www.oreilly.com/

★ "Top 100 Sites on the Web" —*PC Magazine*
★ "Top 5% Web sites" —*Point Communications*
★ "3-Star site" —*The McKinley Group*

Our web site contains a library of comprehensive product information (including book excerpts and tables of contents), downloadable software, background articles, interviews with technology leaders, links to relevant sites, book cover art, and more. File us in your Bookmarks or Hotlist!

2. Join Our Email Mailing Lists

New Product Releases
To receive automatic email with brief descriptions of all new O'Reilly products as they are released, send email to:
listproc@online.oreilly.com
Put the following information in the first line of your message (*not* in the Subject field):
subscribe oreilly-news

O'Reilly Events
If you'd also like us to send information about trade show events, special promotions, and other O'Reilly events, send email to:
listproc@online.oreilly.com
Put the following information in the first line of your message (*not* in the Subject field):
subscribe oreilly-events

3. Get Examples from Our Books via FTP

There are two ways to access an archive of example files from our books:

Regular FTP
* ftp to:
  ftp.oreilly.com
  (login: anonymous
  password: your email address)
* Point your web browser to:
  ftp://ftp.oreilly.com/

FTPMAIL
* Send an email message to:
  ftpmail@online.oreilly.com
  (Write "help" in the message body)

4. Contact Us via Email

order@oreilly.com
To place a book or software order online. Good for North American and international customers.

subscriptions@oreilly.com
To place an order for any of our newsletters or periodicals.

books@oreilly.com
General questions about any of our books.

software@oreilly.com
For general questions and product information about our software. Check out O'Reilly Software Online at **http://software.oreilly.com/** for software and technical support information. Registered O'Reilly software users send your questions to: **website-support@oreilly.com**

cs@oreilly.com
For answers to problems regarding your order or our products.

booktech@oreilly.com
For book content technical questions or corrections.

proposals@oreilly.com
To submit new book or software proposals to our editors and product managers.

international@oreilly.com
For information about our international distributors or translation queries. For a list of our distributors outside of North America check out:
http://www.oreilly.com/www/order/country.html

O'Reilly & Associates, Inc.
101 Morris Street, Sebastopol, CA 95472 USA
TEL   707-829-0515 or 800-998-9938
         (6am to 5pm PST)
FAX   707-829-0104

O'REILLY®

International Distributors

UK, EUROPE, MIDDLE EAST AND AFRICA (EXCEPT FRANCE, GERMANY, AUSTRIA, SWITZERLAND, LUXEMBOURG, LIECHTENSTEIN, AND EASTERN EUROPE)

INQUIRIES
O'Reilly UK Limited
4 Castle Street
Farnham
Surrey, GU9 7HS
United Kingdom
Telephone: 44-1252-711776
Fax: 44-1252-734211
Email: josette@oreilly.com

ORDERS
Wiley Distribution Services Ltd.
1 Oldlands Way
Bognor Regis
West Sussex PO22 9SA
United Kingdom
Telephone: 44-1243-779777
Fax: 44-1243-820250
Email: cs-books@wiley.co.uk

FRANCE

ORDERS
GEODIF
61, Bd Saint-Germain
75240 Paris Cedex 05, France
Tel: 33-1-44-41-46-16 (French books)
Tel: 33-1-44-41-11-87 (English books)
Fax: 33-1-44-41-11-44
Email: distribution@eyrolles.com

INQUIRIES
Éditions O'Reilly
18 rue Séguier
75006 Paris, France
Tel: 33-1-40-51-52-30
Fax: 33-1-40-51-52-31
Email: france@editions-oreilly.fr

GERMANY, SWITZERLAND, AUSTRIA, EASTERN EUROPE, LUXEMBOURG, AND LIECHTENSTEIN

INQUIRIES & ORDERS
O'Reilly Verlag
Balthasarstr. 81
D-50670 Köln
Germany
Telephone: 49-221-973160-91
Fax: 49-221-973160-8
Email: anfragen@oreilly.de (inquiries)
Email: order@oreilly.de (orders)

CANADA (FRENCH LANGUAGE BOOKS)
Les Éditions Flammarion ltée
375, Avenue Laurier Ouest
Montréal (Québec) H2V 2K3
Tel: 00-1-514-277-8807
Fax: 00-1-514-278-2085
Email: info@flammarion.qc.ca

HONG KONG
City Discount Subscription Service, Ltd.
Unit D, 3rd Floor, Yan's Tower
27 Wong Chuk Hang Road
Aberdeen, Hong Kong
Tel: 852-2580-3539
Fax: 852-2580-6463
Email: citydis@ppn.com.hk

KOREA
Hanbit Media, Inc.
Sonyoung Bldg. 202
Yeksam-dong 736-36
Kangnam-ku
Seoul, Korea
Tel: 822-554-9610
Fax: 822-556-0363
Email: hant93@chollian.dacom.co.kr

PHILIPPINES
Mutual Books, Inc.
429-D Shaw Boulevard
Mandaluyong City, Metro
Manila, Philippines
Tel: 632-725-7538
Fax: 632-721-3056
Email: mbikikog@mnl.sequel.net

TAIWAN
O'Reilly Taiwan
No. 3, Lane 131
Hang-Chow South Road
Section 1, Taipei, Taiwan
Tel: 886-2-23968990
Fax: 886-2-23968916
Email: taiwan@oreilly.com

CHINA
O'Reilly Beijing
Room 2410
160, FuXingMenNeiDaJie
XiCheng District
Beijing, China PR 100031
Tel: 86-10-66412305
Fax: 86-10-86631007
Email: beijing@oreilly.com

INDIA
Computer Bookshop (India) Pvt. Ltd.
190 Dr. D.N. Road, Fort
Bombay 400 001 India
Tel: 91-22-207-0989
Fax: 91-22-262-3551
Email: cbsbom@giasbm01.vsnl.net.in

JAPAN
O'Reilly Japan, Inc.
Kiyoshige Building 2F
12-Bancho, Sanei-cho
Shinjuku-ku
Tokyo 160-0008 Japan
Tel: 81-3-3356-5227
Fax: 81-3-3356-5261
Email: japan@oreilly.com

ALL OTHER ASIAN COUNTRIES
O'Reilly & Associates, Inc.
101 Morris Street
Sebastopol, CA 95472 USA
Tel: 707-829-0515
Fax: 707-829-0104
Email: order@oreilly.com

AUSTRALIA
WoodsLane Pty., Ltd.
7/5 Vuko Place
Warriewood NSW 2102
Australia
Tel: 61-2-9970-5111
Fax: 61-2-9970-5002
Email: info@woodslane.com.au

NEW ZEALAND
Woodslane New Zealand, Ltd.
21 Cooks Street (P.O. Box 575)
Waganui, New Zealand
Tel: 64-6-347-6543
Fax: 64-6-345-4840
Email: info@woodslane.com.au

LATIN AMERICA
McGraw-Hill Interamericana
Editores, S.A. de C.V.
Cedro No. 512
Col. Atlampa
06450, Mexico, D.F.
Tel: 52-5-547-6777
Fax: 52-5-547-3336
Email: mcgraw-hill@infosel.net.mx

O'REILLY®

O'REILLY™

O'Reilly & Associates, Inc.
101 Morris Street
Sebastopol, CA 95472-9902
1-800-998-9938

Visit us online at:
**http://www.ora.com/
orders@ora.com**

O'REILLY WOULD LIKE TO HEAR FROM YOU

Which book did this card come from?

_____

Where did you buy this book?
- ❏ Bookstore ❏ Computer Store
- ❏ Direct from O'Reilly ❏ Class/seminar
- ❏ Bundled with hardware/software
- ❏ Other _____

What operating system do you use?
- ❏ UNIX ❏ Macintosh
- ❏ Windows NT ❏ PC(Windows/DOS)
- ❏ Other _____

What is your job description?
- ❏ System Administrator ❏ Programmer
- ❏ Network Administrator ❏ Educator/Teacher
- ❏ Web Developer
- ❏ Other _____

❏ Please send me O'Reilly's catalog, containing a complete listing of O'Reilly books and software.

Name _____ Company/Organization _____

Address _____

City _____ State _____ Zip/Postal Code _____ Country _____

Telephone _____ Internet or other email address (specify network)

Nineteenth century wood engraving
of a bear from the O'Reilly &
Associates Nutshell Handbook®
Using & Managing UUCP.

BUSINESS REPLY MAIL

FIRST CLASS MAIL   PERMIT NO. 80   SEBASTOPOL, CA

Postage will be paid by addressee

O'Reilly & Associates, Inc.
101 Morris Street
Sebastopol, CA 95472-9902